500 Crochet Stitches

500 CROCHET STITCHES
 Printed in Singapore.
For information, address St. Martin's Press,
175 Fifth Avenue, New York, N.Y. 10010.
www.stmartins.com

Library of Congress Cataloging-in-Publication Data
Available Upon Request

ISBN 978-1-250-06730-2

St. Martin's Griffin books may be purchased for educational, business, or promotional use. For information on bulk purchases, please contact Macmillan Corporate and Premium Sales Department at 1-800-221-7945, extension 5442, or write specialmarkets@macmillan.com.

First U.S. Edition: August 2015

10 9 8 7 6 5 4 3 2 1

500 Crochet Stitches

The Ultimate Crochet Stitch Bible

ST. MARTIN'S GRIFFIN
NEW YORK

contents

Introduction	6
Tools & equipment	8
Starting off	10
Basic stitches	34
Motifs	128
Edgings & trims	220
Index	286

Introduction

Crochet is perhaps the most versatile of all crafts. Using just a hook and a ball of yarn, it is possible to create a fabric from almost any length of continuous fiber: wool, cotton, string, ribbon, leather, wire, and even plastic bags cut into strips!

Quite simply, crochet is a series of interlocking loops of thread worked into a chain using a thin rod with a hook at the end. A chain of loops is formed, with each new loop catching the thread and pulling it through the previous loop. After the chain is completed, the thread is then turned to start a second chain, and so on, until a fabric is created—and one that grows rather more quickly than knitting.

Crochet can often prove to be easier than knitting, as working with just one stitch on a crochet hook at a time is simpler than handling a number of stitches on a knitting needle. There are just a handful of basic stitches (see page 10); each one is easily mastered, and the variations and combinations of these are endless.

Crochet is one of the most basic forms of textile, having an affinity with fishermen's nets and medieval lace: the very word "crochet" is French for "hook". The craft also has an affinity with knitting; early knitting frames used a single, hooked needle, and it may well be that the looping effect gave birth to the crochet technique.

In the past, crochet designs were not usually written down, just lovingly remembered, and handed down from generation to generation. Crochet as we recognize it today became popular in the late 1930s and 1940s as a cheaper alternative to lace. Crochet soon adorned utilitarian collars and cuffs, and even snoods, giving femininity and a little glamour to the clothes of the austere war years. A revival in the 1960s took crochet to new heights, with colorful, freeform hangings, even hanging chairs, and of course the quintessential crochet mini-dress.

This edition is just a starting point for your own interpretation. It offers a selection of the very best stitches, including a few new ones and some reinvented for a new generation.

The book is divided into three main sections. The first covers basic crochet stitches (see page 34). The emphasis here is on texture, and we show how combinations of the basic stitches can be used to make a huge variety of different crochet fabrics, featuring shells, chevrons, puff stitches, trellis stitches and loop stitches, among others.

The second section focuses on motifs (see page 128) in a variety of shapes: circular, square, polygonal, triangular as well as leaf and petal shapes. Regular-shaped motifs can be made in multiples and stitched together to create items such as afghans and blankets. Many of the circular or flower-like motifs would work well as embellishments, for example, on hats, or as pins.

The third section covers edgings and trims (see page 220), ranging from simple cords and braids to more elaborate ruffles and frills. Crochet trims can be used to decorate a plain knit or crochet item, adding a special something to a hem, cuff, neckline or plain blanket edge.

Although there is a wealth of ideas in this book, you can think of it as just a starting point for your own creativity. Building on this knowledge, you might find inspiration for your own crochet stitches and designs in many everyday things: the worn walls of buildings, patterned sidewalks, undulating tiles, the delicate stamens of flowers, even tangled and broken wire-mesh fences; seemingly mundane items, but inspiring in their form and design.

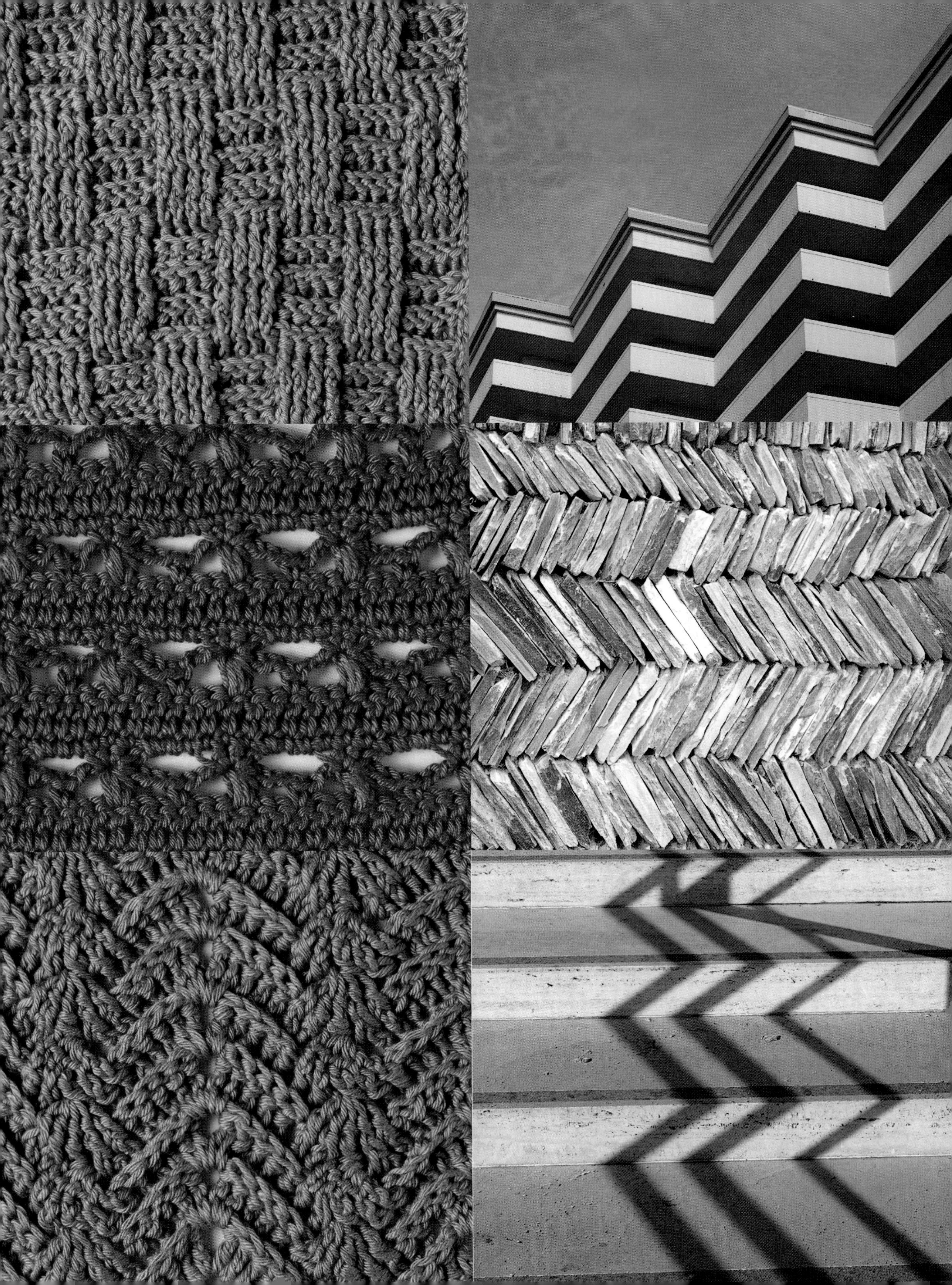

Tools & equipment

It is sometimes hard to believe that beautiful and intricate-looking crochet is created using only two essential tools: a crochet hook and the yarn itself.

Crochet hooks

Crochet hooks are usually made from steel, aluminum or plastic in a range of sizes according to their diameter. As each crochet stitch is worked separately until only one loop remains on the hook, space is not needed to hold stitches.

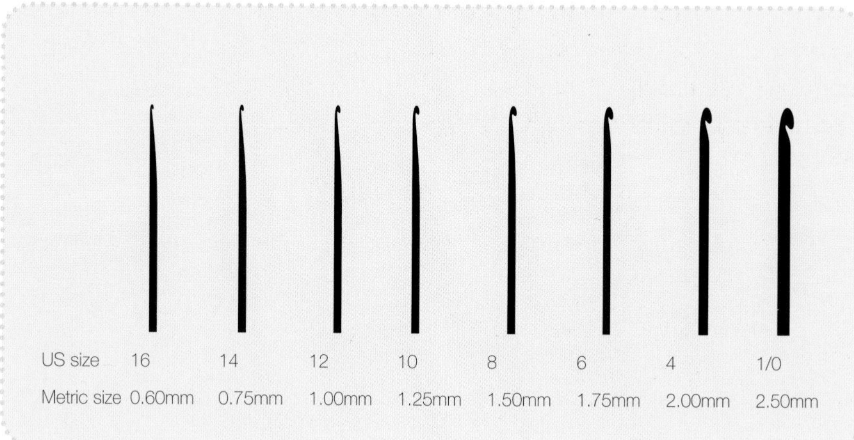

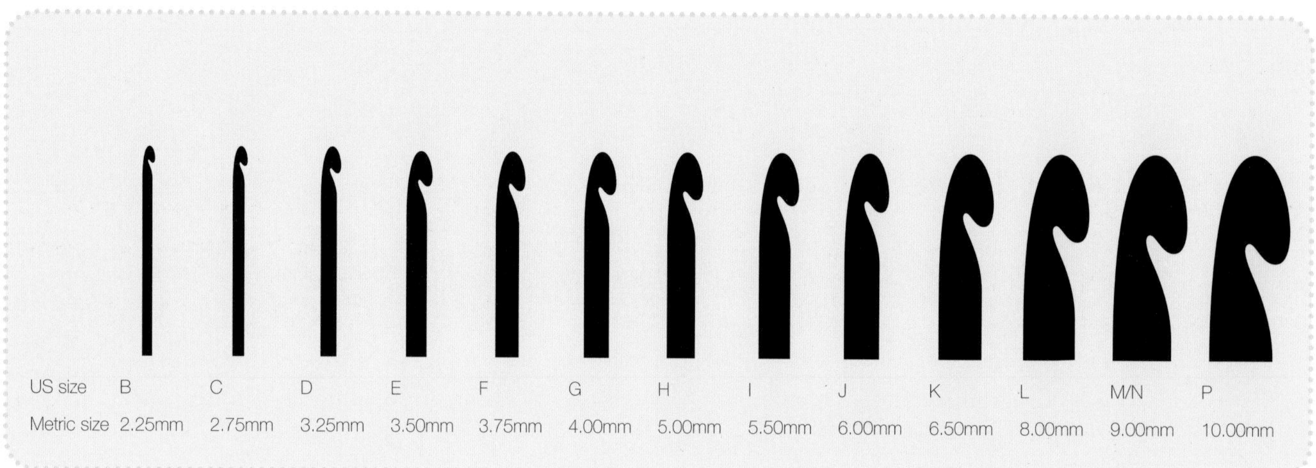

Crochet yarns

Traditionally, crochet was worked almost exclusively in very fine cotton yarn to create or embellish household items such as tablecloths, doilies, cuffs and frills. The samples in this book were worked in a fine mercerized cotton, but may take on a totally different appearance if different yarns are used. Lacier stitches probably look their best in smooth threads, but some of the all-over stitches can be more interesting when worked in tweedy or textured yarns. Crochet yarns can also be found in leather, suede and even fine jewelry wire.

Holding the hook and yarn

There are no hard and fast rules as to the best way to hold the hook and yarn. The diagrams below show one method, but you can choose whichever way you find the most comfortable.

Due to the restrictions of space it is not possible to show diagrams for both right- and left-handed people. Left-handers may find it easier to trace the diagrams and then turn the tracing paper over, thus reversing the image; alternatively, reflect the diagrams in a mirror. Read left for right and right for left where applicable.

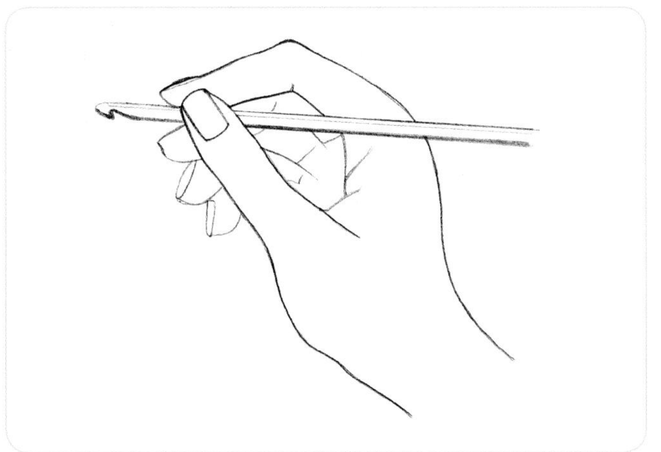

1 The hook is held in the right hand as if holding a pencil.

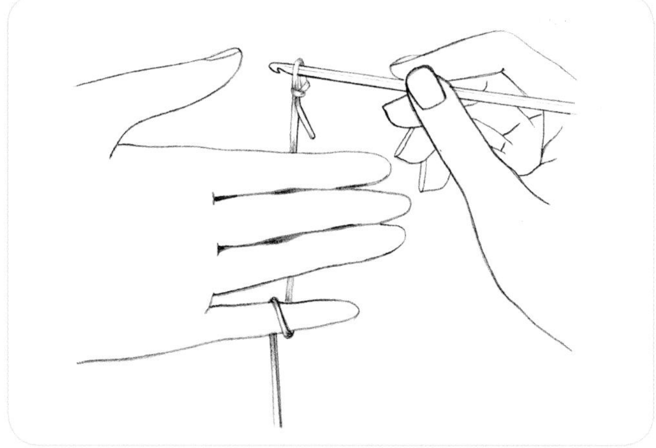

2 To maintain the slight tension in the yarn necessary for easy, even working, it can help to arrange the yarn around the fingers of the left hand in this way.

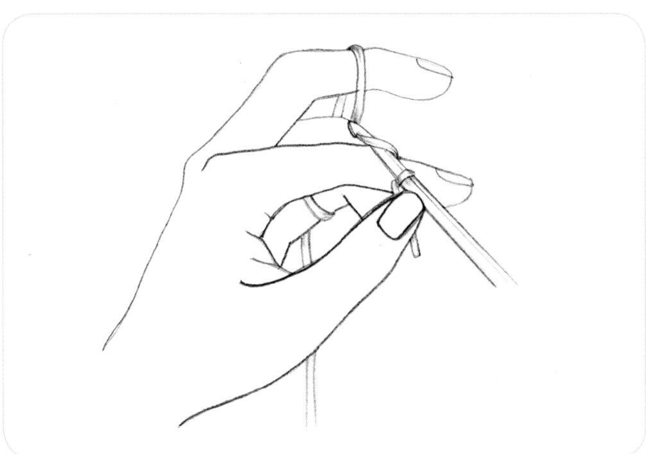

3 The left hand holds the work and at the same time controls the yarn supply. The left-hand middle finger is used to manipulate the yarn, while the index finger and thumb hold on to the work.

Starting off

The patterns in this book use the following basic stitches. They are shown worked into a starting chain, but the method is the same whatever part of the work the stitch is worked into.

The first step

To be able to start a crocheted piece the first step is to secure the working yarn on to the hook. You will need to make a slip knot to create the first loop on the hook, while a yarn over is the way you will make all subsequent loops.

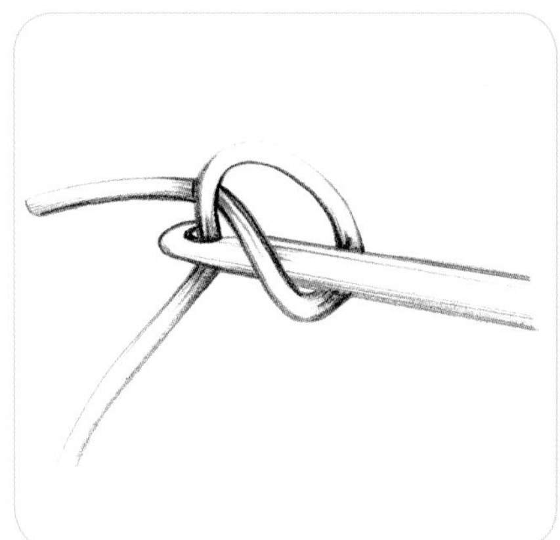

Slip knot

Almost all crochet begins with a slip knot. Make a loop, then hook another loop through it. Tighten gently and slide the knot up to the hook.

Yarn over (yo)

Wrap the yarn from back to front over the hook (or hold the yarn still and maneuver the hook). This movement of the yarn over the hook is used over and over again in crochet, and is usually abbreviated as "yo".

o Chain stitch (ch)

Pretty much every piece of crochet begins with a length of chain stitch. The pattern that you follow will tell you how many chains you will need for your first row (often referred to as the foundation row). To create circular pieces, such as those found in the Motifs section (see page 128), you will work a small number of chains and then join them with a slip stitch (see page 11) to form a round.

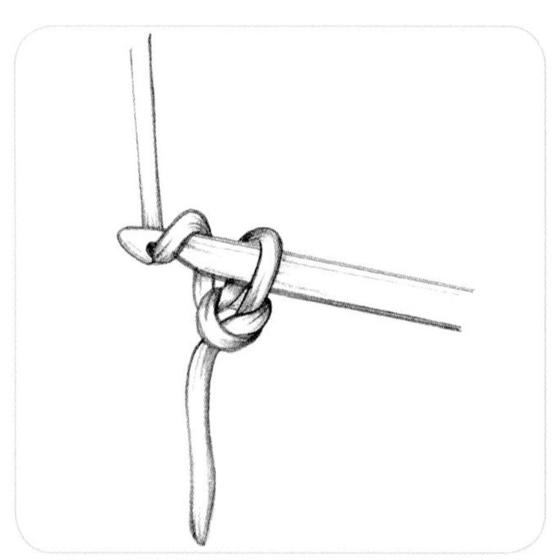

1 Yarn over and draw the yarn through to form a new loop without tightening up the previous one.

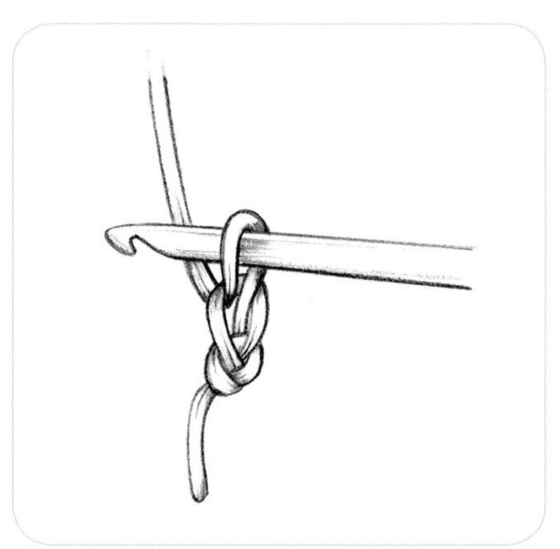

2 Repeat to form as many chains as required. Do not count the slip knot as a stitch. **Note:** Unless otherwise stated, when working into the starting chain always work under two strands of chain loops, as shown in the following diagrams.

• Slip stitch (sl st)

This is the shortest of crochet stitches and, unlike other stitches, is not used on its own to produce a fabric. It is used for joining, shaping and, where necessary, carrying the yarn to another part of the fabric for the next stage.

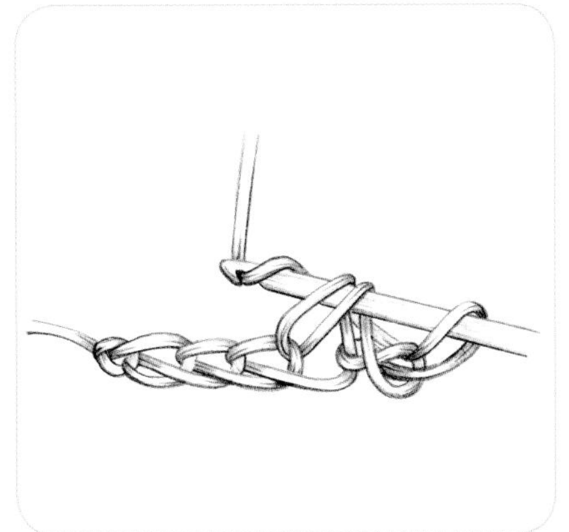

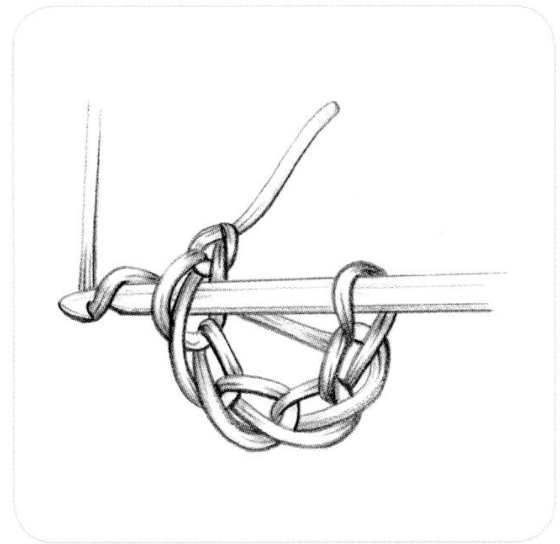

1 Insert the hook into the work (second chain from hook in diagram), yarn over and draw the yarn through both the work and the loop on the hook in one movement.

2 To join a chain ring with a slip stitch, insert the hook into the first chain, yarn over and draw the yarn through the work and the yarn on the hook.

+ Single crochet (sc)

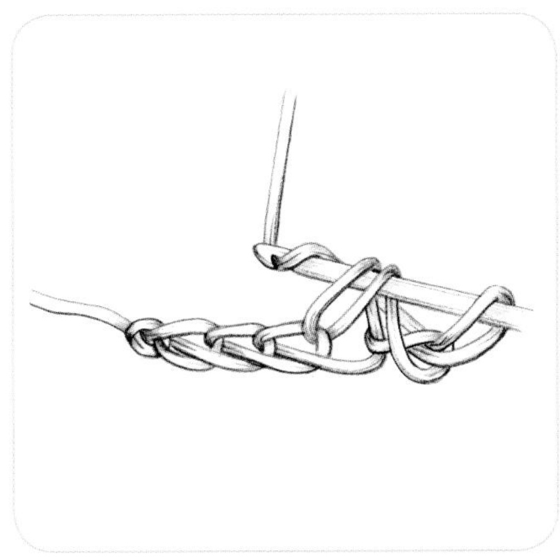

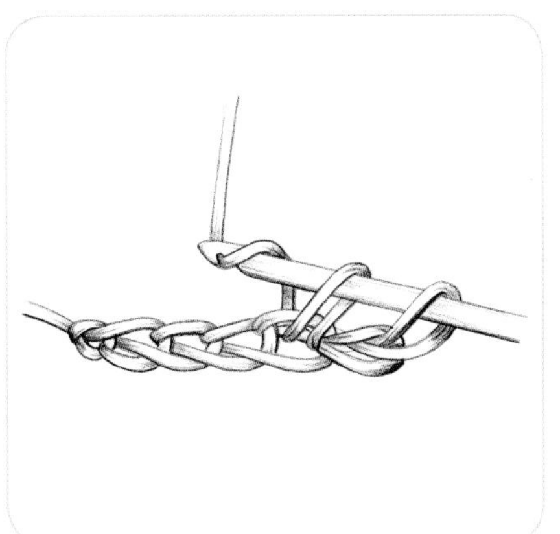

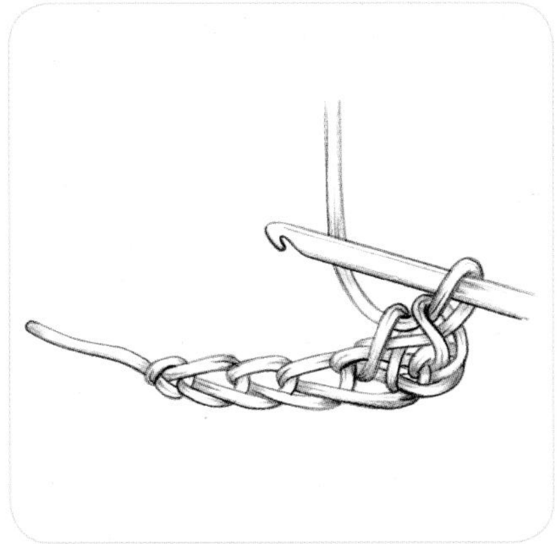

1 Insert the hook into the work (second chain from hook on starting chain), *yarn over and draw the yarn through the work only.

2 Yarn over again and draw the yarn through both loops on the hook.

3 1sc made. Insert hook into next stitch; repeat from * in step 1.

T Half-double crochet (hdc)

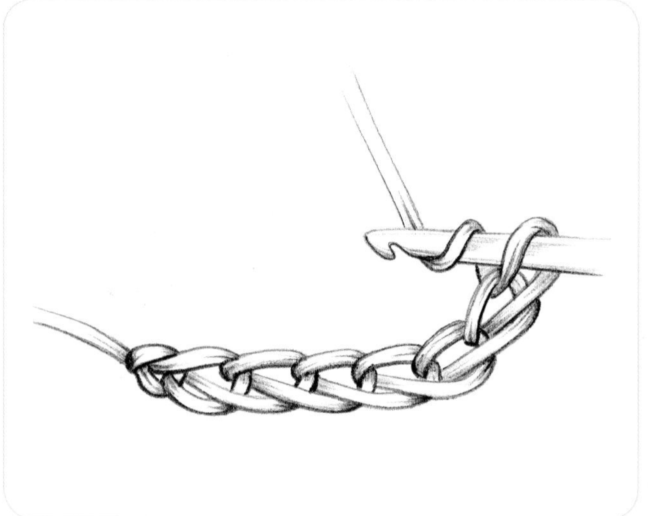

1 Yarn over and insert the hook into the work (third chain from hook on starting chain).

2 *Yarn over and draw through the work only.

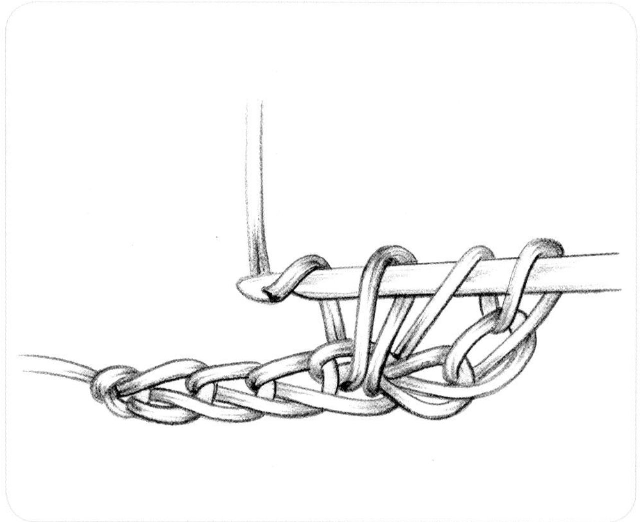

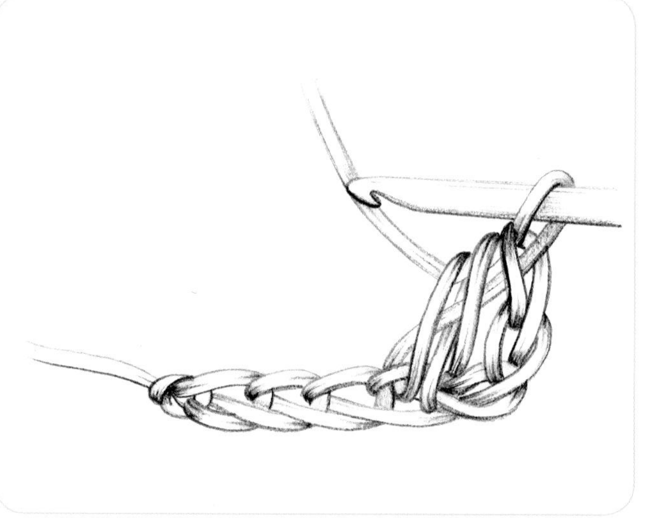

3 Yarn over again and draw through all three loops on the hook.

4 1hdc made. Yarn over, insert hook into next stitch; repeat from * in step 2.

Ŧ Double crochet (dc)

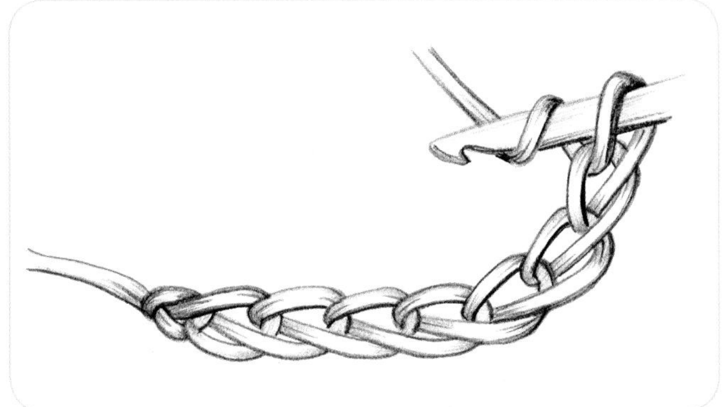

1 Yarn over and insert the hook into the work (fourth chain from hook on starting chain).

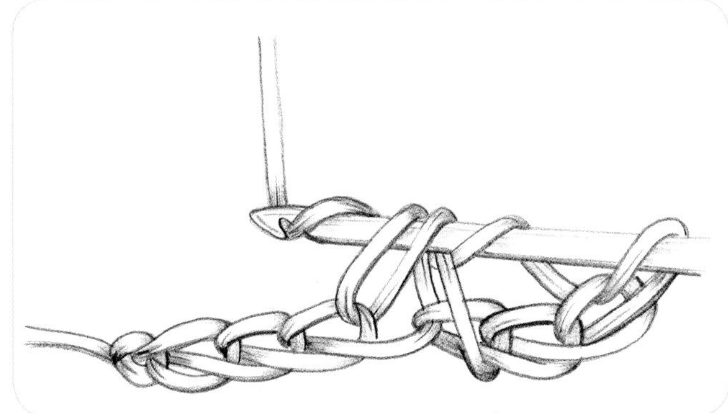

2 *Yarn over and draw through the work only.

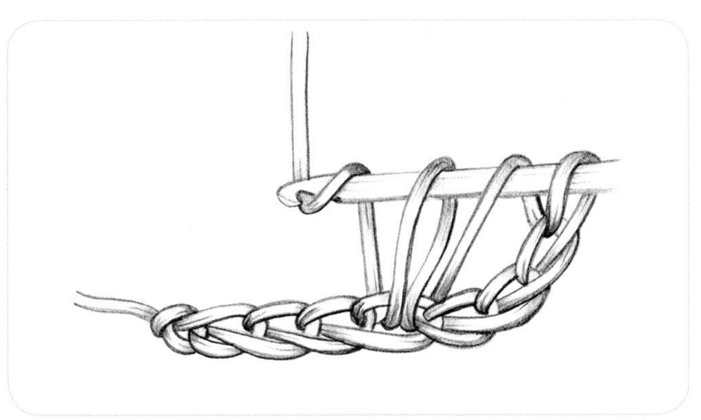

3 Yarn over and draw through the first two loops only.

4 Yarn over and draw through the last two loops on the hook.

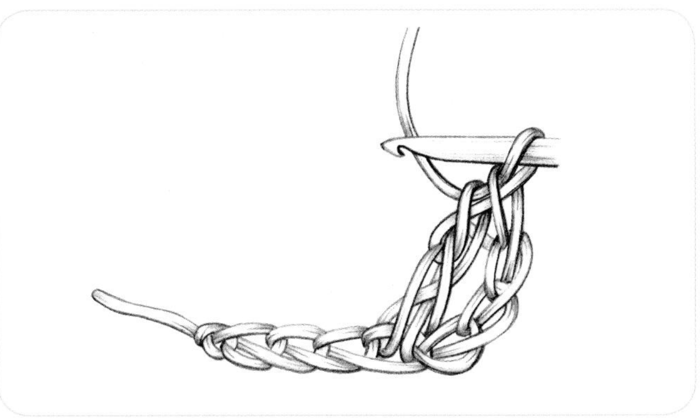

5 1dc made. Yarn over, insert hook into next stitch; repeat from * in step 2.

ⱡ Treble (tr)

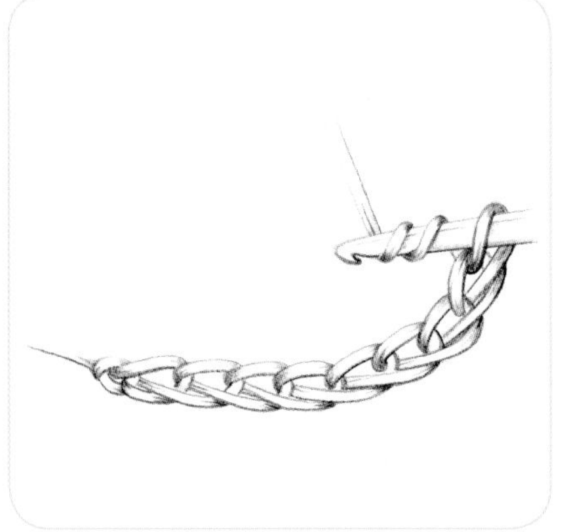

1 Yarn over twice, insert the hook into the work (fifth chain from hook on starting chain).

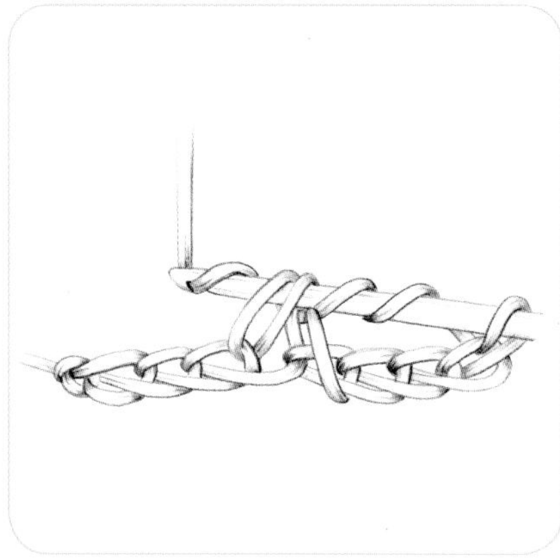

2 *Yarn over and draw through the work only.

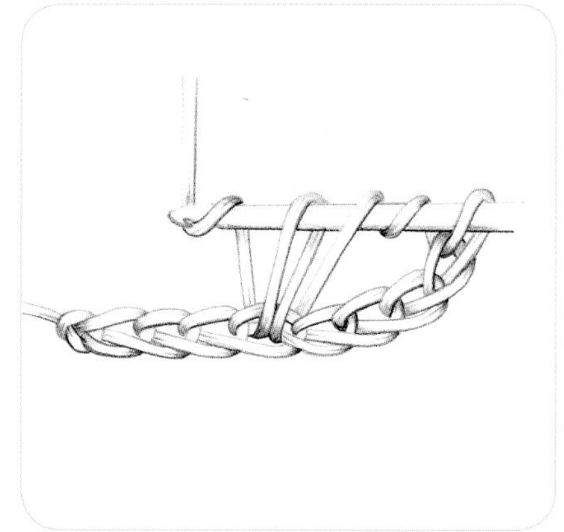

3 Yarn over again and draw through the first two loops only.

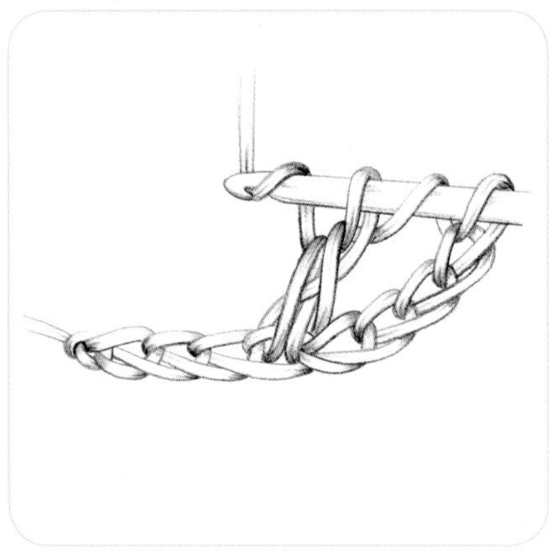

4 Yarn over again and draw through the next two loops only.

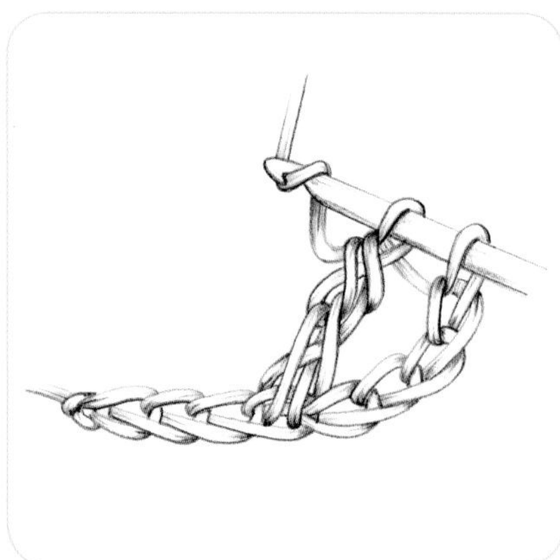

5 Yarn over again and draw through the last two loops on the hook.

6 1tr made. Yarn over twice, insert hook into next stitch; repeat from * in step 2.

Longer basic stitches

Double treble (dtr), triple treble (ttr), and quadruple treble (quadtr) are made by wrapping the yarn over three to five times at the beginning and finishing as for a treble, repeating step 4 until two loops remain on the hook, then finishing with step 5.

Solomon's knot

A Solomon's knot is a lengthened chain stitch locked with a single crochet stitch worked into its back loop.

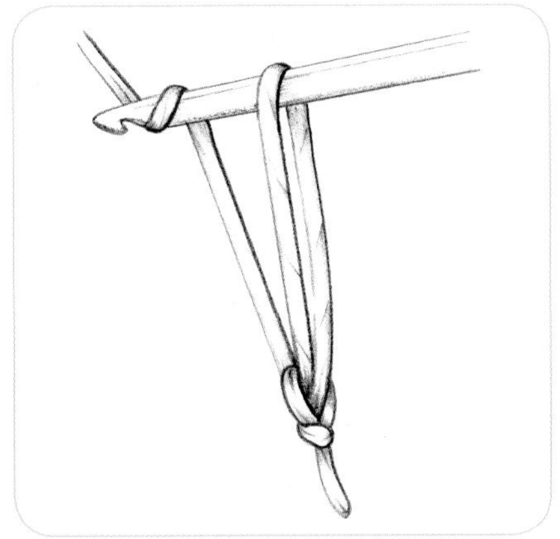

1 Make one chain and lengthen the loop as required. Wrap the yarn over the hook.

2 Draw through the loop on the hook, keeping the single back thread of this long chain separate from the two front threads.

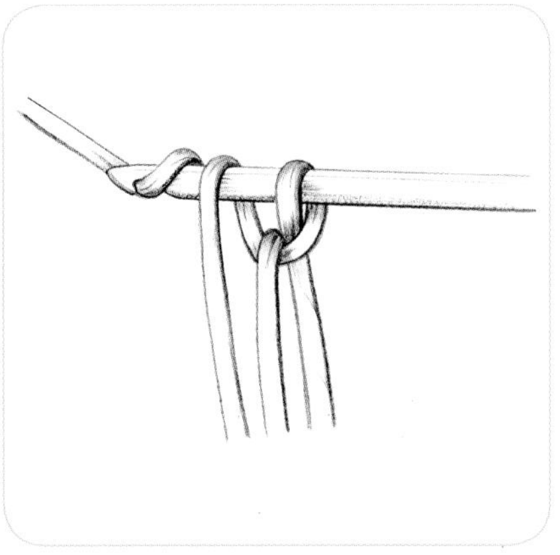

3 Insert hook under the single back thread. Wrap the yarn over the hook.

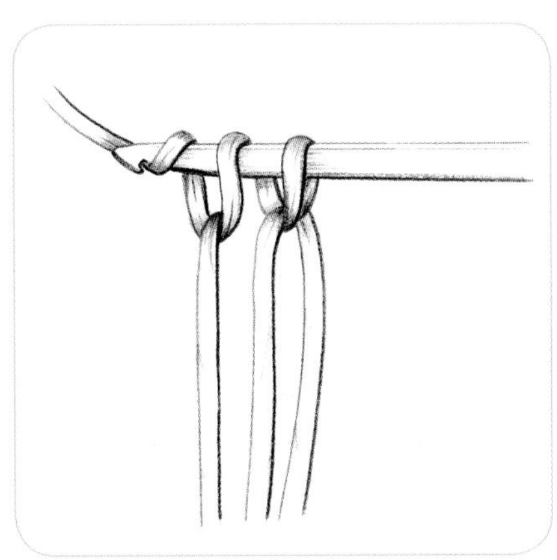

4 Draw a loop through and wrap again.

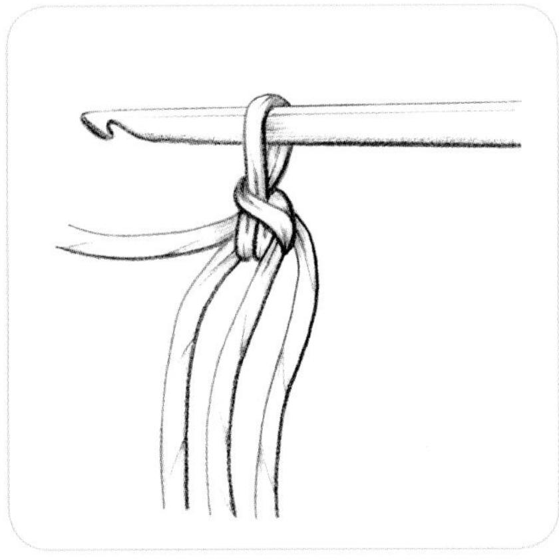

5 Draw through both loops on the hook to complete.

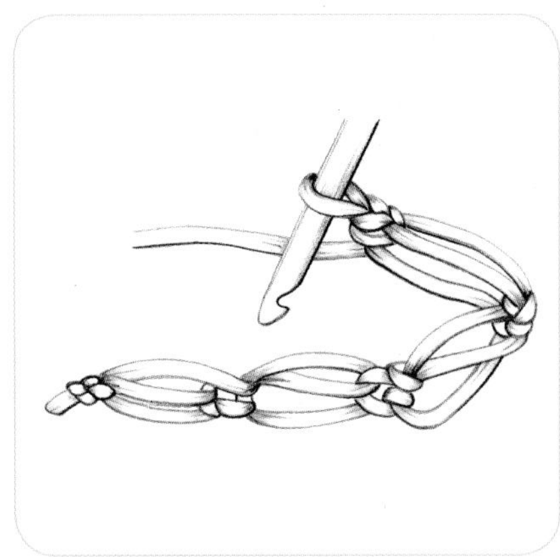

6 It is necessary to work back into the "knots" between the lengthened chains in order to make the classic Solomon's knot fabric.

Making fabric

These are the basic procedures for making crochet fabrics—the things that crochet patterns sometimes assume you know. These principles can be applied to all the patterns in this book.

Starting chain

To make a flat fabric worked in rows, you must begin with a starting chain (also called a foundation chain). The length of the starting chain is the number of stitches needed for the first row of fabric plus the number of chains needed to get to the correct height of the stitches to be used in the first row. All the patterns in this book indicate the length of starting chain required to work one repeat of the design.

When working an edging or trim, this can be worked from a foundation chain or from the edge of the fabric. If working along the edge of a fabric, join in the yarn and work the number of skipped chains specified at the beginning of the first row.

When working a motif in the round, you will need to join your starting chain with a slip stitch to link your chain into a circle and then crochet the first round.

Working in rows

A flat fabric can be produced by turning the work at the end of each row. Right-handers work from right to left and left-handers from left to right. One or more chains must be worked at the beginning of each row to bring the hook up to the height of the first stitch in the row. The number of chains used for turning depends upon the height of the stitch they are to match:

single crochet = 1 chain
half-double crochet = 2 chains
double crochet = 3 chains
treble = 4 chains

When working half-double crochet or longer stitches the turning chain takes the place of the first stitch. Where one chain is worked at the beginning of a row starting with single crochet, it is usually for height only and is in addition to the first stitch.

Basic double crochet fabric

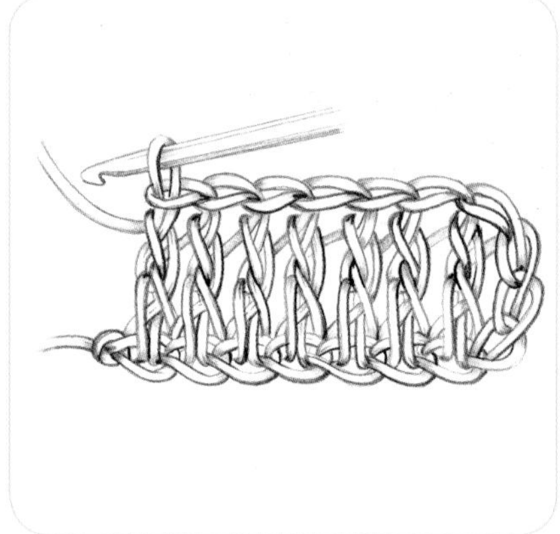

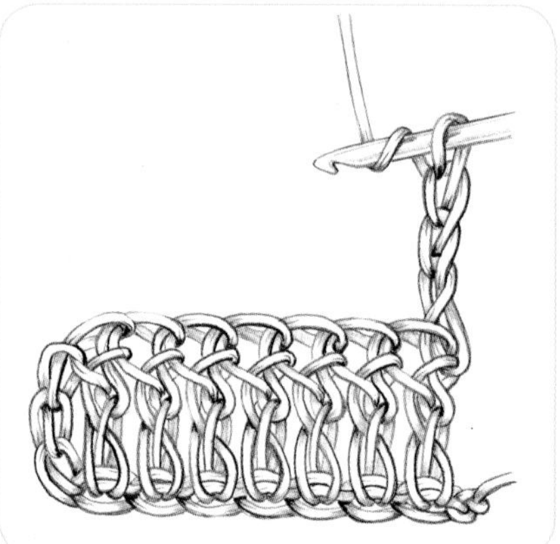

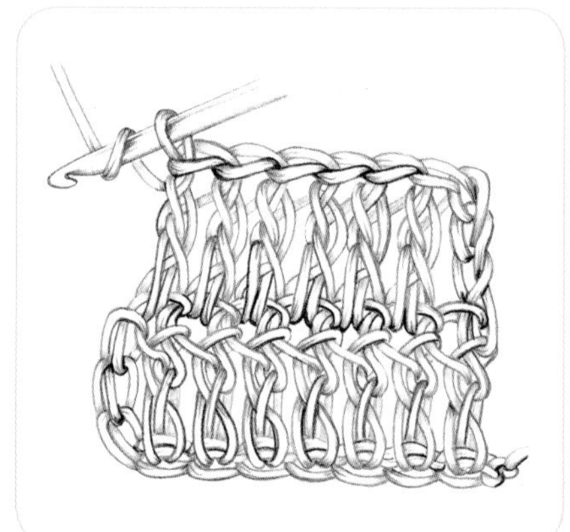

Make a starting chain of the required length plus two chains. Work one double crochet into the fourth chain from hook. The three chains at the beginning of the row form the first double crochet. Work one double crochet into the next and every chain to the end of the row.

At the end of each row, turn the work so that another row can be worked across the top of the previous one. It does not matter which way the work is turned, but be consistent. Make three chains for turning. These turning chains will count as the first double crochet.

Skip the first double crochet in the previous row, work a double crochet into the top of the next and every double crochet including the last double crochet in row, then work a double crochet into the third of three chains at the beginning of the previous row.

Fastening off

Once you have completed a crochet piece you will need to secure the yarn end, or your stitches will unravel. To fasten off the yarn permanently, break off the yarn about 2in (5cm) away from the work (leave a longer length if you need to sew pieces together). Draw the end through the loop on the hook and tighten gently. For a neat finish, you will want to sew the yarn end into the crochet fabric rather than leaving it hanging loose. Thread the yarn through a large-eyed tapestry or darning needle and weave it in and out of a few stitches until the yarn end is lost in the body of the fabric.

Joining in new yarn and changing color

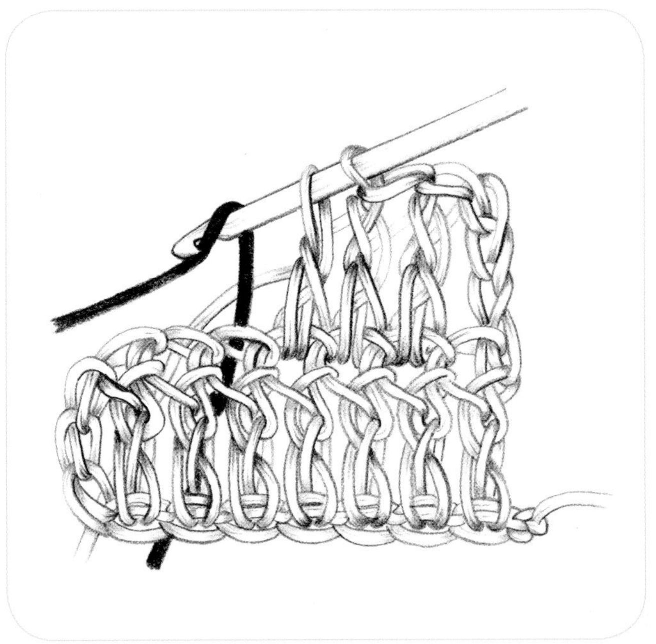

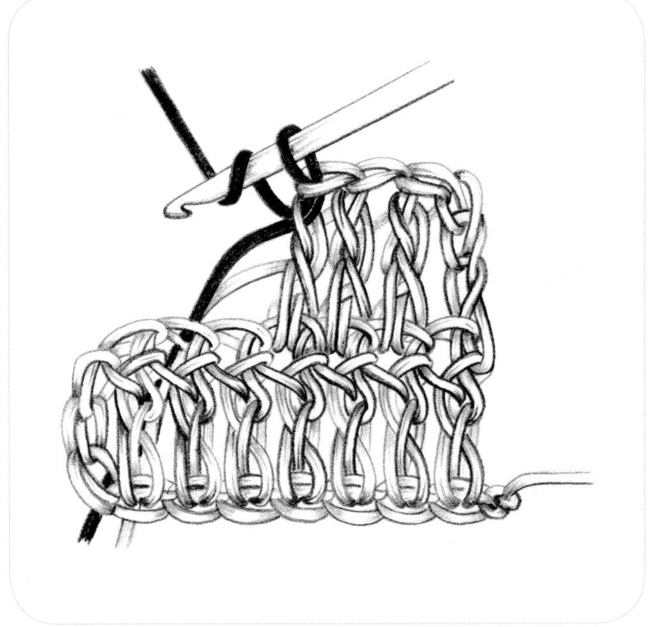

When joining a new yarn or changing color, work in the old yarn until two loops of the last stitch remain in the old yarn or color. Use the new color or yarn to complete the stitch.

Continue to work the following stitches in the new color or yarn, as before.

If you are working whole rows in different colors, make the change during the last stitch in the previous row, so the new color for the next row is ready to work the turning chain.

Do not cut off any yarns that will be needed again later at the same edge, but continue to use them as required, leaving an unbroken "float" thread up the side of the fabric.

If, at the end of a row, the pattern requires you to return to the beginning of the same row without turning and to work another row in a different color in the same direction, complete the first row in the old color and fasten off by lengthening the final loop on the hook, passing the whole ball through it and gently tighten again. That yarn is now available if you need to rejoin it later at this edge (if not, cut it).

Placement of stitches

All crochet stitches (except chains) require the hook to be inserted into existing work. It has already been shown how to work into a chain and into the top of a stitch; however, stitches can also be worked into the following places.

Working into chain spaces

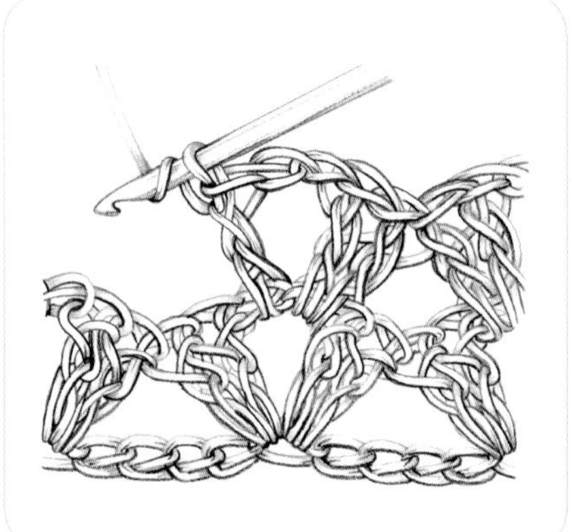

When a stitch, group, shell, cluster or bobble is positioned over a chain or chains, the hook is often inserted into the space under the chain.

It is important to note, however, whether the pattern instructions stipulate working into a particular chain, as this will change the appearance of the design.

If necessary, information of this kind has been given as notes with the diagram.

A bobble, popcorn or cluster that is worked into a chain space is shown in the diagram spread out over more than one stitch; therefore on the diagrams they will not be closed at the base.

Working around the stem

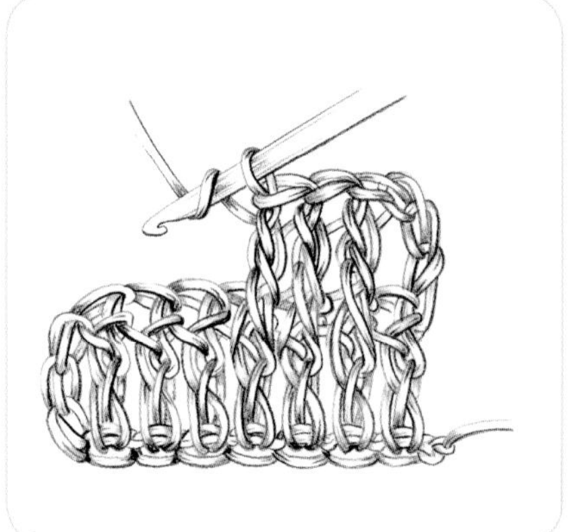

Inserting the hook around the whole stem of a stitch creates raised or relief effects.

Working around the front of the stem (as in the diagram above) gives a stitch that lies on the front of the work.

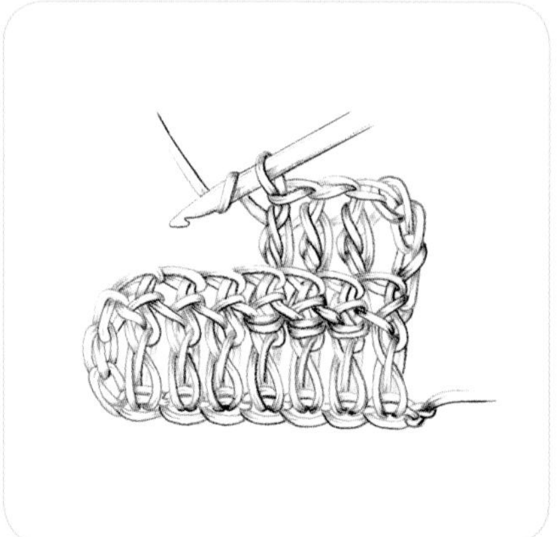

Working around the back of the stem (as in the diagram above) gives a stitch that lies on the back of the work.

Working between stitches

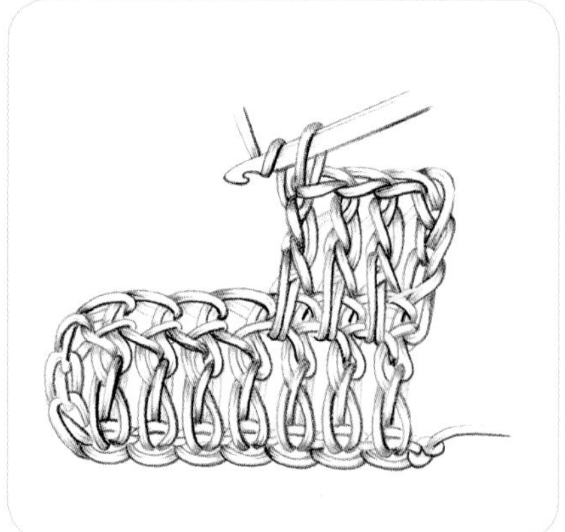

Inserting the hook between the stems of the stitches produces an open effect.

Ensure that the number of stitches remains constant after each row.

Working under the front or back loop only

Inserting the hook under one loop at the top of the stitch leaves the other loop as a horizontal bar.

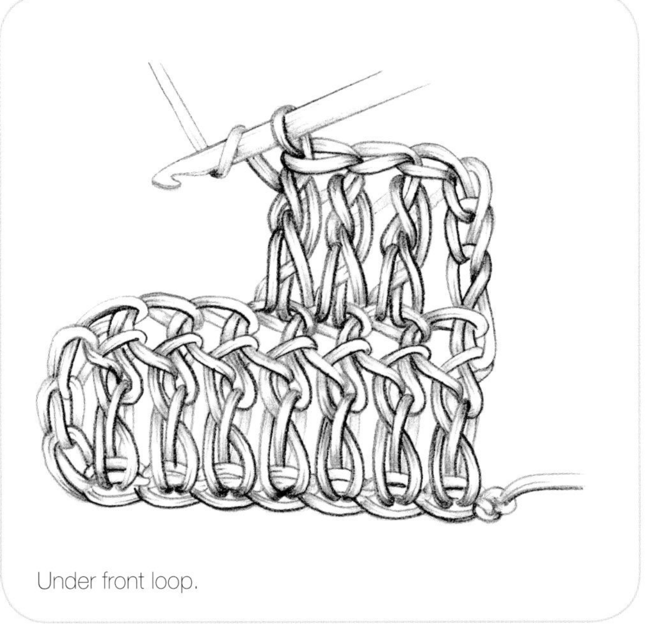

Under front loop.

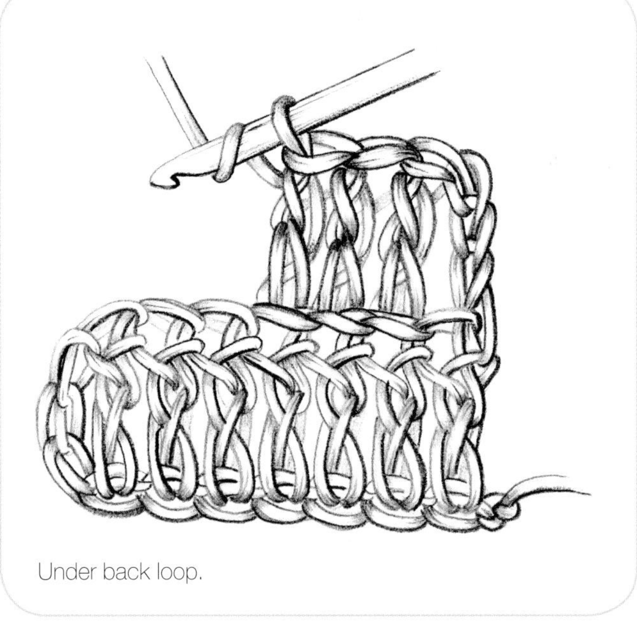

Under back loop.

Working in rows

If you work consistently into the front loop only, you will make a series of ridges alternately on the back and front of the work. Working into the back loop only makes the ridges appear alternately on the front and back of the work.

If, however, you work alternately into the front loop only on one row and then the back loop only on the next row, the horizontal bars will all appear on the same side of the fabric.

Working in rounds

Working always into the front loop only will form a bar on the back of the work, and vice versa.

Tip

When you work into the front or back loop only, you will create a visible ridge in the work on the other side. This can be used for decorative effect, or to create structure. For example, when crocheting an object with a circular base, the ridge line can be used to demarcate the base from the main body of the object.

Starting chains and pattern repeats

The number of starting chains required is given with each pattern. It may be given in the form of a multiple, for example:
Starting chain: Multiple of 7 sts + 3.
This means you can make any length of chain that is a multiple of 7 + 3, such as 14 + 3 ch, 21 + 3 ch or 28 + 3 ch.

In the written instructions the stitches that should be repeated are contained within brackets [ ] or follow an asterisk *. These stitches are repeated across the row or round the required number of times. On the diagrams the stitches that have to be repeated can be easily visualized. The extra stitches not included in the pattern repeat are there to balance the row or make it symmetrical and are worked only once. Obviously, turning chains are worked only at the beginning of each row. Some diagrams consist of more than one pattern repeat, so that you can see more clearly how the design is worked.

Working in color

Capital letters A, B, C, and so on are used to indicate different yarn colors in both the written instructions and the diagrams. They do not refer to any particular color. See page 17 for instructions on changing color within a pattern.

Gauge

Whenever you are following crochet pattern instructions, whatever form they take, probably the most important single factor in your success is obtaining the "gauge" (or "tension" in UK) that the pattern designer worked to. If you do not obtain the same gauge as indicated, your work will not turn out to be the measurement given.

The gauge is usually specified as a number of stitches and a number of rows to a given measurement (usually 4in/10cm). The quick way to check is to make a square of fabric about 6in (15cm) wide in the correct pattern and with the correct yarn and suggested hook size, lay this down on a flat surface and measure it—first horizontally (for stitch gauge) and then vertically (for row gauge). If your square has too few stitches or rows to the measurement, your tension is too loose and you should try again with a smaller hook. If it has too many stitches, try a larger hook. (Hint: Stitch gauge is generally more important than row gauge in crochet.)

Note that the hook size quoted in instructions is a suggestion only. You must use whichever hook gives you the correct gauge.

Tip

Working with color is perhaps one of the most pleasurable and inspiring aspects of a craft such as crochet. One of the creative benefits of working with the stitch designs from this book is that you won't need much yarn to work up a sample design to see if you like it and to see how your ideas for color combinations turn out—try going through your stash and using up leftover scraps of yarn from other projects. The perennial granny square (see page 168) never loses its popularity and is an excellent way of using scraps in a colorful way.

Increasing and decreasing

If you are working crochet to make something that requires shaping, such as decreasing for the neckline of a garment or increasing to add width for a sleeve, you need to know something about shaping.

Increasing is generally achieved by working two or more stitches in the pattern where there would normally be one stitch. Conversely, decreasing is achieved by working two or more stitches together, or skipping one or more stitches. However, it can be difficult to know exactly where these adjustments are best made, and a visual guide would make the work easier!

On the diagrams here we show you some examples of shapings, which cover a variety of possibilities. We recommend that you use this method yourself when planning a project. First, pencil-trace the diagram given with the stitch. If necessary, repeat the tracing to match the repeat of the pattern until you have a large enough area to give you the required shape. Once this is correct, ink it in so that you can draw over it in pencil without destroying it. Now, over this draw the shaping you want, matching as near as possible the style of the particular pattern you are using.

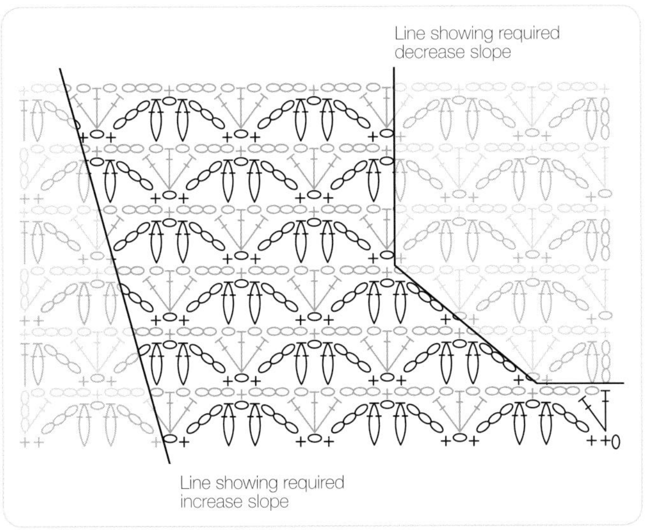

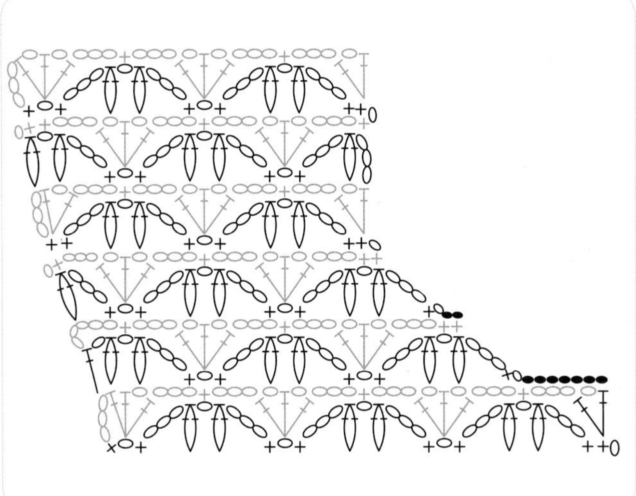

Stitch variations

Different effects can be created by small variations in the stitch-making procedure or by varying the position and manner of inserting the hook into the fabric.

Filet crochet

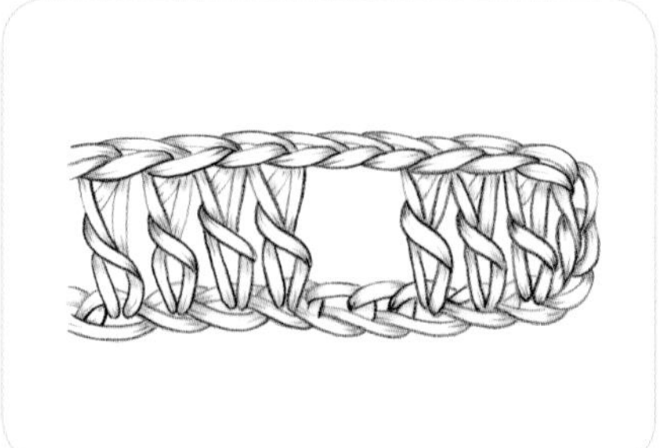

This is a particular technique of crochet based on forming designs from a series of solid and open squares called "blocks" and "spaces". These are more often used in crochet lace patterns made with cotton, but can be worked in knitting yarn.

To work a space, chain 2, skip 2 chains (or 2 stitches on the preceding row), and work 1 double crochet into the next stitch. To work a block, work 1 double crochet into each of the next 3 chains or stitches. When a block follows a space, it will look like 4 double crochets; this is because the first double crochet belongs to the adjacent space.

Groups or shells

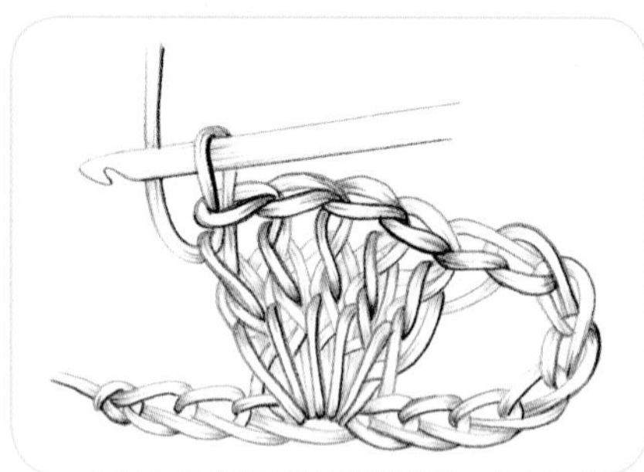

These consist of several complete stitches worked into the same place. They can be worked as part of a pattern or as a method of increasing. On diagrams, the point at the base of the group will be positioned above the space or stitch where the hook is to be inserted.

Clusters

Any combination of stitches may be joined into a cluster by leaving the last loop of each temporarily on the hook until they are worked off together at the end. Working stitches together in this way can also be a method of decreasing. It is important to be sure exactly how and where the hook is to be inserted for each "leg" of the cluster. The "legs" may be worked over adjacent stitches, or stitches may be skipped between "legs".

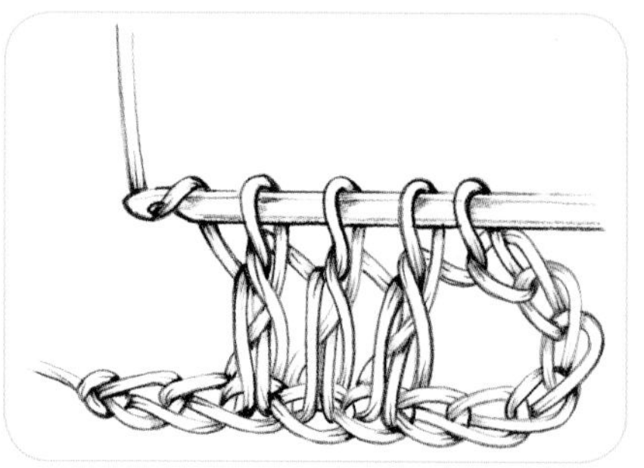

1 Work a double crochet into each of the next three stitches, leaving the last loop of each double crochet on the hook.

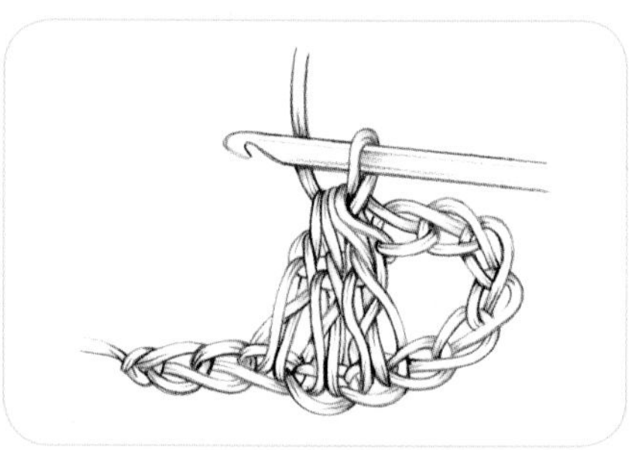

2 Yarn over and draw through all four loops on the hook. On diagrams, each "leg" of the cluster will be positioned above the stitch where the hook is to be inserted.

Bobbles

When a cluster is worked into one stitch, it forms a bobble.

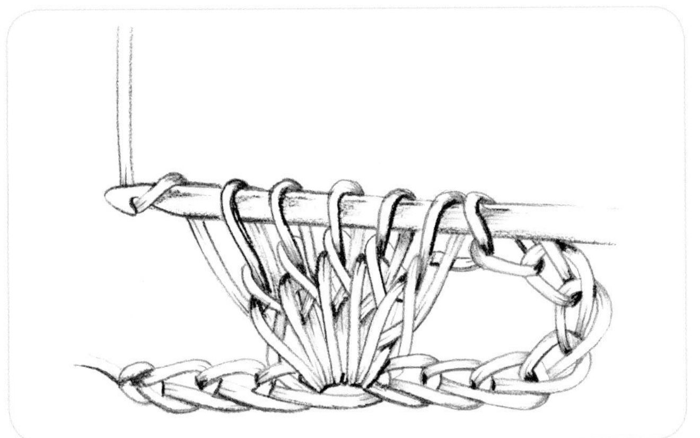

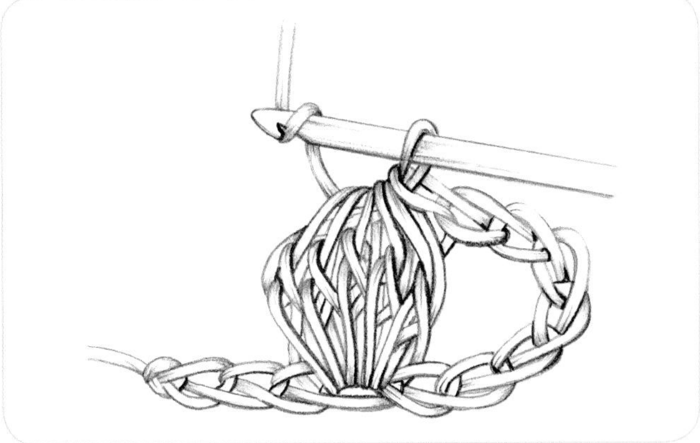

1 Work five double crochet into one stitch, leaving the last loop of each on the hook.

2 Yarn over and draw through all the loops on the hook. More bulky bobbles can be secured with an extra chain stitch. If this is necessary, it will be indicated within the pattern.

Popcorns

Popcorns are groups of complete stitches usually worked into the same place, folded and closed at the top. An extra chain can be worked to secure the popcorn. They're great for adding textural interest to a garment.

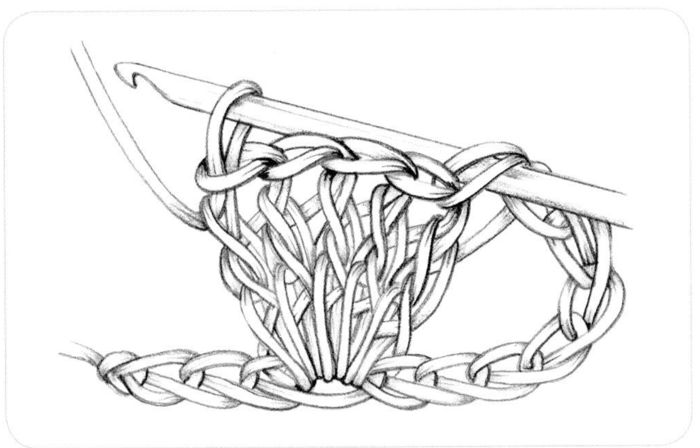

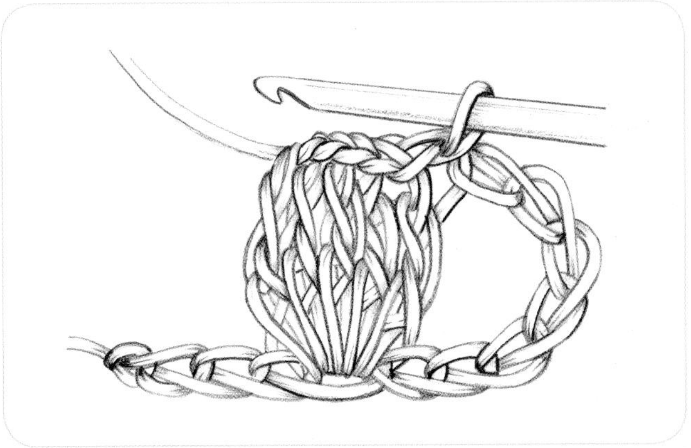

1 Work five trebles into one stitch. Take the hook out of the working loop and insert it into the top of the first treble made, from front to back.

2 Pick up the working loop and draw this through to close the popcorn. If required, work one chain to secure the popcorn. On diagrams, the point at the base of the popcorn will be positioned above the space or stitch where it is to be worked.

Puff stitches

These are similar to bobbles but worked using half double crochets. As half double crochets cannot be worked until one loop remains on the hook, the stitches are not closed until the required number have been worked.

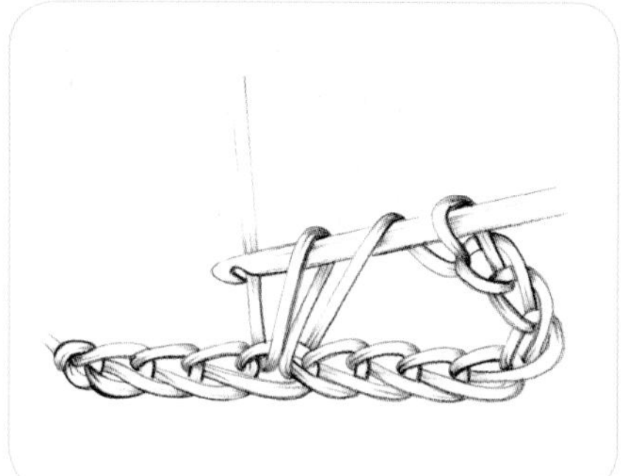

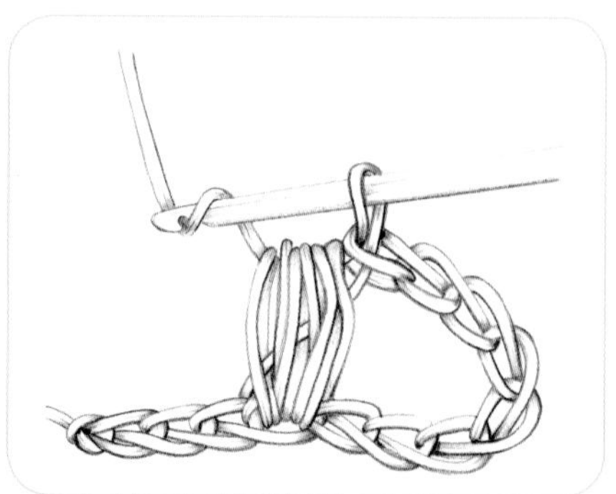

1 Yarn over, insert the hook, yarn over again and draw a loop through (three loops on the hook).

2 Repeat this step twice more, inserting the hook into the same stitch (seven loops on the hook); yarn over and draw through all the loops on the hook.

3 As with popcorns and bulky bobbles, an extra chain stitch is often used to secure the puff stitch firmly. This will be indicated within the pattern if necessary. A cluster of half double crochet stitches is worked in the same way as a puff stitch but each "leg" is worked where indicated.

Picots

A picot is normally a chain loop formed into a closed ring by a slip stitch or single crochet. The number of chains in a picot can vary. When working a picot closed with a slip stitch at the top of a chain arch, the picot will not appear central unless an extra chain is worked after the slip stitch.

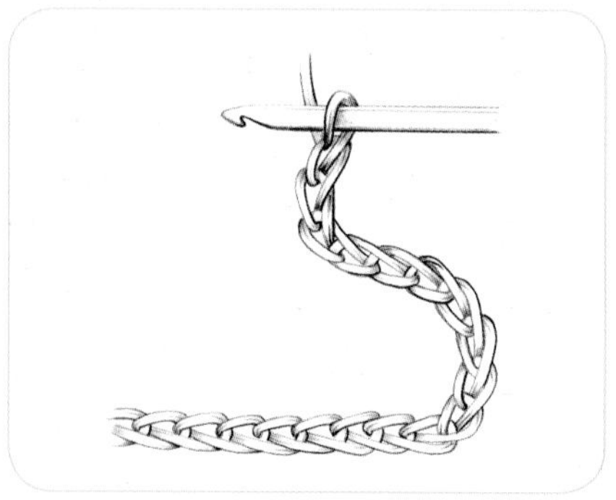

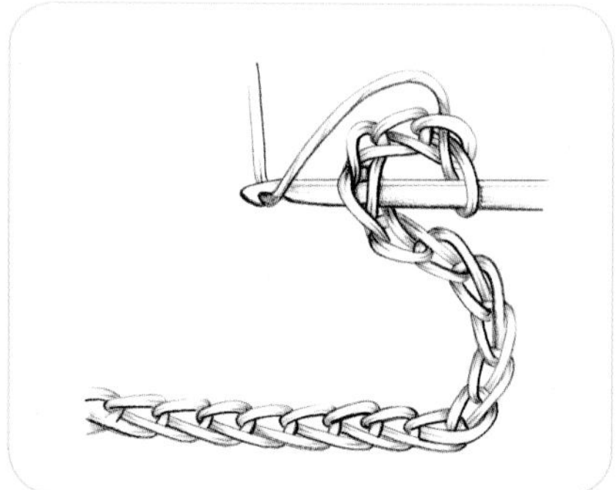

1 Work four chains.

2 Into fourth chain from hook work a slip stitch to close.

3 Continue working chains or required stitch.

Crossed stitches

This method produces stitches that are not entangled with each other and so maintain a clear "X" shape.

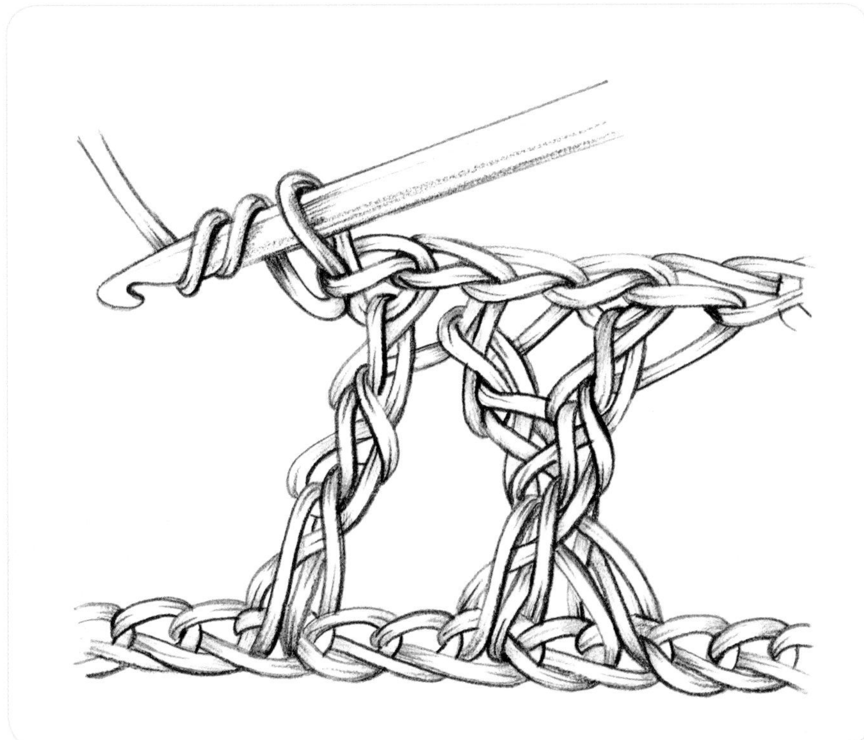

1 Skip two stitches and work the first treble into next stitch. Work one chain, then work second treble into first of skipped stitches, taking the hook behind the first treble before inserting. See individual pattern instructions for variations on crossed stitch.

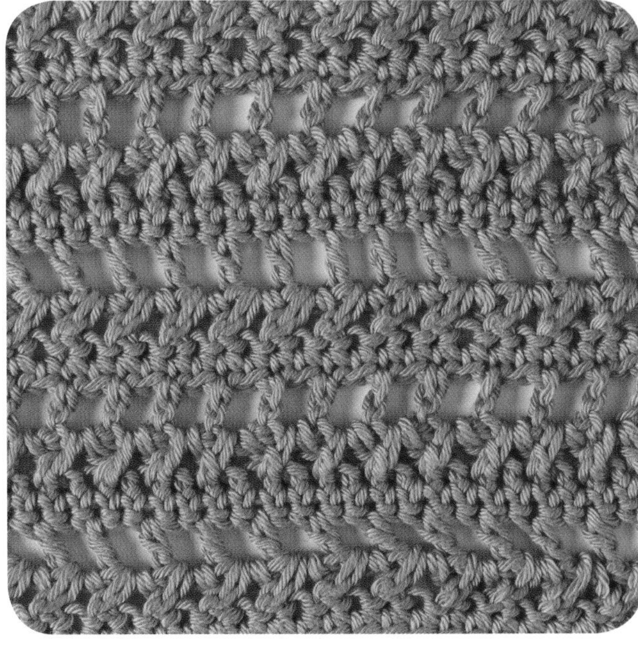

Irish crochet

Of all forms of crochet lace, Irish crochet is the most revered and sought after. This type of lace is comprised of separately crocheted motifs that are assembled into a mesh background.

True Irish crochet is made by first working motifs and then creating a net or mesh background incorporating the motifs and forming the fabric which holds them in position. This is done by placing the motifs in the required position, face down on paper or a scrap of fabric, and temporarily securing them. The background or filling, is then worked progressively, joining in the motifs. After the work is completed the paper or fabric is carefully removed.

Historically, crochet was believed to have been introduced into Ireland in the early part of the 19th century by nuns, probably from Italy or France. It was evolved by them and convent-educated girls into an art form in itself, reaching levels of complexity and delicacy not seen in other styles of crochet work.

Stitches and techniques were developed that are particular to Irish crochet. The use of padding threads, which are held at the edge of the work so that subsequent rows or rounds are worked over them to give a three-dimensional effect, is one example.

Because of the difficulty of giving general instructions for the construction of true Irish crochet and particularly since the various motifs can each be incorporated into almost any crocheted net background, we have simplified the following selection to give you a taste of Irish-style crochet.

Padding threads

Padding threads are used to give a three-dimensional appearance to some Irish crochet motifs. The thread used is usually the same as the thread used for the motif and the number of threads worked over determines the amount of padding. In this book we have usually worked over three thicknesses of thread.

The example below is for padding threads at the beginning of a motif, but they can also be used in other areas of motifs (see Tristar on page 159).

1 Make the required number of chains and join with a slip stitch.

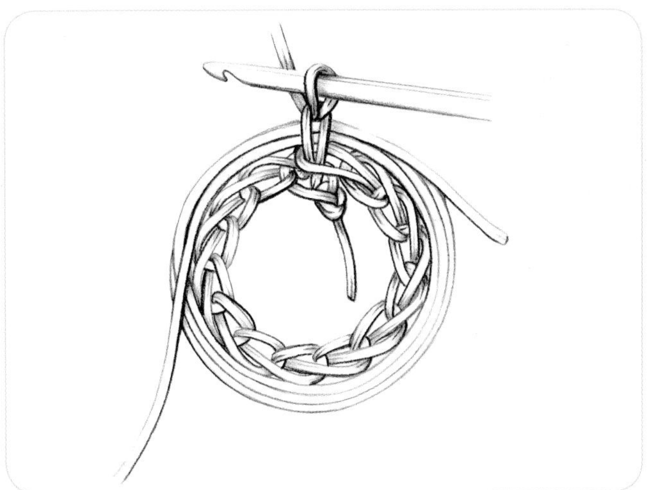

2 Wind a length of thread three or four times around the end of a pencil or finger and hold against the chain.

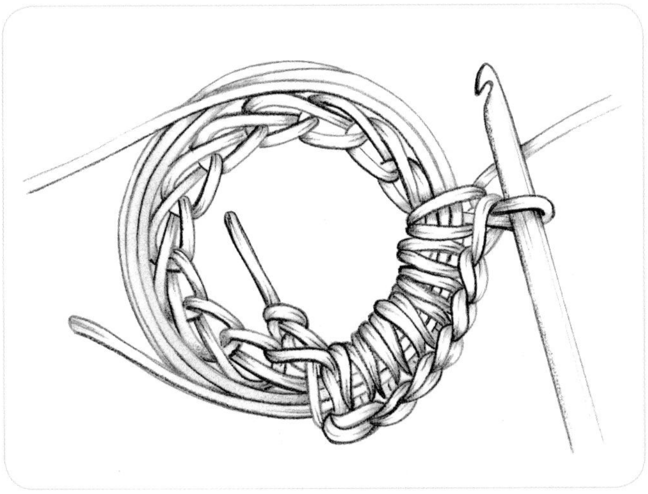

3 The stitches are then worked over the chain and "padding" threads. When the motif is complete, the ends of the padding thread are pulled through several stitches and cut. Instructions and diagrams of individual patterns indicate where it is appropriate to use padding threads. On the diagrams the padding thread is indicated with a thicker line.

Tip

Many of the circular motifs in the Motifs section (see page 128), like the Tristar shown here, can be used singly as doilies or stitched together to make larger items such as tablecloths, runners, placemats or throws. Make them in one single shade or experiment with color combinations to create the most striking effect. Take good care of your crochet masterpieces as they could turn out to be heirlooms of the future. If an item is likely to receive some wear and tear in daily use make sure you use a yarn that can be easily laundered.

Working from patterns

Most crochet pattern instructions are written out in words. In order to follow these, you must be able to understand the simple jargon, abbreviations and standard conventions. You are expected to know how to make the basic stitches and to be familiar with basic fabric-making procedures; anything more advanced or specialized is always spelled out in individual pattern instructions. Important terms and abbreviations with which you should be familiar are explained below.

Abbreviations

alt = alternate
approx = approximate(ly)
beg = begin(ning)
ch sp = chain space
ch(s) = chain(s)
CL = cluster
cm = centimetre(s)
cont = continue
dc = double crochet
dtr = double treble
gr = group
hdc = half double crochet
htr = half treble crochet
in = inch(es)
quad tr = quadruple treble
rem = remains/ing
rep = repeat
RS = right side
sc = single crochet
slip st = slip stitch
sp = space
st(s) = stitch(es)
tch = turning chain
tog = together
tr = treble
trtr = triple treble
WS = wrong side
yo = yarn over

Asterisks (*), square brackets [ ] and round brackets ()

These are used to simplify repetition. Instructions are put inside brackets and these are to be worked the number of times stated, for example: "[1ch, skip 1 ch, 1tr into next st] 5 times."

A sequence of stitches after an asterisk means that the whole sequence between that asterisk and the next semicolon is to be repeated as many times as necessary to reach the end of the row, for example:

"*1ch, skip 1 ch, 1tr into next st, 1ch, skip 1 ch, 1tr into each of next 3 sts; rep from * to end, turn."

If no further details are given, as in this case, the end of the sequence will coincide exactly with the end of the row. If there are stitches remaining unworked after the last complete repeat sequence, details of how to complete the row are given, for example: "Rep from * to last 4 sts, ending 1ch, skip 1ch, 1tr into each of last 3 sts, turn." "Rep from * 4 more times," means work that sequence 5 times in all.

Round brackets either enclose additional information, for example:

"3ch (counts as 1tr), skip first dc"

or group together a sequence of stitches that are to be worked into the same location, for example:

"3ch, in next 4ch-sp (1tr, 2ch, 1tr), 3ch"

Base (foundation) chain

The length of chain made at the beginning of a piece of crochet as a basis for constructing the fabric.

Charts

Filet crochet patterns, which are based on a regular grid of double crochet and chain stitches, are much easier to follow from a squared chart when you understand the basic procedures. This type of chart is also used to indicate different colors in Jacquard and Fair Isle patterns, which are usually based on a plain single crochet fabric.

Color

Capital letters A, B, C, D, etc are used to indicate different yarn colors; when only two colors are involved and one of these is intended to dominate, the terms "main (M)" and "contrast (C)" may be used instead.

Front/back

"Front" and "back" mean the front and back surfaces of a fabric for the time being as you hold and look at it; these change over every time you turn the work.

Note: In garment pattern instructions, the terms "front" and "back" denote the different pieces of the garment.

Group

Several stitches worked into the same place; sometimes called "shell", "fan" etc.

Multiple

All but the simplest crochet stitch patterns are built around repeated sequences of stitches. In order to make sense of the instructions, you must have exactly the right number of stitches in your base row. This number is a multiple of the number of stitches required for one complete sequence—sometimes plus an extra edge stitch or two—and is given at the beginning of each set of instructions.

The number of chains you need for the base chain, in order to be able to create the appropriate number of stitches in the base row, is also given. For example, "Multiple of 2 sts + 1, (add 1 for base chain)' = make 4, 6, 8, etc chains for a base row of 3, 5, 7, etc, stitches" or "Multiple of 8 sts + 3, (add 2 for base chain)' = make 13, 21, 29, etc, chains for a base row of 11, 19, 27, etc, stitches."

Picot

A run of chain stitches normally brought back on itself and fixed into a decorative loop with a slip stitch or double crochet.

Note: Terms such as "group", "cluster", "picot" and even "shell ", "fan", "flower", "petal", "leaf", "bobble", etc, do not denote a fixed arrangement of stitches. Exactly what they mean may be different for each pattern. The procedure is therefore always spelled out at the beginning of each set of instructions and is valid only for that set, unless stated otherwise.

Right/wrong side (RS/WS)

The "right side" is the surface of the fabric intended to be the outside of the finished article and therefore shown in the photographs; the "wrong side" is the inside. If there is a difference, the instructions state which side is facing you as you work the first row and that surface of the fabric is identified and fixed from then on.
Hint: crochet stitches are not the same back and front and so the two sides of a fabric may well be quite different. Even when a stitch pattern has no particular "right side", however, it is wise to make a positive decision in respect of all separate pieces of the same article, so that the "grain" of the rows can be matched exactly when you join the pieces together.

Stitch diagrams

Accurate stitch diagrams show the overall picture at a glance and at the same time indicate precisely every detail of construction. To follow them you need to be familiar with the symbols that represent each individual stitch. Stitch diagrams have been provided for most stitches, depending on the level of complexity.

Turning/starting chain

One or more chains, depending upon the length of stitch required, worked at the beginning of a row (or end of the previous row) as preparation for the new row; sometimes counts as the first stitch in the new row. This is called "starting chain" when working "in the round".

Work even

Work over an existing row of stitches without "increasing" (i.e. adding stitches and so making the fabric wider), or "decreasing" (i.e. reducing the number of stitches and so making the fabric narrower).
Precise methods of increasing and decreasing vary according to each stitch pattern and circumstances and are detailed in pattern instructions.

Yarn over

The stitch-making instruction to wrap the yarn from the ball over the hook (or manipulate the hook around the yarn) in order to make a new loop; always done in a counterclockwise direction, unless otherwise stated.

Stitch diagrams

Stitch diagrams are detailed "maps" of the fabric as viewed from the right side. They enable you to see what you are going to do before you start and also where you are at any moment.

Chain

Slip stitch

Single crochet

Half-double crochet

Double crochet

Treble

Double treble

Triple treble

Quadruple treble

Quintuple treble

Bullion stitch

Lace loop

Solomon's knot

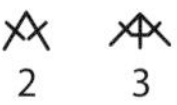

Single crochet cluster

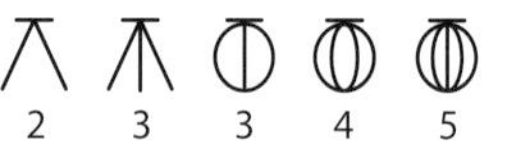

Half-double crochet cluster

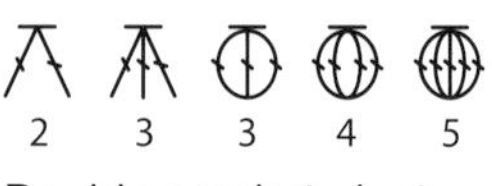

Double crochet cluster

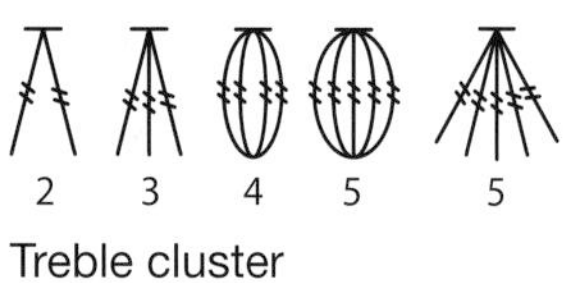

Treble cluster

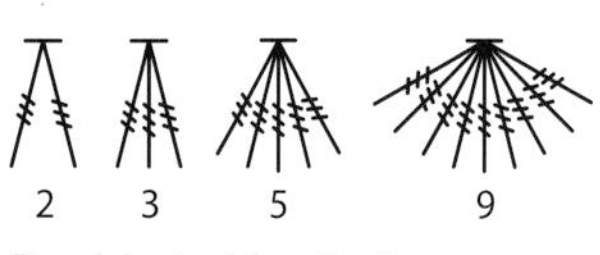

Double treble cluster

Marguerites

The individual parts of the marguerite clusters have barbs.

Popcorns: Half-double crochet

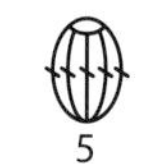

Popcorns: Double crochet

Popcorns: Treble

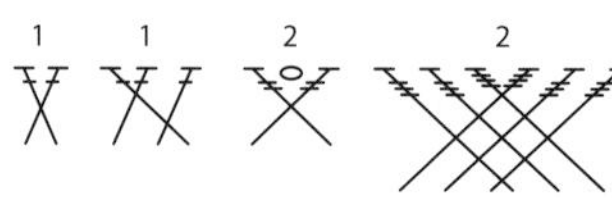

Crossed stitches

X-shape

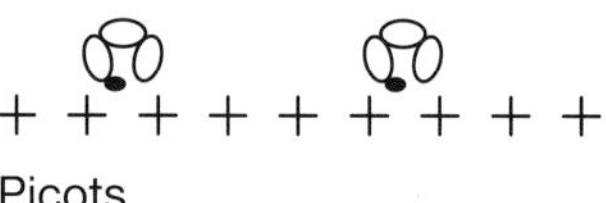

Picots

When a single picot loop occurs after a solid stitch, note the usual method of working the closing slip stitch.

Commence

Rejoin yarn

Bind off

Direction of row

2, 3 and 4 half-double crochet group

Work 2 (3, 4) half-double crochets into same place.

2, 3, 4 and 5 double crochet group

Work 2 (3, 4, 5) double crochets into same place.

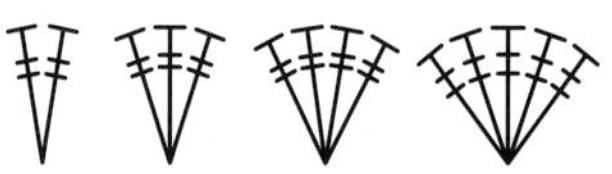

2, 3, 4 and 5 treble group

Work 2 (3, 4, 5) trebles into same place.

  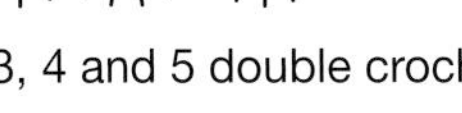

3, 4 and 5 double crochet cluster
Work a double crochet into each of the next 3 (4, 5) stitches leaving the last loop of each on the hook. Yarn over and draw through all loops on hook. On diagrams each "leg" of the cluster will be positioned above the stitch where the hook is to be inserted.

3, 4 and 5 treble cluster
Work a treble into each of the next 3 (4, 5) stitches, leaving the last loop of each on the hook. Yarn over and draw through all loops on hook.

3, 4 and 5 double crochet bobble
Follow instructions as if working a cluster but for each "leg" insert the hook into the same stitch or space. For a 5 double crochet bobble, work five double crochets into one stitch leaving the last loop of each on the hook. Yarn over and draw through all the loops on the hook. More bulky bobbles can be secured with an extra chain stitch. If this is necessary it would be indicated within the pattern.

 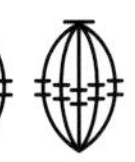  

4, 5, 6 and 7 treble bobble
Follow instructions as if working a cluster but for each "leg" insert the hook into the same stitch or space.

3 and 4 half-double crochet popcorn
Work 3 (4) half-double crochets into the same place, drop loop off hook, insert hook into first half-double crochet, pick up dropped loop and draw through.

3, 4 and 5 double crochet popcorn
Work 3 (4, 5) double crochets into the same place, drop loop off hook, insert hook into first double crochet, pick up dropped loop and draw through.

3, 4 and 5 treble popcorn
Work 3 (4, 5) trebles into the same place, drop loop off hook, insert hook into first treble, pick up dropped loop and draw through.

3 half-double crochet puff stitch
Work 3 half-double crochets into same stitch, leaving the last 2 loops of each on the hook. Yarn over and draw through all loops on hook. If required, work one chain to secure the puff stitch.

Crossed treble
Skip two stitches and work the first treble into next stitch. Work one chain, then work second treble into first of skipped stitches taking the hook behind the first treble before inserting. See individual pattern instructions for variations on crossed stitch.

4-chain picot
(Closed with a slip stitch.) Work four chains. Into fourth chain from hook work a slip stitch to close. Continue working chain or required stitch.

Chart distortions

For the sake of clarity, stitch symbols are drawn and laid out realistically, but are then distorted. Sometimes, for example, single crochet stitches may look extra long. This is only to show clearly where they go; you should not make artificially long stitches. When the diagram represents a fabric that is not intended to lie flat—for instance, a gathered or frilled edging—since the drawing itself has to remain flat, the stitch symbols have to be stretched.

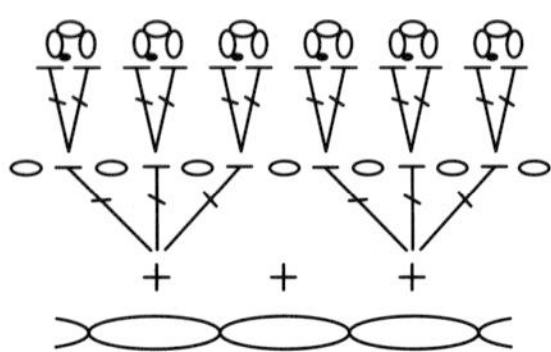

Symbols that accompany stitch symbols

Back/front loop

Stitches that are to be made by inserting the hook under only one of the top two loops are indicated by heavyweight and lightweight stitch symbols with underlining. A lightweight symbol in conjunction with an underline means pick up the loop nearest the right side of the fabric, i.e. front loop on right-side rows, but back loop on wrong-side rows. A heavyweight symbol with an underline means pick up the loop nearest the wrong side, i.e. back loop on right-side rows, but front loop on wrong-side rows.

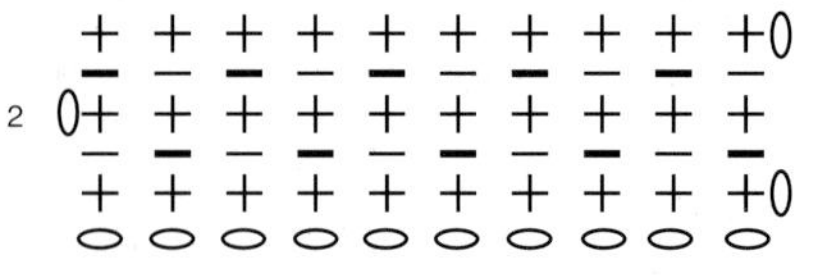

Back and front loop single crochet

Back bar symbol

On the reverse of half-double crochet stitches is a prominent horizontal thread or bar just below the top loops. A tilted lightweight symbol is used to represent this back bar. If stitches are worked into this bar rather than the top loops, both top loops of the stitch appear on the reverse of the side being worked.

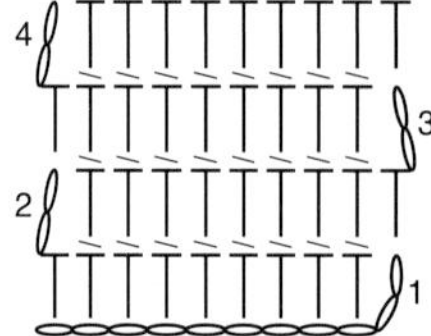

Raised (relief) stitches

When a stitch is to be worked by inserting the hook behind a stem (instead of under the top two loops), the stitch symbol ends in a "crook" around the appropriate stem. The direction of the crook indicates into which side of the fabric the hook is to be inserted. On a RS row, work a raised stitch with a right crook at the front, and one with a left crook at the back.

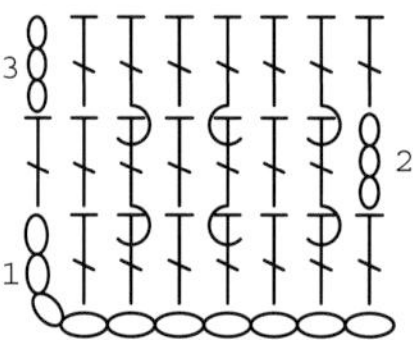

Spikes

The stitch symbol is extended downward to show where the hook is to go through the fabric.

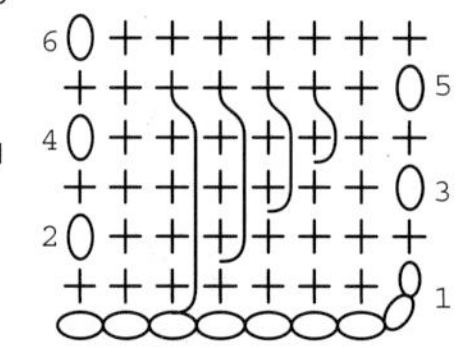

Other elements that appear on charts

Arrows

Once you are familiar with the basic fabric-making procedures, it is usually clear where a stitch pattern diagram begins and ends, which direction a row goes, etc. (Hint: Look for the turning chain). If there is any doubt, additional directions are given with the help of various arrows.

Color

Letters A, B, etc, and also light and heavy stitch symbols confirm changes of color.

Figures

Figures indicate row (or round) numbers.

Foundation rows

These are unlabeled rows that should be worked if an edging is not going to be worked directly along another edge.

Motifs

When the base ring of a motif is drawn as a plain circle, make it by looping the yarn around a finger.

Paler stitches or arrows

These indicate stitches that are worked with the darker stitches or arrows in front.

Basic single crochet

Any number of sts (add 1 for base chain).

Row 1: Skip 1 ch, 1sc into next and each ch to end, turn.

Row 2: Ch1, 1sc into 1st and each st to end, turn.

Rep row 2.

Basic half double crochet

Any number of sts (add 1 for base chain).

Row 1: Skip 2 ch (count as 1hdc), 1hdc into next and each ch to end, turn.

Row 2: Ch2 (count as 1hdc), skip 1 st, 1hdc into next and each st to end working last st into top of tch, turn.

Rep row 2.

Basic double crochet

Any number of sts (add 2 for base chain).

Row 1: Skip 3 ch (count as 1dc), 1dc into next and each ch to end, turn.

Row 2: Ch3 (count as 1dc), skip 1 st, 1dc into next and each st to end working last st into top of tch, turn.

Rep row 2.

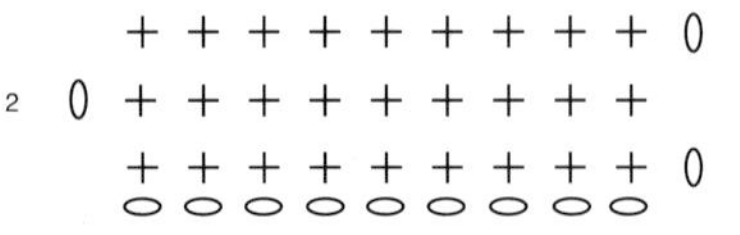

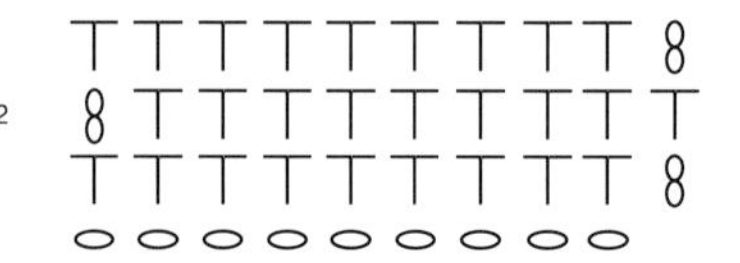

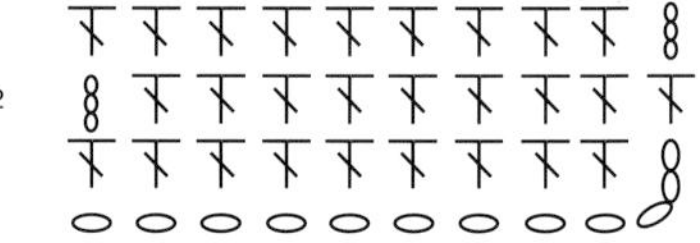

Tip

If you are new to crochet you will find it a relatively beginner-friendly craft. As there is generally only one stitch on the hook, mistakes can easily be unraveled and the stitch worked again.

Basic trebles

Any number of sts (add 3 for base chain).
Row 1: Skip 4 ch (count as 1tr), 1tr into next and each ch to end, turn.
Row 2: Ch4 (count as 1tr), skip 1 st, 1tr into next and each st to end, working last st into top of tch, turn.
Rep row 2.

Back loop single crochet

Work as basic single crochet (see left), but from row 2 insert hook into back loop only of each st.

Mixed cluster stitch

Multiple of 2 sts + 1 (add 1 for base chain).
Special abbreviation:
MC (Mixed Cluster) = yo, insert hook into 1st st as indicated, yo, draw loop through, yo, draw through 2 loops, skip 1 st, [yo, insert hook into next st, yo, draw loop through] twice all into same st, (6 loops on hook), yo, draw through all loops on hook.
Row 1 (WS): Skip 2 ch (count as 1sc), 1sc into next and each ch to end, turn.
Row 2: Ch2 (count as 1hdc), 1MC inserting hook into 1st then 3rd st, *ch1, 1MC inserting hook 1st into same st as previous MC; rep from * ending last rep in top of tch, 1hdc into same place, turn.
Row 3: Ch1, skip 1 st, 1sc into next and each st to end, working last st into top of tch, turn.
Rep rows 2–3.

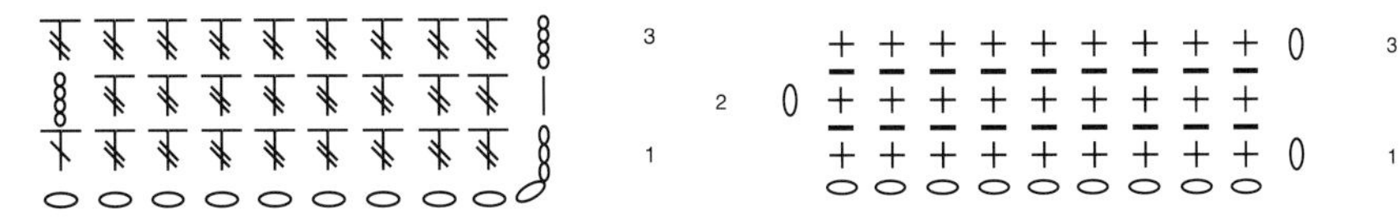

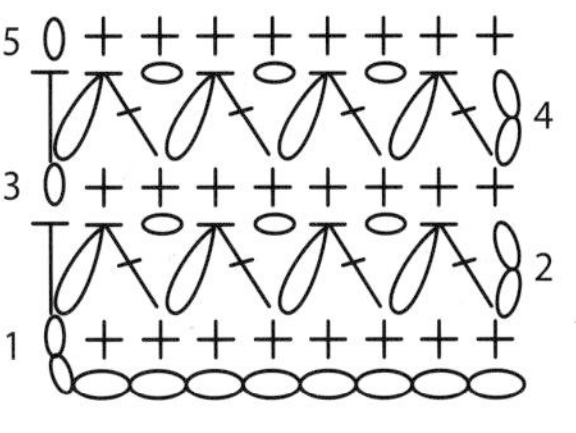

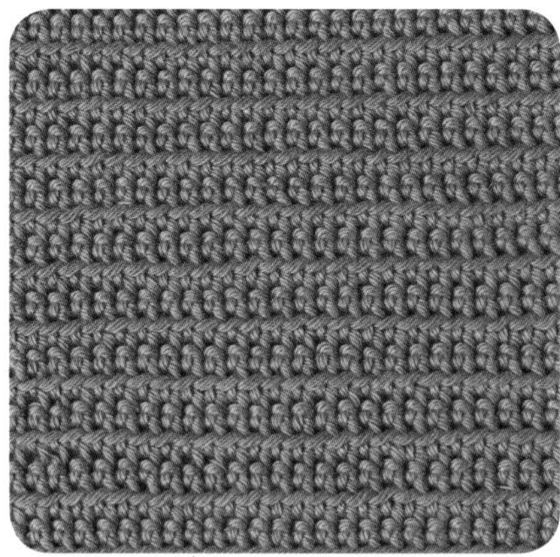

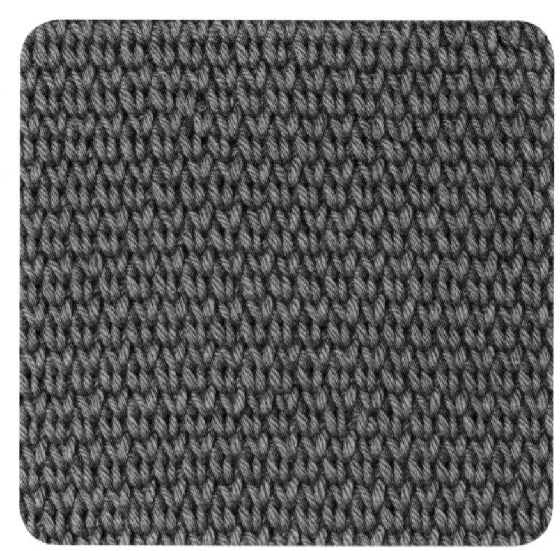

Front loop single crochet

Work as basic single crochet (see page 34), but from row 2 insert hook into front loop only of each st.

Back and front loop single crochet

Multiple of 2 sts (add 1 for base chain).

Row 1: Skip 1 ch, 1sc into next and each ch to end, turn.

Row 2: Ch1, 1sc into back loop only of 1st st, 1sc into front loop only of next st, *1sc into back loop only of next st, 1sc into front loop only of next st; rep from * to end, turn.

Rep row 2.

Shallow single crochet

Work as basic single crochet (see page 34), but from row 2 insert hook low into body of each st, below 3 horizontal loops, and between 2 vertical threads.

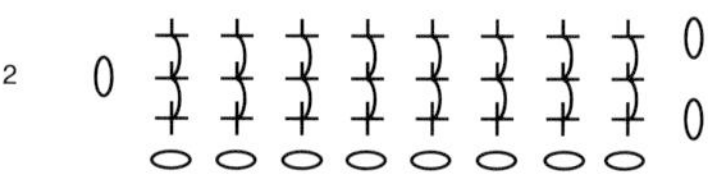

Tip

To make a decorative edging you can work your foundation row into the yarn "bumps" at the reverse of the foundation chain. This can be a little tricky, but creates a nice edge where the foundation chain is clearly visible on the right side.

Back loop half double crochet

Work as basic half double crochet (see page 34), but from row 2 insert hook into back loop only of each st.

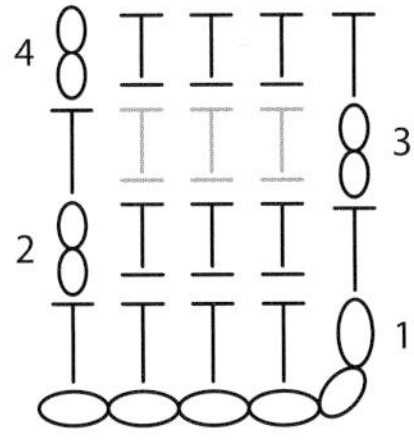

Back and front loop half double crochet

Multiple of 2 sts (add 1 for base chain).

Row 1: Skip 2 ch(count as 1hdc), 1hdc into next and each ch to end, turn.

Row 2: Ch2 (count as 1hdc), skip 1 st, *1hdc into back loop only of next st, 1hdc into front loop only of next st; rep from * ending 1hdc into top of tch, turn.

Rep row 2.

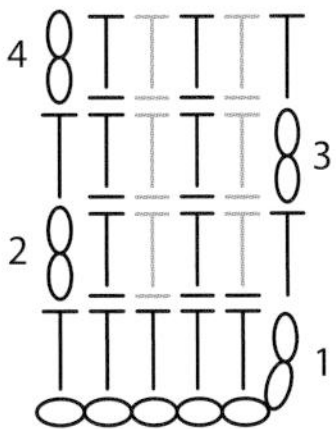

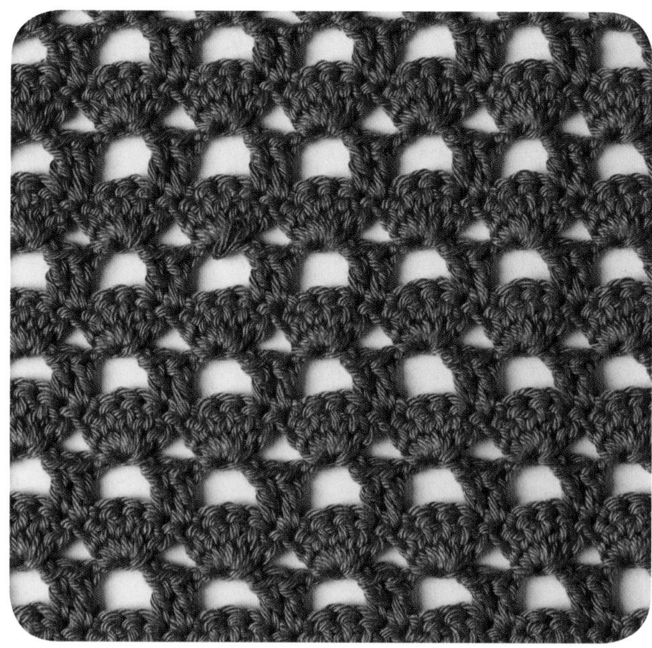

Simple marguerite stitch

Multiple of 2 sts + 1 (add 2 for base chain).

Special abbreviation:

M3C (Marguerite cluster with 3 spike loops) = see text below.

Row 1: Make a spike loop (i.e. yo and draw through) into 2nd, 3rd, and 5th chs from hook, yo and through all 4 loops (1M3C made), *ch1, make 1M3C picking up 1 loop in ch that closed previous M3C, 2nd loop in same place as last spike of previous M3C, skip 1 ch, then last loop in next ch, yo and through all 4 loops; rep from * to end, turn.

Row 2: Ch3, make 1M3C picking up loops in 2nd and 3rd ch from hook and in ch that closed 2nd M3C on previous row, *ch1, work 1M3C picking up 1st loop in ch that closed previous M3C, 2nd loop in same place as last spike of previous M3C and last loop in ch that closed next M3C on previous row; rep from * to end, picking up final loop in top of ch at beg of previous row.

Rep row 2.

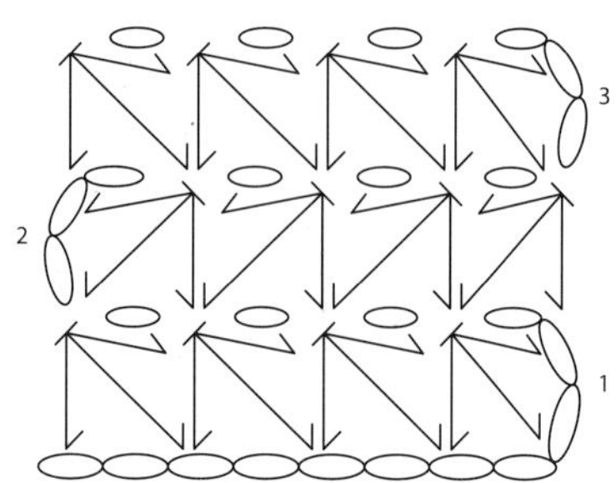

Boxed shell stitch

Multiple of 5 sts + 2 (add 2 for base chain).

Row 1 (RS): Skip 3 ch (count as 1dc), 1dc into next ch, *ch3, skip 3 ch, 1dc into each of next 2 ch; rep from * to end, turn.

Row 2: Ch3 (count as 1dc), skip 1st st, *5dc into 2nd ch of next ch-3 arch; rep from *, ending 1dc into top of tch, turn.

Row 3: Ch3 (count as 1dc), skip 1st st, 1dc into next dc, *ch3, skip 3 dc, 1dc into each of next 2 dc; rep from * to end, turn.

Rep rows 2–3.

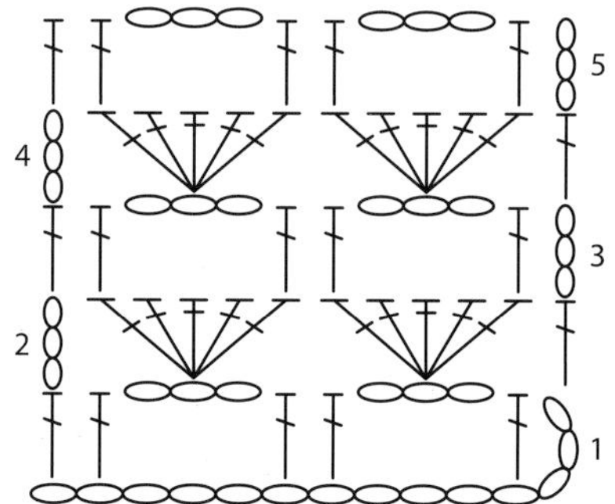

Multi-colored parquet stitch

Multiple of 3 sts + 1 (add 1 for base chain).

Work 1 row each in colors A, B and C alternately throughout.

Row 1 (RS): 1sc into 2nd ch from hook, *ch3, 1dc into same place as previous sc, skip 2 ch, 1sc into next ch; rep from * to end, turn.

Row 2: Ch3 (count as 1dc), 1dc into 1st st, 1sc into next ch-3 arch, *ch3, 1dc into same ch-3 arch, 1sc into next ch-3 arch; rep from * ending ch2, 1dc into last sc, skip tch, turn.

Row 3: Ch1, 1sc into 1st st, ch3, 1dc into next ch-2 sp, *work [1sc, ch3, 1dc] into next ch-3 arch; rep from * ending 1sc into top of tch, turn.

Rep rows 2–3.

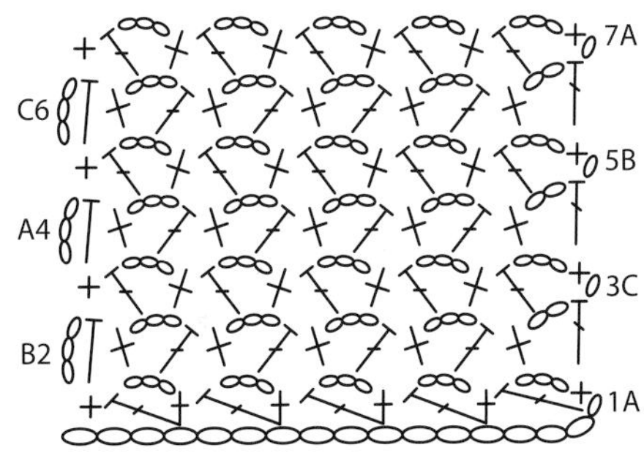

Linked half trebles

Any number of sts (add 1 for base chain).

Special abbreviation:

Lhdc (Linked half double crochet) = insert hook into single vertical thread at left-hand side of previous st, yo, draw loop through, insert hook normally into next st, yo, draw loop through st, yo, draw through all 3 loops on hook.

Note: To make 1st Lhdc at beg of row, treat 2nd ch from hook as a single vertical thread.

Row 1: 1Lhdc into 3rd ch from hook (picking up loop through 2nd ch from hook), 1Lhdc into next and each ch to end, turn.

Row 2: Ch2 (count as 1hdc), skip 1 st, 1Lhdc into next and each st to end, working last st into top of tch, turn.

Rep row 2.

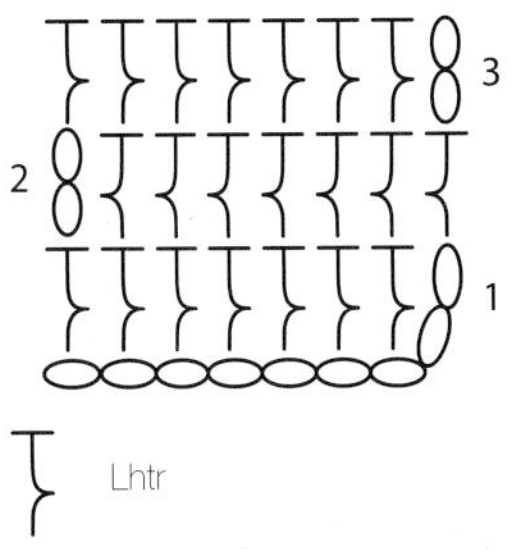

Wide double crochet

Work as basic double crochet (see page 34), but after row 1 insert hook between stems and below all horizontal threads connecting sts.

Note: Base chain should be worked loosely to accommodate extra width.

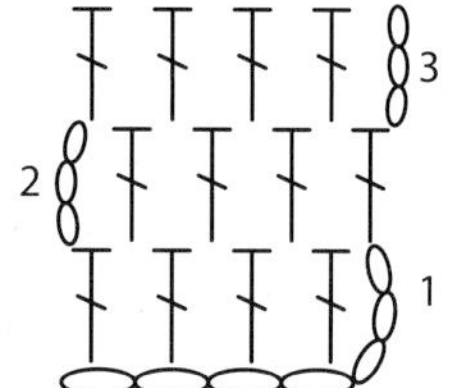

Herringbone half double crochet

Any number of sts (add 1 for base chain).

Special abbreviation:

HBhdc (Herringbone half double crochet) = yo, insert hook, yo, draw through st and 1st loop on hook, yo, draw through both loops on hook.

Row 1: Skip 2 ch (count as 1hdc), 1HBhdc into next and each ch to end, turn.

Row 2: Ch2 (count as 1hdc), skip 1 st, 1HBhdc into next and each st to end working last st into top of tch, turn.

Rep row 2.

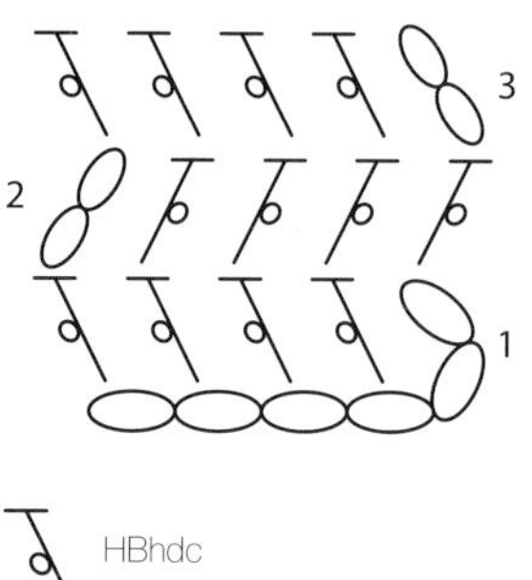

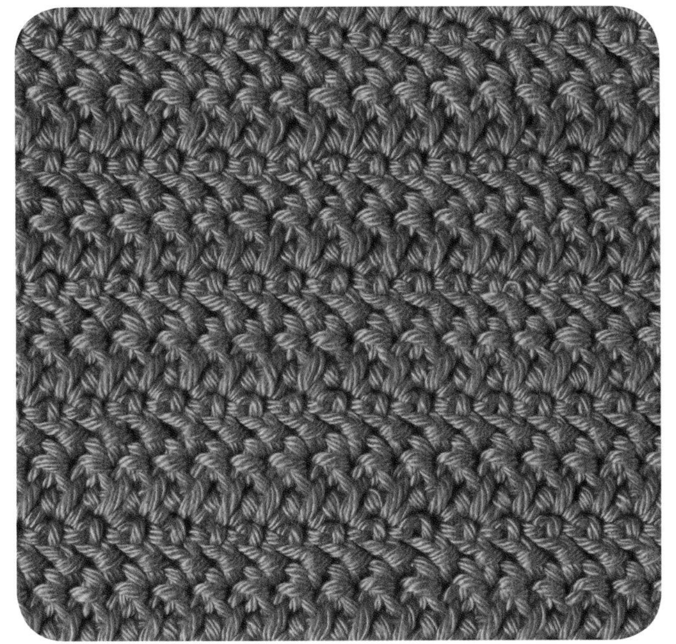

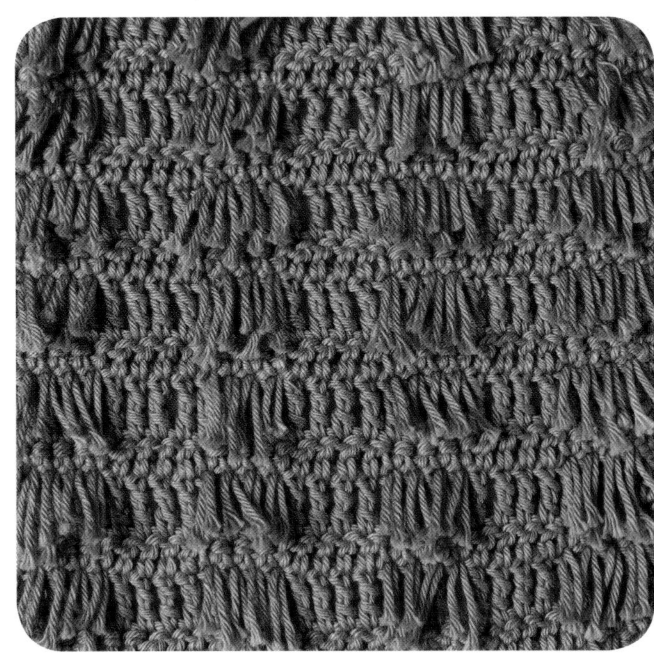

Herringbone double crochets

Any number of sts (add 2 for base chain).

Special abbreviation:

HBdc (Herringbone double crochet) = yo, insert hook, yo, draw through st and 1st loop on hook, yo, draw through 1 loop, yo, draw through both loops on hook.

Row 1: Skip 3 ch (count as 1dc), 1HBdc into next and each ch to end, turn.

Row 2: Ch3 (count as 1dc), skip 1 st, 1HBdc into next and each st to end, working last st into top of tch, turn.

Rep row 2.

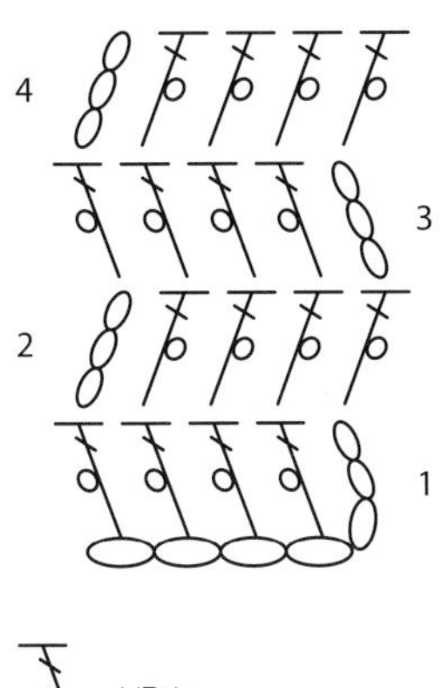

Loop or fur stitch

Multiple of 8 sts (add 2 for base chain).

Note: For plain loop stitch do not cut loops.

Special abbreviation:

Loop stitch = using the left-hand finger to control the loop size, insert the hook, pick up both threads of the loop, and draw these through; wrap the supply of yarn over the hook and draw through all the loops on the hook to complete.

Row 1 (RS): Skip 3 ch (count as 1dc), 1dc into next and each ch to end, turn.

Row 2: Ch1, 1sc into each of 1st 2 sts, *1 Loop st into each of next 4 sts**, 1sc into each of next 4 sts; rep from * ending last rep at **, 1sc into each of last 2 sts including top of tch, turn.

Row 3: Ch3 (count as 1dc), skip 1 st, 1dc into next and each st to end, skip tch, turn.

Rep rows 2–3.

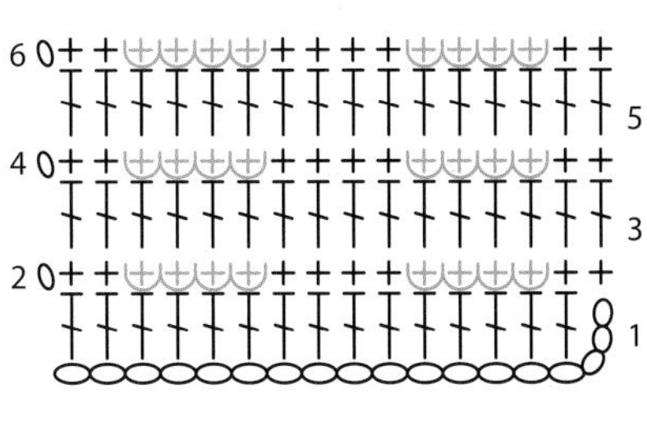

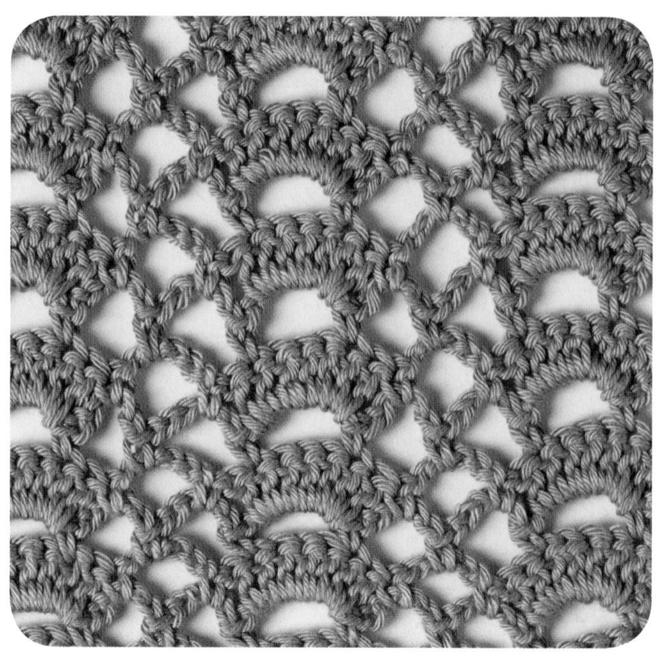

Ridged chevron stitch

Multiple of 12 sts (add 3 for base chain).

Row 1: Skip 3 ch (count as 1dc), 1dc into next ch, *1dc into each of next 3 ch, [over next 2 ch work dc2tog] twice, 1dc into each of next 3 ch, [2dc into next ch] twice; rep from * ending last rep with 2dc once only into last ch, turn.

Row 2: Ch3 (count as 1dc), 1dc into 1st st, always inserting hook into back loop only of each st *1dc into each of next 3 sts, [over next 2 sts work dc2tog] twice, 1dc into each of next 3 sts, [2dc into next st] twice; rep from * ending last rep with 2dc once only into top of tch, turn.

Rep row 2.

Fan trellis stitch

Multiple of 12 sts + 11 (add 1 for base chain).

Row 1 (WS): 1sc into 2nd ch from hook, *ch5, skip 3 ch, 1sc into next ch; rep from * to last 2 ch, ch2, skip 1 ch, 1dc into last ch, turn.

Row 2: Ch1, 1sc into 1st st, skip ch-2 sp, *7dc into next ch-5 arch, 1sc into next arch**, ch5, 1sc into next arch; rep from * ending last rep at **, ch2, 1tr into last dc, skip tch, turn.

Row 3: Ch1, 1sc into 1st st, *ch5, 1sc into 2nd of next 7 dc, ch5, 1sc into 6th dc of same group**, ch5, 1sc into next ch-5 arch; rep from * ending last rep at **, ch2, 1tr into last sc, skip tch, turn.

Rep rows 2–3.

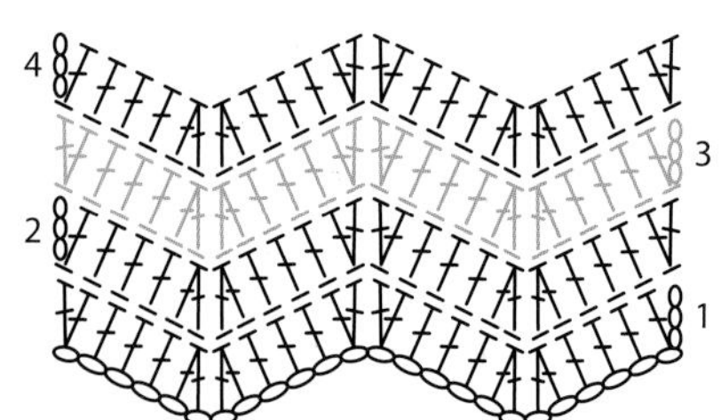

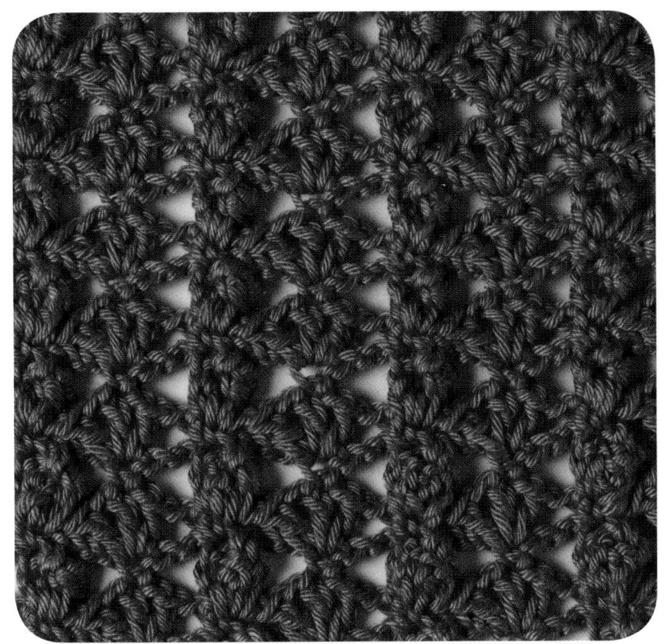

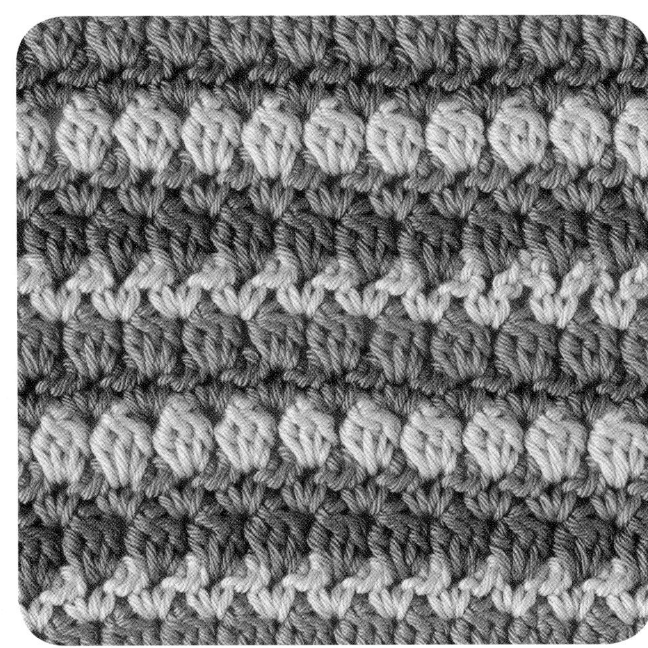

Global connection

Multiple of 8 sts + 2.

Special abbreviation:

Popcorn = work 4dc into next st, drop loop from hook, insert hook from the front into top of 1st of these dc, pick up dropped loop and draw through dc, ch1 to secure popcorn.

Row 1 (RS): Work 1sc into 2nd ch from hook, *ch1, skip 3 ch, 1dc into next ch, ch1, into same ch as last dc work [1dc, ch1, 1dc], ch1, skip 3 ch, 1sc into next ch; rep from * to end, turn.

Row 2: Ch6 (count as 1dc, ch3), skip 1 dc, 1sc into next dc, *ch3, 1 popcorn into next sc, ch3, skip 1 dc, 1sc into next dc; rep from * to last sc, ch3, 1dc into last sc, turn.

Row 3: Ch1, 1sc into 1st dc, *ch1, 1dc into next sc, ch1, into same st as last dc work [1dc, ch1, 1dc], ch1, 1sc into top of next popcorn; rep from * to end, placing last sc into 3rd of ch-6 at beg of previous row, turn.

Rep rows 2–3.

3
2
1

Popcorn

Zigzag lozenge stitch

Multiple of 2 sts + 1 (add 2 for base chain).

Work 1 row each in colors A, B and C alternately throughout.

Row 1 (WS): Skip 2 ch (count as 1hdc), 1hdc into next ch, *skip 1 ch, [1hdc, ch1, 1hdc] into next ch; rep from * to last 2 ch, skip 1 ch, 2hdc into last ch, turn.

Row 2: Ch3, 1dc into 1st st (count as dc2tog), *ch1, work dc3tog into next ch sp; rep from * to last sp, ending ch1, dc2tog into top of tch, turn.

Row 3: Ch2 (count as 1hdc), skip 1st st, *work [1hdc, ch1, 1hdc] into next ch sp; rep from * ending 1hdc into top of tch, turn.

Row 4: Ch3 (count as 1dc), skip 1st st, *work dc3tog into next sp, ch1; rep from * to last sp, work dc3tog into last sp, 1dc into top of tch, turn.

Row 5: Ch2 (count as 1hdc), 1hdc into 1st st, *work [1hdc, ch1, 1hdc] into next ch sp; rep from * ending 2hdc into top of tch, turn.

Rep rows 2–5.

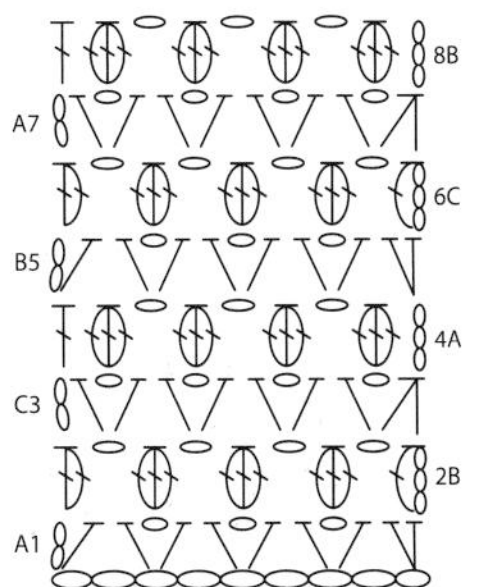

Alternative double crochets

Any number of sts (add 2 for base chain).

Special abbreviation:

Alt dc (Alternative double crochet) = yo, insert hook, yo, draw loop through, yo, draw through 1 loop only, yo, draw through all 3 loops on hook.

Row 1: Skip 3 ch (count as 1dc), 1 Alt dc into next and each ch to end, turn.

Row 2: Ch3 (count as 1dc), skip 1 st, work 1 Alt dc into next and each st to end, working last st into top of tch, turn.

Rep row 2.

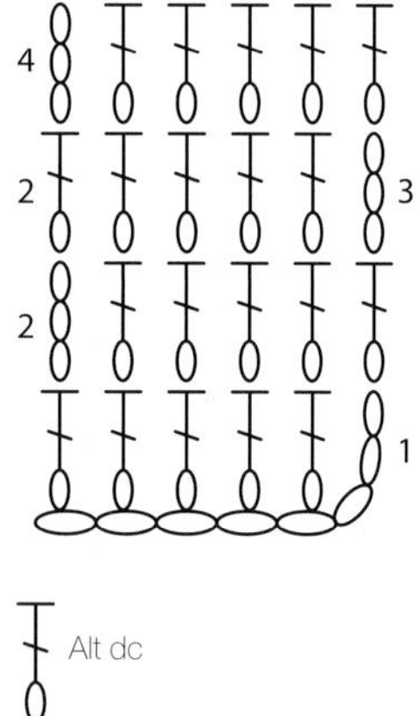

Linked trebles

Any number of sts (add 3 for base chain).

Special abbreviation:

Ltr (Linked trebles) = insert hook down through upper of 2 horizontal loops around stem of last st made, yo, draw loop through, insert hook down through lower horizontal loop of same st, yo, draw loop through, insert hook normally into next st, yo, draw loop through st, (4 loops on hook), [yo, draw through 2 loops] 3 times.

Note: To make 1st Ltr (at beg of row), treat 2nd and 4th chs from hook as upper and lower horizontal loops.

Row 1: 1Ltr into 5th ch from hook (picking up loops through 2nd and 4th chs from hook), 1Ltr into next and each ch to end, turn.

Row 2: Ch4 (count as Ltr), skip 1 st, 1Ltr into next and each st to end, working last st into top of tch, turn.

Rep row 2.

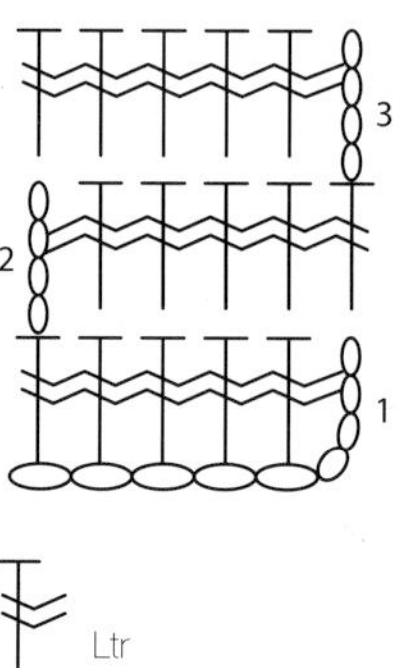

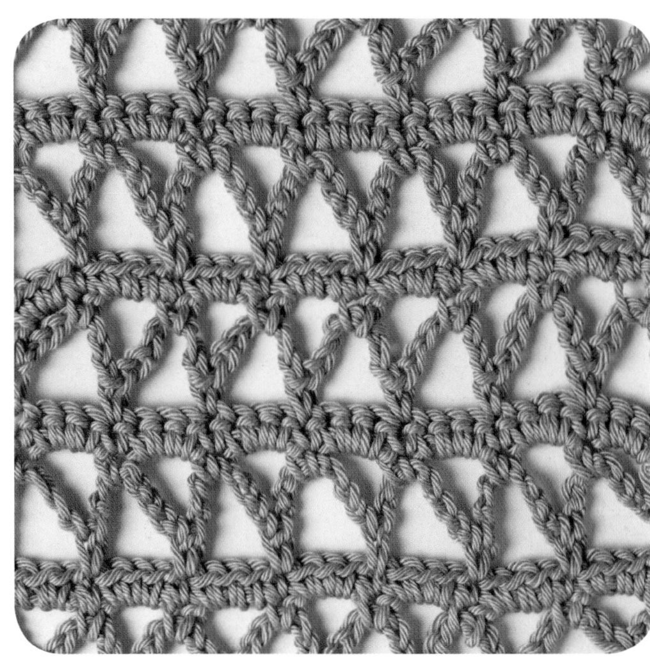

Sedge stitch

Multiple of 3 sts + 1 (add 2 for base chain).

Row 1: Skip 2 ch (count as 1sc), work [1hdc, 1dc] into next ch, *skip 2 ch, work [1sc, 1hdc, 1dc] into next ch; rep from * to last 3 ch, skip 2 ch, 1sc into last ch, turn.

Row 2: Ch1 (count as 1sc), work [1hdc, 1dc] into 1st st, *skip [1dc and 1hdc], work [1sc, 1hdc, 1dc] into next sc; rep from * to last 3 sts, skip [1dc and 1hdc], 1sc into top of tch, turn.

Rep row 2.

Ruled lattice

Multiple of 4 sts + 1 (add 1 for base chain).

Row 1 (RS): 1sc into 2nd ch from hook, 1sc into each ch to end, turn.

Row 2: Ch7, skip 1st 2 sts, 1sc into next st, *ch7, skip 3 sts, 1sc into next st; rep from * to last 2 sts, ch3, skip 1 st, 1dc into last st, skip tch, turn.

Row 3: Ch1, 1sc into 1st st, *ch3, 1sc into next ch-7 arch; rep from * to end, turn.

Row 4: Ch1, 1sc into 1st st, *3sc into next ch-3 arch, 1sc into next sc; rep from * to end, skip tch, turn.

Rep rows 2–4.

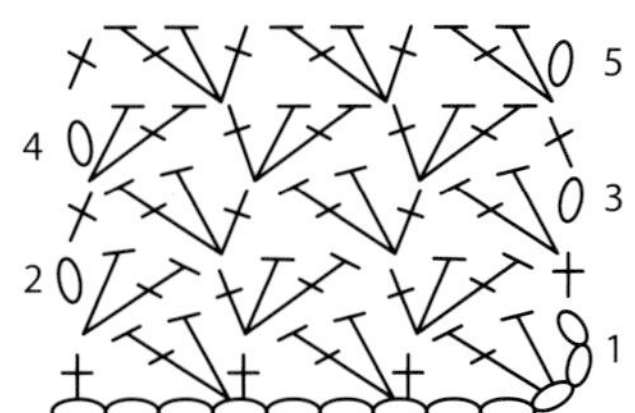

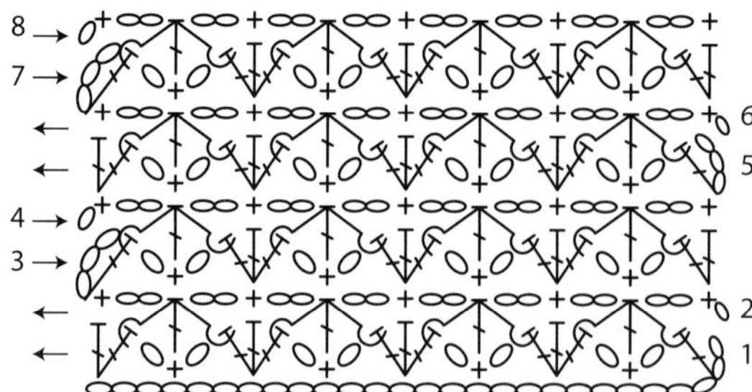

Fleur de lys stitch

Multiple of 6 sts + 1 (add 2 for base chain).

Special abbreviations:

FC/rf (Fleur Cluster raised at front) = leaving last loop of each st on hook work 1dc/rf around next dc, skip 1 ch, 1dc into top of next sc, skip 1 ch, 1dc/rf around next dc (4 loops on hook), yo, draw through all loops.

FC/rb (Fleur Cluster raised at back) = as for FC/rf except insert hook at back for 1st and 3rd legs.

Work 1 row each in colors A and B alternately throughout. Do not break yarn when changing color, but fasten off temporarily and begin row at same end as new color.

Row 1 (RS in A): Skip 2 ch (count as 1dc), 1dc into next ch, *ch1, skip 2 ch, 1sc into next ch, ch1, skip 2 ch**, 3dc into next ch; rep from * ending last rep at **, 2dc into last ch. Do not turn.

Row 2 (RS in B): Join new yarn into top of tch, ch1, 1sc into same place, *ch2, FC/rb, ch2, 1sc into next dc; rep from * to end, turn.

Row 3 (WS in A): Ch3 (count as 1dc), 1dc into 1st st, *ch1, skip 2 ch, 1sc into next cluster, ch1, skip 2 ch**, 3dc into next sc; rep from * ending last rep at **, 2dc into last sc. Do not turn.

Row 4 (WS in B): Rejoin new yarn at top of ch-3, ch1, 1sc into same place, *ch2, FC/rf, ch2, 1sc into next dc; rep from * to end, turn.

Row 5 (RS in A): Ch3 (count as 1dc), 1dc into 1st st, *ch1, skip 2 ch, 1sc into next cluster, ch1, skip 2 ch**, 3dc into next sc; rep from * ending last rep at **, 2dc into last sc. Do not turn.

Rep rows 2–5.

Leafhopper stitch

Multiple of 4 sts + 1 (add 2 for base chain).

Special abbreviation:

LCL (Leafhopper Cluster) = *[yo, insert hook at front and from right to left behind stem of st before next st, yo, draw loop through and up to height of htr] twice, yo, draw through 4 loops**, skip next st, rep from * to ** around stem of next st, ending yo, draw through all 3 loops on hook.

Row 1 (WS): Skip 3 ch (count as 1dc), 1dc into next and each ch to end, turn.

Row 2: Ch3 (count as 1dc), skip 1st st, 1dc into next st, *1LCL over next st, 1dc into each of next 3 sts; rep from * omitting 1dc from end of last rep, turn.

Row 3: Ch3 (count as 1dc), skip 1st st, 1dc into next and each st to end, working last st into top of tch, turn.

Row 4: Ch3 (count as 1dc), skip 1st st, *1dc into each of next 3 sts, 1LCL over next st; rep from * ending 1dc into each of last 4 sts, working last st into top of tch, turn.

Row 5: As row 3.

Rep rows 2–5.

Sharp chevron stitch

Multiple of 14 sts (add 2 for base chain).

Row 1: Skip 2 ch (count as 1dc), 2dc into next ch, *1dc into each of next 3 ch, [over next 3 ch work dc3tog] twice, 1dc into each of next 3 ch, [3dc into next st] twice; rep from * ending last rep with 3dc once only into last ch, turn.

Row 2: Ch3 (count as 1dc), 2dc into 1st st, *1dc into each of next 3 sts, [over next 3 sts work dc3tog] twice, 1dc into each of next 3 sts, [3dc into next st] twice; rep from * ending last rep with 3dc once only into top of tch, turn.

Rep row 2.

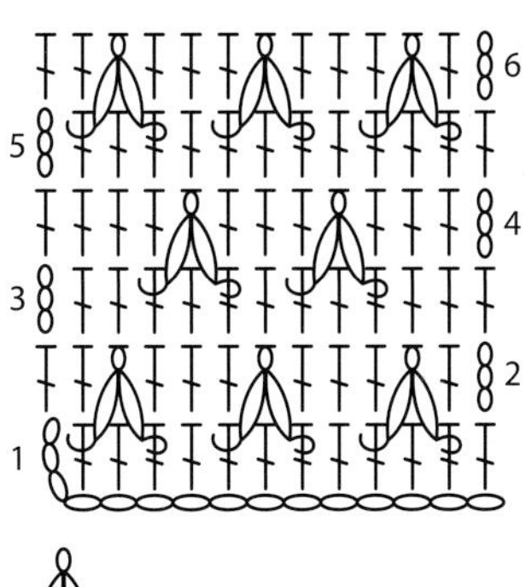

Leafhopper stitch

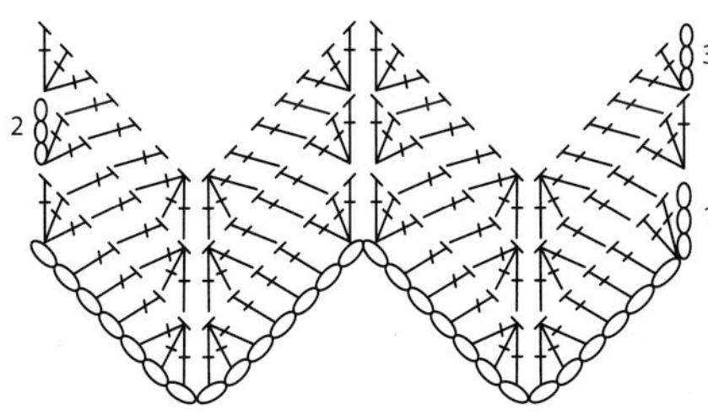

Sharp chevron stitch

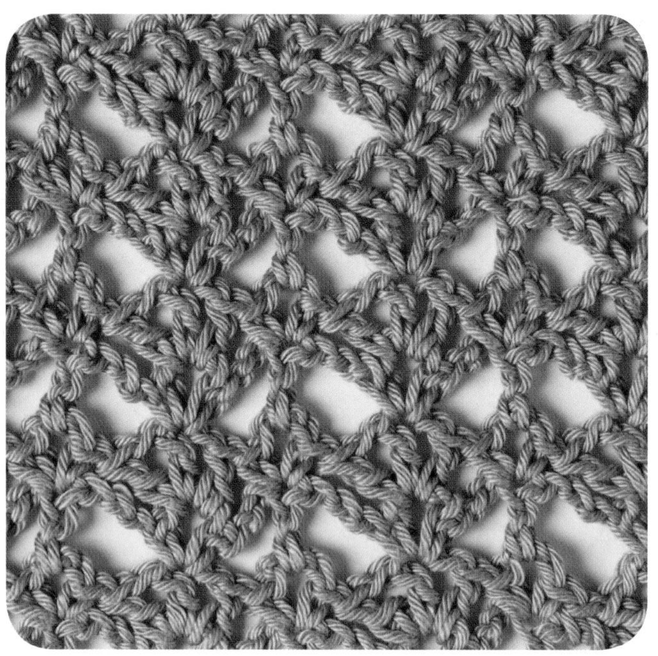

Open shell and picot stitch

Multiple of 7 sts (add 1 for base chain).

Row 1 (RS): 1sc into 2nd ch from hook, *skip 2 ch, work a shell of [1dc, ch1, 1dc, ch1, 1dc] into next ch, skip 2 ch, 1sc into next ch**, ch3, 1sc into next ch; rep from * ending last rep at **, turn.

Row 2: Ch7 (count as 1tr, ch3), *work a picot of [1sc, ch3, 1sc] into center dc of next Shell, ch3**, 1dc into next ch-3 arch, ch3; rep from * ending last rep at **, 1tr into last sc, skip tch, turn.

Row 3: Ch1, 1sc into 1st st, *skip next ch-3 sp, shell into center of next picot, skip next ch-3 sp**, picot into next dc; rep from * ending last rep at **, 1sc into next ch of tch, turn.

Rep rows 2–3.

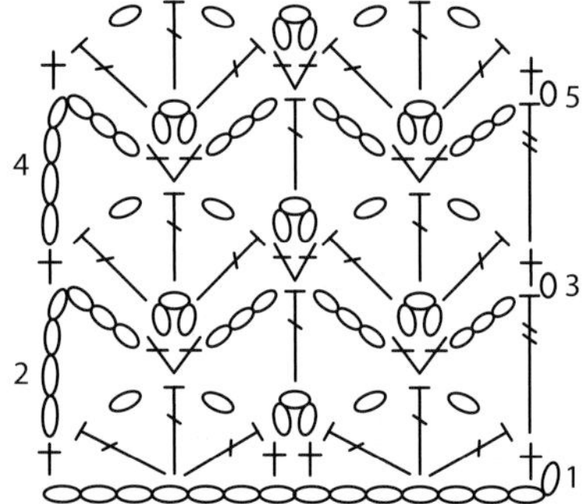

Broadway

Multiple of 8 sts + 2.

Special abbreviations:

Cr3L (Cross3Left) = skip 1 sc, work 1dc into each of next 2 sc, working in front of last 2 dc work 1tr into skipped sc.

Cr3R (Cross3Right) = skip 2 sc, work 1tr into next sc, working behind last tr work 1dc into each of 2 skipped sc.

Row 1 (WS): Work 1sc into 2nd ch from hook, 1sc into each ch to end, turn.

Row 2: Ch3 (count as 1dc), skip 1st sc, *Cr3R, 1dc into next sc, Cr3L, 1dc into next sc; rep from * to end, turn.

Row 3: Ch1, work 1sc into each st to end placing last sc into 3rd of ch-3 at beg of previous row, turn.

Rep rows 2–3.

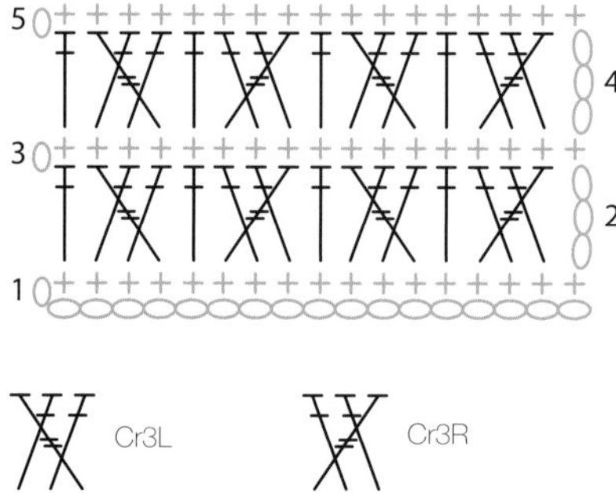

Close chevron stitch

Multiple of 11 sts +1 (add 1 for base chain).

Work 4 rows each in colors A and B alternately throughout.

Row 1 (RS): 2sc into 2nd ch from hook, *1sc into each of next 4 ch, skip 2 ch, 1sc into each of next 4 ch, 3sc into next ch; rep from * ending last rep with 2sc only into last ch, turn.

Row 2: Ch1, 2sc into 1st st, *1sc into each of next 4 sts, skip 2 sts, 1sc into each of next 4 sts, 3sc into next st; rep from * ending last rep with 2sc only into last st, skip tch, turn.

Rep row 2.

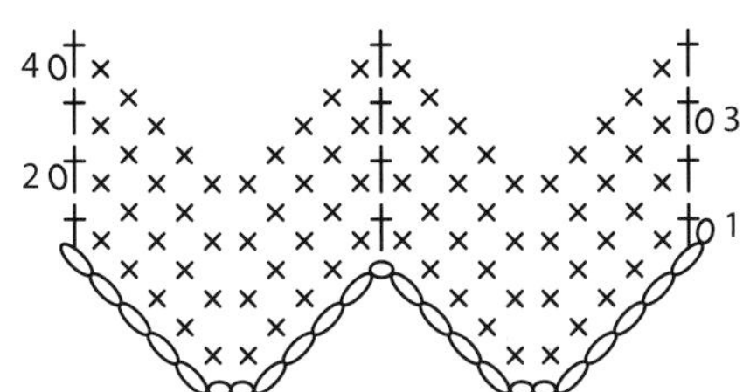

Picot ridge stitch

Multiple of 10 sts + 2 (add 2 for base chain).

Special abbreviation:

Dc/rf = wrap the yarn around the hook, insert the hook from in front and from right to left around the stem of the appropriate stitch, and complete the stitch normally.

Row 1 (RS): Skip 3 ch (count as 1dc), *1dc into each of next 5 ch, ch3, skip 2 ch, [1sc, ch4, 1sc] into next ch, ch3, skip 2 ch; rep from * ending 1dc into last ch, turn.

Row 2: Ch8 (count as 1dc, ch5), skip 1st st and next 3 arches, *1dc/rf around each of next 5 sts, ch5, skip next 3 arches; rep from * ending 1dc/rf around each of last 5 dcs, 1dc into top of tch, turn.

Row 3: Ch6, skip 1st 3 sts, *[1sc, ch4, 1sc] into next st, ch3, skip 2 sts, 1dc into each of next 5 ch**, ch3, skip 2 sts; rep from * ending last rep at **, 1dc into next ch of tch, turn.

Row 4: Ch3 (count as 1dc), skip 1st st, *1dc/rf around each of next 5 sts, ch5**, skip next 3 arches; rep from * ending last rep at **, skip next 2 arches, 1dc into tch arch, turn.

Row 5: Ch3 (count as 1dc), skip 1st st, *1dc into each of next 5 ch, ch3, skip 2 sts, [1sc, ch4, 1sc] into next st, ch3, skip 2 sts; rep from * ending 1dc into top of tch, turn.

Rep rows 2–5.

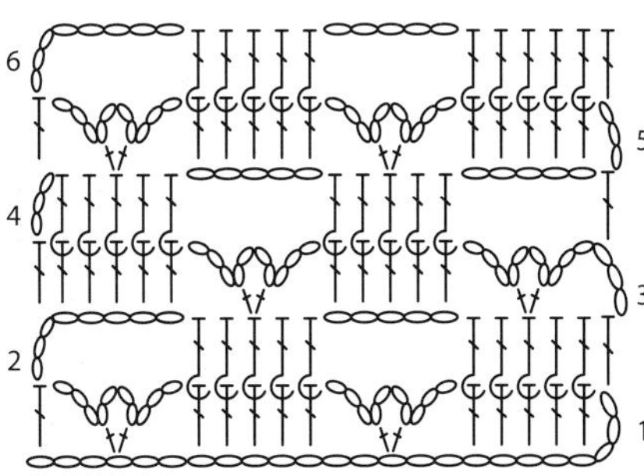

Single crochet cluster stitch I

Multiple of 2 sts + 1 (add 1 for base chain).

Row 1 (WS): 1sc into 2nd ch from hook, *ch1, skip 1 ch, 1sc into next ch; rep from * to end, turn.

Row 2: Ch1, 1sc into 1st st, ch1, sc2tog inserting hook into each of next 2 ch sps, ch1, *sc2tog inserting hook 1st into same ch sp as previous st then into next ch sp, ch1; rep from * ending 1sc into last st, skip tch, turn.

Row 3: Ch1, 1sc into 1st st, *ch1, skip 1 ch, 1sc into next st; rep from * to end, skip tch, turn.

Rep rows 2–3.

Single crochet cluster stitch II

Multiple of 2 sts + 1 (add 1 for base chain).

Row 1: Skip 1 ch, *sc2tog inserting hook into each of next 2 ch, ch1; rep from * ending 1sc into last ch, turn.

Row 2: Ch1, sc2tog inserting hook into 1st st then into next ch sp, ch1, *sc2tog inserting hook 1st before and then after the vertical thread between the next 2 clusters, ch1; rep from * ending 1sc into last sc, skip tch, turn.

Rep row 2.

Single crochet cluster stitch III

Multiple of 2 sts (add 1 for base chain).

Row 1: Skip 2 ch (count as 1hdc), *sc2tog inserting hook into each of next 2 ch, ch1; rep from * ending with 1hdc into last ch, turn.

Row 2: Ch2 (count as 1hdc), skip 1 st, *sc2tog inserting hook into back loop only of next ch then into back loop only of next st, ch1; rep from * ending with 1hdc into top of tch, turn.

Rep row 2.

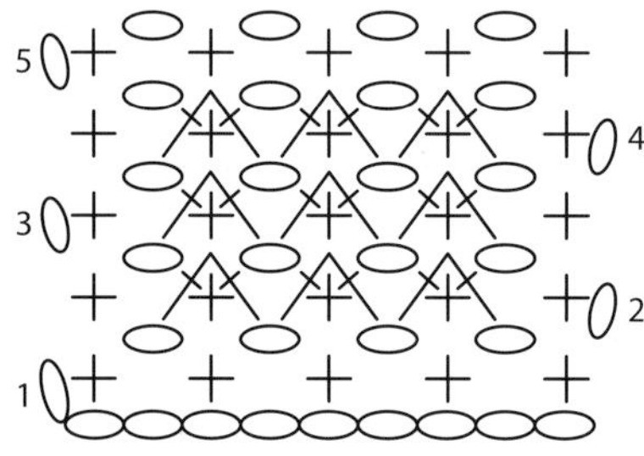

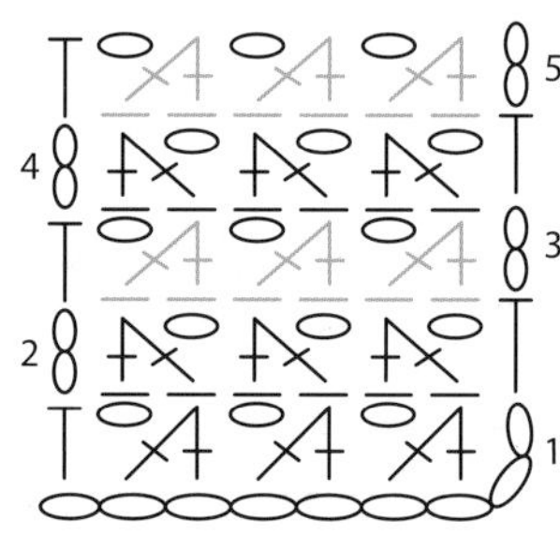

Single crochet cluster stitch IV

Multiple of 2 sts + 1 (add 1 for base chain).

Special abbreviation:

SC (Slip Cluster) = insert hook into ch or st as indicated, yo, draw loop through, insert hook again, yo, draw loop through st and through next loop on hook, yo, draw through last 2 loops on hook.

Row 1: 1SC inserting hook into 2nd and then 3rd ch from hook, ch1, *1SC inserting hook into each of next 2 ch, ch1; rep from * ending with 1sc into last ch, turn.

Row 2: Ch1, skip 1 st, *1SC inserting hook into front loop only of next ch then front loop only of next st, ch1; rep from * ending 1sc into top of tch, turn.

Rep row 2.

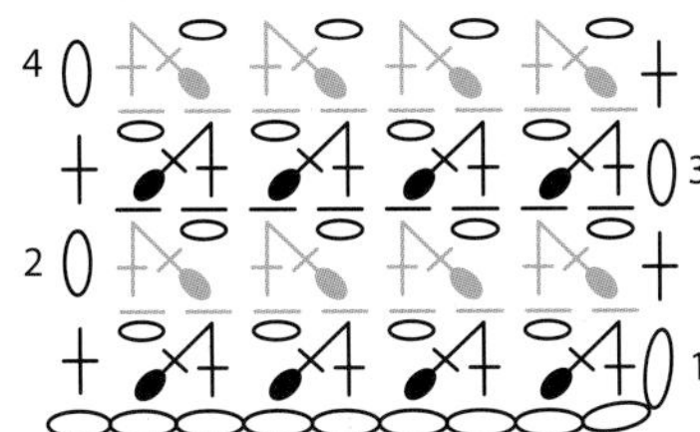

Ridged string network

Multiple of 4 sts + 1 (add 1 for base chain).

Row 1 (RS): 1sc into 2nd ch from hook, *ch3, skip 3 ch, 1sc into next ch; rep from * to end, turn.

Row 2: Ch1, working into back loop only of each st work 1sc into 1st st, *ch3, skip ch-3, 1sc into next sc; rep from * to end, skip tch, turn.

Rep row 2.

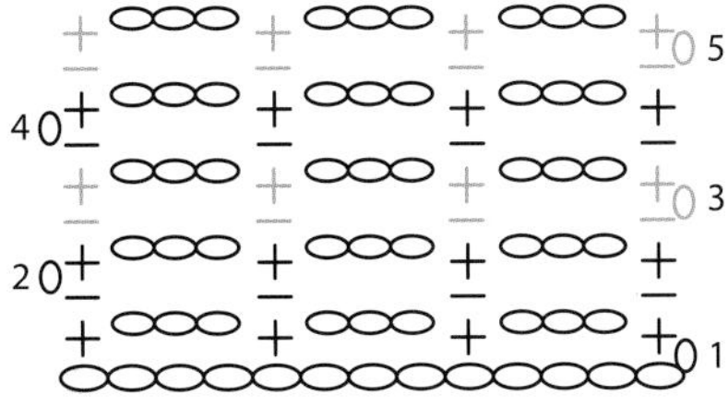

Spatter pattern

Multiple of 6 sts + 2.

Row 1 (RS): Work 1sc into 2nd ch from hook, *skip 2 ch, 1dc into next ch, ch2, into same ch as last dc work [1dc, ch2, 1dc], skip 2 ch, 1sc into next ch; rep from * to end, turn.

Row 2: Ch5 (count as 1dc, ch2), 1dc into 1st sc, skip 1 dc, 1sc into next dc, *1dc into next sc, ch2, into same st as last dc work [1dc, ch2, 1dc], skip 1 dc, 1sc into next dc, rep from * to last sc, into last sc work [1dc, ch2, 1dc], turn.

Row 3: Ch1, 1sc into 1st dc, *1dc into next sc, ch2, into same st as last dc work [1dc, ch2, 1dc], skip 1 dc, 1sc into next dc; rep from * to end placing last sc into 3rd of ch-5 at beg of previous row, turn.

Rep rows 2–3.

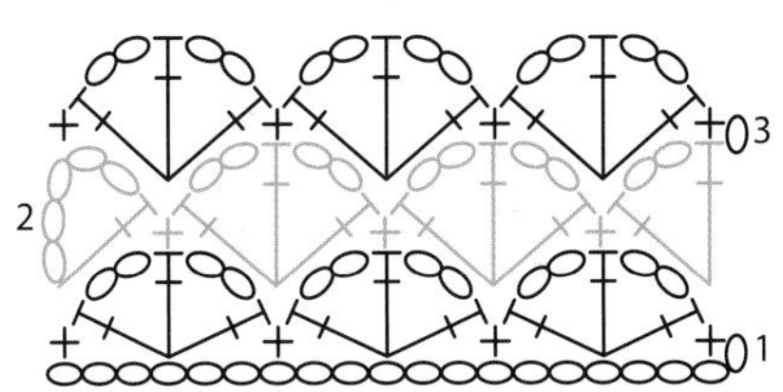

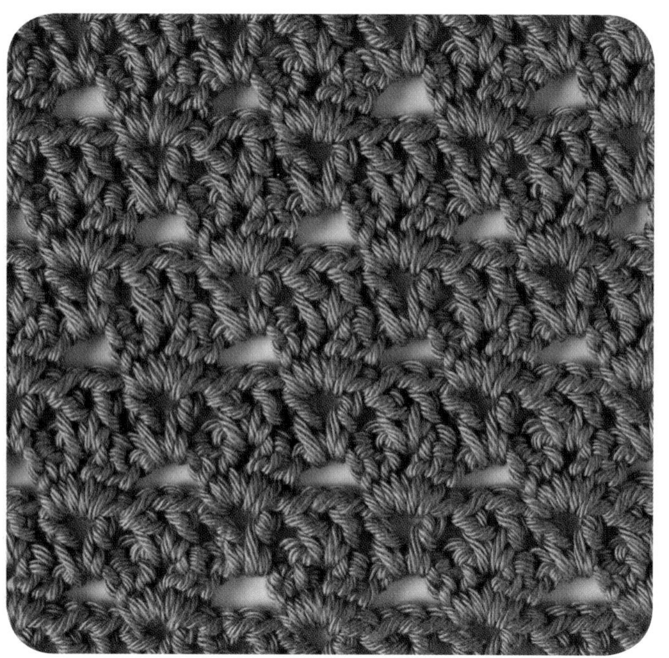

Basket stitch

Multiple of 6 sts + 5 (add 2 for base chain).

Row 1 (WS): Work a V st of [1dc, ch1, 1dc] into 5th ch from hook, *skip 2 ch, work V st into next ch; rep from * to last 2 ch, skip 1 ch, 1dc into last ch, turn.

Row 2: Ch3, skip 2 sts, work a Double V st of [2dc, ch1, 2dc] into ch sp at center of V st, *ch1, skip next V st, work a Double V st into sp at center of next V st; rep from * leaving last loop of last dc of last Double V st on hook and working it together with 1dc into top of tch, turn.

Row 3: Ch3, work a V st into each sp to end, finishing with 1dc into top of tch, turn.

Row 4: Ch3, 1dc into 1st st, *ch1, skip next V st, work a Double V st into sp at center of next V st; rep from * until 1 V st remains, ch1, skip V st, 2dc into top of tch, turn.

Row 5: As row 3.

Rep rows 2–5.

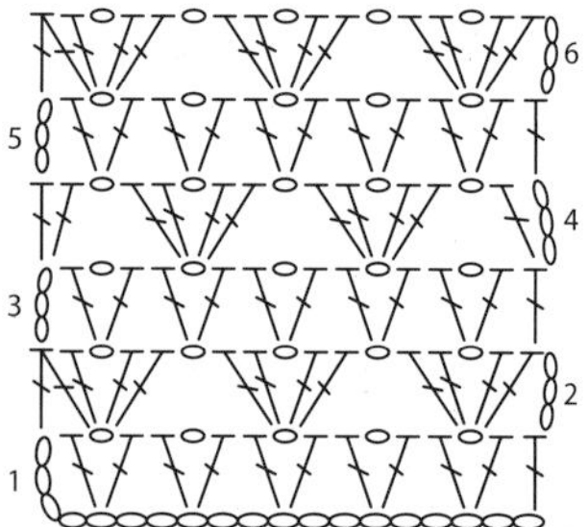

Connected spiral

Multiple of 3 sts + 5.

Special abbreviation:

Cluster4 = work 3dc over stem of dc just worked but leaving last loop of each dc on hook, then work 4th dc as indicated leaving last loop as before (5 loops on hook), yo and through all 5 loops.

Row 1 (RS): Work 1dc into 6th ch from hook, *ch3, skip 2 ch, work cluster4 placing 4th dc into next ch; rep from * to last 2 ch, ch3, work cluster4 placing 4th dc in last ch, turn.

Row 2: Ch3 (count as 1dc), 1dc into next ch-3 sp, *ch3, work cluster4 placing 4th dc into next ch-3 sp; rep from * to end, placing final dc into top of ch at beg of previous row, turn.

Rep row 2.

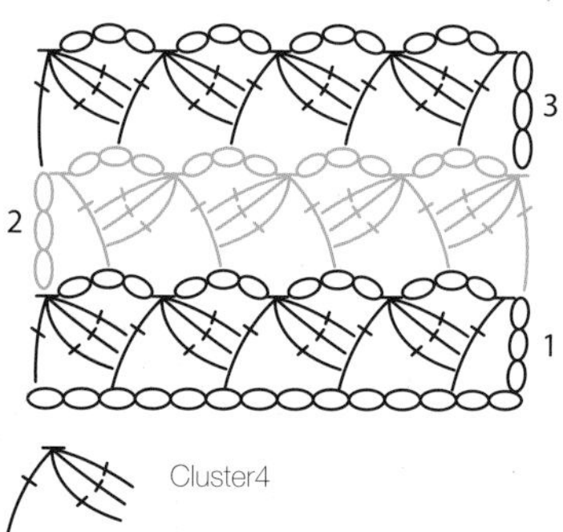

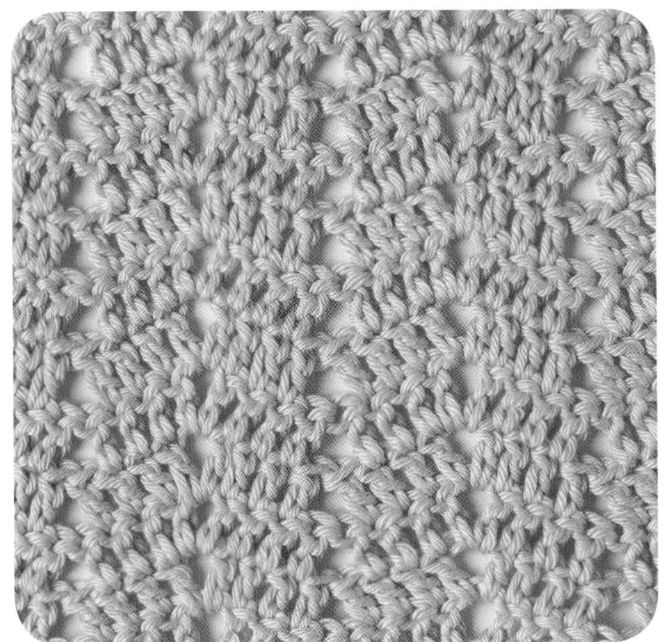

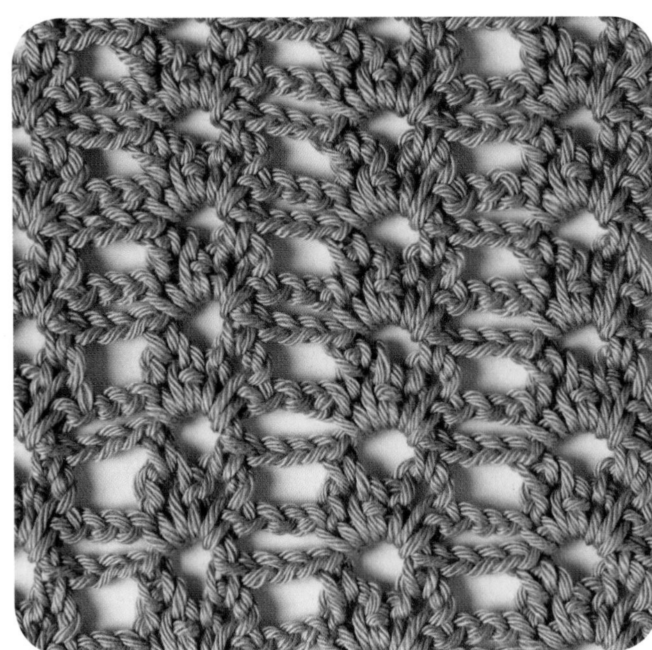

Peephole chevron stitch

Multiple of 10 sts (add 2 for base chain).

Row 1: Skip 2 ch (count as 1dc), 1dc into each of next 4 ch, *skip 2 ch, 1dc into each of next 4 ch, ch2, 1dc into each of next 4 ch; rep from * to last 6 ch, skip 2 ch, 1dc into each of next 3 ch, 2dc into last ch, turn.

Row 2: Ch3 (count as 1dc), 1dc into 1st st, 1dc into each of next 3 sts, *skip 2 sts, 1dc into each of next 3 sts, [1dc, ch2, 1dc] into ch-2 sp, 1dc into each of next 3 sts; rep from * to last 6 sts, skip 2 sts, 1dc into each of next 3 sts, 2dc into top of tch, turn.

Rep row 2.

Treble picot string network

Multiple of 6 sts + 5 (add 1 for base chain).

Row 1 (WS): 1sc into 2nd ch from hook, ch3, skip 4 ch, work a picot of [1sc, ch3, 1sc] into next ch, *ch3, skip 5 ch, picot into next ch; rep from * to last 5 ch, ch3, skip 4 ch, 1sc into last ch, turn.

Row 2: Ch1, 1sc into 1st st, *ch3, skip 3 ch, 2 picots into next ch-3 arch; rep from * ending ch3, skip 3 ch, 1sc into last sc, turn.

3rd row: Ch6 (count as 1dc, ch3), skip 3 ch, *1sc into next picot arch, ch3, 1sc into next picot arch, ch3, skip 3 ch; rep from * ending 1dc into last sc, skip tch, turn.

Rep rows 2–3.

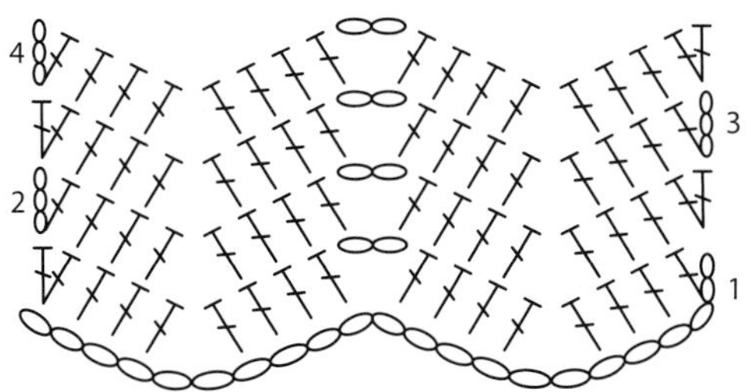

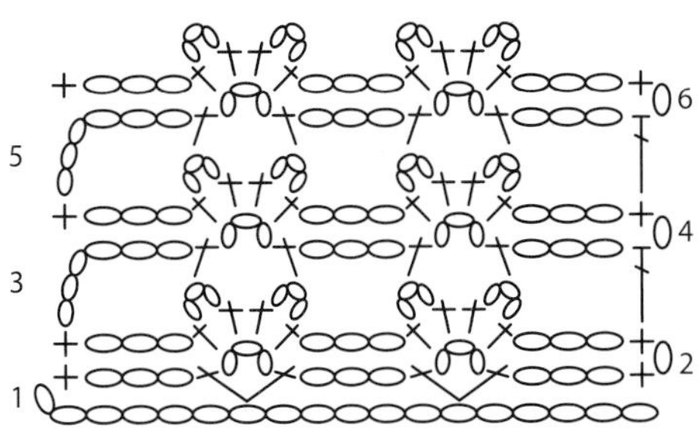

Tooth pattern

Multiple of 4 sts + 4.

Row 1 (RS): Using A, work 1dc into 4th ch from hook, 1dc into each ch to end, turn.

Row 2: Using A, ch1, work 1sc into each dc to end, working last sc into top of ch-3, turn.

Row 3: Using B, ch3 (count as 1dc), skip 1st sc, 1dc into next sc, *ch2, skip 2 sc, 1dc into each of next 2 sc; rep from * to end, turn.

Row 4: Using B, ch1, work 1sc into each of 1st 2 dc, *ch2, 1sc into each of next 2 dc; rep from * to end, working last sc into 3rd of ch-3 at beg of previous row, turn.

Row 5: Using C, ch1, 1sc into each of 1st 2 sc, *1tr into each of the 2 skipped sc 3 rows below, 1sc into each of next 2 sc; rep from * to end, turn.

Row 6: Using C, ch1, 1sc into each sc and each tr to end, turn.

Row 7: Using A, ch3, skip 1st sc, 1dc into each sc to end, turn.

Row 8: Using A, ch1, 1sc into each dc to end, working last sc into 3rd of ch-3 at beg of previous row, turn.

Rep rows 3–8.

Granule stitch

Multiple of 4 sts + 1 (add 1 for base chain).

Special abbreviation:

Psc (Picot single crochet) = insert hook, yo, draw loop through, [yo, draw through 1 loop] 3 times to make ch-3, yo, draw through both loops on hook.

Note: Draw picot chain loops to the back (RS) of fabric.

Row 1 (RS): 1sc into 2nd ch from hook, 1sc into each ch to end, turn.

Row 2: Ch1, 1sc into 1st st, *1Psc into next st, 1sc into next st; rep from * to end, skip tch, turn.

Row 3: Ch1, 1sc into 1st and each st to end, skip tch, turn.

Hint: Hold down the picot chains at the front and you will see the top 2 loops of the Psc where you are to insert the hook.

Row 4: Ch1, 1sc into each of 1st 2 sts, *1Psc into next st, 1sc into next st; rep from * to last st, 1sc into last st, skip tch, turn.

Row 5: As row 3.

Rep rows 2–5.

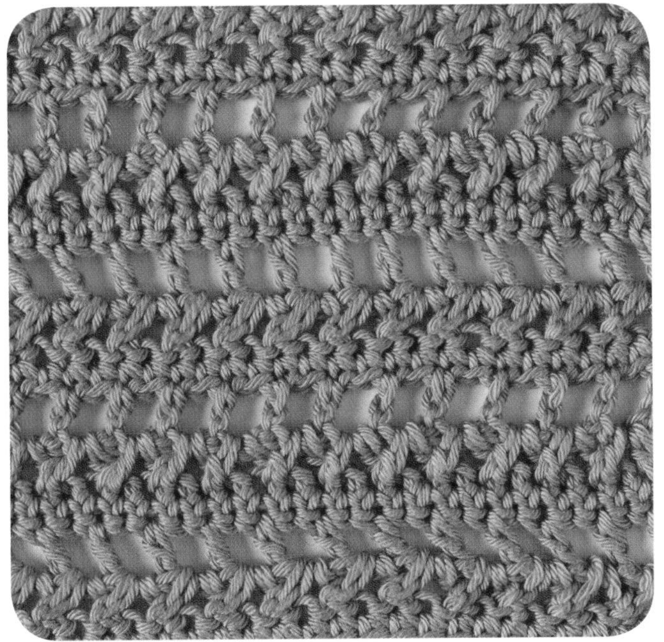

Zeros and crosses stitch

Multiple of 2 sts + 1 (add 3 for base chain).

Row 1 (RS): 1dc into 6th ch from hook, *ch1, skip 1 ch, 1dc into next ch; rep from * to end, turn.

Row 2: Ch3, skip next ch sp, work 2 crossed sts as follows: 1dc forward into next ch sp, 1dc back into ch sp just skipped going behind forward dc so as not to catch it, *1dc forward into next unoccupied ch sp, 1dc back into previous ch sp going behind forward dc as before; rep from * to end when last forward dc occupies tch, 1dc into next ch, turn.

Row 3: Ch1, 1dc into 1st st, 1dc into next and each st to end, working last st into top of tch, turn.

Row 4: Ch4 (count as 1sc, ch1), skip 2 sts, 1dc into next st, *ch1, skip 1 st, 1sc into next st; rep from * ending last rep in tch, turn.

Rep rows 2–4.

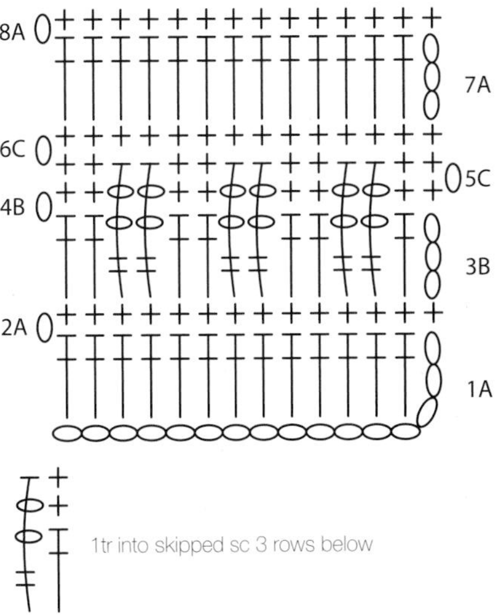

Tooth pattern

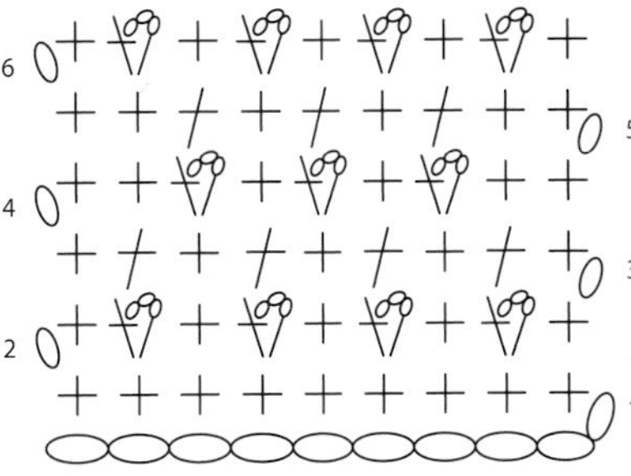

Granule stitch

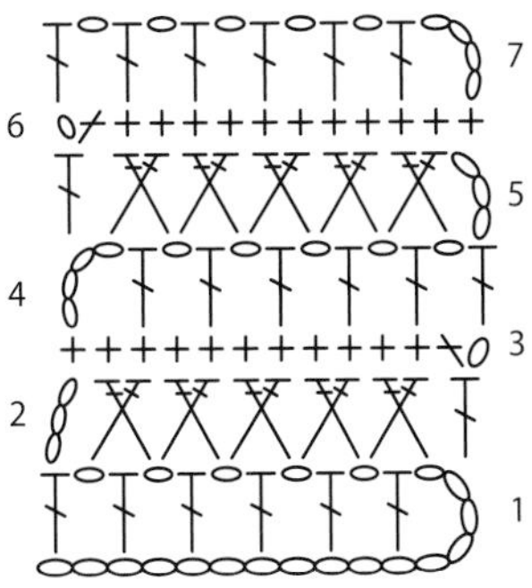

Zeros and crosses stitch

Half double crochet cluster stitch I

Any number of sts (add 1 for base chain).

Row 1: Skip 2 ch (count as 1hdc), *hdc2tog all into next ch; rep from * to end, turn.

Row 2: Ch2 (count as 1hdc), skip 1 st, hdc2tog all into next and each st, ending with hdc2tog into top of tch, turn.

Rep row 2.

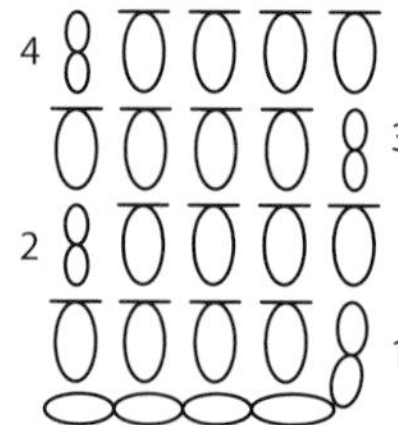

Half double crochet cluster stitch II

Any number of sts (add 2 for base chain).

Row 1: Skip 2 ch (count as 1hdc), hdc2tog inserting hook into each of next 2 ch, *hdc2tog inserting hook 1st into same ch as previous cluster then into next ch; rep from * until 1 ch remains, 1hdc into last ch, turn.

Row 2: Ch2 (count as 1hdc), hdc2tog inserting hook 1st into 1st st then into next st, *hdc2tog inserting hook 1st into same st as previous cluster then into next st; rep from * ending 1hdc into top of tch, turn.

Rep row 2.

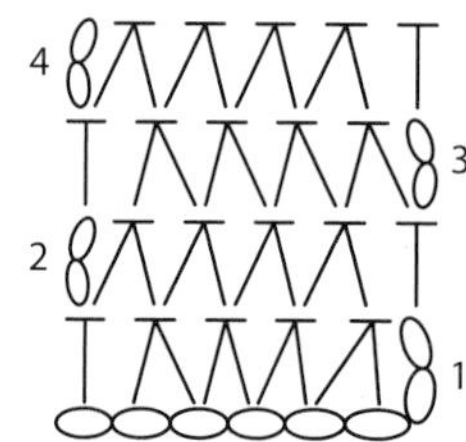

Half double crochet cluster stitch III

Multiple of 2 sts (add 1 for base chain).

Row 1: Skip 2 ch (count as 1hdc), *hdc2tog inserting hook into each of next 2 ch, ch1; rep from * ending 1hdc into last ch, turn.

Row 2: Ch2 (count as 1hdc), skip 1 st, *hdc2tog inserting hook into next ch sp then into next st, ch1; rep from * ending 1hdc into top of tch, turn.

Rep row 2.

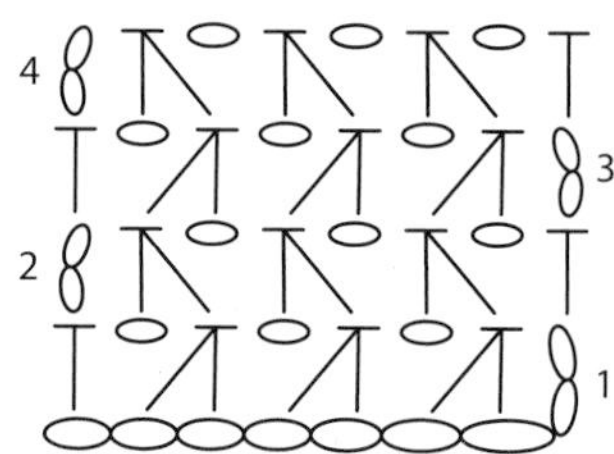

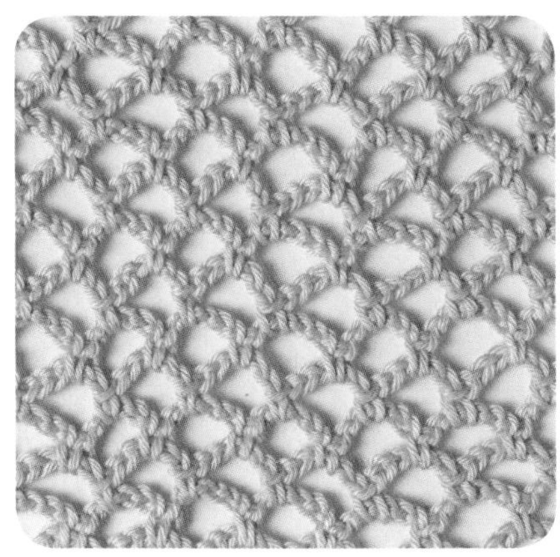

Plain trellis stitch

Multiple of 4 sts + 3 (add 3 for base chain).

Row 1: 1sc into 6th ch from hook, *ch5, skip 3 ch, 1sc into next ch; rep from * to end, turn.

Row 2: *Ch5, 1sc into next ch-5 arch; rep from * to end, turn.

Rep row 2.

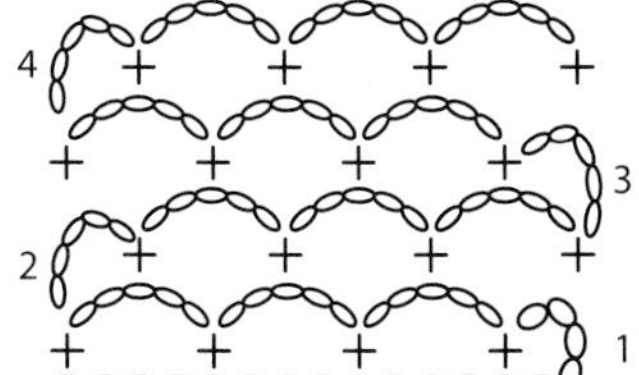

Wattle stitch

Multiple of 3 sts + 2 (add 1 for base chain).

Row 1: Skip 2 ch (count as 1sc), *work [1sc, ch1, 1dc] into next ch, skip 2 ch; rep from * ending 1sc into last ch, turn.

Row 2: Ch1 (count as 1sc), skip 1st sc and next dc, *work [1sc, ch1, 1dc] into next ch sp, skip sc and dc; rep from * ending with [1sc, ch1, 1dc] into last ch sp, skip next sc, 1sc into top of tch, turn.

Rep row 2.

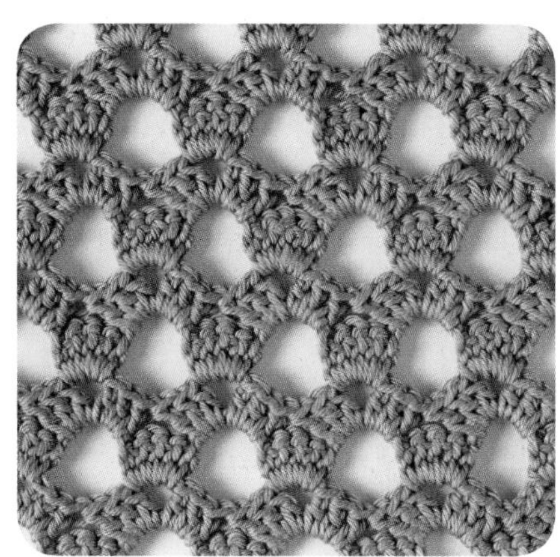

Acrobatic stitch

Multiple of 6 sts + 1 (add 2 for base chain).

Row 1 (RS): 2dc into 3rd ch from hook, *ch4, skip 5 ch, 5dc into next ch; rep from * working only 3dc at end of last rep, turn.

Row 2: Ch2 (count as 1dc), skip 1st 3 sts, *work [3dc, ch3, 3dc] into next ch-4 arch**, skip next 5 dc; rep from * ending last rep at **, skip 2 dc, 1dc into top of tch, turn.

Row 3: Ch6 (count as 1dtr, ch1), *5dc into next ch-3 arch**, ch4; rep from * ending last rep at **, ch1, 1dtr into top of tch, turn.

Row 4: Ch5 (count as 1tr, ch1), 3dc into next ch-1 sp, *skip 5 dc, work [3dc, ch3, 3dc] into next ch-4 arch; rep from * ending skip 5 dc, work [3dc, ch1, 1tr] into tch, turn.

Row 5: Ch3 (count as 1dc), 2dc into next ch-1 sp, *ch4, 5dc into next ch-3 arch; rep from * ending ch4, 3dc into tch, turn.

Rep rows 2–5.

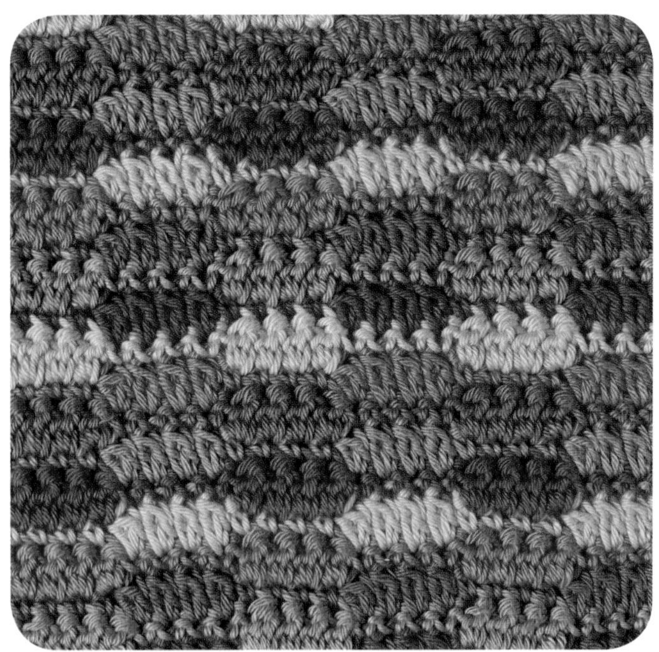

Crunchy chevron stitch

Multiple of 8 sts (add 1 for base chain).

Work 1 row each in colors A, B, C, D and E throughout.

Row 1: 1sc into 2nd ch from hook, 1sc into each of next 3 ch, *hdc2tog all into each of next 4 ch, 1sc into each of next 4 ch; rep from * to last 4 ch, hdc2tog all into each of last 4 ch, turn.

Row 2: Ch1, then starting in 1st st, *1sc into each of next 4 sts, hdc2tog all into each of next 4 sc; rep from * to end, skip tch, turn.

Rep row 2.

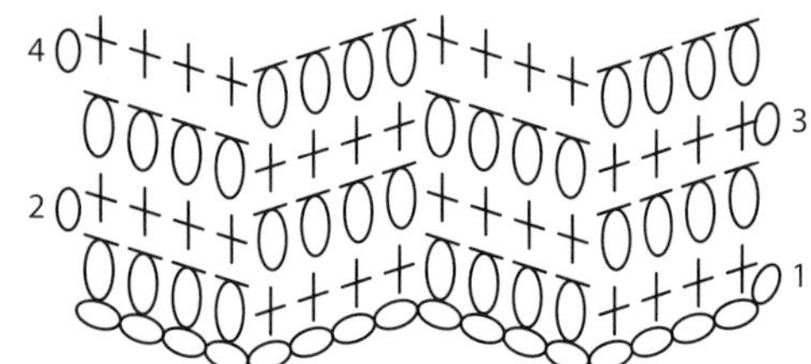

Forked cluster stitch

Any number of sts (add 2 for base chain).

Special abbreviation:

FC (Forked Cluster) = [yo, insert hook into ch or st as indicated, yo, draw loop through] twice (5 loops on hook), [yo, draw through 3 loops] twice.

Row 1: Skip 2 ch (count as 1dc), work 1FC inserting hook into each of next 2 ch, *work 1FC inserting hook into same ch as previous FC then into next ch; rep from * until 1 ch remains, 1dc into last ch, turn.

Row 2: Ch3 (count as 1dc), 1FC inserting hook into each of 1st 2 sts, *1FC inserting hook into same st as previous FC then into next st; rep from * ending 1dc into top of tch, turn.

Rep row 2.

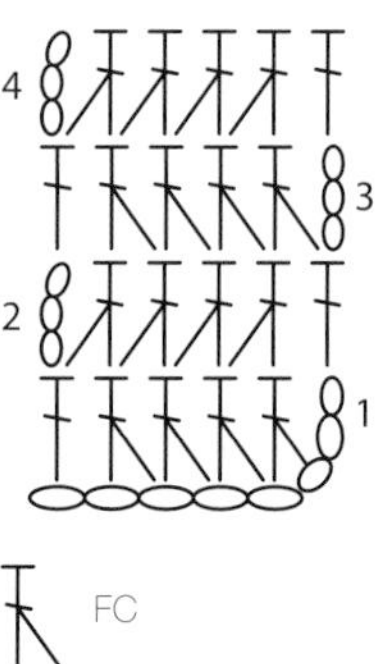

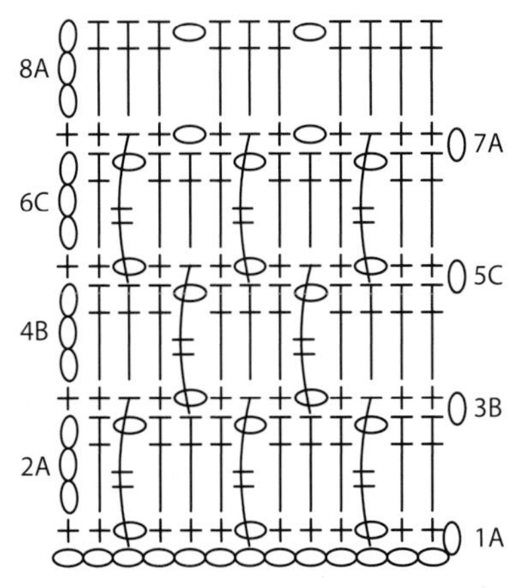

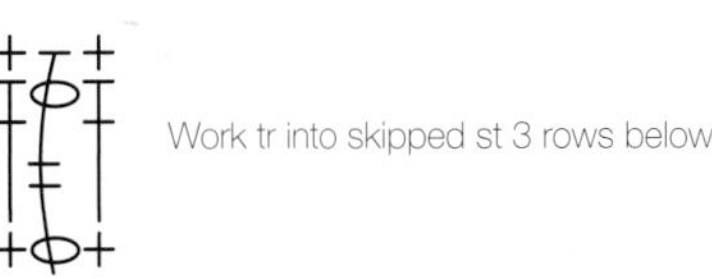

Mirror stitch

Multiple of 4 sts + 2.

Row 1 (RS): Using A, work 1sc into 2nd ch from hook, 1sc into next ch, *ch1, skip 1 ch, 1sc into each of next 3 ch; rep from * to end omitting 1sc at end of last rep, turn.

Row 2: Using A, ch3 (count as 1dc), skip 1st sc, work 1dc into next sc, *ch1, skip 1 ch, 1dc into each of next 3 sc; rep from * to end omitting 1dc at end of last rep, turn.

Row 3: Using B, ch1, work 1sc into each of 1st 2 dc, 1tr into 1st skipped starting ch, *1sc into next dc, ch1, skip 1 dc, 1sc into next dc, 1tr into next skipped starting ch; rep from * to last 2 dc, 1sc into next dc, 1sc into 3rd of ch-3 at beg of previous row, turn.

Row 4: Using B, ch3, skip 1st sc, work 1dc into each of next 3 sts, *ch1, skip 1 ch, 1dc into each of next 3 sts; rep from * to last sc, 1dc into last sc, turn.

Row 5: Using C, ch1, work 1sc into each of 1st 2 dc, *ch1, skip 1 dc, 1sc into next dc, 1tr into next skipped dc 3 rows below, 1sc into next dc; rep from * to last 3 dc, ch1, skip 1 dc, 1sc into next dc, 1sc into 3rd of ch-3 at beg of previous row, turn.

Row 6: Using C, ch3, skip 1st sc, 1dc into next sc, *ch1, skip 1 ch, 1dc into each of next 3 sts; rep from * to end omitting 1dc at end of last rep, turn.

Row 7: Using A, ch1, 1sc into each of 1st 2 dc, 1tr into next skipped dc 3 rows below, *1sc into next dc, ch1, skip 1 dc, 1sc into next dc, 1tr into next skipped dc 3 rows below; rep from * to last 2 dc, 1sc into each of last 2 dc, turn.

Row 8: As row 4 but using A instead of B.

Rep rows 5–8 continuing to work 2 rows each in colors B, C and A as set.

Berry

Aran style

Multiple of 8 sts + 4.

Row 1: Into 3rd ch from hook work 1sc, 1sc into each ch to end, turn.

Row 2: Ch1 (count as first sc), skip first st, 1sc into each st to end, turn.

Row 3: Ch1, skip first st, 1sc into each of next 3 sts, *slip st into next st, yo and insert into next st, yo and draw through a loop, yo and draw through first loop on hook, yo and insert into same st, yo and draw through a loop, yo and draw through all loops on hook, ch1 to secure st – berry st made, slip st into next st, 1sc into each of next 5 sts; rep from * ending last rep with 1sc into each of next 4 sts, turn.

Row 4: Ch1, skip first st, 1sc into each of next 3 sts, *1sc into next slip st, slip st into next berry st, 1sc into next slip st, 1sc into each of next 5 sts; rep from * ending last rep with 1sc into each of next 4 sts, turn.

Row 5: Ch1, skip first st, 1sc into each of next 2 sts, *slip st into next sc, berry st into next sc, slip st into next slip st, berry st into next sc, slip st into next sc, 1sc into each of next 3 sts; rep from * to end, turn.

Row 6: Ch1, skip first st, 1sc into each of next 3 sts, *slip st into next berry st, 1sc into next slip st, slip st into next berry st, 1sc into each of next 5 sts; rep from * ending last rep with 1sc into each of next 4 sts, turn.

Rows 7–8: As rows 3–4.

Row 9: Ch1, skip first st, berry st into next sc, slip st into next st, *1sc into each of next 5 sts, slip st into next st, berry st into next sc, slip st into next st; rep from * to end, turn.

Row 10: Ch1, skip first st, slip st into next berry st, *1sc into each of next 7 sts, slip st into next berry st; rep from * ending with 1sc into last st, turn.

Row 11: Ch1, skip first st, *slip st into next sl st, berry st into next sc, slip st into next sc, 1sc into each of next 3 sts, slip st into next sc, berry st into next sc; rep from * to last 2 sts, slip st into next slip st, 1sc into last st, turn.

Row 12: Ch1, skip first st, 1sc into next slip st, slip st into next berry st, *1sc into each of next 5 sts, slip st into next berry st, 1sc into next slip st **, slip st into next berry st; rep from *, ending last rep at **, 1sc into last st, turn.

Rows 13–14: As rows 9–10.

Rep rows 3–14.

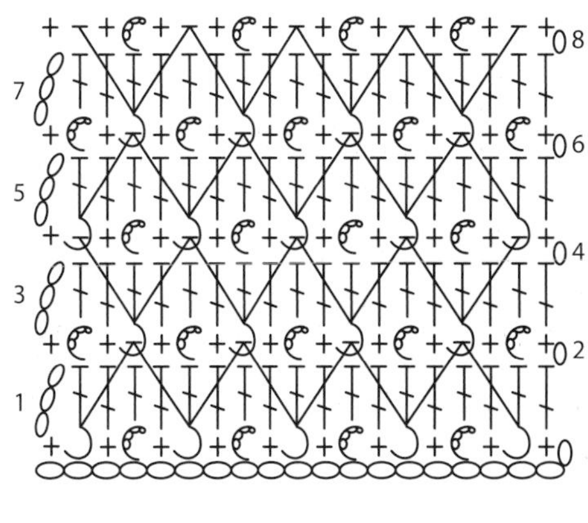

Psc

Dots and diamonds

Multiple of 4 sts + 3 (add 1 for base chain).

Special abbreviations:

Psc (Picot single crochet) = insert hook, yo, draw loop through, [yo, draw through 1 loop] 3 times, yo, draw through both loops on hook. Draw picot ch loops to front (RS) of fabric.

Tr/rf2tog = *yo twice, insert hook as indicated, yo, draw loop through, (yo, draw through 2 loops) twice*.

Base row (RS): 1sc into 2nd ch from hook, 1sc into each of next 2 ch, *Psc into next ch, 1sc into each of next 3 ch; rep from * to end, turn.

Row 1: Ch3 (count as 1dc), skip 1st st, 1dc into each st to end, skip tch, turn.

Row 2: Ch1, 1sc into 1st st, *Psc into next st, 1sc into next st**, tr/rf2tog over next st inserting hook around 2nd sc in second-to-last row for 1st leg and around following 4th sc for 2nd leg (skipping 3 sts between), 1sc into next st; rep from * ending last rep at ** in top of tch, turn.

Row 3: As row 1.

Row 4: 1ch, 1sc into 1st st, 1tr/rf over next st inserting hook around top of 1st raised cluster 2 rows below, *1sc into next st, Psc into next st, 1sc into next st**, tr/rf2tog over next st inserting hook around same cluster as last raised st for 1st leg and around top of next raised cluster for 2nd leg; rep from * ending last rep at ** when 2 sts remain, tr/rf over next st inserting hook around top of same cluster as last raised st, 1sc into top of tch, turn.

Row 5: As row 1.

Row 6: As row 2, except to make new raised clusters insert hook around previous raised clusters instead of scs.

Rep rows 3–6.

Mat stitch

Multiple of 6 sts + 2.

Row 1 (RS): Work 1sc into 2nd ch from hook, *skip 2 ch, 1dc into next ch, ch1, into same ch as last dc work [1dc, ch1, 1dc], skip 2 ch, 1sc into next ch; rep from * to end, turn.

Row 2: Ch4 (count as 1dc, ch1), 1dc into 1st sc, skip 1 dc, 1sc into next dc, *1dc into next sc, ch1, into same st as last dc work [1dc, ch1, 1dc], skip 1 dc, 1sc into next dc; rep from * to last sc, into last sc work [1dc, ch1, 1dc], turn.

Row 3: Ch1, 1sc into 1st sc, *1dc into next sc, ch1, into same st as last dc work [1dc, ch1, 1dc], skip 1 dc, 1sc into next dc; rep from * to end placing last sc into 3rd of ch-4 at beg of previous row, turn.

Rep rows 2–3.

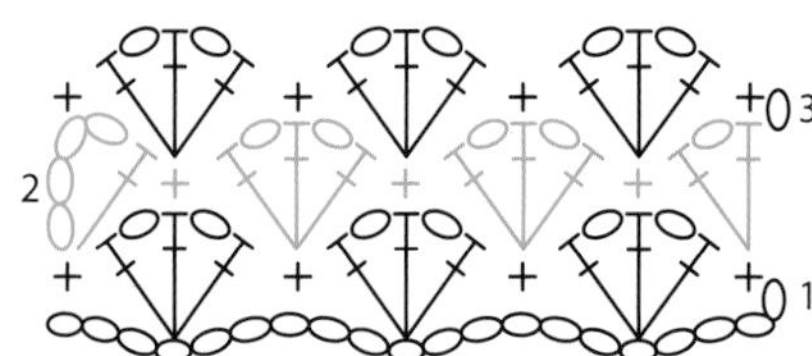

Simple chevron stitch

Multiple of 10 sts + 1 (add 2 for base chain).

Row 1: Skip 2 ch (count as 1dc), 1dc into next ch, *1dc into each of next 3 ch, over next 3 ch work dc3tog, 1dc into each of next 3 ch, 3dc into next ch; rep from * ending last rep with 2dc into last ch, turn.

Row 2: Ch3 (count as 1dc), 1dc into 1st st, *1dc into each of next 3 dc, over next 3 sts work dc3tog, 1dc into each of next 3 dc, 3dc into next dc; rep from * ending last rep with 2dc into top of tch, turn.

Rep row 2.

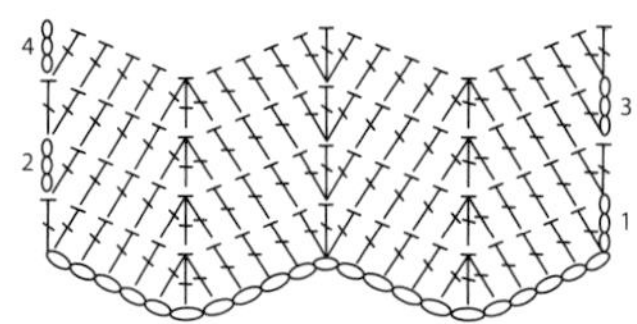

Cabbage patch

Multiple of 4 sts + 7.

Special abbreviation:

Cross2dc = skip 3 dc, work 1dc into next dc, ch2, working behind last dc work 1dc into the 1st of the skipped dc.

Row 1 (RS): Work 4dc into 5th ch from hook, *skip 3 ch, 4dc into next ch; rep from * to last 2 ch, 1dc into last ch, turn.

Row 2: Ch3 (count as 1dc), skip 1st dc, *cross2dc; rep from * to end, 1dc into top of ch-3 at beg of previous row, turn.

Row 3: Ch3, work 4dc into each ch-2 sp to end, 1dc into 3rd of ch-3 at beg of previous row, turn.

Rep rows 2–3.

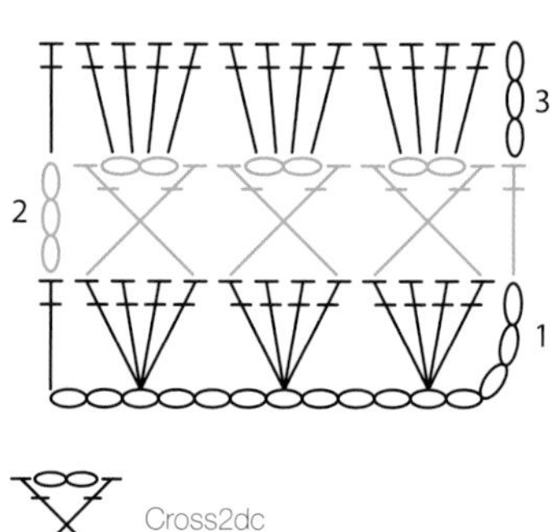

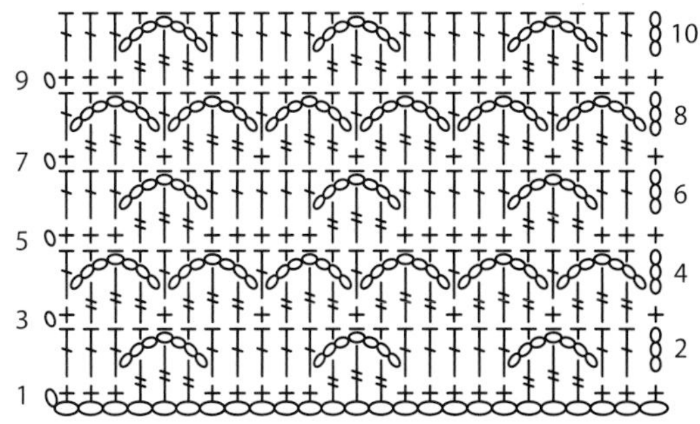

Relief arch stitch

Multiple of 8 sts + 1 (add 1 for base chain).

Row 1 (WS): 1sc into 2nd ch from hook, 1sc into each of next 2 ch, *ch7, skip 3 ch, 1sc into each of next 5 ch; rep from * to last 6 ch, ch7, skip 3 ch, 1sc into each of last 3 ch, turn.

Row 2: Ch3 (count as 1dc), skip 1 st, 1dc into each of next 2 sts, *going behind ch-7 loop work 1tr into each of next 3 base ch**, 1dc into each of next 5 sc; rep from * ending last rep at ** when 3 sts rem, 1dc into each of last 3 sts, skip tch, turn.

Row 3: Ch1, 1sc into 1st st, *ch7, skip 3 sts, 1sc into next st at same time catching in center of ch-7 loop of second-to-last row, ch7, skip 3 sts, 1sc into next st; rep from * to end, turn.

Row 4: Ch3 (count as 1dc), skip 1 st, * going behind ch-7 loop of last row work 1tr into each of next 3 sts of second-to-last row, 1dc into next sc; rep from * to end, skip tch, turn.

Row 5: Ch1, 1sc into each of 1st 2 sts, *1sc into next st at same time catching in center of ch-7 loop of second-to-last row, ch7, skip 3 sts, 1sc into next st at same time catching in center of ch-7 loop of second-to-last row**, 1sc into each of next 3 sts; rep from * ending last rep at ** when 2 sts rem, 1sc into each of last 2 sts, turn.

Row 6: As row 2 working trs into second-to-last row.

Rep rows 3–6.

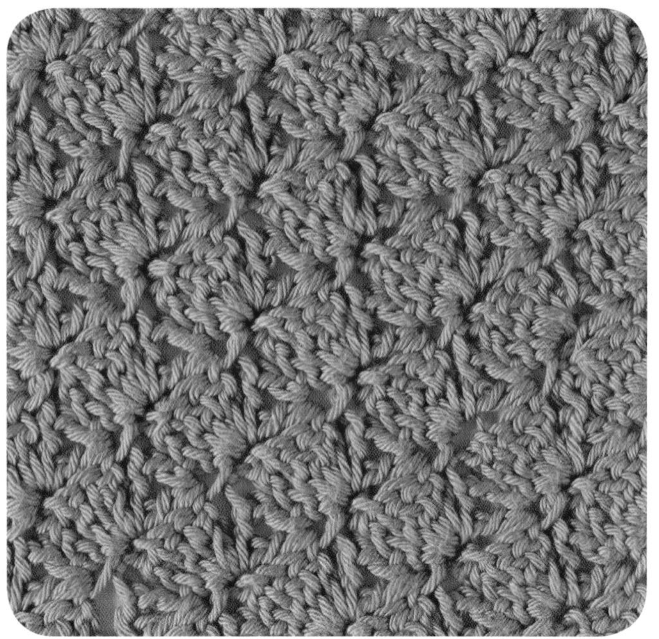

Flying shell stitch

Multiple of 4 sts + 1 (add 1 for base chain).

Row 1 (RS): Work a Flying shell (called FS) of [1sc, ch3, 3dc] into 2nd ch from hook, *skip 3 ch, 1FS into next ch; rep from * to last 4ch, skip 3 ch, 1sc into last ch, turn.

Row 2: Ch3, 1dc into 1st st, *skip 3 sts, 1sc into top of ch-3**, work a V st of [1dc, ch1, 1dc] into next sc; rep from * ending last rep at **, 2dc into last sc, skip tch, turn.

Row 3: Ch3, 3dc into 1st st, skip next st, *1FS into next sc, skip next V st; rep from * ending 1sc into last sc, ch3, dc2tog over last dc and top of tch, turn.

Row 4: Ch1, *V st into next sc, skip 3 sts, 1sc into top of ch-3; rep from * to end, turn.

Row 5: Ch1, FS into 1st st, *skip next V st, FS into next sc; rep from * ending skip last V st, 1sc into tch, turn.

Rep rows 2–5.

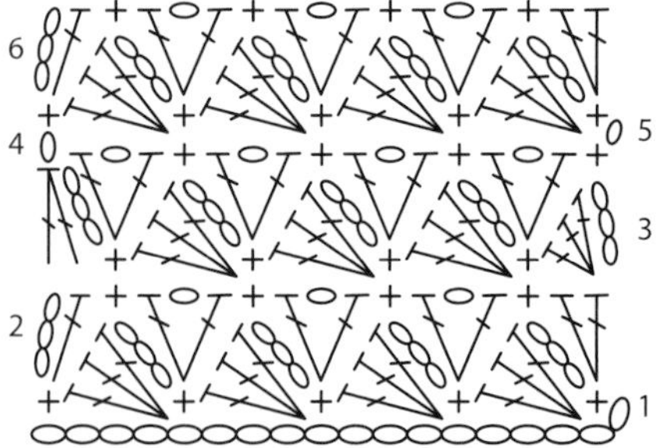

Corded ridge stitch

Any number of sts (add 2 for base chain).

Note: Work all rows with RS facing—for example, work even-numbered rows from left to right.

Row 1 (RS): Skip 3 ch (count as 1dc), 1dc into next and each ch to end. Do not turn.

Row 2: Ch1, 1sc into front loop only of last dc made, *1sc into front loop only of next dc to right; rep from * ending sl st into top of tch at beg of row. Do not turn.

Row 3: Ch3 (count as 1dc), skip 1 st, 1dc into back loop only of next and each st of second-to-last row to end. Do not turn.

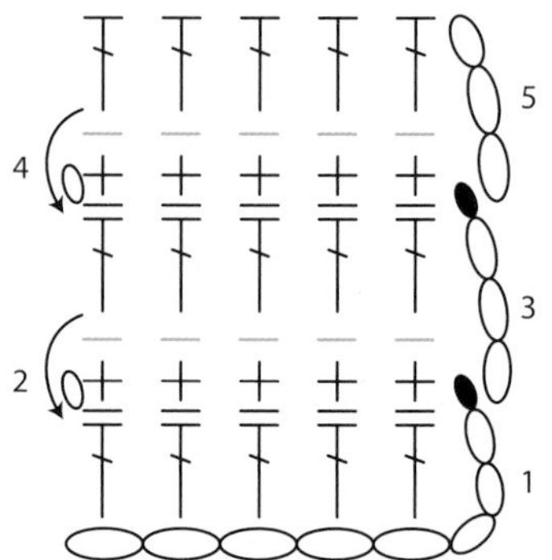

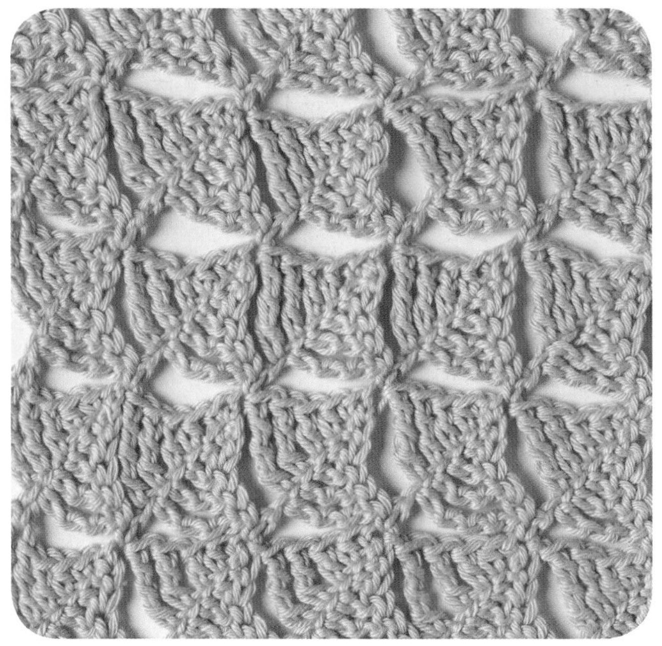

Wedge stitch I

Multiple of 6 sts + 1 (add 1 for base chain).

Special abbreviation:

WP (Wedge Picot) = ch6, 1sc into 2nd ch from hook, 1hdc into next ch, 1dc into next ch, 1tr into next ch, 1dtr into next ch.

Row 1 (WS): 1sc into 2nd ch from hook, *1WP, skip 5 ch, 1sc into next ch; rep from * to end, turn.

Row 2: Ch5 (count as 1dtr), *1sc into top of WP, over next ch-5 at underside of WP work 1sc into next ch, 1hdc into next ch, 1dc into next ch, 1tr into next ch, 1dtr into next ch, skip next sc; rep from * omitting 1dtr at end of last rep when 2 sts rem, **[yo] 3 times, insert hook into last ch at underside of WP, yo, draw loop through, [yo, draw through 2 loops] 3 times, rep from ** into next sc, yo, draw through all 3 loops on hook, skip tch, turn.

Row 3: Ch1, 1sc into 1st st, *1WP, skip next 5 sts, 1sc into next st; rep from * ending last rep with 1sc into top of tch, turn.

Rep rows 2–3.

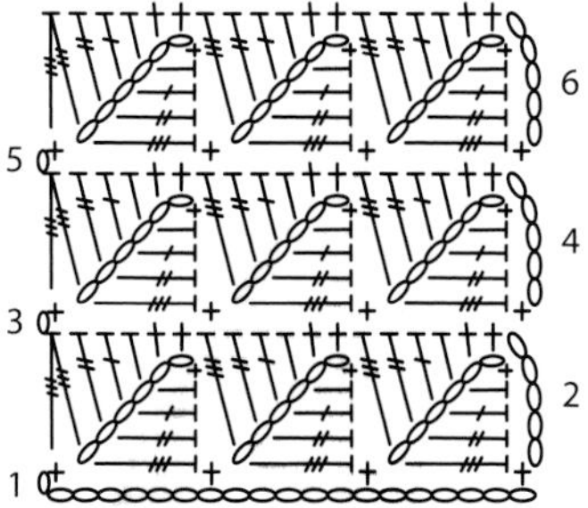

Wedge stitch II

Work as Wedge stitch I (see left).

Make base chain and work 1st row in color A.

Thereafter, work 2 rows each in color B and color A.

Half moon stitch

Multiple of 10 sts +12.

Special abbreviation:

1 circle = rotating work as required, work 6dc down and around stem of next dc 1 row below, then work 6dc up and around stem of previous dc 1 row below.

Row 1 (RS): Work 1dc into 4th ch from hook, 1dc into each ch to end, turn.

Row 2: Ch3 (count as 1dc), skip first dc, work 1dc into each dc to end, working last dc into 3rd of ch-3 at beg of previous row, turn.

Row 3: Ch3, skip first dc, work 1dc into each of next 4 dc, *work 1 circle, working behind circle work 1dc into each of next 10 dc; rep from * to end, omitting 5dc at end of last rep and working last tr into 3rd of ch-3 at beg of previous row, turn.

Rows 4–6: Ch3, skip first dc, work 1dc into each dc to end, working last dc into 3rd of ch-3 at beg of previous row, turn.

Row 7: Ch3, skip first dc, work 1dc into each of next 9 dc, *work 1 circle, 1dc into each of next 10 dc; rep from * to end, working last dc into 3rd of ch-3, turn.

Rows 8– 9: Ch3, skip first dc, work 1dc into each dc to end working last dc into 3rd of ch-3, turn.

Rep rows 2–9.

Crown pattern

Multiple of 8 sts + 7.

Special abbreviation:

Bobble = work 3dc into next sc until last loop of each dc remains on hook, yo and through all 4 loops.

Note: Count each sc, ch sp and bobble as 1 st throughout.

Row 1 (WS): Using A, work 1dc into 4th ch from hook, 1dc into each of next 3 ch, *ch3, skip 1 ch, 1sc into next ch, ch3, skip 1 ch, 1dc into each of next 5 ch; rep from * to end, turn.

Row 2: Using B, ch1, work 1sc into each of 1st 5 dc, *ch1, 1 bobble into next sc, ch1, 1sc into each of next 5 dc; rep from * to end placing last sc into top of ch-3, turn.

Row 3: Using B, ch6 (count as 1dc, ch3), skip 1st 2 sc, 1sc into next sc, ch3, *skip 1 sc, 1dc into each of next 5 sts (see note above), ch3, skip 1 sc, 1sc into next sc, ch3; rep from * to last 2 sc, skip 1 sc, 1dc into last sc, turn.

Row 4: Using A, ch1, work 1sc into 1st dc, ch1, 1 bobble into next sc, ch1, *1sc into each of next 5 dc, ch1, 1 bobble into next sc, ch1; rep from * to last dc, 1sc into 3rd of ch-6 at beg of previous row, turn.

Row 5: Using A, ch3 (count as 1dc), skip 1st sc, 1dc into each of next 4 sts, *ch3, skip 1 sc, 1sc into next sc, ch3, skip 1 sc, 1dc into each of next 5 sts; rep from * to end, turn.

Rep rows 2–5.

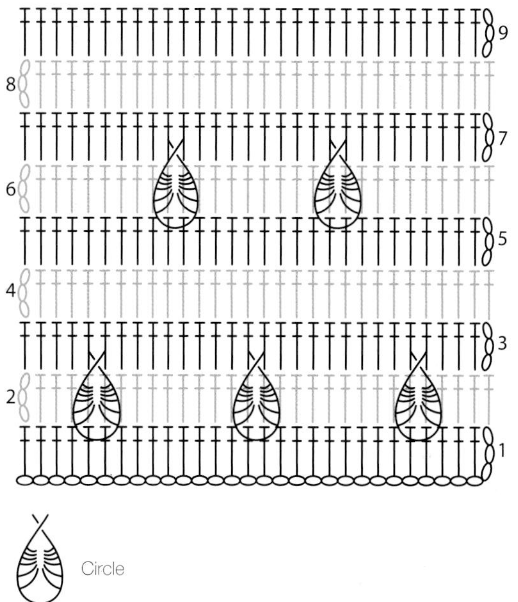

Half moon stitch

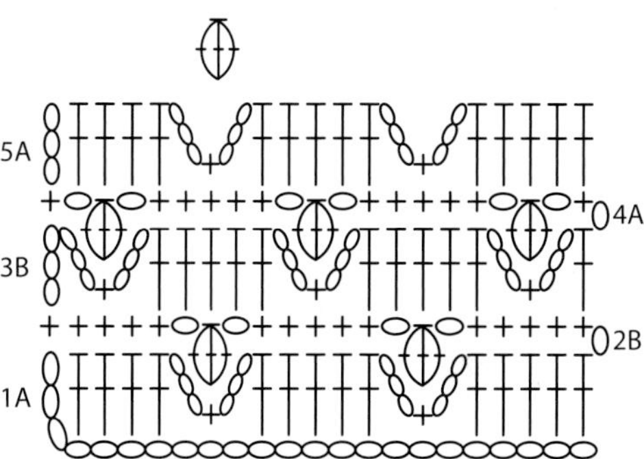

Crown pattern

Pebble lace stitch

Multiple of 4 sts + 3 (add 1 for base chain).

Note: Close tr7tog clusters with ch1 drawn tightly (this does not count as part of following ch loop).

Clusters always occur on WS rows. Be sure to push them all out to the back (RS) of the fabric as you complete them.

Row 1 (WS): 1sc into 2nd ch from hook, *ch2, skip 1 ch, work tr7tog into next ch, ch2, skip 1 ch, 1sc into next ch; rep from * to last 2 ch, ch2, skip 1 ch, 1hdc into last ch, turn.

Row 2: Ch1, 1sc into 1st st, *ch3, 1sc into next cluster; rep from * ending ch1, 1hdc into last sc, skip tch, turn.

Row 3: Ch4, skip 1st hdc and ch, 1sc into next sc, *ch2, tr7tog into 2nd of next ch-3, ch2, 1sc into next sc; rep from * to end, skip tch, turn.

Row 4: Ch3, skip 1st st and ch-2, 1sc into next cluster, *ch3, 1sc into next cluster; rep from * ending ch3, 1sc into last ch-4 arch, turn.

Row 5: Ch1, 1sc into 1st st, *ch2, tr7tog into 2nd of next ch-3, ch2, 1sc into next sc; rep from * ending ch2, skip 1 ch, 1hdc into next ch of tch, turn.

Rep rows 2–5.

Pebble lace stitch

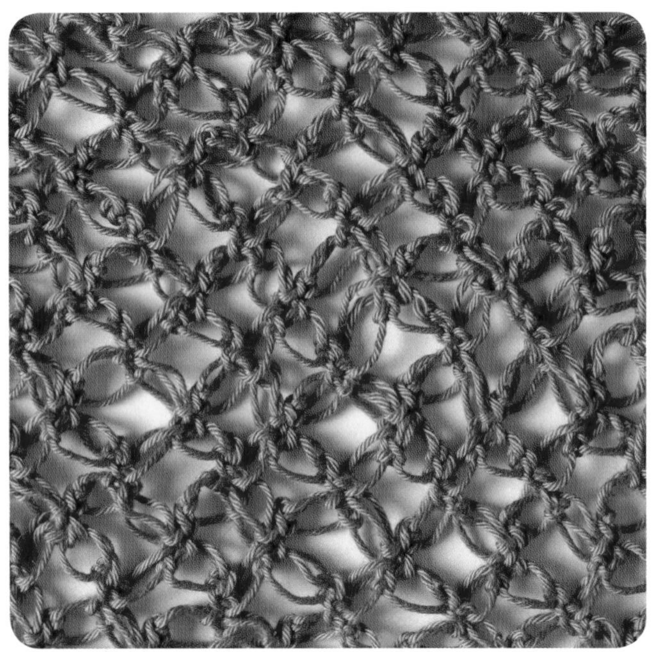

Solomon's knot

Multiple of 2 Solomon's knots + 1 (add 2 Solomon's knots for base "chain").

Special abbreviations:

ESK (Edge Solomon's Knot) = these form the base "chain" and edges of the fabric and are only two-thirds the length of MSKs.

MSK (Main Solomon's Knot) = these form the main fabric and are half as long again as ESKs.

Base chain: Ch2, 1sc into 2nd ch from hook, now make a multiple of 2 ESKs (approx ¾in/2cm), ending with 1 MSK (approx 1¼in/3cm).

Row 1: 1sc into sc between 3rd and 4th loops from hook, *2 MSK, skip 2 loops, 1sc into next sc; rep from * to end, turn.

Row 2: 2 ESK and 1 MSK, 1sc into sc between 4th and 5th loops from hook, *2 MSK, skip 2 loops, 1sc into next sc; rep from * ending in top of ESK, turn.

Rep row 2.

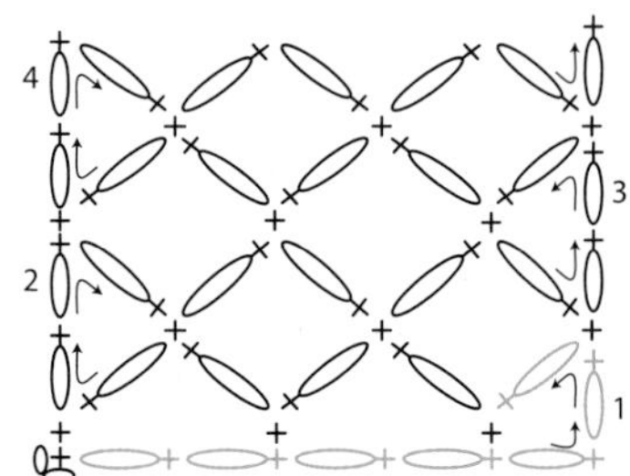

Double crochet cluster stitch I

Multiple of 2 sts (add 2 for base chain).

Special abbreviation:

DcC (Double crochet Cluster) = *yo, insert hook into ch or st as indicated, yo, draw loop through, yo, draw through 2 loops*, skip 1 ch or st, rep from * to * into next st, yo, draw through all 3 loops on hook.

Row 1: Skip 2 ch (count as 1dc), work 1DcC inserting hook 1st into 3rd ch, ch,1 *work 1DcC inserting hook 1st into same ch as previous DcC, ch1; rep from * ending 1dc into last ch, turn.

Row 2: Ch3 (count as 1dc), 1DcC inserting hook first into 1st st, ch1, *1DcC inserting hook first into same st as previous DcC, ch1; rep from * ending 1dc into top of tch, turn.

Rep row 2.

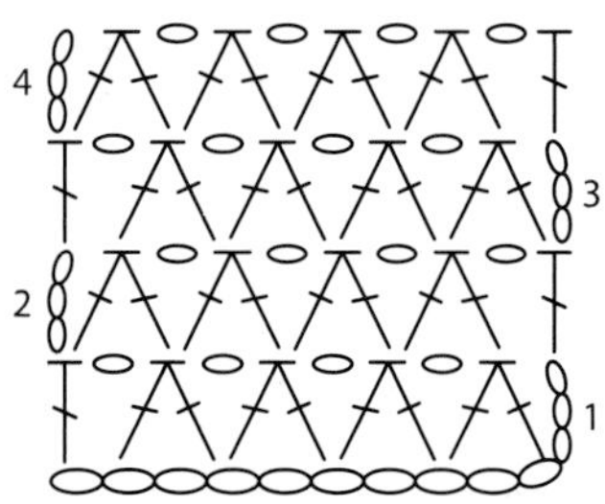

Double crochet cluster stitch II

Multiple of 2 sts (add 2 for base chain).

Special abbreviation:

DcC (Double crochet Cluster) = work as under Double crochet cluster stitch I.

Row 1 (RS): Skip 2 ch (count as 1sc), work 1DcC inserting hook into 3rd ch then 5th ch, ch1, *work 1DcC inserting hook first into same ch as previous DcC, ch1; rep from * ending 1dc into last ch, turn.

Row 2: Ch1, skip 1 st, *1sc into next ch sp, ch1, skip 1 st; rep from * ending 1sc into top of tch, turn.

Row 3: Ch3 (count as 1dc), 1DcC inserting hook first into 1st st, ch1, *1DcC inserting hook first into same st as previous DcC, ch1; rep from * ending 1dc into top of tch, turn.

Rep rows 2–3.

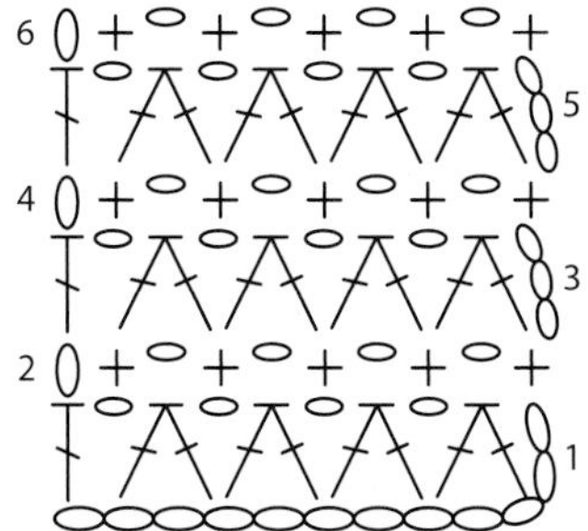

Double crochet cluster stitch III

Any number of sts (add 2 for base chain).

Row 1: Skip 3 ch (count as 1dc), work dc2tog into next and each ch until 1 ch rem, 1dc into last ch, turn.

Row 2: Ch3 (count as 1dc), dc2tog between 1st dc and next cluster, *dc2tog between next 2 clusters; rep from * ending 1dc into top of tch, turn.

Rep row 2.

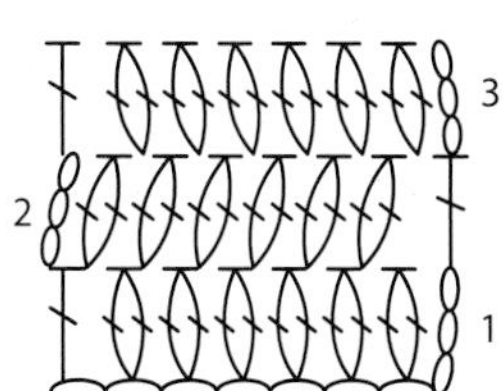

Thistle pattern

Multiple of 10 sts + 1 (add 1 for base chain).

Special abbreviation:

Catch loop = Catch ch-10 loop of Thistle by inserting hook under ch at tip of loop at the same time as under the next st.

Base row (WS): Skip 2 ch (count as 1sc), 1sc into each of next 4 ch, *into next st work a Thistle of 1sc, [ch10, 1sc] 3 times**, 1sc into each of next 9 ch; rep from * ending last rep at **, 1sc into each of last 5 ch, turn.

Commence pattern

Note: Hold loops of Thistle down at front of work on RS rows.

Row 1: Ch1 (count as 1sc), skip 1 sc, 1sc into each of next 4 sc, *skip 1 sc of Thistle, work sc2tog over next 2 sc, skip last sc of Thistle**, work 1sc into each of next 9 sts; rep from * ending last rep at **, 1sc into each of next 4 sc, 1sc into tch, turn.

Rows 2, 4, 8 and 10: Ch1, skip 1 st, 1sc into each st to end, turn.

Row 3: Ch1, skip 1 st, 1sc into next sc, *catch 1st loop of Thistle in next sc, 1sc into each of next 5 sc, skip center loop of Thistle, catch 3rd loop in next st**, 1sc into each of next 3 sc; rep from * ending last rep at **, 1sc into each of last 2 sts, turn.

Row 5: Ch1, skip 1 st, 1sc into each of next 4 sc, *work 6dc into next sc and at the same time catch center loop**, 1sc into each of next 9 sc; rep from * ending last rep at **, 1sc into each of last 5 sts, turn.

Row 6: Ch1, skip 1 st, 1sc into each of 1st 4 sc, *ch1, skip 6 dc, 1sc into each of next 4 sc**, work a Thistle into next sc, 1sc into each of next 4 sc; rep from * ending last rep at **, 1sc into last st, turn.

Row 7: Ch1, skip 1 st, 1sc into each of next 9 sts, *work sc2tog over center 2 of next 4 sc, skip 1 sc, 1sc into each of next 9 sts; rep from * to last st, 1sc into last st, turn.

Row 9: Ch1, skip 1 st, 1sc into each of next 6 sc, *catch 1st loop into next sc, 1sc into each of next 5 sc, catch 3rd loop into next sc**, 1sc into each of next 3 sc; rep from * ending last rep at **, 1sc into each st to end, turn.

Row 11: Ch1, skip 1 st, 1sc into each of next 9 sts, *work 6dc into next sc and catch center loop at the same time, 1sc into each of next 9 sc; rep from * to last st, 1sc in last st, turn.

Row 12: Ch1, skip 1 st, 1sc into each of next 4 sc, *work a Thistle into next sc, 1sc into each of next 4 sc**, ch1, skip 6 dc, 1sc into each of next 4 sc; rep from * ending last rep at **, 1sc into last st, turn.

Rep these 12 rows.

Floret stitch I

Multiple of 2 sts + 1 (add 2 for base chain).

Row 1 (RS): Skip 3 ch (count as 1dc), 1dc into next and each ch to end, turn.

Row 2: Ch1, skip 1 st, *1dc into next st, slip st into next st; rep from * ending last rep into top of tch, turn.

Row 3: Ch3 (count as 1dc), skip 1 st, *1dc into next dc, 1dc into next slip st; rep from * ending last rep into tch, turn.

Rep rows 2–3.

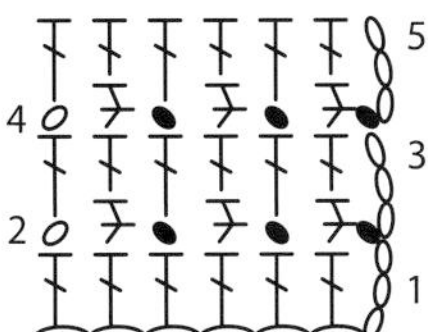

Floret stitch II

Work as Floret stitch I (see left).

Work 1 row each in colors A and B alternately throughout.

Floret stitch III

Work as Floret stitch I (see above left).

Work 1 row each in colors A, B and C throughout.

Crunch stitch

Multiple of 2 sts (add 1 for base chain).

Row 1: Skip 2 ch (count as 1hdc), *slip st into next ch, 1hdc into next ch; rep from * ending slip st into last ch, turn.

Row 2: Ch2 (count as 1hdc), skip 1 st, *slip st into next hdc, 1hdc into next slip st; rep from * ending slip st into top of tch, turn.

Rep row 2.

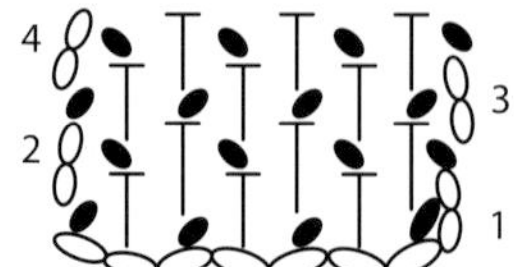

Griddle stitch

Multiple of 2 sts (add 2 for base chain).

Row 1: Skip 3 ch (count as 1dc), *1sc into next ch, 1dc into next ch; rep from * ending 1sc into last ch, turn.

Row 2: Ch3 (count as 1dc), skip 1 st, *1sc into next dc, 1dc into next sc; rep from * ending 1sc into top of tch, turn.

Rep row 2.

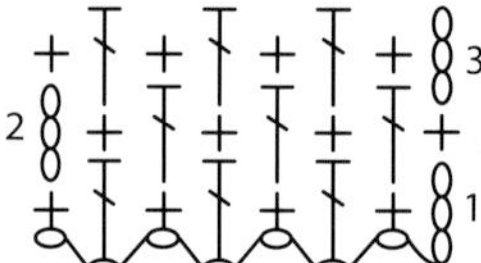

Crumpled griddle stitch

Multiple of 2 sts + 1 (add 2 for base chain).

Row 1: Skip 3 ch (count as 1dc), *1sc into next ch, 1dc into next ch; rep from * to end, turn.

Row 2: Ch3 (count as 1dc), skip 1 st, *1sc into next sc, 1dc into next dc; rep from * ending last rep into top of tch, turn.

Rep row 2.

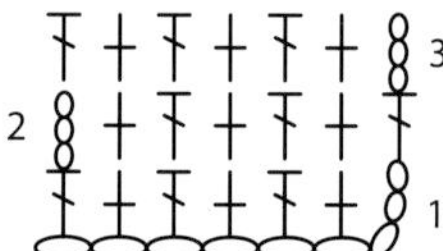

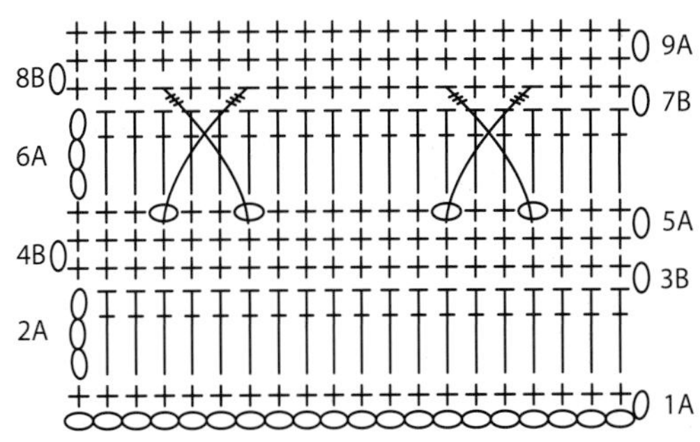

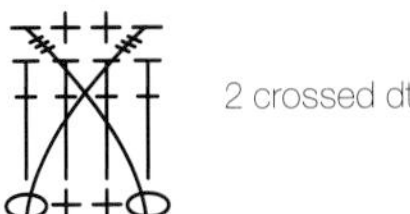

2 crossed dtr

Slot stitch

Multiple of 10 sts + 1.

Using A make required number of chains.

Row 1 (RS): Using A, work 1sc into 2nd ch from hook, 1sc into each ch to end, turn.

Row 2: Using A, ch3 (count as 1dc), skip 1st sc, work 1dc into each sc to end, turn.

Row 3: Using B, ch1, work 1sc into each dc to end placing last sc into 3rd of ch-3 at beg of previous row, turn.

Row 4: Using B, ch1, work 1sc into each sc to end, turn.

Row 5: Using A, ch1, work 1sc into each of 1st 3 sc, *ch1, skip 1 sc, 1sc into each of next 2 sc, ch1, skip 1 sc, 1sc into each of next 6 sc; rep from * to end omitting 3sc at end of last rep, turn. On row 6 work dc into ch not ch space.

Row 6: Using A, ch3 (count as 1dc), skip 1st sc, 1dc into each sc and into each ch to end, turn.

Row 7: Using B, ch1, 1sc into each of 1st 3 dc, *work 1dtr into 2nd skipped sc 3 rows below, skip 1 dc, 1sc into each of next 2 dc, 1dtr into 1st skipped sc 3 rows below (thus crossing 2dtr), skip 1 dc, 1sc into each of next 6 dc; rep from * to end omitting 3sc at end of last rep and placing last sc into 3rd of ch-3 at beg of previous row, turn.

Row 8: Using B, ch1, work 1sc into each st to end, turn.

Row 9: Using A, ch1, work 1sc into each sc to end, turn.

Rep rows 2–9.

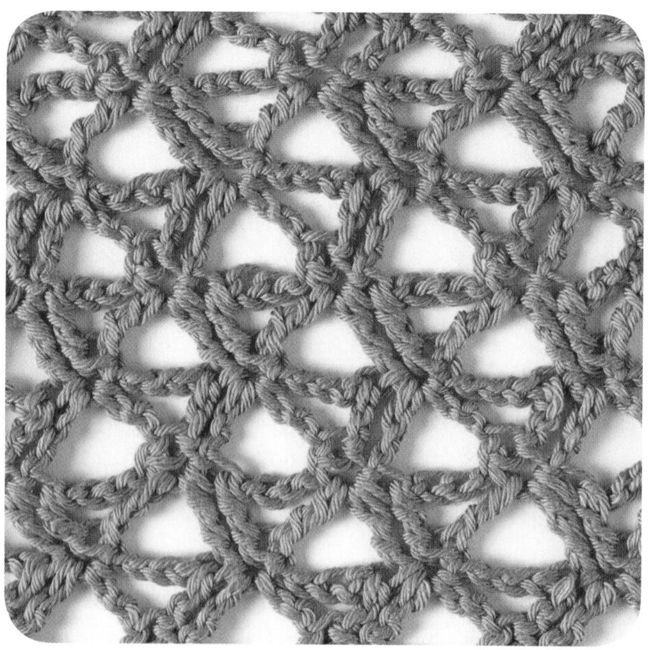

Doubled lattice stitch

Multiple of 6 sts + 2 (add 3 for base chain).

Row 1 (RS): Skip 6 ch, 1tr into next ch (counts as edge cluster), ch4, 1tr into same ch as tr just made, *tr2tog inserting hook into next ch for 1st leg and then into following 5th ch for 2nd leg (skipping 4 ch between), ch4, 1tr into same ch as 2nd leg of cluster just made; rep from * to last 4 ch, tr2tog inserting hook into next ch for 1st leg and into last ch for 2nd leg (skipping 2 ch between), turn.

Row 2: Ch6 (count as 1tr, ch2), 1tr into 1st st, *tr2tog inserting hook into next tr for 1st leg and then into next cluster for 2nd leg**, ch4, 1tr into same place as 2nd leg of cluster just made; rep from * ending last rep at ** when 2nd leg is in edge cluster, ch2, 1tr into same place, turn.

Row 3: Ch4, skip 2 ch, 1tr into next cluster (counts as edge cluster), *ch4, 1tr into same place as tr just made**, tr2tog inserting hook into next tr for 1st leg and then into next cluster for 2nd leg; rep from * ending last rep at **, tr2tog inserting hook into next tr for 1st leg and then into following 3rd ch for 2nd leg, turn.

Rep rows 2–3.

Zigzag pip stitch

Multiple of 4 sts + 1 (add 1 for base chain).

Note: Work 1 row each in colors A, B, C, D, and E throughout.

Row 1 (RS): 1sc into 2nd ch from hook, *ch1, skip 1 ch, 1sc into next ch; rep from * to end, turn.

Row 2: Ch3, 1dc into next ch sp (counts as dc2tog), *ch1, dc2tog inserting hook into same sp as previous st for first leg and into next sp for 2nd leg; rep from * to last sp, ending ch1, dc2tog over same sp and last sc, skip tch, turn.

Row 3: Ch1, 1sc into first st, *1sc into next sp, ch1, skip next cluster; rep from * ending 1sc into last sp, 1sc into last st, skip tch, turn.

Row 4: Ch3 (count as 1dc), dc2tog inserting hook into first st for first leg and into next sp for 2nd leg, *ch1, dc2tog inserting hook into same sp as previous st for first leg and into next sp for 2nd leg; rep from * ending with 2nd leg of last cluster in last sc, 1dc into same place, skip tch, turn.

Row 5: Ch1, 1sc into first st, *ch1, skip next cluster, 1sc into next sp; rep from * working last sc into top of tch, turn.

Rep rows 2-5.

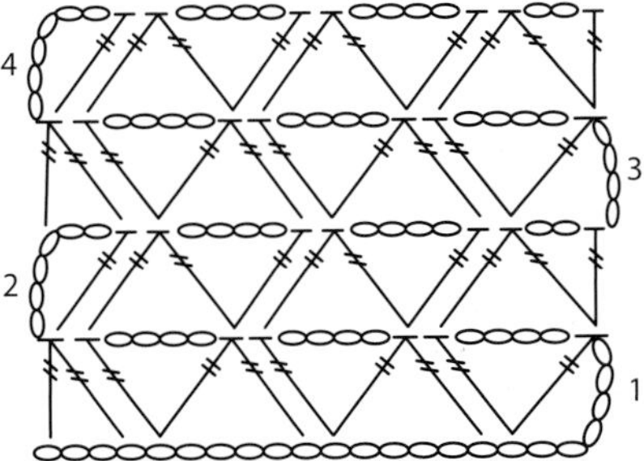

Doubled lattice stitch

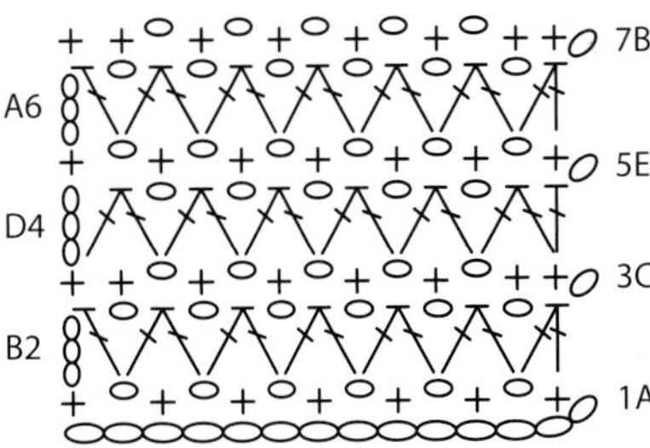

Zigzag pip stitch

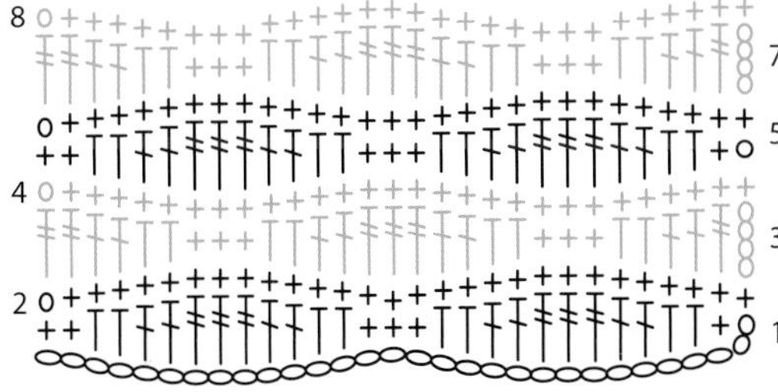

Long wave stitch

Long wave stitch

Multiple of 14 sts + 1 (add 1 for base chain).

Special abbreviations:

Gr (Group) (worked over 14 sts) = 1sc into next st, [1hdc into next st] twice, [1dc into next st] twice, [1tr into next st] 3 times, [1dc into next st] twice, [1hdc into next st] twice, [1sc into next st] twice.

Rev Gr (Reverse Group) (worked over 14 sts) = 1tr into next st, [1dc into next st] twice, [1hdc into next st] twice, [1sc into next st] 3 times, [1hdc into next st] twice, [1dc into next st] twice, [1tr into next st] twice.

Work 2 rows each in colors A and B alternately throughout.

Row 1 (RS): Skip 2 ch (count as 1sc), *1 Gr over next 14 ch; rep from * to end, turn.

Row 2: Ch1 (count as 1sc), skip 1st st, 1sc into next and each st to end working last st into top of tch, turn.

Row 3: Ch4 (count as 1tr), skip 1st st, *1 Rev Gr over next 14 sts; rep from * ending last rep in tch, turn.

Row 4: As row 2.

Row 5: Ch1 (count as 1sc), skip 1st st, *1 Gr over next 14 sts; rep from * ending last rep in tch, turn.

Row 6: As row 2.

Rep rows 3–6.

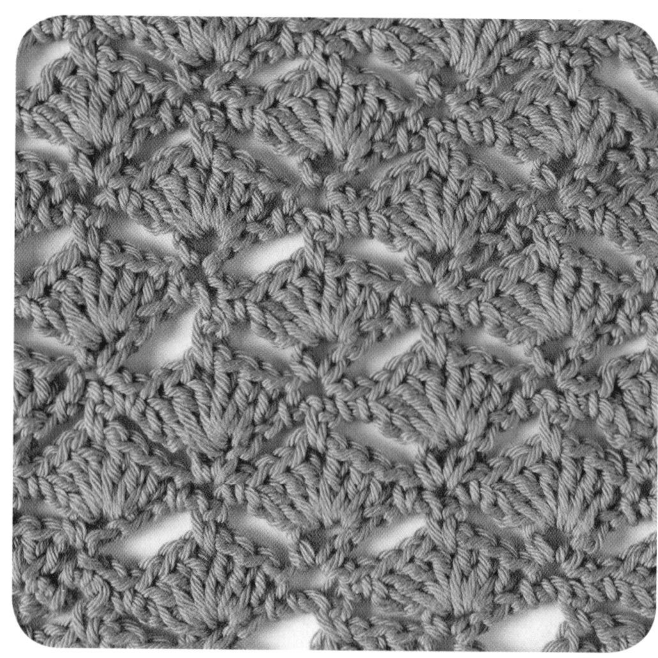

Embossed pockets

Multiple of 3 sts + 1 (add 2 for base chain).

Special abbreviation:

PGr (Pocket Group) = work [1sc, 1hdc, 3dc] around stem of indicated st.

Row 1 (WS): Skip 3 ch (count as 1dc), 1dc into each ch to end, turn.

Row 2: 1PGr around 1st st, skip 2 sts, slip st into top of next st, *1PGr around same st as sl st, skip 2 sts, slip st into top of next st; rep from * to end, turn.

Row 3: Ch3 (count as 1dc), skip 1 st, 1dc into each st to end, turn.

Rep rows 2–3.

Fantail stitch

Multiple of 10 sts + 1.
(add 1 for base chain)

Row 1 (RS): 1sc into 2nd ch from hook, 1sc into next ch, *skip 3 ch, work a Fan of [3dc, ch1, 3dc] into next ch, skip 3 ch, 1sc into next ch**, ch1, skip 1 ch, 1sc into next ch; rep from * ending last rep at **, 1sc into last ch, turn.

Row 2: Ch2 (count as 1hdc), 1hdc into first st, *ch3, 1sc into ch sp at center of next Fan, ch3**, work a V st of [1hdc, ch1, 1hdc] into next sp; rep from * ending last rep at **, 2hdc into last sc, skip tch, turn.

Row 3: Ch3, 3dc into first st, *1sc into next ch-3 arch, ch1, 1sc into next arch**, work a Fan into sp at center of next V st; rep from * ending last rep at **, 4dc into top of tch, turn.

Row 4: Ch1, 1sc into first st, *ch3, V st into next sp, ch3, 1sc into sp at center of next Fan; rep from * ending last rep into top of tch, turn.

Row 5: Ch1, 1sc into first st, *1sc into next arch, Fan into sp at center of next V st, 1sc into next arch**, ch1; rep from * ending last rep at **, 1sc into last sc, skip tch, turn.

Rep rows 2–5.

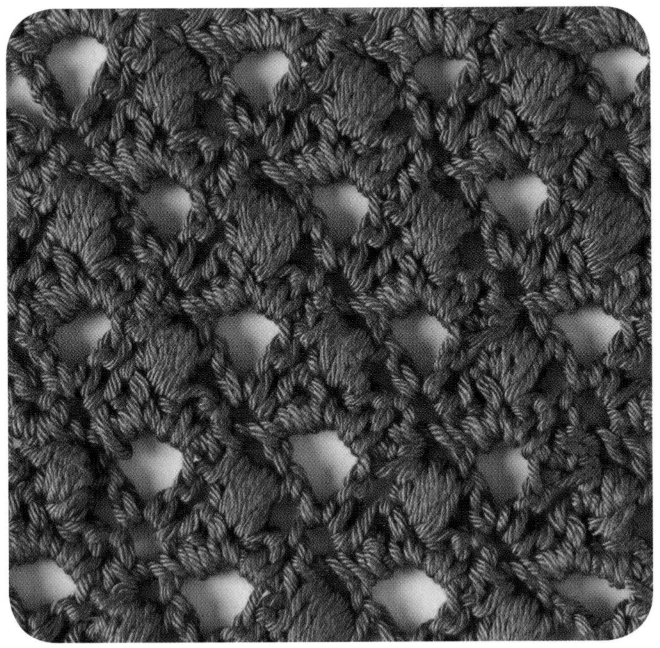

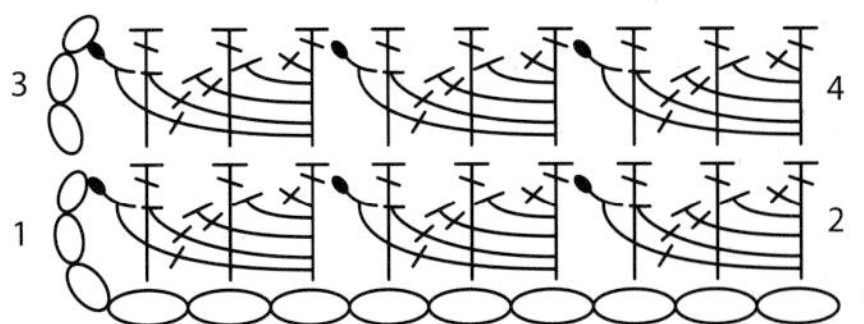

Embossed pockets

Fantail stitch

Crown puff lattice

Crown puff lattice

Multiple of 6 sts + 1 (add 2 for base chain).

Row 1 (RS): 1hdc into 3rd ch from hook, *1sc into next ch, sc3tog over next 3 ch, 1sc into next ch, [1hdc, 1dc, 1hdc] into next ch; rep from * omitting 1hdc at end of last rep, turn.

Row 2: Ch3 (count as 1dc), skip 1st 3 sts, *[1tr, ch3, 1tr] into next sc cluster, skip 2 sts**, work hdc5tog into next dc; rep from * ending last rep at **, 1dc into top of tch, turn.

Row 3: Ch1, skip 1 st, 1sc into next tr (all counts as sc cluster), *[1sc, 1hdc, 1dc, 1hdc, 1sc] into next ch-3 arch**, sc3tog over next

3 sts; rep from * ending last rep at **, sc2tog over last st and top of tch, turn.

Row 4: Ch5 (count as 1tr, ch1), 1tr into 1st st, *skip 2 sts, hdc5tog into next dc, skip 2 sts**, [1tr, ch3, 1tr] into next sc cluster; rep from * ending last rep at **, [1tr, ch1, 1tr] into top of tch, turn.

Row 5: Ch3 (count as 1dc), 1hdc into 1st st, 1sc into next ch sp, *sc3tog over next 3 sts**, [1sc, 1hdc, 1dc, 1hdc, 1sc] into next ch-3 arch; rep from * ending last rep at **, 1sc into next ch of tch, [1hdc, 1dc] into next ch, turn.

Rep rows 2–5.

Wave and chevron stitch

Multiple of 6 sts + 1 (add 1 for base chain).
Work 2 rows each in colors A, B, C and D throughout.
Base row (RS): Skip 2 ch (count as 1sc), 1sc into next and each ch to end, turn.

Commence pattern
Row 1: Ch1 (count as 1sc), skip 1 st, *1hdc into next st, 1dc into next st, 3tr into next st, 1dc into next st, 1hdc into next st, 1sc into next st; rep from * to end, turn.
Row 2: Ch1, skip 1 st, 1sc into next st (count as sc2tog), 1sc into each of next 2 sts, *3sc into next st, 1sc into each of next 2 sts, over next 3 sts work sc3tog, 1sc into each of next 2 sts; rep from * to last 5 sts, 3sc into next st, 1sc into each of next 2 sts, over last 2 sts work sc2tog, skip tch, turn.
Row 3: As row 2.
Row 4: Ch4, skip 1 st, 1tr into next st (count as tr2tog), *1dc into next st, 1hdc into next st, 1sc into next st, 1hdc into next st, 1dc into next st**, over next 3 sts work tr3tog; rep from * ending last rep at **, over last 2 sts work tr2tog, skip tch, turn.
Row 5: Ch1 (count as 1sc), skip 1 st, 1sc into next and each st to end, turn.
Row 6: As row 5.
Rep rows 1–6.

Single rib

Multiple of 2 sts (add 2 for base chain).
Special abbreviations:
Dc/rf (raised double crochet at the front of the fabric) = wrap the yarn around the hook, insert the hook from in front and from right to left around the stem of the appropriate stitch, and complete the stitch normally.
Dc/rb (raised double crochet at the back of the fabric) = wrap the yarn around the hook, insert the hook from behind and from right to left around the stem of the appropriate stitch, and complete the stitch normally.
Row 1 (WS): Skip 3 ch (count as 1dc), 1dc into next and each ch to end, turn.
Row 2: Ch2 (count as 1dc), skip 1st st, *1dc/rf around next st, 1dc/rb around next st; rep from * ending 1dc into top of tch, turn.
Rep row 2.

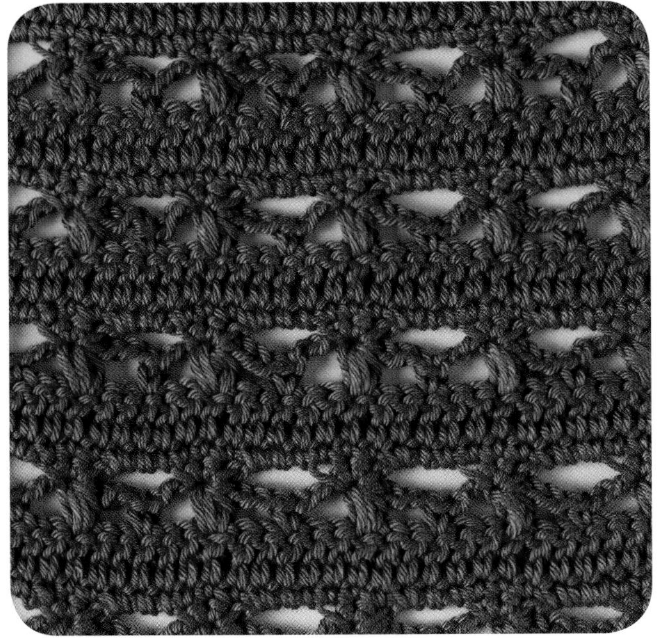

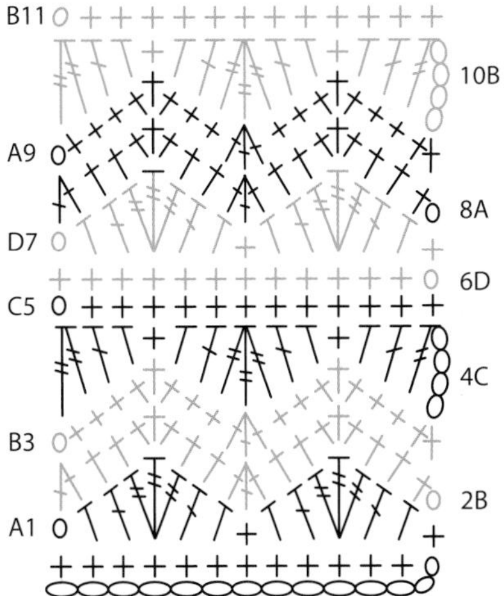

Wave and chevron stitch

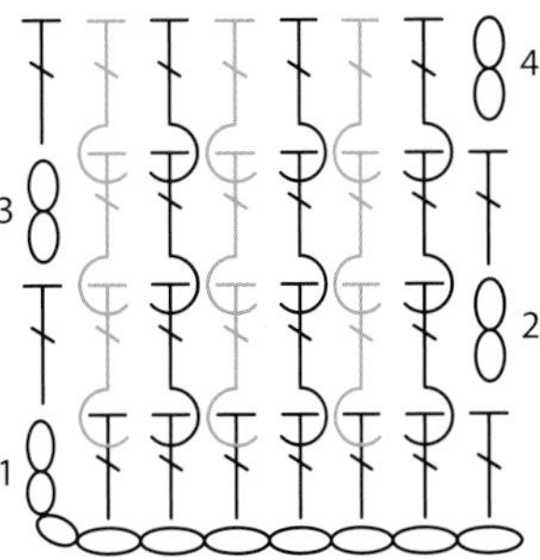

Single rib

Theatre box

Multiple of 6 sts + 4.

Special abbreviation:

Puff st = [yo, insert hook into next st, yo and draw a loop through] 3 times into same st, yo and draw through 7 loops on hook, work 1 firm ch to close puff st.

Row 1 (RS): Work 1sc into 2nd ch from hook, 1sc into each ch to end, turn.

Row 2: Ch3 (count as 1dc), skip 1st sc, 1dc into each sc to end, turn.

Row 3: Ch1, 1sc into each of 1st 2 dc, *ch3, skip 2 dc, 1 puff st into next dc, ch3, skip 2 dc, 1sc into next dc; rep from * to last dc, 1sc into 3rd of ch-3 at beg of previous row, turn.

Row 4: Ch5 (count as 1dc, ch2), work 3sc into closing ch of next puff st, *ch3, 3sc into closing ch of next puff st; rep from * to last 2 sc, ch2, 1dc into last dc, turn.

Row 5: Ch1, 1sc into 1st dc, 2sc into 1st ch-2 sp, *1sc into each of next 3 sc, 3sc into next ch-3 sp; rep from * to end working last sc into 3rd of ch-5 at beg of previous row, turn.

Rep rows 2–5.

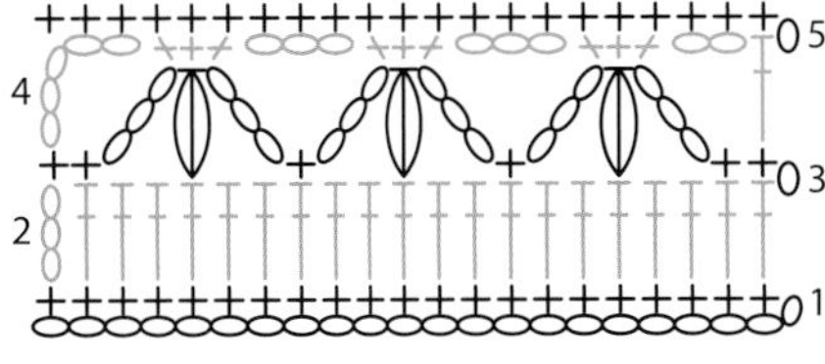

Puff st

Theatre box

Crow's foot lattice

Multiple of 6 sts + 1 (add 4 for base chain).

Row 1 (WS): Skip 4 ch (count as 1tr, ch1), 1dc into next ch, ch1, skip 2 ch, 1sc into next ch, *ch1, skip 2 ch, work [1dc, ch1, 1tr, ch1, 1dc] into next ch, ch1, skip 2 ch, 1sc into next ch; rep from * to last 3 ch, ch1, skip 2 ch, [1dc, ch1, 1tr] into last ch, turn.

Row 2: Ch1, 1sc into 1st st, *ch1, skip 2 sps, 1tr into next sc, ch1, 1dc into base of tr just made, ch1, skip 2 sps, 1sc into next tr; rep from * ending last rep in tch, turn.

Row 3: Ch1, 1sc into 1st st, *ch1, skip sp, work [1dc, ch1, 1tr, ch1, 1dc] into next sp, ch1, skip sp, 1sc into next sc; rep from * to end, turn.

Row 4: Ch4 (count as 1tr), 1dc into 4th ch from hook, *ch1, skip 2 sps, 1sc into next tr, ch1, 1tr into next sc**, ch1, 1dc into base of tr just made; rep from * ending last rep at **, 1dc into base of tr just made, turn.

Row 5: Ch5 (count as 1tr, ch1), 1dc into 1st st, ch1, skip sp, 1sc into next sc, *ch1, skip sp, work [1dc, ch1, 1tr, ch1, 1dc] into next sp, ch1, skip sp, 1sc into next sc; rep from * ending ch1, skip sp, [1dc, ch1, 1tr] into top of tch, turn.

Rep rows 2–5.

Interlocking diamonds

Multiple of 6 sts + 1 (add 1 for base chain).

Work row 1 in color A, then 2 rows each in colors B and A alternately throughout.

Row 1 (WS): Slip st into 2nd ch from hook, *ch3, skip 2 ch, 1dc into next ch, ch3, skip 2 ch, slip st into next ch; rep from * to end, turn.

Row 2: Ch4 (count as 1dc, ch1), 1dc into first sl st, *skip 3 ch, slip st into next dc**, skip 3 ch, work [1dc, ch1, 1dc, ch1, 1dc] into next slip st; rep from * ending last rep at ** in last dc, skip 3 ch, work [1dc, ch1, 1dc] into last slip st, turn.

Row 3: Ch6 (count as 1dc, ch3), skip [first st, 1 ch and 1 dc], *sl st into next slip st**, ch3, skip 1 dc and 1 ch, 1dc into next dc, ch3, skip 1 ch and 1 dc; rep from * ending last rep at ** in last slip st, ch3, skip 1 dc and 1 ch, 1dc into next ch to tch, turn.

Row 4: Slip st into first st, *skip 3 ch, [1dc, ch1, 1dc, ch1, 1dc] all into next slip st, skip 3 ch, slip st into next dc; rep from * ending in 3rd ch of tch loop, turn.

Row 5: *Ch3, skip 1 dc and 1 ch, 1dc into next dc, ch3, skip 1 ch and 1 dc, slip st into next slip st; rep from * to end, turn.

Rep rows 2–5.

Crow's foot lattice

Solid shell stitch

Multiple of 6 sts + 1 (add 1 for base chain).

Row 1: 1sc into 2nd ch from hook, *skip 2 ch, 5dc into next ch, skip 2 ch, 1sc into next ch; rep from * to end, turn.

Row 2: Ch3 (count as 1dc), 2dc into 1st st, *skip 2 dc, 1sc into next dc, skip 2 dc, 5dc into next sc; rep from * ending last rep with 3dc into last sc, skip tch, turn.

Row 3: Ch1, 1sc into 1st st, *skip 2 dc, 5dc into next sc, skip 2 dc, 1sc into next dc; rep from * ending last rep with 1sc into top of tch, turn.

Rep rows 2–3.

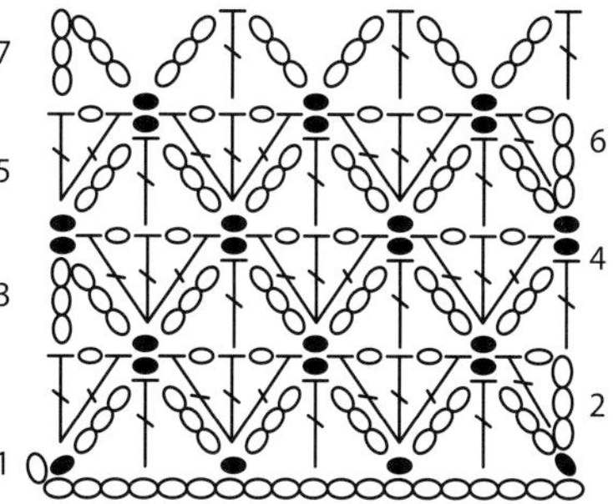
Interlocking diamonds

Solid shell stitch

Wavy shell stitch I

Multiple of 14 sts + 1 (add 2 for base chain).

Row 1 (RS): Skip 2 ch (count as 1dc), 3dc into next ch, *skip 3 ch, 1sc into each of next 7 ch, skip 3 ch, 7dc into next ch; rep from * ending last rep with 4dc into last ch, turn.

Row 2: Ch1, 1sc into 1st st, 1sc into each st to end, finishing with 1sc into top of tch, turn.

Row 3: Ch1, 1sc into each of 1st 4 sts, *skip 3 sts, 7dc into next st, skip 3 sts, 1sc into each of next 7 sts; rep from * to last 11 sts, skip 3 sts, 7dc into next st, skip 3 sts, 1sc into each of last 4 sc, skip tch, turn.

Row 4: Ch1, 1sc into 1st st, 1sc into next and each st to end, skip tch, turn.

Row 5: Ch3 (count as 1dc), 3dc into 1st st, *skip 3 sts, 1sc into each of next 7 sts, skip 3 sts, 7dc into next st; rep from * ending last rep with 4dc into last sc, skip tch, turn.

Rep rows 2–5.

Wavy shell stitch II

Work as Wavy shell stitch I (see left).

Work 1 row each in colors A, B and C throughout.

Wheatsheaf

Multiple of 5 sts + 2.

Row 1 (WS): Work 1sc into 2nd ch from hook, 1sc into next ch, *ch3, skip 2 ch, 1sc into each of next 3 ch; rep from * to end omitting 1sc at end of last rep, turn.

Row 2: Ch1, 1sc into 1st sc, *5dc into next ch-3 arch, skip 1 sc, 1sc into next sc; rep from * to end, turn.

Row 3: Ch3 (count as 1hdc, ch1), skip 1st 2 sts, 1sc into each of next 3 dc, *ch3, skip next 3 sts, 1sc into each of next 3 dc; rep from * to last 2 sts, ch1, 1hdc into last sc, turn.

Row 4: Ch3 (count as 1dc), 2dc into 1st ch sp, skip 1 sc, 1sc into next sc, *5dc into next ch-3 arch, skip 1 sc, 1sc into next sc; rep from * to last sp, 2dc into last sp, 1dc into 2nd of ch-3 at beg of previous row, turn.

Row 5: Ch1, 1sc into each of 1st 2 dc, *ch3, skip 3 sts, 1sc into each of next 3 dc; rep from * to end omitting 1sc at end of last rep and placing last sc into 3rd of ch-3 at beg of previous row, turn.

Rep rows 2–5.

Woven shell stitch

Multiple of 6 sts + 1 (add 2 for base chain).

Special abbreviation:

CGr (Crossed Group) = skip 3 dc and next st, 3dc into 2nd of next 3 dc, ch3, 3dc into 2nd of 3 dc just skipped working back over last 3dc.

Row 1: Skip 3 ch (count as 1dc), *skip next 3 ch, 3dc into next ch, ch3, 3dc into 2nd of 3 ch just skipped working back over last 3 dc made, skip 1 ch, 1dc into next ch; rep from * to end, turn.

Row 2: Ch3 (count as 1dc), 3dc into 1st st, 1sc into next ch-3 arch, *1CGr, 1sc into next ch-3 arch; rep from * ending 4dc into top of tch, turn.

Row 3: Ch3 (count as 1dc), skip 1 st, 1CGr, *1sc into next ch-3 loop, 1CGr; rep from * ending 1dc into top of tch, turn.

Rep rows 2–3.

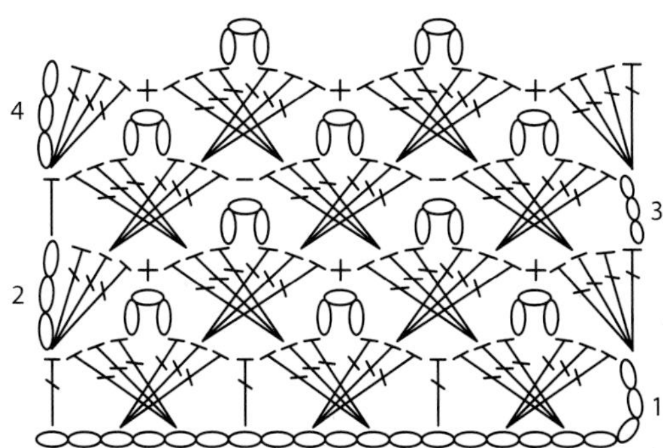

Catherine wheel I

Multiple of 10 sts + 6 (add 1 for base chain).

Special abbreviation:

CL (Cluster) = work [yo, insert hook, yo, draw loop through, yo, draw through 2 loops] over the number of sts indicated, yo, draw through all loops on hook.

Row 1 (WS): 1sc into 2nd ch from hook, 1sc into next ch, *skip 3 ch, 7dc into next ch, skip 3 ch, 1sc into each of next 3 ch; rep from * to last 4 ch, skip 3 ch, 4dc into last ch, turn.

Row 2: Ch1, 1sc into 1st st, 1sc into next st, *ch3, 1CL over next 7 sts, ch3, 1sc into each of next 3 sts; rep from * to last 4 sts, ch3, 1CL over last 4 sts, skip tch, turn.

Row 3: Ch3 (count as 1dc), 3dc into 1st st, *skip ch-3, 1sc into each of next 3 sc, skip ch-3, 7dc into loop that closed next CL; rep from * to end finishing with skip ch-3, 1sc into each of last 2 sc, skip tch, turn.

Row 4: Ch3 (count as 1dc), skip 1st st, 1CL over next 3 sts, *ch3, 1sc into each of next 3 sts, ch3, 1CL over next 7 sts; rep from * finishing with ch3, 1sc into next st, 1sc into top of tch, turn.

Row 5: Ch1, 1sc into each of 1st 2 sc, *skip ch-3, 7dc into loop that closed next CL, skip ch-3, 1sc into each of next 3 sc; rep from * ending skip ch-3, 4dc into top of tch, turn.

Rep rows 2–5.

Catherine wheel II

Work as Catherine wheel I (see left).

Work 1 row each in colors A, B and C throughout.

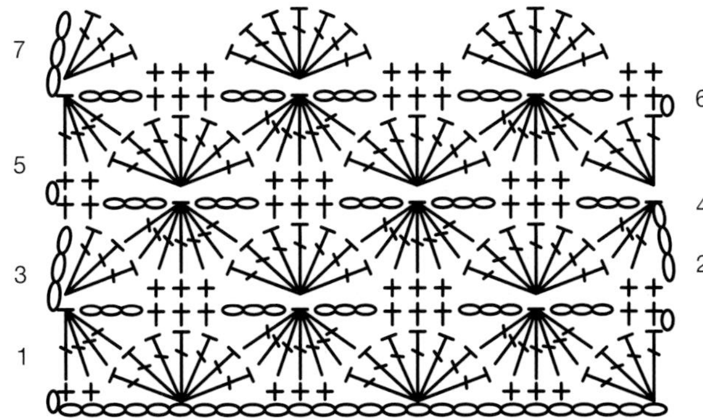

Catherine wheel III

Catherine wheel III

Multiple of 8 sts +1 (add 1 for base chain).

Special abbreviation:

CL (Cluster) = worked as under Catherine wheel I (see left).

Row 1 (RS): 1sc into 2nd ch from hook, *skip 3 ch, 9dc into next ch, skip 3 ch, 1sc into next ch; rep from * to end, turn.

Row 2: Ch3 (count as 1dc), skip 1st st, 1CL over next 4 sts, *ch3, 1sc into next st, ch3, 1CL over next 9 sts; rep from * ending last rep with 1CL over last 5 sts, skip tch, turn.

Row 3: Ch3 (count as 1dc), 4dc into 1st st, *skip ch-3, 1sc into next sc, skip ch-3, 9dc into loop that closed next CL; rep from * ending last rep with 5dc into top of tch, turn.

Row 4: Ch1, 1sc into 1st st, *ch3, 1CL over next 9 sts, ch3, 1sc into next st; rep from * ending last rep with 1sc into top of tch, turn.

Row 5: Ch1, 1sc into 1st st, *skip ch-3, 9dc into loop that closed next CL, skip ch-3, 1sc into next sc; rep from * to end, skip tch, turn.

Rep rows 2–5.

Smooth wave stitch

Multiple of 8 sts + 4 (add 1 for base chain).

Work 2 rows each in colors A and B alternately throughout.

Row 1 (RS): Skip 2 ch (count as 1sc), 1sc into each of next 3 ch, *1dc into each of next 4 ch, 1sc into each of next 4 ch; rep from * to end, turn.

Row 2: Ch1 (count as 1sc), skip 1st st, 1sc into each of next 3 sts, *1dc into each of next 4 sts, 1sc into each of next 4 sts; rep from * to end working last st into top of tch, turn.

Row 3: Ch3 (count as 1dc), skip 1st st, 1dc into each of next 3 sts, *1sc into each of next 4 sts, 1dc into each of next 4 sts; rep from * to end working last st into top of tch, turn.

Row 4: As row 3.

Rows 5–6: As row 2.

Rep rows 3–6.

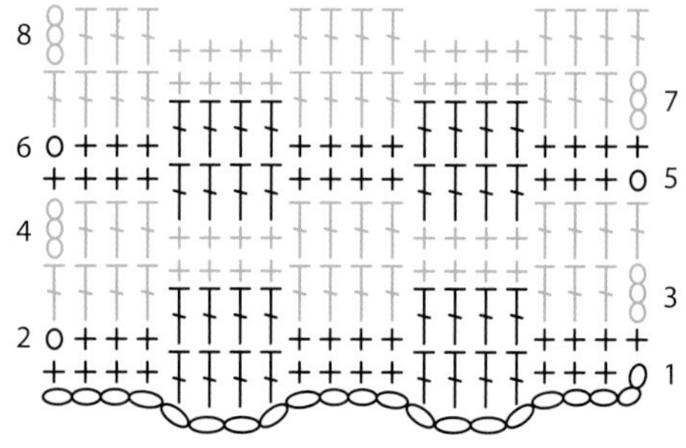

Silt stitch

Multiple of 3 sts + 1 (add 2 for base chain).

Row 1 (RS): Skip 3 ch (count as 1dc), 1dc into next and each ch to end, turn.

Row 2: Ch1 (count as 1sc), 2dc into 1st st, *skip 2 sts, work [1sc, 2dc] into next st; rep from * to last 3 sts, skip 2 sts, 1sc into top of tch, turn.

Row 3: Ch3 (count as 1dc), skip 1 st, 1dc into next and each st to end, working last st into top of tch, turn.

Rep rows 2–3.

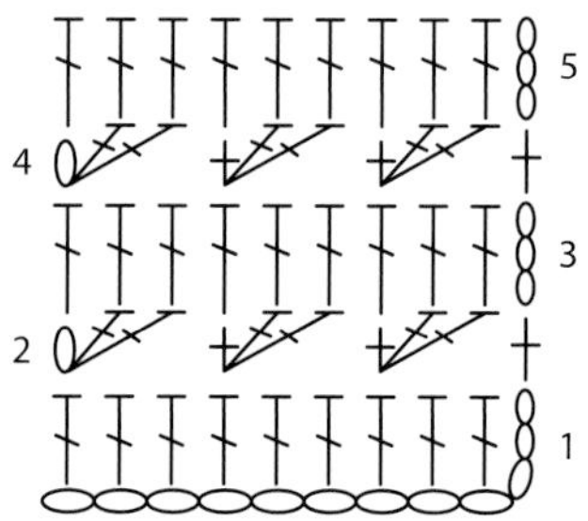

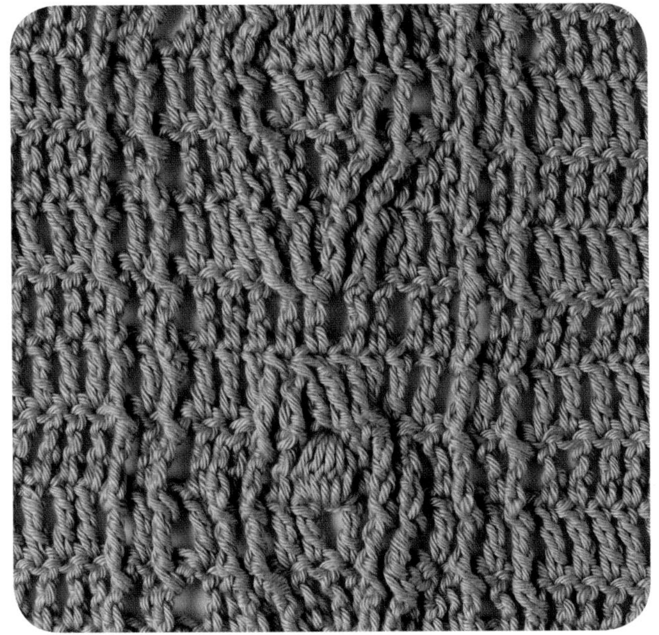

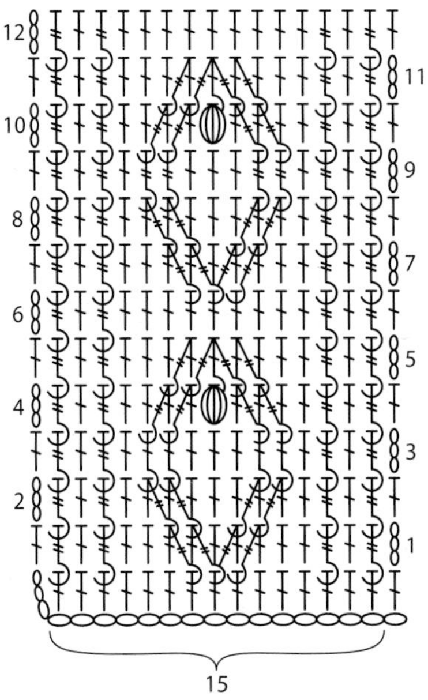

Tulip cable

Worked over 15 sts on a background of basic double crochets with any number of sts.

Special abbreviations:

FCL (Forward Cluster) = leaving last loop of each st on hook, work 1dc into next st and 1tr/rf or rb (see Note below) around next st after that, ending yo, draw through all 3 loops on hook.

BCL (Backward Cluster) = leaving last loop of each st on hook, work 1tr/rf or rb around st below dc just made and 1dc into next st.

Note: Raised legs of these clusters are to be worked at front (rf) on RS rows and at back (rb) on WS rows as indicated in the text thus: FCL/rf, FCL/rb, BCL/rf, BCL/rb.

TCL (Triple Cluster) = leaving last loop of each st on hook work, 1tr/rf around st below dc just made, 1tr/rf around next puff st, and 1tr/rf around next st, ending yo, draw through all 4 loops on hook.

Row 1 (RS): 1tr/rf around next st, 1dc into next st, 1tr/rf around next st, 1dc into each of next 2sts, [1FCL/rf] twice, 1dc into next st, [1BCL/rf] twice, 1dc into each of next 2 sts, 1tr/rf around next st, 1tr into next st, 1tr/rf around next st.

Row 2: [1tr/rb around next st, 1dc into next st] twice, [1FCL/rb] twice, 1dc into each of next 3 sts, [1BCL/rb] twice, [1dc into next st, 1tr/rb around next st] twice.

Row 3: [1tr/rf around next st, 1dc into next st] twice, 1tr/rf around each of next 2 sts, 1dc into each of next 3 sts, 1tr/rf around each of next 2 sts, [1dc into next st, 1tr/rf around next st] twice.

Row 4: 1tr/rb around next st, 1dc into next st, 1tr/rb around next st, 1dc into each of next 2 sts, [1BCL/rb] twice, work a puff st of hdc5tog all into next st, [1FCL/rb] twice, 1dc into each of next 2 sts, 1tr/rb around next st, 1dc into next st, 1tr/rb around next st.

Row 5: 1tr/rf around next st, 1dc into next st, 1tr/rf around next st, 1dc into each of next 3 sts, 1BCL/rf, 1TCL, 1FCL/rf, 1dc into each of next 3 sts, 1tr/rf around next st, 1dc into next st, 1tr/rf around next st.

Row 6: *1tr/rb around next st, 1dc into next st, 1tr/rb around next st**, 1dc into each of next 9 sts, rep from * to **.

Rep rows 1–6.

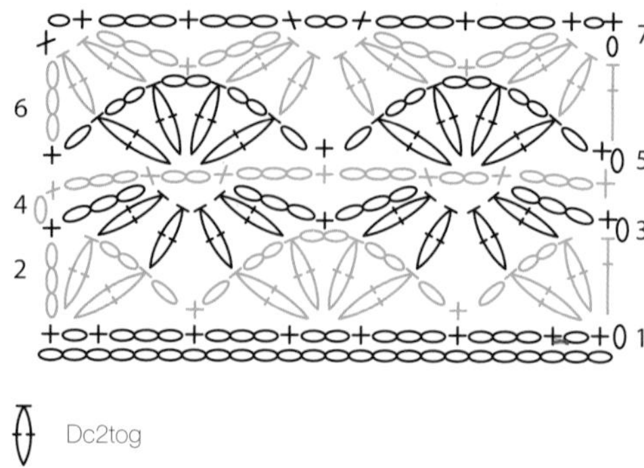

Petal pattern I

Multiple of 11 sts + 3.

Special abbreviation:

Dc2tog = work 2dc into next st until 1 loop of each remains on hook, yo and through all 3 loops on hook.

Row 1 (RS): Work 1sc into 2nd ch from hook, ch1, skip 1 ch, 1sc into next ch, [ch3, skip 3 ch, 1sc into next ch] twice, *ch2, skip 2 ch, 1sc into next ch, [ch3, skip 3 ch, 1sc into next ch] twice; rep from * to last 2 ch, ch1, skip 1 ch, 1sc into last ch, turn.

Row 2: Ch3 (count as 1dc), into 1st ch sp work [dc2tog, ch2, dc2tog], ch1, skip 1 sc, 1sc into next sc, *ch1, skip ch-3 sp, dc2tog into next ch-2 sp, into same sp as last dc2tog work [ch2, dc2tog] 3 times, ch1, skip ch-3 sp, 1sc into next sc; rep from * to last 2 sps, ch1, skip ch-3 sp, into last ch sp work [dc2tog, ch2, dc2tog], 1dc into last sc, turn.

Row 3: Ch1, 1sc into 1st dc, *ch3, work 1dc2tog into top of each of next 4 dc2tog, ch3, 1sc into next ch-2 sp; rep from * to end placing last sc into 3rd of ch-3 at beg of previous row, turn.

Row 4: Ch1, 1sc into 1st sc, *ch3, 1sc into top of next dc2tog, ch2, skip 2 dc2tog, 1sc into top of next dc2tog, ch3, 1sc into next sc; rep from * to end, turn.

Row 5: Ch1, work 1sc into 1st sc, *ch1, skip ch-3 sp, dc2tog into next ch-2 sp, into same sp as last dc2tog work [ch2, dc2tog] 3 times, ch1, skip ch-3 sp, 1sc into next sc; rep from * to end, turn.

Row 6: Ch3, work 1dc2tog into top of each of next 2 dc2tog, ch3, 1sc into next ch-2 sp, ch3, *dc2tog into top of next 4 dc2tog, ch3, 1sc into next ch-2 sp, ch3; rep from * to last 2 dc2tog, work 1dc2tog into each of last 2 dc2tog, 1dc into last sc, turn.

Row 7: Ch1, 1sc into 1st dc, ch1, skip 1 dc2tog, 1sc into next dc2tog, ch3, 1sc into next sc, ch3, *1sc into top of next dc2tog, ch2, skip 2 dc2tog, 1sc into top of next dc2tog, ch3, 1sc into next sc, ch3; rep from * to last 2 dc2tog, 1sc into next dc2tog, ch1, skip 1 dc2tog, 1sc into 3rd of ch-3 at beg of previous row, turn.

Rep rows 2–7.

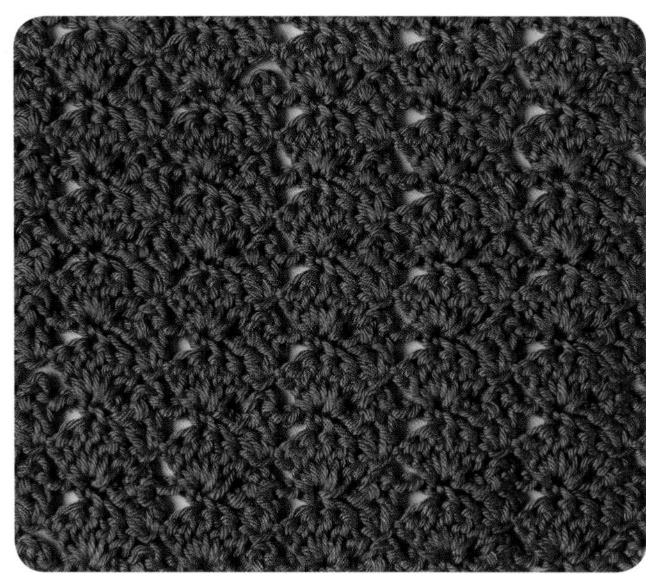

Petal pattern II

Work as Petal pattern I (see left) but working rows 1 and 2 in A, then 3 rows each in B and A throughout.

Note: Cut yarn after each color change.

Petal pattern III

Work as Petal pattern I (see left) but working rows 1 and 2 in A, then work 3 rows each in B, C and A throughout.

Shell filigree stitch

Multiple of 5 sts + 1 (add 2 for base chain).

Row 1 (WS): 2dc into 3rd ch from hook, *ch1, skip 4 ch, 5dc into next ch; rep from * working only 3dc at end of last rep, turn.

Row 2: Ch1, 1sc into first st, *ch2, skip 2 dc, work a Picot V st of [1dc, ch3, insert hook down through top of dc just made and work a slip st to close, 1dc] into next ch-1 sp, ch2, skip 2 dc, 1sc into next dc; rep from * ending last rep in top of tch, turn.

Row 3: Ch3 (count as 1dc), 2dc into first sc, *ch1, skip ch-2, Picot V st and ch-2, work 5dc into next sc; rep from * finishing with only 3dc at end of last rep, skip tch, turn.

Rep rows 2–3.

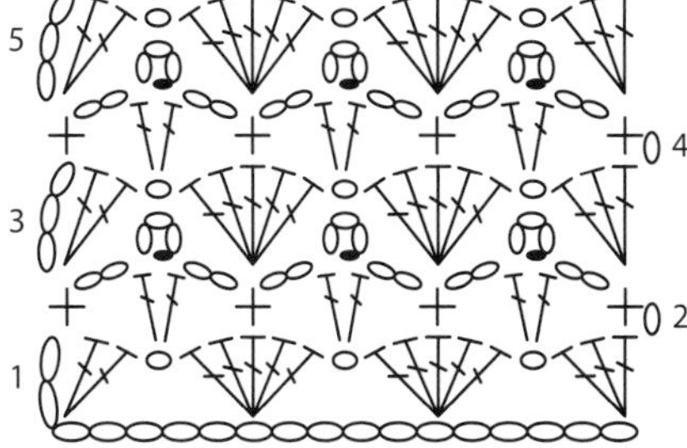

Crosshatch stitch I

Multiple of 7 sts + 4 (add 3 for base chain).

Row 1: Skip 2 ch (count as 1dc), 2dc into next ch, *skip 3 ch, 1sc into next ch, ch3, 1dc into each of next 3 ch; rep from * to last 4 ch, skip 3 ch, 1sc into last ch, turn.

Row 2: Ch3 (count as 1dc), 2dc into 1st sc, *skip 3 dc, 1sc into 1st ch of ch-3, ch3, 1dc into each of next 2 ch, 1dc into next sc; rep from * ending skip 2 dc, 1sc into top of tch, turn.

Rep row 2.

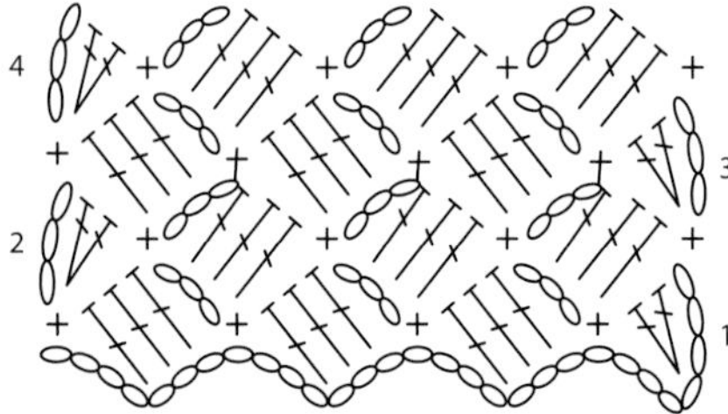

Crosshatch stitch II

Work as Crosshatch stitch I (see left). Work 1 row each in colors A, B and C throughout.

Crossed double crochet stitch

Multiple of 2 sts (add 2 for base chain).

Special abbreviation:

2Cdc (2 crossed double crochet) = skip next st, 1dc into next st, 1dc into skipped st working over previous dc.

Row 1 (RS): Skip 3 ch (count as 1dc), *2Cdc over next 2 ch; rep from * ending 1dc into last ch, turn.

Row 2: Ch1 (count as 1sc), skip 1 st, 1sc into next and each st to end, working last st into top of tch, turn.

Row 3: Ch3 (count as 1dc), skip 1 st, *work 2Cdc over next 2 sts; rep from * ending 1dc into tch, turn.

Rep rows 2–3.

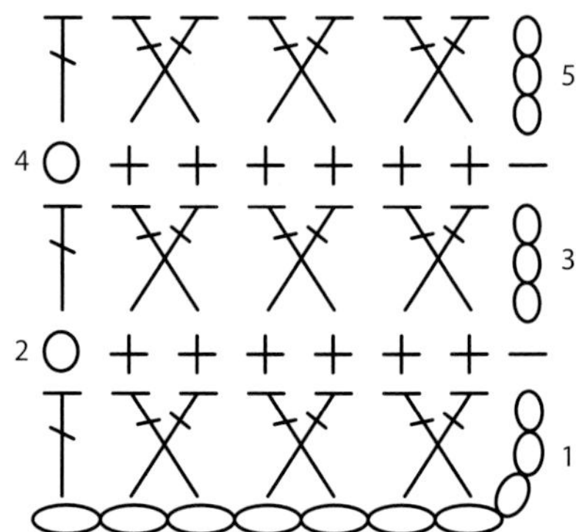

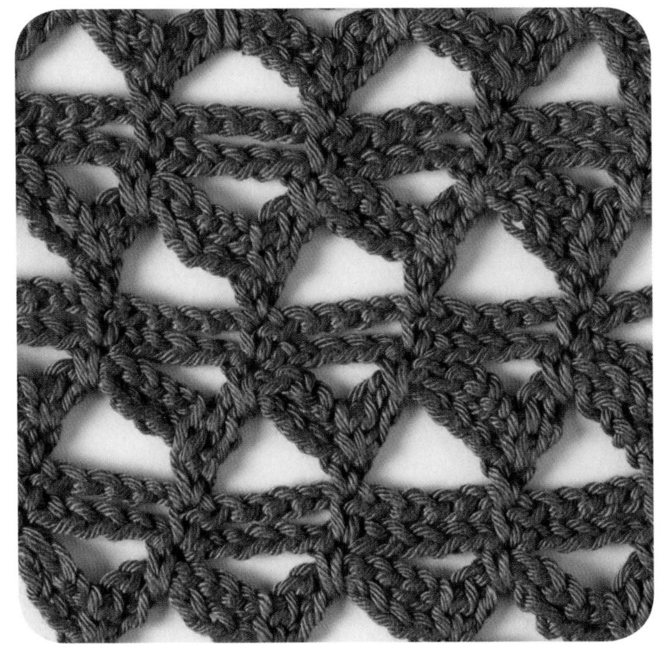

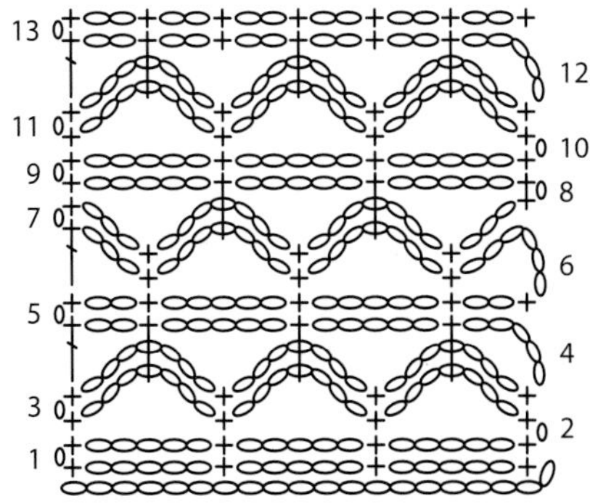

Zigzag double string network

Multiple of 6 sts + 1 (add 1 for base chain).

Base row (RS): 1sc into 2nd ch from hook, *ch5, skip 5 ch, 1sc into next ch; rep from * to end, turn.

Commence pattern

Row 1: Ch1, 1sc into 1st st, *ch5, skip ch-5, 1sc into next sc; rep from * to end, skip tch, turn.

Row 2: Ch1, 1sc into 1st st, *ch7, skip ch-5, 1sc into next sc; rep from * to end, skip tch, turn.

Row 3: Ch1, 1sc into 1st st, *ch7, skip ch-7, 1sc into next sc; rep from * to end, skip tch, turn.

Row 4: Ch5 (count as 1dc, ch2), inserting hook under the ch-7 arch made in row 2, work 1sc thus binding the arches of rows 2 and 3 together, *ch5, 1sc under next pair of arches as before; rep from * ending ch2, 1dc into last sc, skip tch, turn.

Row 5: Ch1, 1sc into 1st st, ch2, skip ch-2, 1sc into next sc, *ch5, skip ch-5, 1sc into next sc; rep from * ending ch2, skip next 2 ch of tch, 1sc into next ch, turn.

Row 6: Ch6 (count as 1dc, ch3), skip ch-2, 1sc into next sc, *ch7, skip ch-5, 1sc into next sc; rep from * ending ch3, skip ch-2, 1dc into last sc, skip tch, turn.

Row 7: Ch1, 1sc into 1st st, ch3, skip ch-3, 1sc into next sc, *ch7, skip ch-7, 1sc into next sc; rep from * ending ch3, skip next 3 ch of tch, 1sc into next ch, turn.

Row 8: Ch1, 1sc into 1st st, *ch5, 1sc under next pair of arches together; rep from * ending last rep with 1sc into last sc, skip tch, turn.

Rep rows 1–8.

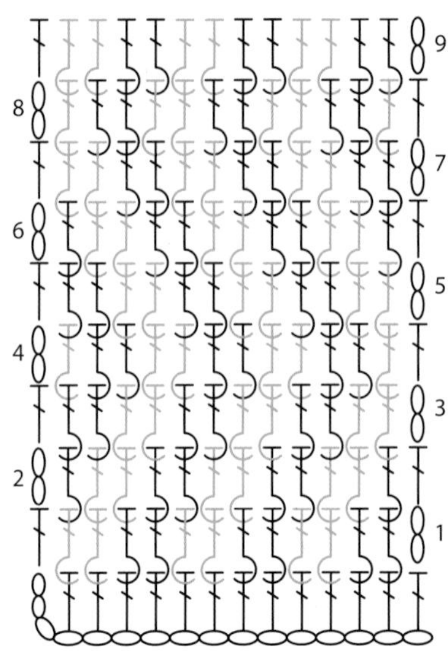

Zigzag rib

Multiple of 4 sts + 2 (add 2 for base chain).

Special abbreviations:

Dc/rf (raised double crochet at the front of the fabric) = wrap the yarn around the hook, insert the hook from in front and from right to left around the stem of the appropriate stitch, and complete the stitch normally.

Dc/rb (raised double crochet at the back of the fabric) = wrap the yarn around the hook, insert the hook from behind and from right to left around the stem of the appropriate stitch, and complete the stitch normally.

Base row (WS): Skip 3 ch (count as 1dc), 1dc into next and each ch to end, turn.

Commence pattern

Row 1: Ch2 (count as 1sc), skip 1st st, *1dc/rf around each of next 2 sts, 1dc/rb around each of next 2 sts; rep from * ending 1dc into top of tch, turn.

Row 2: Ch2 (count as 1dc), skip 1st st, 1dc/rb around next st, *1dc/rf around each of next 2 sts**, 1dc/rb around each of next 2 sts; rep from * ending last rep at ** when 2 sts rem, 1dc/rb around next st, 1dc into top of tch, turn.

Row 3: Ch2 (count as 1dc), skip 1st st, *1dc/rb around each of next 2 sts, 1dc/rf around each of next 2 sts; rep from * ending 1dc into top of tch, turn.

Row 4: Ch2 (count as 1dc), skip 1st st, 1dc/rf around next st, *1dc/rb around each of next 2 sts**, 1dc/rf around each of next 2 sts; rep from * ending last rep at ** when 2 sts rem, 1dc/rf around next st, 1dc into top of tch, turn.

Row 5: As row 3.

Row 6: As row 2.

Row 7: As row 1.

Row 8: As row 4.

Rep rows 1–8.

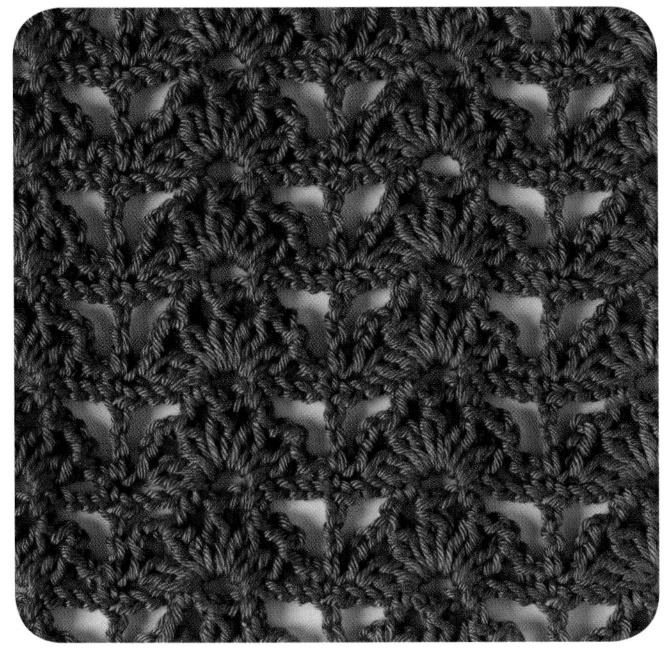

Dc2tog

Flame stitch

Multiple of 10 sts + 2.

Special abbreviation:

Dc2tog = work 2dc into next ch-3 arch until 1 loop of each remains on hook, yo and through all 3 loops on hook.

Row 1 (WS): Work 1sc into 2nd ch from hook, *ch3, skip 3 ch, 1sc into next ch, ch3, skip 1 ch, 1sc into next ch, ch3, skip 3 ch, 1sc into next ch; rep from * to end, turn.

Row 2: Ch1, 1sc into 1st sc, *ch1, skip next ch-3 sp, dc2tog into next ch-3 arch, into same arch as last dc2tog work [ch3, dc2tog] 4 times, ch1, skip next ch-3 sp, 1sc into next sc; rep from * to end, turn.

Row 3: Ch7 (count as 1tr, ch3), skip next ch-3 arch, 1sc into next ch-3 arch, ch3, 1sc into next ch-3 arch, ch3, 1tr into next sc, *ch3, skip next ch-3 arch, 1sc into next ch-3 arch, ch3, 1sc into next ch-3 arch, ch3, 1tr into next sc; rep from * to end, turn.

Row 4: Ch1, 1sc into 1st dc, *ch1, skip next ch-3 sp, dc2tog into next ch-3 arch, into same arch as last dc2tog work [ch3, dc2tog] 4 times, ch1, 1sc into next dc; rep from * to end, working last sc into 4th of ch-7 at beg of previous row, turn.

Rep rows 3–4.

Tip

Think about how the stitch samples would look worked in a different weight of yarn. With the flame stitch above, the cotton yarn is crisp enough to show the intricate detail of the pattern. However, there is enough "space" in this design that it could also look effective in a thicker yarn such as a DK-weight merino.

Ripple stitch I

Multiple of 2 sts +1 (add 2 for base chain).

Special abbreviations:

Tr/rf (raised treble at the front of the fabric) = wrap the yarn around the hook, insert the hook from in front and from right to left around the stem of the appropriate stitch, and complete the stitch normally.

Tr/rb (raised treble at the back of the fabric) = wrap the yarn around the hook, insert the hook from behind and from right to left around the stem of the appropriate stitch, and complete the stitch normally.

Row 1 (RS): Skip 3 ch (count as 1dc), 1dc into each ch to end, turn.

Row 2: Ch1 (count as 1sc), skip 1st st, 1sc into each st to end, working last st into top of tch, turn.

Row 3: Ch3 (count as 1dc), skip 1st st, *1tr/rf around dc below next st, 1dc into next st; rep from * to end, turn.

Row 4: As row 2.

Row 5: Ch3 (count as 1dc), skip 1st st, *1dc into next st, 1tr/rf around dc below next st; rep from * to last 2 sts, 1dc into each of last 2 sts, turn.

Rep rows 2–5.

Ripple stitch II

Work as Ripple stitch I (see left).

Work 2 rows each in colors A and B alternately throughout.

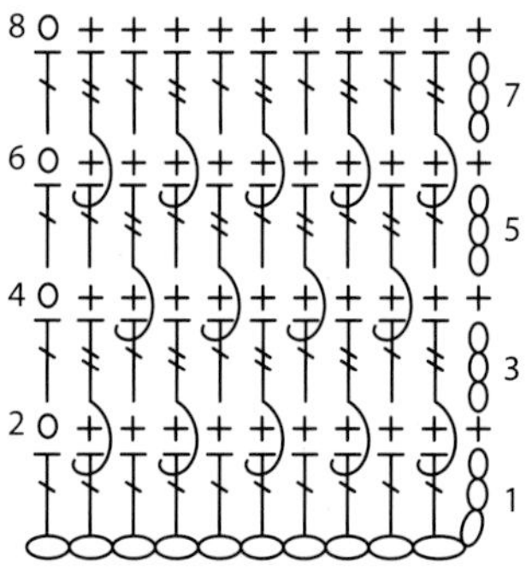

Trinity stitch I

Multiple of 2 sts + 1 (add 1 for base chain).

Row 1: 1sc into 2nd ch from hook, sc3tog inserting hook 1st into same ch as previous sc, then into each of next 2 ch, *ch1, sc3tog inserting hook 1st into same ch as 3rd leg of previous cluster, then into each of next 2 ch; rep from * to last ch, 1sc into same ch as 3rd leg of previous cluster, turn.

Row 2: Ch1, 1sc into 1st st, sc3tog inserting hook 1st into same place as previous sc, then into top of next cluster, then into next ch sp, *ch1, sc3tog inserting hook 1st into same ch sp as 3rd leg of previous cluster, then into top of next cluster, then into next ch sp; rep from * to end working 3rd leg of last cluster into last sc, 1sc into same place, skip tch, turn.

Rep row 2.

Trinity stitch II

Work as Trinity stitch I (see left).

Work 1 row each in colors A, B and C throughout.

Note: Normally the maximum number of stitches that may be worked together into a single crochet cluster is 3. (Longer stitches may have more.) Remember that working stitches together into clusters is often the best way to decrease.

Open fan stitch

Multiple of 10 sts + 6 (add 1 for base chain).

Row 1 (RS): 1sc into 2nd ch from hook, *ch1, skip 4 ch, into next ch work a Fan of 1tr, [ch2, 1tr] 4 times, then ch1, skip 4 ch, 1sc into next ch; rep from * to last 5 ch, ch1, skip 4 ch, into last ch work [1tr, ch2] twice and 1tr, turn.

Row 2: Ch1, 1sc into 1st st, *ch3, skip next ch-2 sp, 1dc into next sp**, ch2, skip next tr, sc and tr and work 1dc into 1st ch-2 sp of next Fan, ch3, work 1sc into center tr of Fan; rep from * ending last rep at **, ch1, 1tr into last sc, skip tch, turn.

Row 3: Ch7 (count as 1tr, ch2), skip 1st tr, work [1tr, ch2, 1tr] into next ch-1 sp, ch1, skip ch-3 sp, 1sc into next sc, *ch1, skip next ch-3 sp, work a Fan into next ch-2 sp, ch1, skip next ch-3 sp, 1sc into next sc; rep from * to end, skip tch, turn.

Row 4: Ch6 (count as 1tr, ch1), skip 1st tr, work 1dc into next ch-2 sp, ch3, 1sc into center tr of Fan, *ch3, skip next ch-2 sp, 1dc into next ch-2 sp, ch2, skip next tr, sc and tr, work 1dc into next ch-2 sp, ch3, 1sc into center tr of Fan; rep from * ending last rep in 3rd ch of tch, turn.

Row 5: Ch1, *1sc into sc, ch1, skip next ch-3 sp, Fan into next ch-2 sp, ch1, skip next ch-3 sp; rep from * to last sc, 1sc into sc, ch1, skip next ch-3 sp, work [1tr, ch2] twice and 1tr all into top of tch, turn.

Rep rows 2–5.

Interweave stitch

Multiple of 2 sts + 1 (add 2 for base chain).

Note: Work 1 row each in colors A, B, and C throughout.

Special abbreviations:

Tr/rf (raised treble at the front of the fabric) = wrap the yarn around the hook, insert the hook from in front and from right to left around the stem of the appropriate stitch, and complete the stitch normally.

Tr/rb (raised treble at the back of the fabric) = wrap the yarn around the hook, insert the hook from behind and from right to left around the stem of the appropriate stitch, and complete the stitch normally.

Row 1 (RS): Skip 3 ch (count as 1dc), 1dc into next and each ch to end, turn.

Row 2: Ch3 (count as 1dc), skip first st, *1tr/rf around next st, 1dc into next st; rep from * ending last rep in top of tch, turn.

Rep row 2.

Rack stitch

Multiple of 7 sts + 4.

Row 1 (RS): Work 1dc into 4th ch from hook, *skip 2 ch, into next ch work [3dc, ch1, 3dc], skip 2 ch, 1dc into each of next 2 ch; rep from * to end, turn.

Row 2: Ch3 (count as 1dc), skip 1st dc, 1dc into next dc, *skip 2 dc, 1dc into next dc, ch1, into next ch sp work [1dc, ch1, 1dc], ch1, 1dc into next dc, skip 2 dc, 1dc into each of next 2 dc; rep from * to end placing last dc into 3rd of ch-3 at beg of previous row, turn.

Row 3: Ch3, skip 1st dc, 1dc into next dc, *skip next ch sp, into next ch sp work [2dc, ch3, 2dc], skip 2 dc, 1dc into each of next 2 dc; rep from * to end placing last dc into 3rd of ch-3 at beg of previous row, turn.

Row 4: Ch3, skip 1st dc, 1dc into next dc, * into next ch-3 sp work [3dc, ch1, 3dc], skip 2 dc, 1dc into each of next 2 dc; rep from * to end placing last dc into 3rd of ch-3 at beg of previous row, turn.

Rep rows 2–4.

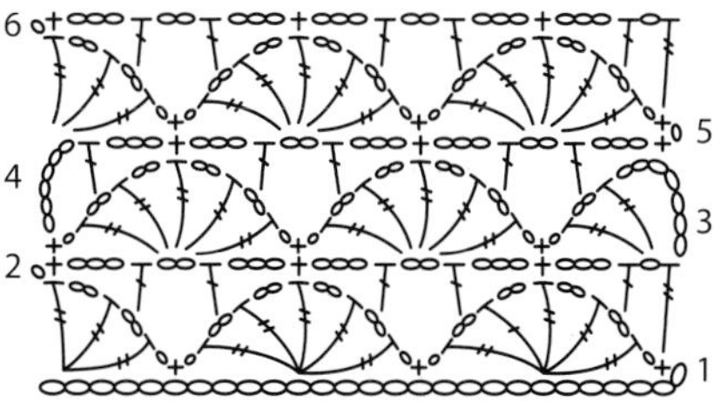

Open fan stitch

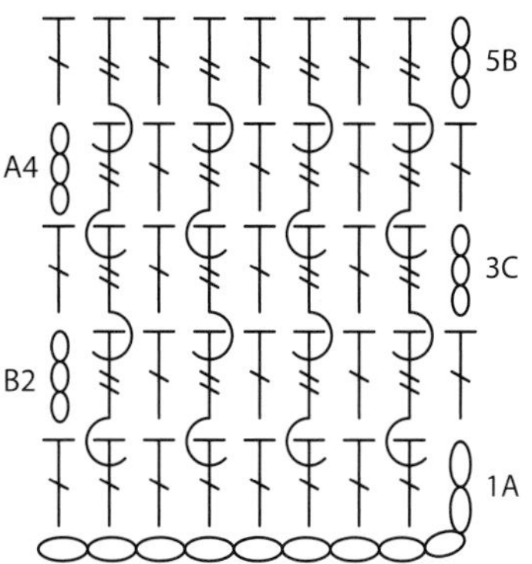

Interweave stitch

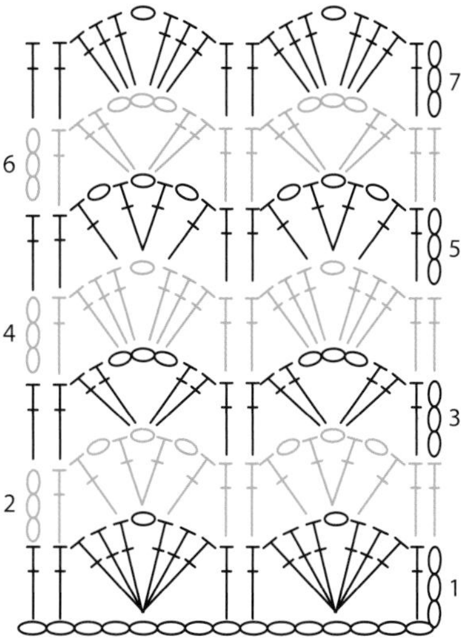

Rack stitch

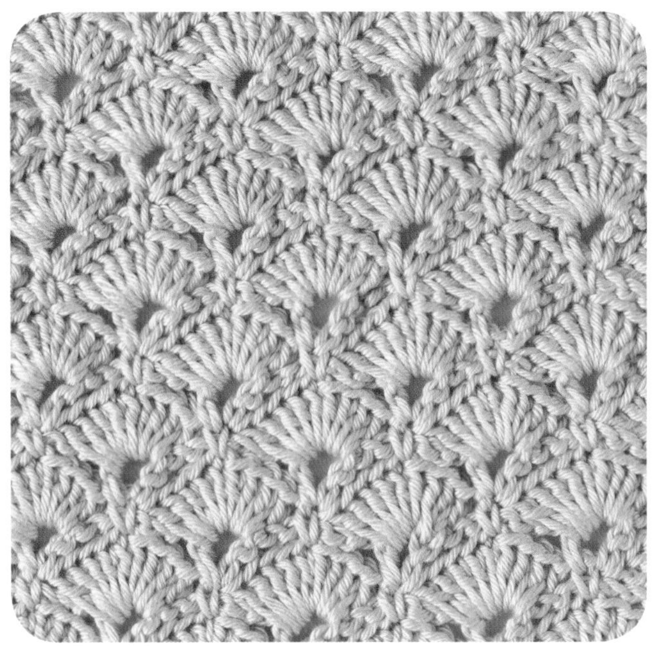

Fan and V stitch

Multiple of 8 sts + 1 (add 1 for base chain).

Row 1 (RS): 1sc into 2nd ch from hook, *skip 3 ch, 9dc into next ch, skip 3 ch, 1sc into next ch; rep from * to end, turn.

Row 2: Ch3 (count as 1dc), 1dc into 1st st, *ch5, skip 9dc group, work a V st of [1dc, ch1, 1dc] into next sc; rep from * ending ch5, skip last 9dc group, 2dc into last sc, skip tch, turn.

Row 3: Ch3 (count as 1dc), 4dc into 1st st, *working over next ch-5 so as to enclose it, work 1sc into 5th dc of group in row below**, 9dc into sp at center of next V st; rep from * ending last rep at **, 5dc into top of tch, turn.

Row 4: Ch3, skip 5 dc, V st into next sc, *ch5, skip 9dc group, V st into next sc; rep from * ending ch2, slip st to top of tch, turn.

Row 5: Ch1, 1sc over slip st into 1st st of row below, *9dc into sp at center of next V st**, working over next ch-5 so as to enclose it work 1sc into 5th dc of group in row below; rep from * ending last rep at **, 1sc into 1st ch of tch, turn.

Rep rows 2–5.

End with a WS row, working [ch2, slip st to 5th dc of group, ch2] in place of ch5 between the V sts.

Norman arch stitch

Multiple of 9 sts + 1 (add 1 for base chain).

Row 1 (WS): 1sc into 2nd ch from hook, *ch3, skip 3 ch, 1sc into next ch, ch7, 1sc into next ch, ch3, skip 3 ch, 1sc into next ch; rep from * to end, turn.

Row 2: Ch1, 1sc into 1st sc, *skip 3 ch, work 13dc into next ch-7 arch, skip 3 ch, 1sc into next st; rep from * to end, skip tch, turn.

Row 3: Ch5 (count as 1dtr), skip 1st sc and next 5 dc, *[1dc into next dc, ch3] twice, 1dc into next dc **, skip [next 5 dc, 1sc and 5 dc]; rep from * ending last rep at **, skip next 5 dc, 1dtr into last sc, skip tch, turn.

Row 4: Ch3 (count as 1dc), skip 1st st and next dc, *1dc into next ch, ch1, skip 1 ch, 1dc into next ch, ch3, skip 1 dc, 1dc into next ch, ch1, skip 1 ch, 1dc into next ch**, skip next 2 dc; rep from * ending last rep at **, skip next dc, 1dc into top of tch, turn.

Row 5: Ch6 (count as 1dc, ch3), *skip next ch-1 sp, work [1sc, ch7, 1sc] into next ch-3 sp, ch3, skip next ch-1 sp**, 1dc between next 2 dc, ch3; rep from * ending last rep at **, 1dc into top of tch, turn.

Rep rows 2–5.

Crossbill stitch

Multiple of 4 sts + 1 (add 2 for base chain).

Special abbreviation:

2Cdc (2 crossed double crochet) = skip 2 sts, 1dc into next st, ch1, 1dc into 1st of 2 sts just skipped working back over last dc made.

Row 1: Skip 3 ch (count as 1dc), *work 2Cdc over next 3 ch, 1dc into next ch; rep from * to end, turn.

Row 2: Ch3 (count as 1dc), 1dc into 1st st, skip 1 dc, *1dc into next ch, work 2Cdc over next 3 dc, rep from * ending 1dc into last ch, skip 1 dc, 2dc into top of tch, turn.

Row 3: Ch3 (count as 1dc), skip 1 st, *work 2Cdc over next 3 dc, 1dc into next ch; rep from * ending last rep into top of tch, turn.

Rep rows 2–3.

Fan and V stitch

Norman arch stitch

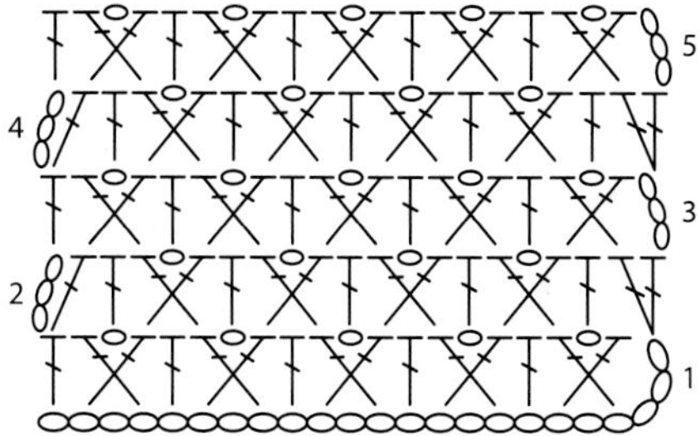

Crossbill stitch

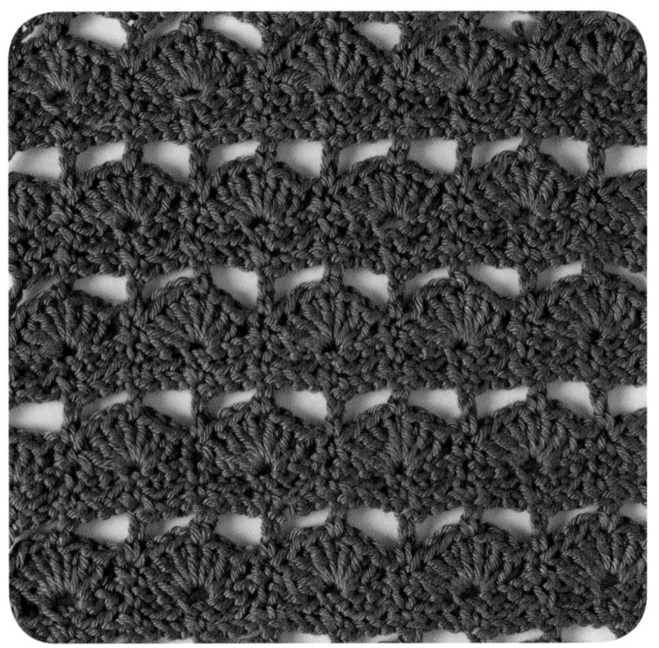

Cool design

Multiple of 8 sts + 4.

Row 1 (RS): Work 3dc into 4th ch from hook, skip 3 ch, 1sc into next ch, *skip 3 ch, 7dc into next ch, skip 3 ch, 1sc into next ch; rep from * to last 4 ch, skip 3 ch, 4dc into last ch, turn.

Row 2: Ch6 (count as 1dc, ch3), 1dc into next sc, *ch3, skip 3 dc, 1dc into next dc, ch3, 1dc into next sc; rep from * to last 4 sts, ch3, 1dc into top of ch-3 at beg of previous row, turn.

Row 3: Ch1, *1sc into next dc, ch3; rep from * to last st, 1sc into 3rd of ch-6 at beg of previous row, turn.

Row 4: Ch1, 1sc into 1st sc, *ch3, 1sc into next sc; rep from * to end, turn.

Row 5: Ch1, 1sc into 1st sc, *7dc into next sc, 1sc into next sc; rep from * to end, turn.

Row 6: Ch6, skip 3 dc, 1dc into next dc, ch3, 1dc into next sc, *ch3, skip 3 dc, 1dc into next dc, ch3, 1dc into next sc; rep from * to end, turn.

Rows 7–8: As rows 3–4.

Row 9: Ch3 (count as 1dc), 3dc into 1st sc, 1sc into next sc, *7dc into next sc, 1sc into next sc; rep from * to last sc, 4dc into last sc, turn.

Rep rows 2–9.

Sidesaddle cluster stitch

Multiple of 5 sts + 1 (add 1 for base chain).

Row 1: 1sc into 2nd ch from hook, *ch3, dc4tog over next 4 ch, ch1, 1sc into next ch; rep from * to end, turn.

Row 2: Ch5, 1sc into next cluster, *ch3, dc4tog all into next ch-3 arch, ch1, 1sc into next cluster; rep from * ending ch3, dc4tog all into next ch-3 arch, 1dc into last sc, skip tch, turn.

Row 3: Ch1, skip 1 st, 1sc into next CL, *ch3, 1CL into next ch-3 arch, ch1, 1sc into next CL; rep from * ending last rep with 1sc into tch arch, turn.

Rep rows 2–3.

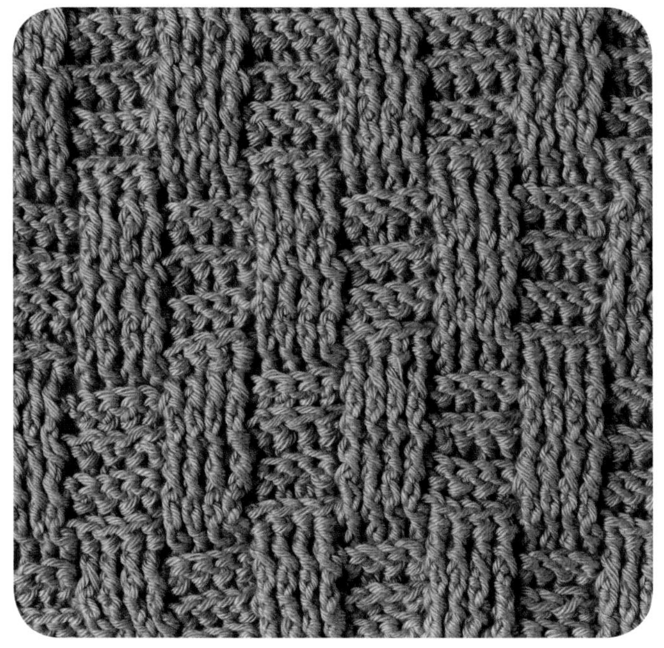

Cool design

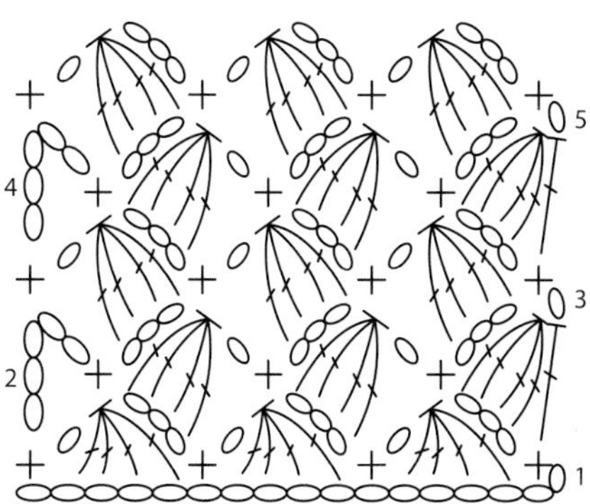

Sidesaddle cluster stitch

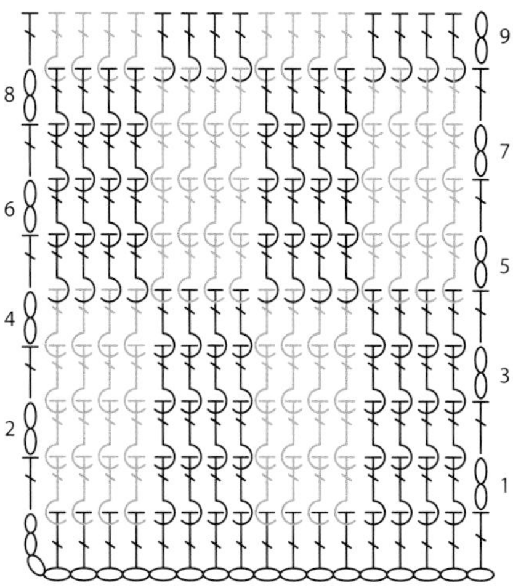

Basketweave stitch

Basketweave stitch

Multiple of 8 sts + 2 (add 2 for base chain).

Special abbreviations:

Dc/rf (raised double crochet at the front of the fabric) = wrap the yarn around the hook, insert the hook from in front and from right to left around the stem of the appropriate stitch, and complete the stitch normally.

Dc/rb (raised double crochet at the back of the fabric) = wrap the yarn around the hook, insert the hook from behind and from right to left around the stem of the appropriate stitch, and complete the stitch normally.

Base row (WS): Skip 3 ch (count as 1dc), 1dc into next and each ch to end, turn.

Row 1: Ch2 (count as 1dc), skip 1st st, *1dc/rf around each of next 4 sts, 1dc/rb around each of next 4 sts; rep from * ending 1dc into top of tch, turn.

Rep the last row 3 times.

Row 5: Ch2 (count as 1dc), skip 1st st, *1dc/rb around each of next 4 sts, 1dc/rf around each of next 4 sts; rep from * ending 1dc into top of tch, turn.

Rep the last row 3 times.

Rep these 8 rows.

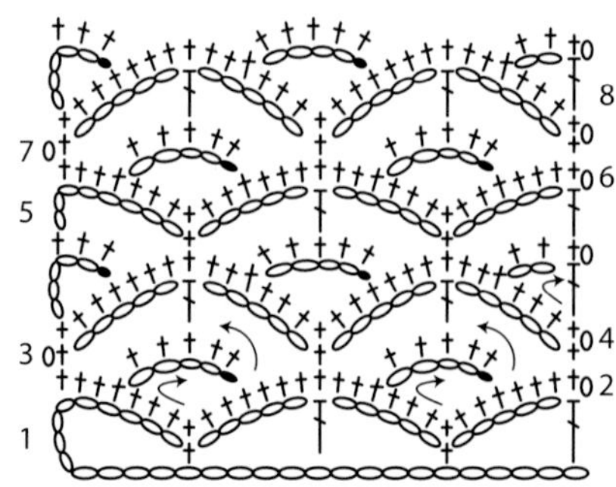

Treble arch ground

Multiple of 10 sts + 1 (add 8 for base chain).

Row 1 (WS): 1sc into 14th ch from hook, *ch5, skip 4 ch, 1dc into next ch**, ch5, skip 4 ch, 1sc into next ch; rep from * ending last rep at **, turn.

Row 2: Ch1, 1sc into 1st dc, *6sc into next ch-5 arch, 1sc into next sc, 3sc into beg of next ch-5 arch, work a "back double crochet" of [ch4, then without turning work, skip 6 previous sc and work a slip st back into previous sc, now work 5sc in the normal direction into ch-4 arch just worked], 3sc into rem part of ch-5 arch**, 1sc into next dc; rep from * ending last rep at **, 1sc into next ch, turn.

Row 3: Ch1, 1sc into 1st st, *ch5, 1dc into 3rd of 5 sc of next 'back double crochet', ch5, 1sc into sc over dc of previous row; rep from * ending last rep in last sc, turn.

Row 4: Ch1, 1sc into 1st st, 3sc into beg of next ch-5 arch, turn, ch2, skip 3 previous sc, work 1dc into 1st sc, ch1, turn, 1sc into dc, 2sc into ch-2 arch, 3sc into rem part of ch-5 arch, *1sc into next dc, 6sc into next ch-5 arch, 1sc into next sc**, 3sc into beg of ch-5 arch, 1 "back double crochet" as before, 3sc into rem part of ch-5 arch; rep from * ending last rep at **, ch5, skip 3 previous sc, sl st back into next sc, 3sc in normal direction into beg of ch-5 arch, turn.

Row 5: Ch8, *1sc into sc over dc of previous row, ch5**, 1dc into 3rd of 5sc of next "back double crochet", ch5; rep from * ending last rep at **, 1dc into last sc, skip tch, turn.

Rep rows 2–5.

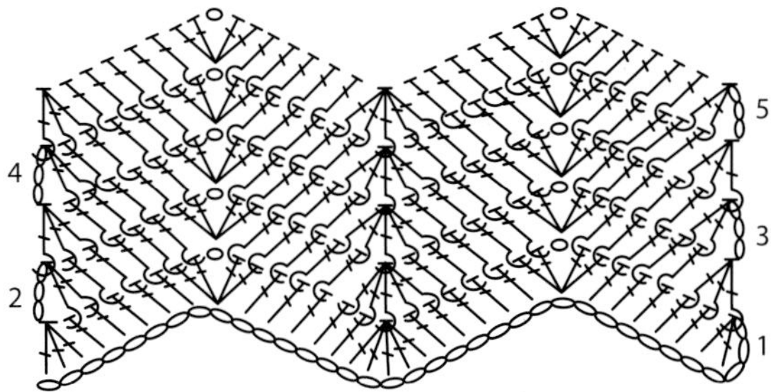

Raised chevron stitch

Multiple of 16 sts + 1 (add 2 for base chain).

Special abbreviation:

Dc/rf (raised double crochet at the front of the fabric) = wrap yarn around hook, insert the hook from in front and from right to left around the stem of the appropriate stitch, and complete the stitch normally.

Dc/rb (raised double crochet at the back of the fabric) = wrap yarn around hook, insert the hook from behind and from right to left around the stem of the appropriate stitch, and complete the stitch normally.

Row 1 (RS): Skip 3 ch, dc2tog over next 2 ch (count as dc3tog), *1dc into each of next 5 ch, [2dc, ch1, 2dc] into next ch, 1dc into each of next 5 ch**, dc5tog over next 5 ch; rep from * ending last rep at ** when 3 ch rem, dc3tog, turn.

Row 2: Ch3, skip 1st st, dc/rb2tog over next 2 sts (all counts as dc/rb3tog), *1dc/rf around each of next 5 sts, [2dc, ch1, 2dc] into next ch sp, 1dc/rf around each of next 5 sts**, dc/rb5tog over next 5 sts; rep from * ending last rep at ** when 3 sts remain, dc/rb3tog, turn.

Row 3: Ch3, skip 1st st, dc/rf2tog over next 2 sts (all counts as dc/rf3tog), *1dc/rb around each of next 5 sts, [2dc, ch1, 2dc] into next ch sp, 1dc/rb around each of next 5 sts**, dc/rf5tog over next 5 sts; rep from * ending last rep at ** when 3 sts remain, dc/rf3tog, turn.

Rep rows 2–3.

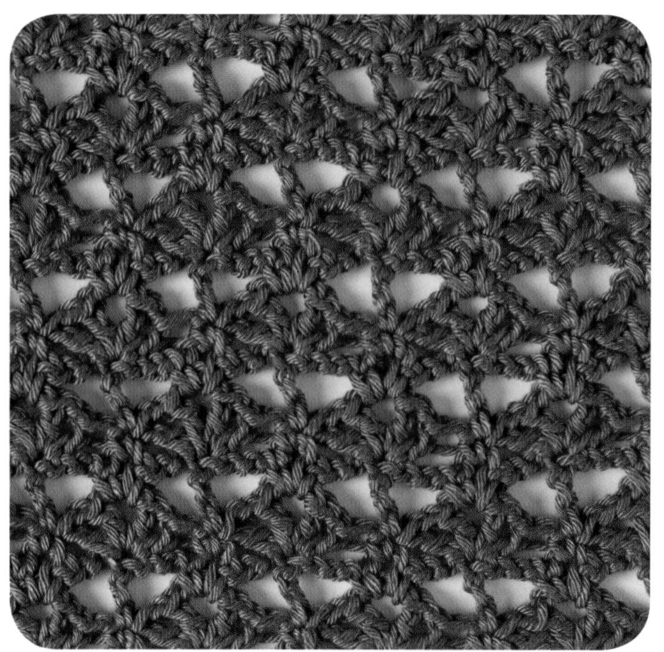

Garland pattern

Multiple of 8 sts + 2.

Row 1 (RS): Work 1sc into 2nd ch from hook, *skip 3 ch, into next ch work [1dc, ch1, 1dc, ch3, 1dc, ch1, 1dc], skip 3 ch, 1sc into next ch; rep from * to end, turn.

Row 2: Ch7 (count as 1tr, ch3), *skip ch-1 sp, into next ch-3 sp work [1sc, ch3, 1sc], ch3, 1tr into next sc, ch3; rep from * to end omitting ch3 at end of last rep, turn.

Row 3: Ch4 (count as 1dc, ch1), into 1st tr work [1dc, 1h1, 1dc], skip ch-3 sp, 1sc into next ch-3 sp, *into next tr work [1dc, ch1, 1dc, ch3, 1dc, ch1, 1dc], skip ch-3 sp, 1sc into next ch-3 sp; rep from * to last sp, skip 3 ch, 1dc into next ch, work [ch1, 1dc] twice into same ch as last dc, turn.

Row 4: Ch1, 1sc into 1st dc, 1sc into 1st ch sp, ch3, 1tr into next sc, *ch3, skip ch-1 sp, into next ch-3 sp work [1sc, ch3, 1sc], ch3, 1tr into next sc; rep from * to last 3 dc, ch3, skip ch-1 sp, 1sc into each of next 2 ch, turn.

Row 5: Ch1, 1sc into 1st sc, *into next tr work [1dc, ch1, 1dc, ch3, 1dc, ch1, 1dc], skip ch-3 sp, 1sc into next ch-3 sp; rep from * to end placing last sc into last sc, turn.

Rep rows 2–5.

Tortoise shell

Multiple of 5 sts + 2.

Row 1 (WS): Work 1sc into 2nd ch from hook, *ch5, skip 4 ch, 1sc into next ch; rep from * to end, turn.

Row 2: Ch5 (count as 1tr, ch1), *into next ch-5 arch work [1tr, 1dc, ch4, slip st into 4th ch from hook, 1dc, 1tr], ch2; rep from * to end omitting 1 ch at end of last rep, 1tr into last sc, turn.

Row 3: Ch1, 1sc into 1st tr, *ch5, 1sc into next ch-2 sp; rep from * to end placing last sc into 4th of ch-5 at beg of previous row, turn.

Rep rows 2–3.

Hexagon stitch

Multiple of 8 sts + 4 (add 1 for base chain).

Special abbreviation:

CL (Cluster) = work [yo, insert hook, yo, draw loop through loosely] over number and position of sts indicated, ending yo, draw through all loops, ch1 tightly to close cluster.

Picot = ch5, 1sc into 2nd ch from hook, 1sc into each of next 3 ch.

Row 1 (WS): 1sc into 2nd ch from hook, 1sc into each of next 3 ch (count as picot), skip 3 ch, 3dc into next ch, skip 3 ch, 1sc into next ch, *skip 3 ch, into next ch work [3dc, 1 picot, 3dc], skip 3 ch, 1sc into next ch; rep from * to end, turn.

Row 2: Ch4 (count as 1tr), 1CL over each of 1st 8 sts, ch3, 1sc into top of picot, *ch3, 1CL over next 15 sts inserting hook into underside of each of 4 ch of picot, into next 3 dc, 1 sc, 3 dc and 4 sc of next picot, then ch3, 1sc into top of picot; rep from * to end, turn.

Row 3: Ch1, 1sc into 1st st, *skip 3 ch, into loop that closed next CL work [3dc, 1 picot, 3dc], skip 3 ch, 1sc into next sc; rep from * ending skip 3 ch, 4dc into loop that closed last CL, skip tch, turn.

Row 4: Ch7 (count as 1tr, ch3), starting into 5th ch from hook work 1CL over next 15 sts as before, *ch3, 1sc into top of picot, ch3, 1CL over next 15 sts; rep from * ending last rep with 1CL over last 8 sts, skip tch, turn.

Row 5: Ch8, 1sc into 2nd ch from hook, 1sc into each of next 3 ch (count as 1dc, 1 picot), 3dc into 1st st, skip 3 ch, 1sc into next sc, *skip 3 ch, into loop that closed next CL work [3dc, 1 picot, 3dc], skip 3 ch, 1sc into next sc; rep from * ending last rep with 1sc into 4th ch of tch, turn.

Rep rows 2–5.

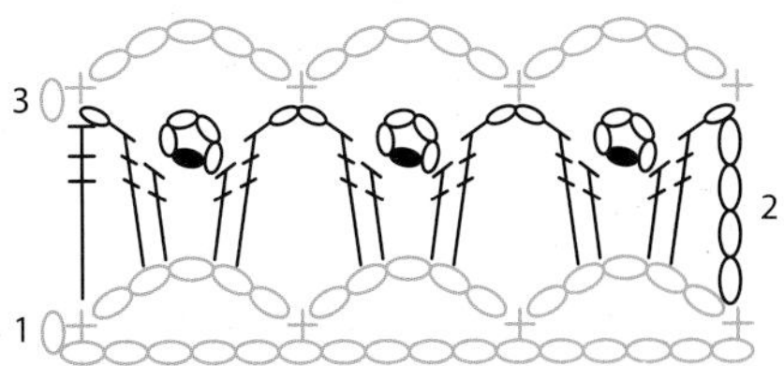

Garland pattern

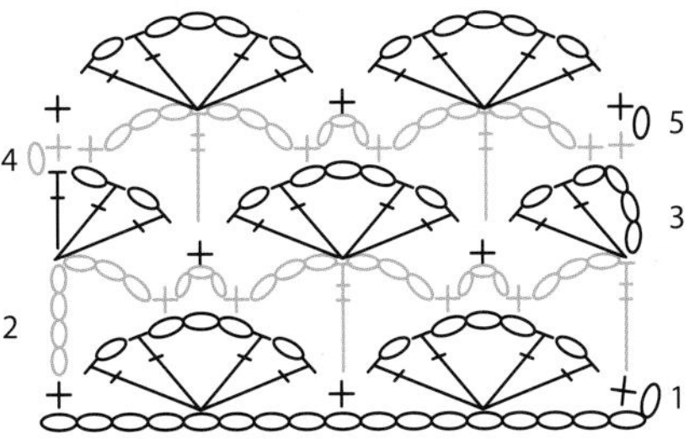

Tortoise shell

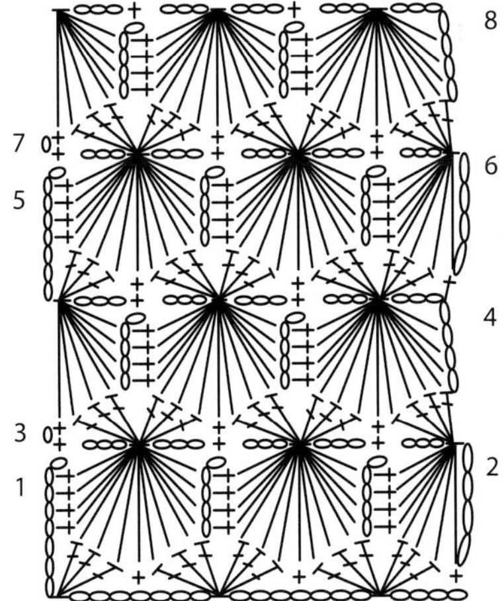

Hexagon stitch

Crinkle stitch

Multiple of 2 sts (add 1 for base chain).

Special abbreviation:

Sc/rf (raised single crochet at the front of the fabric) = wrap yarn around hook, insert the hook from in front and from right to left around the stem of the appropriate stitch, and complete the stitch normally.

Sc/rb (raised single crochet at the back of the fabric) = wrap yarn around hook, insert the hook from behind and from right to left around the stem of the appropriate stitch, and complete the stitch normally.

Row 1 (WS): Skip 2 ch (count as 1hdc), 1hdc into each ch to end, turn.

Row 2: Ch1, 1sc into 1st st, *1sc/rf around next st, 1sc/rb around next st; rep from * ending 1sc into top of tch, turn.

Row 3: Ch2 (count as 1hdc), skip 1st st, 1hdc into next and each st to end, skip tch, turn.

Row 4: Ch1, 1sc into 1st st, *1sc/rb around next st, 1sc/rf around next st; rep from * ending 1sc into top of tch, turn.

Row 5: As row 3.

Rep rows 2–5.

Boxed block stitch

Work as Boxed shell stitch (see page 38), except that on row 2 and every alt row 5dc are worked under ch-3 arch instead of into the actual st, thus making a block rather than a shell.

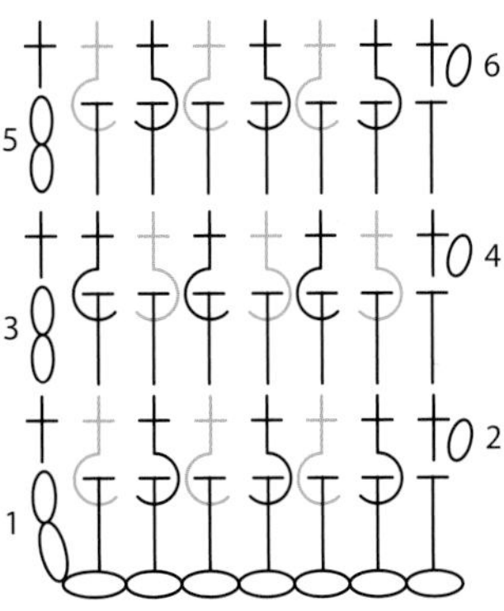

Crinkle stitch

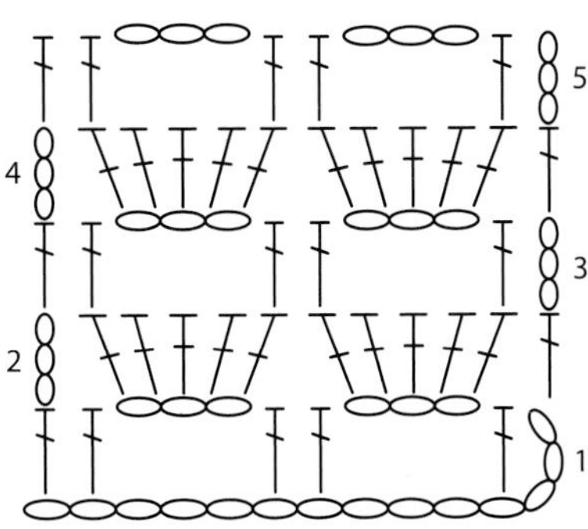

Boxed block stitch

Crossed cluster stitch

Multiple of 8 sts + 4 (add 1 for base chain).

Special abbreviation:

2CC (2 crossed clusters) = skip 1 st, into next st work *[yo, insert hook, yo, draw loop through] twice, yo, draw through all 5 loops on hook; rep from * into st just skipped, working over previous cluster.

Row 1 (WS): Skip 2 ch (count as 1sc), 1sc into next and each ch to end, turn.

Row 2: Ch3 (count as 1dc), skip 1 st, *2CC over next 2 sts, 1dc into each of next 6 sts, rep from * to last 3 sts, 2CC over next 2 sts, 1dc into tch, turn.

Row 3: Ch1 (count as 1sc), skip 1 st, 1sc into next and each st to end, working last st into top of tch, turn.

Row 4: Ch3 (count as 1dc), skip 1 st, 1dc into each of next 4 sts, *2CC over next 2 sts, 1dc into each of next 6 sts; rep from * to last 7 sts, 2CC over next 2 sts, 1dc into each of last 5 sts, working last st into tch, turn.

Row 5: As row 3.

Rep rows 2–5.

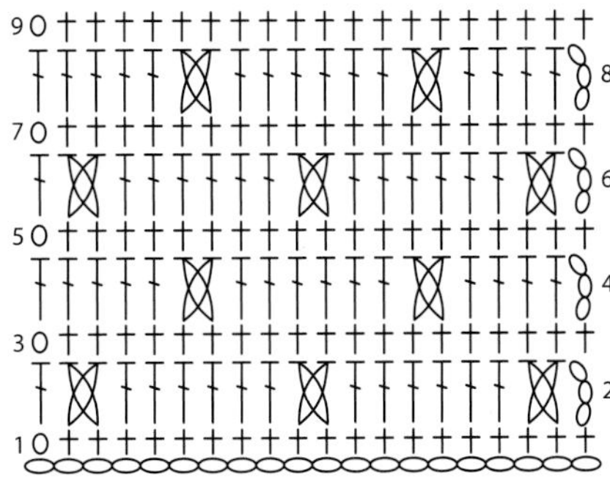

2CC

Crossed cluster stitch

Diagonal shell stitch

Multiple of 4 sts + 1 (add 1 for base chain).
Special abbreviation:
Shell = [1sc, ch3, 4dc] all into same st.
Row 1 (RS): Work 1 shell into 2nd ch from hook, *skip 3 ch, 1 shell into next ch; rep from * to last 4 ch, skip 3 ch, 1sc into last ch, turn.
Row 2: Ch3 (count as 1dc), skip 1 st, *skip 1 dc, over next 2 sts work dc2tog, ch3, skip 1 dc, 1sc into top of ch-3; rep from * to end, turn.
Row 3: Ch1, 1 shell into 1st st, *skip 3 ch and next st, 1 shell into next sc; rep from * ending skip 3 ch and next st, 1sc into top of tch, turn.
Rep rows 2–3.

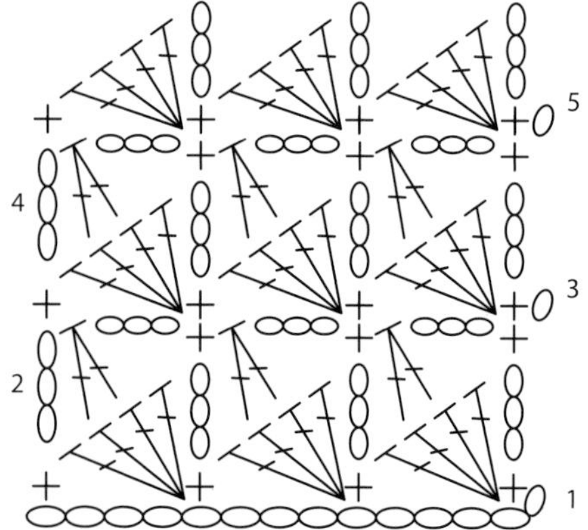

Singles and doubles

Any number of sts (add 1 for base chain).
Row 1 (WS): Skip 2 ch (count as 1sc), 1sc into next and each ch to end, turn.
Row 2: Ch3 (count as 1dc), skip 1 st, 1dc into next and each st to end, working last st into top of tch, turn.
Row 3: Ch1 (count as 1sc), skip 1 st, 1sc into next and each st to end, working last st into top of tch, turn.
Rep rows 2–3.
Note: This is one of the simplest and most effective combination stitch patterns. It is also one of the easiest to get wrong! Concentration is required as you work the ends of the rows to avoid increasing or decreasing, or working two rows of the same stitch in succession by mistake.

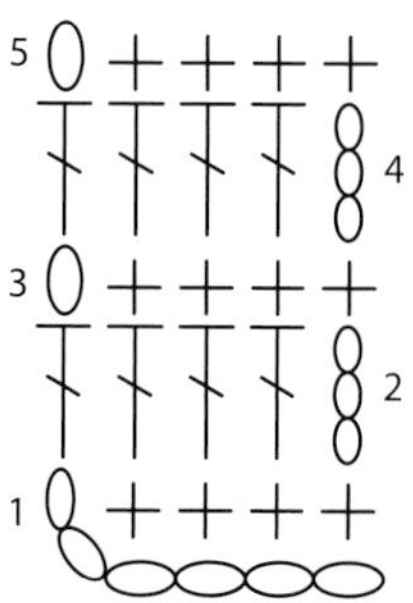

Shell and V stitch

Multiple of 8 sts + 1 (add 2 for base chain).
Row 1 (RS): Skip 2 ch (count as 1dc), 2dc into next ch, *skip 3 ch, work a V st of [1dc, 1h1, 1dc] into next ch, skip 3 ch**, 5dc into next ch; rep from * ending last rep at **, 3dc into last ch, turn.
Row 2: Ch3 (count as 1dc), 1dc into 1st st, *5dc into sp at center of next V st **, V st into 3rd of next 5 dc; rep from * ending last rep at **, 2dc into top of tch, turn.
Row 3: Ch3 (count as 1dc), 2dc into 1st st, *V st into 3rd of next 5 dc**, 5dc into sp at center of next V st; rep from * ending last rep at **, 3dc into top of tch, turn.
Rep rows 2–3.

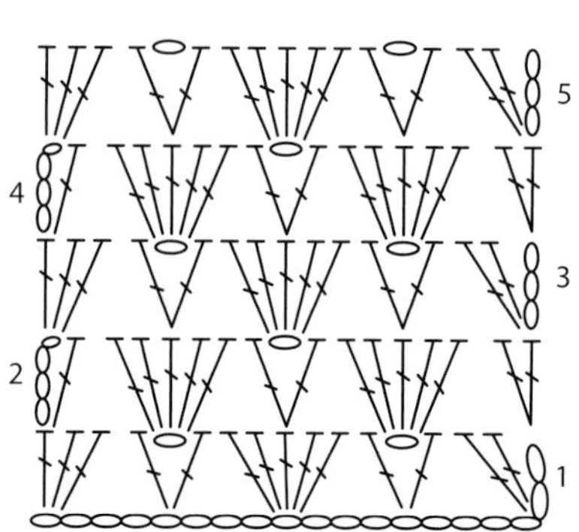

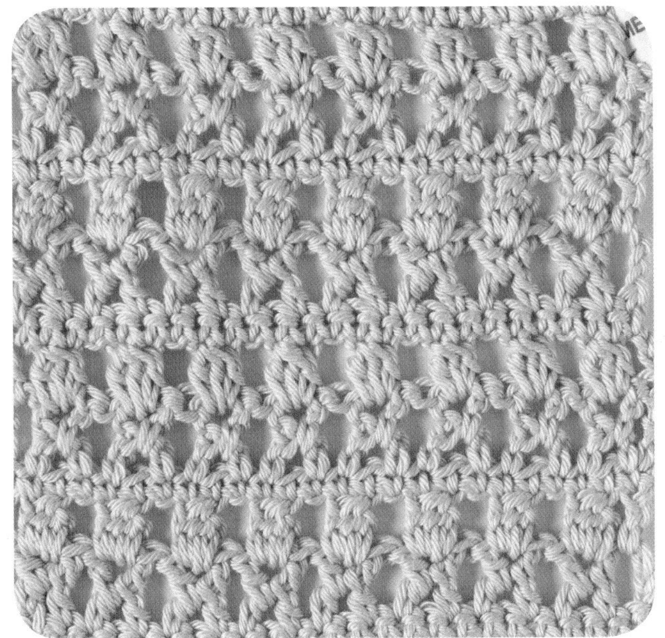

Hotcross bun stitch

Multiple of 3 sts + 2 (add 1 for base chain).

Special abbreviation:

TrX (treble "X" shape – worked over 3 sts) = [yo] twice, insert hook into next st, yo, draw loop through, yo, draw through 2 loops, skip next st, yo, insert hook into next st, yo, draw loop through, [yo, draw through 2 loops] 4 times, ch1, yo, insert hook half way down st just made where lower "legs" join, yo, draw loop through, [yo, draw through 2 loops] twice.

Row 1 (WS): 1sc into 2nd ch from hook, 1sc into next and each ch to end, turn.

Row 2: Ch4 (count as 1tr), skip 1st st, *TrX over next 3 sts; rep from * ending 1tr into last st, skip tch, turn.

Row 3: Ch4 (count as 1dc, ch1), *work dc3tog into next ch-1 sp**, ch2; rep from * ending last rep at **, ch1, 1dc into top of tch, turn.

Row 4: Ch1, 1sc into 1st st, 1sc into next ch, *1sc into next cluster, 1sc into each of next 2 ch; rep from * to end, turn.

Rep rows 2–4.

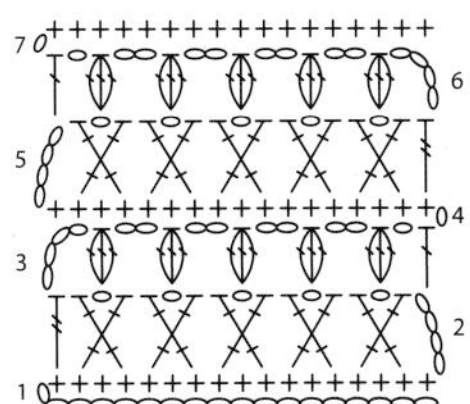

Tread pattern

Multiple of 8 sts + 3 (add 2 for base chain).

Row 1 (RS): Skip 3 ch (count as 1dc), 1dc into each of next 2 ch, *skip 2 ch, 1dc into next ch, ch3, work a block of 3dc evenly spaced into side of dc just made, skip 2 ch, 1dc into each of next 3ch; rep from * to end, turn.

Row 2: Ch3 (count as 1dc), skip 1st st, 1dc into each of next 2 dc, *ch2, 1sc into top of ch-3 at corner of next block, ch2, skip dc that forms base of same block, 1dc into each of next 3 dc; rep from * ending last rep in top of tch, turn.

Row 3: Ch3 (count as 1dc), skip 1st st, 1dc into each of next 2 dc, *skip 2 ch, 1dc into next sc, ch3, 3dc evenly spaced into side of dc just made, skip 2 ch, 1dc into each of next 3 dc; rep from * ending last rep in top of tch, turn.

Rep rows 2–3.

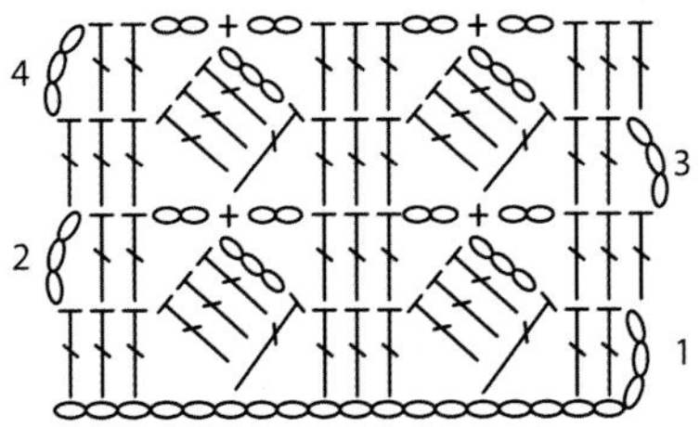

Chevron stitch I

Multiple of 16 sts + 2.

Row 1 (RS): Work 2sc into 2nd ch from hook, *1sc into each of next 7 ch, skip 1 ch, 1sc into each of next 7 ch, 3sc into next ch; rep from * to end omitting 1sc at end of last rep, turn.

Row 2: Ch1, work 2sc into 1st sc, *1sc into each of next 7 sc, skip 2 sc, 1sc into each of next 7 sc, 3sc into next sc; rep from * to end, omitting 1sc at end of last rep, turn.

Rep row 2 only.

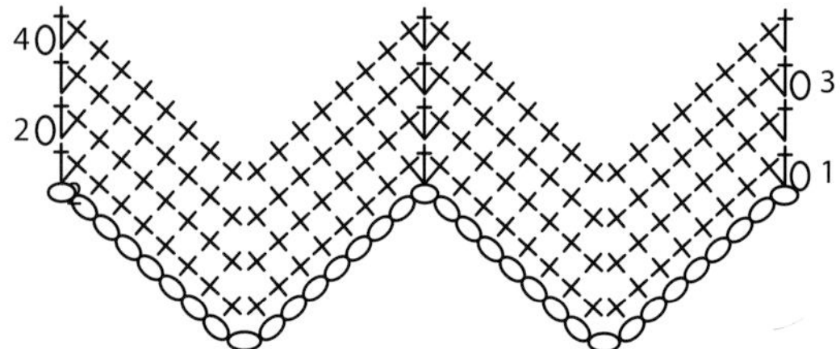

Chevron stitch II

Work as given for Chevron stitch I (see left), working 1 row each in colors A, B and C throughout.

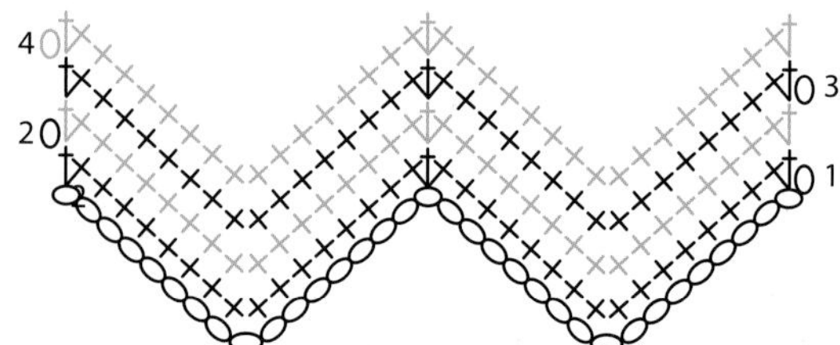

Interlocking block stitch I

Multiple of 6 sts + 3 (add 2 for base chain).

Special abbreviation:

Sdc (Spike double crochet) = work dc over ch sp by inserting hook into top of next row below (or base chain).

Work 1 row each in colors A, B and C throughout.

Row 1: Skip 3 ch (count as 1dc), 1dc into each of next 2 ch, *ch3, skip 3 ch, 1dc into each of next 3 ch; rep from * to end, turn.

Row 2: *Ch3, skip 3 sts, 1Sdc over each of next 3 sts; rep from * to last 3 sts, ch2, skip 2 sts, sl st into top of tch, turn.

Row 3: Ch3 (count as 1Sdc), skip 1 st, 1Sdc over each of next 2 sts, *ch3, skip 3 sts, 1Sdc over each of next 3 sts; rep from * to end, turn.

Rep rows 2–3.

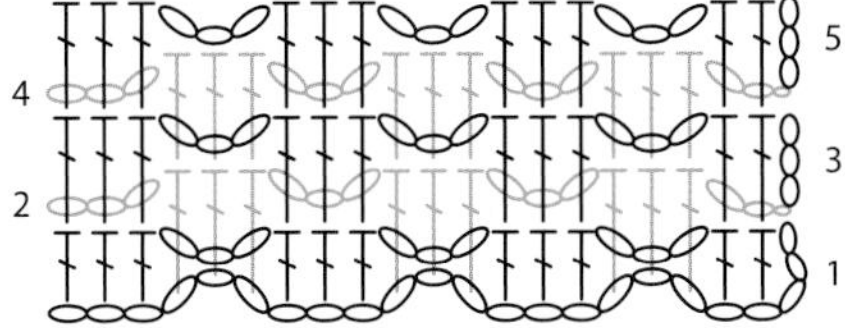

Interlocking block stitch II

Work as Interlocking block stitch I (see left). Work 1 row each in colors A and B alternately throughout. Do not break yarn when changing color, but begin row at same end as color.

Track stitch

Any number of sts (add 1 for base chain).

Row 1 (WS): Skip 2 ch (count as 1sc), 1sc into next and each ch to end, turn.

Row 2: Ch5 (count as 1dtr), skip 1 st, 1dtr into next and each st to end, working last st into top of tch, turn.

Rows 3–5: Ch1 (count as 1sc), skip 1 st, 1sc into next and each st to end, working last st into top of tch, turn.

Rep rows 2–5.

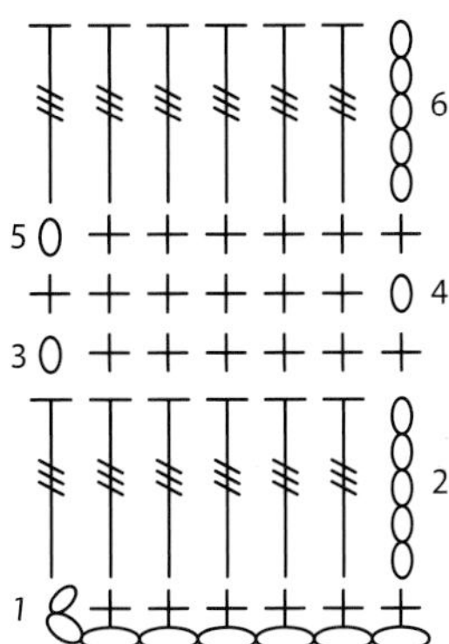

Crossed ripple stitch

Multiple of 3 sts + 2 (add 1 for base chain).
Special abbreviation:
Dc/rf (raised double crochet at the front of the fabric) = wrap the yarn around the hook, insert the hook from in front and from right to left around the stem of the appropriate stitch, and complete the stitch normally.
Base row 1 (WS): 1sc into 2nd ch from hook, 1sc into each ch to end, turn.
Base row 2: Ch3 (count as 1dc), skip 1st st, *skip next 2 sts, 1dc into next st, ch1, 1dc back into 1st of 2 sts just skipped – called Crossed Pair; rep from * ending 1dc into last st, skip tch, turn.

Commence pattern
Row 1: Ch1, 1sc into 1st st, 1sc into next and each st and each ch sp to end, working last st into top of tch, turn.
Row 2: As 2nd base row, except as 2nd st of each Crossed Pair work 1dc/rf loosely around 1st st of corresponding Crossed Pair 2 rows below.
Rep these 2 rows.

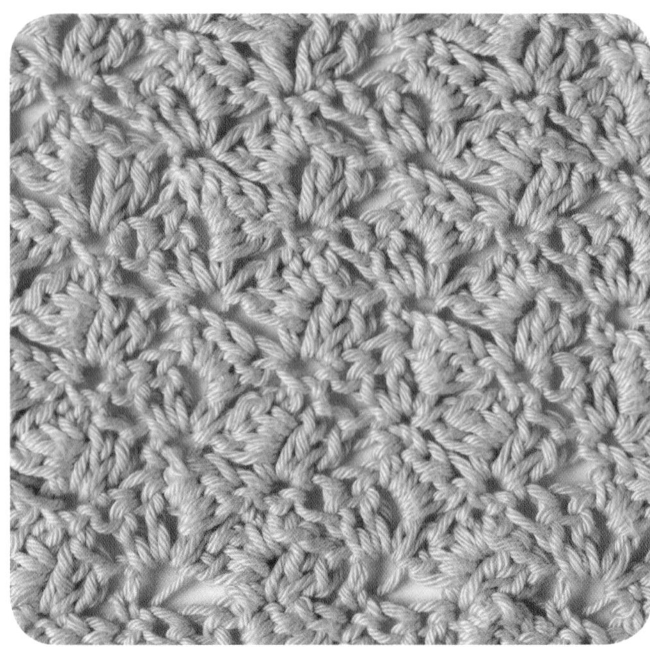

Sidesaddle shell stitch

Multiple of 6 sts + 1 (add 3 for base chain).
Special abbreviation:
Shell = 3dc, ch1, [1sc, 1hdc, 1dc] all into side of last of 3dc just made.
Row 1 (WS): Skip 3 ch (count as 1dc), 3dc into next ch, skip 2 ch, 1sc into next ch, *skip 2 ch, Shell into next ch, skip 2 ch, 1sc into next ch; rep from * to last 3 ch, skip 2 ch, 4dc into last ch, turn.
Row 2: Ch1 (count as 1sc), skip 1 st, *skip next 3 sts, Shell into next sc, skip 3 sts, 1sc into next ch sp; rep from * ending last rep with 1sc into top of tch, turn.
Row 3: Ch3 (count as 1dc), 3dc into 1st st, skip 3 sts, 1sc into next ch sp, *skip 3 sts, Shell into next sc, skip 3 sts, 1sc into next ch sp; rep from * ending skip 3 sts, 4dc into tch, turn.
Rep rows 2–3.

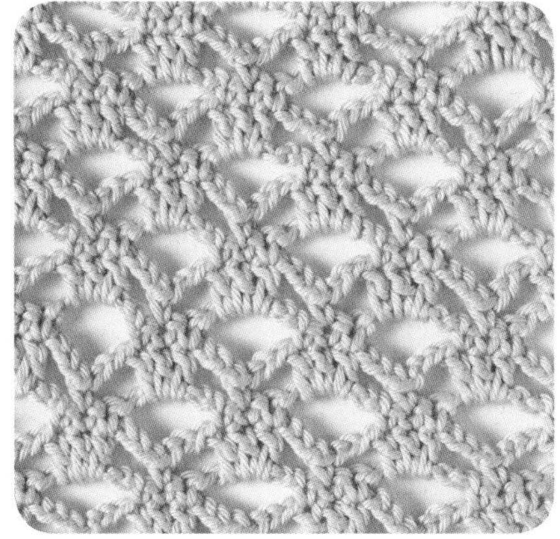

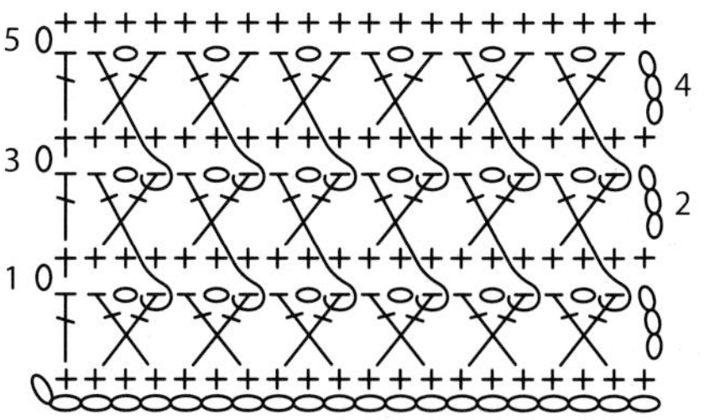

Crossed ripple stitch

Gwenyth's cable

Worked over 19 sts on a background of basic double crochets with any number of sts.

Special abbreviation:

Tr/rf (raised treble at the front of the fabric) = wrap the yarn around the hook, insert the hook from in front and from right to left around the stem of the appropriate stitch, and complete the stitch normally.

Tr/rb (raised treble at the back of the fabric) = wrap the yarn around the hook, insert the hook from behind and from right to left around the stem of the appropriate stitch, and complete the stitch normally.

Row 1 (RS): 1tr/rf around 1st st, 1dc into next st, skip next 3 sts, 1dtr into each of next 3 sts, going behind last 3dtrs work 1dtr into each of 3 sts just skipped, 1dc into next st, 1tr/rf around next st, 1dc into next st, skip next 3 sts, 1dtr into each of next 3 sts, going in front of last 3dtrs but not catching them work 1dtr into each of 3 sts just skipped, 1dc into next st, 1tr/rf around next st.

Row 2: As 1st row, except work 1tr/rb instead of rf over 1st, 10th and 19th sts to keep raised ridges on right side of fabric.

Rep rows 1–2.

Arched lace stitch

Multiple of 8 sts + 1 (add 1 for base chain).

Row 1 (RS): 1sc into 2nd ch from hook, 1sc into next ch, *ch5, skip 5 ch, 1sc into each of next 3 ch; rep from * omitting 1sc at end of last rep, turn.

Row 2: Ch1, 1sc into 1st st, *ch3, skip next sc, 3dc into next ch-5 arch, ch3, skip 1 sc, 1sc into next sc; rep from * to end, skip tch, turn.

Row 3: Ch6 (count as 1tr, ch2), skip 3 ch, *1sc into each of next 3 dc**, ch5, skip [3 ch, 1sc and 3 ch]; rep from * ending last rep at **, ch2, skip 3 ch, 1tr into last sc, skip tch, turn.

Row 4: Ch3 (count as 1dc), skip 1st st, 1dc into ch-2 sp, *ch3, skip next sc, 1sc into next sc, ch3, skip 1sc**, 3dc into next ch-5 arch; rep from * ending last rep at **, skip 1ch, 1dc into each of next 2 ch of tch, turn.

Row 5: Ch1, 1sc into 1st st, 1sc into next st, *ch5, skip [3ch, 1sc and 3ch], 1sc into each of next 3 dc; rep from * to end, omitting 1sc at end of last rep, turn.

Rep rows 2–5.

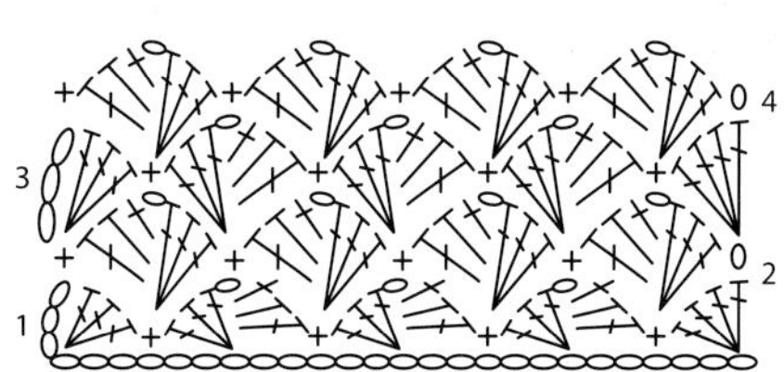

Sidesaddle shell stitch

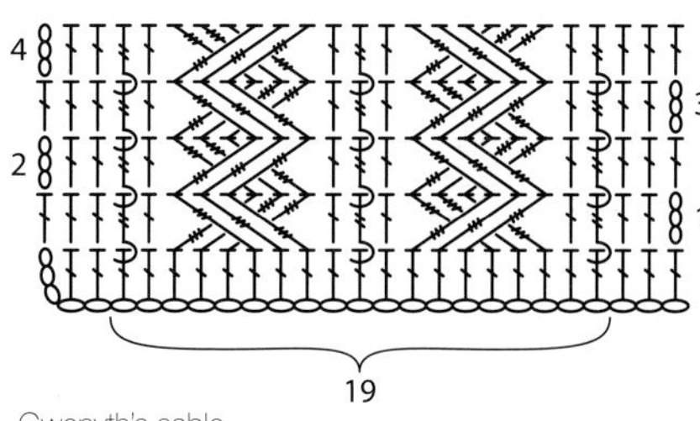

Gwenyth's cable

Arched lace stitch

Crossed puff cables

Worked over 11 sts on a background of basic double crochets with any number of sts.

Special abbreviations:

Tr/rf (treble at the front of the fabric) = wrap the yarn around the hook, insert the hook from in front and from right to left around the stem of the appropriate stitch, and complete the stitch normally.

Tr/rb (treble at the back of the fabric) = wrap the yarn around the hook, insert the hook from behind and from right to left around the stem of the appropriate stitch, and complete the stitch normally.

Row 1 (RS): 1dc into each st.

Row 2: *1tr/rb around next st, work a Puff st of hdc5tog all into next st, 1tr/rb around next st**, 1dc into next st; rep from * once and from * to ** again.

Row 3: *Leaving last loop of each st on hook work [1dc into next st, skip puff st, work 1tr/rf around next st] ending yo, draw through all 3 loops on hook, 1dc into top of puff st, leaving last loop of each st on hook work [1tr/rf around st before same puff st and 1dc into top of st after puff st] ending yo, draw through all 3 loops on hook**, 1dc into next st; rep from * once and from * to ** again.

Row 4: As row 2, but make new tr/rbs by inserting hook under raised stems only of previous sts.

Rep rows 3–4.

Peacock fan stitch

Multiple of 12 sts + 1 (add 1 for base chain).

Row 1 (RS): 1sc into 2nd ch from hook, *skip 5 ch, 13dtr into next ch, skip 5 ch, 1sc into next ch; rep from * to end, turn.

Row 2: Ch5 (count as 1dtr), 1dtr into 1st st, *ch4, skip 6 dtr, 1sc into next dtr, ch4, skip 6 dtr**, work [1dtr, ch1, 1dtr] into next sc; rep from * ending last rep at **, 2dtr into last sc, skip tch, turn.

Row 3: Ch1, 1sc into 1st st, *skip [1dtr and ch-4], 13dtr into next sc, skip [ch-4 and 1dtr], 1sc into next ch; rep from * to end, turn.

Rep rows 2–3.

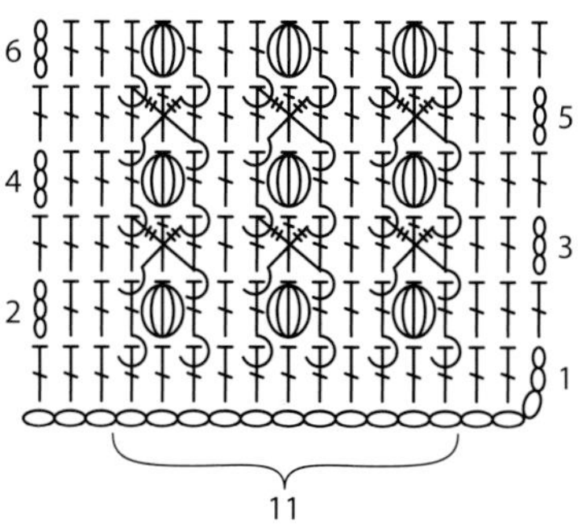

Crossed puff cables

Petal stitch

Multiple of 8 sts + 1 (add 1 for base chain).

Row 1 (WS): 1sc into 2nd ch from hook, *ch2, skip 3 ch, 4tr into next ch, ch2, skip 3 ch, 1sc into next ch; rep from * to end, turn.

Row 2: Ch1, 1sc into 1st st, *ch3, skip ch-2 and 1 tr, 1sc into next tr, ch3, skip 2 tr and ch-2, 1sc into next sc; rep from * to end, skip tch, turn.

Row 3: Ch4 (count as 1tr), 1tr into 1st st, *ch2, skip ch-3, 1sc into next sc, ch2, skip ch-3, 4tr into next sc; rep from * to end omitting 1tr at end of last rep, skip tch, turn.

Row 4: Ch1, 1sc into 1st st, *ch3, skip 2 tr and ch-2, 1sc into next sc, ch3, skip ch-2 and 1tr, 1sc into next tr; rep from * ending last rep in top of tch, turn.

Row 5: Ch1, 1sc into 1st st, *ch2, skip ch-3, 4tr into next sc, ch2, skip ch-3, 1sc into next sc; rep from * to end, skip tch, turn.

Rep rows 2–5.

Odd forked cluster stitch

Any number of sts (add 2 for base chain).

Special abbreviation:

OFC (Odd Forked Cluster) = yo, insert hook into ch or st as indicated, yo, draw loop through, yo, draw through 2 loops, insert hook into next ch or st, yo, draw loop through, yo, draw through all 3 loops on hook.

Row 1: Skip 2 ch (count as 1hdc), 1OFC inserting hook 1st into 3rd then 4th ch from hook, *1OFC inserting hook 1st into same ch as previous OFC then into next ch; rep from * until 1 ch rem, 1hdc into last ch, turn.

Row 2: Ch2 (count as 1hdc), 1OFC inserting hook into 1st st then into next st, *1OFC inserting hook into same st as previous OFC then into next st; rep from * ending 1hdc into top of tch, turn.

Rep row 2.

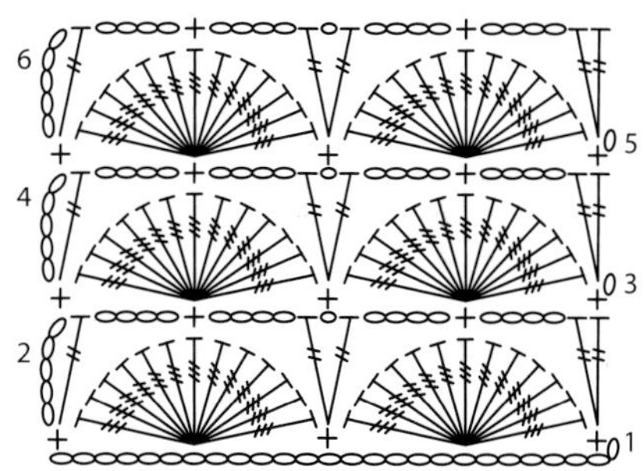

Peacock fan stitch

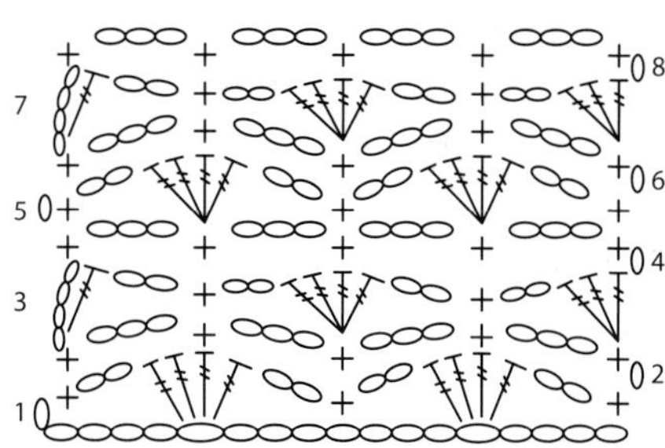

Petal stitch

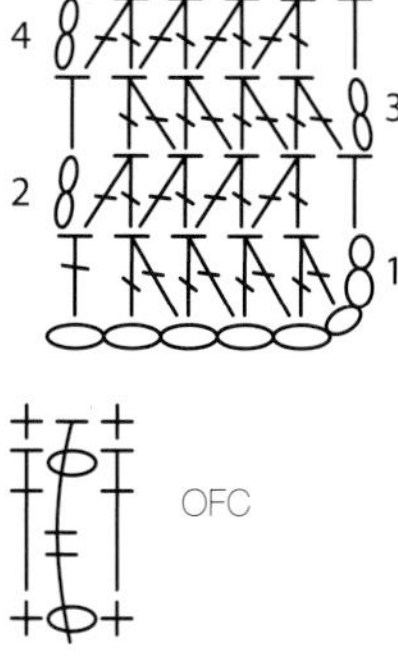

Odd forked cluster stitch

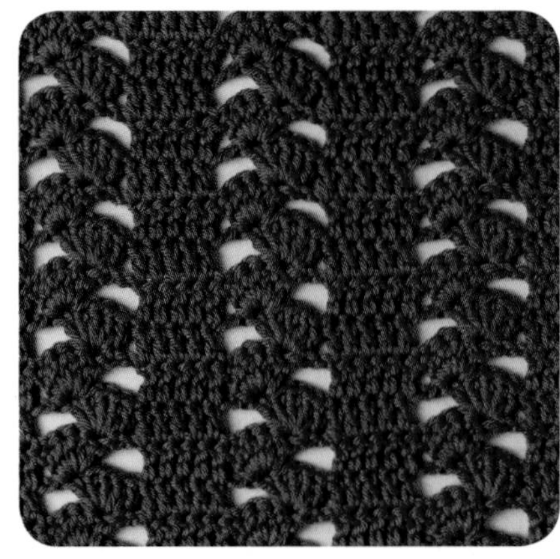

Diagonal spike stitch

Multiple of 4 sts + 2 (add 2 for base chain).

Special abbreviation:

Sdc (Spike double crochet) = yo, insert hook into same place that 1st dc of previous 3dc block was worked, yo, draw loop through and up so as not to crush 3dc block, [yo, draw through 2 loops] twice.

Row 1: Skip 3 ch (count as 1dc), *1dc into each of next 3 ch, skip next ch and work 1Sdc over it instead; rep from * ending 1dc into last ch, turn.

Row 2: Ch3 (count as 1dc), skip 1 st, *1dc into each of next 3 sts, skip next st and work 1Sdc over it instead; rep from * ending 1dc into top of tch, turn.

Rep row 2.

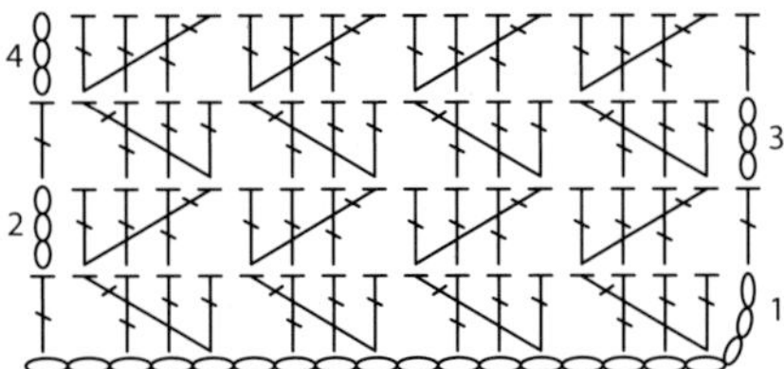

Block and offset shell stitch

Multiple of 11 sts + 5 (add 2 for base chain).

Row 1 (RS): Skip 3 ch (count as 1dc), 1dc into each of next 4 ch, *skip 2 ch, 5dc into next ch, ch2, skip 3 ch, 1dc into each of next 5 ch; rep from * to end, turn.

Row 2: Ch3 (count as 1dc), skip 1st st, 1dc into each of next 4 sts, *skip ch-2, 5dc into next dc, ch2, skip 4 dc, 1dc into each of next 5 sts; rep from * to end, turn.

Rep row 2.

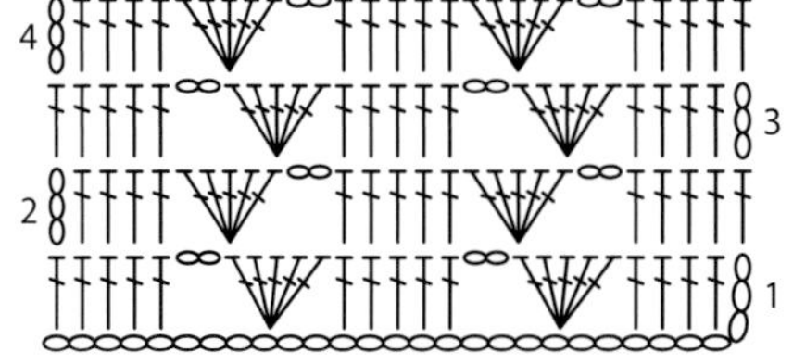

Aligned cobble stitch

Multiple of 2 sts + 1 (add 1 for base chain).

Row 1 (RS): 1sc into 2nd ch from hook, 1sc into each ch to end, turn.

Row 2: Ch1, 1sc into 1st st, *1tr into next st, 1sc into next st; rep from * to end, skip tch, turn.

Row 3: Ch1, 1sc into 1st st, 1sc into next and each st to end, skip tch, turn.

Rep rows 2–3.

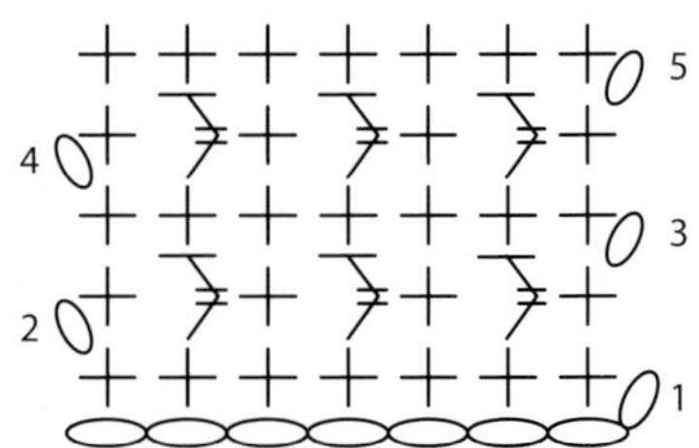

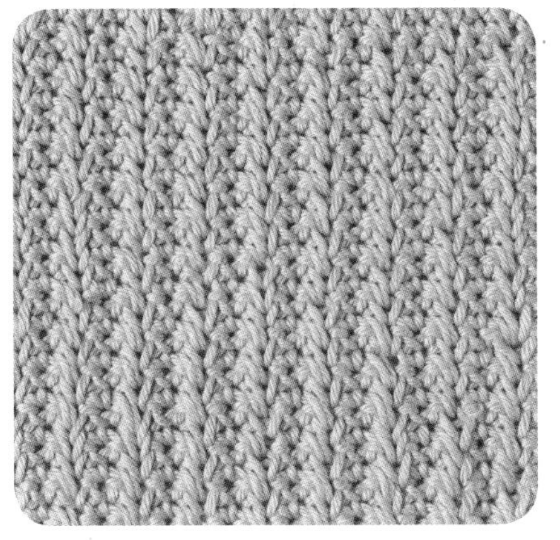

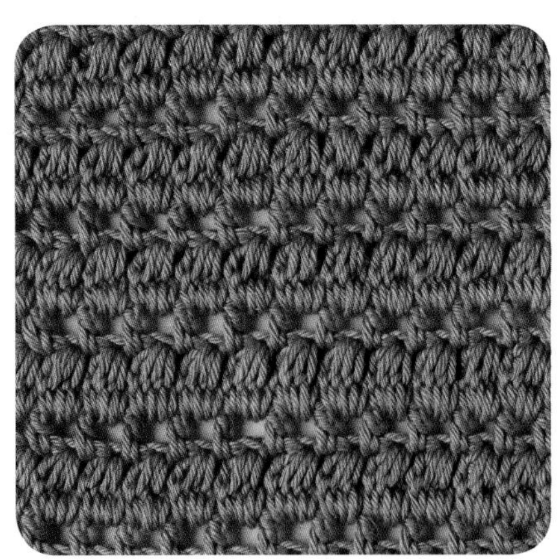

Alternating spike stitch I

Multiple of 2 sts (add 1 for base chain).

Special abbreviation:

Ssc (Spike single crochet) = insert hook below next st 1 row down (i.e. into same place as that st was worked), yo, draw loop through and up to height of present row, yo, draw through both loops on hook.

Row 1: Skip 2 ch (count as 1sc), 1sc into next and each ch to end, turn.

Row 2: Ch1 (count as 1sc), skip 1 st, *1sc into next st, 1Ssc over next st; rep from * ending 1sc into tch, turn.

Rep row 2.

Alternating spike stitch II

Work as Alternating spike stitch I (see left). Work 1 row each in colors A, B and C throughout.

Aligned puff stitch

Multiple of 2 sts + 1 (add 1 for base chain).

Row 1 (RS): 1sc into 2nd ch from hook, *ch1, skip 1 ch, 1sc into next ch; rep from * to end, turn.

Row 2: Ch2 (count as 1hdc), skip 1st st, *hdc4tog all into next ch sp, ch1, skip 1sc; rep from * ending hdc4tog into last ch sp, 1hdc into last sc, skip tch, turn.

Row 3: Ch1, 1sc into 1st st, *ch1, skip 1 st, 1sc into next ch sp; rep from * ending in top of tch, turn.

Rep rows 2–3.

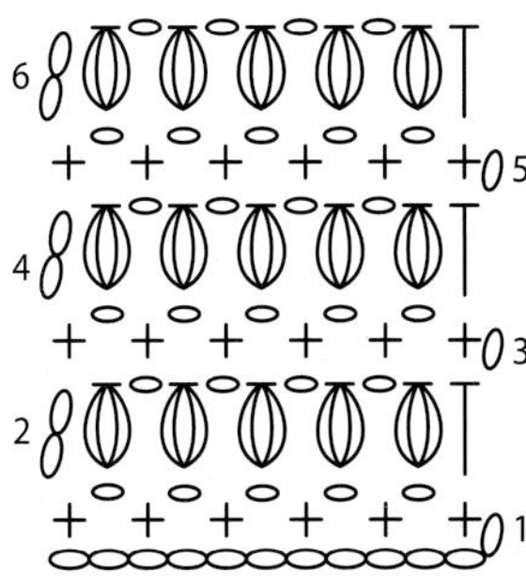

Triple picot V stitch

Multiple of 11 sts + 7 (add 3 for base chain).

Row 1 (RS): 1dc into 4th ch from hook, *ch3, skip 3 ch, 1sc into next ch**, work a picot of [ch3, 1sc into next ch] 3 times, ch3, skip 3 ch, [1dc, ch2, 1dc] into next ch; rep from * ending last rep at ** when 2 ch rem, ch3, 1sc into next ch, ch1, 1hdc into last ch, turn.

Row 2: Ch4 (count as 1dc, ch1), 1dc into 1st st, *ch3, skip 1 Picot and ch-3**, into next ch-2 sp work 1sc, [ch3, 1sc] 3 times, then ch3, skip ch-3 and 1 Picot, [1dc, ch2, 1dc] into next Picot; rep from * ending last rep at **, work [1sc, ch3, 1sc] into top of tch, ch1, 1hdc into next ch, turn.

Rep row 2.

Broomstick lace

Multiple of 4 sts (add 1 for base chain).

Row 1 (RS): 1sc into 2nd ch from hook, 1sc into next and each ch to end, turn.

Row 2: Ch1, 1sc into 1st st, 1sc into next and each st to end, skip tch, turn.

Row 3: *Ch1, draw loop on hook up to approx height of dtr, keeping loop on hook and not allowing it to change size through yarn slippage, insert hook into next st, yo, draw loop through; rep from * to end, keeping all lace loops on hook.

At end remove all except last lace loop from hook, yo, draw loop through, turn.

Row 4: *Always inserting hook through next 4 lace loops together work 4sc; rep from * to end, turn.

Rep rows 2–4.

Arch gallery

Multiple of 3 sts + 2.

Row 1 (RS): Work 1sc into 2nd ch from hook, 1sc into next ch, *ch4, slip st into 4th ch from hook (1 picot made), 1sc into each of next 3 ch; rep from * to end omitting 1sc at end of last rep, turn.

Row 2: Ch5 (count as 1dc, ch2), skip 2 sc, 1dc into next sc, *ch2, skip 2 sc, 1dc into next sc; rep from * to end, turn.

Row 3: Ch1, 1sc into 1st dc, *into next ch-2 sp work [1sc, 1picot, 1sc], 1sc into next dc; rep from * to end placing last sc into 3rd of ch-5 at beg of previous row, turn.

Rep rows 2–3.

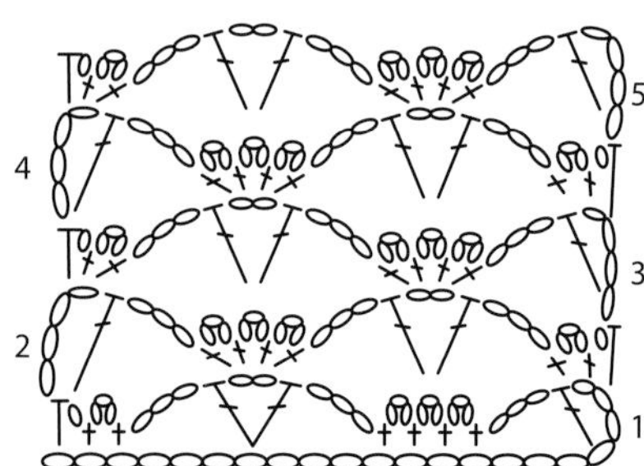

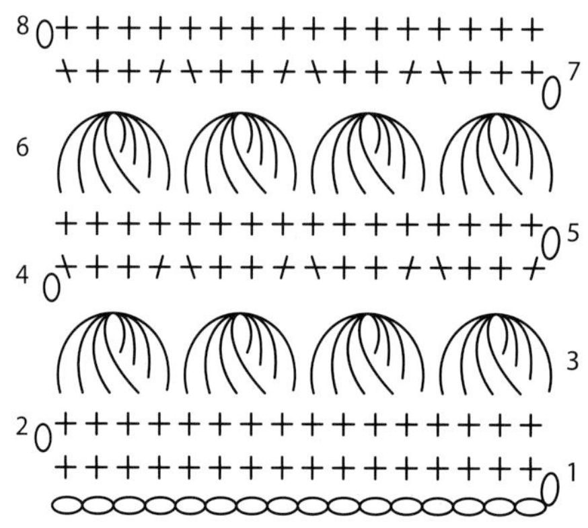

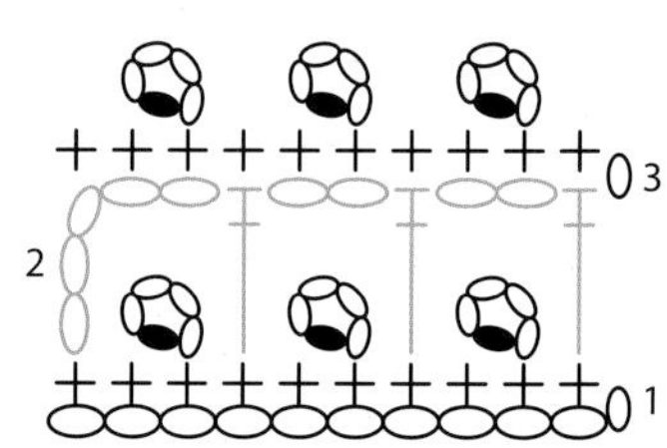

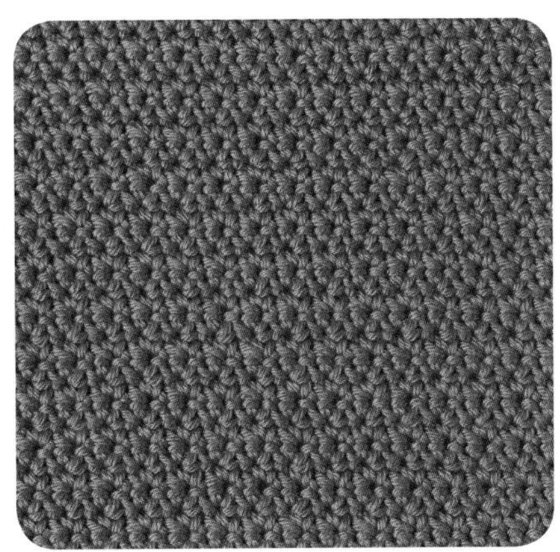

Boxed puff stitch

Multiple of 3 sts + 1 (add 4 for base chain).

Special abbreviation:

Puff st = hdc4tog all into same st and closed with 1ch drawn tightly.

Row 1 (RS): Puff st into 5th ch from hook, *skip 2 ch, [1dc, ch2, puff st] all into next ch; rep from * ending skip 2 ch, 1dc into last ch, turn.

Row 2: Ch1, skip 1st st, *work 1dc loosely over next row into 1st of 2 skipped sts in row below, 1sc into puff st, 1sc into next ch-2 sp; rep from * ending 1sc into 3rd ch of tch, turn.

Row 3: Ch5 (count as 1dc, ch2), puff st into 1st st, *skip 2 sc, [1dc, ch2, puff st] all into next dc; rep from * ending skip 2 sc, 1dc into last dc, skip tch, turn.

Rep rows 2–3.

Grit stitch I

Multiple of 2 sts + 1 (add 2 for base chain).

Row 1: Skip 2 ch (count as 1sc), 1sc into next ch, *skip 1 ch, 2sc into next ch; rep from * to last 2 ch, skip 1 ch, 1sc into last ch, turn.

Row 2: Ch1 (count as 1sc), 1sc into 1st st, *skip 1 sc, 2sc into next sc; rep from * to last 2 sts, skip 1 sc, 1sc into top of tch, turn.

Rep row 2.

Grit stitch II

Multiple of 2 sts + 1 (add 2 for base chain).

Row 1: Skip 2 ch (count as 1sc), 1dc into next ch, *skip 1 ch, work [1sc and 1dc] into next ch; rep from * to last 2 ch, skip 1ch, 1sc into last ch, turn.

Row 2: Ch1 (count as 1sc), 1dc into 1st st, *skip 1 dc, work [1sc and 1dc] into next sc; rep from * to last 2 sts, skip 1 dc, 1sc into top of tch, turn.

Rep row 2.

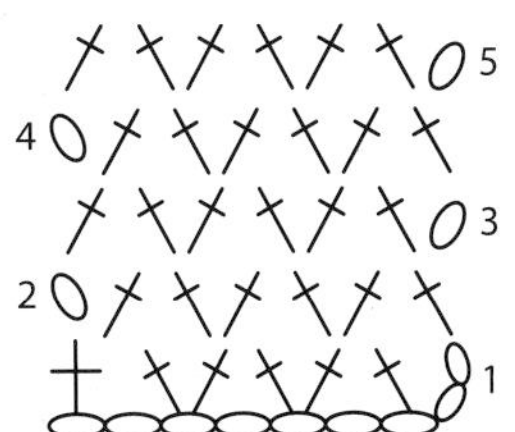

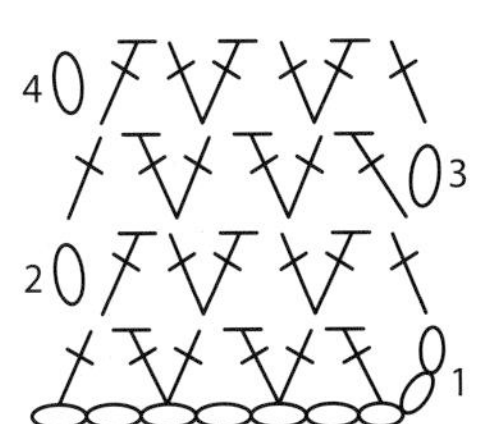

Picot fan stitch

Multiple of 12 sts + 1 (add 1 for base chain).

Row 1 (RS): 1sc into 2nd ch from hook, *ch5, skip 3 ch, 1sc into next ch; rep from * to end, turn.

Row 2: Ch5 (count as 1dc, ch2), *1sc into next ch-5 arch, 8dc into next arch, 1sc into next arch**, ch5; rep from * ending last rep at ** in last arch, ch2, 1dc into last sc, skip tch, turn.

Row 3: Ch1, 1sc into 1st st, skip ch-2 and 1sc, *work a picot of [1dc into next dc, ch3, insert hook down through top of dc just made and slip st to close] 7 times, 1dc into next dc, 1sc into next arch; rep from * to end, turn.

Row 4: Ch8, skip 2 picots, *1sc into next picot, ch5, skip 1 picot, 1sc into next picot, ch5, skip 2 picots, 1dc into next sc**, ch5, skip 2 picots; rep from * ending last rep at **, skip tch, turn.

Row 5: Ch5 (count as 1dc, ch2), *1sc into next ch-5 arch, 8dc into next arch, 1sc into next arch**, ch5; rep from * ending last rep at ** in last arch, ch2, 1dc into 3rd ch of tch, turn.

Rep rows 3–5.

Lacy wave stitch

Multiple of 11 sts + 1 (add 1 for base chain).

Row 1 (RS): 1sc into 2nd ch from hook, *ch2, skip 2 ch, 1dc into each of next 2 ch, ch2, skip 2 ch, 1sc into each of next 5 ch; rep from * to end, turn.

Row 2: Ch5 (count as 1dc, ch2), 1dc into 1st st, *[ch1, skip 1 st, 1dc into next st] twice, ch1, 1dc into next ch-2 sp, skip 2 dc**, 5dc into next ch-2 sp, ch2, 1dc into next st; rep from * ending last rep at **, 4dc into last ch-2 sp, 1dc into last sc, skip tch, turn.

Row 3: Ch5 (count as 1dc, ch2), 1dc into 1st st, *[ch1, skip 1 st, 1dc into next st] twice, ch1, skip 1 st, 1dc into next ch, skip [1dc, ch1, 1dc, ch1 and 1dc], 5dc into next ch-2 sp**, ch2, 1dc into next st; rep from * ending last rep at ** in tch, turn.

Rep row 3.

Picot fan stitch

Spiked squares

Multiple of 10 sts + 2 (add 1 for base chain).

Special abbreviation:

Ssc (Spike single crochet) = insert hook below next st 1 row down, yo, draw loop through and up to height of present row, yo, draw through both loops on hook.

Note: when working Sscs over previous Sscs, insert hook in centers of previous Sscs.

Work 2 rows each in colors A, B and C throughout.

Base row (RS): 1sc into 2nd ch from hook, 1sc into next and each ch to end, turn.

Commence pattern

Row 1: Ch1, 1sc into 1st and each st to end, skip tch, turn.

Row 2: Ch1, 1sc into 1st st, *1Ssc over each of next 5 sts, 1sc into each of next 5 sts; rep from * ending 1sc into last sc, skip tch, turn.

Rep the last 2 rows 3 more times.

Row 9: As row 1.

Row 10: 1sc into 1st st, *1sc into each of next 5 sts, 1Ssc over each of next 5 sts; rep from * ending 1sc into last sc, skip tch, turn.

Rep the last 2 rows 3 times more.

Rep these 16 rows.

Puff stitch plaits

Multiple of 8 sts + 1 (add 1 for base chain).

Row 1 (RS): Skip 2 ch (count as 1hdc), 1hdc into each of next 2 ch, *ch1, skip 1 ch, hdc3tog all into next ch, ch1, skip 1 ch**, 1hdc into each of next 5 ch; rep from * ending last rep at ** when 3 ch remain, 1hdc into each of last 3 ch, turn.

Row 2: Ch2 (count as 1hdc), skip 1st st, 1hdc into each of next 2 sts, *hdc3tog into next ch sp, ch1, skip 1 st, hdc3tog into next ch sp**, 1hdc into each of next 5 sts; rep from * ending last rep at ** when 3 sts remain including tch, 1hdc into each of last 3 sts, turn.

Row 3: Ch2 (count as 1hdc), skip 1st st, 1hdc into each of next 2 sts, *ch1, skip 1 st, hdc3tog into next ch sp, ch1, skip 1 st**, 1hdc into each of next 5 sts; rep from * ending last rep at ** when 3 sts rem including tch, 1hdc into each of last 3 sts, turn.

Rep rows 2–3.

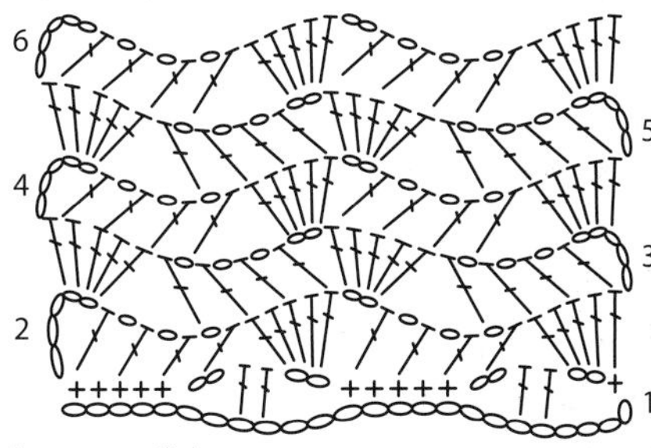

Lacy wave stitch

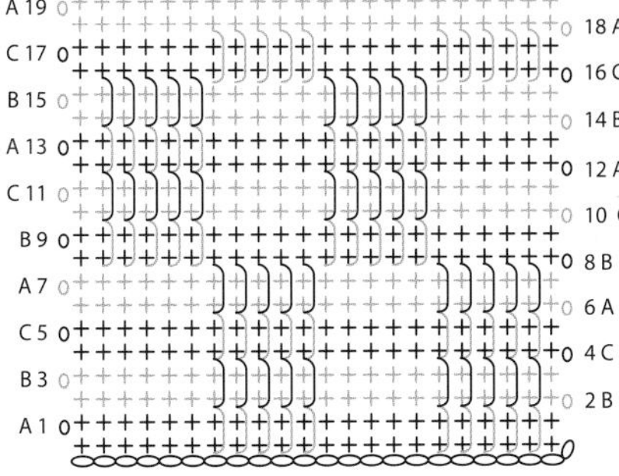

Spiked squares

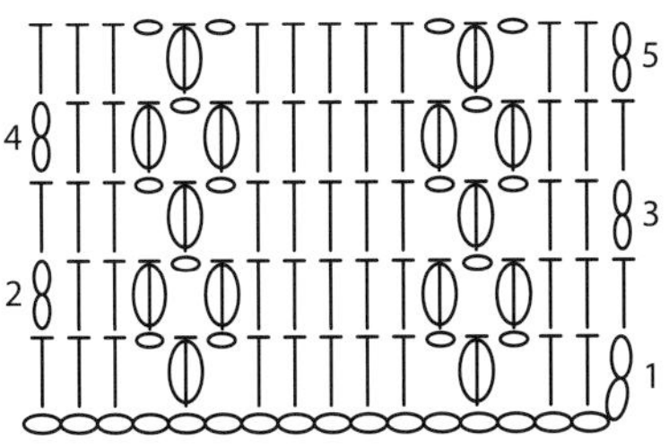

Puff stitch plaits

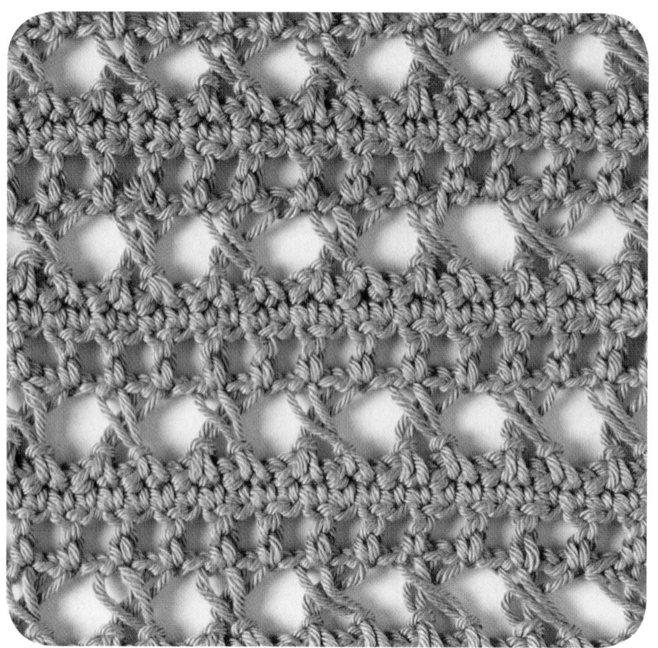

Crossed lace loop stitch

Multiple of 4 sts + 3 (add 3 for base chain).

Row 1 (RS): 1dc into 6th ch from hook, *ch1, skip 1 ch, 1dc into next ch; rep from * to end, turn.

Row 2: Ch1, 1sc into 1st st, *1sc into next ch, 1sc into next dc; rep from * ending 1sc into each of next 2 ch of tch, turn.

Row 3: *Ch1, draw loop on hook up to approx height of tr, keeping loop on hook and not allowing it to change size through yarn slippage, insert hook into next st, yo, draw loop through, slip st into next st; rep from * to end, keeping all lace loops on hook. At end remove all except last lace loop from hook, yo, draw loop through, insert hook under back thread as though for Solomon's knot (see page 15), but make slip st to lock last lace loop, turn.

Row 4: Skip 1st lace loop, *ch1, skip 1 lace loop, slip st into top of next loop, ch1, bring forward loop just skipped and slip st into top of it; rep from * ending ch1, slip st into top of last loop, turn.

Row 5: Ch4 (count as 1dc, ch1), skip 1 ch, 1dc into next slip st, *ch1, skip 1 ch, 1dc into next sl st; rep from * to end, turn.

Rep rows 2–5.

Basic patchwork

Multiple of 5 sts + 1.

Note: The color not in use is held along the line of work and this is kept in place by the crochet stitch being worked over the yarn. This avoids ugly loops appearing on the work and also ensures that the work is completely reversible.

Row 1: Using color A, into 3rd ch from hook work 1sc, 1sc into each of next 2 ch, insert hook into next ch, yo and draw through a loop, yo with color B and draw through both loops on hook, using color B, work 1sc into each of next 5 ch, using color A work 1sc into each of next 5 ch, continue in this way working 5 sts alternately in A and B to end of row. Turn.

Row 2: Using same color as last 5 sc of previous row and working over color not in use as before, work ch1 to count as first sc, 1sc into each of next 4 sc, change color, 1sc into each of next 5 sc, continue in this way to end of row, working last sc into tch. Turn.

Rows 3–5: Work as row 2.

Rows 6–10: Work as row 2, working a square of color A over color B and a square of color B over color A.

Row 11: Work as row 2.

Repeat rows 2–11, ending with a row 5 or 10.

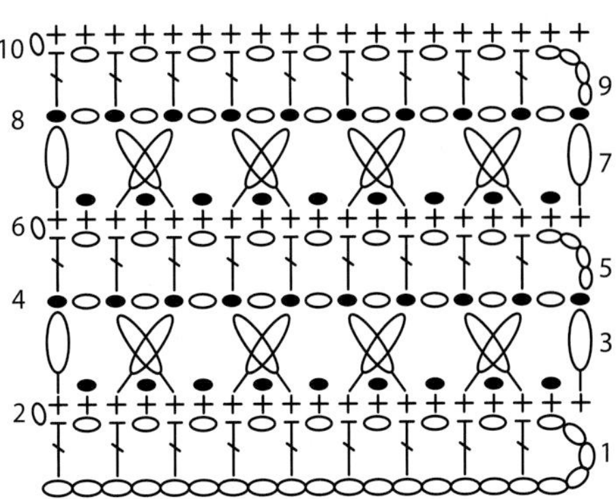

Crossed lace loop stitch

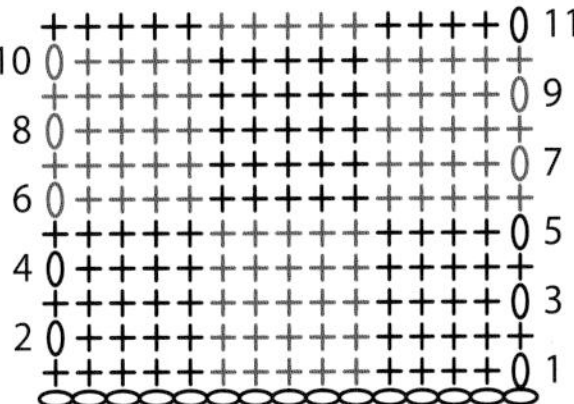

Basic patchwork

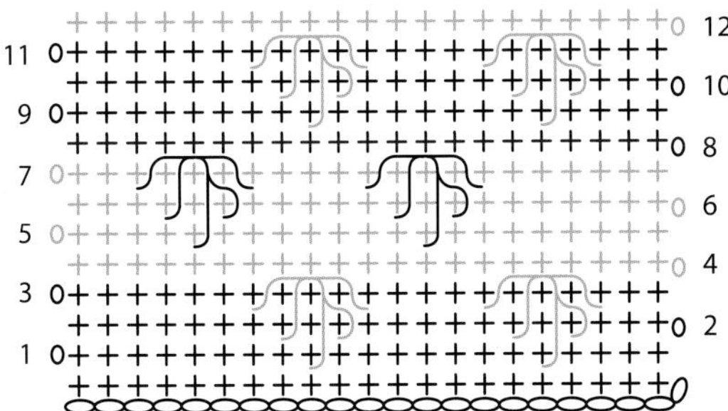

Spike cluster stitch

Spike cluster stitch

Multiple of 8 sts + 5 (add 1 for base chain).

Special abbreviation:

SPC (Spike Cluster) = over next st pick up 5 spike loops by inserting hook as follows: 2 sts to right of next st and 1 row down; 1 st to right and 2 rows down; directly below and 3 rows down; 1 st to left and 2 rows down; 2 sts to left and 1 row down (6 loops on hook); now insert hook into top of next st itself, yo, draw loop through, yo, draw through all 7 loops on hook.

Work 4 rows each in colors A and B alternately throughout.

Base row (RS): 1sc into 2nd ch from hook, 1sc into each ch to end, turn.

Commence pattern

Row 1: Ch1, 1sc into 1st and each st to end, skip tch, turn.

Rows 2 and 3: As row 1.

Row 4: Ch1, 1sc into each of 1st 4 sts, *1SPC over next st, 1sc into each of next 7 sts (be careful not to pick up any of the spikes of the previous SPC); rep from * ending 1sc into last st, skip tch, turn.

Rows 5, 6 and 7: As row 1.

Row 8: Ch1, 1sc into each of 1st 8 sts, *1SPC over next st, 1sc into each of next 7 sts; rep from * to last 5 sts, 1SPC over next st, 1sc into each of last 4 sts, skip tch, turn.

Rep these 8 rows.

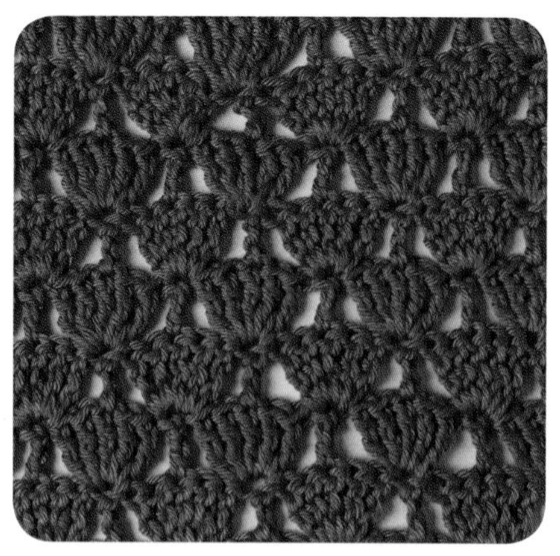

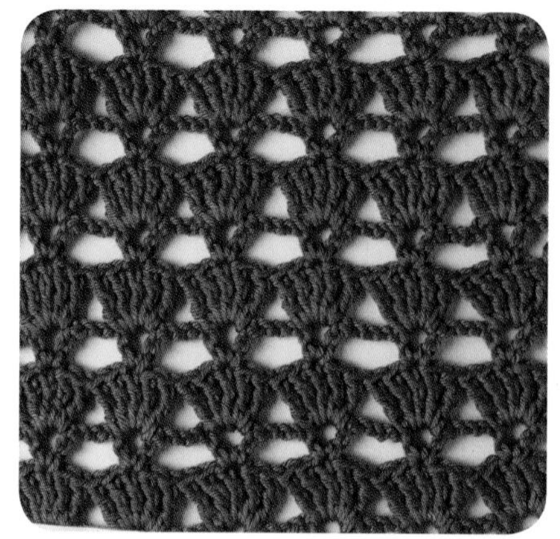

Column and bowl

Multiple of 8 sts + 12.

Row 1 (RS): Work 5tr into 8th ch from hook, skip 3 ch, 1tr into next ch, *skip 3 ch, 5tr into next ch, skip 3 ch, 1tr into next ch; rep from * to end, turn.

Row 2: Ch4 (count as 1tr), 2tr into 1st tr, skip 2 tr, 1tr into next tr, *skip 2 tr, 5tr into next tr, skip 2 tr, 1tr into next tr; rep from * to last 3 sts, skip 2 tr, 3tr into next ch, turn.

Row 3: Ch4, skip 1st tr, *skip 2 tr, 5tr into next tr, skip 2 tr, 1tr into next tr; rep from * to end placing last tr into 4th of ch-4 at beg of previous row, turn.

Rep rows 2–3.

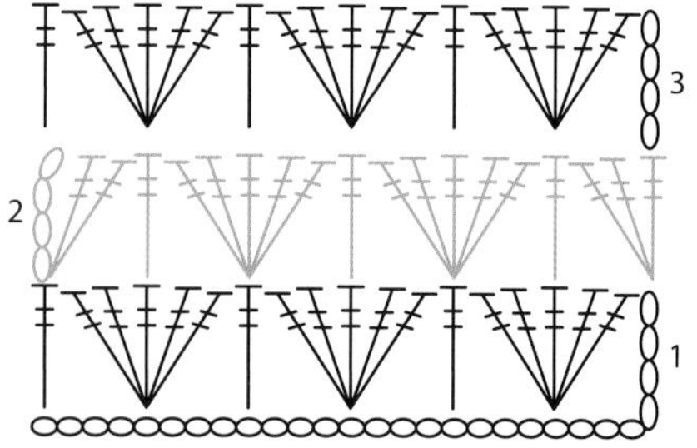

Column stitch

Multiple of 5 sts + 6.

Row 1 (WS): Work [1dc, ch2, 1dc] into 8th ch from hook, *ch3, skip 4 ch, work [1dc, ch2, 1dc] into next ch; rep from * to last 3 ch, ch2, 1dc into last ch, turn.

Row 2: Ch4 (count as 1tr), skip 1st ch-2 sp, work 5tr into next ch-2 sp, *skip ch-3 sp, work 5tr into next ch-2 sp; rep from * to last sp, skip 2 ch, 1tr into next ch, turn.

Row 3: Ch5 (count as 1dc, ch2), skip 1st 3 tr, into next tr work [1dc, ch2, 1dc], *ch3, skip 4 tr, into next tr work [1dc, ch2, 1dc]; rep from * to last 3 tr, ch2, 1dc into 4th of ch-4 at beg of previous row, turn.

Rep rows 2–3.

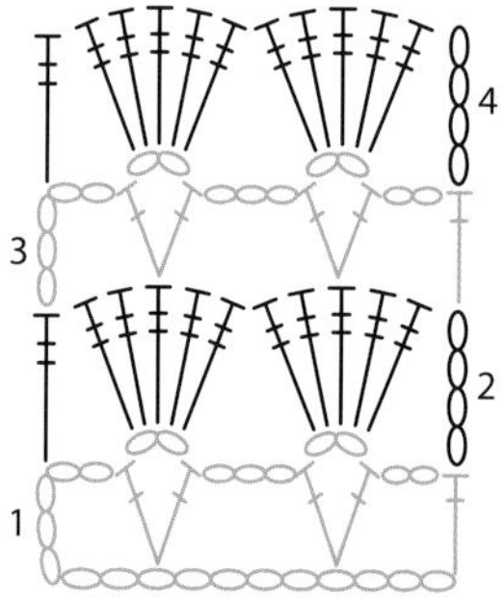

Carpet bag stitch

Multiple 5 sts + 6.

Special abbreviation:

Dc2tog = work 2dc into next st until 1 loop of each remains on hook, yo and through all 3 loops on hook.

Row 1 (RS): Work dc2tog into 6th ch from hook, (count as 1dc, ch-2 sp), *skip 4 ch, dc2tog into next ch, ch2, into same ch as last dc2tog work [dc2tog, ch2, dc2tog]; rep from * to last 5 ch, skip 4 ch, into last ch work [dc2tog, ch2, 1dc], turn.

Row 2: Ch1, 1sc into 1st dc, *ch4, skip 2 dc2tog, 1sc into top of next dc2tog; rep from * to end placing last sc into 3rd ch, turn.

Row 3: Ch5 (count as 1dc, ch2), dc2tog into 1st sc, *dc2tog into next sc, ch2, into same st as last dc2tog work [dc2tog, ch2, dc2tog]; rep from * to last sc, into last sc work [dc2tog, ch2, 1dc], turn.

Rep rows 2–3.

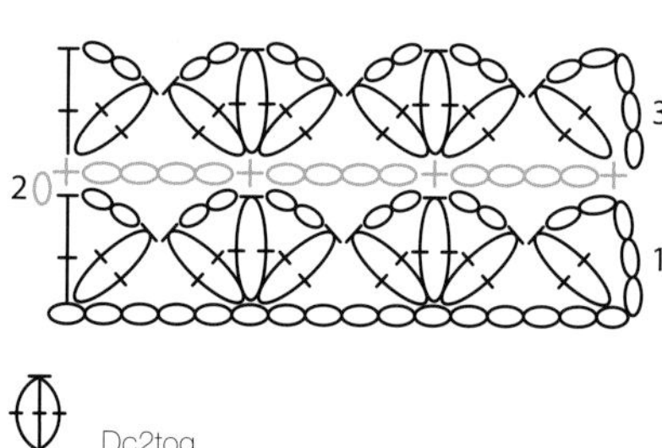

Zigzag popcorn network

Multiple of 10 sts + 1 (add 4 for base chain).

Note: Popcorns occur on both RS and WS rows. Be sure to push them all out on the right side of the fabric as you complete them.

Row 1 (RS): 1sc into 9th ch from hook, 1sc into each of next 2 ch, *ch3, skip 3 ch, 5dc popcorn into next ch, ch3, skip 3 ch, 1sc into each of next 3 ch; rep from * to last 4 ch, ch3, skip 3 ch, 1dc into last ch, turn.

Row 2: Ch1, 1sc into 1st st, *1sc into next arch, ch3, 5dc popcorn into 2nd of next 3 sc, ch3**, 1sc into next arch, 1sc into next popcorn; rep from * ending last rep at **, skip 2 ch of tch arch, 1sc into each of next 2 ch, turn.

Row 3: Ch6 (count as 1dc, ch3), *1sc into next arch, 1sc into next popcorn, 1sc into next arch, ch3**, 5dc popcorn into 2nd of next 3 sc, ch3; rep from * ending last rep at **, 1dc into last sc, skip tch, turn.

Rep rows 2–3.

5-star marguerite stitch

Multiple of 2 sts + 1 (add 1 for base chain).

Special abbreviation:

M5C (Marguerite Cluster with 5 spike loops) = pick up spike loops (i.e.: yo and draw through) inserting hook as follows: into loop that closed previous M5C, under 2 threads of last spike loop of same M5C, into same place that last spike loop of same M5C was worked, into each of next 2 sts (6 loops on hook), yo, draw through all loops on hook.

Row 1 (WS): 1sc into 2nd ch from hook, 1sc into next and each ch to end, turn.

Row 2: Ch3, 1M5C inserting hook into 2nd and 3rd chs from hook and then 1st 3 sts to pick up 5 spike loops, *ch1, 1M5C; rep from * to end, skip tch, turn.

Row 3: Ch1, 1sc into loop that closed last M5C, *1sc into next ch, 1sc into loop that closed next M5C; rep from * ending 1sc into each of next 2 ch of tch, turn.

Rep rows 2–3.

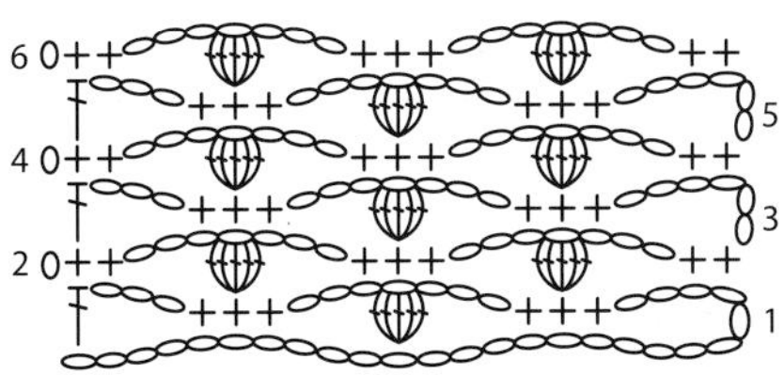

Zigzag popcorn network

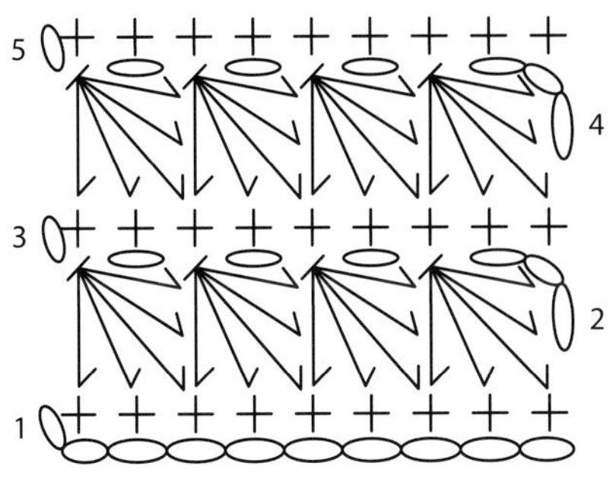

5-star marguerite stitch

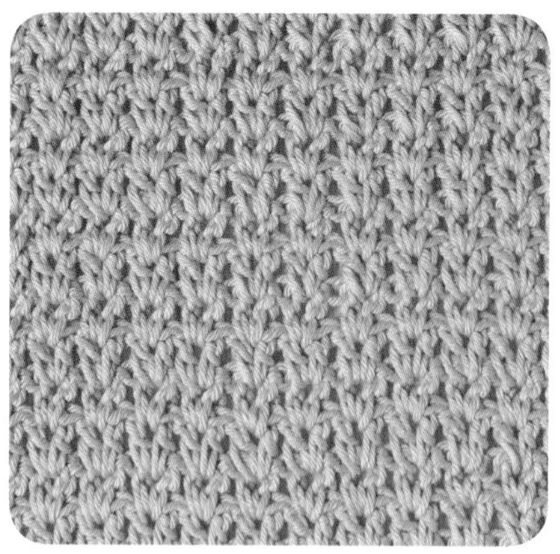

Double crochet V stitch

Multiple of 2 sts.
(add 2 for base chain)

Row 1 (RS): 2dc into 4th ch from hook, *skip 1 ch, 2dc into next ch; rep from * to last 2 ch, skip 1 ch, 1dc into last ch, turn.

Row 2: Ch3, *skip 2 sts, 2dc between 2nd skipped st and next st; rep from * to last 2 sts, skip 1 st, 1dc into top of tch, turn.

Rep Row 2.

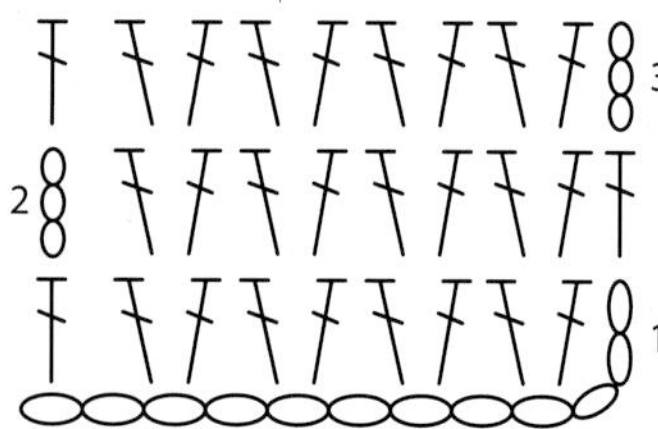

Three-and-two stitch

Multiple of 6 sts + 2.
(add 2 for base chain)

Row 1 (RS): Work a V st of [1dc, ch1, 1dc] into 5th ch from hook, *skip 2 ch, 3dc into next ch, skip 2 ch, work a V st into next ch; rep from * to last 5 ch, skip 2 ch, 3dc into next ch, skip 1 ch, 1dc into last ch, turn.

Row 2: Ch3, *skip 2 sts, work 3dc into center dc of next 3 dc, work a V st into ch sp at center of next V st; rep from * ending 1dc into top of tch, turn.

Row 3: Ch3, *V st into sp of next V st, 3dc into center dc of next 3 dc; rep from * ending 1dc into top of tch, turn.

Interlocking shell stitch

Multiple of 6 sts + 1.
(add 2 for base chain)

Note: Work 1 row each in colors A and B alternately; fasten off each color at the end of each row.

Row 1 (RS): Skip 2 ch (count as 1dc), 2dc into next ch, skip 2 ch, 1sc into next ch, *skip 2 ch, 5dc into next ch, skip 2 ch, 1sc into next ch; rep from * to last 3 ch, skip 2 ch, 3dc into last ch, turn.

Row 2: Ch1, 1sc into first st, *ch2, dc5tog over next 5 sts, ch2, 1sc **into next st; rep from * ending last rep in top of tch, turn.**

Row 3: Ch3 (count as 1dc), 2dc into first st, skip 2 ch, 1sc into next cluster, *skip 2 ch, 5dc into next sc, skip 2 ch, 1sc into next cluster; rep from * to last 2 ch, skip 2 ch, 3dc into last sc, skip tch, turn.

Rep rows 2–3.

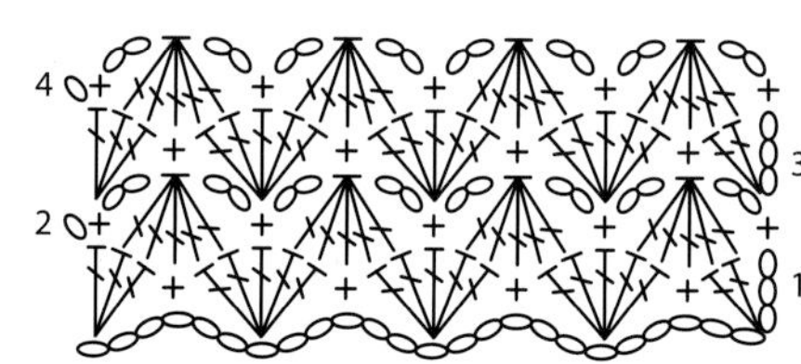

Offset V stitch

Multiple of 3 sts + 1.
(add 3 for base chain)
Row 1 (RS): 1dc into 4th ch from hook, *skip 2 ch, work a V st of [1dc, ch1, 1dc] into next ch; rep from * to last 3 ch, skip 2 ch, 1dc into last ch, turn.
Row 2: Ch4, 1dc into first st, *V st into 2nd dc of next V st; rep from * until 1 dc and tch remain, skip dc and 1 ch, 1dc into next ch, turn.
Rep row 2.

Bar stitch

Multiple of 3 sts + 3.
Special abbreviation:
1dc/rf = work 1dc around stem of next st 2 rows below, inserting hook around stem from right to left to draw up loops.
Row 1 (RS): Work 1sc into 2nd ch from hook, 1sc into each ch to end, turn.
Row 2: Ch1, work 1sc into each sc to end, turn.
Row 3: Ch1, work 1sc into each of first 2 sc, *1dc/rf around next sc 2 rows below, 1sc into each of next 2 sc; rep from * to end, turn.
Row 4: Ch1, work 1sc into each st to end, turn.
Row 5: Ch1, work 1sc into each of first 2 sc, *1dc/rf around stem of next dc/rf 2 rows below, 1sc into each of next 2 sc; rep from * to end, turn.
Rep rows 4–5.

Picot V stitch

Multiple of 3 sts + 1.
(add 2 for base chain)
Row 1 (RS): Skip 3 ch (count as 1dc), 1dc into next ch, skip 1 ch, 1dc into next ch, work a picot of [ch3, insert hook down through top of dc just made and work a slip st], 1dc into same ch as last dc, *skip 2 ch, [1dc, picot, 1dc] into next ch; rep from * to last 3 ch, skip 2 ch, 1dc into last ch, turn.
Row 2: Ch3 (count as 1dc), 1dc into first st, *skip 1 dc and picot, [1dc, picot, 1dc] into next dc; rep from * to last 2 sts, skip next dc, 1dc into top of tch, turn.
Rep row 2.

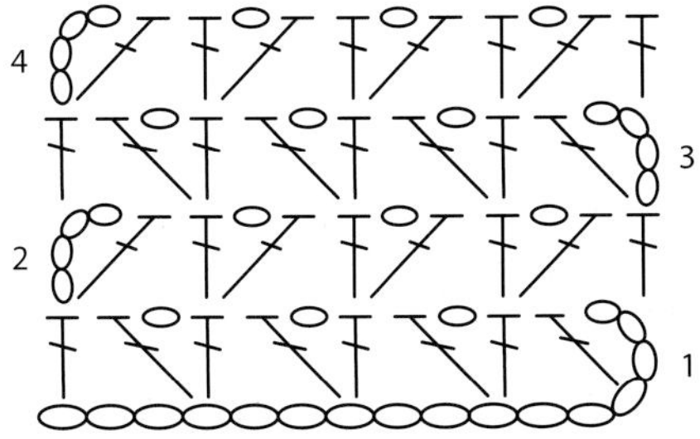

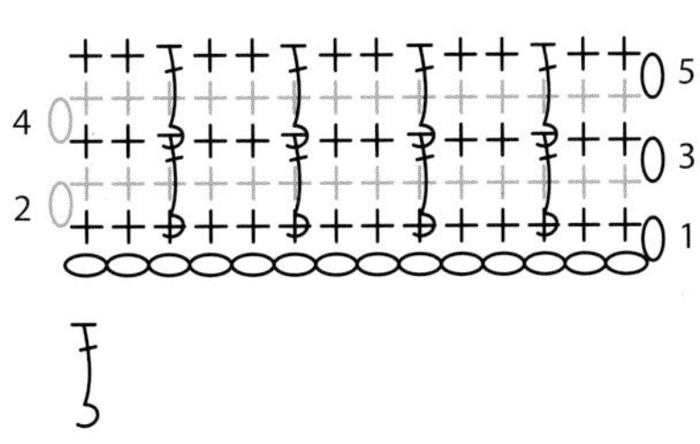

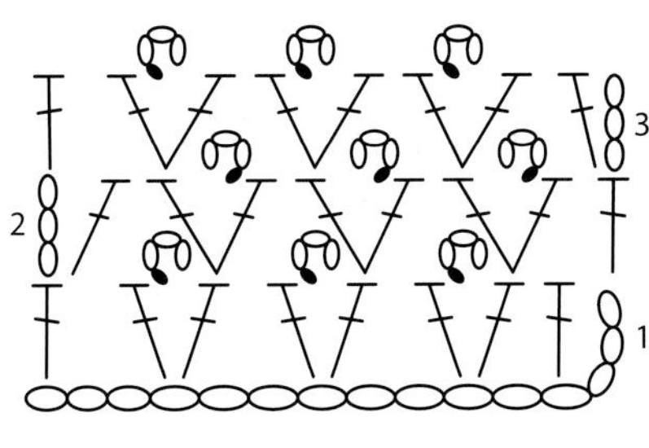

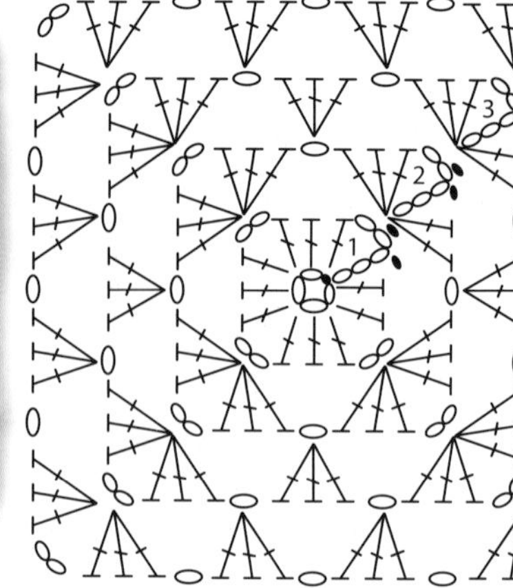

Traditional square I

Traditional square I

Base ring: Ch4, join with slip st.

Round 1: Ch5 (count as 1dc, ch2), [3dc into ring, ch2] 3 times, 2dc into ring, slip st to 3rd of ch-5.

Round 2: Slip st into next sp, ch5 (count as 1dc, ch2), 3dc into same sp, *ch1, skip 3 dc, [3dc, ch2, 3dc] into next sp; rep from * twice more, ch1, skip 3 sts, 2dc into same sp as ch-5 at beg of round, slip st to 3rd of ch-5.

Round 3: Slip st into next sp, ch5 (count as 1dc, 2ch), 3dc into same sp, *ch1, skip 3 dc, 3dc into next sp, ch1, skip 3 dc**, [3dc, ch2, 3dc] into next sp; rep from * twice more and from * to ** again, 2dc into same sp as ch-5, slip st to 3rd of ch-5.

Round 4: Slip st into next sp, ch5 (count as 1dc, ch2), 3dc into same sp, *[ch1, skip 3 dc, 3dc into next sp] twice, ch1, skip 3 dc**, [3dc, ch2, 3dc] into next sp; rep from * twice more and from * to ** again, 2dc into same sp as ch-5, slip st to 3rd of ch-5.

Fasten off.

Traditional square II

Worked as Traditional square I (see left). Work 1 round each in colors A, B, C and D.

Traditional square II

Tip

Since you can crochet with almost any yarn or continuous length fiber, you can experiment with unusual materials such as torn T-shirts, leather cords and even plastic bags torn into strips. Take some time to familiarize yourself with an unconventional fiber such as hemp or raffia. These yarns have no elasticity so it may be quite tricky to achieve a correct gauge.

Double crochet square I

Base ring: Ch4, join with slip st.

Round 1: Ch5 (count as 1dc, ch2), [3dc into ring, ch2] 3 times, 2dc into ring, slip st to 3rd of ch-5. (4 groups of 3dc)

Round 2: Slip st into next sp, ch7 (count as 1dc, ch4), *2dc into same sp, 1dc into each dc across side of square**, 2dc into next sp, ch4; rep from * twice more and from * to ** again, 1dc into same sp as ch-7, slip st to 3rd of ch-7. (4 groups of 7dc)

Round 3: As round 2. (4 groups of 11dc)

Round 4: As round 2. (4 groups of 15dc)

Fasten off.

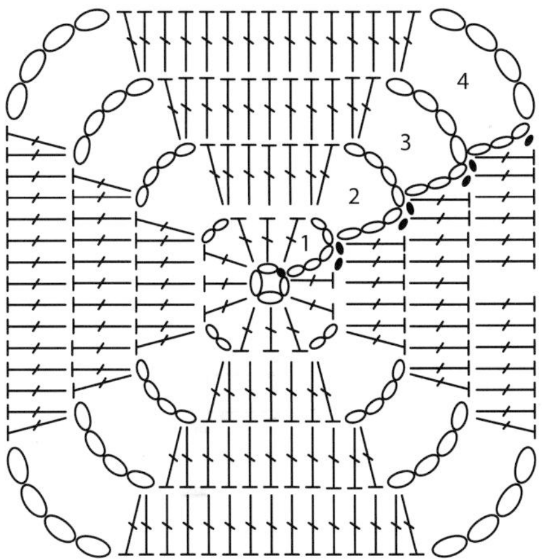

Double crochet square II

Worked as Double crochet square I (see left).

Work 1 round each in colors A, B, C and D.

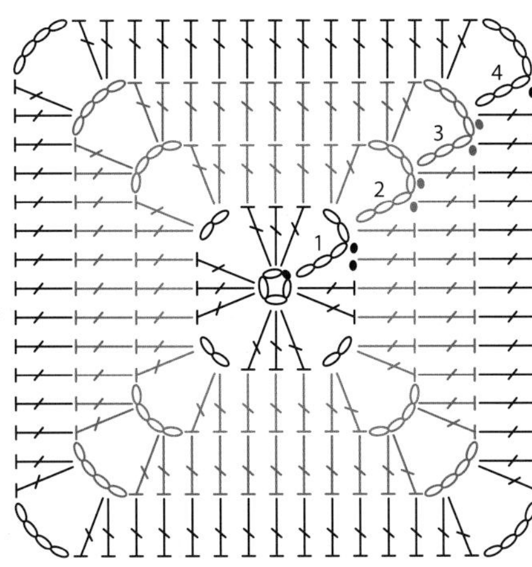

Painter's palette

Base ring: Ch4, join with slip st.

Round 1: Work 8sc into ring, slip st to 1st sc.

Round 2: Ch5, 1hdc and ch3, skip sc at base of ch-5, hdc into next sc, *ch3, hdc into next sc; rep from * 5 more times, ch3, slip st to 2nd ch of ch-5.

Round 3: Ch1, work 1sc into each hdc and 4sc into each sp around, slip st to 1st sc.

Fasten off.

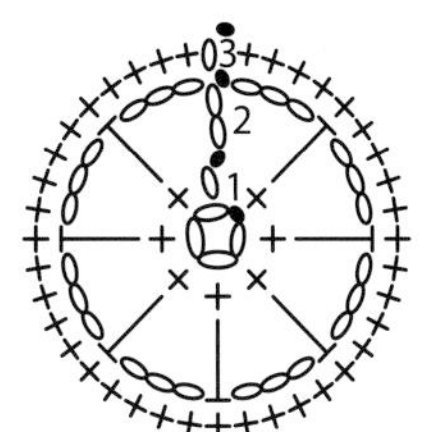

French square

Special abbreviation:

Puff st = [yo, insert hook into sp, yo and draw loop through] 4 times, yo and draw through all loops on hook.

Base ring: Ch6, join with slip st.

Round 1: Ch4 (count as 1dc, ch1), [1dc into ring, ch1] 11 times, slip st to 3rd of ch-4. (12 sps)

Round 2: Slip st into next sp, ch3, work puff st into same sp (counts as puff st), *ch2, work puff st into next sp, ch3, 1tr into next dc, ch3, work puff st into next sp, ch2**, puff st into next sp; rep from * twice more and from * to ** again, slip st to top of 1st puff st.

Round 3: Ch1, 1sc into same place, *ch2, skip next ch-2 sp, 4dc into next ch-3 sp, ch2, 1tr into next tr, ch3, insert hook down through top of last tr and work slip st, ch2, 4dc into next ch-3 sp, ch2, skip next ch-2 sp, 1sc into next puff st; rep from * 3 more times, omitting sc at end of last rep, slip st to 1st sc.
Fasten off.

Christmas rose square

Special abbreviation:

Bobble = work 4dc into same sp leaving last loop of each on hook, yo and draw through all loops on hook.

Base ring: Using A, ch6, join with slip st.

Round 1: Ch5 (count as 1dc , ch2), [1dc into ring, ch2] 7 times, slip st to 3rd of ch-5. (8 sps)

Round 2: Slip st into next sp, ch3, work dc3tog into same sp (count as bobble), [ch5, work bobble into next sp] 7 times, ch5, slip st to top of 1st bobble. Fasten off.

Round 3: Using B join into same place, ch1, 1sc into same place, *ch2, working over the ch-5 sp so as to enclose it work 1dc into next dc of 1st round, ch2, 1sc into top of next cluster; rep from * all around omitting sc at end, slip st to 1st sc.

Round 4: Slip st into next sp, ch1, 1sc into same sp, *ch3, 1sc into next sp; rep from * all around omitting sc at end, slip st to 1st sc.

Round 5: Slip st into next sp, ch3 (count as 1dc), [1dc, ch2, 2dc] into same sp, *ch2, 1sc into next sp, [ch3, 1sc into next sp] twice, ch2**, [2dc, ch2, 2dc] into next sp ; rep from * twice more and from * to ** again, slip st to top of ch-3. Fasten off.

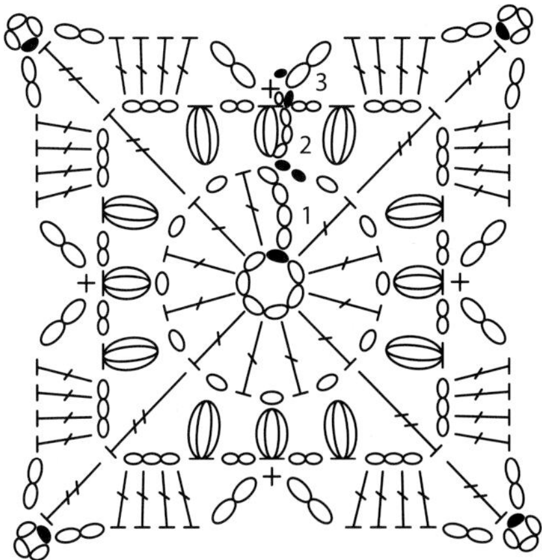

French square

Christmas rose square

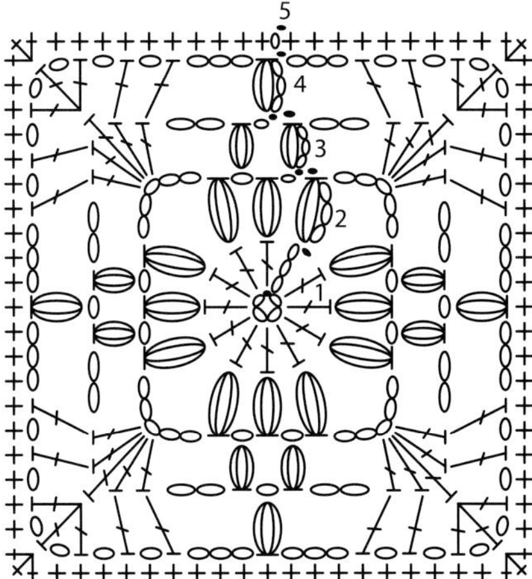

Italian square

Italian square

Special abbreviation:

Puff st = [yo, insert hook into sp, yo and draw loop through] 4 times, yo and draw through all loops on hook.

Base ring: Ch4, join with slip st.

Round 1: Ch3 (count as 1dc), 11dc into ring, slip st to top of ch-3. (12 sts)

Round 2: Ch3, work hdc3tog into same place as ch-3 (counts as puff st), *[ch1, work puff st into next st] twice, ch5**, puff st into next st; rep from * twice more and from * to ** again, slip st to top of 1st puff st.

Round 3: Slip st into next sp, ch3, work hdc3tog into same sp (counts as puff st), *ch1, puff st into next sp, ch2, 5dc into next ch-5 sp, ch2**, hdc4tog into next sp; rep from * twice more and from * to ** again, slip st to top of 1st puff st.

Round 4: Slip st into next sp, ch3, work hdc3tog into same sp (counts as puff st), *ch3, skip ch-2, [1dc into next dc, ch1] twice, work [1dc, ch1, 1dc, ch1, 1dc] into next dc, [ch1, 1dc into next dc] twice, ch3, skip ch-2**, work puff st into next sp; rep from * twice more and from * to ** again, slip st to top of 1st puff st.

Round 5: Ch1, 1sc into each ch and each st all around, but working 3sc into 2nd/center dc of each corner group at each corner, ending slip st to 1st sc.

Fasten off.

Baltic square

Special abbreviation:

Popcorn = work 5dc into same sp. Remove hook from working loop and insert it into the top of the 1st dc made from front to back, pick up working loop and draw through to close popcorn.

Base ring: Ch8, join with slip st.

Round 1: Ch3, 4dc popcorn into ring (counts as 5dc popcorn), [ch5, 5dc popcorn into ring] 3 times, ch5, slip st to top of 1st popcorn.

Round 2: Ch3 (count as 1dc), *work [2dc, ch2, 5dc popcorn, ch2, 2dc] into next ch-5 sp**, 1dc into next popcorn; rep from * twice more and from * to ** again, slip st to top of ch-3.

Round 3: Ch3 (count as 1dc), 1dc into each of next 2 sts, *2dc into next sp, ch2, 5dc popcorn into next popcorn, ch2, 2dc into next sp**, 1dc into each of next 5 dc; rep from * twice more and from * to ** again, 1dc into each of last 2 dc, slip st to top of ch-3.

Round 4: Ch3 (count as 1dc), 1dc into each of next 4 dc, *2dc into next sp, ch2, 5dc popcorn into next popcorn, ch2, 2dc into next sp**, 1dc into each of next 9 dc; rep from * twice more and from * to ** again, 1dc into each of last 4 dc, slip st to top of ch-3. Fasten off.

Cranesbill lace square

Special abbreviation:

Bobble = work 4dc into same sp leaving last loop of each on hook, yo and draw through all loops on hook.

Base ring: Ch6, join with slip st.

Round 1: Ch3, dc2tog into ring (counts as bobble), [ch3, bobble into ring] 7 times, ch3, slip st to top of 1st bobble.

Round 2: Slip st to center of next ch-3 sp, ch1, 1sc into same sp, [ch5, 1sc into next sp] 7 times, ch2, 1dc into 1st sc.

Round 3: *Ch5, [bobble, ch3, bobble] into next sp**, ch5, 1sc into next sp; rep from * twice and from * to ** again, ch2, 1dc into dc that closed round 2.

Round 4: *Ch5, 1sc into next sp, ch5, [1sc, ch5, 1sc] into corner ch-3 sp, ch5, 1sc into next ch-5 sp; rep from * 3 more times, ending last rep into dc that closed 3rd round, slip st to 1st ch. Fasten off.

Rose square

Special abbreviation:

Picot = ch3, slip st down through top of last sc made.

Base ring: Using A, ch12, join with slip st.

Round 1: Ch1, 18sc into ring, slip st to 1st sc. (18 sts)

Round 2: Ch1, beginning into same st as ch-1 [1sc, ch3, skip 2 sts] 6 times, slip st to 1st sc.

Round 3: Ch1, work a petal of [1sc, ch3, 5dc, ch3, 1sc] into each of next 6 ch-3 sps, slip st to 1st sc.

Round 4: Ch1, [1sc between 2 sc, ch5 behind petal of 3rd round] 6 times, slip st to 1st sc.

Round 5: Ch1, work a petal of [1sc, ch3, 7dc, ch3, 1sc] into each of next 6 ch-5 sps, slip st to 1st sc. Fasten off.

Round 6: Using B, join between 2 sc, ch1, [1sc between 2 sc, ch6 behind petal of Round 5] 6 times, slip st to 1st sc.

Round 7: Slip st into next sp, ch3 (count as 1dc), *[4dc, ch2, 1dc] all into same sp, 6dc into next sp, [2dc, ch2, 4dc] all into next sp**, 1dc into next sp; rep from * to **, slip st to top of ch-3.

Round 8: Ch3 (count as 1dc), 1dc into each dc all around with [3dc, ch2, 3dc] into each ch-2 corner sp, ending slip st to top of ch-3. Fasten off.

Round 9: Using C, join into same place, ch1, 1sc into same st as ch-1, *[1sc into next st, picot] twice, 1sc into each of next 3 sts, work [picot, 1sc into next st] twice, [1sc, ch7, 1sc] into corner ch-2 sp, [1sc into next st, picot] twice, 1sc into each of next 3 sts, [picot, 1sc into next st] twice, 1sc into next st; rep from * 3 more times omitting sc at end of last rep, slip st to 1st sc.

Round 10: Slip st across to top of next ch-3 picot, ch1, 1sc into same picot, *ch5, skip next picot, 1sc into next picot, ch5, (sc, ch5, sc) in next ch-7 sp, [ch5, skip next picot, 1sc into next picot] twice, ch5, 1sc into next picot; rep from * 3 more times omitting sc at end of last rep, slip st to 1st sc.

Fasten off.

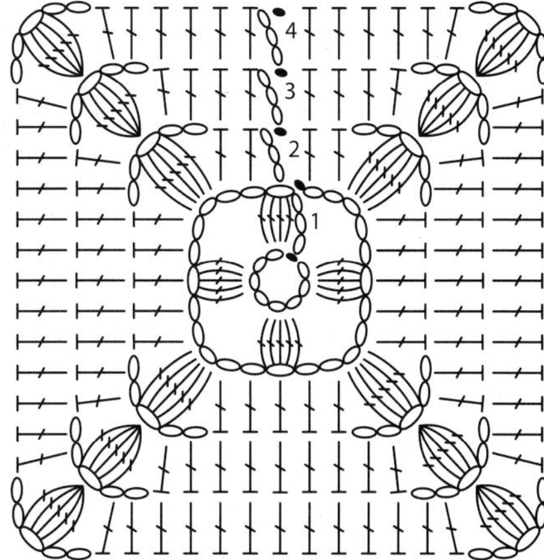

Baltic square

Cranesbill lace square

Rose square

Saturn motif

Special abbreviation:

Bobble = work 3dc into same sp leaving last loop of each on hook, yo and draw through all loops on hook.

Base ring: Using A, ch8, join with slip st.

Round 1: Ch1, 12sc into ring, slip st to 1st sc. (12 sts)

Round 2: Ch3, 1dc into same place as ch-3 (counts as dc2tog), [ch3, dc2tog into next st] 11 times, ch3, slip st to 1st bobble.

Round 3: Slip st into each of next 2 ch, ch1, 1sc into same place as ch-1, [ch4, 1sc into next ch-3 sp] 11 times, ch4, slip st to 1st sc.

Round 4: Ch1, *[2sc, ch3, 2sc] all into next ch-4 sp; rep from * 11 more times, slip st to 1st sc. Fasten off.

Round 5: Join B into next ch-3 sp, ch3, dc2tog into same sp (counts as 1st bobble), ch4, bobble all into same sp, *[bobble, ch4, bobble] all into next ch-3 sp; rep from * 10 more times, slip st to 1st bobble.

Round 6: Ch1, 1sc into same place as ch-1, *[2sc, ch3, 2sc] all into next ch-4 sp, miss next bobble**, 1sc into next bobble; rep from * 10 more times and from * to ** again, slip st to 1st sc. Fasten off.

Thai orchid

Special abbreviation:

3 picot cluster = work ch4, slip st into 1st ch, [ch3, slip st into same ch as 1st slip st] twice.

Base ring: Ch6, slip st to 1st ch.

Round 1: With yarn A ch1, work 12sc into ring, slip st into 1st sc.

Round 2: With yarn A ch3 (count as 1dc), 1dc into same st as last slip st, work 2dc into each of next 11 sc, slip st into 3rd of ch-3 at beg of round.

Round 3: With yarn A ch1, 1sc into same st as last slip st, 1sc into each of next 23 dc, slip st into 1st sc.

Round 4: With yarn B ch1, 1sc into same sc as last slip st, ch5, skip 2 sc, [1sc into next sc, ch5, skip 2 sc] 7 times, slip st into 1st sc.

Round 5: With yarn B ch1, 1sc into same st as last slip st, *into next ch-5 sp work [1hdc, 3dc, 3 picot cluster, 3dc, 1hdc], 1sc into next sc; rep from * 7 more times omitting 1sc at end of last rep, slip st into 1st sc.

Round 6: With yarn C ch1, 1sc into same st as last slip st, *ch7, 1sc into center picot of 3 picot cluster, ch7, 1sc into next sc; rep from * 7 more times omitting 1sc at end of last rep, slip st into 1st sc.

Round 7: With yarn C slip st into 1st ch-7 sp, ch1, [work 8sc into next ch-7 sp, 3 picot cluster, 8sc into same ch-7 sp] 8 times, slip st into 1st sc.

Fasten off.

Saturn motif

Thai orchid

Dandelion

Petals: Ch12, 1sc in 2nd ch from hook, 1hdc in each of next 3 ch, 1dc in each of next 3 ch, 1tr in each of next 3 ch, 10tr in last ch – work along opposite side of ch, 1tr in each of next 3 ch, 1dc in each of next 3 ch, 1hdc in each of next 3 ch, 1sc in next ch. Fasten off. Make 5 more petals.

After 6th petal, do not fasten off but work 2sc across base of petal, *ch1, 2sc across base of next petal; rep from * 4 more times, ch1, join with slip st to 1st sc of 1st petal. Fasten off.

Center motif: Ch4, join with slip st.

Round 1: Ch3 (count as 1dc), 17dc into ring, slip st to top of ch-3. Fasten off.

Sew together on WS.

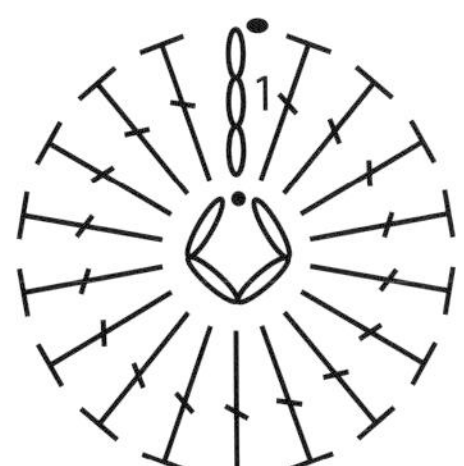

Dandelion centre

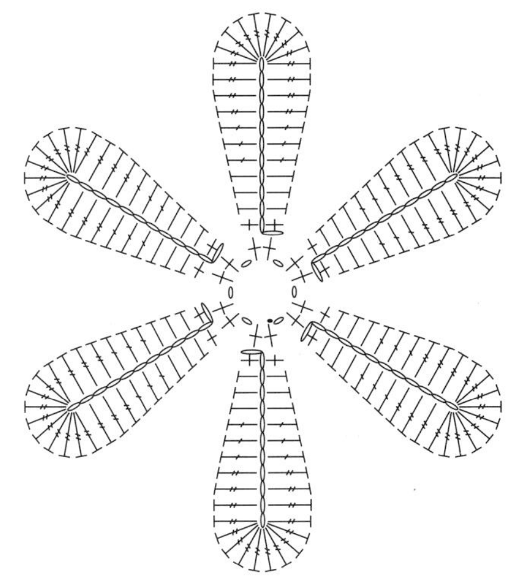

Dandelion petals

Floribunda

Base ring: Using A, ch6, join with slip st.
Round 1: Ch1, 16sc into ring, sl ipst to 1st sc. (16 sts)
Round 2: Ch6 (count as 1dc, ch-3 sp), skip 1st 2 sts, [1dc into next st, ch3, skip 1 st] 7 times, slip st to 3rd of ch-6.
Round 3: Ch1, work a petal of [1sc, 1hdc, 5dc, 1hdc, 1sc] into each of next 8 ch-3 sps, slip st to 1st sc. Fasten off.
Round 4: Using B join between 2 sc, ch1, [1sc between 2 sc, ch6 behind petal of 3rd round] 8 times, slip st to 1st sc.
Round 5: Ch1, work a petal of [1sc, 1hdc, 6dc, 1hdc, 1sc] into each of next 8 sps, slip st to 1st sc. Fasten off.
Round 6: Using C join into 2nd dc of petal of round 5, ch1, 1sc into same place as ch-1, ch6, skip 2 dc, 1sc into next dc, [ch6, 1sc into 2nd dc of next petal, ch6, skip 2 dc, 1sc into next dc] 7 times, ch3, 1dc into 1st sc.
Round 7: Ch3 (count as 1dc), 3dc into sp formed by dc that closed round 6, *ch4, 1sc into next sp, [ch6, 1sc into next sp] twice, ch4**, [4dc, ch4, 4dc] into next sp; rep from * twice more and from * to ** again, ending [4dc, ch4] into last ch sp, slip st to top of ch-3.
Fasten off.

Spring zinnia

Paisley: Ch70, 2dc in 4th ch from hook, *skip 2 ch, slip st in next ch, ch3, 2dc in same sp (shell); rep from * 15 times, skip next 2 ch, hook in next ch and in base of 1st shell, yo and draw through all loops, ch3, 2dc in same sp, skip 2 ch, slip st in next ch, **ch3, 2dc in same sp, skip 2 ch, slip st in next ch; rep from ** 3 times. Fasten off.
Flower: Ch8, join with slip st.
Round 1: Ch3 (counts as dc), 1dc in ring, *ch4, slip st in 1st ch for picot, 2dc in ring; rep from * 7 times, ch4 picot, join with slip st to top of ch-3. Attach another strand of yarn and ch5, for stem *with single strand ch5 and join with slip st in base of 4th shell from bottom of paisley, ch2, 1dc in 2nd ch, 1tr in each of next 2 ch, 1dc in next ch, slip st in stem; rep from * with 2nd strand attaching to base of shell opposite the 4th shell. End with slip st in stem. Fasten off. Sew 7 picots of flower to paisley on WS leaving bottom 2
picots free.

Floribunda

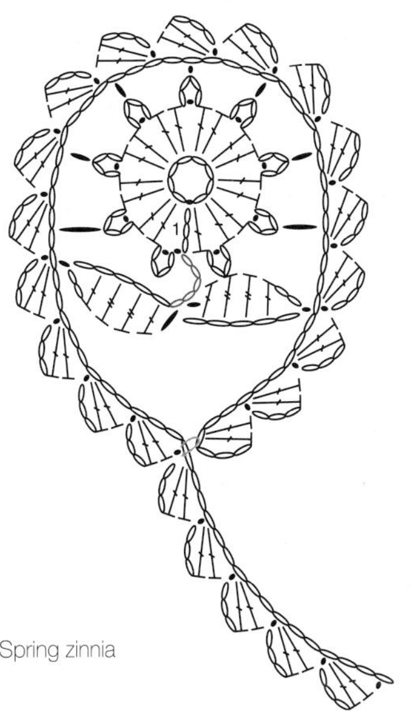

Spring zinnia

Sow thistle square

Special abbreviation:

Cluster = yo, insert hook in st and draw up a loop, yo and draw through 2 loops. (Yo, insert hook in next st and draw up a loop. Yo, draw through 2 loops) twice, yo and draw through all loops on hook.

Base ring: Using A, ch4, join with slip st.

Round 1: Ch4 (count as 1dc, ch1), [1dc, ch1] 11 times into ring, slip st to 3rd of ch-4. Fasten off.

Round 2: Using B join into same sp, ch3, dc2tog into same sp (counts as cluster), [ch3, cluster into next sp] 11 times, ch3, slip st to top of 1st cluster. Fasten off.

Round 3: Using A join into ch-3 sp, ch1, 1sc into same sp, [ch5, 1sc into next sp] 11 times, ch2, 1dc into 1st sc. Fasten off.

Round 4: Using B join into sp formed by dc, 1h1, 1sc into same place, *ch5, 1sc into next sp, ch1, [5dc, ch3, 5dc] into next sp, ch1, 1sc into next sp; rep from * 3 more times, omitting sc at end of last rep, slip st to 1st sc.

Fasten off.

Sow thistle square

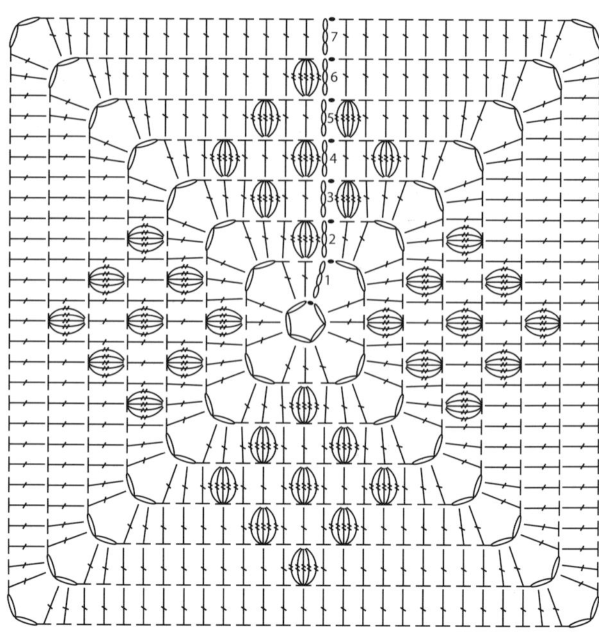

Diamond cluster motif

Special abbreviation:

5tr bobble = leaving last loop of each st on hook, work 5tr into next dc, yo and draw through all loops on hook.

Base ring: Ch6, join with slip st.

Round 1: Ch3 (count as 1dc), 2dc into ring, [ch2, 3dc into ring] 3 times, ch2, slip st to top of ch-3. (4 blocks of 3dc)

Round 2: Ch3, *5tr bobble into next dc, 1dc into next dc, [2dc, ch2, 2dc] into next ch-2 sp, 1dc into next dc; rep from * to end omitting 1dc at end of last rep, slip st to top of ch-3.

Round 3: Ch3, *1dc into top of bobble, 1dc into next dc, 5tr bobble into next dc, 1dc into next dc, [2dc, ch2, 2dc] into next ch-2 sp, 1dc into next dc, 5tr bobble into next dc, 1dc into next dc; rep from * to end omitting 1dc at end of last rep, slip st to top of ch-3.

Round 4: Ch3, *5tr bobble into next dc, 1dc into next dc, 1dc into top of next bobble, 1dc into next dc, 5tr bobble into next dc, 1dc into next dc, [2dc, ch2, 2dc] into ch-2 sp, 1dc into next dc, 5tr bobble into next dc, 1dc into next dc, 1dc into top of next bobble, 1dc into next dc; rep from * to end omitting 1dc at end of last rep, slip st to top of ch-3.

Round 5: Ch3, *1dc into top of next bobble, 1dc into next dc, 5tr bobble into next dc, 1dc into each of next 5 sts, [2dc, ch2, 2dc] into next ch-2 sp, 1dc into each of next 5 sts, 5tr bobble into next dc, 1dc into next dc; rep from * to end omitting 1dc at end of last rep, slip st to top of ch-3.

Round 6: Ch3, *5tr bobble into next dc, 1dc into each of next 9 sts, [2dc, ch2, 2dc] into next ch-2 sp, 1dc into each of next 9 sts; rep from * to end omitting 1dc at end of last rep, slip st to top of ch-3.

Round 7: Ch3, *1dc into each of next 12 sts, [2dc, ch2, 2dc] into next ch-2 sp, 1dc into each of next 11 sts; rep from * to end omitting 1dc at end of last rep, slip st to top of ch-3. Fasten off.

Trefoil I

Leaf (make 3 alike)
Base chain: Ch17.
Row 1 (RS): Skip 2 ch (count as 1sc), 1sc into each ch to last ch, work 3sc into last ch for point, then work back along underside of base chain with 1sc into each ch to end, turn.
Row 2: Ch1 (counts as 1sc), skip 1 st, 1sc into each st up to st at center of point, work 3sc into center st, 1sc into each st to last 3 sts and tch, turn.
Rows 3–7: As row 2. Fasten off.

Stem
Ch22 (or as required), slip st to point of center Leaf (2nd) as diagram, work back along base chain in sc and at same time join in side Leaves (1st and 3rd) at, say, 6th and 7th sts as follows: *insert hook through point of 1st Leaf and base chain, make 1sc, slip st to point of 3rd Leaf to match; rep from * once more. Continue to end of base chain in sc. Fasten off.

Trefoil II

Round 1: Ch16, slip st into 1st ch (1st loop formed), [ch15, slip st into same ch as last slip st] twice.
Round 2: Ch1, work [28sc into next loop, 1slip st into same ch as slip sts of 1st round] 3 times.
Round 3: Slip st into each of 1st 3 sc, ch1, 1sc into same st as last slip st, 1sc into each of next 23 sc, [skip 4 sc, 1sc into each of next 24 sc] twice, ch17, work 1sc into 2nd ch from hook, 1sc into each of next 15 ch, slip st into 1st sc.
Fasten off.

Daisy time

Special abbreviation:
Dc2tog = work 1dc into each of next 2sc until 1 loop of each remains on hook, yo and draw through all 3 loops on hook.
Base ring: Ch6, join with slip st.
Round 1: Ch1, work 15sc into ring, slip st into 1st sc.
Round 2: [Ch3, dc2tog over next 2 sc, ch3, slip st into next sc] 5 times placing last slip st into 1st sc of previous round.
Fasten off.

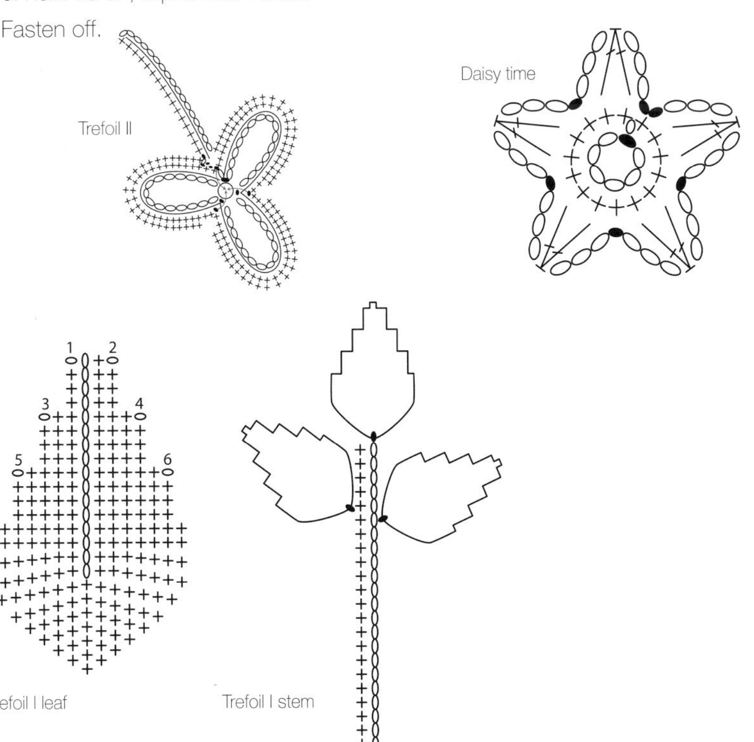

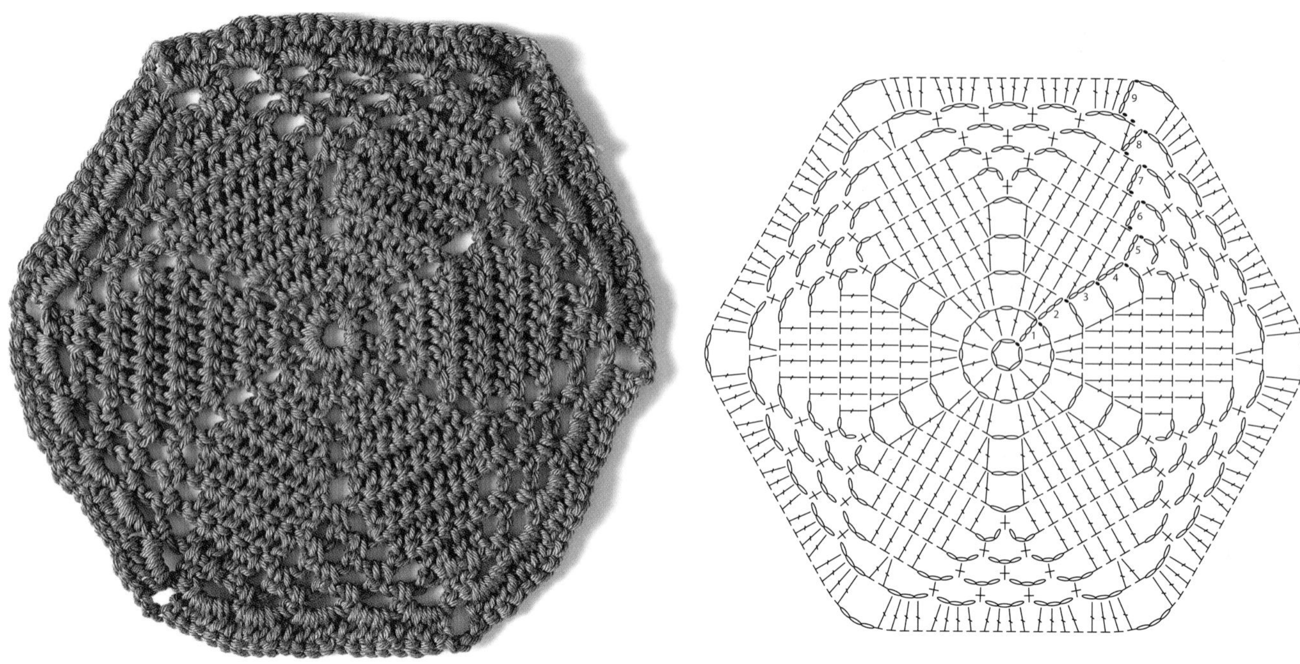

Flower hexagon

Base ring: Ch6, join with slip st.
Round 1: Ch4, [1dc into ring, ch1] 11 times, slip st to 3rd of ch-4.
Round 2: Ch3, 2dc into next sp, 1dc into next dc, ch2, *1dc into next dc, 2dc into next sp, 1dc into next dc, ch2; rep from * 4 more times, slip st to top of ch-3.
Round 3: Ch3, 1dc into same place as last slip st, 1dc into each of next 2 dc, 2dc into next dc, ch2, *2dc into next dc, 1dc into each of next 2 dc, 2dc into next dc, ch2; rep from * 4 more times, slip st to top of ch-3.
Round 4: Ch3, 1dc into same place as last slip st, 1dc into each of next 4 dc, 2dc into next dc, ch2, *2dc into next dc, 1tr into each of next 4 dc, 2dc into next dc, ch2; rep from * 4 more times, slip st to top of ch-3.
Round 5: Ch3, 1dc into each of next 7 dc, *ch3, 1sc into next ch-2 sp, ch3, 1dc into each of next 8 dc; rep from * 4 more times, ch3, 1sc into next ch-2 sp, ch3, slip st to top of ch-3.
Round 6: Slip st into next dc, ch3, 1dc into each of next 5 dc, *ch3, [1sc into next ch-3 sp, ch3] twice, skip next dc, 1dc into each of next 6 dc; rep from * 4 more times, ch3, [1sc into next ch-3 sp, ch3] twice, slip st to top of ch-3.
Round 7: Slip st into next dc, ch3, 1dc into each of next 3 dc, *ch3, [1sc into next ch-3 sp, ch3] 3 times, skip next dc, 1dc into each of next 4 dc; rep from * 4 more times, ch3, [1sc into next ch-3 sp, ch3] 3 times, slip st to top of ch-3.
Round 8: Slip st between 2nd and 3rd dc of 1st group, ch3, 1dc into same place, *ch3, [1sc into next ch-3 sp, ch3] 4 times, 2dc between 2nd and 3rd dc of next group; rep from * 4 more times, ch3, [1sc into next ch-3 sp, ch3] 4 times, slip st to top of ch-3.
Round 9: Slip st into next ch-3 sp, ch3, 3dc into same sp, [4dc into next ch-3 sp] 4 times, *ch3, skip 2 dc, [4dc into next ch-3 sp] 5 times; rep from * 4 more times, ch3, slip st to top of ch-3. Fasten off.

Tip

When approaching a new design, consider the previous successes you have had, the yarn you are working with, and your goal for the project. Careful planning will be rewarded. Think about what purpose the final project will have and choose the most appropriate yarn for the best effect. Take into consideration whether the item will be mostly decorative, or whether you need to choose a practical yarn, for example, for an item that will need to be laundered.

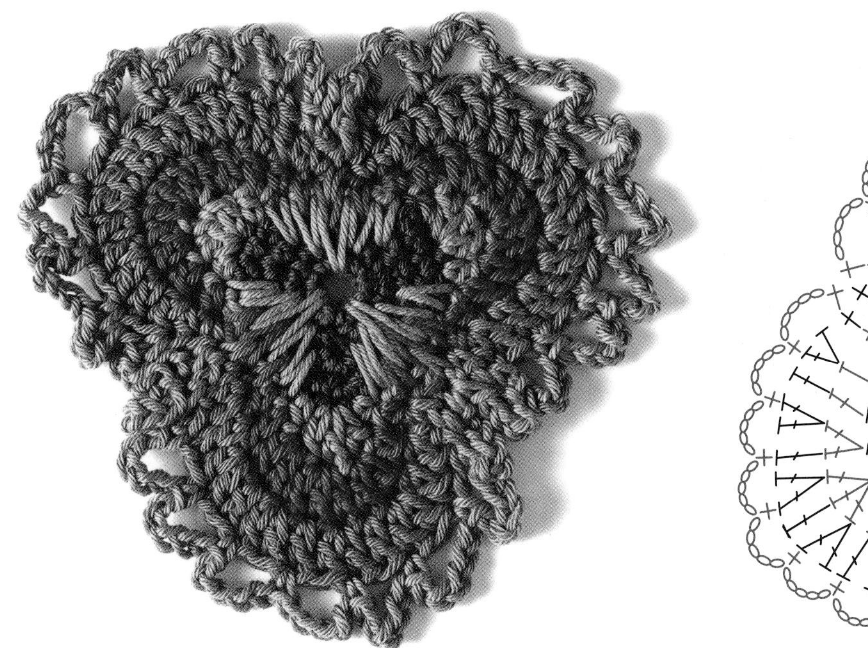

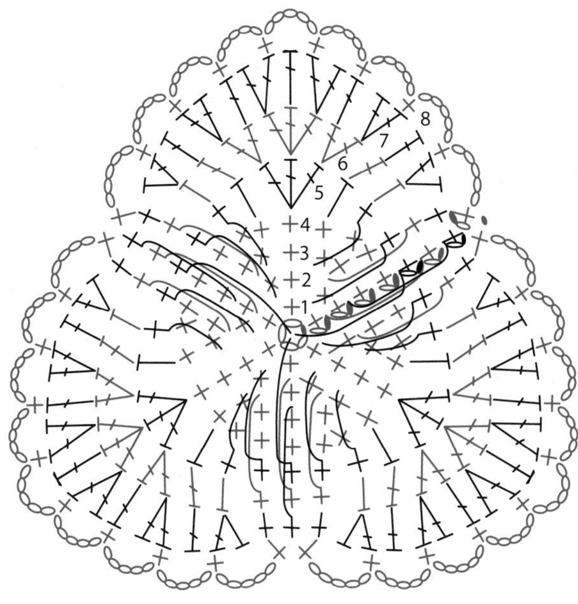

Viola

Special abbreviation:

Ssc (Spike single crochet) = insert hook lower than usual (as indicated), yo, draw loop through and up to height of current row, yo, draw through both loops on hook.

Base ring: Using A, ch4, join with slip st.

Round 1: Ch1, 6sc into ring, slip st to 1st sc. (6 sts)

Round 2: Ch1, 2sc into each sc, slip st to 1st sc. (12 sts)

Round 3: Ch1, 1sc into 1st st, [2sc into next st, 1sc into next st] 5 times, 2sc into last st, slip st to 1st sc. (18 sts)

Round 4: Ch1, 1sc into 1st st, [2sc into next st, 1sc into each of next 2 sts] 5 times, 2sc into next st, 1sc into last st, slip st to 1st sc. (24 sts) Fasten off.

Round 5: Using B join into same place, ch1, then starting in same st as ch-1 work *1Ssc inserting hook into base ring, [1Ssc over next st inserting hook to left of last sc, but 1 round higher] twice, 1hdc into next st, 3dc into next st, 1hdc into next st, 1Ssc over next st inserting hook through top of 2nd round, 1Ssc over next st inserting hook through top of 1st round; rep from * twice more, slip st to 1st Ssc. Fasten off.

Round 6: Using C join into same place, ch1, then starting in same st as ch-1 work *1Ssc inserting hook between threads of previous Ssc and through top of 1st round, 1Ssc over next st inserting hook between vertical threads of previous Ssc and through top of 2nd round, 1hdc into next st, 1dc into next st, 2dc into next st, 3dc into next st, 2dc into next st, 1dc into next st, 1hdc into next st, 1Ssc over next st inserting hook between threads of 2nd of 5 previous Sscs and 1 round higher; rep from * twice more, slip st to 1st Ssc.

Fasten off.

Round 7: Using D join into same place, ch1, starting in same st as ch-1 *1Ssc inserting hook between threads of previous Sscs and through top of 2nd round, 1sc into next st, [1hdc, 1dc] into next st, [1dc into next st, 2dc into next st] 4 times, 1dc into next st, [1dc, 1hdc] into next st, 1sc into next st; rep from * twice more, slip st to 1st Ssc. Fasten off.

Round 8: Using B, join into next st, ch1, 1sc into same st as ch-1, *[ch5, skip next st, 1sc into next st] 9 times, skip next st**, 1sc into next st; rep from * and from * to ** again, slip st to 1st sc. Fasten off.

Daisy cluster square

Special abbreviation:
Bobble = yo, insert hook in st and draw up a loop, yo and draw through 2 loops. [Yo, insert hook in same st and draw up a loop. yo, draw through 2 loops] twice, yo and draw through all loops on hook.
Base ring: Wrap yarn around finger.
Round 1: Ch1, 8sc into ring, slip st to 1st sc. (8 sts)
Round 2: Ch3, dc2tog into 1st st (counts as cluster), [ch3, cluster into next st] 7 times, ch3, slip st to top of 1st cluster.
Round 3: Ch3, 1dc into 1st st (counts as dc2tog), *skip ch-3, [dc2tog, ch5, dc2tog] all into next cluster; rep from * 6 more times, dc2tog into 1st clutter from 2nd row, ch5, slip st to top of ch-3.
Round 4: Slip st into next cluster, ch7 (counts as 1dc, ch4), [1sc into next ch-5 sp, ch4, skip 1 cluster, 1dc into next cluster, ch4] 7 times, 1sc into next ch-5 sp, ch4, slip st to 3rd of ch-7.
Round 5: Ch1, 1sc into same place as ch-1, *ch4, skip ch-4, [1tr, ch4, 1tr] into next dc, ch4, skip ch-4, 1sc into next dc, ch4, skip ch-4, 1hdc into next sc, ch4, skip ch-4, 1sc into next dc; rep from * 3 more times, omitting sc at end of last rep, slip st to 1st sc.
Fasten off.

Garden balsam

Special abbreviation:
Cluster = [yo, insert hook in next st, yo and draw up loop, yo and draw through 2 loops on hook] as many times as indicated, yo and draw through all loops on hook.
Base ring: Ch10, join with slip st.
Round 1: Ch3 (count as 1dc), 4dc into ring, [ch9, 5dc into ring] 3 times, ch9, slip st to top of ch-3.
Round 2: Ch3, 1dc into each of next 2 dc, *ch2, 1dc into same dc as last dc, 1dc into each of next 2 dc, ch2, into next ch-9 sp work [3dc, ch3, 3dc] for corner, ch2**, 1dc into each of next 3 dc, rep from * 3 times more, ending last rep at **, slip st to top of ch-3.
Round 3: Ch3 (count as 1dc), cluster over next 5 dc, *ch5, skip 1 dc, 1dc into next dc, ch3, into next ch-3 sp work [2dc, ch2, 2dc], ch3, skip 1 dc, 1dc into next dc, ch5, skip 1 dc, cluster over next 6 dc; rep from * twice more, ch5, skip 1 dc, 1dc into next dc, ch3, into next ch-3 sp work [2dc, ch2, 2dc], ch3, skip 1 dc, 1dc into next dc, ch5, slip st to top of 1st cluster.
Round 4: 1sc in each ch and in back loop of each dc, working 2dc into ch-2 sp at each corner, slip st to 1st sc.
Fasten off.

Daisy cluster square

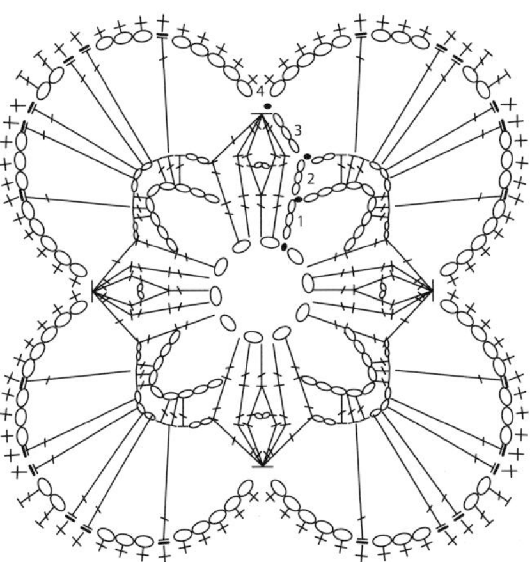
Garden balsam

Spandrel motif

Spandrel motif

Base ring: Using A, ch4, join with slip st.

Round 1: Ch1, 1sc into ring, [ch4, 1dtr into ring, ch4, 1sc into ring] 4 times omitting sc at end of last rep, slip st to 1st sc. Fasten off.

Round 2: Join B into same place, ch11 (count as 1tr, ch7), skip 4 ch, 1sc into next dtr, *ch7, skip 4 ch**, 1tr into next sc, ch7, skip 4 ch, 1sc into next dtr; rep from * twice more and from * to ** again, slip st to 4th ch of ch-11. Fasten off.

Round 3: Join C into same place, ch4 (count as 1tr), 2tr into same place as ch-4, *ch1, 1sc into next ch-7 sp, ch1, work [2dtr, ch2, 2dtr] into next sc, ch1, 1sc into next ch-7 sp, ch1**, 3tr into next tr; rep from * twice more and from * to ** again, slip st to top of ch-4. Fasten off.

Round 4: Rejoin B into same place, ch1, 1sc into same place as ch-1, 1sc into next and each ch and each st all around, except 3sc into each ch-2 sp at corners, ending slip st to 1st sc. Fasten off.

Round 5: Rejoin A into next sc, ch6 (count as 1tr, ch2), skip 1st 2 sc, *1tr into next sc, ch2, skip 1 sc, 1dc into next sc, ch2, skip 1 sc, 1hdc into next sc, ch2, skip 1 sc, 1sc into next sc, ch2, skip 1 sc, 1hdc into next sc, ch2, skip 1 sc, 1dc into next sc, ch2, skip 1 sc, 1tr into next sc, ch2, skip 1 sc**, 1tr into next sc, ch2, skip 1 sc; rep from * twice more and from * to ** again, slip st to 4th ch of ch-6.

Round 6: Ch1, into 1st st work a trefoil of [1sc, ch5, 1sc, ch7, 1sc, ch5, 1sc], *[2sc into next ch-2 sp, 1sc into next st] twice, work a picot of [ch3, insert hook down through top of sc just made and work slip st to close], [2sc into next ch-2 sp, 1sc into next st] 4 times, picot, 2sc into next ch-2 sp, 1sc into next st, 2sc into next ch-2 sp**, trefoil into next st; rep from * twice more and from * to ** again, slip st to 1st sc. Fasten off.

Clockwork

Base ring: Ch8, join with slip st.

First motif: Ch3 (count as 1dc), 1dc in ring, *ch3, slip st in top of last dc (picot), 2dc in ring; rep from * until 12th picot is completed, slip st in top of ch-3. Fasten off.

Second motif: Ch8, join with slip st, ch3, 1dc in ring, ch2, drop loop from hook, insert hook in any picot of 1st motif and in dropped loop, draw loop through, ch1, complete picot on 2nd motif, 2dc in ring of 2nd motif, join with picot to next free picot on 1st motif, continue as in 1st motif until 12th picot is completed (including the 2 joined picots), slip st in top of ch-3. Fasten off. Rep 2nd motif, joining 1st 2 picots to 7th and 8th picot of previous motif.

Row 2 – first motif: Follow directions for 2nd motif of row 1, but join the 1st 2 picots of this motif to the 4th and 5th picots of the 1st motif in row 1.

Row 2 – second motif: Work as before, joining 1st 2 picots to 10th and 11th picots of next motif in row 1 and the 4th and 5th picots to 4th and 5th picots of 1st motif of row 2.

Continue, 1 picot of each motif remains free between joinings.

Puff stitch square

Special abbreviation:

Puff st = hdc5tog.

Base ring: Ch8, join with slip st.

Round 1: Ch2, hdc4tog into ring (counts as 1 puff st), ch2, work [puff st, ch2] 7 times into ring, slip st to 1st puff st.

Round 2: Ch5 (count as 1dc, ch2), 1dc into same puff st, *ch2, [puff st into next sp, ch2] twice**, work a V st of [1dc, ch2, 1dc] into next puff st; rep from * twice more and from * to ** again, slip st to 3rd of ch-5.

Round 3: Slip st into next ch sp, ch5 (count as 1dc, ch2), 1dc into same sp, *ch2, [puff st into next sp, ch2] 3 times**, V st into next sp at corner; rep from * twice more and from * to ** again, slip st to 3rd of ch-5.

Round 4: As for round 3, but work 4 puff sts along each side of square.

Round 5: As for round 3, but work 5 puff sts along each side of square. Fasten off.

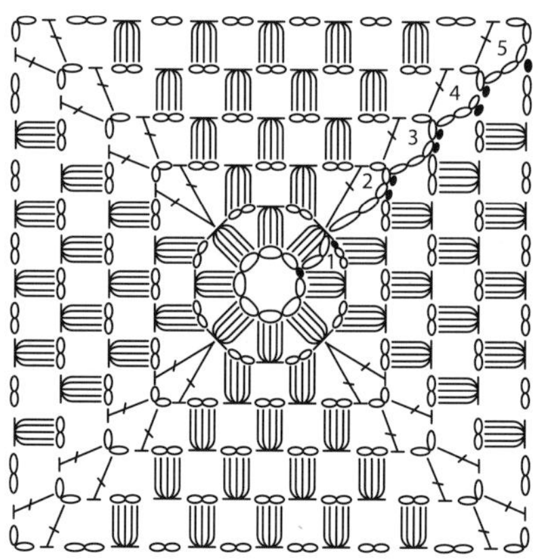

Halley's comet

Special abbreviation:

Ssc (Spike single crochet) = insert hook below st indicated 1 row down, i.e. into top of 1st round, yo, draw loop through and up to height of current round, yo, draw through both loops on hook.

Base ring: Using A, ch4, join with slip st.

Round 1: Ch5 (count as 1dc, ch2), [1dc into ring, ch2] 7 times, slip st to 3rd of ch-5. (8 sps)

Round 2: Ch3 (count as 1dc), 3dc into next sp, [1dc into next dc, 3dc into next sp] 7 times, slip st to top of ch-3. Fasten off. (32 sts)

Round 3: Join B into same place, ch1, 1Ssc over 1st st, work a picot of [ch3, insert hook down through top of sc just made and work slip st to close], *1sc into next st, 2sc into next st, 1sc into next st**, 1Ssc over next st, picot; rep from * 6 more times and from * to ** again, slip st to 1st Ssc. Fasten off.

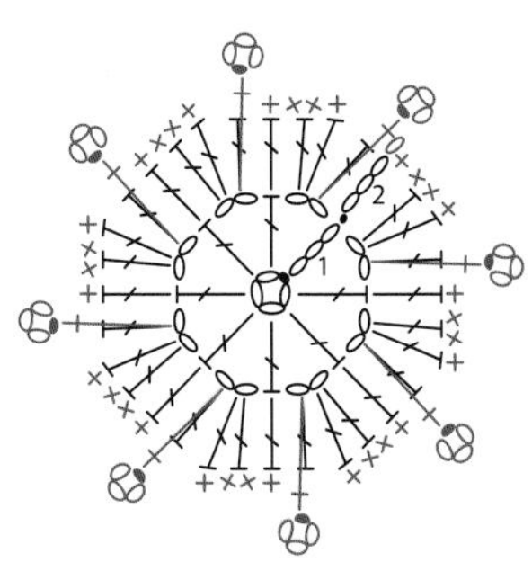

Daisy wheel square

Base ring: Ch8, join with slip st.

Round 1: Ch1, 12sc into ring, slip st to 1st sc. (12 sts)

Round 2: Ch6 (count as 1tr, ch2), skip 1st st, [1tr into next st, ch2] 11 times, slip st to 4th of ch-6.

Round 3: Ch5 (counts as 1dc, ch2), *[1sc into next sp, ch2] twice, [3dc, ch2, 3dc] into next sp, ch2; rep from *3 more times, omitting 1dc and ch2 at end of last rep, slip st to 3rd of ch-5.

Round 4: Ch1, *[1sc into next sp, ch2] 3 times, [3dc, ch2, 3dc] into corner sp, ch2; rep from *3 more times, slip st to 1st sc.

Round 5: Ch1, work 2sc into each sp and 1sc into each st all around, but working 3sc into each corner sp, slip st to 1st sc. Fasten off.

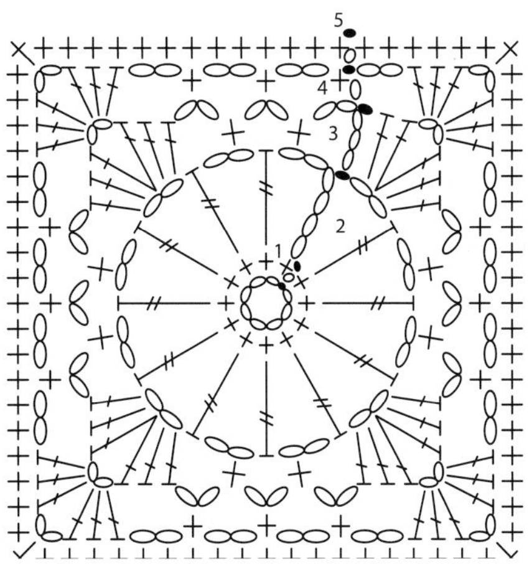

Cluster wheel

Base ring: Ch6, join with slip st.

Round 1: Ch4 (count as 1dc, ch1), (3dc into ring, ch1) 5 times, 2dc into ring, slip st to 3rd of ch-4.

Round 2: Slip st into next ch sp, ch3 (count as 1dc), [2dc, ch1, 3dc] into same sp, *ch1, [3dc, ch1, 3dc] into next ch-1 sp; rep from * 4 more times, ch1, slip st to top of ch-3.

Round 3: Slip st in next 2 sts, slip st into next ch sp, ch3 (count as 1dc), [2dc, ch1, 3dc] into same ch sp, *ch1, 3dc into next ch sp, ch1, [3dc, ch1, 3dc] into next ch sp, rep from * 4 more times, ch1, slip st into top of ch-3.

Fasten off.

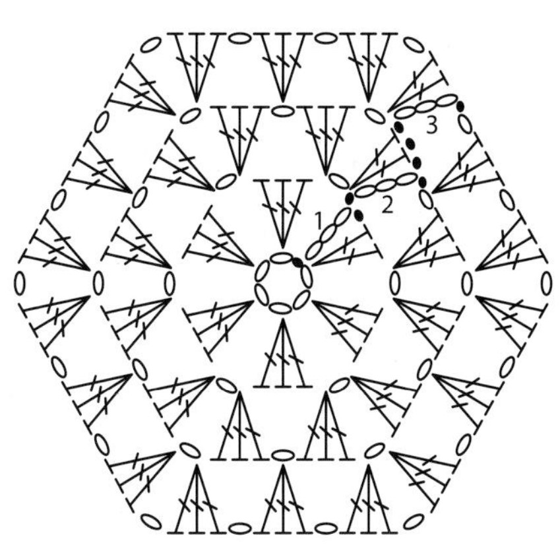

Four petal

Special abbreviation:

Bobble = 3tr into next sc until 1 loop of each remains on hook, yo and draw through all 4 loops on hook.

Base ring: Ch5, join with slip st.

Round 1: Ch1, 12sc into ring, slip st into 1st sc.

Round 2: *Ch4, 1 bobble into next sc, ch4, slip st into each of next 2 sc; rep from * 3 more times, omitting 1slip st at end of last rep, ch7, 1sc into 2nd ch from hook, 1sc into each of next 5 ch, slip st into 1st sc on 1st round. Fasten off.

Two-tone hexagon

Base ring: Using A, ch6, join with slip st.

Round 1: Ch3 (count as 1dc), 2dc into ring, *ch3, 3dc into ring; rep from * 4 more times, ch3, slip st to top of 1st ch-3. Fasten off.

Round 2: Join B to any ch-3 sp, ch5 (count as 1dtr), [2dtr, ch2, 3dtr] into same sp, *[3dtr, ch2, 3dtr] into next ch-3 sp; rep from * 4 more times, slip st to top of ch-5. Fasten off.

Round 3: Join A to same place as slip st, ch3 (count as 1dc), 1dc into each of next 2 dtr, *[2dc, ch2, 2dc] into next ch-2 sp, 1dc into each of next 6 dtr; rep from * 4 more times, [2dc, ch2, 2dc] into next ch-2 sp, 1dc into each of next 3 dtr, slip st to top of ch-3. Fasten off.

Round 4: Join B into any st, ch3 (count as 1dc), 1dc into previous st, *skip 1 st, 1dc into next st, 1dc into the skipped st; rep from * all around, slip st to top of ch-3. Fasten off.

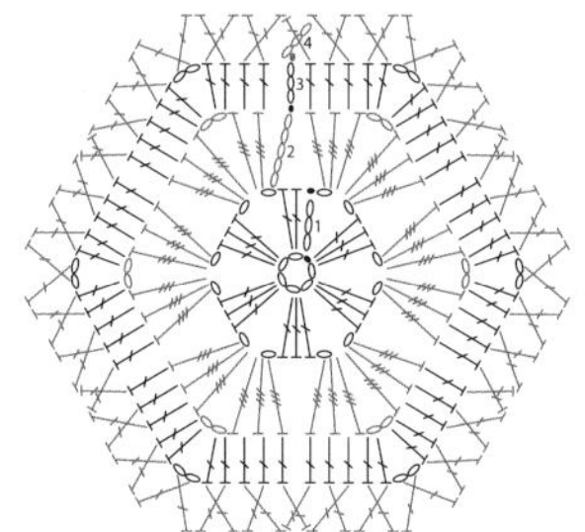

Begonia wheel

Base chain: Ch6, join with slip st.

Round 1: Ch3 (count as 1dc), 13dc into ring, slip st to top of ch-3.

Round 2: Ch3 (count as 1dc), 2dc into 1st st, *ch1, skip 1 dc, 3dc into next dc; rep from * 5 more times, ch1, skip 1 dc, slip st to top of ch-3.

Round 3: Slip st into next dc, ch3 (count as 1dc), 1dc into same dc, *ch1, 2dc into next ch-1 sp, ch1, skip 1 dc, 2dc into next dc; rep from * 5 more times, ch1, 2dc into next ch-1 sp, ch1, slip st to top of ch-3.

Round 4: [Ch4, 1sc into next ch-1 sp] 13 times, ch2, 1dc into base of 1st ch-4.

Round 5: [Ch4, 1sc into center of next ch-4 sp] 13 times, ch2, 1dc into dc at end of previous round.

Round 6: Ch3 (count as 1dc), 3dc into same sp, 4dc into each of next 13 sps, slip st to top of ch-3.

Round 7: Slip st to center of 1st dc group, ch1, 1sc into same place, [ch6, 1sc into center of next dc group] 13 times, ch6, slip st to 1st sc.

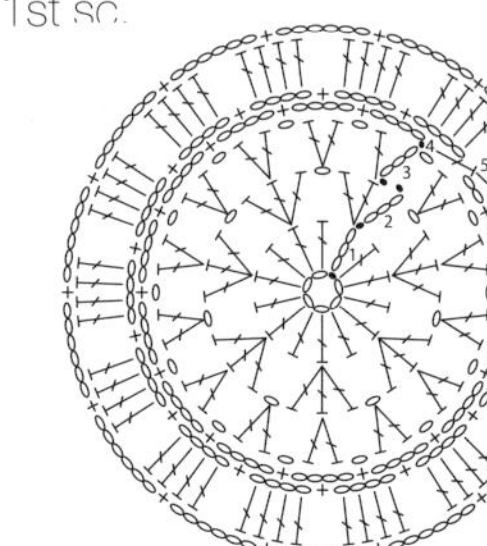

Primula circle

Base ring: Ch4, join with slip st.
Round 1: Ch1, 12sc into ring, slip st to 1st ch.
Round 2: Ch1, 2sc into same place, inserting hook into back loop of each st work 2sc into each st to end, slip st to 1st ch. (24sc)
Round 3: Ch1, 1sc in same st, ch2, *skip 1 sc, 1sc into back loop of next sc, ch2; rep from * to end, slip st to 1st of ch-3.
Round 4: [1sc, 1dc, 2tr, 1dc, 1sc] into each ch-2 sp, slip st to 1st sc.
Fasten off.

Eastern star

Base ring: Ch6, join with slip st.
Round 1: Ch1, [1sc into ring, ch3] 12 times, slip st to 1st sc.
Round 2: Slip st into each of next 2 ch, ch1, 1sc into same ch-3 sp, [ch3, 1sc into next ch-3 sp] 11 times, ch1, 1hdc into top of 1st sc.
Round 3: *Ch6, 1sc into next ch-3 sp**, ch3, 1sc into next ch-3 sp; rep from * 4 more times and from * to ** again, ch1, 1dc into hdc that closed previous round.
Round 4: *[5dc, ch2, 5dc] into next ch-6 sp, 1sc into next ch-3 sp; rep from * 5 more times ending last rep in dc that closed previous round, slip st to next st.
Fasten off.

Incan star

Note: Pattern is worked in a spiral, do not join at the end of rounds 1–6.
Base ring: Ch6, join with slip st.
Round 1: 8sc into ring.
Round 2: 3sc in each st. (24 sts)
Rounds 3 and 4: 1sc in each st.
Round 5: *1sc in next sc, 2sc in next sc; rep from * around. (36 sts)
Round 6: 1sc in each st.
Round 7: *Ch9, slip st in 2nd ch from hook, 1sc in next ch, 1dc in each of next 3 ch, 1tr in each of next 3 ch, skip next 3 sts of previous round, slip st in next st; rep from * around, join with slip st.
Fasten off.

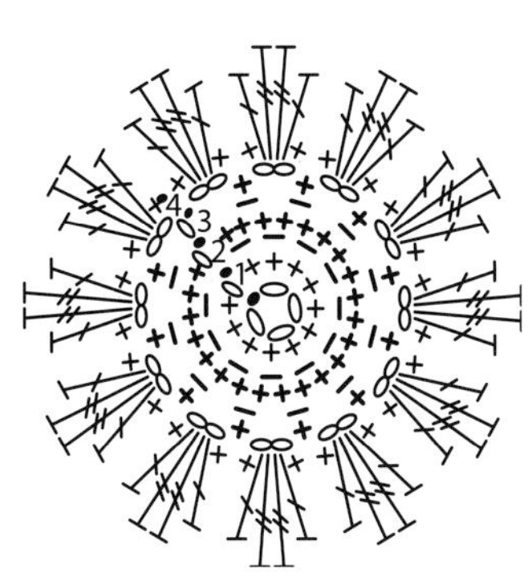

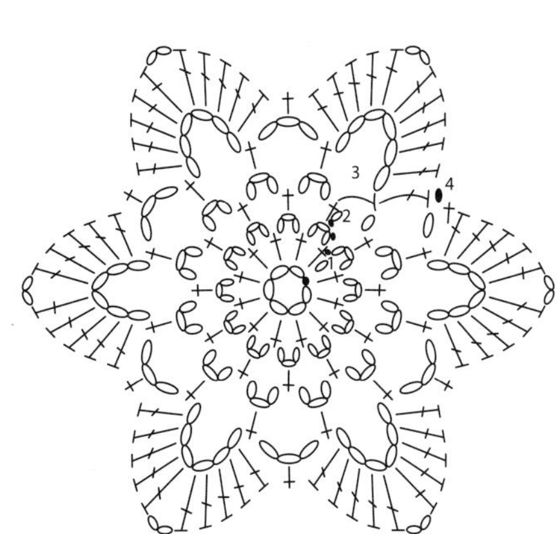

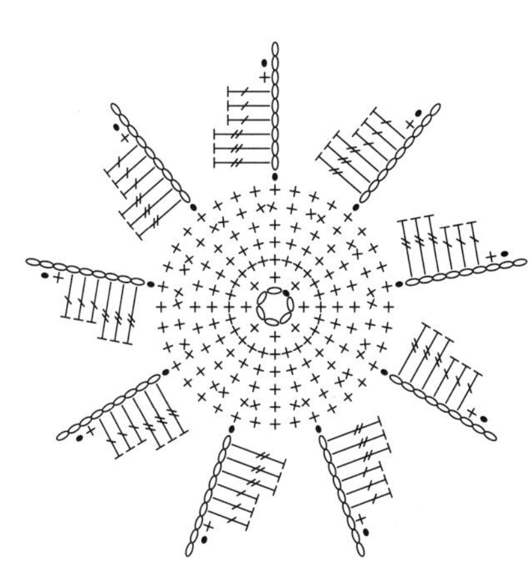

Flower square

Base ring: Ch4, join with slip st.

Round 1: *Ch2, 4dc into ring, slip st into ring; rep from * 3 times more. (4 petals)

Round 2: Slip st into back of 2nd dc, * keeping yarn at back of work, ch4, slip st into back of 2nd dc of next petal; rep from * twice more, ch4, slip st to 1st slip st.

Round 3: [1slip st, 5dc, 1slip st] into each loop.

Round 4: *Ch6, 1slip st into back of slip st between petals; rep from * 3 times more.

Round 5: Ch3 (count as 1dc), [2dc, ch3, 3dc] into 1st loop, *ch1, [3dc, ch3, 3dc] into next loop; rep from * twice more, ch1, slip st to top of ch-3.

Round 6: Slip st across next 2 dc and into next ch-3 sp, ch3 (count as 1dc), [2dc, ch3, 3dc] into same sp, *ch1, 3dc into next ch-1 sp, ch1, [3dc, ch3, 3dc] into next ch-3 sp; rep from * twice more, ch1, 3dc into next ch-1 sp, ch1, slip st to top of ch-3.

Round 7: Slip st across next 2 dc and into next ch-3 sp, ch3 (count as 1dc), [2dc, ch3, 3dc] into same sp, *[ch1, 3dc into next ch-1 sp] twice, ch1, [3dc, ch3, 3dc] into next ch-3 sp; rep from * twice more, [ch1, 3dc into next ch-1 sp] twice, ch1, slip st to top of ch-3.

Fasten off.

Vintage square

Base ring: Ch5, join with slip st.

Round 1: Ch3 (count as 1dc), 2dc into ring, [ch1, 3dc into ring] 3 times, ch1, slip st into top of ch-3.

Round 2: Slip st into each of next 2 dc, *[1sc, ch3, 1sc] into next sp for a corner, ch3; rep from * 3 times more, slip st to 1st sc.

Round 3: Slip st into corner sp, [ch3 (count as 1dc), 2dc, ch1, 3dc] into same sp, *3dc into next ch-3 sp, [3dc, ch1, 3dc] into next corner sp; rep from * twice more, 3dc into next ch-3 sp, slip st to top of ch-3.

Round 4: Slip st into each of next 2 dc, *[1sc, ch3, 1sc] into next corner sp, [ch3, skip 3 dc, 1sc between last dc and next dc] twice, ch3, skip 3 dc, rep from * 3 times more, slip st to 1st sc.

Round 5: Slip st into next corner sp, [ch3 (count as 1dc), 2dc, ch1, 3dc] into same sp, *[3dc into next ch-3 sp] 3 times, [3dc, ch1, 3dc] into next corner sp; rep from * twice more, [3dc into next ch-3 sp] 3 times, slip st to top of ch-3.

Round 6: Rep round 4, working 4 [ch-3] sps between corner sps.

Round 7: Rep round 5, working 3dc into each ch-3 loop along sides between [3dc, ch1, 3dc] at corners.

Fasten off.

Moorish medallion

Special abbreviation:

Ssc (Spike single crochet) = insert hook 2 rounds below st indicated, i.e. into top of 1st round, yo, draw loop through and up to height of current round, yo, draw through both loops on hook.

Base ring: Ch6, join with slip st.

Round 1: Ch1, 16sc into ring, slip st to 1st sc. (16 sts)

Round 2: Ch1, 1sc into same place as ch-1, 1sc into next sc, *[1sc, ch9, 1sc] into next sc**, 1sc into each of next 3 sc; rep from * twice more and from * to ** again, 1sc into next sc, slip st to 1st sc.

Round 3: Ch1, 1sc into same place as ch-1, *skip next 2 sc, [2hdc, 17dc, 2hdc] into next ch-9 sp, skip next 2 sc, 1sc into next sc; rep from * 3 more times, omitting 1sc at end of last rep and ending slip st to 1st sc.

Round 4: Ch1, 1Ssc over 1st st, *ch5, skip 5 sts, 1sc into next st, work picot of [ch3, slip st into 3rd ch from hook], [ch5, skip 4 sts, 1sc into next st, ch3, slip st into 3rd ch from hook] twice, ch5, skip 5 sts, 1Ssc over next st; rep from * 3 more times, omitting Ssc at end of last rep and ending slip st to 1st Ssc. Fasten off.

Flower square

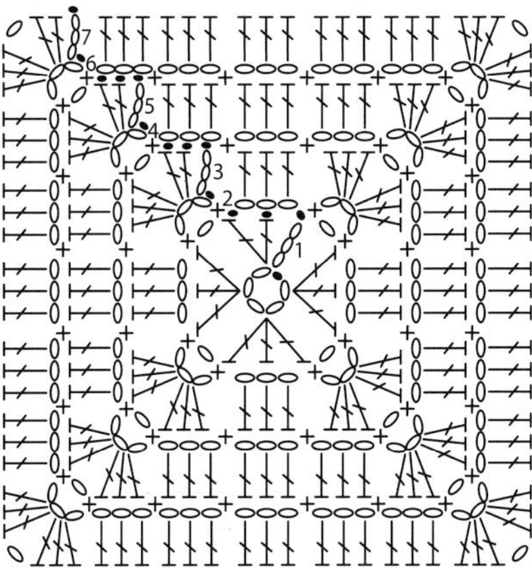

Vintage square

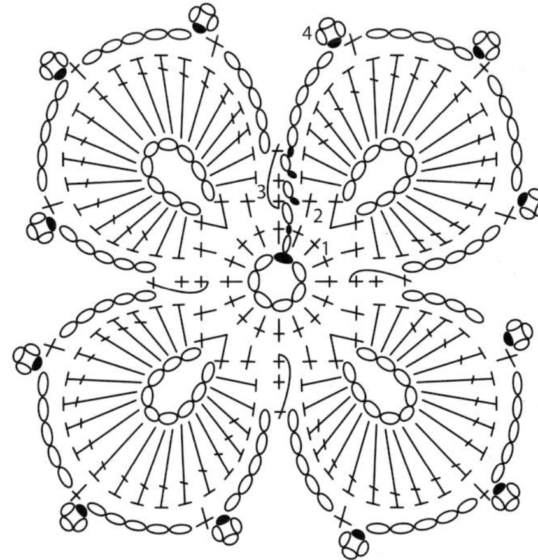

Moorish medallion

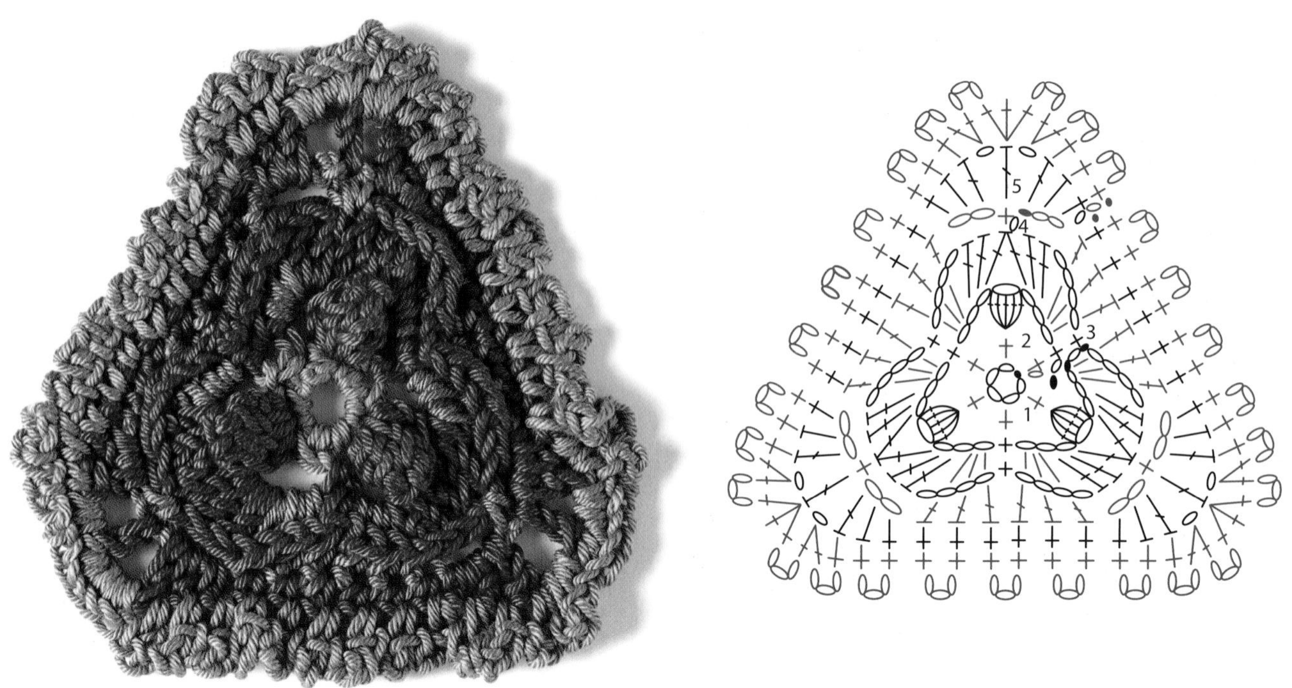

Popcorn trefoil

Special abbreviations:

Cluster = dc2tog.

Popcorn = see page 23.

Base ring: Using A, ch5, join with slip st.

Round 1: Ch1, 6sc into ring, slip st to 1st sc. Fasten off.

Round 2: Join B in same st, ch1, 1sc into same place as ch-1, *ch3, 5dc popcorn into next st, ch3**, 1sc into next st; rep from once more and from * to ** again, slip st to 1st sc.

Round 3: Ch1, 1sc into same place as ch-1, *ch4, 2dc into next ch-3 sp, dc2tog inserting hook into same ch sp for 1st leg and into next ch sp for 2nd leg, 2dc into same ch sp, ch4**, 1sc into next sc; rep from * once more and from * to ** again, slip st to 1st sc. Fasten off.

Round 4: Using C join into corner cluster, ch1, 1sc into same place as ch-1, *ch2, skip 2 dc, going behind ch sps of round 3, [3dc into next ch sp of round 2] twice, ch2, skip 2 dc**, 1sc into corner cluster; rep from * once more and from * to ** again, slip st to 1st sc. Fasten off.

Round 5: Using B join into last ch-2 sp of round 4, ch1, *[1sc, 1hdc, 1dc] into ch-2 sp, ch1, 1dc into next sc, ch1, [1dc, 1hdc, 1sc] into next ch-2 sp, 1sc into each of next 6 dc; rep from * twice more, slip st to 1st sc.

Fasten off.

Round 6: Using A join into same place, ch1, 1sc into same place as ch-1, ch3, 1sc into each of next 2 sts, ch3, *2sc into next ch sp, ch3, 3sc into dc at corner, ch3, 2sc into next ch sp, ch3**, [1sc into each of next 2 sts, ch3] 6 times; rep from * once more and from * to ** again, [1sc into each of next 2 sts, ch3] 4 times, 1sc into next st, slip st to 1st sc.

Fasten off.

Frozen star

Special abbreviation:

Cluster = dtr4tog.

Base ring: Ch12, join with slip st.

Round 1: Ch1, 24sc into ring, slip st to 1st sc. (24 sts)

Round 2: Ch6, dtr3tog over next 3 sts (counts as dtr4tog), [ch7, dtr4tog over same st as last leg of previous cluster and next 3 sts] 7 times, ch7, slip st to top of 1st cluster.

Round 3: Ch1, 1sc into same place as ch-1, *[ch3, skip 1 ch, 1sc into next ch] 3 times, ch3, skip 1 ch, 1sc into top of next cluster; rep from * 7 more times, omitting sc at end of last rep, slip st to 1st sc.

Round 4: Slip st to center of next ch-3 sp, ch1, 1sc into same sp, *ch3, 1dc into next sp; rep from * to end, omitting sc at end of last rep, slip st to 1st sc.

Round 5: As round 4.

Round 6: Slip st to center of next ch-3 sp, ch1, 1sc into same sp, *[ch3, 1sc into next sp] 4 times, ch3, skip next sp, [tr3tog, ch5, dtr4tog, ch4, slip st to top of last cluster, ch5, tr3tog] into next sp, ch3, skip next sp, 1sc into next sp; rep from * 3 more times, omitting sc at end of last rep, slip st to 1st sc.

Fasten off.

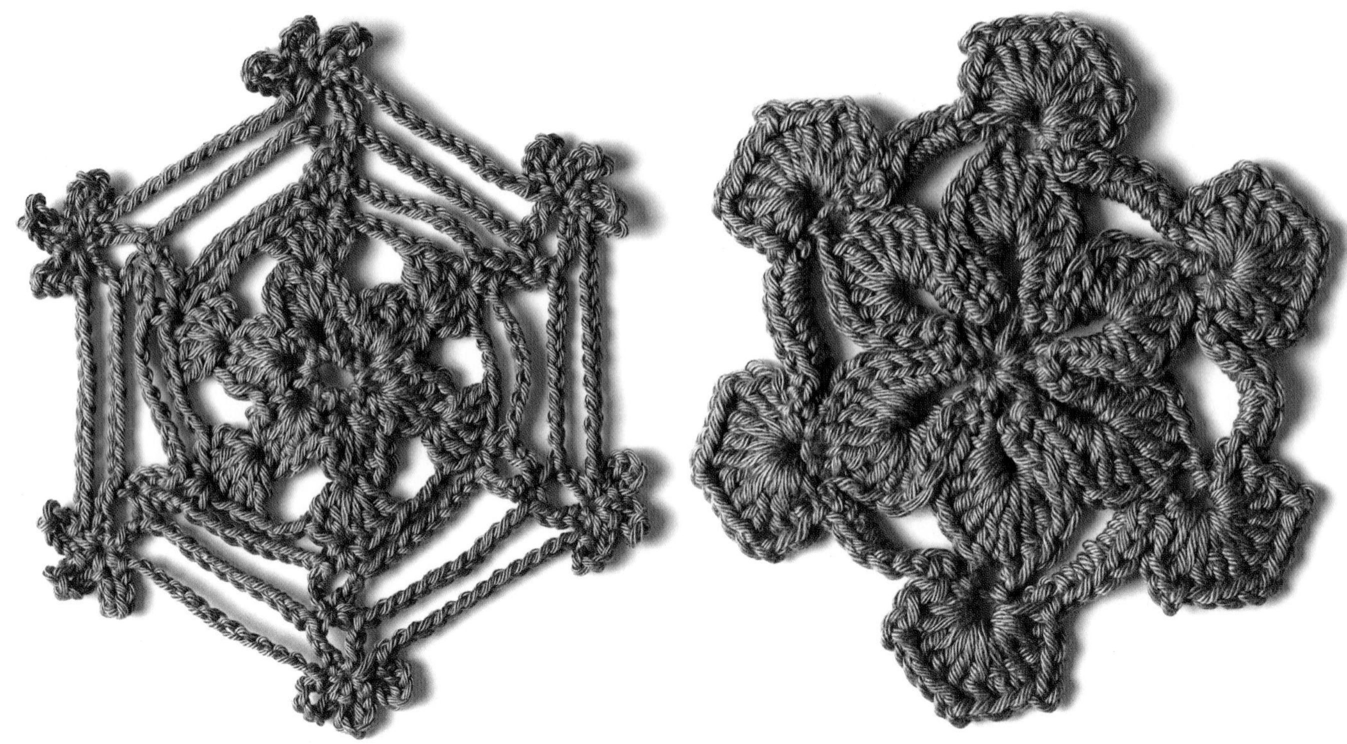

Snowflake I

Base ring: Ch6, join with slip st.

Round 1: Ch1, into ring work [1sc, ch2] 6 times, slip st into 1st sc.

Round 2: Ch1, into each ch-2 sp work [2sc, 1hdc, 3dc, 1hdc, 2sc], slip st to 1st sc. (6 petals)

Round 3: 3slip sts to center dc, ch3 (count as 1dc), 4dc into same st, *ch3, 5dc in center of dc of next petal; rep from * 4 more times, ch3, slip st to 3rd of 1st ch-3.

Round 4: Slip st to center dc, ch1, [1sc, ch7, 1sc] into same st, *ch8, skip 4 dc, [1sc, ch7, 1sc] into next dc; rep from * 4 more times, ch8, slip st to 1st sc.

Round 5: Slip st to 4th ch of ch-7 loop, ch1, [1sc, ch7, 1sc] into same st, *ch10, [1sc, ch7, 1sc] into 4th ch of next ch-7 loop; repeat from * 4 more times, ch10, slip st to 1st sc.

Round 6: 3slip sts to 4th ch of ch-7 loop, ch1, into same st work (1sc, ch6, [1slip st, ch6] twice, 1sc), *ch12, into 4th ch of next ch-7 loop work (1sc, ch6, [1slip st, ch6] twice, 1sc); rep from * 4 more times, ch12, slip st to 1st sc.

Fasten off.

Snowflake II

Base ring: Ch6, join with slip st.

Round 1: Ch1, [1sc into ring, ch7] 6 times, slip st to 1st sc (6 loops).

Round 2: *Ch1, into next ch-7 sp work [2sc, 1hdc, 3dc, 3tr, 3dc, 1hdc, 2sc], ch1, slip st into next sc; rep from * 5 times more.

Round 3: 7slip sts to center tr, *ch4, slip st into same tr, ch8, slip st on top of next tr; rep from * around.

Round 4: Slip st into ch-4 loop, *ch1, work 1sc, 2dc, ch2, [3dc, ch2] twice, 2dc, 1sc into same sp, ch1, 6sc into next ch-8 sp; rep from * around, slip st to 1st sc.

Fasten off.

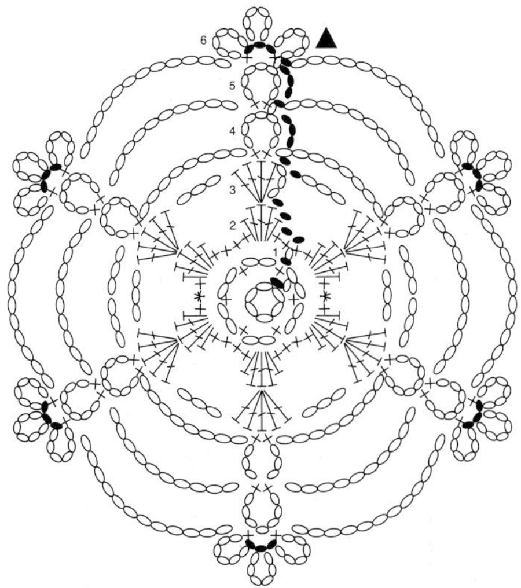

Snowflake I

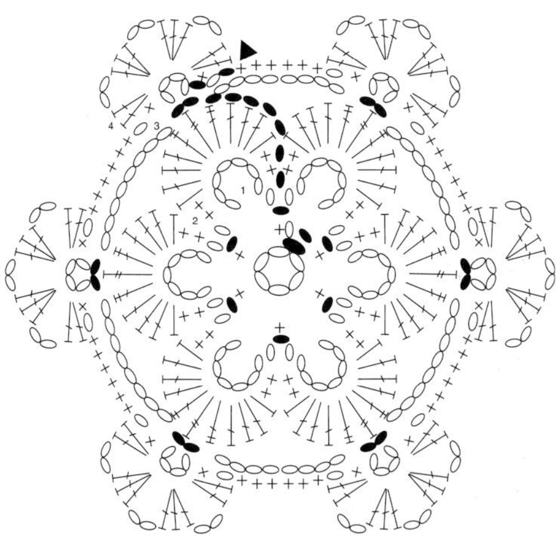

Snowflake II

Spiral pentagram

Spiral pentagram

Base ring: Ch5, join with slip st.
Round 1: [Ch6, 1sc into ring] 5 times.
Note: mark last sc of each round with contrasting thread.
Round 2: [Ch6, 3sc into next ch-6 sp] 5 times.
Round 3: [Ch6, 3sc into next ch-6 sp, 1sc into each of next 2 sc] 5 times. (5 blocks of 5sc each)
Round 4: [Ch6, 3sc into next ch-6 sp, 1sc into each sc of next block skipping last sc] 5 times. (5 blocks of 7sc each)
Continue as given on round 4 for 3 more rounds finishing with 5 blocks of 13sc each.
Round 8: *Ch5, 1sc into center of next ch-6 sp, ch5, skip 1 sc, 1sc into each sc of next block skipping last sc; rep from * 4 more times.
Round 9: *[Ch5, 1sc into next sp] twice, ch5, skip 1 sc, 1sc into each sc of next block skipping last sc; rep from * 4 more times.
Continue as given on round 9 for 3 more rounds, but work 1 more ch-5 sp in each segment on each round at same time as number of sc in each block reduces, finishing with 6 sps and 3sc in each of 5 segments.
Round 13: Ch5, 1sc into next sp, *[ch3, 1sc into next sp] 5 times, ch3, 1dc into 2nd of next 3 sc, ch3, 1sc into next sp; rep from * 4 more times, omitting sc at end of last rep, slip st to 1st sc.
Fasten off.

Traditional hexagon I

Special abbreviation:

Cluster = dc3tog.

Base ring: Ch6, join with slip st.

Round 1: Ch3, dc2tog into ring (counts as dc3tog), [ch3, dc3tog into ring] 5 times, ch1, 1hdc into top of 1st cluster.

Round 2: Ch3, dc2tog into sp formed by hdc (counts as dc3tog), *ch3, [dc3tog, ch3, dc3tog] into next sp; rep from * 4 more times, ch3, dc3tog into last sp, ch1, 1hdc into top of 1st cluster.

Round 3: Ch3, dc2tog into sp formed by hdc (counts as dc3tog), *ch3, [dc3tog, ch3, dc3tog] into next sp**, ch3, dc3tog into next sp; rep from * 4 more times and from * to ** again, ch1, 1hdc into top of 1st cluster.

Round 4: Ch3 (counts as 1dc), 1dc into sp formed by hdc, *3dc into next sp, [3dc, ch2, 3dc] into next sp**, 3dc into next sp; rep from * 4 more times and from * to ** again, 1dc into next sp, slip st to top of ch-3.

Round 5: Ch1, 1sc into same place, 1sc into each dc and each ch all around, ending slip st to 1st sc. Fasten off.

Traditional hexagon II

Worked as Traditional hexagon I (see left).
Work 1 round each in colors A, B, C, D and E.

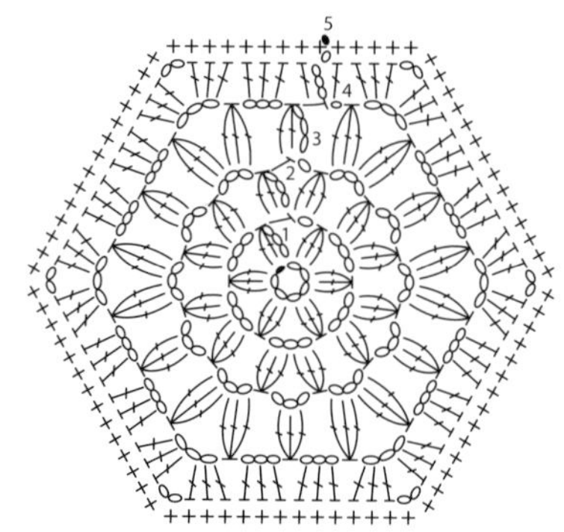

Traditional hexagon I

Traditional hexagon II

Scalloped circle

Base ring: Ch6, join with slip st.

Round 1: Ch3 (count as 1dc), 23dc into ring, join with slip st to top of ch-3.

Round 2: Ch5 (count as 1dc, ch2), 1dc into slip st, ch1, *skip 2 dc, [1dc, ch2, 1dc] into next dc, ch1; rep from * 6 times more, slip st to 3rd of ch-5.

Round 3: Slip st into next ch-2 sp, ch3 (count as 1dc), [1dc, ch2, 2dc] into same sp, *1sc into next ch-1 sp, [2dc, ch2, 2dc] into next ch-2 sp; rep from * 6 times more, 1sc into next ch-1 sp, slip st to top of ch-3.

Round 4: Slip st into next ch-2 sp, ch3 (count as 1dc), [2dc,ch1, 3dc] into same sp, *1sc in sp before next sc, 1sc in sp after the same sc, [3dc, ch1, 3dc] into next ch-2 sp; rep from * 6 times more, 1sc in sp before next sc, 1sc in sp after the same sc, slip st to top of ch-3.

Fasten off.

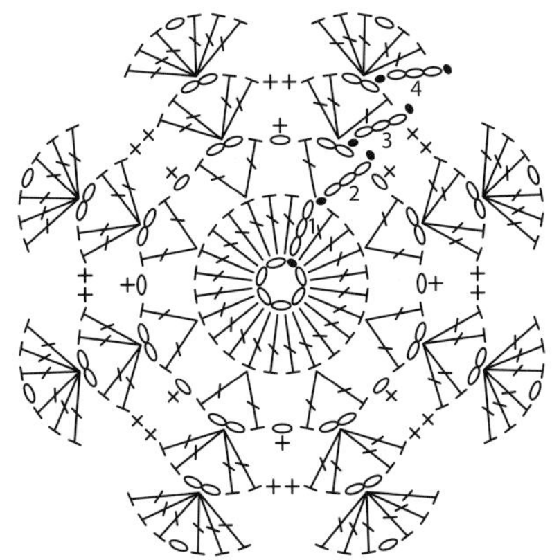

Five-point star

Note: Pattern is worked in a spiral; do not join at the end of each round.

Base chain: Ch2.

Round 1: 5sc in 2nd ch from hook.

Round 2: 3sc in each sc. (15 sts)

Round 3: [1sc in next st, ch6, slip st in 2nd ch from hook, 1sc in next ch, 1hdc in next ch, 1dc in next ch, 1tr in next ch, 1tr in bottom of base sc, skip 2 sc] 5 times, slip st in 1st dc.

Fasten off.

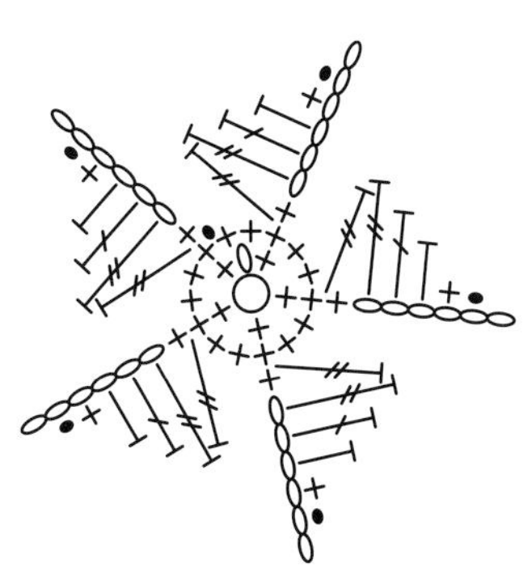

Citrus ring

Base ring: Ch4, join with slip st.

Round 1: Ch4 (count as 1dc, ch1), *1dc into ring, ch1; rep from * 6 times more, slip st in 3rd of ch-4.

Round 2: Ch2, [1dc, 1tr, 1dc, 1hdc] in same sp, *[1hdc, 1dc, 1ddc, 1dc, 1hdc] in next sp; rep from * around, slip st to top of ch-2.

Fasten off.

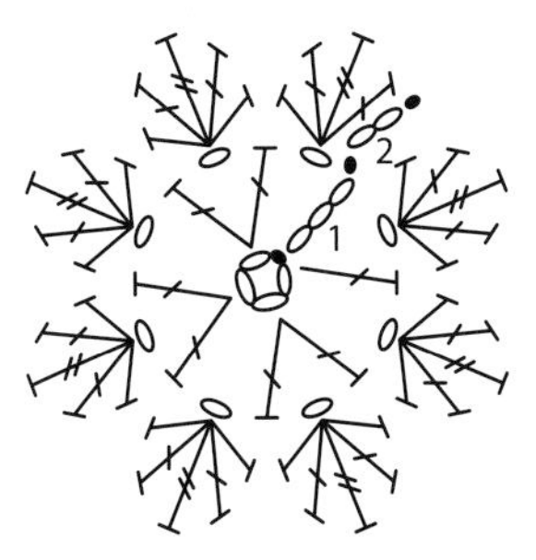

Flower crystal

Special abbreviation:
Popcorn = 5dc into next st, drop loop off hook, insert hook into 1st of these dc, pick up dropped loop and draw through.
Base ring: Ch5, join with slip st.
Round 1: Ch4 (count as 1dc, ch1), [1dc, ch1] 11 times into ring, slip st into 3rd of ch-4.
Round 2: Ch6 (count as 1dc, ch3), 1 popcorn into next dc, ch3, [1dc into next dc, ch3, 1 popcorn into next dc, ch3] 5 times, slip st into 3rd of ch-6 at beg of round.
Round 3: Ch1, 1sc into same st as last slip st, ch4, 1sc into top of next popcorn, ch4, [1sc into next dc, ch4, 1sc into top of next popcorn, ch4] 5 times, slip st into 1st sc.
Round 4: Slip st into 1st ch-4 sp, ch2 (count as 1hdc), [1dc, 1tr, 1dtr, 1tr, 1dc, 1hdc] into same sp, [1hdc, 1dc, 1tr, 1dtr, 1tr, 1dc, 1hdc] into each of next 11 ch-4 sps, slip st to top of ch-2. Fasten off.

Russian square

Special abbreviations:
Dc/rf = insert hook around the post of the stitch indicated from the front, around the back and to the front again and complete the dc as usual.
Dc/rb = insert hook around the post of the stitch indicated from the back, around the front and to the back again and complete the dc as usual. See raised stitches, page 32.
Base ring: Using A, ch8, join with slip st.
Round 1: Ch6 (count as 1dc, ch3), [3dc into ring, ch3] 3 times, 2dc into ring, slip st to 3rd of ch-6. Fasten off.
Round 2: Using B, join into a different corner ch-3 sp, ch3 (count as 1dc), 2dc into same corner sp, *1dc/rf around each of next 3 sts**, [3dc, ch3, 3dc] into next corner sp; rep from * twice more and from * to ** again, [3dc, ch3] into last corner sp, slip st to top of ch-3. Fasten off.
Round 3: Using C, join into a different corner sp, ch6 (count as 1dc and ch3), 3dc into same corner sp, *1dc/rb around each of next 3 sts, 1dc/rf around each of next 3 sts, 1dc/rb around each of next 3 sts**, [3dc, ch3, 3dc] into next corner sp; rep from * twice more and from * to ** again, 2dc into last corner sp, slip st to 3rd of ch-6. Fasten off.
Round 4: Using D, join into a different corner sp, ch3 (count as 1dc), 2dc into same corner sp, *[1dc/rf around each of next 3 sts, 1dc/rb around each of next 3 sts] twice, 1dc/rf around each of next 3 sts**, [3dc, ch3, 3dc] into next corner sp; rep from * twice more and from * to ** again, [3dc, ch3] into last corner sp, slip st to top of ch-3. Fasten off.

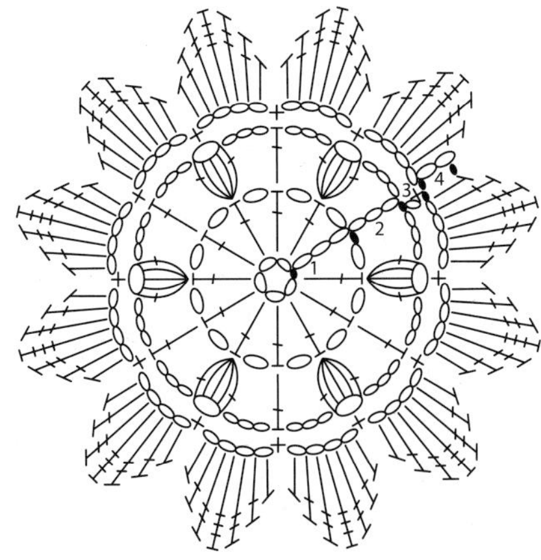

Flower crystal

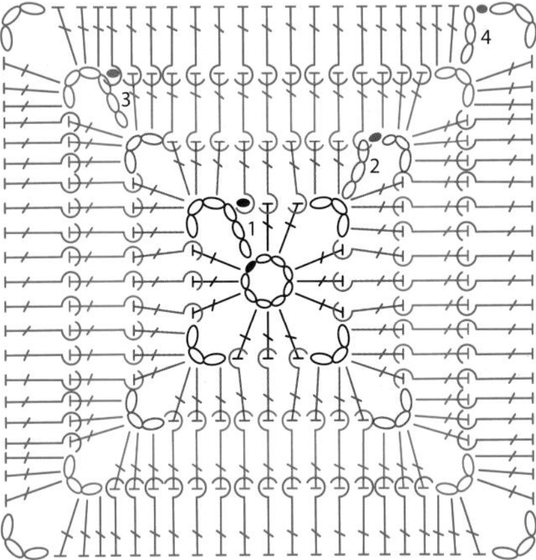

Russian square

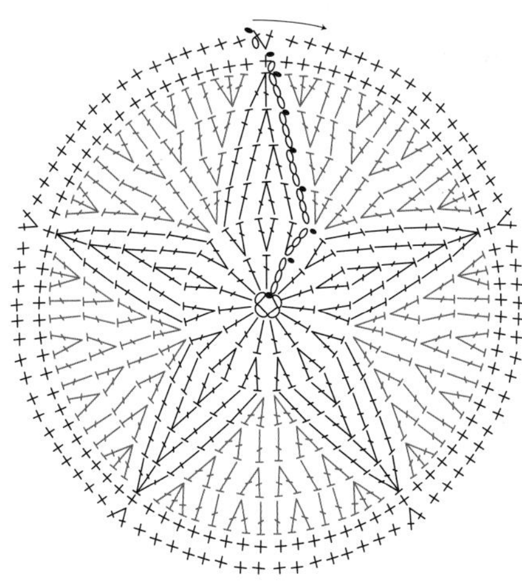
Two-color star

Two-color star

Special abbreviation:

Cluster = dc3tog.

Base ring: Using A, ch4, join with slip st.

Round 1: Ch3 (count as 1dc), 14dc into ring, slip st to top of ch-3. (15 sts)

Round 2: Ch3 (count as 1dc), 1dc into same place as ch-3, 2dc into next and each dc all around, slip st to top of ch-3. (30 sts)

Round 3: Ch3 (count as 1dc), *1dc into next st, dc2tog over next 2 sts, 1dc into each of next 2 sts, change to B, 2dc into same place as last dc with A, 2dc into next st, change to A**, 1dc into same place as last dc with B; rep from * 3 more times and from * to ** again, slip st to top of ch-3.

Round 4: Ch3 (count as 1dc), *dc2tog over next 2 sts, 1dc into each of next 2 sts, change to B, 2dc into next st, 1dc into each of next 2 sts, 2dc into next st, change to A**, 1dc into next st; rep from * 3 more times and from * to ** again, slip st to top of ch-3.

Round 5: Ch3 (count as 1dc), *dc2tog over next 2 sts, 1dc into next st, change to B, 2dc into next st, 1dc into next st, 2dc into each of next 2 sts, 1dc into next st, 2dc into next st, change to A**, 1dc into next st; rep from * 3 more times and from * to ** again, slip st to top of ch-3.

Round 6: Ch3, dc2tog over next 2 sts (counts as dc3tog), *change to B, 3dc into next st, [1dc into each of next 2 sts, 2dc into next st] twice, 1dc into each of next 2 sts, 3dc into next st, change to A**, dc3tog over next 3 sts; rep from * 3 more times and from * to ** again, slip st to top of 1st cluster. Fasten off B.

Round 7: Continue using A only ch1, 1sc into same place as ch-1, 1sc into next and each st all around, slip st to 1st sc, turn.

Round 8 (WS): Ch1, 2sc into same place as ch-1, 1sc into next and each st all around, except 2sc into each of 4 sts corresponding to rem points of Star, ending slip st to 1st sc. Fasten off.

Spider square

Special abbreviation:
Cluster = dc3tog.
Base ring: Ch6, join with slip st.
Round 1: Ch1, [1sc into ring, ch15] 12 times, slip st to 1st sc.
Round 2: Slip st along to center of next ch-15 sp, ch3, dc2tog into same sp (counts as dc3tog), *ch4, dc3tog into same sp, [ch4, 1sc into next sp] twice, ch4, dc3tog into next sp; rep from * 3 more times, omitting dc3tog at end of last rep, slip st to 1st cluster.
Round 3: Slip st into next ch-4 sp, ch3, dc2tog into same sp (counts as dc3tog), *ch4, dc3tog into same sp, [ch4, 1sc into next ch-4 sp, ch4, dc3tog into next ch-4 sp] twice; rep from * 3 more times, omitting dc3tog at end of last rep, slip st to 1st cluster. Fasten off.

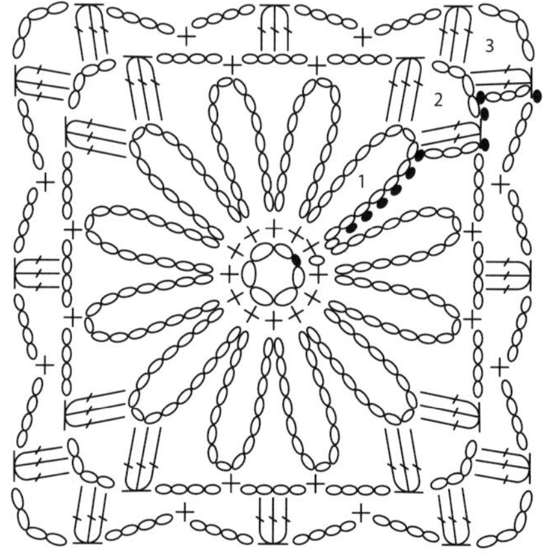

Mosaic tile

Base ring: Using A, ch6, join with slip st.
Round 1: Ch4, [1dc, ch1] 11 times into ring, slip st to 3rd of ch-4, draw B through loop, drop A.
Round 2: [1sc into next sp, ch2] 12 times, slip st to 1st sc, draw A through loop, drop B.
Round 3: *[1sc into next sp, ch2] twice, [2dc, ch2] twice into next sp for corner; rep from * 3 times more, slip st to 1st sc, draw B through loop, cast off A.
Round 4: *(1sc, ch3) into each sp to corner, [1sc, ch3] twice into corner sp; rep from * 3 times more, slip st to 1st sc. Fasten off.

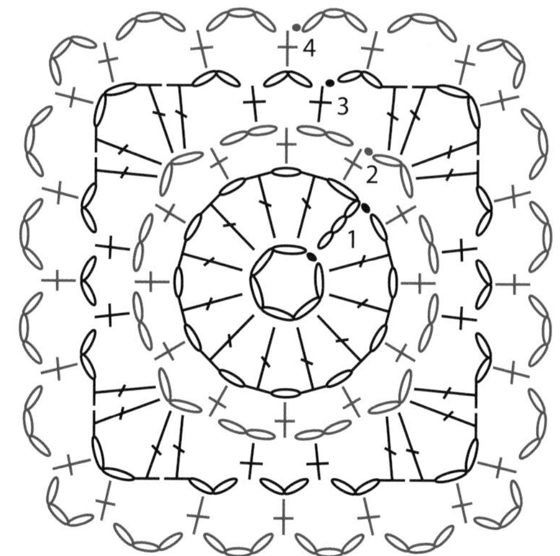

Tristar

Special abbreviation:

Picot = ch3, slip st into 1st of these ch.

Round 1: Ch10, slip st into 1st ch, [ch9, slip st into same ch as last slip st] twice. (3 loops formed)

Round 2: *Ch1, working into next ch-9 sp work [2sc, 1hdc, 11dc, 1hdc, 2sc], ch1, slip st into same ch as slip sts of 1st round; rep from * twice more.

Round 3: Slip st into each of 1st 9 sts of 1st loop, [ch16, skip 1st 8 sts on next loop, slip st into next dc] twice, ch16, slip st into same dc as last slip st at beg of round.

Round 4: Ch1, 1sc into same dc as last slip st of previous round, 19sc into 1st ch-16 sp, [1sc into same dc as next slip st of previous round, 19sc into next ch-16 sp] twice, slip st to 1st sc. (60sc)

Round 5: Ch8 (count as 1dc, ch5), skip next 3 sc, [1dc into next sc, ch5, skip 3 sc] 14 times, slip st to 3rd of ch-8 at beg of round.

Round 6: Slip st into 1st ch-3 of 1st ch-5 sp, ch1, 4sc into 1st sp, 7sc into each of next 14 sps, 3sc to same sp as 1st 4sc, slip st into 1st sc.

Round 7: [Ch6, skip next 6 sc, slip st into next sc] 14 times, ch6, slip st to same sc as last slip st of previous round.

Round 8: Ch1, into each ch-6 sp work 2sc, [1 picot, 2sc] 3 times, slip st to 1st sc.

Fasten off.

Magic circle

Base ring: Ch16, join with slip st.

Round 1: Ch2 (count as 1hdc), 35hdc into ring, slip st into 2nd of ch-2 at beg of round.

Round 2: Ch1, 1sc into same st as last slip st, [ch5, skip 2 hdc, 1sc into next hdc] 11 times, ch5, slip st to 1st sc. Fasten off.

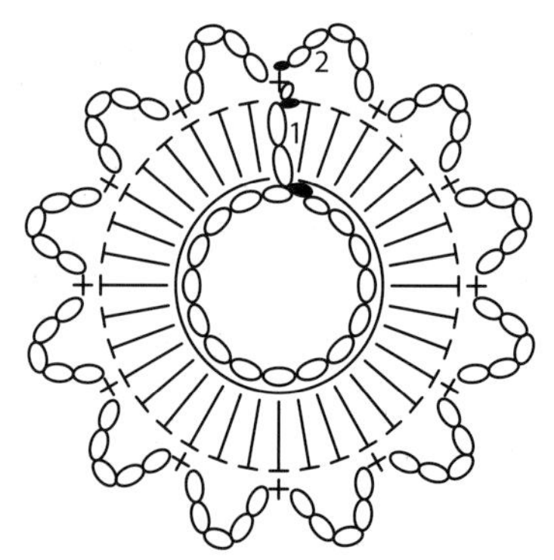

Green leaf

Special abbreviation:

Picot = ch3, slip st into 1st of these ch.

Base chain: Ch15, work in a spiral as follows:

1sc into 2nd ch from hook, working 1 st into each ch, 1hdc, 3dc, 4tr, 3dc, 1hdc and 1sc, ch3, then working 1 st into each ch on other side of base chain, 1sc, 1hdc, 3dc, 4tr, 3dc, 1hdc, 1sc, ch3, 1sc into 1st sc at beg of spiral, 1sc into next hdc, 1 picot, [1sc into each of next 2 sts, 1 picot] 6 times, [1sc, ch4, slip st into 3rd ch from hook, ch1, 1sc] into ch-3 sp at point of leaf, [1 picot, 1sc into each of next 2 sts] 7 times, slip st into ch-3 sp. Fasten off.

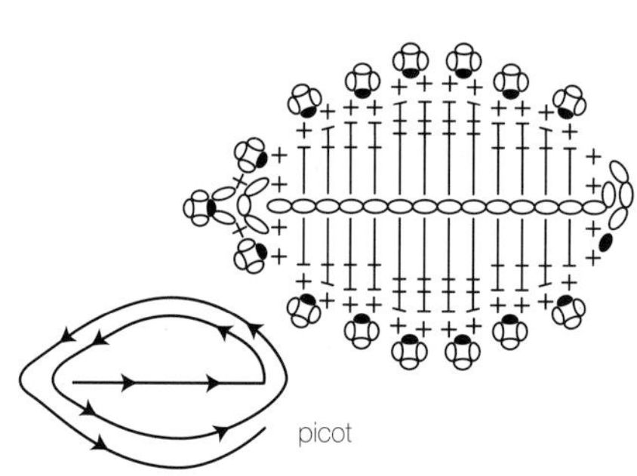

Canterbury bell

Special abbreviation:

Bobble = 5dc into next sc until 1 loop of each remains on hook, yo and draw through all 6 loops on hook.

Base ring: Ch6, join with slip st.

Round 1: Ch1, 12sc into ring, slip st to 1st sc.

Round 2: Ch3, 4dc into same st as last slip st until 1 loop of each dc remains on hook, yo and draw through all 5 loops on hook (1 bobble made at beg of round), *ch5, skip 1 sc, 1 bobble into next sc; rep from * 4 times more, ch5, slip st to top of 1st bobble. Fasten off.

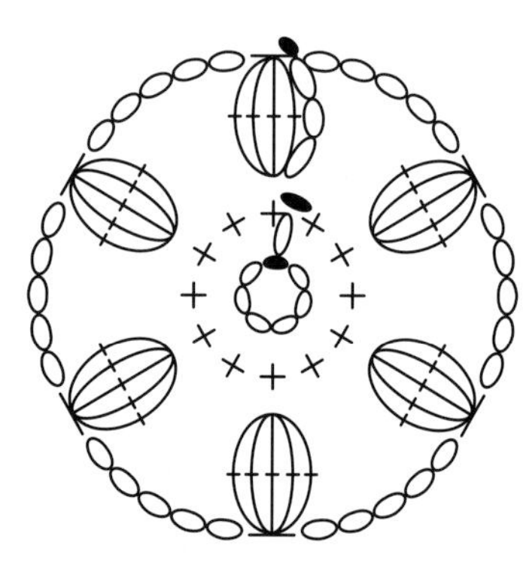

Scallop flower

Base ring: Using A, ch6, join with slip st.
Round 1: Ch3 (count as 1dc), 17dc into ring, slip st to top of ch-3 (18 sts).
Round 2: Ch1, 1sc into same place as ch-1, *ch3, skip next 2 sts, 1sc into next st; rep from * 5 more times omitting last sc and ending slip st to 1st sc. Fasten off.
Round 3: Using B join into next ch, ch1, *work a Petal of [1sc, 1hdc, 3dc, 1hdc, 1sc] into next ch-3 sp, slip st into next sc; rep from * 5 more times. (6 petals)
Round 4: Slip st into each of next 4 sts to center dc of next Petal, ch1, 1sc into same place as ch-1, *ch8, 1sc into center dc of next Petal; rep from * 5 more times omitting last sc and ending slip st to 1st sc. Fasten off.
Round 5: Using A join into next ch, ch1, *[1sc, 3hdc, 5dc, 3hdc, 1sc] into next sp; rep from * 5 more times, ending slip st into 1st sc. Fasten off.

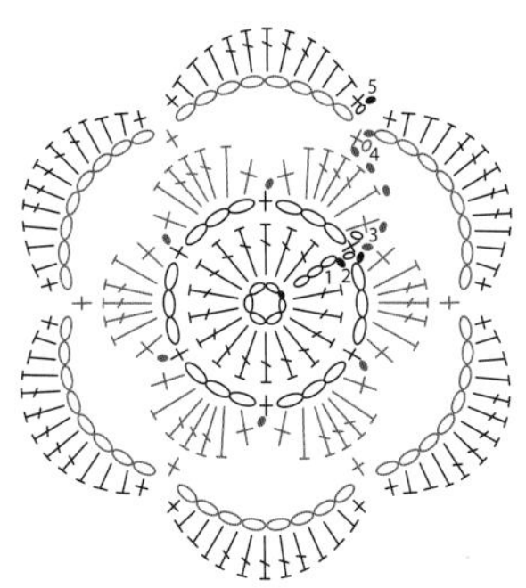

Sun fire

Base ring: Ch5, join with slip st.
Round 1: Ch7 (count as 1tr, ch3), [1tr into ring, ch3] 7 times, slip st to 4th of ch-7. (8 sps)
Round 2: Ch3 (count as 1dc), [4dc into next sp, 1dc into next tr] 7 times, 4dc into next sp, slip st to top of ch-3. (40 sts)
Round 3: Ch1, 1sc into same place as last slip st, *ch6, 1sc into 2nd ch from hook, 1hdc into next ch, 1dc into next ch, 1tr into next ch, 1dtr into next ch, skip 4 sts, 1sc into next st; rep from * 7 more times omitting sc at end of last rep, slip st to 1st sc. Fasten off.

Elephant's ear

Work as given for Flower crystal (see page 156), but working rounds 1 and 2 in A and rounds 3 and 4 in B.

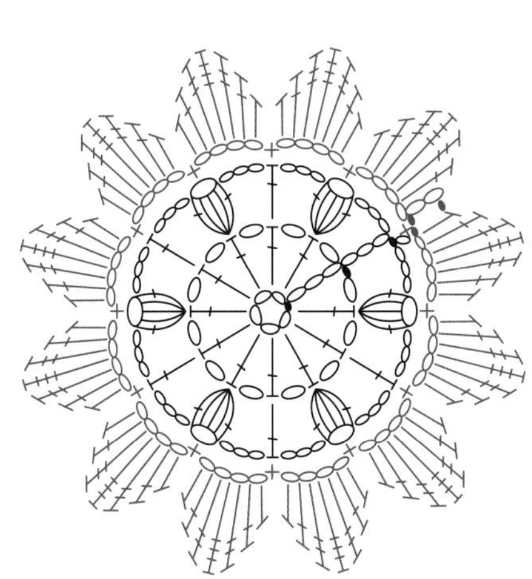

Little gem

Special abbreviation:
Cluster = dc3tog.
Base ring: Using A, ch5, join with slip st.
Round 1: Ch4 (count as 1tr), 2dc into 4th ch from hook, *ch3, 1tr into ring, 2dc into base of stem of tr just made; rep from * 4 more times, ch3, slip st to top of ch-4.
Round 2: Ch3, dc2tog over next 2 dc (count as cluster), *ch6, skip ch-3, cluster over next 3 sts; rep from * 5 more times omitting last cluster and ending slip st to top of 1st cluster. Fasten off.
Round 3: Using B, join into center of ch-3 sp of 1st round to enclose ch-6 sp of round 2, ch1, 1sc into same place as ch-1, *ch5, 1dc into top of next cluster, ch5, 1sc into ch-3 sp of 1st round at same time enclosing ch-6 sp of round 2; rep from * 5 more times omitting last sc and ending slip st to 1st sc. Fasten off.
Round 4: Using C join into same place, ch1, 1sc into same place as ch1, *ch5, skip ch-5, 3sc into next dc, ch5, skip ch-5, 1sc into next sc; rep from * 5 more times omitting last sc and ending with slip st to 1st sc. Fasten off.

Arcade diamond

Base ring: Ch6, join with slip st.
Round 1: Ch3 (count as 1dc), 15dc into ring, slip st to 3rd of ch-3. (16dc)
Round 2: Ch5 (count as 1dc, ch2), *1dc into next dc, ch2; rep from * 14 more times, slip st to 3rd of ch-5.
Round 3: Slip st into 1st sp, ch3 (count as 1dc), [1dc, ch3, 2dc] into same sp, *[ch2, 1sc into next sp] 3 times, ch2, [2dc, ch3, 2dc] into next sp; rep from * twice more, [ch2, 1sc into next sp] 3 times, ch2, slip st to top of ch-3.
Round 4: Slip st into next ch-3 sp, ch3 (count as 1dc), [2dc, ch3, 3dc] into same sp, *[ch2, 1sc into next ch-2 sp] 4 times, ch2, [3dc, ch3, 3dc] into next ch-3 sp; rep from * twice more, [ch2, 1sc into next ch-2 sp] 4 times, ch2, slip st to top of ch-3.
Round 5: Slip st into next ch-3 sp, ch3 (count as 1dc), [2dc, ch2, 3dc] into same sp, *[ch1, 2dc into ch-2 sp] 5 times, ch1, [3dc, ch2, 3dc] into next ch-3 sp; rep from * twice more, [ch1, 2dc into ch-2 sp] 5 times, ch1, slip st to top of ch-3. Fasten off.

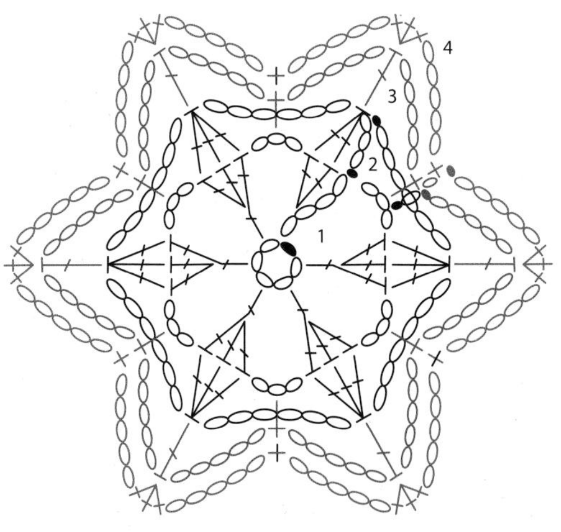

Little gem

Arcade diamond

Crystal snowflake

Crystal snowflake

Base ring: Ch12, join with slip st.

Round 1: Ch1, 24sc into ring, slip st to 1st sc. (24 sts)

Round 2: Ch1, 1sc into same place as ch-1, *1sc into next st, [ch3, insert hook down through top of sc just made and work sl st] (one picot made)**, 1sc into next st; rep from * 10 more times and from * to ** again, slip st to 1st sc.

Round 3: Ch8 (count as 1tr, ch4), miss picot, [1tr into next sc between picots, ch4] 11 times, slip st to 4th of ch-8.

Round 4: Ch1, [5sc into next ch-4 sp] 12 times, slip st to 1st sc.

Round 5: Ch1, *1sc into back loop only of each of next 5 sc, ch15, skip next 5 sc; rep from * 5 more times, slip st to 1st sc.

Round 6: Ch1, *1sc into back loop only of each of next 5 sc, 15sc into next ch-15 sp; rep from * 5 more times, slip st to 1st sc.

Round 7: Slip st into back loop only of next st, ch1, 1sc into same place as ch-1, 1sc into back loop only of each of next 2 sc, *skip 1 sc, [1sc into each of next 3 sc, picot] 4 times, 1sc into each of next 3 sc, miss 1 sc**, 1sc into back loop only of each of next 3 sc; rep from * 4 more times and from * to ** again, slip st to 1st sc. Fasten off.

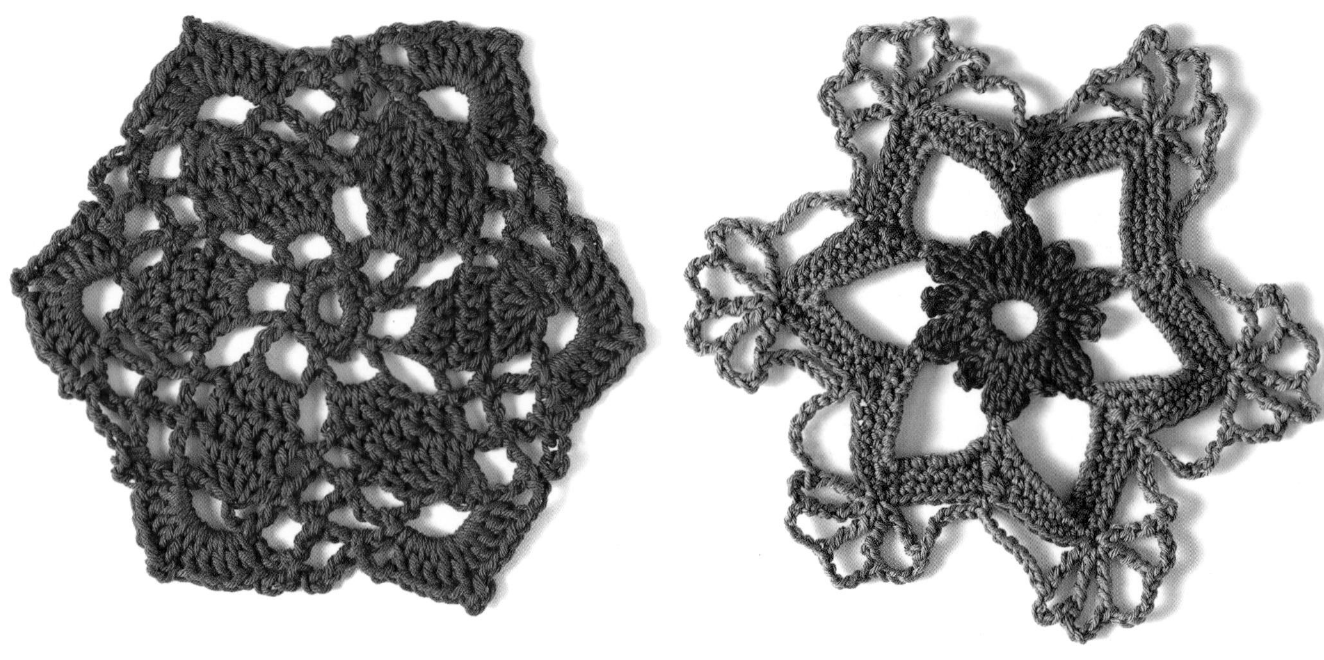

Ice crystal

Special abbreviation:
Cluster = 1dc into each of next 5 dc until 1 loop of each remains on hook, yo and draw through all 6 loops on hook. –
Base ring: Ch6, join with slip st.
Round 1: Ch1, 12sc into ring, slip st to 1st sc. (12 sts)
Round 2: Ch1, 1sc into same place as ch-1, [ch7, skip 1 sc, 1sc into next sc] 5 times, ch3, skip 1 sc, 1tr into top of 1st sc.
Round 3: Ch3 (count as 1dc), 4dc into sp formed by tr, [ch3, 5dc into next ch-7 sp] 5 times, ch3, slip st to top of ch-3.
Round 4: Ch3 (count as 1dc), 1dc into each of next 4 dc, *ch3, 1sc into next ch-3 sp, ch3**, 1dc into each of next 5 dc; rep from * 4 more times and from * to ** again, slip st to top of ch-3.
Round 5: Ch3, dc4tog over next 4 dc (count as cluster), *[ch5, 1sc into next ch-3 sp] twice, ch5**, cluster over next 5 dc; rep from * 4 more times and from * to ** again, slip st to 1st cluster.
Round 6: Slip st into each of next 3 ch, ch1, 1sc into same space, *ch5, 1sc into next ch-5 sp; rep from * all around omitting last sc and ending slip st to 1st sc.
Round 7: Slip st into each of next 3 ch, ch1, 1sc into same space, *ch5, 1sc into next ch-5 sp, ch3, [5dc, ch3, 5dc] into next sp, ch3, 1sc into next sp; rep from * 5 more times omitting last sc and ending slip st to 1st sc.
Fasten off.

Crystal motif

Special abbreviation:
Cluster = sc3tog.
Base ring: Using A, ch12, join with slip st.
Round 1: Ch1, 1sc into ring, *[ch7, 1sc, ch4, 1dtr, ch4, 1sc] into ring; rep from * 5 more times omitting sc at end of last rep, slip st to 1st sc. Fasten off.
Round 2: Join B into top of any dtr, ch1, 1sc into same place as ch-1, *ch13, skip ch-7 sp, 1sc into top of next dtr; rep from * 5 more times omitting sc at end of last rep, slip st to 1st sc.
Round 3: Ch1, skip next ch, 1sc into each of next 5 ch, *3sc into next ch, 1sc into each of next 5 ch**, sc3tog over [next ch, next sc and next ch], 1sc into each of next 5 ch; rep from * 4 more times and from * to ** again, slip st to 1st sc.
Round 4: Ch1, skip 1st st, *1sc into each of next 5 sts, 3sc into next st, 1sc into each of next 5 sts**, sc3tog over next 3 sts; rep from * 4 more times and from * to ** again, slip st to 1st sc.
Round 5: As round 4. Fasten off.
Round 6: Join C into same place, ch1, 1sc into same place, *ch7, skip 6 sc, (1dtr, [ch5, 1dtr] 4 times) into next sc at tip of star, ch7, skip 6 sc, 1sc into next sc cluster; rep from * 5 more times omitting sc at end of last rep, slip st to 1st sc.
Fasten off.

Ice crystal

Crystal motif

Astrolabe motif

Astrolabe motif

Base ring: ch4, join with slip st.

Round 1: Ch4 (count as 1dc, ch1), [1dc into ring, ch1] 7 times, slip st to 3rd of ch-4. (8 spaces)

Round 2: Ch1, 1sc into same place as ch-1, [ch3, skip 1 ch, 1sc into next dc] 8 times omitting sc at end of last rep, slip st to 1st sc.

Round 3: Slip st into each of next 2 ch, ch1, 1sc into same sp as ch-1, [ch6, 1sc into next ch-3 sp] 8 times omitting sc at end of last rep, slip st to 1st sc.

Round 4: Slip st into each of next 3 ch, ch1, 1sc into same sp as ch-1, [ch6, 1sc into next ch-6 sp] 8 times omitting sc at end of last rep, slip st to 1st sc.

Round 5: Ch1, 1sc into same place as ch-1, *[2dc, ch4, 2dc] into next sp, 1sc into next sc; rep from * 7 more times omitting sc at end of last rep, slip st to 1st sc.

Round 6: Slip st into each of next 2 dc and next 2 ch, ch1, 1sc into same place as ch-1, [ch8, 1sc into next ch-4 sp] 8 times omitting sc at end of last rep, slip st to 1st sc.

Round 7: Ch1, *work a Wave of [1sc, 1hdc, 2dc, 1tr, 2dc, 1hdc, 1sc] into next ch-8 sp; rep from * 7 more times, slip st to 1st sc.

Round 8: Slip st into each of next 4 sts to tr, ch1, 1sc into same place as ch-1, [ch11, 1sc into tr at center of next Wave] 8 times omitting sc at end of last rep, slip st to 1st sc.

Round 9: Ch1, *[2sc, 2hdc, 2dc, 4tr, 2dc, 2hdc, 2sc] into next ch-11 sp; rep from * 7 more times, slip st to 1st sc.

Fasten off.

Five branches

Base ring: Ch7, join with slip st.

Round 1: Ch1, 16sc into ring, slip st to 1st sc.

Round 2: Ch1, 1sc into 1st sc, [ch5, skip 1 sc, 1sc into next sc] 7 times, ch5, slip st to 1st sc.

Round 3: Slip st into 1st ch-5 sp, ch1, [1sc, 5hdc, 1sc] into each ch-5 sp to end, slip st into 1st sc. (8 petals)

Round 4: Ch1, working behind each petal, 1sc into 1st sc on round 2, [ch6, 1sc into next sc on Round 2] 7 times, ch6, slip st to 1st sc.

Round 5: Slip st into 1st ch-6 sp, ch1, [1sc, 6hdc, 1sc] into each ch-6 sp to end, slip st to 1st sc.

Round 6: Ch1, working behind each petal, 1sc into 1st sc on round 4, [ch7, 1sc into next sc on Round 4] 7 times, ch7, slip st to 1st sc.

Round 7: Slip st into 1st ch-7 sp, ch1, [1sc, 7hdc, 1sc] into each ch-7 sp to end, slip st to 1st sc.

Round 8: Ch1, working behind each petal, 1sc into 1st sc on round 6, *[ch9, slip st into 6th ch from hook (1 picot made)] twice, ch4, 1sc into next sc on Round 6, [ch13, slip st into 6th ch from hook (1 picot made)] twice, ch8, 1sc into same sc as last sc, [ch9, slip st into 6th ch from hook] twice, ch4, 1sc into next sc on round 6; rep from * 3 more times omitting 1sc at end of last rep, slip st to 1st sc.

Round 9: Slip st into each of 1st 3 ch, behind 1st picot and into next ch of sp between picots, ch1, 1sc into same sp as slip st, **[ch10, slip st into 6th ch from hook] twice, ch5, 1sc into corner loop between 2 picots, *[ch10, slip st into 6th ch from hook] twice, ch5, 1sc into sp between 2 picots; rep from * once more; rep from ** 3 more times omitting 1sc at end of last rep, slip st to 1st sc.

Round 10: Slip st into each of 1st 4 ch, behind 1st picot and into next ch-2 of sp between 2 picots, ch1, 1sc into same sp between 2 picots, **[ch10, slip st into 6th ch from hook] twice, ch5, 1sc into next sc at top of loop, *[ch10, slip st into 6th ch from hook] twice, ch5, 1sc into next sp between 2 picots; rep from * twice more; rep from ** 3 more times omitting 1sc at end of last rep, slip st to 1st sc.

Fasten off.

Sylvan circles

Base ring: Ch8, join with slip st.

Round 1: Ch3 (count as 1dc), 31dc into ring, slip st to top of ch-3. (32 sts)

Round 2: Ch3, 1dc into same place as ch-3 (count as dc2tog), ch3, dc2tog into same place as last dc2tog, *ch7, skip 3 sts, [dc2tog, ch3, dc2tog] into next st; rep from * 6 more times, ch7, skip 3 sts, slip st to top of 1st dc2tog.

Round 3: Slip st into next ch-3 sp, ch3, 1dc into same place as ch-3 (count as dc2tog), ch3, dc2tog into same ch-3 sp, *ch7, skip 7 ch, [dc2tog, ch3, dc2tog] into next ch-3 sp; rep from * 6 more times, ch7, skip 7 ch, slip st to top of 1st dc2tog.

Round 4: Slip st into next ch-3 sp, ch3, 1dc into same place as ch-3 (count as dc2tog), ch3, dc2tog into same ch-3 sp, *ch4, 1sc under ch-7 sp of 2nd round to enclose ch-7 sp of 3rd round, ch4**, [dc2tog, ch3, dc2tog] into next ch-3 sp; rep from * 6 more times and from * to ** again, slip st to top of 1st dc2tog.

Round 5: Slip st into next ch-3 sp, ch3, 1dc into same place as ch-3 (count as dc2tog), ch3, dc2tog into same ch-3 sp, *ch15, slip st into 12th ch from hook, ch3, slip st to top of previous dc2tog, 6dc into ch-12 ring, skip 4 ch, slip st to next sc, 8dc into ring, skip 4 ch, (inner half of Sylvan Circle completed)**, [dc2tog, ch3, dc2tog] into next ch-3 sp; rep from * 6 more times and from * to ** again, slip st to top of 1st dc2tog.

Round 6: *Ch1, [dc2tog, ch6, sl st to 5th ch from hook, ch1, dc2tog] into next ch-3 sp, ch1, slip st to top of next dc2tog, 16dc into ch-12 ring (outer half of Sylvan circle completed), slip st to top of next dc2tog; rep from * 7 more times.

Fasten off.

Briar rose

Base ring: Using A, ch3, join with slip st.

Round 1: Ch5 (count as 1dc, ch2), [1dc into ring, ch2] 7 times, slip st to 3rd of ch-5. Fasten off. (8 sps)

Round 2: Join B into a sp, ch8, slip st into 4th ch from hook, work a picot of [ch5, slip st into 4th ch from hook], ch1, *1dc into next sp, work a picot twice, ch1; rep from * 6 more times, slip st to 3rd of ch-4 at beg of round. Fasten off.

Round 3: Join C into ch-1 between 2 picots, ch1, 1sc into same place as ch-1, *ch7, skip [1 picot, 1dc and 1 picot], 1sc into next ch between picots; rep from * 7 more times omitting sc at end of last rep, slip st to 1st sc.

Round 4: Slip st into next ch, ch1, *[1sc, 1hdc, 9dc, 1hdc, 1sc] into next sp; rep from * 7 more times, slip st into 1st sc. Fasten off.

Granny square

Base ring: Ch4, join with slip st.

Round 1: Ch3 (count as 1dc), 2dc into ring, *ch1, 3dc into ring; rep from * twice more, ch1, slip st into top of ch-3.

Round 2: Slip st into each of next 2 dc and next ch-1 sp, ch3, 4dc into same sp for a corner, *1dc into center of next 3 dc group, 5dc into next ch-1 sp for a corner; rep from * twice more, 1dc into center of next 3dc group, slip st to top of ch-3. Fasten off.

Round 3: Join into center of any corner group, ch3, 5dc into same place for corner, *3dc into next dc, 6dc into center of next corner group; rep from * twice, 3dc into next dc, slip st to top of ch-3. Fasten off.

Round 4: Join into center sp of any corner group, ch3, 5dc into same place for corner, *1dc into last dc of same corner group, 1dc into center of next 3dc group, 1dc into 1st dc of next corner group**, 6dc into center sp of same corner group; rep from * twice more, then from * to ** again, slip st to top of ch-3. Fasten off.

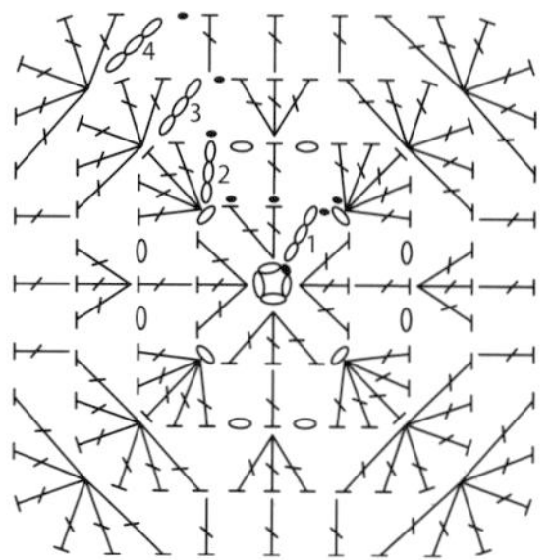

Springtime

Base ring: Ch5, join with slip st.

Round 1: Ch1, 10sc into ring, slip st into 1st sc.

Round 2: Ch1, 1sc into each sc, slip st to 1st sc.

Round 3: Ch2 (count as 1hdc), skip 1st sc, 2hdc into each of next 9 sc, 1hdc into 1st sc, slip st into 2nd of ch-2.

Round 4: *Ch2, working into front loop only of each hdc, 2dc into each of next 3 hdc, ch2, slip st into next hdc; rep from * 4 times more placing last slip st into 2nd of ch-2 at beg of previous round. (5 petals made)

Round 5: Working behind each petal of previous round and into back loop of each hdc on round 3, slip st into 1st 2 hdc, *ch4, 2dtr into each of next 3 hdc, ch4, slip st into next hdc; rep from * 3 times more, ch4, 2dtr into next hdc, 2dtr into 2nd of ch-2 at beg of round 3, 2dtr into next hdc, ch4, slip st to next hdc. Fasten off.

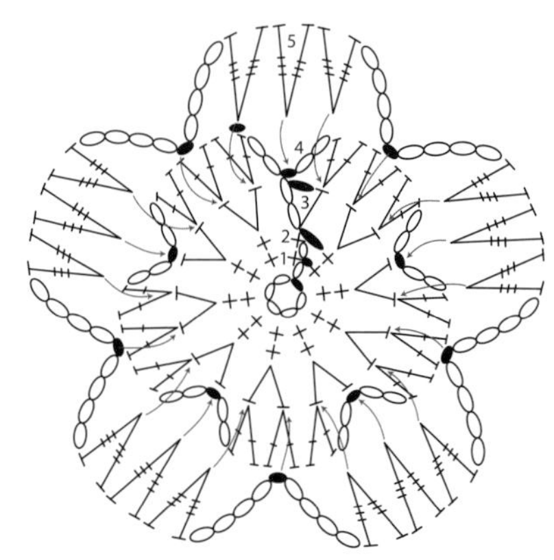

Gardenia bloom

Base ring: Ch5, join with slip st.
Round 1: Ch6 (count as 1dc, ch3), [1dc into ring, ch3] 5 times, slip st to 3rd of ch-6.
Round 2: Ch1, 1sc into slip st, *[1dc, ch1, 1dc, ch1, 1dc] into next ch-3 sp, 1sc into next dc; rep from * 5 more times omitting sc at end of last rep, slip st to 1st sc.
Round 3: Ch1, 1sc into 1st sc, *ch1, skip 1 dc, [1dc, ch1] 5 times into next dc, skip 1 dc, 1sc into next sc; rep from * 5 more times omitting sc at end of last rep, slip st to 1st sc. Fasten off.

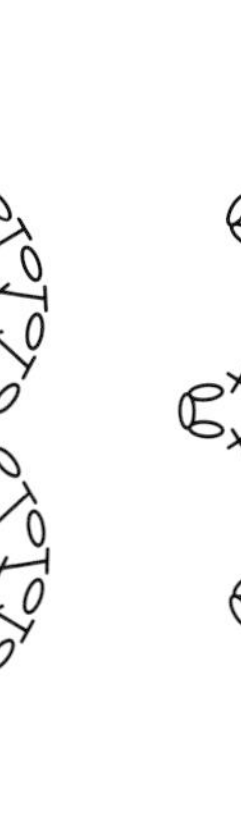

Granite wheel

Special abbreviation:
Puff st = see page 24, work 3hdc leaving last loop on hook, yo and draw through all loops on hook.
Base ring: Ch7, join with slip st.
Round 1: Ch1, 12sc into ring, slip st to 1st sc. (12 sts)
Round 2: Ch3 (count as 1dc), 1dc into next sc, *ch3, 1dc into each of next 2 sts; rep from * 4 more times, ch3, slip st to top of ch-3.
Round 3: Slip st into next dc and next ch, ch3, hdc2tog into same sp (counts as puff st), ch4, puff st into same sp, *ch4, [puff st, ch4, puff st] into next sp; rep from * 4 more times, ch4, slip st to top of 1st puff st. (12 puff sts)
Round 4: Ch1, *[2sc, ch3, 2sc] into next sp; rep from * 11 more times, slip st to 1st sc. Fasten off.

Mayfair square

Special abbreviation:
Bobble = work 4dc into same sp leaving last loop of each dc on hook, yo and draw through all 5 loops on hook.
Base ring: Ch8, join with slip st.
Round 1: Ch3, 3dc into ring (hold back last loop of each dc, yo and draw through all 4 loops on hook), *ch4, bobble into ring; rep from * twice more, ch4, slip st to top of 1st bobble.
Round 2: Slip st into next ch-4 sp, ch3 (count as 1dc), [2dc, ch3, 3dc] into same sp, *1dc into top of next bobble, [3dc, ch3, 3dc] into next ch-4 sp; rep from * twice more, 1dc into top of next bobble, slip st to top of ch-3.
Round 3: Ch3, 1dc into each of next 2 dc, [2dc, ch3, 2dc] into next ch-3 sp, *1dc into each of next 7 dc, [2dc, ch3, 2dc] into next ch-3 sp; rep from * twice more, 1dc into each of next 4 dc, slip st to top of ch-3.

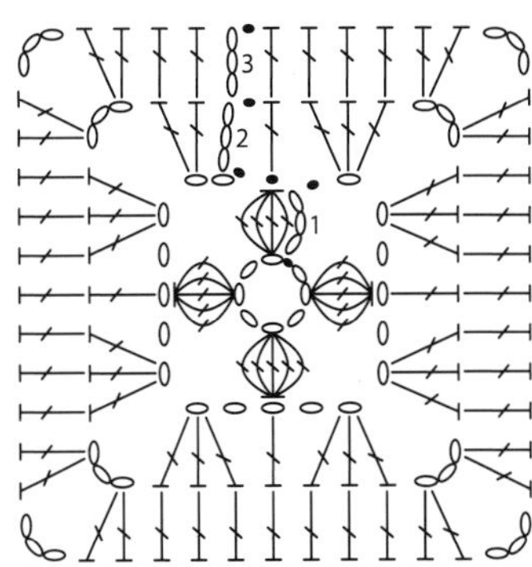

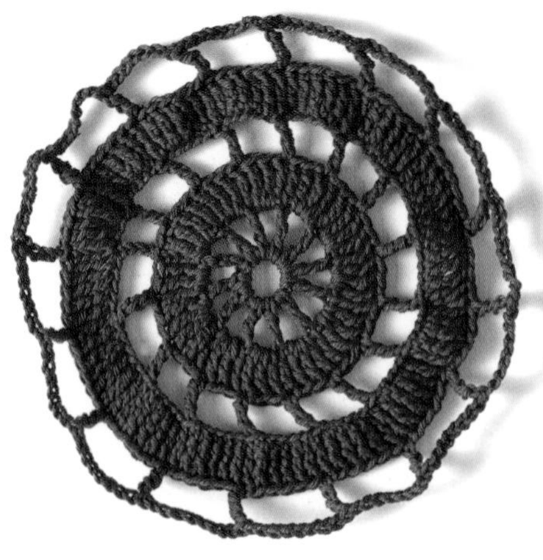

Ring web

Base ring: Ch10, join with slip st.

Round 1: Ch6 (count as 1tr, ch2), [1tr into ring, ch2] 11 times, slip st to 4th of ch-6.

Round 2: Ch4, 3tr into next sp, [1tr into next tr, 3tr into next sp] 11 times, slip st to top of ch-4.

Round 3: Ch9, skip next 2 tr, [1tr into next tr, ch5, skip next 2 tr] 15 times, slip st to 4th of ch-9.

Round 4: Ch4, 1tr into each of next 5 ch, [1tr into next tr, 1tr into each of next 5 ch] 15 times, slip st to top of ch-4.

Round 5: Ch12 (count as 1tr, ch8), [skip next 5 tr, 1tr into next tr, ch8] 15 times, skip next 5 tr, slip st to 4th of ch-12. Fasten off.

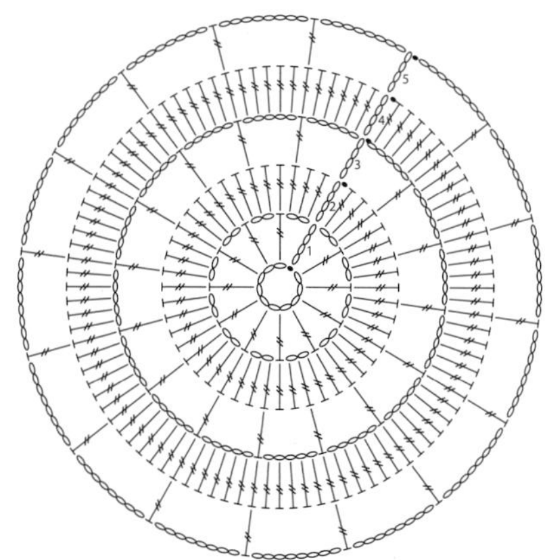

Barnacle motif

Base ring: Ch8, join with slip st.

Round 1: Ch1, [1sc into ring, ch3, 1tr into ring, ch3] 8 times, slip st to 1st sc.

Round 2: Slip st into each of next 3 ch and into tr, [ch12, 1dc into 9th ch from hook, ch3, slip st to top of next tr] 8 times.

Round 3: Slip st into each of next 4 ch, ch3 (count as 1dc), *[1hdc, 7sc, 1hdc] into next ch-8 sp, 1dc into next dc, skip last ch-3 of same segment and 1st ch-3 of next segment**, 1dc into next ch, (i.e. opposite side of same ch as dc of round 2); rep from * 6 more times and from * to ** again, slip st to top of ch-3.

Round 4: Ch1, 1sc inserting hook under slip st which joined round 3, *ch3, skip [1hdc and 1sc], 1sc into next sc, ch3, skip 1 sc, [1sc, ch4, 1sc] into next sc, ch3, skip 1 sc, 1sc into next sc, ch3, skip [1sc, 1hdc and 1dc]**, 1sc between 2 dc, skip 1 dc; rep from * 6 more times and from * to ** again, slip st to 1st sc. Fasten off.

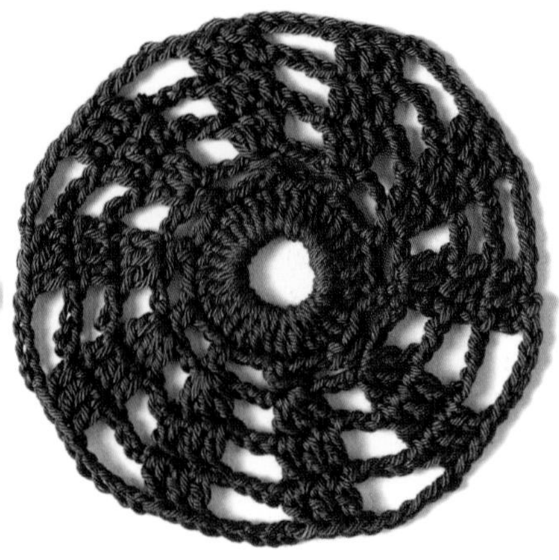

Geometric circle

Base ring: Ch10, join with slip st.

Round 1: Ch3 (count as 1dc), 29dc into ring, slip st to top of ch-3. (30dc)

Round 2: Ch6 (count as 1dc, ch3), skip next 2 dc, [1dc into next dc, ch3, skip next 2 dc] 9 times, slip st to 3rd of ch-5.

Round 3: Ch3 (count as 1dc), 2dc into same place as last slip st, ch3, [3dc into next dc, ch3] 9 times, slip st to top of ch-3.

Round 4: Ch3 (count as 1dc), 1dc into each of next 2 dc, ch4, [1dc into each of next 3 dc, ch4] 9 times, slip st to top of ch-3.

Round 5: Ch3 (count as 1dc), 1dc into each of next 2 dc, ch5, [1dc into each of next 3 dc, ch5] 9 times, slip st to top of ch-3. Fasten off.

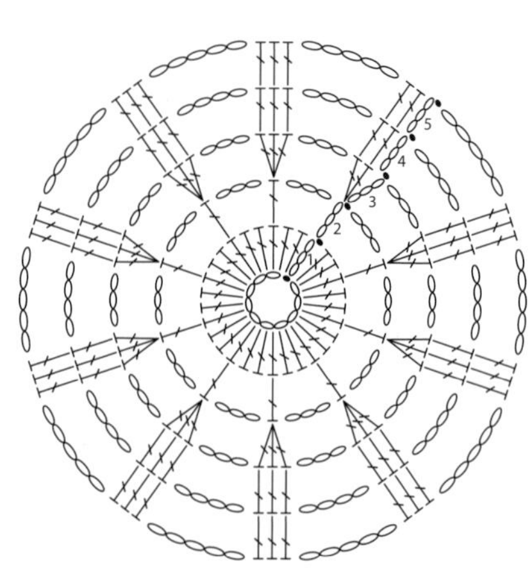

Spiral hexagon

Base ring: Ch5, join with slip st.
Round 1: [Ch6, 1sc into ring] 6 times, slip st into 1st 3 ch of 1st sp.
Round 2: [Ch4, 1sc into next ch-6 sp] 6 times, working last sc into slip st before the 1st ch-4 sp.
Round 3: [Ch4, 2sc into next ch-4 sp, 1sc into next sc] 6 times, working last sc into last sc at end of last round.
Round 4: *Ch4, 2sc into next ch-4 sp, 1sc into each of next 2 sc; rep from * to end.
Round 5: *Ch4, 2sc into next ch-4 sp, 1sc into each of next 3 sc; rep from * to end.
Continue in this way, working 1 more sc in each group on each round until motif is the required size, ending with a slip st into next sc. Fasten off.

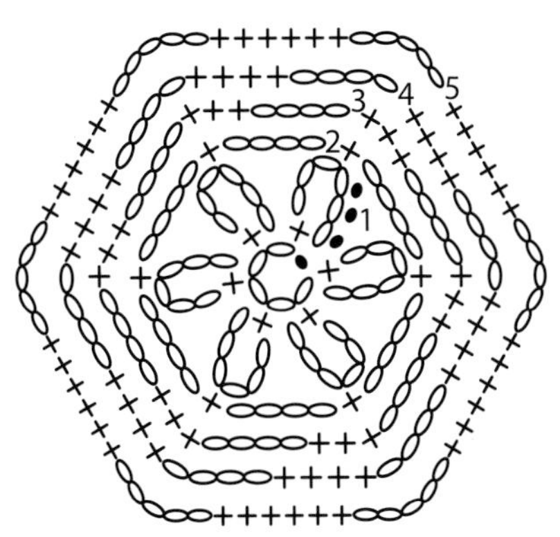

Popcorn wheel square

Special abbreviation:
Popcorn = see page 23.
Round 1: Ch3, 4dc popcorn into ring (counts as 5dc popcorn), [ch3, 5dc popcorn into ring] 7 times, ch3, slip st to 1st popcorn.
Round 2: Ch3 (count as 1dc), 2dc into next ch-3 sp, [9dc into next sp, 2dc into next sp] 3 times, 8dc into last sp, slip st to top of ch-3.
Round 3: Ch1, 1sc into same place as ch-1, 1sc into each of next 2 sts, *into next 9dc group work 1sc into each of 1st 3 dc, skip 1 dc, [1hdc, 4dc, 1hdc] into next dc, skip 1 dc, **1sc into each of last 3 dc, 1sc into each of next 2 sts; rep from * twice more and from * to ** again, 1sc into each of last 2 dc, slip st to 1st sc. Fasten off.

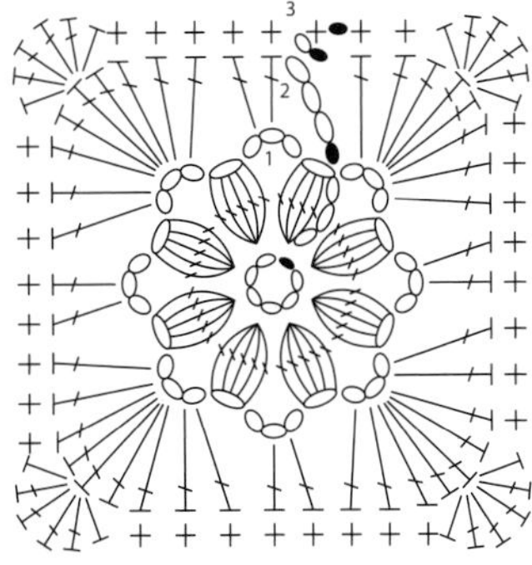

popcorn

Hydrangea

Special abbreviation:
Bobble = tr4tog.
Base ring: Ch7, join with slip st.
Round 1: Ch3 (count as 1dc), 13dc into ring, slip st to top of ch-3. (14dc)
Round 2: Ch9 (count as 1tr, ch5), 1tr into next dc, [ch5, 1tr into next dc] 12 times, ch5, slip st to 4th of ch-9.
Round 3: Ch4, hold back last loop of each tr, 3tr into 1st sp, yo and draw through all 4 sps on hook (count as 1st bobble), [ch5, bobble into next ch-5 sp] 13 times, ch5, slip st to top of 1st bobble.
Round 4: Slip st into next ch-5 sp, ch3 (count as 1dc), 2dc into same sp, [ch5, 3dc into next ch-5 sp] 13 times, slip st to top of ch-3. Fasten off.

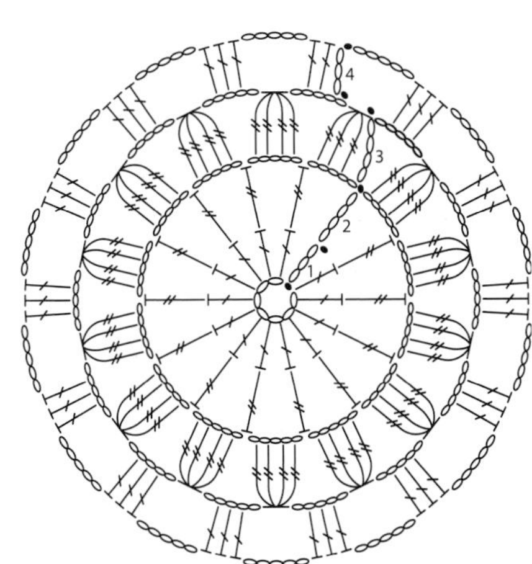

Cross panel

Special abbreviations:

4dc cluster = 1dc into each of next 4dc until 1 loop of each remains on hook, yo and through all 5 loops on hook.

4dc bobble or 5dc bobble = 4dc (or 5dc) into next ch until 1 loop of each remains on hook, yo and through all 5 (or 6) loops on hook.

Base ring: Ch6, join with slip st.

Round 1: Ch3 (count as 1dc), 15dc into ring, slip st to top of ch-3.

Round 2: Ch3, 1dc into each of next 3 dc, [ch7, 1dc into each of next 4 dc] 3 times, ch7, slip st to top of ch-3.

Round 3: Ch3, 1dc into each of next 3 dc until 1 loop of each remains on hook, yo and through all 4 loops on hook (1 cluster made at beg of round), ch5, skip 3 ch, [1dc, ch5, 1dc] into next ch, ch5, *4dc cluster over next 4 dc, ch5, skip 3 ch, [1dc, ch5, 1dc] into next ch, ch5; rep from * twice more, slip st into top of 1st cluster.

Round 4: Ch1, *1sc into top of cluster, 1sc into each of next 5 ch, 1sc into next dc, ch2, 4dc bobble into next ch, ch5, skip 1 ch, 5dc bobble into next ch, ch5, skip 1 ch, 4dc bobble into next ch, ch2, 1sc into next dc, 1sc into each of next 5 ch; rep from * 3 times more, slip st to 1st sc. Fasten off.

Crystal hexagon

Base ring: Ch6, join with slip st.

Round 1: Ch5 (count as 1dc, ch2), [1dc into ring, ch2] 5 times, slip st to 3rd of ch-5.

Round 2: Ch4, 2tr in same place as slip st, *ch2, 1tr into next sp, ch3, slip st into last tr, ch2**, 3tr into next tr; rep from * 4 more times, then from * to ** again, slip st to top of ch4. Work in back loop only of each tr from now on.

Round 3: Ch4, 1tr into same place as slip st, *1tr into next tr, 2tr in next tr, ch7**, 2tr in 1st tr of next 3 tr group; rep from * 4 more times, then from * to ** again, slip st to top of ch-4.

Round 4: Ch4, 1tr into same place as slip st, *1tr into each of next 3 tr, 2tr into next tr, ch4, skip 1st 3 ch of next ch-7, 1sc into next ch, ch3, 1sc into same sp, ch4**, 2tr into next tr; rep from * 4 more times, then from * to ** again, slip st to top of ch-4. Fasten off.

Galaxy motif

Special abbreviations:

Puff st = see page 24, work 5hdc leaving last loop of each st on hook, yo and draw through all loops on hook.

Cluster = see page 22, work 3dc over sts indicated leaving last loop on hook, yo and draw through all loops on hook.

Base ring: Ch6, join with slip st.

Round 1: Ch6 (count as 1tr, ch2), [1tr into ring, ch2] 7 times, slip st to 4th of ch-6. (8 sps)

Round 2: Ch2, hdc4tog into next sp (counts as puff st), [ch7, puff st into next sp] 7 times, ch7, slip st to top of 1st puff st.

Round 3: Slip st into each of next 3 ch, ch1, 3sc into same sp, [ch9, 3sc into next sp] 7 times, ch8, 1sc into 1st sc.

Round 4: Ch3, dc2tog over next 1sc and next ch skipping sc between (counts as cluster), *ch2, skip 1 ch, 1dc into next ch, ch2, skip 1 ch, [1dc, ch3, 1dc] into next ch, ch2, skip 1 ch, 1dc into next ch, ch2, skip 1 ch**, cluster over [next ch, 2nd of next 3 sc and next ch]; rep from * 6 more times and from * to ** again, slip st to top of 1st cluster. Fasten off.

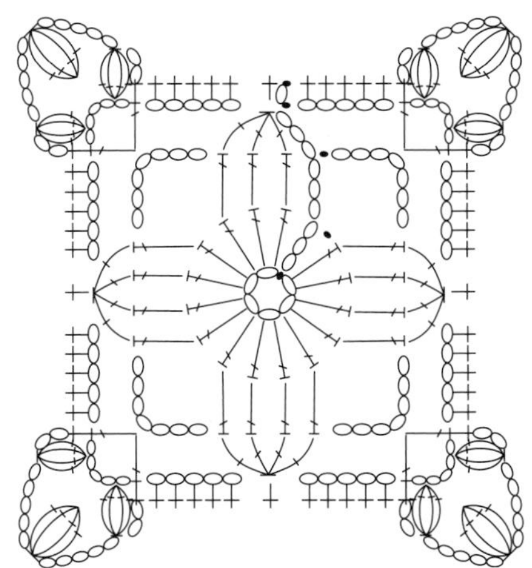

4dc cluster

4dc bobble

5dc bobble

Cross panel

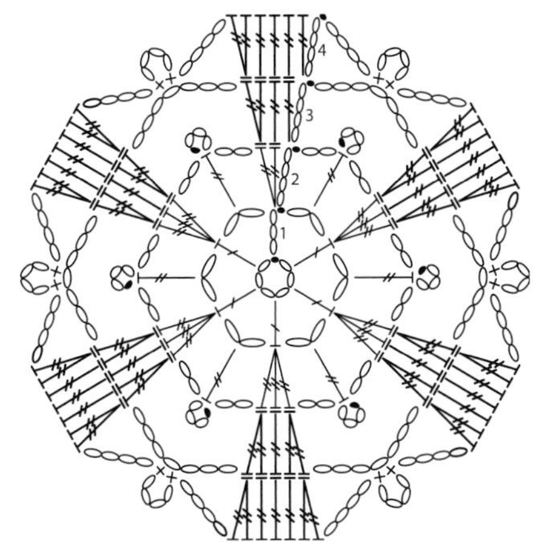

Crystal hexagon

Galaxy motif

Flemish motif

Base ring: Ch8, join with slip st.

Round 1: Ch1, 16sc into ring, slip st to 1st sc. (16 sts)

Round 2: Ch12 (count as 1tr, ch8), skip 1st 2 sc, [1tr into next sc, ch8, skip 1 sc] 7 times, slip st to 4th of ch-12.

Round 3: Ch1, *[1sc, 1hdc, 1dc, 3tr, ch4, insert hook down through top of tr just made and work a slip st to close, 2tr, 1dc, 1hdc, 1sc] into next ch-8 sp; rep from * 7 more times, slip st to 1st sc. Fasten off.

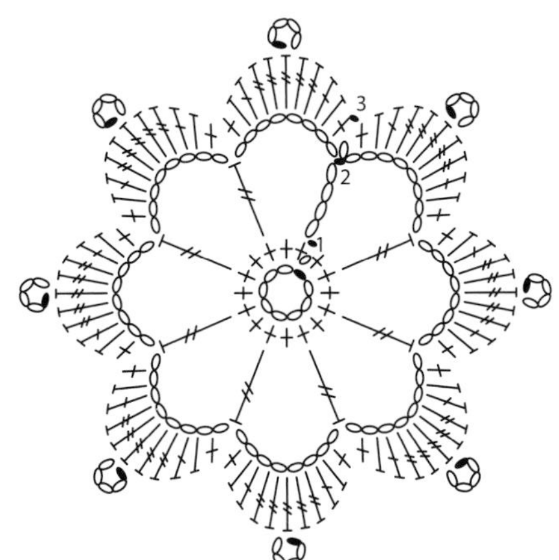

Boat steer

Base ring: Ch4, join with slip st.

Round 1: Ch1, 10sc into ring, slip st to 1st sc.

Round 2: Ch1, 1sc into same place as last slip st, [ch4, skip 1 sc, 1sc into next sc] 4 times, ch4, skip 1 sc, slip st to 1st sc.

Round 3: [Slip st into next ch-4 sp, 5sc into same loop] 5 times, slip st to 1st slip st.

Fasten off.

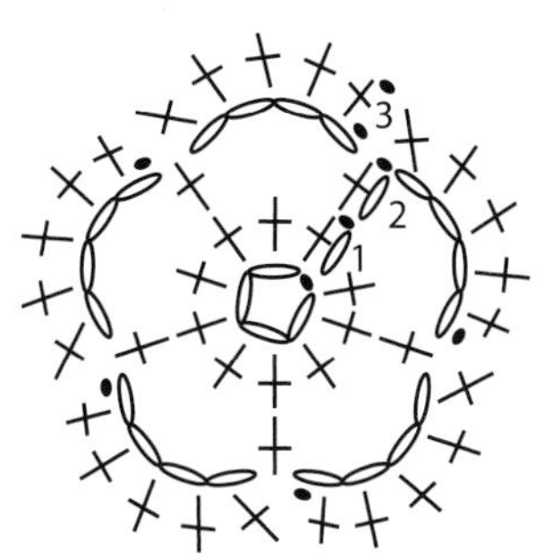

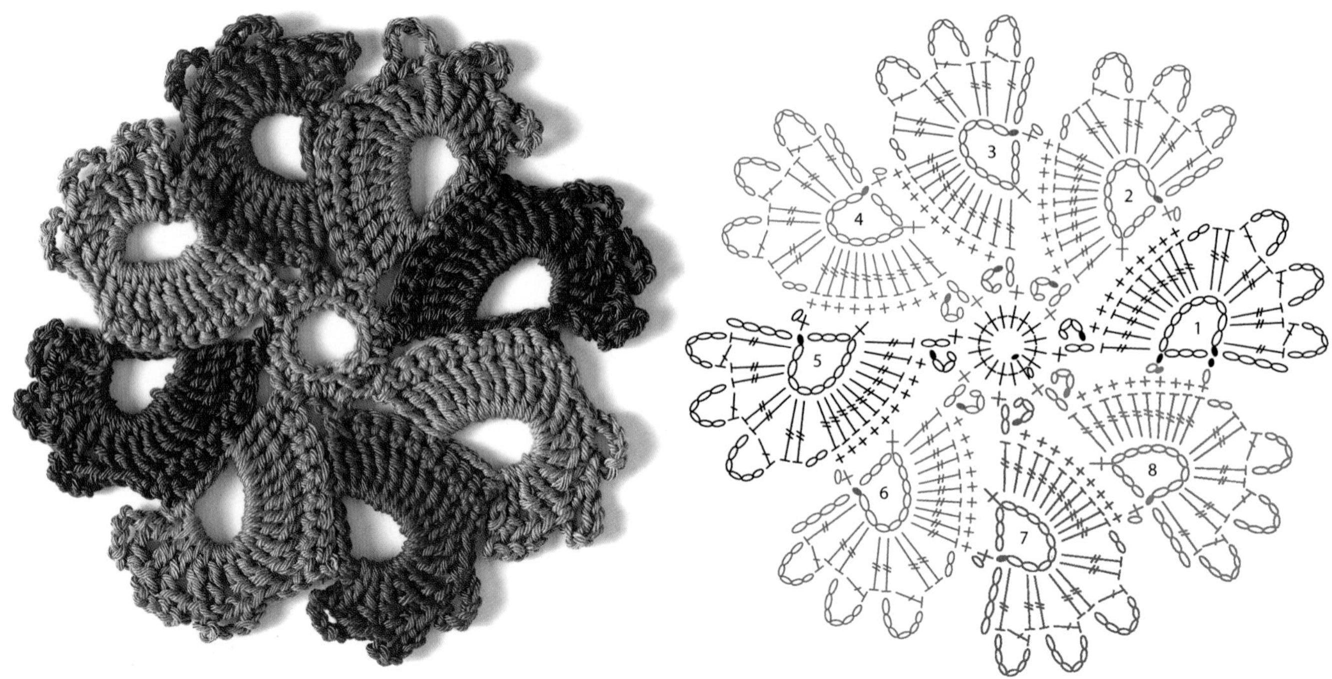

Amanda whorl

Segment 1

Base ring: Using A, ch12, join with slip st.

Row 1 (RS): Ch4 (count as 1tr), [1tr into ring, ch6, 1dc into top of tr just made, 1tr into ring] 3 times, 1tr into ring, ch2, 10tr into ring, turn.

Row 2: Work a picot of [ch5, slip st to 5th ch from hook], *skip 1st tr, 1sc into each of next 9 tr, change to next color, turn.

Segment 2

Ch1, 1sc into same place as ch-1, ch3, skip 3 sc, 1sc into next sc, 9ch, slip st to 1st sc to complete joined base ring.

Row 1: As given for Segment 1.

Row 2: Ch2, 1sc into picot of previous Segment, ch3, slip st to 1st ch of row to complete picot, continue as for Segment 1 from *.

Work 5 more Segments as Segment 2 using C, D, A, B and C.

Segment 8

Using D, work as for previous Segments, except also join to Segment 1 during row 2 as follows: ch2, 1sc into picot of Segment 7, ch1, 1sc into picot of Segment 1, ch2, slip st to 1st ch of row to complete picot, skip 1st tr, 1sc into each of next 5 tr, slip st to Segment 1, 1sc into each of next 4 tr, slip st to Segment 1. Fasten off.

Center ring

Using A, work inward round center to make edging as follows: join into any sc, ch1, 1sc into same place as ch-1, [1sc into next picot, 1sc into side of next sc] 7 times, 1sc into next picot, slip st to 1st sc.

Fasten off.

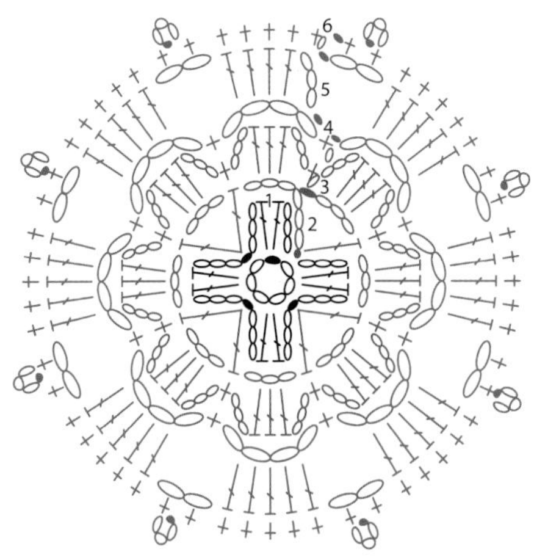

Celtic motif

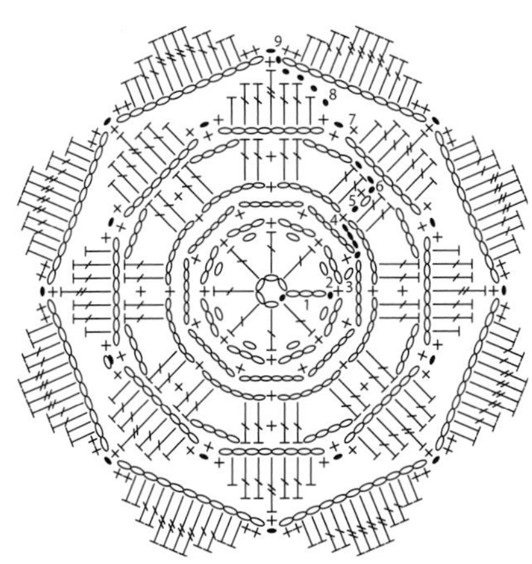

Astro waves

Celtic motif

Base ring: Using A, ch6, join with slip st.

Round 1: Work a Leaf of [ch3, 2dc into ring, ch3, slip st into ring] 4 times. Fasten off.

Round 2: Join B into same place, ch6 (count as 1dc, ch3), skip next Leaf, *[1dc, ch3, 1dc] into slip st, ch3, skip next Leaf; rep from * twice more, 1dc into next slip st, ch3, slip st to 3rd of ch-6.

Round 3: Ch1, 1sc into same place as ch-1, *work a Leaf of [ch3, 3dc into next ch-3 sp, ch3, 1sc into next dc]; rep from * 7 more times omitting sc at end of last rep, slip st to 1st sc. Fasten off.

Round 4: Join C into same place, ch1, 1sc into same place as ch-1, *ch4, skip next Leaf, 1sc into next sc; rep from * 7 more times omitting sc at end of last rep, slip st to 1st sc.

Round 5: Ch3 (count as 1dc), 4dc into next ch-4 sp, [ch2, 5dc into next sp] 7 times, ch2, slip st to top of ch-3.

Round 6: Ch1, 1sc into same place as ch-1, 1sc into each of next 4 dc, *[1sc, ch3, insert hook down through top of sc just made and work slip st to close, 1sc] into next ch-2 sp**, 1sc into each of next 5 dc; rep from * 6 more times and from * to ** again, slip st to 1st sc.
Fasten off.

Astro waves

Base ring: Ch5, join with slip st.

Round 1: Ch4, [1dc into ring, ch1] 7 times, slip st to 3rd of ch-4.

Round 2: [Ch3, 1sc into next dc] 8 times, working last sc into 1st of 1st ch-3. (8 ch-3 loops).

Round 3: Ch1, [1sc into next ch-3 sp, ch6] 8 times, slip st to 1st sc. (8 ch-6 sps)

Round 4: Slip st into each of 1st 3 ch of next ch-6 sp, 1sc into same ch-6 sp, ch6, [1sc into next ch-6 sp] 7 times, slip st to 1st sc.

Round 5: Ch1, 1sc into same place, *[2dc, ch4, 2dc] into next ch-6 sp, 1sc into next sc; rep from * 6 more times, [2dc, ch4, 2dc] into next ch-6 sp, slip st to 1st sc.

Round 6: Slip st into each of 1st 2 dc, [1sc into next ch-4 sp, ch8] 8 times, slip st to 1st sc.

Round 7: *[1sc, 1hdc, 2dc, 1tr, 2dc, 1hdc, 1sc] into next ch-8 sp, slip st into next sc; rep from * 7 more times, working last slip st into 1st sc.

Round 8: Slip st into each of 1st sc, hdc, 2dc and tr, 1sc in same tr, ch11, [1sc in next tr, ch11] 7 times, slip st to 1st sc.

Round 9: *[2sc, 2hdc, 2dc, 4tr, 2dc, 2hdc, 2sc] into next ch-11 loop, slip st into next sc; rep from * 7 more times, working last slip st into 1st sc. Fasten off.

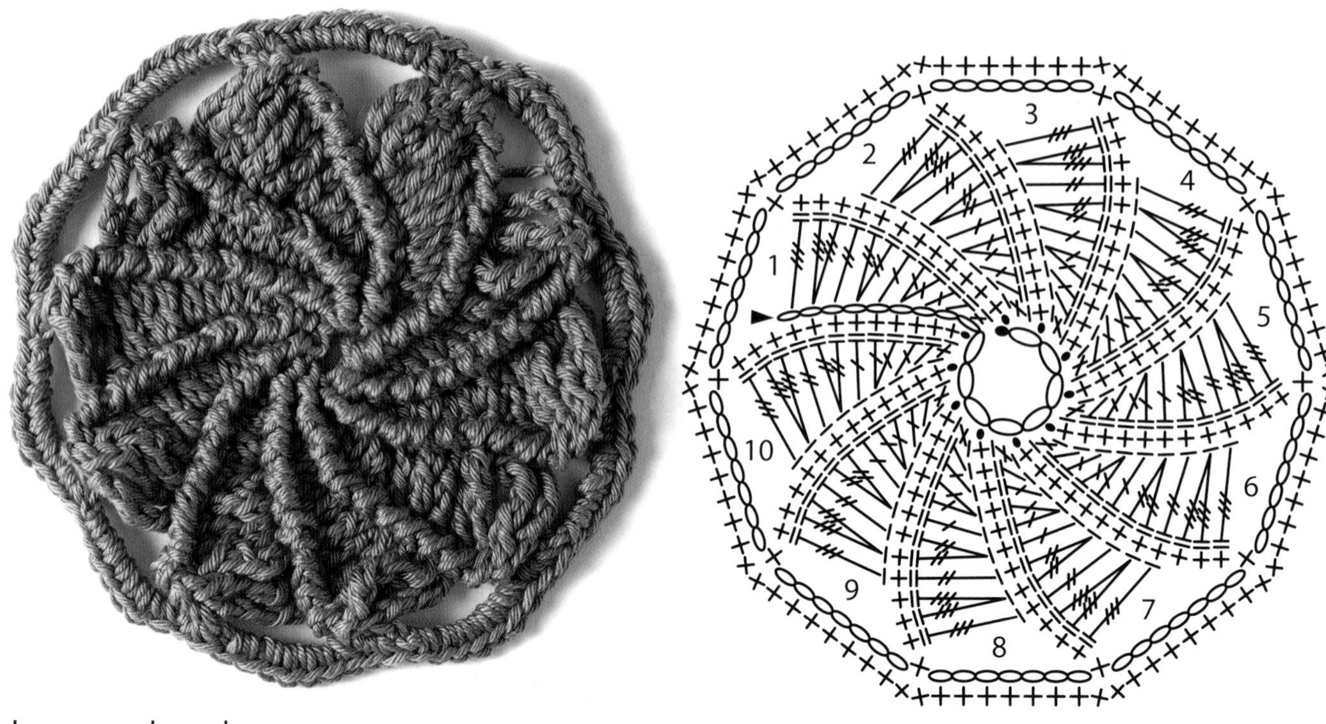

Lazy wheel

Special abbreviation:

Corded sc = working from left to right, insert hook into each stitch and complete as for sc.

Segment 1

Ch17, slip st into 8th ch from hook.

Row 1: 1sc into next ch, 1hdc into next ch, 1dc into next ch, 2dc into next ch, 1dc into next ch, 2tr into next ch, 1tr into next ch, 2dtr into next ch, 1dtr into last ch, ch1. Do not turn.

Row 2: Work corded sc back from left to right inserting hook under front loop only of each st, ending slip st into ring.

Segment 2

Row 1: Working behind corded sc row into back loop only of row 1 of previous Segment, 1sc into 1st st, 1hdc into next st, 1dc into next st, 2dc into next st, 1dc into next st, 2tr into next st, 1tr into next st, 2dtr into next st, 1dtr into next st, ch1. Do not turn.

Row 2: Complete as for Segment 1.

Segments 3–10

Work as given for Segment 2.

Fasten off, leaving enough yarn to sew Segment 10 to Segment 1 on WS.

Edging

Row 1 (RS): Rejoin yarn at tip of any Segment in corded edge row, ch1, 1sc into same place as ch-1, [ch7, 1sc into tip of next Segment] 9 times, ch7, slip st to 1st sc.

Row 2: Ch1, 2sc into same place as ch-1, *7sc into next sp**, 2sc into next sc; rep from * 8 more times and from * to ** again, slip st to 1st sc.

Fasten off.

Tea rose

Base ring: Ch8, join with slip st.

Round 1: Ch1, 16sc into ring, slip st into 1st sc.

Round 2: Ch5 (count as 1dc, ch2), skip next sc, [1dc into next sc, ch2, skip 1sc] 7 times, slip st into 3rd of ch-5.

Round 3: Slip st into next ch-2 sp, ch1, [1sc, 1hdc, 1dc, 1hdc, 1sc] into each of the 8 ch-2 sps, slip st to 1st sc. (8 petals)

Round 4: Working behind each petal, slip st into base of each of next 2 sts, ch1, 1sc into base of same dc as last slip st, [ch3, skip 4 sts, 1sc into base of next dc] 7 times, ch3, slip st into 1st sc.

Round 5: Slip st into next ch-3 sp, ch1, [1sc, 1hdc, 3dc, 1hdc, 1sc] into each of the 8 ch-3 sps, slip st to 1st sc.

Round 6: Working behind each petal, slip st into base of each of next 3 sts, ch1, 1sc into base of same dc as last slip st, [ch5, skip 6 sts, 1sc into base of next dc] 7 times, ch5, slip st to 1st sc.

Round 7: Slip st into next ch-5 sp, ch1, [1sc, 1hdc, 5dc, 1hdc, 1sc] into each of the 8 ch-5 sps, slip st to 1st sc.

Round 8: Working behind each petal, slip st into base of each of next 4 sts, ch1, 1sc into base of same dc as last slip st, [ch7, skip 8 sts, 1sc into base of next dc] 7 times, ch7, slip st to 1st sc.

Round 9: Slip st into next ch-7 sp, ch1, [1sc, 1hdc, 7dc, 1hdc, 1sc] into each of the 8 ch-7 sps, slip st to 1st sc.

Round 10: Working behind each petal, slip st into base of each of next 5 sts, ch1, 1sc into base of same dc as last slip st, [ch9, skip 10 sts, 1sc into base of next dc] 7 times, ch9, slip st to 1st sc.

Round 11: Slip st into next ch-9 sp, ch1, [1sc, 1hdc, 9dc, 1hdc, 1sc] into each of the 8 ch-9 sps, slip st to 1st sc.
Fasten off.

Celestial cluster

Base ring: Ch3, join with slip st.
Round 1: 10sc into ring, slip st to 1st sc.
Round 2: [Ch3, skip 1 sc, 1sc into next sc] 5 times, working last sc into base of 1st ch-3.
Round 3: *[1sc, 1hdc, 1dc, ch2, 1dc, 1hdc, 1sc, ch1] into each ch-3 sp around, slip st to 1st sc.
Round 4: Slip st into last ch-1 sp, ch4 (count as 1dc, ch1), *[3dc, ch2, 3dc] into next ch-2 sp, ch1**, 1dc into next ch-1 sp, ch1; rep from * 3 more times, then from * to ** again, slip st to 3rd of ch-4.
Round 5: Ch4 (count as 1dc, ch1), 1dc into same place, ch3, *[1sc, ch3, 1sc] into next ch-2 sp, ch3, skip next 3 dc and ch-1 sp**, [1dc, ch1, 1dc] into next dc, ch3; rep from * 3 more times, then from * to ** again, slip st to 3rd of ch-4.
Fasten off.

Window pane

Base chain: Ch8, join with slip st.
Round 1: Ch1, 12sc into ring, slip st to 1st sc.
Round 2: Ch7 (count as 1tr, ch3), 1tr into same sc as slip st, *ch10, skip 2 sc, [1tr, ch3, 1tr] into next sc; rep from * twice more, ch5, 1tr into 4th of ch-7.
Round 3: *3tr into next ch-3 sp, ch4, slip st into last tr (picot) [4tr, picot, 4tr, picot, 3tr] into same ch-3 sp, 1sc into next ch-10 sp; rep from * 3 times more working last sc into sp formed by last tr of previous round, slip st to 1st tr of round.
Fasten off.

Samosa motif

Note: On rounds 1 and 2, draw dc loops up to ½in (1.3cm).
Base ring: Ch6, join with slip st.
Round 1: Ch4 (count as 1dc, ch1), 1dc into ring, *[ch2, 1dc, ch1, 1dc] 5 times, ch2, slip st to 3rd of ch-4.
Round 2: *1sc into next sp, [1dc, ch1] twice into next sp, 1dc into same sp; rep from * 5 more times, slip st to 1st sc.
Round 3: Ch4 (count as 1dc, ch1), *[1sc into next ch-1 sp, ch1] twice, (1 long dc drawing loop up to 1in (2.5cm), ch1, 1 long dc, ch5, 1 long dc, ch1, 1 long dc) into next sc for a corner group, [ch1, 1sc into next ch-1 sp] twice, ch1**, 1dc into next sc, ch1; rep from * once more, then from * to ** again, slip st to 3rd of ch-4.
Fasten off.

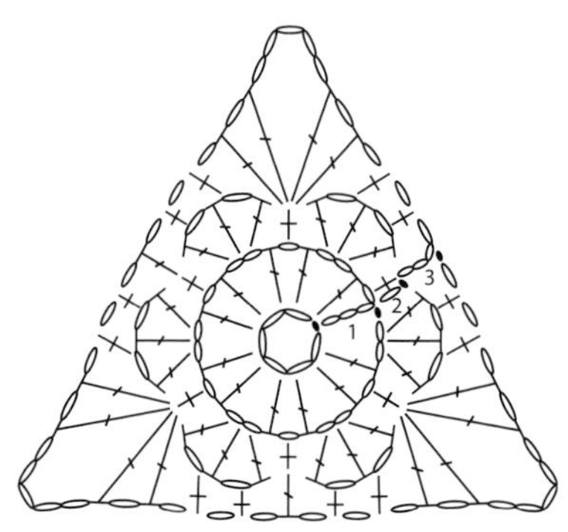

Tribal star

Base ring: Ch9, join with slip st.

Round 1: Ch3 (count as 1dc), 23dc into ring, slip st to top of ch-3.

Round 2: Ch10 (count as 1dc, ch8), 1sc into 4th ch from hook, 1dc into each of next 4 ch, skip 1 dc in ring, 1dc into next dc, *ch8, 1sc in 4th ch from hook, 1dc into each of next 4 ch, skip 1 dc in ring, 1dc into next dc; rep from * 9 more times, ch8, 1sc into 4th ch from hook, 1dc into each of next 4 ch, slip st to 3rd of ch-10. Fasten off.

Gemini

Base ring: Ch8, join with slip st.

Round 1: Ch4 (count as 1dc, ch1), [1dc, ch1] 11 times into ring, slip st to 3rd of ch-4. (12dc)

Round 2: Ch1, 1sc into 1st ch-1 sp, ch4, [skip 2 dc, 1sc into next ch-1 sp, ch4] 5 times, slip st to 1st sc. (6 ch-4 sps)

Round 3: Ch1, 1sc into same sc as last slip st, *ch1, [1 long dc drawing loop up to 1in (2.5cm), ch1] 4 times into next ch-4 sp, 1sc into next sc; rep from * 4 more times, ch1, [1 long dc, ch1] 4 times into next ch-4 sp, slip st to 1st sc.

Round 4: Ch5 (count as 1tr, ch1), 1tr into same place as last slip st, ch1, *skip 2 long dc, 1sc into next ch-1 sp, ch1, [1tr, ch1] 4 times into next sc; rep from * 5 more times, ending [1tr, ch1] twice into same place as last slip st of previous round, slip st to 4th of ch-5. Fasten off.

Bean cluster

Special abbreviation:

Puff = [yo, insert hook in sp indicated and pull up loop] twice, yo and draw through all 5 loops on hook.

Base ring: Ch5, join with slip st.

Round 1: Ch1, [puff into ring, ch1] 8 times, slip st to top of 1st puff.

Round 2: Ch1, *[puff, ch1] twice into next ch sp; rep from * 7 more times, slip st to top of 1st puff.

Round 3: Slip st into ch sp between 1st 2 puffs, ch3 (count as 1dc), 4dc into same ch sp, [skip next ch sp, 5dc into next ch sp] 7 times, slip st to top of ch-3. Fasten off.

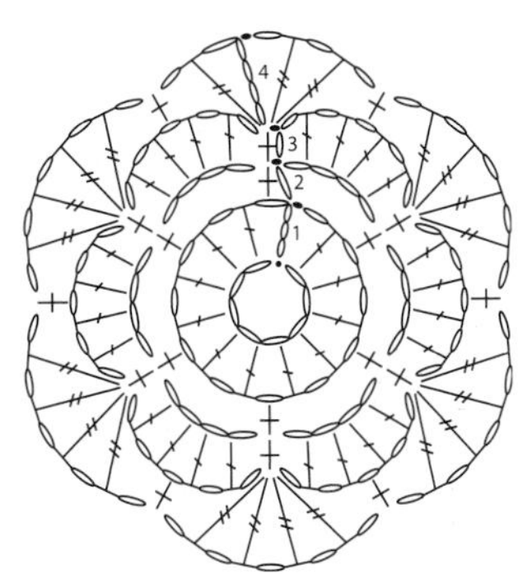

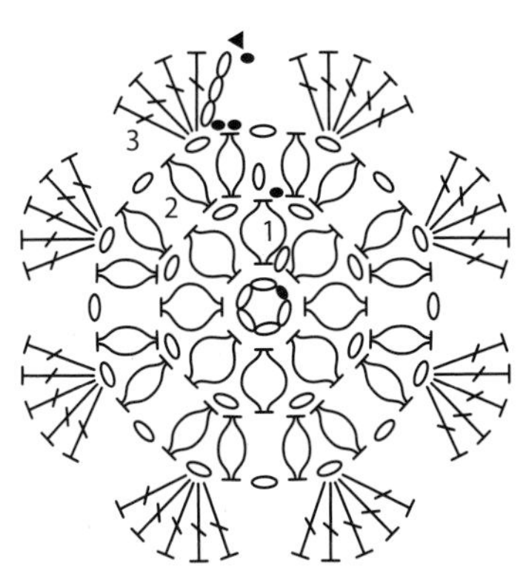

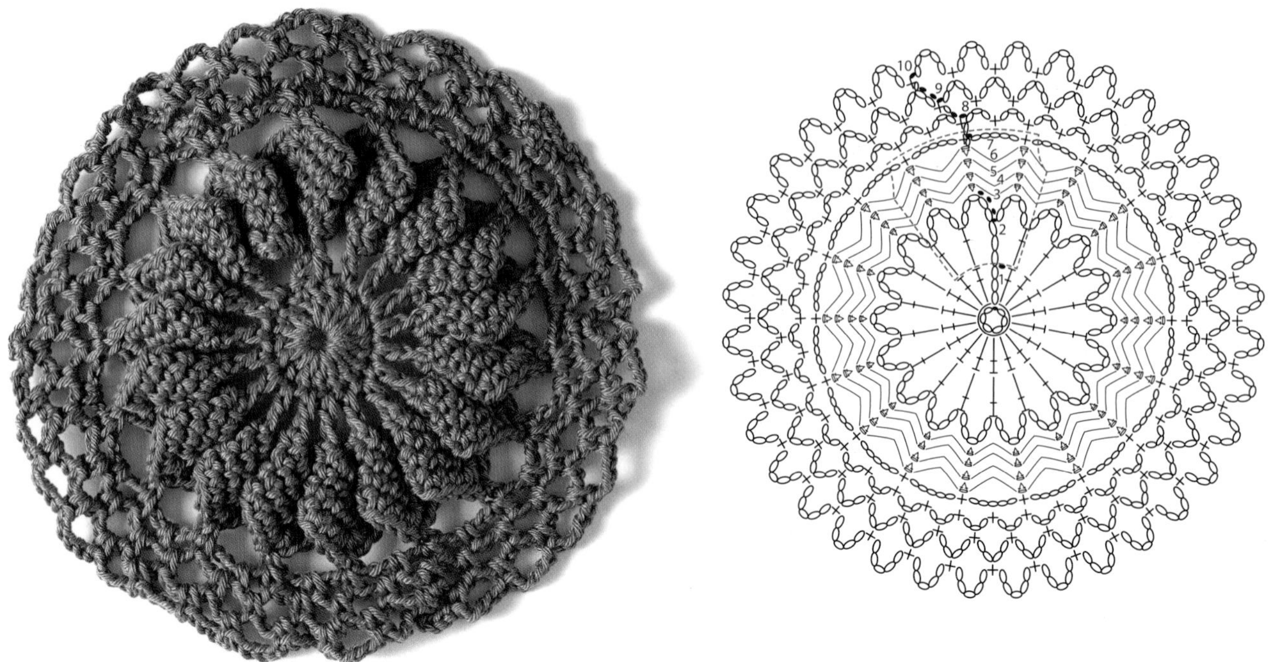

Windmills

Base ring: Ch6, join with slip st.

Round 1: Ch3 (count as 1dc), 17dc into ring, slip st to top of ch-3.

Round 2: Ch8 (count as 1dc, ch5), [1dc into next dc, ch5] 17 times, slip st to 3rd of ch-8.

Round 3: Slip st into each of next 3 ch of 1st sp, ch1, [1sc, ch1, 1sc] into same ch as last slip st, *2sc into 2nd part of sp and 2sc into 1st part of next sp, [1sc, ch1, 1sc] into center ch of same sp; rep from * 16 more times, 2sc into 2nd part of last sp, 2sc into 1st part of 1st sp, slip st to 1st sc.

Round 4: Slip st into 1st ch sp, ch1, [1sc, ch1, 1sc] into same sp as last slip st, 1sc into each of next 6 sc, *[1sc, ch1, 1sc] into next ch sp, 1sc into each of next 6 sc; rep from * 16 more times, slip st to 1st sc.

Round 5: Slip st into 1st ch sp, ch1, [1sc, ch1, 1sc] into same sp as last slip st, 1sc into each of next 8 sc, *[1sc, ch1, 1sc] into next ch sp, 1sc into each of next 8 sc; rep from * 16 more times, slip st to 1st sc.

Round 6: Slip st into 1st ch sp, ch1, [1sc, ch1, 1sc] into same sp as last slip st, 1sc into each of next 10 sc, *[1sc, ch1, 1sc] into next ch sp, 1sc into each of next 10 sc; rep from * 16 more times, slip st to 1st sc.

Round 7: Slip st into 1st ch sp, ch1, 1sc into same sp as last slip st, ch5, [1sc into next ch sp, ch5] 17 times, slip st to 1st sc.

Round 8: Ch1, 1sc into 1st sc of previous round, ch3, 1sc into next ch-5 sp, [ch3, 1sc into next sc, ch3, 1sc into next ch-5 sp] 17 times, ch3, slip st to 1st sc.

Round 9: Slip st into 1st ch of 1st ch-3 sp, ch1, 1sc into same sp as last slip st, *ch4, 1sc into next ch-3 sp; rep from * to end, ch4, slip st to 1st sc.

Round 10: Slip st into each of 1st 2 ch of 1st ch-4 sp, ch1, 1sc into same sp as last slip sts, *ch5, 1sc into next ch-4 sp; rep from * to end, ch5, slip st to 1st sc.

Fasten off.

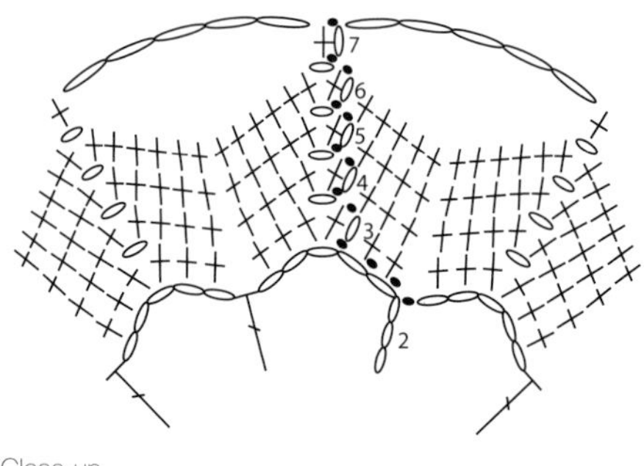

Close-up

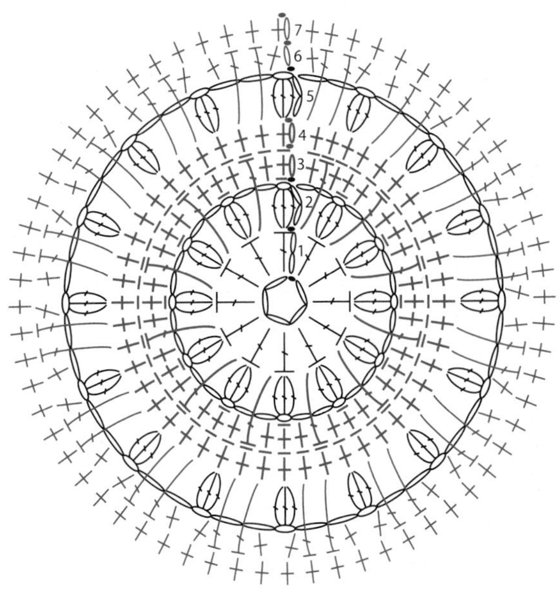

Snail shell

Special abbreviations:

Popcorn = work 3dc into st, drop loop from hook and insert hook into the 1st of these 3dc and pick up dropped loop, tighten and draw loop through, ch1.

Long dc (long double crochet) = yo, insert hook in designated st or row, pull up long loop on hook, (yo, pull through 2 loops on hook) 2 times.

Base ring: Using A, ch5, join with slip st.

Round 1: Ch2, 12dc into ring, slip st to 1st dc (not in ch-2).

Round 2: Ch2, popcorn into same place as slip st, [ch2, popcorn into next dc] 11 times, ch2 (12 popcorns), draw B through, slip st to back loop of 1st popcorn.

Round 3: Ch1, 1sc into same place as last slip st, [1sc into next ch-2 sp, 1 long dc into base of next popcorn, 1sc into same ch-2 sp, 1sc into back loop of top of same popcorn as last long dc] 12 times, omitting 1sc at end of last rep, slip st to back loop of 1st sc.

Round 4: Ch1, 1sc into back loop of each st around, slip st to 1st sc, drop B, draw A through loop.

Round 5: Ch2, 1 popcorn into same place as last slip st, [ch2, skip 2 sc, 1 popcorn into next sc] 15 times, ch2 (16 popcorns), slip st to back loop of 1st popcorn, draw B through loop. Fasten off A.

Round 6: Ch1, 1sc into same place as last slip st, [1sc in next ch-2 sp, 1 long dc into each of 2 sc between popcorns, 1sc into same ch-2 sp] 16 times, slip st to 1st sc.

Round 7: Ch1, 1sc into each st around, slip st to 1st sc. Fasten off.

Chrysanthemum

Special abbreviation:

Dtr2tog = 2dtr into next sp until 1 loop of each remains on hook, yo and draw through all 3 loops on hook.

Round 1: Ch5 (count as 1dtr), 19dtr into 1st ch, slip st to 5th ch of ch-5. (20dtr)

Round 2: Ch8 (count as 1dtr, ch3), [1dtr into next dtr, ch3] 19 times, slip st to 5th of ch-8. (20 sps)

Round 3: Slip st into 1st sp, ch5 (count as 1dtr), 1dtr into same sp as slip st, ch6, [1dtr2tog into next sp, ch6] 19 times, slip st to top of 1st dtr.

Round 4: Slip st into each of 1st 3 ch of 1st sp, ch1, 1sc into same sp as slip sts, [ch8, 1sc into next ch-6 sp] 19 times, ch4, 1dtr to 1st sc.

Round 5: Ch1, 1sc into sp just formed, ch9, [1sc into next ch-8 sp, ch9] 19 times, slip st into 1st sc.

Fasten off.

cluster

Bird of paradise

Flower petals: *Ch20, skip 2 ch, 1sc into each of next 2 ch, 1hdc into next ch, 1dc into each of next 2 ch, 1tr into each of next 2 ch, holding back last loop of each tr, 1tr into each of next 2 ch, yo and draw through all 3 loops on hook, 1dc into each of next 3 ch, 1hdc into next ch, slip st into each of last 5 ch; rep from * 5 more times. (6 petals made)

Flower base: Ch1, 1sc in base of each of 6 petals, ch5, turn. Holding back last loop of each tr, 1tr into each of 1st 5 sc, 2tr into last sc, yo and through all 8 loops on hook.

Stem: Ch30, skip 2 ch, 1hdc into each ch to base of flower, slip st to base of flower.

Fasten off.

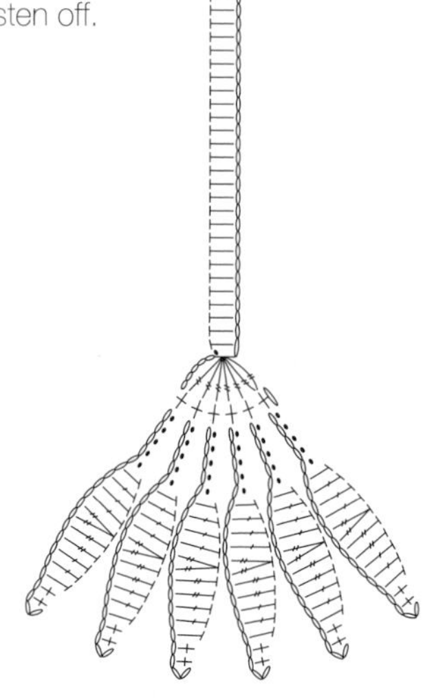

Six-point motif

Special abbreviations:

Bobble = 3dc into next st until 1 loop of each remains on hook, yo and draw through all 4 loops on hook.

Picot = ch3, slip st into 1st of these ch.

Round 1: Ch2, 12sc into 2nd ch from hook, slip st to 1st sc.

Round 2: Ch3 (count as 1dc), skip 1st sc, 1dc into next sc, ch3, [1dc into each of next 2 sc, ch3] 5 times, slip st to top of ch-3.

Round 3: Slip st into next dc and ch-3 sp, ch3 (count as 1dc), [2dc until 1 loop of each remains on hook, yo and through all 3 loops on hook (bobble made at beg of round), ch3, 1 bobble] into same ch-3 sp, ch7, *[1 bobble, ch3, 1 bobble] into next ch-3 sp, ch7; rep from * 4 more times, slip st to top of 1st bobble.

Round 4: 2slip sts into 1st ch-3 sp, ch1, 1sc into same sp, *[6dc, 1 picot, 6dc] into next ch-7 sp, 1sc into next ch-3 sp; rep from * 5 more times, omitting sc at end of last rep, slip st to 1st sc.

Fasten off.

bobble

picot

Shamrock

Base ring: Ch9, join with slip st.
Round 1: Ch1, 16sc into ring, slip st to 1st sc.
Round 2: Ch5 (count as 1tr), 2tr into same st as last slip st, 3tr into next sc, [ch7, skip 2 sc, 3tr into each of next 2 sc] 3 times, ch7, slip st to top of ch-5.
Round 3: Ch1, 1sc into same st as last slip st, *1dc into next tr, 2dc into next tr, ch4, slip st through top of last dc (picot), 2dc into next tr, 1dc into next tr, 1sc into next tr, 7sc into next ch-7 sp, 1sc into next tr; rep from * 3 times more, omitting 1sc at end of last rep, slip st to 1st sc.
Fasten off.

Blossom

Base ring: Ch6, join with slip st.
Round 1: 12sc into ring, slip st to 1st sc.
Round 2: Ch1, 1sc into same sc, [ch3, skip 1 sc, 1sc into next sc] 5 times, ch3, skip 1 sc, slip st to 1st sc.
Round 3: *[1sc, 1hdc, 3dc, 1hdc, 1sc] into next ch-3 sp; rep from * 5 more times, slip st to 1st sc. Fasten off.
Round 4: Working in back of petals, join yarn in back loop of sc on round 2 below last and 1st petals, [ch5, 1sc in back loop of next sc on round 2 below next 2 petals] 5 times, ch5, 1sc into joining st.
Round 5: *[1sc, 1hdc, 5dc, 1hdc, 1sc] into next ch-5 sp; rep from * 5 more times, slip st to 1st sc.
Fasten off.
Round 6: Rep round 4 with ch7 instead of ch5 for each ch sp.
Round 7: 11sc into each ch-7 sp, slip st to 1st sc. Fasten off.

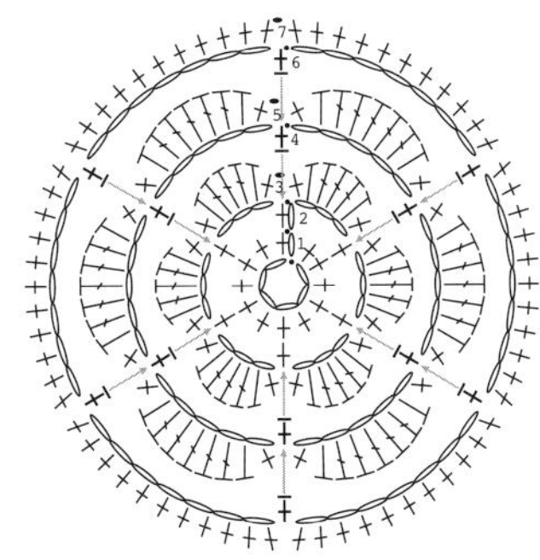

Hamster wheel

Base ring: Ch12, join with slip st.
Round 1: Ch1, 24sc into ring, slip st to 1st sc.
Round 2: Ch12, skip next sc, 1sc into next sc, turn, *ch3 (count as 1dc), 1dc into each of 1st 7 ch of ch-12 sp, turn, ch3, skip 1st dc, 1dc into each of next 6 dc, 1dc into top of ch-3, (one block made)**, skip next sc on ring, 1tr into next sc, ch8, skip 1 sc, 1sc into next sc, turn; rep from * 4 more times, then from * to ** again, slip st to 4th of ch-12.
Round 3: Slip st to 3rd of ch-3 at top corner of 1st block, ch1, 1sc into top of ch-3, ch13, [1sc into 3rd of ch-3 at top of next block, ch13] 5 times, slip st to 1st sc.
Round 4: Ch6 (count as 1dc, ch3), 1dc into same place as last slip st, [ch1, skip 1 ch, 1dc into next ch] 6 times, ch1, *[1dc, ch3, 1dc] into next sc, [ch1, skip 1 ch, 1dc into next ch] 6 times, ch1; rep from * 4 more times, slip st to 3rd of ch-6.
Fasten off.

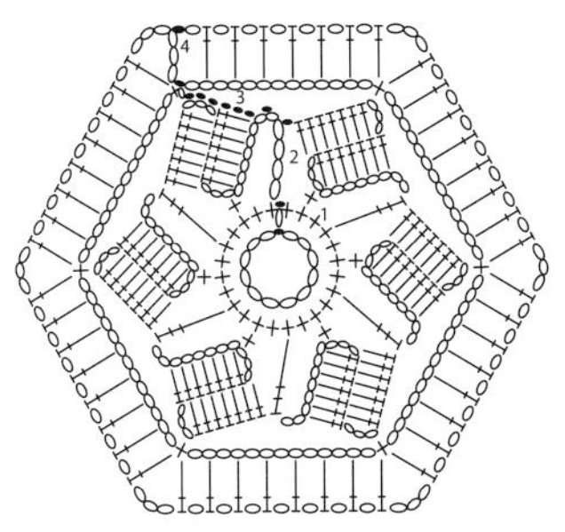

Appliqué square

Base ring: Ch6, join with slip st.

Round 1: Ch3 (count as 1dc), 15dc into ring, slip st to top of ch-3.

Round 2: Ch1, 1sc into same st as last slip st, 1sc into next dc, *[1sc, ch7, 1sc] into next dc, 1sc into each of next 3 dc; rep from * 3 more times omitting 2sc at end of last rep, slip st to 1st sc.

Round 3: Ch1, 1sc into same st as last slip st, *[2hdc, 17dc, 2hdc] into next ch-7 sp (1 shell made), skip 2 sc, 1sc into next sc; rep from * 3 more times omitting 1sc at end of last rep, slip st to 1st sc.

Round 4: Slip st into each of 1st 2hdc and 6dc of 1st shell, ch1, 1sc into same st as last slip st, ch9, skip 5 dc, 1sc into next dc, *ch7, skip 1st 2 hdc and 5 dc on next shell, 1sc into next dc, ch9, skip 5 dc, 1sc into next dc; rep from * twice more, ch7, slip st to 1st sc.

Round 5: Ch3, *[8dc, 1tr, 8dc] into next ch-9 sp, 1dc into next sc, 7dc into next ch-7 sp, 1dc into next tr; rep from * 3 more times omitting 1dc at end of last rep, slip st to top of ch-3.
Fasten off.

Solar system

Special abbreviation:

Picot = ch3, slip st to 1st of these ch.

Base ring: Ch10, join with slip st.

Round 1: Ch1, 5sc into ring, 1 picot, [8sc into ring, 1 picot] twice, 3sc into ring, slip st into 1st sc.

Round 2: Ch1, 1sc into same st as last slip st, *ch12, skip [4sc, 1 picot, 3sc], 1sc into next sc; rep from * once more, ch12, slip st to 1st sc.

Round 3: Slip st into 1st ch-12 sp, ch1, [1sc, 1hdc, 2dc, 9tr, 2dc, 1hdc, 1sc] into each of the 3 sps, slip st to 1st sc.

Round 4: *Ch1, 1sc into next hdc, ch1, [1dc into next st, ch1] 13 times, 1sc into next hdc, ch1, slip st into each of next 2 sc; rep from * twice more omitting 1slip st at end of last rep.

Round 5: Slip st into each of 1st [slip st, ch sp, sc and ch sp], ch1, [1sc, ch4, 1sc] into same ch sp as last slip st, [1sc, ch4, 1sc] into each of next 13 ch sps, *ch1, slip st into each of next [sc, ch sp, 2slip sts, ch sp, sc and ch sp], ch1, [1sc, ch4, 1sc] into same sp as last slip st, [1sc, ch4, 1sc] into each of next 13 ch sps; rep from * once more, ch1, slip st into each of last [sc, ch sp and slip st].
Fasten off.

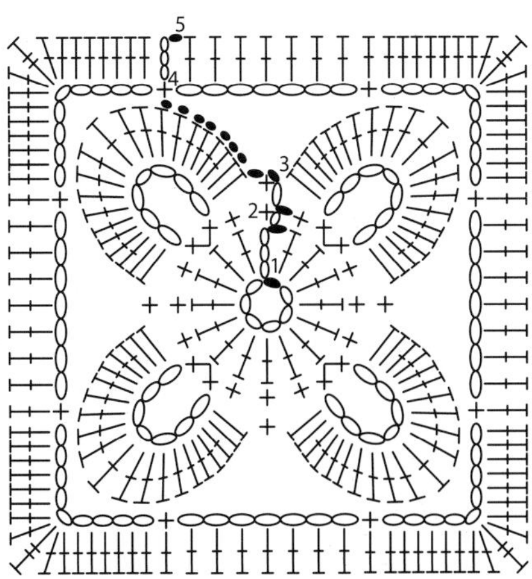

Appliqué square

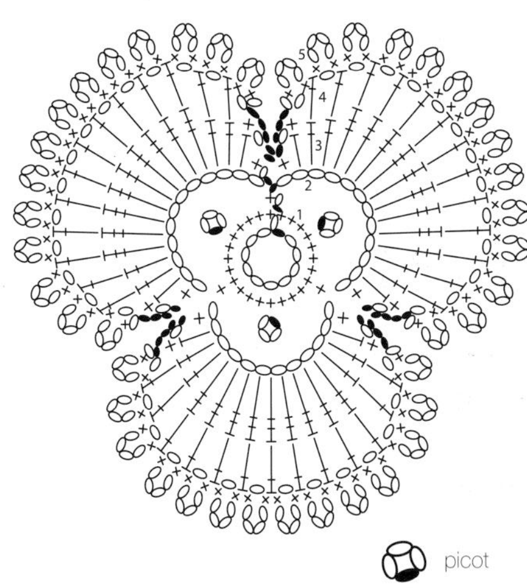

picot

Solar system

Pulsar motif

Pulsar motif

Special abbreviations:

Picot = ch5, insert hook through top of last dc made, slip st to close.

V st = [2dc, ch2, 2dc].

Base ring: Ch8, join with slip st.

Round 1: Ch8, slip st into 6th ch from hook (counts as 1dc, picot), *4dc into ring, picot; rep from * 6 more times, 3dc into ring, slip st to 3rd of ch-8. (8 picots)

Round 2: Slip st into each of next 2 ch, ch3 (count as 1dc), [1dc, ch2, 2dc] into same picot, *ch4, V st into next picot; rep from * 6 more times, ch4, slip st to top of ch-3.

Round 3: Slip st into next dc and next ch sp, ch3 (count as 1dc), [1dc, ch2, 2dc] into same sp, *ch6, V st into next V st ch sp; rep from * 6 more times, ch6, slip st to top of ch-3.

Round 4: Slip st into next dc and next ch sp, ch3 (count as 1dc), [1dc, ch2, 2dc] into same sp, *ch8, V st into next V st ch sp; rep from * 6 more times, ch8, slip st to top of ch-3.

Round 5: Slip st into next dc and ch-2 sp, ch3 (count as 1dc), 4dc into same ch sp, *1sc into each of next 8 ch, 5dc into next ch-2 sp; rep from * 6 more times, 1sc into each of next 8 ch, slip st to top of ch-3.

Fasten off.

Showtime

Base ring: Ch8, join with slip st.

Round 1: Ch1, 15sc into ring, slip st to 1st sc.

Round 2: Ch5, skip 1st 3 sc, [slip st into next sc, ch5, skip 2 sc] 4 times, slip st into slip st at end of previous round.

Round 3: Slip st into 1st ch-5 sp, ch1, [1sc, 1hdc, 5dc, 1hdc, 1sc] into same sp and each of next 4 sps, slip st to 1st sc. (5 petals)

Round 4: Ch1, working behind each petal of previous round, 1slip st into last slip st on round 2, ch8, [1slip st into next slip st on round 2, ch8] 4 times, slip st to same st as 1st slip st at beg of round.

Round 5: Slip st into 1st ch-8 sp, ch1, [1sc, 1hdc, 8dc, 1hdc, 1sc] into same sp and each of next 4 sps, slip st to 1st sc.

Round 6: Ch2, working behind each petal of previous round 1slip st into last slip st on round 2, ch10, [1slip st into next slip st on round 2, ch10] 4 times, slip st to same st as 1st slip st at beg of round.

Round 7: Slip st into 1st ch-10 sp, ch1, 15sc into same sp and into each of next 4 sps, slip st to 1st sc.

Round 8: Slip st into next sc, *[ch4, skip 1 sc, slip st into next sc] 6 times, turn, 2slip sts into 1st ch-4 sp, [ch4, slip st into next ch-4 sp] 5 times, turn, 2slip sts into 1st ch-4 sp, [ch4, slip st into next ch-4 sp] 4 times, turn, 2slip sts into 1st ch-4 sp, [ch4, slip st into next ch-4 sp] 3 times, turn, 2slip sts into 1st ch-4 sp, [ch4, slip st into next ch-4 sp] twice, turn, 2slip sts into 1st ch-4 sp, ch4, slip st into next sp and fasten off*. [With RS facing, skip next 2 sc on round 7, rejoin yarn to next sc and rep from * to *] 4 more times.

Spanish square

Base ring: Ch8, join with slip st.

Round 1: Ch1, 16sc into ring, slip st to 1st sc. (16 sts)

Round 2: Ch1, 1sc into same place as ch-1, [ch7, skip 3 sts, 1sc into next st] 3 times, ch7, skip 3 sts, slip st to 1st sc.

Round 3: Slip st across to 3rd ch of next ch-7 sp, ch3 (count as 1dc), 1dc into same sp, *[ch3, 2dc] into same sp, ch3, dc2tog inserting hook into same sp for 1st leg and into next sp for 2nd leg, ch3, 2dc into same sp; rep from * 3 more times, omitting 2dc at end of last rep, slip st to top of ch-3.

Round 4: Slip st into next dc and next ch sp, ch3 (count as 1dc), 1dc into same sp, *[ch3, 2dc] into same sp, ch3, skip 2 dc, 1dc into each of next 3 ch, 1dc into next dc2tog, 1dc into each of next 3 ch, ch3, skip 2 dc, 2dc into next sp; rep from * 3 more times, omitting 2dc at end of last rep, slip st to top of ch-3.

Round 5: Slip st into next dc and next ch sp, ch3, 2dc into same sp, *[ch3, 3dc] into same sp, ch6, skip [2dc, ch3, 1dc], 1dc into each of next 5 dc, ch6, skip [1dc, ch3, 2dc], 3dc into next ch-3 sp; rep from * 3 more times, omitting 3dc at end of last rep, slip st to top of ch-3.

Round 6: Ch3 (count as 1dc), 1dc into each of next 2 dc, *[3dc, ch5, 3dc] into next ch-3 sp, 1dc into each of next 3 dc, ch6, skip [ch-6 and 1dc], 1dc into each of next 3 dc, ch6, skip [1dc and ch-6], 1dc into each of next 3 dc; rep from * 3 more times, omitting 3dc at end of last rep, slip st to top of ch-3.

Fasten off.

Traffic lights

Base ring: Ch6, join with slip st.
Round 1: Ch1, 2sc into ring, *ch13, slip st into 6th ch from hook, ch3, skip 3 ch, slip st into next ch, ch3, slip st into side of last sc worked, 4sc into ring; rep from * 3 more times omitting 2sc at end of last rep, slip st to 1st sc. (4 points made)
Round 2: *[1sc, 3dc, 1sc] into each of 1st 2 sps on next point, 1sc into top sp of same point, [3dc, 1sc] twice into same top sp, then working on other side of loop [1sc, 3dc, 1sc] into each of next 2 sps, 1slip st into each of next 3 sc on 1st round; rep from * 3 more times omitting 1 slip st at end of last rep.
Round 3: Ch1, 1sc into same sc as last slip st, *ch16, 1sc into center sc at top of point, ch16, 1sc into center slip st between 2 points on 1st round; rep from * 3 more times omitting 1sc at end of last rep, slip st to 1st sc.
Round 4: Ch1, *1sc into each of next 16 ch, 1sc into next sc, 1sc into each of next 16 ch, skip 1 sc; rep from * 3 more times, slip st to 1st sc.
Fasten off.

La fleur de vie

Base ring: Ch10, join with slip st.
Round 1: Ch3 (count as 1dc), 23dc into ring, slip st to top of ch-3.
Round 2: Ch3 (count as 1dc), 1dc into next dc, 2dc into next dc, [1dc into each of next 2 dc, 2dc into next dc] 7 times, slip st to top of ch-3.
Round 3: Ch3, 2dc into next dc, ch2, [1dc into each of next 3 dc, 2dc into next dc, ch2] 7 times, 1dc into each of last 2 dc, slip st to top of ch-3.
Round 4: Ch3, 1dc into each of next 2 dc, ch2, 1dc into next ch-2 sp, ch2, [1dc into each of next 5 dc, ch2, 1dc into next ch-2 sp, ch2] 7 times, 1dc into each of last 2 dc, slip st to top of ch-3.
Round 5: Ch3, 1dc into next dc, ch5, skip 1 dc, 1dc into next dc, [ch5, skip 1 dc, 1dc into each of next 3 dc, ch5, skip 1 dc, 1dc into next dc] 7 times, ch5, skip 1 dc, 1dc into last dc, slip st to top of ch-3.
Round 6: Ch11 (count as 1dc, ch8), skip next dc, 1dc into next dc, [ch8, skip 1 dc, 1dc into next dc] 14 times, ch8, slip st to 3rd of ch-11. Fasten off.

Traffic lights

La fleur de vie

Anemone

Special abbreviation:

Picot = ch3, slip st into 1st of these ch.

Base ring: Ch8, join with slip st.

Round 1: Ch3 (count as 1dc), 15dc into ring, slip st into top of ch-3.

Round 2: Ch5 (count as 1dc, ch2), [1dc into next dc, ch2] 15 times, slip st to 3rd of ch-5.

Round 3: Ch1, 3sc into each of the 16 ch-2 sps, slip st to 1st sc.

Round 4: Ch1, 1sc into same sc as last slip st, *ch6, skip 5 sc, 1sc into next sc; rep from * 6 more times, ch6, slip st to 1st sc.

Round 5: Slip st into 1st ch-6 sp, ch1, [1sc, 1hdc, 6dc, 1hdc, 1sc] into each of the 8 ch-6 sps, slip st to 1st sc. (8 petals worked)

Round 6: Ch1, working behind each petal of previous round, 1sc into 1st sc on round 4, *ch7, 1sc into next sc on round 4; rep from * 6 more times, ch7, slip st to 1st sc.

Round 7: Slip st into 1st ch-7 sp, ch1, [1sc, 1hdc, 7dc, 1hdc, 1sc] into each of the 8 ch-7 sps, slip st to 1st sc.

Round 8: Ch1, working behind each petal of previous round, 1sc into 1st sc on round 6, *ch8, 1sc into next sc on round 6; rep from * 6 more times, ch8, slip st to 1st sc.

Round 9: Slip st into 1st ch-8 sp, ch1, [1sc, 1hdc, 3dc, 1 picot, 3dc, 1 picot, 3dc, 1hdc, 1sc] into each of the 8 ch-8 sps, slip st to 1st sc.

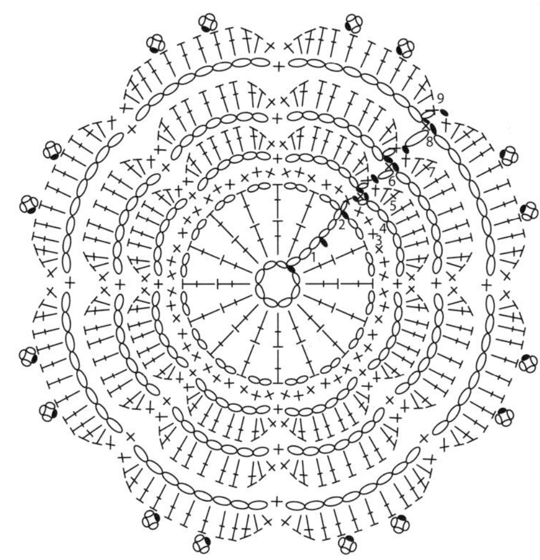

Anemone

 picot

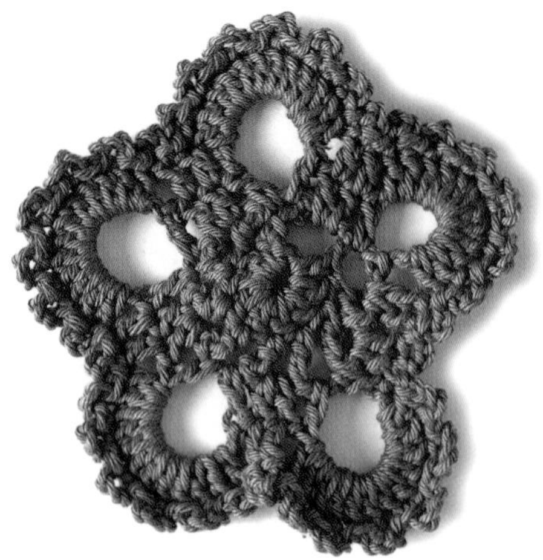

Star bright

Base ring: Ch5, join with slip st.
Round 1: Ch3 (count as 1dc), 9dc into ring, slip st to top of ch-3.
Round 2: Ch5 (count as 1tr, ch1), [1tr into next dc, ch1] 9 times, slip st to 4th of ch-5.
Round 3: Slip st into 1st sp, ch11 (count as 1dc, ch8), [1dc into same sp, 2dc into next sp, 1dc into next sp, ch8] 4 times, 1dc into same sp, 2dc into next sp, slip st to 3rd of ch11.
Round 4: Slip st into 1st ch-8 sp, ch3, 11dc into same sp, [skip 1 dc, 1dc into each of next 2 dc, skip 1 dc, 12dc into next sp] 4 times, skip 1 dc, 1dc into each of next 2 dc, slip st to top of ch-3.
Round 5: *[Ch3, slip st into each of next 2 dc] 5 times, ch3, slip st into each of next 4 dc; rep from * 4 times more omitting 1dc at end of last rep, slip st to 1st of 1st ch-3.
Fasten off.

Eyelet square

Base ring: Ch8, join with slip st.
Round 1: Ch1, 16sc into ring, slip st to 1st sc.
Round 2: Ch1, 1sc into same place as last slip st, [ch10, skip 3 sc, 1sc into next sc] 3 times, ch10, skip 3 sc, slip st to 1st sc.
Round 3: Ch1, 1sc into same place as last slip st, [11sc into next ch-10 sp, 1sc into next sc] 3 times, 11sc into next ch-10 sp, slip st to 1st sc.
Round 4: Ch1, 1sc into same place as last slip st, 1sc into each of next 5 sc, [2sc into next sc to form corner, 1sc into each of next 11 sts] 3 times, 2sc into next sc, 1sc into each of next 5 sc, slip st to 1st sc.
Round 5: Ch1, 1sc into each sc and 2sc in 1st sc of increase at each corner, slip st to 1st sc.
Rep round 5 for desired size.
Fasten off.

Magdalene motif

Base ring: Ch5, join with slip st.
Round 1: Ch6 (count as 1tr, ch2), *1tr in ring, ch2; rep from * around 6 times more, join with slip st in 4th of ch-6.
Round 2: Slip st in next sp, ch4 (count as 1tr), 4tr in same sp, *ch2, 5tr in next sp; rep from * around, ch2, slip st to top of ch-4.
Round 3: Ch4 (count as 1tr), 1tr in same place as sl st, 1tr into each of next 4 tr, *1tr in 1st ch of ch-2, ch3, 1tr in next ch of same ch-2, 1tr into each of next 5 tr; rep from * around to last ch-2 sp, 1tr in 1st ch of ch-2, ch3, slip st to top of ch-4.
Fasten off.

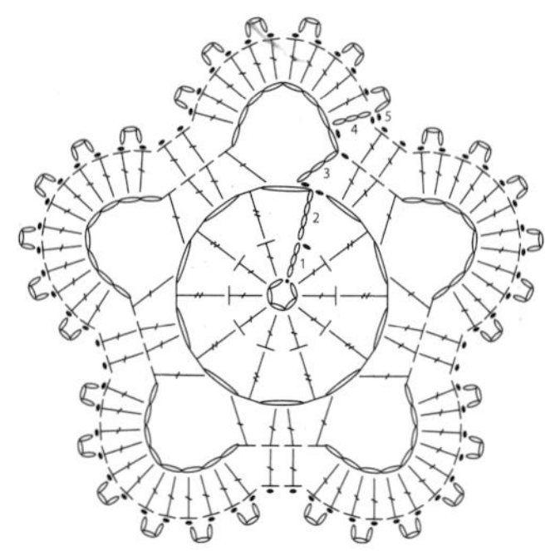

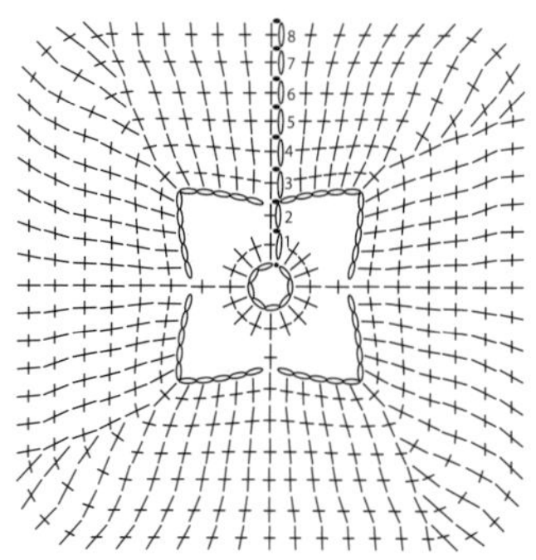

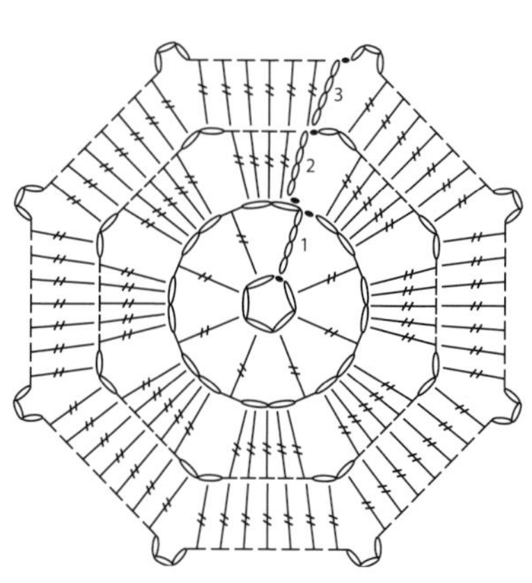

Starfish

Base ring: Ch9, join with slip st.
Round 1: Ch1, 18sc into ring, slip st to 1st sc.
Round 2: Ch9, 1sc into 4th ch from hook, 1hdc into each of next 2 ch, 1dc into each of next 3 ch, skip 1st 3 sc on ring, slip st into next sc, *ch9, 1sc into 4th ch from hook, 1hdc into each of next 2 ch, 1dc into each of next 3 ch, skip next 2 sc on ring, slip st into next sc; rep from * 4 times more placing last slip st into same st as slip st of previous round. Fasten off.

Begonia square

Special abbreviation:
Bobble = work 5tr until 1 loop of each remains on hook, yo and draw through all 6 loops on hook.
Base ring: Using A, ch4, join with slip st.
Round 1: Using A, ch4, work 4tr until loop of each remains on hook, yo and draw through all 5 loops on hook (count as 1st bobble), ch4, *[bobble, ch4 into ring] 7 times, slip st to top of 1st bobble. Fasten off A.
Round 2: Join B to a ch-4 sp, ch3 (count as 1dc), 3dc into same sp, *4dc into next sp, ch6, 4dc into next sp; rep from * twice more, 4dc into next sp, ch6, slip st to top of ch-3. Fasten off.

Summer spiral

Base ring: Ch6, join with slip st.
Round 1: Ch6 (count as 1tr, ch2), [1tr into ring, ch2] 7 times, slip st to 4th of ch-6.
Round 2: Slip st into next sp, ch4 (count as 1tr), 4tr into same sp, [ch2, 5tr into next sp] 7 times, ch2, slip st to top of ch-4.
Round 3: Ch4, 1tr into each of next 4 tr, [1tr into 1st ch of next ch-2, ch3, 1tr into next ch of same ch-2, 1tr into each of next 5 tr] 7 times, 1tr into 1st ch of next ch-2, ch3, 1tr into next ch of same ch-2, slip st to top of ch-4. Fasten off.

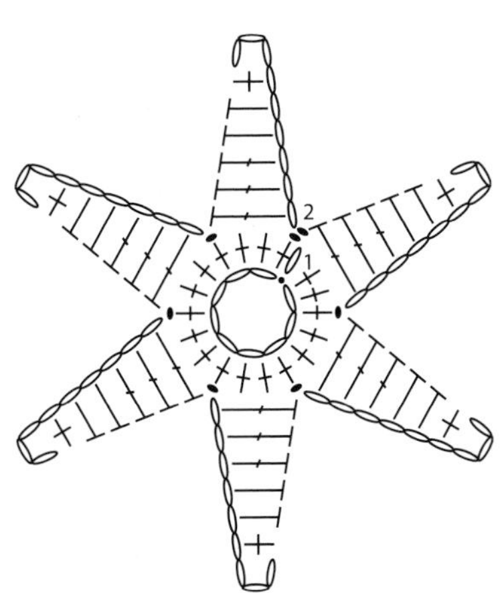

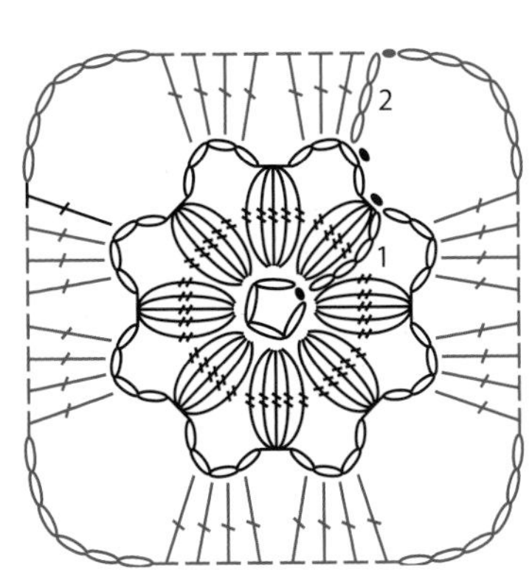

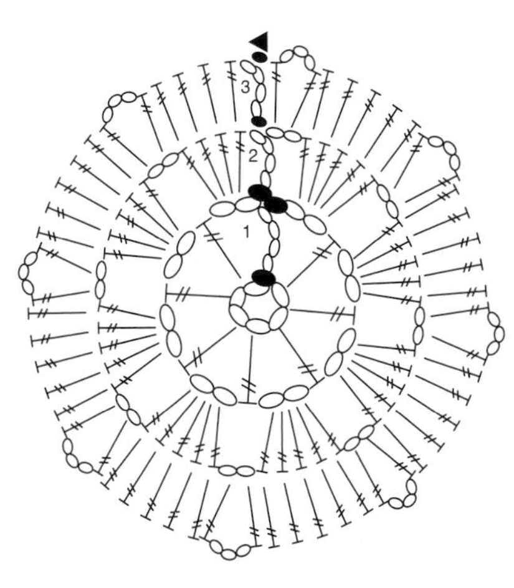

Prairie motif

Special abbreviation:

Popcorn = 4dc into next ch sp, drop loop from hook, insert hook under 2 loops at top of 1st of the 4dc and through dropped loop, draw loop through dc.

Base ring: Using A, ch12, join with slip st.

Round 1: Ch5 (count as 1tr, ch1), [1tr in ring, ch1] 15 times, slip st to 4th of ch-5. (16 ch sps)

Round 2: Ch4, 3dc into 1st ch sp, drop loop from hook, insert hook in 4th of ch-4 and through dropped loop, draw loop through ch (count as 1st popcorn), ch2, [popcorn, ch2] 15 times, slip st to top of ch-4. Fasten off A.

Round 3: Join B in any ch-2 sp, ch3 (count as 1dc), 3dc into same sp, ch2, 4dc into same sp (corner), *[ch3, 1sc into next ch-2 sp] 3 times, ch3, [4dc, ch2, 4dc] into next ch-2 sp for corner; rep from * twice more, [ch3, 1sc into next ch-2 sp] 3 times, ch3, slip st to top of ch-3.

Round 4: Slip st to 1st ch-2 sp, ch3 (count as 1dc), [3dc, ch2, 4dc] into same sp, *ch1, skip next ch-3 sp, [4dc into next ch-3 sp, ch1] twice, [4dc, ch2, 4dc] into corner sp; rep from * twice more, ch1, skip next ch-3 sp, [4dc into next ch-3 sp, ch1] twice, slip st to top of ch-3. Fasten off B.

Round 5: Join A in a corner ch-2 sp, ch3 (count as 1dc), [3dc, ch2, 4dc] into same sp, *[4dc into next ch-1 sp] 3 times, [4dc, ch2, 4dc] into corner sp; rep from * twice more, [4dc into next ch-1 sp] 3 times, slip st to top of ch-3. Fasten off.

Wagon wheel

Special abbreviation:

Puff st = [yo, insert hook into ring, draw up a loop] twice, yo and through all 5 loops on hook.

Base ring: Ch4, join with slip st.

Round 1: Ch3, 1hdc into ring (counts as 1st puff st), ch1, [puff st, ch1] 7 times into ring, slip st to top of 1st puff st. (8 petals)

Round 2: Slip st into next ch sp, ch3, 1dc into 1st ch sp, ch2, [2dc, ch2] into each of next 7 ch sps, slip st into top of ch-3.

Round 3: Slip st into next ch sp, ch3, [1dc, ch1, 2dc, ch1] into same ch sp, [2dc, ch1] twice into each of next 7 ch sps, slip st to top of ch-3.

Round 4: Slip st into next ch sp, ch3, 2dc into same ch sp, ch1, [3dc, ch1] into each of next 15 ch sps, slip st to top of ch-3.

Round 5: Slip st into next ch sp, ch3, 3dc into same ch sp, ch1, [4dc, ch1] into each of next 15 ch sps, slip st to top of ch-3.

Rep rounds 4 and 5 as many times as desired for size but, after round 5, ch2 between dc groups.

Fasten off.

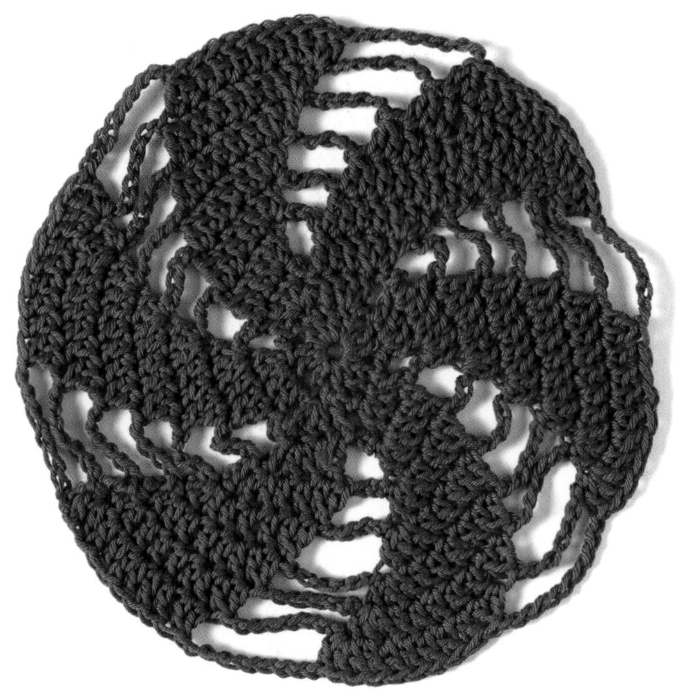

Water wheel

Base ring: Ch4, join with slip st.

Round 1: Ch3 (count as 1dc), 1dc into ring, [ch2, 2dc into ring] 5 times, ch2, slip st to top of ch-3.

Round 2: Ch3 (count as 1dc), 2dc into same place as ch-3, 1dc into next dc, *ch3, skip 2 ch, 3dc into next dc, 1dc into next dc; rep from * 4 more times, ch3, skip 2 ch, slip st to top of ch-3. (6 segments of 4dc and ch-3).

Round 3: Ch3 (count as 1dc), 2dc into same place as ch-3, 1dc into next dc, dc2tog over next 2 dc, *ch4, skip 3 ch, 3dc into next dc, 1dc into next dc, dc2tog over next 2 dc; rep from * 4 more times, ch4, skip 3 ch, slip st to top of ch-3.

Round 4: Ch3 (count as 1dc), 2dc into same place as ch-3, 1dc in each of next 2 dc, dc2tog over next 2 dc, *ch5, skip 4 ch, 3dc into next dc, 1dc in each of next 2 dc, dc2tog over next 2 dc; rep from * 4 more times, ch5, skip 4 ch, slip st to top of ch-3.

Round 5: Ch3 (count as 1dc), 2dc into same place as ch-3, 1dc in each of next 3 dc, dc2tog over next 2 dc, *ch6, skip 5 ch, 3dc into next dc, 1dc in each of next 3 dc, dc2tog over next 2 dc; rep from * 4 more times, ch6, skip 5 ch, slip st to top of ch-3.

Rounds 6, 7 and 8: As round 5, but adding 1 more single dc in each dc block and 1 more ch in each ch sp on each round. Fasten off.

Prairie motif

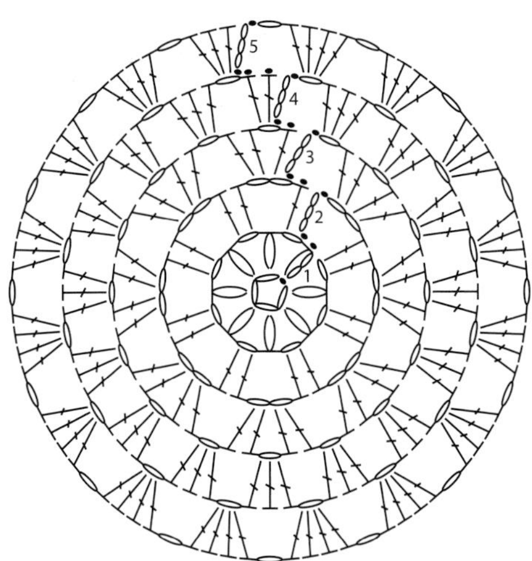

Wagon wheel

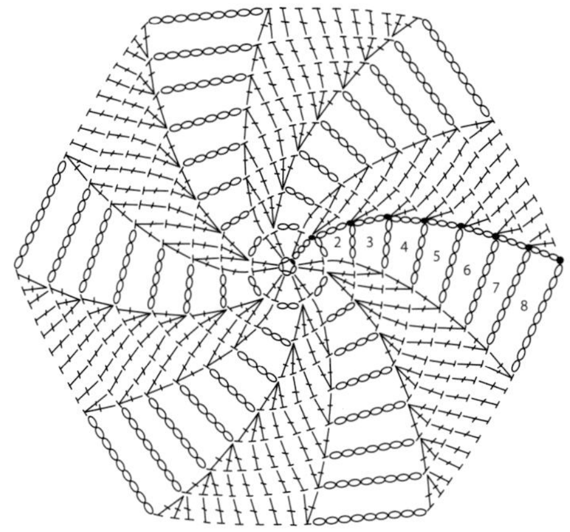

Water wheel

Dutch medallion

Special abbreviations:

2tr bobble = leaving last loop of each on hook, work 2tr into ring, yo, draw through all 3 loops on hook.

3tr bobble = leaving last loop of each st on hook, work 3tr into ring, yo and draw through all 4 loops on hook.

Base ring: Ch10, join with slip st.

Round 1: Ch4, 2tr bobble into ring, *ch6, 3tr bobble into ring; rep from * 6 more times, ch6, slip st to top of 1st bobble.

Round 2: Slip st into each of next 3 ch, ch4, [2tr bobble, ch5, 3tr bobble] into same sp, *ch5, [3tr bobble, ch7, 1dc] into next sp, ch7**, [3tr bobble, ch5, 3tr bobble] into next sp; rep from * twice more, then from * to ** again, slip st to top of 1st bobble. Fasten off.

Maui orchid

Base ring: Ch8, join with slip st.

Round 1: Ch3 (count as 1dc), 19dc into ring, slip st to top of ch-3.

Round 2: [Ch11, skip next dc, slip st into next dc] 9 times, ch6, 1trtr into slip st at end of previous round.

Round 3: Slip st into loop just formed by trtr, ch3, [2dc, ch3, 3dc] into same loop, [3dc, ch3, 3dc] into each of next 9 loops, slip st to top of ch-3. Fasten off.

Note: After working round 3 it may be necessary to ease the shells of [3dc, ch3, 3dc] to the center of the loop formed in the previous round.

Petit point

Base ring: Ch6, join with slip st.

Round 1: Ch1, 12sc into ring, slip st to 1st sc.

Round 2: Ch1, [1sc into next sc, 2sc into next sc] 6 times, slip st to 1st sc.

Round 3: Ch1, [1sc into next sc, ch3, skip 2 sc] 6 times, slip st to 1st sc.

Round 4: [(1sc, 1hdc, 1dc, 1tr, 1dc, 1hdc, 1sc) into next ch-3 sp] 6 times, slip st to 1st sc. Fasten off.

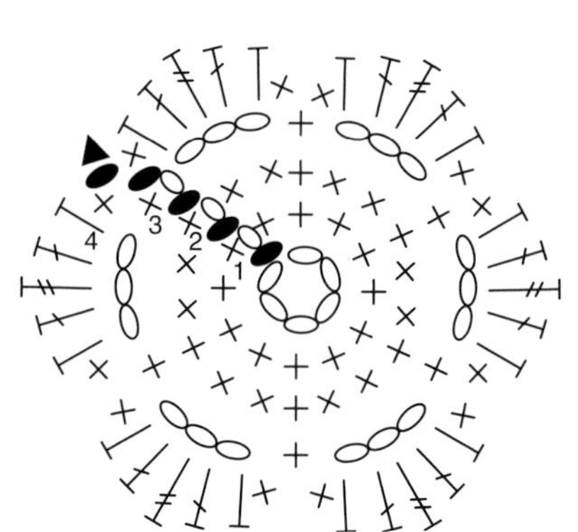

Maui wheel

Work as given for Maui Orchid (see left) but working 1 round each in colors A, B and C.

Old American square

Base ring: Ch6, join with slip st.

Round 1: Ch3 (count as 1dc), 2dc into ring, [ch2, 3dc into ring] 3 times, ch2, slip st to top of ch-3.

Round 2: Slip st into 1st ch-2 sp, ch3, [2dc, ch2, 3dc] into same sp to form corner, *ch1, [3dc, ch2, 3dc] into next ch-2 sp to form corner; rep from * twice more, ch1, slip st to top of ch-3.

Round 3: Slip st into 1st ch-2 sp, ch3, [2dc, ch2, 3dc] into same sp to form corner, *[ch1, 3dc] into each ch-1 sp along the side, [ch1, 3dc, ch2, 3dc] into next ch-2 sp to form corner; rep from * twice more, [ch1, 3dc] into each ch-1 sp along the side, ch1, slip st to top of ch-3.

Rep round 3 for desired size. Fasten off.

Daisy bloom

Base ring: Ch8, join with slip st.

Round 1: Ch3 (count as 1dc), 1dc into ring, [ch6, 3dc into ring] 5 times, ch6, 1dc into ring, slip st to top of ch-3.

Round 2: *Ch1, [1sc, 1hdc, 7dc, 1hdc, 1sc] into next ch-6 sp, ch1, skip 1 dc, 1 slip st into next dc; rep from * 5 more times placing last slip st into top of ch-3 at beg of previous round. Fasten off.

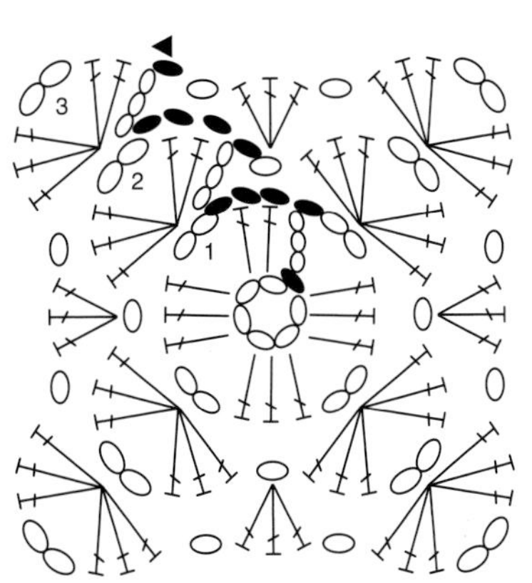

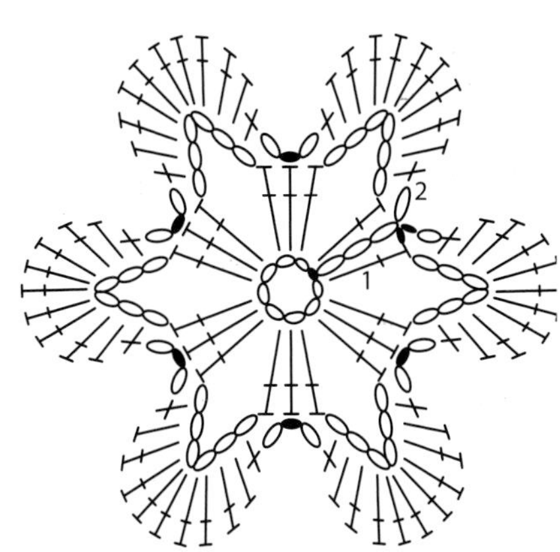

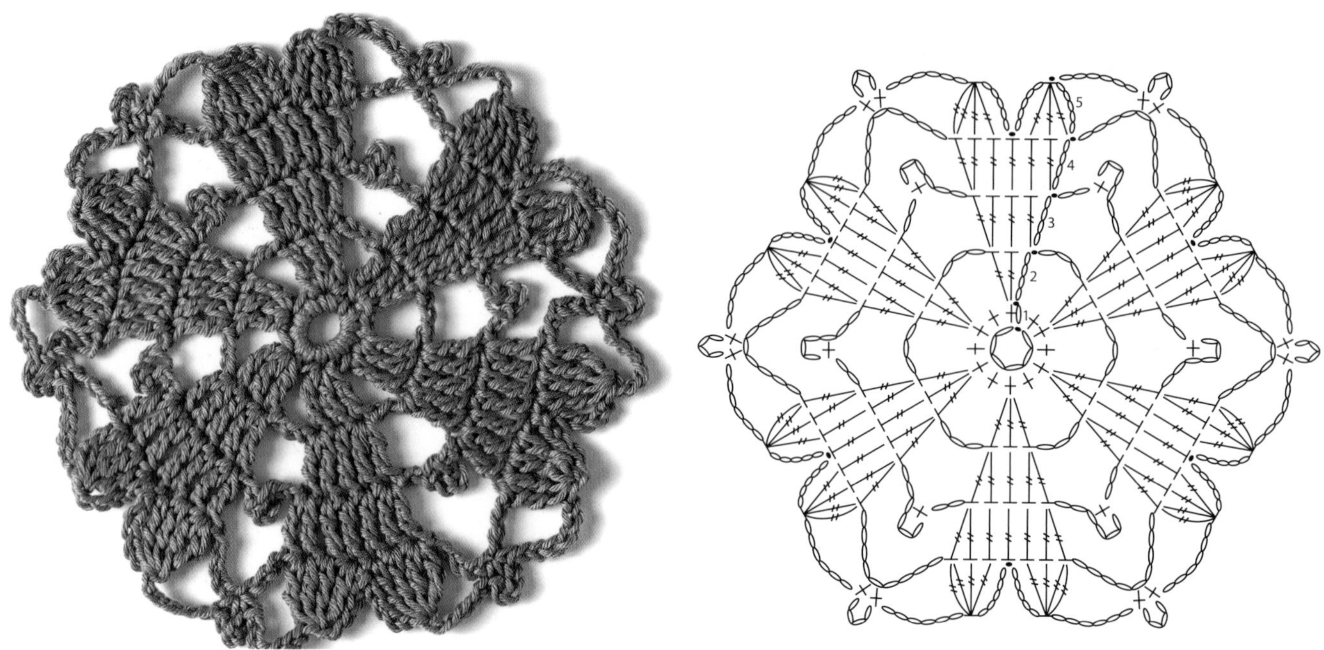

Six-spoked wheel

Special abbreviations:

Picot = ch6, 1sc in 4th ch from hook.

3tr cluster = yo twice, insert hook into same place as last slip st, yo and pull through, [yo and pull through 2 loops on hook] twice, [yo twice, insert hook into next tr, yo and pull through, (yo and pull through 2 loops on hook) twice] twice, yo and pull through last 4 loops on hook.

Left cluster = [yo twice, insert hook into next tr, yo and pull through, (yo and pull through 2 loops on hook) twice] 3 times, yo twice, insert hook into same tr, yo and pull through, [yo and pull through 2 loops on hook] twice, yo and pull through last 5 loops on hook.

Right cluster = yo twice, insert hook into next tr, yo and pull through, [yo and pull through 2 loops on hook] twice, yo twice, insert hook into same tr, yo and pull through, [yo and pull through 2 loops on hook] twice, [yo twice, insert hook into next tr, yo and pull through, (yo and pull through 2 loops on hook) twice], twice, yo and pull through last 5 loops on hook.

Base ring: Ch6, join with slip st.

Round 1: Ch1, 12sc into ring, slip st to 1st sc.

Round 2: Ch4 (count as 1tr), 2tr into same place as last slip st, [ch3, skip 1 sc, 3tr into next sc] 5 times, ch3, slip st to top of ch-4.

Round 3: Ch4, 1tr into same place as last slip st, [1tr into next tr, 2tr into next tr, picot, ch2, 2tr into next tr] 5 times, 1tr into next tr, 2tr into next tr, picot, ch2, slip st to top of ch-4.

Round 4: Ch4, 1tr into same place as last slip st, [1tr into each of next 3 tr, 2tr into next tr, ch9, 2tr into next tr] 5 times, 1tr into each of next 3 tr, 2tr into next tr, ch9, slip st to top of ch-4.

Round 5: Ch4, 3tr cluster *ch5, slip st into next tr, ch5, left cluster, ch6, skip 4 ch, [1sc, ch4, 1sc] into next ch, ch6, skip 4 ch, right cluster; rep from * 4 more times, ch5, slip st into next tr, ch5, 1 left cluster over next 3 tr, ch6, skip 4 ch, [1sc, ch4, 1sc] into next ch, ch6, skip 4 ch, slip st to top of 1st cluster.

Fasten off.

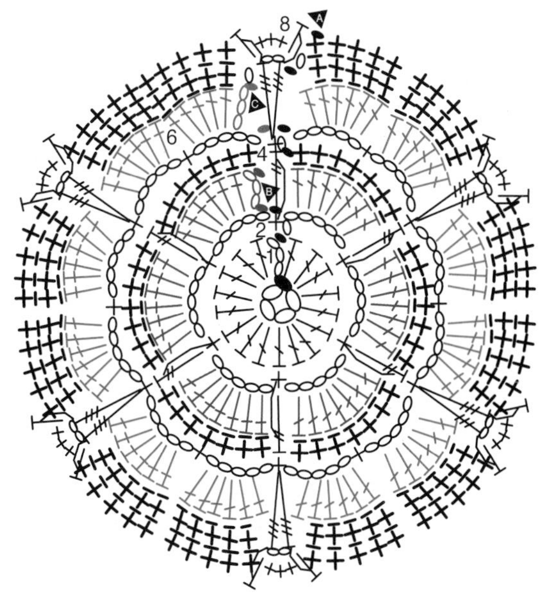

Astro motif

Base ring: Using A, ch4, join with slip st.

Round 1: Ch3 (count as 1dc), 17dc into ring, slip st to top of ch-3.

Round 2: Ch1, 1sc into same place as last sl st, [ch5, skip 2 dc, 1sc into next dc] 5 times, ch5, slip st to 1st sc. (6 loops)

Drop A, draw B through loop on hook.

Round 3: Slip st into 1st ch-5 sp, ch3 (count as 1dc), 6dc into same ch-5 sp, [7dc into next ch-5 sp] 5 times, slip st to top of ch-3.

Draw A through loop on hook, tighten B. Fasten off.

Round 4: *Yo twice, insert hook from right to left behind next sc of round 2, yo and draw up loop to height of dc of round 3, [yo and draw through 2 loops] 3 times (1st tr made), 1sc into each of next 7 dc through back loops; rep from * 5 more times, slip st to top of 1st tr.

Round 5: Ch1, 1sc into same place as last sl st, [ch5, skip 3 sts, 1sc in next st] 11 times, ch5, slip st to 1st sc. (12 loops)

Drop A, draw C through loop on hook.

Round 6: Slip st into 1st ch-5 sp, ch3, 5dc into same ch-5 sp, [6dc into next ch-5 sp] 11 times, slip st to top of ch-3, draw A through loop on hook, tighten C and fasten off.

Round 7: Ch1, yo 3 times, insert hook under dc of round 4, yo and draw up long loop, [yo and through 2 loops] 4 times (dtr worked around tr), ch2, dtr around same tr, skip 1 st, *working through back loops, 1sc into each of next 10 sts, (1dtr, ch2, 1dtr) around next tr of round 4, skip 2 sts; rep from * 4 more times, 1sc into back loop of each of next 10 sts, slip st to 1st dtr.

Round 8: Ch1, *yo, insert hook behind 1st dtr, yo and draw up loop, yo and draw through 3 loops on hook (1hdc worked around dtr), 3sc into next ch-2 sp, 1hdc around next dtr, 1sc into back loop of each of next 10 sts; rep from * 5 more times, slip st to 1st hdc.

Fasten off.

Nanna square

Base ring: Ch6, join with slip st.
Round 1: Ch3 (count as 1dc), 15dc into ring, slip st to top of ch-3.
Round 2: Ch5 (count as 1dc, ch2), (1dc into next dc, ch2) 15 times, slip st to 3rd of ch-5. (16 spokes)
Round 3: Ch3, [1dc, ch3, 2dc] into 1st ch-2 sp, *[ch2, 1sc into next ch-2 sp] 3 times, ch2**, [2dc, ch3, 2dc] into next ch-2 sp; rep from * twice more, then from * to ** again, slip st to top of ch-3.
Round 4: Slip st into next ch-3 sp, ch3, [1dc, ch3, 2dc] into same ch sp, *[ch2, 1sc into next ch-2 sp] 4 times, ch2 ** [2dc, ch3, 2dc] into next ch-2 sp; rep from * twice more, then from * to ** again, slip st to top of ch-3.
Round 5: Slip st into next ch-3 sp, ch3, [1dc, ch3, 2dc] into same ch sp, *[ch2, 1sc into next ch sp] 5 times, ch2** [2dc, ch3, 2dc] into next ch-2 sp; rep from * twice more, then from * to ** again, slip st to top of ch-3.
Fasten off.

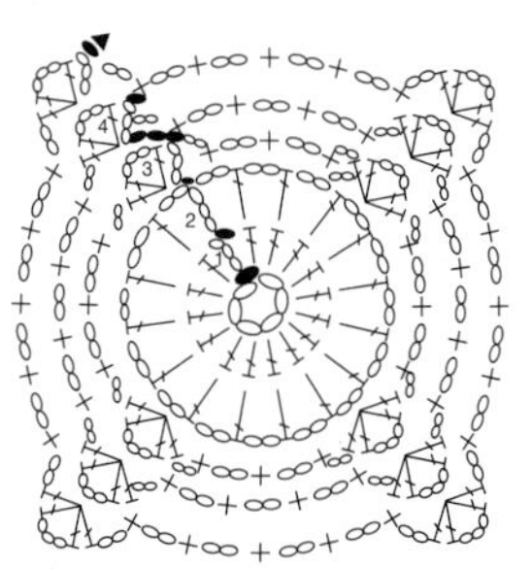

Springtime blossom

Base ring: Ch6, join with slip st.
Round 1: Ch3 (count as 1dc), 15dc into ring, slip st to top of ch-3.
Round 2: Ch5 (count as 1dc, ch2), 1dc into same st as last slip st, *ch1, skip 1 dc, [1dc, ch2, 1dc] into next dc; rep from * 6 more times, ch1, slip st to 3rd of ch-5.
Round 3: Slip st into 1st ch-2 sp, ch3 (count as 1dc), [1dc, ch2, 2dc] into same sp, *ch1, [2dc, ch2, 2dc] into next ch-2 sp; rep from * 6 more times, ch1, slip st to top of ch-3.
Round 4: Slip st into next dc and 1st ch-2 sp, ch3, 6dc into same sp as last sl st, 1sc into next ch sp, [7dc into next ch-2 sp, 1sc into next ch sp] 7 times, slip st into top of ch-3.
Fasten off.

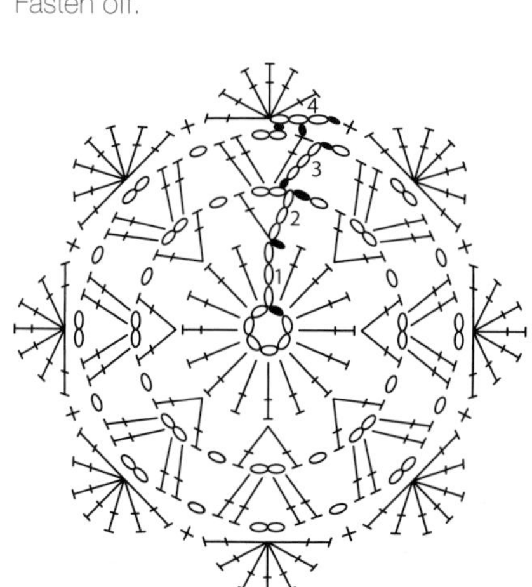

Leaf over

Row 1: Ch10, 1sc into 2nd ch from hook and into each of next 7 ch, 3sc into last ch, work on opposite side of ch, 1sc into each of next 6 ch, turn.
Row 2: Ch3, skip 1st st, working into back loops of sts, 1sc into each of next 6 sc, 3sc into next sc, 1sc into each of next 6 sc, turn.
Rep row 2 a further 3 times.
Fasten off.

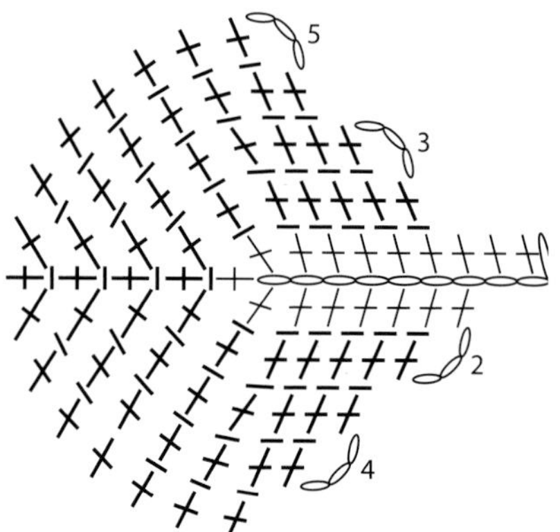

Treasury

Base ring: Using A, ch4, join with slip st.
Round 1: Ch1, [1sc in ring, ch10] 8 times, slip st to 1st sc. Fasten off A.
Round 2: Join B at top of any ch-10 sp, ch3 (count as 1dc), 2dc into same sp, *[3dc, ch2, 3dc] into next sp for corner, 3dc into next sp; rep from * twice more, [3dc, ch2, 3dc] into next sp, slip st to top of ch-3. Fasten off B.
Round 3: Join C in ch-2 of any corner, ch3, 2dc into same ch-2 sp, [1dc into each of next 9 dc, 3dc into next ch-2 sp] 3 times, 1dc into each of next 9 dc, slip st to top of ch-3.
Fasten off.

Fern leaf

Round 1: Ch18, slip st into 2nd ch from hook, 1sc into next ch, 1hdc into next ch, 1dc into each of next 4 ch, 1tr into each of next 5 ch, 1dc into each of next 2 ch, 1hdc into next ch, 1sc in next ch, slip st into next ch. Fasten off. Do not turn.
Round 2: Join yarn in 1st sc, 1sc into next st, 1hdc into next st, 1dc into each of next 5 sts, 1hdc into each of next 3 sts, 1sc into each of next 2 sts, slip st into each of next 3 sts.
Fasten off.

Webbed flower

Special abbreviation:
Bobble = holding back last loop of each tr, 5tr into next sp, yo and draw through all 6 loops on hook.
Base ring: Ch4, join with slip st.
Round 1: Ch5 (count as 1dc and ch2), [1dc, ch2] 5 times into ring, slip st to 3rd of ch-5.
Round 2: Sl st into next sp, ch4, holding back last loop of each tr, 4tr into same sp, yo and draw through all 5 loops on hook, *ch9, bobble in next sp; rep from * 4 more times, ch9, slip st to top of 1st bobble.
Round 3: Ch1, 1sc into same place as last slip st, *ch9, skip 4 ch, work bobble into next ch of ch-9, ch9, 1sc into top of next bobble; rep from * 5 more times skipping 1sc at end of last rep, slip st to 1st sc.
Fasten off.

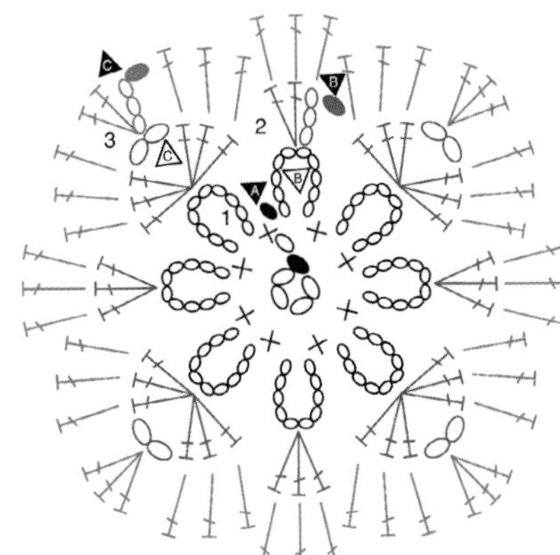

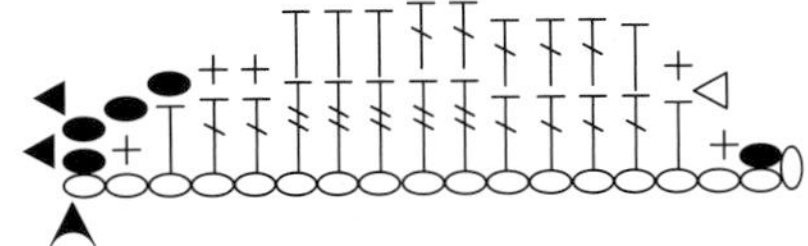

Genesa crystal

Special abbreviations:

Petal = ch1, 1tr into next sc, ch2, 1tr into stem of last tr two-thirds of the way down, ch2, [1dc, ch2] twice into stem of last tr (two-thirds of the way down as before), 1dc two-thirds of the way down stem of 1st tr, ch1, 1sc into next dc.

Bobble = 3dc into next sc until 1 loop of each remains on hook, yo and through all 4 loops on hook.

Base ring: Ch8, join with slip st.

Round 1: Ch1, 16sc into ring, slip st to 1st sc.

Round 2: Ch3, 2dc into same place as last sl st until 1 loop of each dc remains on hook, yo and draw through all 3 loops, (1 bobble made at beg of round), [ch3, skip next sc, 1 bobble into next sc] 7 times, ch3, slip st to top of ch-3 at beg of round.

Round 3: Ch6 (count as 1dc and ch3), 1sc into next ch-3 sp, ch3, [1dc into next bobble, ch3, 1sc to next ch-3 sp, ch3] 7 times, slip st into 3rd of ch-6.

Round 4: Ch1, 1sc into same place as last slip st, work 8 petals omitting sc at end of last petal, slip st to 1st sc.

Fasten off.

Framed star

Base ring: Ch5, join with slip st.

Round 1: Ch6 (count as 1dc, ch3), [1dc into ring, ch3] 7 times, slip st to 3rd of ch-6. (8dc)

Round 2: Ch3 (count as 1dc), [4dc into next ch-3 sp, 1dc into next dc] 7 times, 4dc into last ch-3 sp, slip st to top of ch-3 (40dc made). Fasten off.

Round 3: Working behind all dc of round 2, attach yarn to top of any dc of round 1, *ch8 (count as 1 long sc, ch6), 1sc into 2nd ch from hook, 1hdc into next ch, 1dc into next ch, 1tr into next ch, 1dtr into last ch, [1 long sc into top of next dc of round 1, ch6, 1sc into 2nd ch from hook, 1hdc into next ch, 1dc into next ch, 1tr into next ch, 1dtr into last ch] 7 times, slip st to 2nd of 1st ch-8. Fasten off.

Round 4: Attach yarn to turning ch of any star point, ch4, [1tr, ch3, 2tr] into same ch, *ch6, 1sc into turning ch of next star point, ch6, [2tr, ch3, 2tr] into turning ch of next star point (corner made); rep from * twice more, ch6, 1sc into turning ch of next star point, ch6, slip st to top of ch-4.

Round 5: Ch3 (count as 1dc), 1dc into next tr, [5dc into next ch-3 sp (corner made), 1dc into each of next 2 tr, 6dc into next ch-6 sp, 1dc into next sc, 6dc into next ch-6 sp, 1dc into each of next 2 tr]

4 times skipping 2 dc at end of last rep, slip st to top of ch-3.

Round 6: Ch4 (count as 1dc, ch1), skip 1 dc, 1dc into next dc, ch1, skip 1 dc, *[1dc, ch3, 1dc] into next dc (corner made), [ch1, skip 1 dc, 1dc into next dc] 10 times, ch1, skip 1 dc; rep from * twice more, [1dc, ch3, 1dc] into next dc, [ch1, miss 1dc, 1dc into next dc] 8 times, ch1, skip 1 dc, slip st to 3rd of ch-4.

Fasten off.

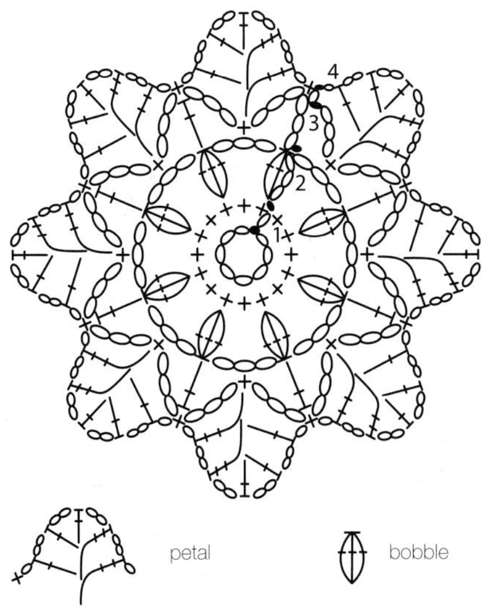

Genesa crystal

Solidarity plaque

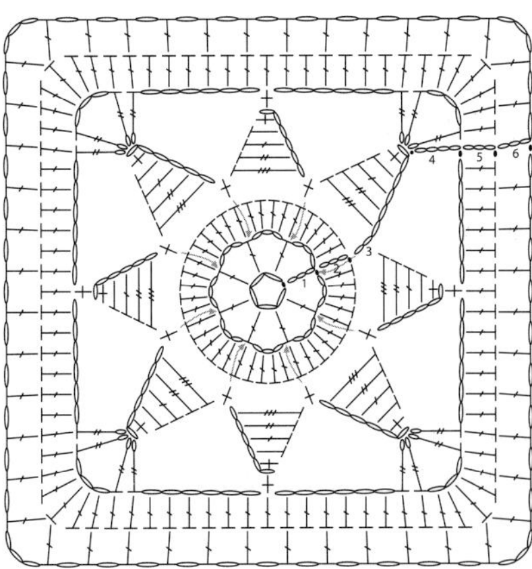

Framed star

Motif 1

Base ring: Ch4, join with slip st.

Round 1: Ch1, 8sc into ring, slip st to 1st sc.

Round 2: Ch2, 1dc into same place as slip st, *ch3, 1sc into next sc, ch3, dc2tog in next sc; rep from * twice more, ch3, 1sc into next sc, ch3, slip st to top of ch-3.

Round 3: Ch6 (count as 1dc, ch3), [1dc, ch3] twice into same place as last slip st, 1dc into next sc, ch3, *[1dc, ch3] 3 times into top of next dc2tog, 1dc into next sc, ch3; rep from * twice more, slip st to 3rd of ch-6.

Motif 2

Follow pattern for 1st motif through round 2.

Round 3: Ch5 (count as 1dc and ch2), slip st in ch-3 sp of 1st motif corner group, ch1, [1dc, ch3] twice into same place as last slip st from previous round, 1dc into next sc, ch3, *[1dc, ch3] 3 times into top of next dc2tog, 1dc into next sc, ch3; rep from * once more, (1dc, ch3, 1dc) in next dc2tog, ch2, slip st in ch-3 sp of corresponding corner of motif 1, (ch1, 1dc) in same dc2tog, ch3, 1dc in next sc, ch3, slip st to 3rd of ch-6.

Join motif 3 to bottom edge of motif 1 as for motif 2.

Join motif 4 as for motif 2 except also join corresponding corner sps to motif 2.

Fasten off.

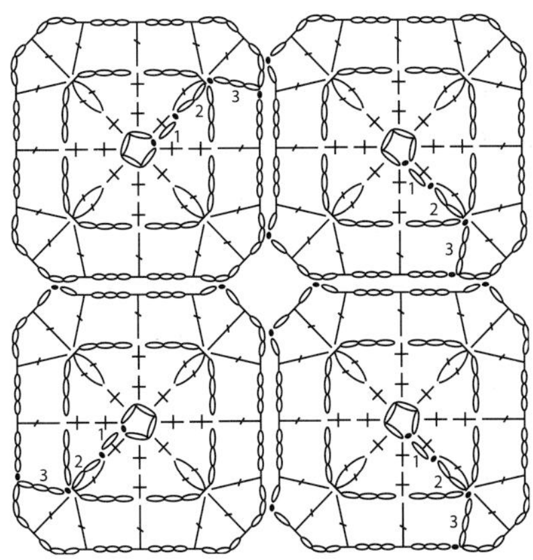

Solidarity plaque

Ripples

Base ring: Ch8, join with slip st.

Round 1: Ch8, slip st into 5th ch from hook (picot), *4dc into ring, ch5, slip st into top of last dc made (picot); rep from * 6 more times, ending 3dc into ring, slip st to 3rd of ch-8.

Round 2: Slip st into center of 1st picot, ch3 (count as 1dc), [1dc, ch2, 2dc] into same picot, *ch4, [2dc, ch2, 2dc] into next picot (shell); rep from * 6 more times, ch4, slip st to top of ch-3.

Round 3: Slip st into next dc and into next ch-2 sp, ch3 (count as 1dc), [1dc, ch2, 2dc] into same sp, *ch6, shell into ch-2 sp of next shell; rep from * 6 more times, ch6, slip st to top of ch-3.

Round 4: Slip st into next dc and into next ch-2 sp, ch3, [1dc, ch2, 2dc] into same ch sp, *ch8, shell into ch-2 sp of next shell; rep from * 6 more times, ch8, slip st to top of ch3.

Round 5: Slip st into next dc and into next ch-2 sp, ch3, 3dc into same sp, *1sc into each ch of next ch-8, 4dc into next ch-2 sp; rep from * 6 more times, ending 1sc into each ch of next ch-8, slip st to top of ch-3.

Fasten off.

Sunflower

Special abbreviations:

2tr bobble = 2tr into next sc until 1 loop of each remains on hook, yo and draw through all 3 loops on hook.

3tr bobble = 3tr into next sc until 1 loop of each remains on hook, yo and draw through all 4 loops on hook.

Base ring: Ch6, join with slip st.

Round 1: Ch1, 12sc into ring, slip st to 1st sc.

Round 2: Ch1, [1sc into next sc, 2sc into next sc] 6 times, slip st to 1st sc. (18sc made)

Round 3: Ch1, [1sc into each of next 2 sc, 2sc into next sc] 6 times, slip st to 1st sc. (24 sc made)

Round 4: Ch1, [1sc into each of next 3 sc, 2sc into next sc] 6 times, slip st to 1st sc. (30 sc made)

Round 5: Ch1, [1sc into each of next 4 sc, 2sc into next sc] 6 times, slip st to 1st sc. (36 sc made)

Round 6: Ch1, [1sc into each of next 5 sc, 2sc into next sc] 6 times, slip st to 1st sc. (42 sc made)

Round 7: Ch1, [1sc into each of next 6 sc, 2sc into next sc] 6 times, slip st to 1st sc. (48 sc made)

Round 8: Ch4, 2tr bobble in same sc as last slip st, *ch5, skip 2 sc, 3tr bobble in next sc; rep from * 14 more times, ch5, slip st to top of 1st bobble.

Round 9: Slip st to center of ch-5, ch7, [1sc in next ch-5 sp, ch6] 16 times, slip st to 1st of ch-7.

Fasten off.

Doily square

Special abbreviations:

Tr2tog = 2tr into ring until 1 loop of each remains on hook, yo and draw through all 3 loops on hook.

Bobble = work 3dc into sp until 1 loop of each remains on hook, yo and draw through all 4 loops on hook.

Base ring: Ch10, join with slip st.

Round 1: Ch4, 1tr into ring, ch2, [tr2tog, ch2] 11 times into ring, slip st to 1st tr.

Round 2: Slip st into next ch-2 sp, ch3, into same ch-2 sp as slip st, work 2dc until 1 loop of each remains on hook, yo and draw through all 3 loops on hook (1st bobble made), ch3, [1 bobble into next ch-2 sp, ch3] 11 times, slip st to top of 1st bobble.

Round 3: Ch5 (count as 1hdc and ch3), skip 1st ch-3 sp, [1 bobble, ch2, 1 bobble, ch4, 1 bobble, ch2, 1 bobble] into next ch-3 sp, ch3, *skip next ch-3 sp, 1hdc into top of next bobble, ch3, skip next ch-3 sp, [1 bobble, ch2, 1 bobble, ch4, 1 bobble, ch2, 1 bobble] into next ch-3 sp, ch3; rep from * twice more, slip st to 2nd of ch-5.

Round 4: Ch1, 1sc into same place as last slip st, *3sc into next ch-3 sp, 1sc into next bobble, 2sc into next ch-2 sp, 1sc into next bobble, 5sc into next ch-4 sp, 1sc into next bobble, 2sc into next ch-2 sp, 1sc into next bobble, 3sc into next ch-3 sp, 1sc into next hdc; rep from * 3 more times skipping 1 sc at end of last rep, slip st to 1st sc.

Fasten off.

Ripples

Sunflower

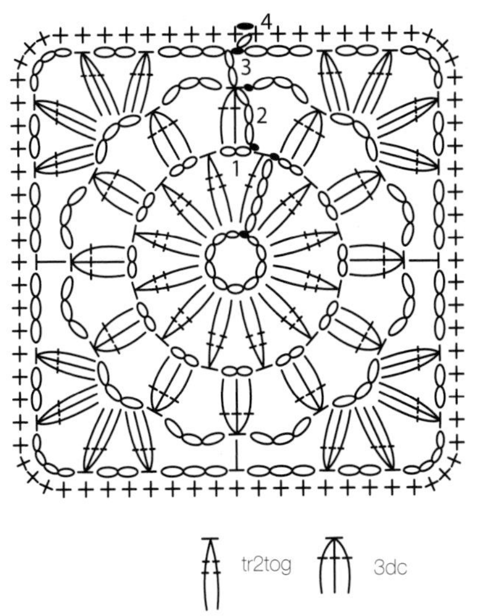

Doily square

Aquarius stitch

Base ring: Ch8, join with slip st.

Round 1: Ch1, 16sc into ring, slip st to 1st sc.

Round 2: Ch4 (count as 1tr), 2tr into 1st sc, 3tr into next sc, ch5, [skip 2 sc, 3tr into each of next 2 sc, ch5] 3 times, slip st to top of ch-4.

Round 3: Ch1, 1sc into same place as last slip st, *[1hdc, 1dc] into next tr, 2tr into each of next 2 tr, [1dc, 1hdc] into next tr, 1sc into next tr, 1sc into each of next 2 ch, 3sc into next ch, 1sc into each of next 2 ch, 1sc into next tr; rep from * 3 more times skipping 1 sc at end of last rep, slip st to 1st sc. Fasten off.

Daisy motif

Base ring: Ch6, join with slip st.

Round 1: Ch1, 15sc into ring, slip st to 1st sc.

Round 2: Ch1, 1sc into same place as last slip st, *[2dc, 1tr, 2dc] into next sc, 1sc into each of next 2 sc; rep from * 4 more times skipping 1 sc at end of last rep, slip st to 1st sc. Fasten off.

Mandala

Work as given for Six-point motif (see page 182) but working and rounds 1 and 2 in A, round 3 in B, and round 4 in C.

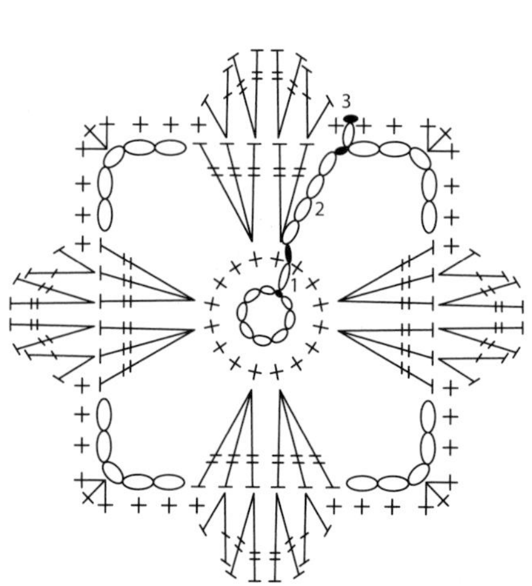

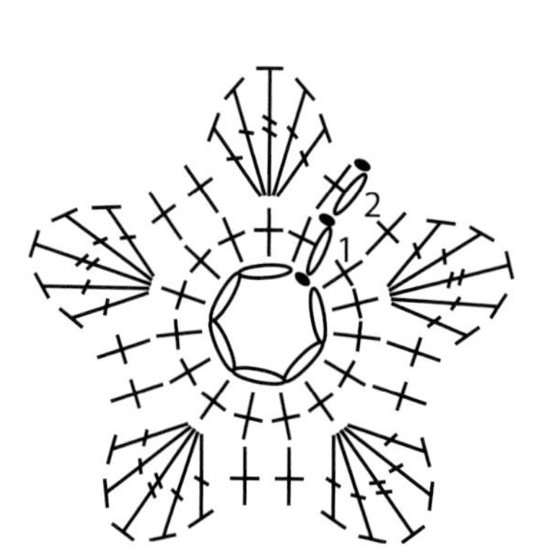

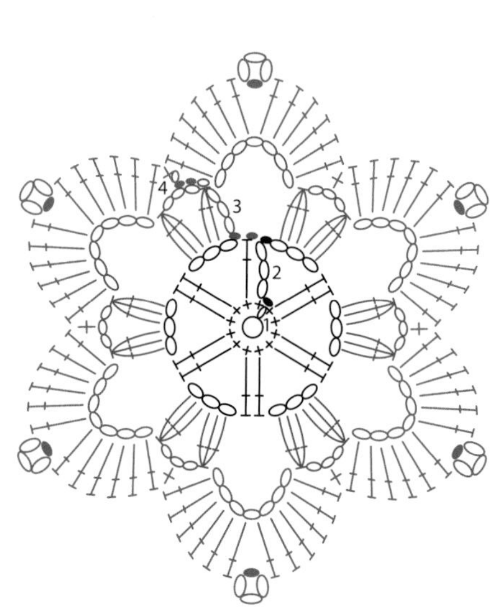

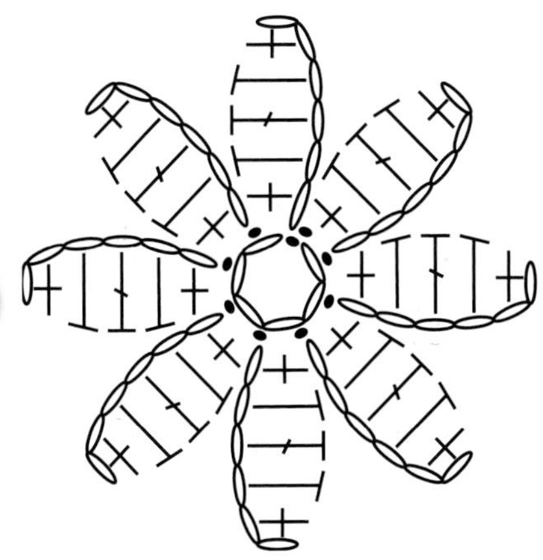

Orchid blossom

Orchid blossom

Base ring: Ch6, join with slip st.
Petal: [Ch6, 1sc into 2nd ch from hook, 1hdc into next ch, 1dc into next ch, 1hdc into next ch, 1sc into next ch, slip st into ring] 8 times. Fasten off.

Popcorn cluster

Base ring: Ch6, join with slip st.
Round 1: Ch5 (count as 1dc, ch2), [1dc into ring, ch2] 7 times, slip st to 3rd of ch-5.
Round 2: Ch3, holding back last loop of each dc, *[3dc, yo and draw through all loops on hook] into next ch-2 sp, ch1; rep from * 7 more times, slip st top of ch-3. Fasten off.

Swirl motif

Note: This motif is worked as a continuous spiral; the size can therefore be increased or decreased as required.
Round 1: Ch2, 6sc into 2nd ch from hook, slip st to 1st sc.
Cont in a spiral as follows:
ch1, 1sc into same st as last slip st, ch3, [1sc into next sc, ch3] 5 times, [1sc into next sc, 1sc into next sp, ch3] 6 times, [skip 1 sc, 1sc into next sc, 2sc into next sp, ch3] 6 times, [skip 1 sc, 1sc into each of next 2 sc, 2sc into next sp, ch4] 6 times, [skip 1 sc, 1sc into each of next 3 sc, 2sc into next ch-4 sp, ch4] 6 times, [skip 1 sc, 1sc into each of next 4 sc, 2sc into next ch-4 sp, ch5] 6 times, [skip 1 sc, 1sc into each of next 5 sc, 2sc into next ch-5 sp, ch5] 6 times, [skip 1 sc, 1sc into each of next 6 sc, 2sc into next ch-5 sp, ch6] 6 times, [skip 1 sc, 1sc into each of next 7 sc, 2sc into next ch-6 sp, ch6] 6 times, [skip 1 sc, 1sc into each of next 8 sc, 2sc into next ch-6 sp, ch7] 6 times, skip 1 sc, sl st to next sc.
Fasten off.

Popcorn cluster

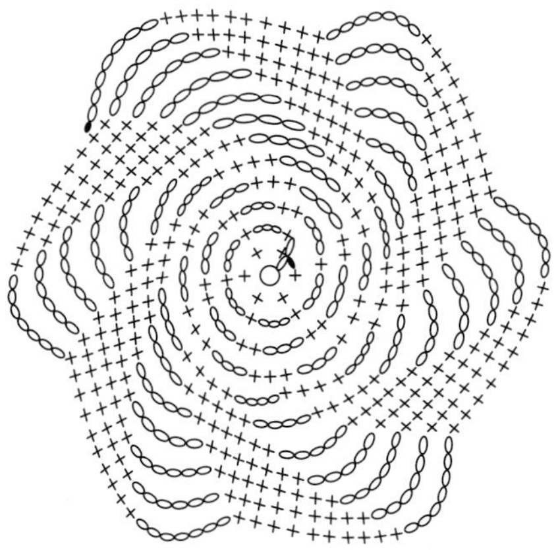

Swirl motif

Granny Mae

Special abbreviation:

3-picot cluster = ch4, slip st into 1st ch, [ch3, slip st into same ch as 1st slip st] twice.

Base ring: Ch6, join with slip st.

Round 1: Ch1, 12sc into ring, slip st to 1st sc.

Round 2: Ch3 (count as 1dc), 1dc into same place as last slip st, 2dc into each of next 11 sc, slip st to top of ch-3.

Round 3: Ch1, 1sc into same place as last slip st, 1sc into each of next 23 dc, slip st to 1st sc.

Round 4: Ch1, 1sc into same place as last slip st, ch5, skip 2 sc, [1sc into next sc, ch5, skip 2 sc] 7 times, slip st to 1st sc.

Round 5: Ch1, 1sc into same place as last slip st, *[1hdc, 3dc, 3-picot cluster, 3dc, 1hdc] into next ch-5 sp, 1sc into next sc; rep from * 7 more times skipping 1 sc at end of last rep, slip st to 1st sc.

Round 6: Ch1, 1sc into same place as last slip st, *ch7, 1sc into center picot of 3-picot cluster, ch7, 1sc into next sc; rep from * 7 more times skipping 1 sc at end of last rep, slip st to 1st sc.

Round 7: Slip st into next ch-7 sp, ch1, [8sc into next ch-7 sp, 3-picot cluster, 8sc into next ch-7 sp] 8 times, slip st to 1st sc. Fasten off.

Tunisia flower

Base ring: Using A, ch4, join with slip st.

Round 1: Ch3 (count as 1dc), 9dc into ring, slip st to top of ch-3.

Round 2: Ch1, 1sc into same place as last slip st, 2sc into next dc, [1sc into next dc, 2sc into next dc] 4 times, slip st to 1st sc.

Round 3: Ch1, 1sc into same place as last slip st, 1sc into next sc, 2sc into next sc, [1sc into each of next 2 sc, 2sc into next sc] 4 times, slip st to 1st sc. (20 sc)

Round 4: [Ch7, 1sc into 2nd ch from hook and into each of next 5 ch, slip st into next sc, 1sc into next sc] 10 times, skipping 1 sc at end of last rep, slip st to sc of 1st point, turn.

Round 5: *Skip slip st and next sc, 1sc into back loop of each of next 6 sc, [1sc, ch1, 1sc] into top of point, 1sc into each of next 6 ch on other side of ch; rep from * 9 more times, slip st to slip st between points, draw B through loop, fasten off A, turn.

Round 6: Skip 1st sc, *1sc into back loop of each of next 6sc, [1sc, ch2, 1sc] into ch-1 of point, 1sc into back loop of each of next 6sc, skip next 2 sc; rep from * 9 more times skipping 1sc at end of last rep, slip st to 1st sc, turn.

Rounds 7, 8 and 9: Work as round 6, through back loops of 6 sts at each side of points with [1sc, ch2, 1sc] into ch-2 sp at each point.

Fasten off.

Granny Mae

Tunisia flower

Floral lace

Special abbreviation:

Dc2tog = 1dc into next dc until 2 loops remain on hook, skip 2 dc, 1dc into next dc until 3 loops remain on hook, yo and draw through all 3 loops on hook.

Base ring: Ch10, join with slip st.

Round 1: Ch3 (count as 1dc), 31dc into ring, slip st to top of ch-3.

Round 2: [Ch7, skip 3 dc, slip st into next dc] 7 times, ch3, 1tr into same st as last slip st of previous round.

Round 3: Ch3 (count as 1dc), 6dc into top of tr, [7dc into 4th ch of next ch-7 sp] 7 times, slip st to top of ch-3.

Round 4: Slip st into next dc, ch6 (count as 1dc and ch3), *skip 1 dc, [1tr, ch5, 1tr] into next dc, ch3, skip 1 dc, dc2tog, ch3, skip 1 dc, 1sc into next dc, ch3, skip 1 dc, dc2tog, ch3; rep from * 3 more times skipping 1 dc2tog and ch3 at end of last rep, skip 1 dc, 1dc into next dc, slip st to 3rd of ch-6.

Round 5: Ch1, 1sc into same place as last slip st, *3sc into next ch-3 sp, 1sc into next tr, 6sc into ch-5 sp, 1sc into next tr, 3sc into next ch-3 sp, 1sc into top of next dc2tog, 3sc into next ch-3 sp, 1sc into next sc, 3sc into next ch-3 sp, 1sc into top of next dc2tog; rep from * 3 more times skipping 1 sc at end of last rep, slip st to 1st sc.

Fasten off.

Floral lace

Posey

Base ring: Ch6, join with sl st.

Round 1: Ch1, 24sc into ring, slip st to 1st sc.

Round 2: Ch5 (count as1dc, ch2), 1dc into next dc, [ch1, skip 1 dc, 1dc into next dc, ch2, 1dc into next dc] 7 times, ch1, skip 1 dc, slip st to 3rd of ch-5.

Round 3: Slip st into 1st ch-2 sp, ch2 (count as 1hdc), [1hdc, ch2, 2hdc] into same ch-2 sp, 1sc into next ch-1 sp, *[2hdc, ch2, 2hdc] into next ch-2 sp, 1sc into next ch-1 sp; rep from * 6 more times, slip st to top of ch-2.

Round 4: Slip st into next dc and into next ch-2 sp, ch3, [2dc, ch1, 3dc] into same ch-2 sp, 1sc on each side of next sc, *[3dc, ch1, 3dc] into next ch-2 sp, 1sc on each side of next sc; rep from * 6 more times, slip st to top of ch-3.

Fasten off.

African violet

Special abbreviation:

Bobble = 3dtr into ch until 1 loop of each remains on hook, yo and draw through all 4 loops on hook.

Round 1: Ch6, dtr2tog into 1st ch (count as 1st bobble), [ch5, 1 bobble] 7 times into same ch, ch2, 1dc into top of 1st bobble.

Round 2: Ch1, 1sc into sp just formed, ch6, [1sc into next ch-5 sp, ch6] 7 times, slip st to 1st sc.

Round 3: Slip st into 1st ch-6 sp, ch3 (count as 1dc), 5dc into same sp, ch3, [6dc into next ch-6 sp, ch3] 7 times, slip st to top of ch-3 at beg of round.

Fasten off.

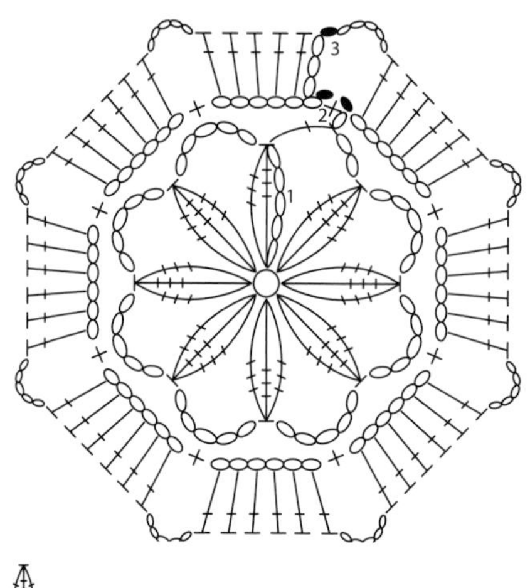

bobble

Gemini spoke

Base ring: Ch8, join with slip st.

Round 1: Ch1, 16sc into ring, slip st to 1st sc.

Round 2: Ch6 (count as 1dc, ch3), skip next sc, [1dc into next sc, ch3, skip 1 sc] 7 times, slip st to 3rd of ch-6.

Round 3: Ch1, 1sc into same place as last slip st, [4dc into next ch-3 sp, 1sc into next dc] 7 times, 4dc into next ch-3 sp, slip st to 1st sc.

Fasten off.

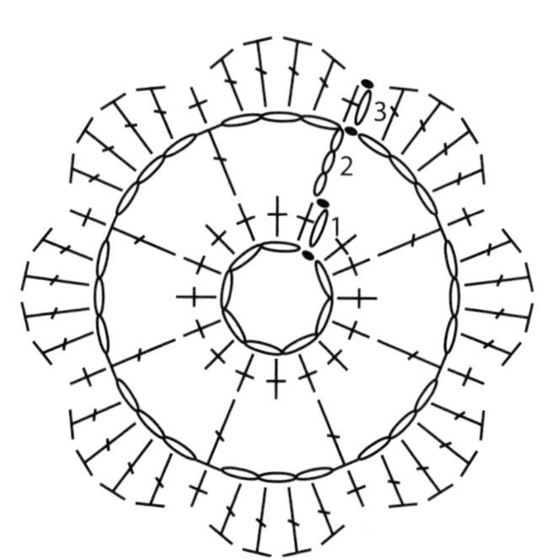

Five-point starfish

Base chain: Ch2.

Round 1: 5sc into 2nd ch from hook, slip st to 1st sc.

Round 2: Ch1, 3sc into each sc, slip st to 1st sc. (15sc)

Round 3: Ch1, 1sc into same place as last slip st, [ch6, slip st into 2nd ch from hook, 1sc into next ch, 1hdc into next ch, 1dc into next ch, 1tr into next ch, 1tr into base of last sc worked into circle, skip 2 sc, 1sc into next sc] 5 times skipping 1 sc at end of last rep, slip st to 1st sc. Fasten off.

Bull's eye

Special abbreviation:

Bobble = leaving last loop of each dc on hook, 3dc in same sp, yo and draw through all 4 loops on hook.

Base ring: Using A, ch8, join with slip st.

Round 1: Ch1, 20sc into ring, slip st to 1st sc.

Round 2: Working through front loops only, 1sc into same place as last slip st, [ch3, 1sc into next sc] 19 times, ch3, slip st to 1st sc. Fasten off.

Round 3: Attach B behind A to any sc on 1st round. Working through back loops only of each sc in 1st round, holding the ch-3 loops forward, ch4 (count as 1dc, ch1), [1dc into next sc, ch1] 19 times, slip st to 3rd of ch-4.

Round 4: Slip st in next ch-1 sp, ch3, dc2tog in same sp (count as 1st bobble), ch5, bobble in same ch sp, *bobble in next sp, (bobble, ch3, bobble) in next sp, bobble in next sp**, (bobble, ch5, bobble) in next sp; rep from * 3 more times and from * to ** once more, slip st to top of 1st bobble. Fasten off.

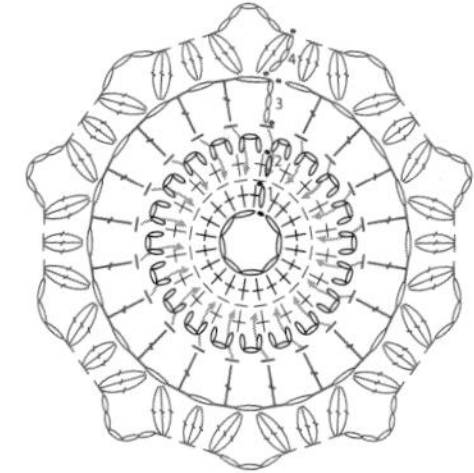

Circle of life

Special abbreviation:

Bobble = 3dc into next dc (leaving last loop of each dc on hook), yo and draw through all 4 loops on hook.

Base ring: Ch6, join with slip st.

Round 1: Ch3 (count as 1dc), 15dc into ring, slip st to top of ch-3.

Round 2: Ch3, dc2tog in same place as last slip st (count as 1st bobble), [ch2, skip 1 dc, 1sc into next dc, ch2, skip 1 dc, bobble into next dc] 3 times, ch2, skip 1 dc, 1sc into next dc, ch2, slip st to top of ch-3.

Round 3: Ch3, [2dc into next ch-2 sp, 3dc into next sc, 2dc into next ch-2 sp, 1dc into next bobble] 4 times skipping 1dc at end of last rep, slip st to top of ch-3. Fasten off.

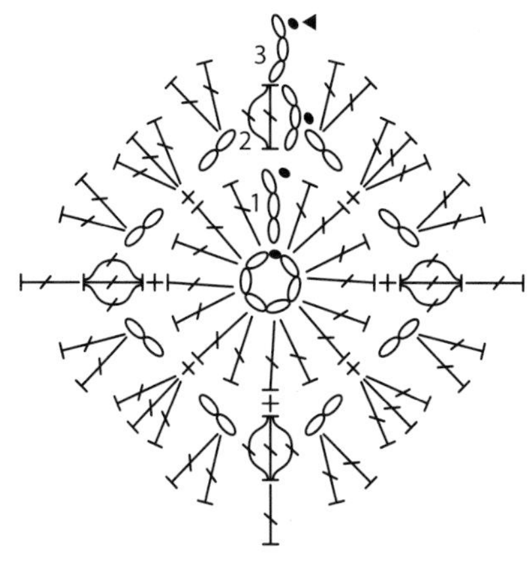

Flower in hexagon

Special abbreviation:

Puff st = [yo, insert hook from front and from right to left around post of next tr, yo, pull up a long loop] 5 times, yo and pull through 11 loops on hook, ch1 to tighten.

Base ring: Ch6, join with slip st.

Round 1: Ch4, 23tr into ring, slip st to top of ch-4.

Round 2: Ch5, [yo, insert hook from front and from right to left around ch-4 of previous round, yo, pull up a long loop] 4 times, yo and pull through 9 loops on hook, ch1, *skip 1 tr, (2dc, 1tr, 2dc) into next tr, skip 1 tr, puff st in next tr; rep from * 4 more times, skip 1 tr, (2dc, 1tr, 2dc) into next tr, skip 1 tr, slip st to top of 1st puff st. (6 puff sts).

Round 3: Ch1, *1sc into each of next 2 dc, 3sc into next tr (corner made), 1sc into each of next 2 dc, 1sc into top of next puff st; rep from * 5 more times, slip st to 1st sc.

Faste

Buttercup

Base ring: Ch5, join with slip st.

Round 1: Ch1, 12sc into ring, slip st to first sc.

Round 2: [Ch3, skip 1sc, 1sc into next sc] 5 times, ch3, skip 1sc, slip st to first of ch-3.

Round 3: [1sc, 1hdc, 3dc, 1hdc, 1sc] into each ch-3 sp, slip st to first sc. (6 petals)

Round 4: *Ch3, 1sc around bar of first sc of next petal; rep from * 4 more times, ch3, slip st to first of first ch-3.

Round 5: Rep round 3.

Fasten off.

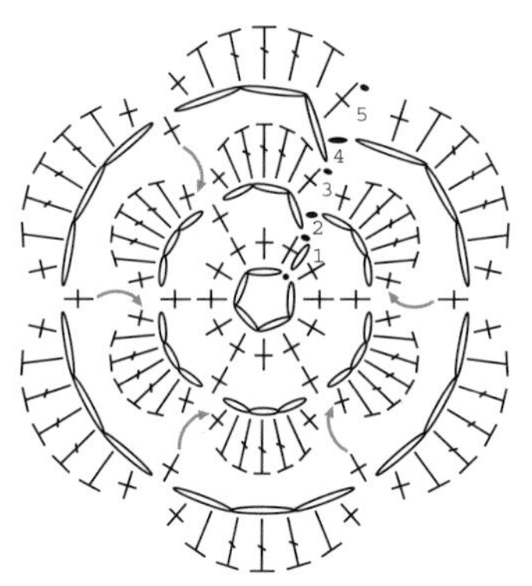

Mediterranean circle

Round 1: Using A, ch7 (count as 1tr, ch2), [1tr, ch2] 5 times into 7th ch from hook, slip st into 4th ch of 7h-7, turn.

Round 2: Ch1, 1sc into same place as last slip st, *[3sc into next ch-2 sp, 1sc into next tr] 5 times, 3sc into next ch-2 sp, slip st to back loop of 1st sc, draw B through loop. Fasten off A.

Round 3: Ch8, drop B from hook, join C in next sc, ch8, *drop C loop, pick up B loop in back of C, 1tr into next sc, ch5, drop B, pick up C loop in back of B, 1tr into next sc, ch5; rep from * around, ending with 1st B ch in front, 1st C ch in back, join last C ch-5 with slip st to 3rd ch of 1st C ch-8 and fasten off C, keeping 1st B ch at back, join last B ch-5 with slip st to 3rd ch of 1st B ch-8. Fasten off.

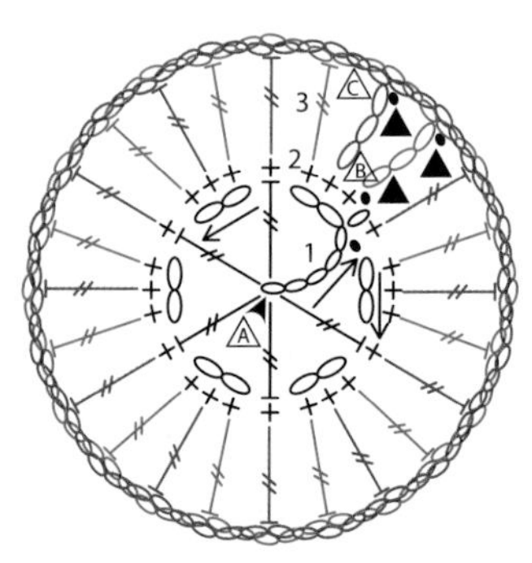

Dahlia

Base ring: Ch5, join with slip st.
Round 1: Ch1, 12sc into ring, slip st to 1st sc.
Round 2: Working into back loop only of each sc, ch12, slip st into 1st sc, *slip st into next sc, ch12, slip st into same sc; rep from * to end.
Round 3: Work as for round 2, but into the front loop only of each sc and ch8 only between slip sts. Fasten off.

Orient motif

Special abbreviation:
Puff = [yo, insert hook, yo and draw up loop] twice, yo and draw through all 5 loops on hook.
Base ring: Ch4, join with slip st.
Round 1: Ch3 (count as 1dc), 1dc into ring, [ch1, 2dc into ring] 4 times, ch1, slip st to top of ch-3.
Round 2: Slip st into next dc and next ch sp, puff into same ch sp, [ch4, puff into next ch sp] 4 times, ch4, slip st to top of 1st puff.
Round 3: Ch1, 1sc into same place as last slip st, [5sc into next ch-4 sp, 1sc into top of next puff] 4 times, 5sc into next ch-4 sp, slip st to 1st sc.
Fasten off.

Druid motif

Base ring: Using A, ch6, join with slip st.
Round 1: Ch2, 1hdc into ring (count as hdc2tog), [ch3, hdc2tog into ring] 7 times, ch3, slip st to 1st hdc2tog.
Round 2: Slip st into each of next 2 ch, ch1, 1sc into same ch sp, [ch5, 1sc into next ch-3 sp] 7 times, ch5, slip st to 1st sc.
Round 3: Ch1, [5sc into next ch-5 sp] 8 times, slip st to 1st sc. Fasten off.
Round 4: Join B to 3rd of next 5 sc, ch1, 1sc into same place as ch-1, *ch7, skip 4 sc, 1sc into next sc; rep from * 7 more times skipping sc at end of last rep, slip st to 1st sc.
Round 5: Ch1, *[4sc, ch3, 4sc] all into next ch-7 sp; rep from * 7 more times, slip st to 1st sc. Fasten off.

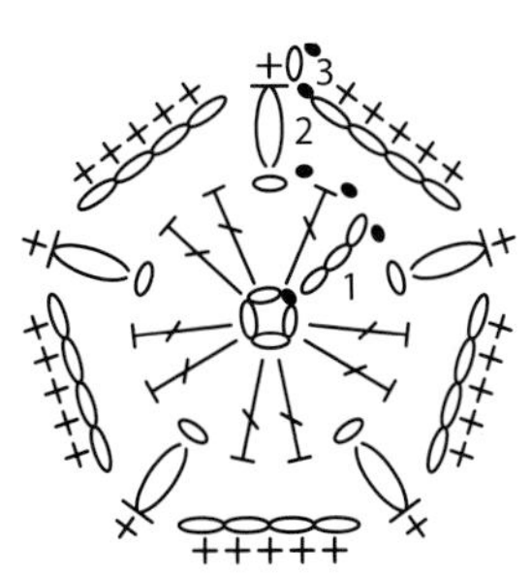

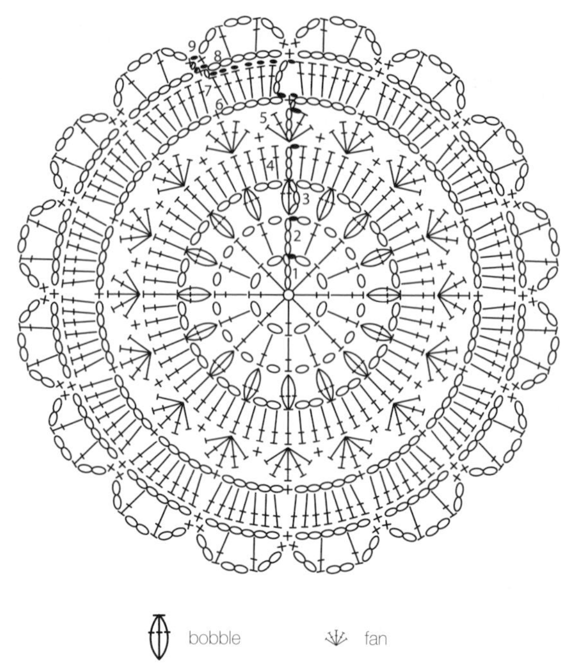

Granny Jane

Special abbreviations:

Bobble = 3dc into next st until 1 loop of each remains on hook, yo and draw through all 4 loops on hook.

Fan = [1hdc, 3dc, 1hdc] into next dc.

Round 1: Ch5, [1dc, ch1] 7 times into 1st ch, slip st to 4th of ch-5.

Round 2: Ch4 (count as 1dc and ch1), 1dc into 1st ch sp, ch1, [1dc into next dc, ch1, 1dc into next ch sp, ch1] 7 times, slip st to 3rd of ch-4.

Round 3: Ch3 (count as 1dc), dc2tog in same place as last slip st (count as bobble), ch2, [1 bobble into next dc, ch2] 15 times, slip st to top of 1st bobble.

Round 4: Ch3 (count as 1dc), 3dc into 1st ch-2 sp, [1dc into next bobble, 3dc into next ch-2 sp] 15 times, slip st to top of ch-3.

Round 5: Ch3, [1dc, 1hdc] into same place as last slip st, skip 1 dc, 1sc into next dc, [skip 1 dc, 1 fan into next dc, skip 1 dc, 1sc into next dc] 15 times, skip last dc, [1hdc, 1dc] into same place as slip st at end of previous round, slip st to top of ch-3.

Round 6: Ch1, 1sc into same place as last slip st, ch5, [1sc into center dc of next fan, ch5] 15 times, slip st into 1st sc.

Round 7: Slip st into 1st ch-5 sp, ch3, 6dc into same sp as slip st, 7dc into each of next 15 ch-5 sps, slip st to top of ch-3.

Round 8: Sl st into each of 1st 6 dc, ch1, 1sc between last dc worked into and next dc, ch6, [skip 7dc, 1sc between last dc skipped and next dc, ch6] 14 times, skip 7 dc, 1sc between last dc skipped and ch-3 at beg of previous round, ch6, slip st into 1st sc.

Round 9: Ch1, 1sc into same place as last slip st, [ch2, 1dc into next ch-6 sp] twice ch2, 2sc into next sc; rep from * 15 more times skipping 1sc at end of last rep, slip st to 1st sc.

Fasten off.

Shells and popcorns

Special abbreviation:

Popcorn = 5dc into next st, withdraw hook from working loop and insert through top of 1st of 5dc, insert hook back into working loop and draw through 1st of 5dc.

Base ring: Ch6, join with slip st.

Round 1: Ch3 (count as 1dc), 1dc into ring, [ch3, 3dc into ring] 3 times, ch3, 1dc into ring, slip st to top of ch-3. (4 3dc blocks)

Round 2: Ch3, popcorn into next dc, *[5dc into next ch-3 sp, popcorn into next dc, 1dc into next dc, popcorn into next dc] 3 times, 5dc into next ch-3 sp, popcorn into next dc, slip st to top of ch-3.

Round 3: Ch5, *skip popcorn, popcorn into next dc, 1dc into next dc, 3dc into next dc, 1dc into next dc, popcorn into next dc, ch2, skip popcorn, 1dc into next dc, ch2; rep from * 3 more times skipping 1dc and ch-2 at end of last rep, slip st to 3rd of ch-5.

Round 4: Slip st into next ch-2 sp, ch5, *skip popcorn, popcorn into next dc, 1dc into next dc, 3dc into next dc, 1dc into next dc, popcorn into next dc, ch2, skip next popcorn, 1dc into next ch-2 sp, ch2, 1dc into next ch-2 sp, ch2; rep from * three more times skipping 1dc and ch-2 at end of last rep, slip st to 3rd of ch-5.

Round 5: Slip st into next ch-2 sp, ch5, *skip popcorn, popcorn into next dc, 1dc into next dc, 3dc into next dc, 1dc into next dc, popcorn into next dc, ch2, [1dc into next ch-2 sp, ch2] 3 times; rep from * 3 more times skipping 1dc and ch-2 at end of last rep, slip st to 3rd of ch-5.

Round 6: Work as round 5, but working section in brackets 4 times instead of 3.

Round 7: As round 5, but working section in brackets 5 times instead of 3.

Continue working in this way until motif is required size.

Fasten off.

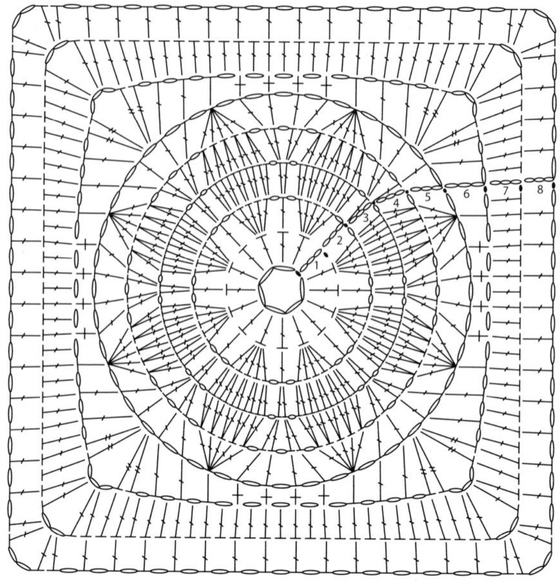

Embossed motif

Base ring: Ch6, join with slip st.

Round 1: Ch3 (count as 1st dc), 15dc into ring, slip st to top of ch-3. (16dc)

Round 2: Ch4, [5dc into next dc, ch1, 1dc into next dc, ch1] 7 times, 5dc into next dc, ch1, slip st to 3rd of ch-4.

Round 3: Ch4, 1dc into same place as last slip st, ch1, [2dc into each of next 5 dc, ch1, 1dc into next dc, ch1, 1dc into same place as last dc, ch1] 7 times, 2dc into each of next 5 dc, ch1, slip st to 3rd of ch-4.

Round 4: Ch3, 1dc into same place as last slip st, ch1, 2dc into next dc, ch1, [dc2tog 5 times over next 10 dc, ch1, 2dc into next dc, ch1, 2dc into next dc, ch1] 7 times, dc2tog 5 times over next 10 dc, ch1, slip st to top of ch-3.

Round 5: Ch4, [1dc into next dc, ch1] 3 times, *work dc5tog over next 5 dc, ch1, [1dc into next dc, ch1] 4 times; rep from * 6 more times, work dc5tog over next 5 dc, ch1, slip st to 3rd of ch-4.

Round 6: Ch4, *1dc into next dc, ch1, [2tr, ch3, 2tr] into next ch-1 sp, [ch1, 1dc into next dc] twice, ch1, 1hdc into top of next cluster, [ch1, 1sc into next dc] 4 times, ch1, 1hdc into top of next cluster, ch1, 1dc into next dc, ch1; rep from * 3 more times skipping 1dc and ch-1 at end of last rep, slip st to 3rd of ch-4.

Round 7: Ch3, *1dc into next ch sp, 1dc into next dc, 1dc into next

ch sp, 1dc into each of next 2 tr, [2dc, ch2, 2dc] into next ch-3 sp, 1dc into each of next 2 tr, [1dc into next ch sp, 1dc into next dc] twice, 1dc into next ch sp, 1dc into next hdc, [1dc into next ch sp, 1dc into next sc] 4 times, 1dc into next ch sp, 1dc into next hdc, 1dc into next ch sp, 1dc into next dc; rep from * 3 more times skipping 1dc at end of last rep, slip st to top of ch-3.

Round 8: Ch4, skip next dc, 1dc into next dc, [ch1, skip next dc, 1dc into next dc] twice, *ch1, skip next dc, [2dc, ch2, 2dc] into ch-2 sp, [ch1, skip next dc, 1dc into next dc] 14 times; rep from * 3 more times working [ch1, skip next dc, 1dc into next dc] 10 times, ch1 at end of last rep, slip st to 3rd of ch-4.

Fasten off.

Six-point snowflake motif

Special abbreviations:

Picot = ch4, slip st into 4th ch from hook.

Dc rice st = ch3, 2dc into indicated base st while holding back last loop of each dc, yo and pull through all 3 loops on hook, ch3, sl st into same base st.

Dtr rice st = ch5, 2dtr into indicated base st while holding back last loop of each dtr, yo and pull through all 3 loops on hook, ch5, sl st into same base st.

Base ring: Ch6, join with slip st.

Round 1: Ch1, 12sc into ring, join with slip st to 1st sc.

Round 2: Dtr rice st in same place as slip st, slip st into next sc, *dc rice st in next sc, slip st in next sc, dtr rice st in next sc, slip st in next sc; rep from * 4 more times, dc rice st in next sc.

Round 3: 5 slip sts to top of dtr rice st, ch1, 1sc into same st, *ch7, 1sc on top of next dtr rice st; rep from * 4 times more, ch7, join with slip st to 1st sc.

Round 4: Ch6 (count as 1dc, ch3), 1dc into same st, *7dc into next ch-7 sp, [1dc, ch3, 1dc] into next sc; rep from * 4 times more ending with 7dc into last ch-7 sp, join with slip st to 3rd of ch-6.

Round 5: Slip st into ch-3 sp, ch3 (count as 1dc), *1dtr into ch-3 sp, 1 picot, ch8, slip st into 8th ch from hook, ch10, slip st into 10th ch from hook, ch14, slip st into 14th ch from hook, 3 picots, ch4, (from now on work on the other side of the picots just made and slip st into base ch of respective picot of the other side after completing each one), 3 picots, ch14, slip st into 14th ch from hook, ch10, slip st into 10th ch from hook, ch8, slip st into 8th ch from hook, 1 picot, slip st on top of dtr just made, 1dc into same ch-3 sp, 1dc into next dc, 1sc into each of next 3 dc, into next sc work 4dc while holding back last loop of each dc, yo and and pull through all 5 loops on hook, 1sc into each of next 3 dc, 1dc into next dc, 1dc into next ch-3 sp; rep from * 5 times more omitting last dc, end with slip st into 3rd of 1st ch-3.

Fasten off.

Garden party

Special abbreviation:

Picot = ch3, slip st in 3rd ch from hook.

Base ring: Ch6, join with slip st.

Round 1: Ch3 (count as 1dc), 1dc into ring, [picot, 2dc into ring] 7 times, picot, slip st to top of ch-3.

Round 2: Ch3 (count as 1dc), 1dc into next dc, [ch6, 1dc into each of next 2 dc] 7 times, ch6, slip st to top of ch-3.

Round 3: Slip st into next dc and into next ch-6 sp, ch1, 8sc into same ch-6 space, [8sc into next ch-6 sp] 7 times, slip st to 1st sc. Fasten off.

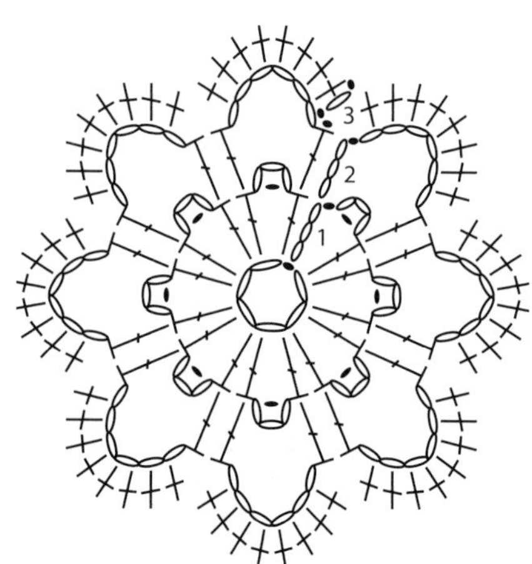

Star hexagon

Base ring: Using A, ch6, join with slip st.

Round 1: Ch4 (count as 1tr), 2tr into ring, [ch1, 3tr into ring] 5 times, ch1, slip st to top of ch-4, turn.

Round 2: [1sc into next ch-1 sp, ch6] 6 times, slip st to 1st sc. Fasten off.

Round 3: Join B to a ch-7 sp, [1hdc, 2dc, 3tr, 2dc, 1hdc] into each ch-7 sp, slip st to 1st hdc (6 petals). Fasten off.

Round 4: Turn, join C to 1st hdc of a petal, ch4 (count as 1tr), *1dc into each of next 2 dc, 1hdc into each of next 3 tr, 1dc into each of next 2 dc, 1tr into each of next 2 hdc; rep from * around skipping last hdc, slip st to top of ch-4. Fasten off.

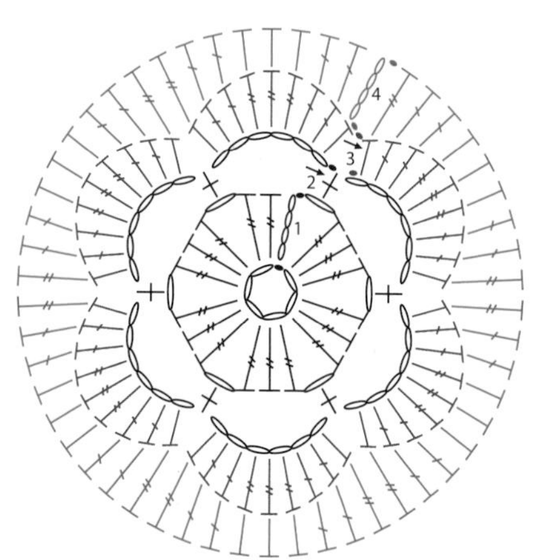

Catherine medallion

Base ring: Ch6, join with slip st.

Round 1: Ch5 (count as 1dc, ch2), [1dc into ring, ch2] 7 times, slip st to 3rd of ch-5.

Round 2: Ch3 (count as 1dc), [2dc into next ch-2 sp, 1dc into next dc] 7 times, 2dc into next ch-2 sp, slip st to top of ch-3.

Round 3: Ch3 (count as 1dc), 2dc in next dc, 1dc in next dc, [1dc in next dc, 2dc in next dc, 1dc in next dc] 7 times, slip st to top of ch-3.

Fasten off.

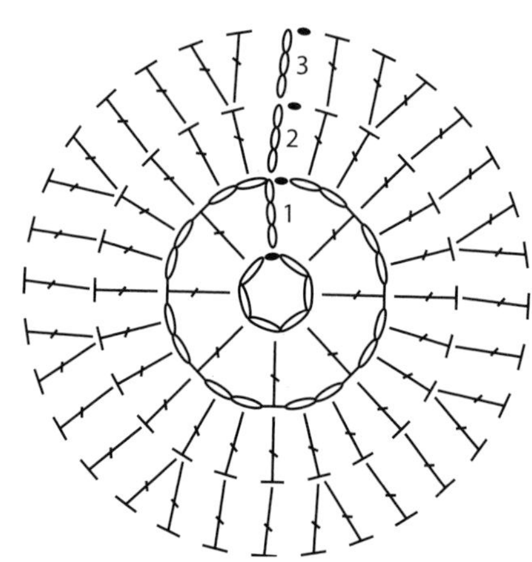

Shamrock motif

Base ring: Ch2, 8sc into 1st ch, slip st to 1st sc, turn.
Petal 1: Ch3 (count as 1dc), 4dc into same place as last slip st, turn.
Row 1: Ch3 (count as 1dc), 1dc into same dc, 1dc into each of next 3 dc, 2dc into top of ch-3, turn.
Round 2: 1dc into 1st dc, 1hdc into next dc, sl st into each of next 3 dc, 1dc into next dc, 1sc into top of ch-3. Fasten off.
Petal 2: Skip 1 sc of 1st row, join yarn in next st, work same as 1st petal.
Work 2 more petals in same manner.

Desert garden

Base ring: Ch4, join with slip st.
Round 1: Ch4 (count as 1dc, ch1), [1dc into ring, ch1] 7 times, slip st to 3rd of ch-4.
Round 2: Sl st into 1st ch-1 sp, ch3, 2dc into same ch-1 sp, ch1, [3dc into next ch-1 sp, ch1] 7 times, slip st to top of of ch-3.
Round 3: Slip st into each of next 2 dc and next ch-1 sp, ch3, 2dc into same ch sp, ch1, *[3dc, ch3, 3dc] into next ch-1 sp, ch1, 3dc into next ch-1 sp, 1ch; rep from * twice more, [3dc, ch3, 3dc] into next ch-1 sp, ch1, slip st to top of ch-3. Fasten off.

Easy polygon

Base ring: Ch3, join with slip st.
Round 1: Ch3 (count as 1dc), 23dc into ring, slip st to top of ch-3.
Round 2: Ch3, [1dc, ch2, 2dc] into same place as last sl st, *skip next 3 dc, [2dc, ch2, 2dc] into next dc; rep from * 4 more times, skip next 3 dc, slip st to top of ch-3. Fasten off.

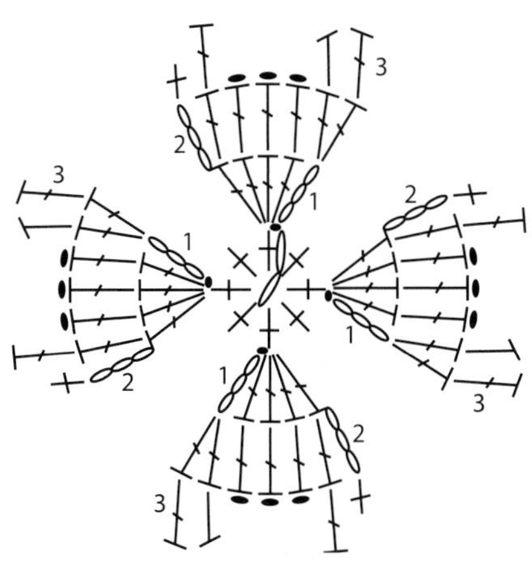

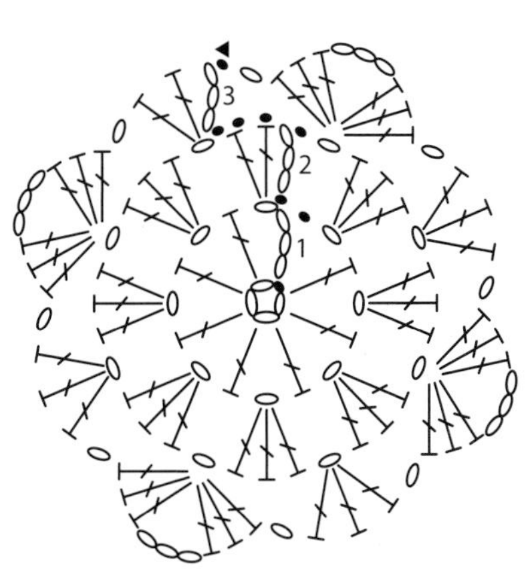

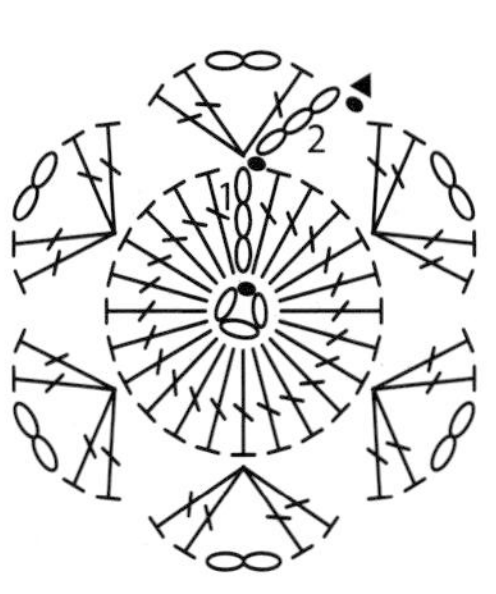

Morning glory

Base ring: Ch4 (count as 1dc), 11dc in 1st ch, slip st to 3rd of ch-4. (12dc)
Round 1: Ch1, 2sc into same place as last sl st, working through back loops 2sc in each dc around, slip st to 1st sc. (24sc)
Round 2: Ch1, 1sc into same place as last slip st *ch10, slip st into 8th ch from hook (forming a ch-8 loop), ch2, miss next 2 sc, 1sc in next sc; rep from * 7 more times, missing 1 sc at end of last rep, slip st to 1st sc.
Round 3: Slip st into each of 1st 2 ch, [1sc, 5dc, 1sc] into 1st ch-8 loop, *[1sc, 5dc, 1sc] into next ch-8 loop; rep from * 6 more times, slip st to 1st sc. Fasten off.

Granny wheel square

Base ring: Ch6, join with slip st.
Round 1: Ch6 (count as 1dc, ch3), [1dc into ring, ch3] 5 times, slip st to 3rd of ch-6.
Round 2: Slip st into 1st ch-3 sp, ch3 (count as 1dc), 3dc into same ch-3 sp, ch2, [4dc into next ch-3 sp, ch2] 5 times, slip st to top of ch-3.
Round 3: Sl st into each of next 3 dc and into next ch-2 sp, ch3, [3dc, ch2, 4dc] into same ch-2 sp, [(4dc, ch2, 4dc) into next ch-2 sp] 5 times, slip st to top of ch-3. Fasten off.

Plain octagon

Base ring: Ch10, join with slip st.
Round 1: Ch3 (count as 1dc), 23dc into ring, slip st to top of ch-3. (24dc)
Round 2: Ch3 (count as 1dc), 1dc into each of next 2 dc, [ch2, 1dc into each of next 3 dc] 7 times, ch2, slip st to top of ch-3. (8 groups)
Round 3: Ch3 (count as 1dc), 1dc into same place as last sl st, 1dc into next dc, 2dc into next dc, [ch2, 2dc into next dc, 1dc into next dc, 2dc into next dc] 7 times, ch2, slip st to top of ch-3.
Round 4: Ch3 (count as 1dc), 1dc into same place as last sl st, 1dc into each of next 3 dc, 2dc into next dc, [ch2, 2dc into next dc, 1dc into each of next 3 dc, 2dc into next dc] 7 times, ch2, slip st to top of ch-3.
Round 5: Ch3 (count as 1dc), 1dc into same place as last sl st, dc into each of next 5 dc, 2dc into next dc, [ch2, 2dc into next dc, 1dc into each of next 5 dc, 2dc into next dc] 7 times, ch2, slip st into top of ch-3. Fasten off.

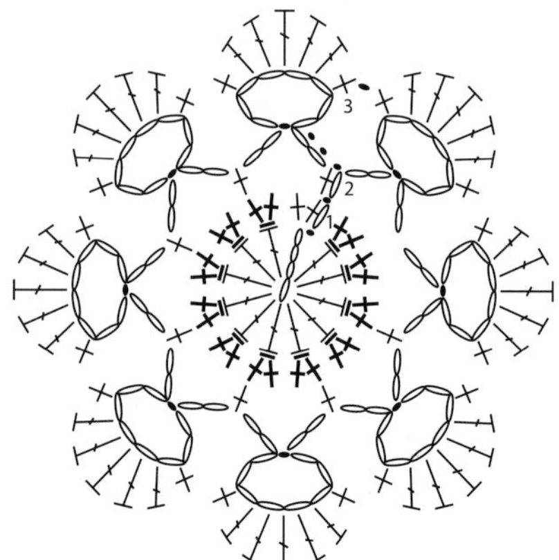

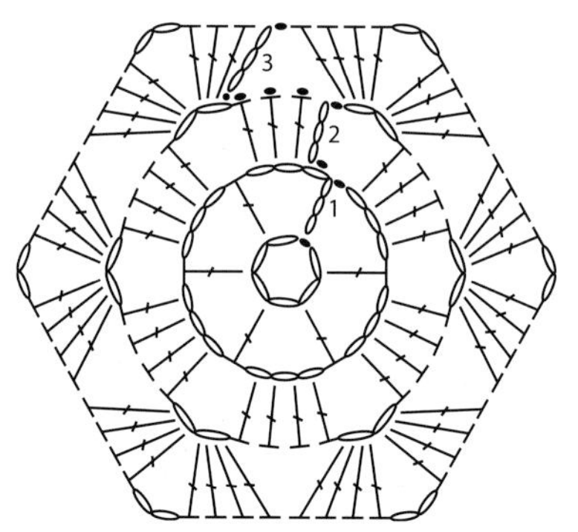

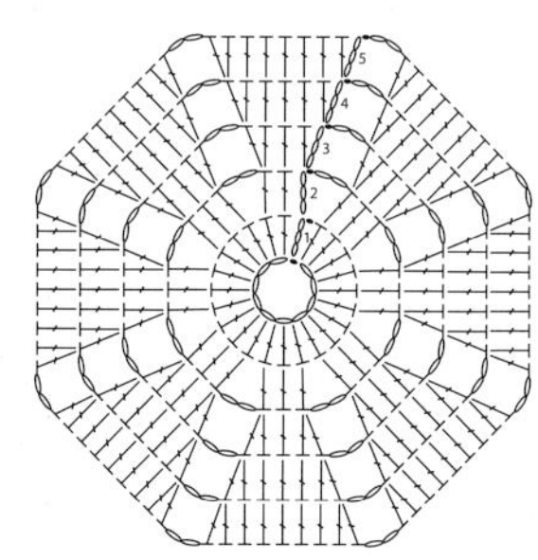

Decorative button

Base ring: Ch6, join with slip st.

Round 1: Ch3 (count as 1dc), 2dc into ring, ch7, [3dc into ring, ch7] 3 times, slip st to top of ch-3.

Round 2: Sl st into each of next 2 dc and into next ch-7 sp, ch3, [2dc, 3tr, 5dtr, 3tr, 3dc] into same ch-7 sp, [3dc, 3tr, 5dtr, 3tr, 3dc] into each of next 3 ch-7 sps, slip st to top of ch-3.

Round 3: Ch1, working through back loops only 1sc in each st around, slip st to 1st sc. Fasten off.

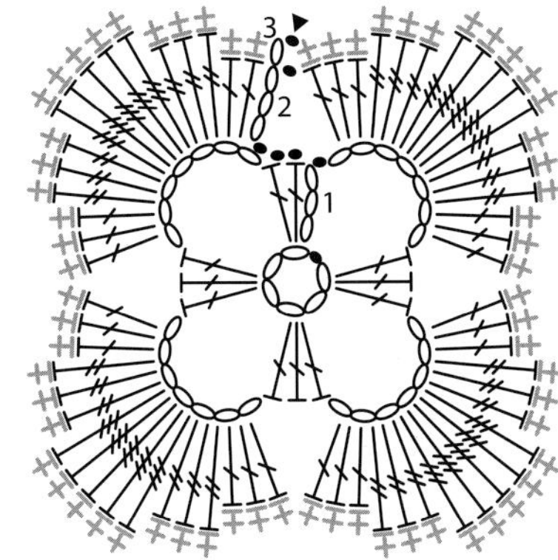

Summer garden motif

Base ring: Ch10, join with slip st.

Round 1: Ch1, 24sc in ring, slip st to 1st sc.

Round 2: Ch12 (count as 1tr, ch8), **skip next sc, 1sc into next sc, ch1, turn, 1sc into each of next 8 ch, ch1, turn, *1sc into each sc across, ch1, turn; rep from * until there are 6 rows of sc, skip next sc of ring, 1tr into next sc, ch8; rep from ** 5 more times ending last rep after 6th row of sc, slip st to 4th of ch-12.

Round 3: Ch12 (count as 1tr, ch8), [1sc into free tip of next sc-block, ch8, 1tr into next tr, ch8] 5 times, 1sc into free tip of next sc-section, ch8, slip st to 4th of ch-12.

Round 4: Ch3, [1dc into each of next 8 ch, 1dc into next sc, 1dc into each of next 8 ch, 1dc into next tr] 6 times skiping 1dc at end of last rep, slip st to top of ch-3. Fasten off.

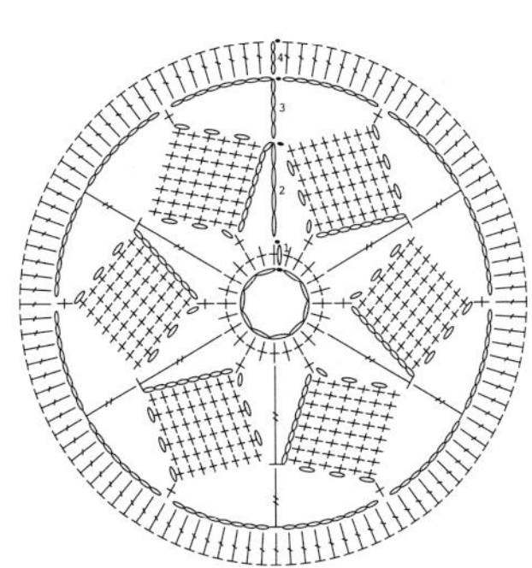

Leafy pinwheel

Base ring: Ch10, join with slip st.

Round 1: Ch1, 16sc into ring, slip st to 1st sc. Fasten off.

Round 2: Ch9, sl st into any sc on ring, hold chain to left, ch1 to right of ch, across ch work 1sc, 1hdc, 5dc, 1hdc, ending 1sc into last ch, *ch17, turn, miss 1sc on ring, sl st into next sc, ch1, turn, across half of ch work 1sc, 1hdc, 5dc, 1hdc, 1sc; rep from * 6 more times, ch8, turn, slip st to end of 1st petal.

Round 3: Ch1, turn, [2sc, 2hdc, 7dc, 2hdc, 2sc] into each ch-8 sp around, slip st to 1st sc. Fasten off.

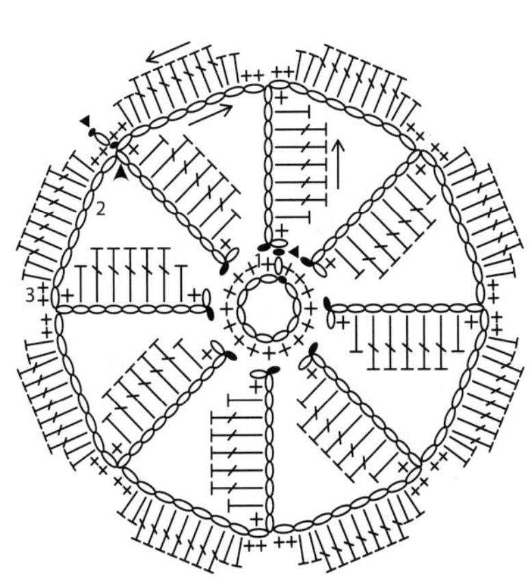

Grouped relief strands

Multiple of 9 sts + 2 sts (add 1 st for base chain).

Row 1 (RS): 1sc into 2nd ch from hook, *1sc in next ch, ch11, skip 7 ch, 1sc into next ch; rep from * to last ch, 1sc into last ch, turn.

Row 2: Ch1, 1sc into 1st st, *1sc into next dc, working in front of ch-11 sp, 1hdc into each of 7 skipped ch of row 1, 1sc into next sc; rep from * to last st, 1sc into last ch, turn.

Row 3: Ch1, 1sc into 1st st, *1sc into next sc, ch9, skip 7 htr, 1sc into next sc; rep from * to last st, 1sc into last ch, turn.

Row 4: Ch1, 1sc into 1st st, *1sc into next sc, working in front of ch-9 sp, 1dc into each of 7 skipped hdc of row 2, 1sc into next sc in row 3; rep from * to last st, 1sc into last ch, turn.

Rep rows 3–4.

Row 7: Ch1, 1sc into 1st st, *1sc into next sc, ch5, insert hook under 3 chain strands of previous rows and work 1sc around the 3 chain strands, ch5, 1sc into next sc; rep from * to last st, 1sc into last ch, turn.

Rep row 2.

Fasten off.

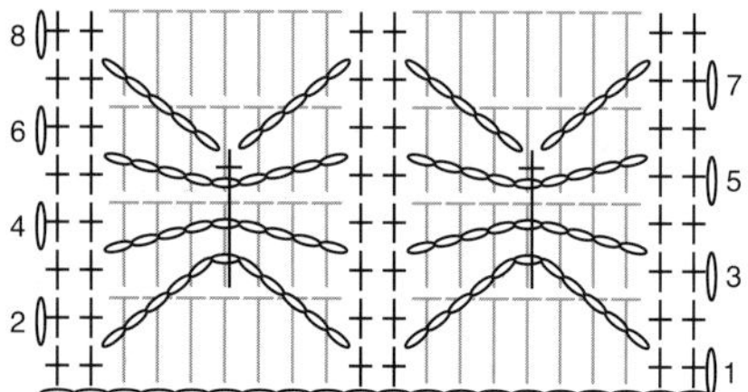

Long-stitch pintucks

Worked lengthwise over any number of sts (add 1 st for base chain).

Row 1 (RS): 1sc into 2nd ch from hook, 1sc into each ch to end, turn.

Row 2: Ch1, 1sc into each sc to end, turn.

Row 3: Ch5 (count as 1dtr) 1dtr into front loop of each sc to last sc, ch5, slip st into last st, turn.

Row 4: Ch1, 1sc into unworked top loop (now front loop) of each sc of row 2, turn.

Row 5: Ch1, *insert hook through next sc and corresponding dtr or tch from row 3, yo, draw loop through the layers, yo, to complete a sc st; rep from * to end, turn.

Row 6: Ch1, 1sc into each sc to end, turn.

Row 7: Ch1, 1sc into each sc to end, turn.

Rep rows 3–7 until required length is reached.

Fasten off.

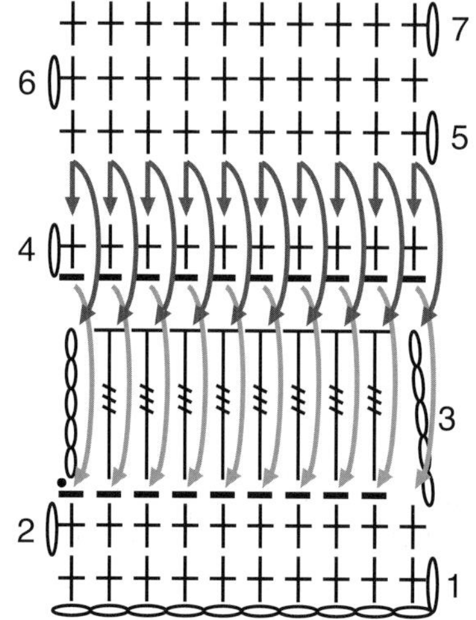

Picot edging

Multiple of 2 sts +1 st (add 1 st for base chain).

Special abbreviation:

Picot = ch3, slip st into 3rd ch from hook.

Note: work foundation row if working from a base chain.

Foundation row: 1sc into 2nd ch from hook and each ch to end, turn.

Row 1 (RS): Ch1, 1sc into 1st st, *picot, skip 1 st, 1sc into next st; rep from * to end.

Fasten off.

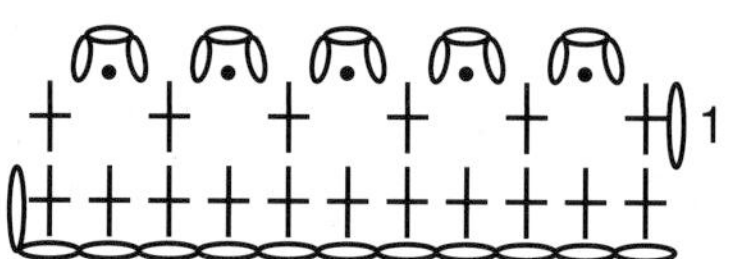

Open shell with picot

Multiple of 7 sts (add 1 st for base chain).

Special abbreviations:

Shell = (1tr, ch1, 1tr, ch1, 1tr) in ch or sp indicated.

Picot = (1sc, ch3, 1sc) in st indicated.

Row 1 (RS): 1sc into 2nd ch from hook, *skip 2 ch, work a shell into next ch, skip 2 ch, 1sc into next ch**, ch3, 1sc into next ch; rep from * ending last rep at **, turn.

Row 2: Ch7 (count as 1tr, ch3), *skip 1 dc and 1 ch, work a picot into next dc of shell, ch3**, 1dc into next ch-3 arch, ch3; rep from * ending last rep at **, 1tr into last sc, skip tch, turn.

Row 3: Ch1, 1sc into 1st st, *skip next ch-3 sp, shell into next picot**, skip next ch-3 sp, picot into next dc; rep from * ending last rep at **, 1sc into 4th ch of tch. Fasten off.

Beaded pintuck

Multiple of any number of sts (add 1 st for base chain).

Special abbreviation:

Beaded dc = yo, insert hook into next st, yo, draw loop through, yo, draw yarn through 2 loops, slide bead along yarn to base of hook, yo, draw yarn through remaining 2 loops.

Note: thread beads onto yarn before starting.

Row 1 (RS): 1sc into 2nd ch from hook, work 1sc into each ch to end, turn.

Row 2: Ch3 (count as 1 dc), skip st at base of ch, * 1 beaded dc into front loop of each sc to end, turn.

Row 3: Ch1, *insert hook through next dc and corresponding back loop from the st on row 2, yo, draw loop through the layers to complete a slip st; rep from * to end. Fasten off.

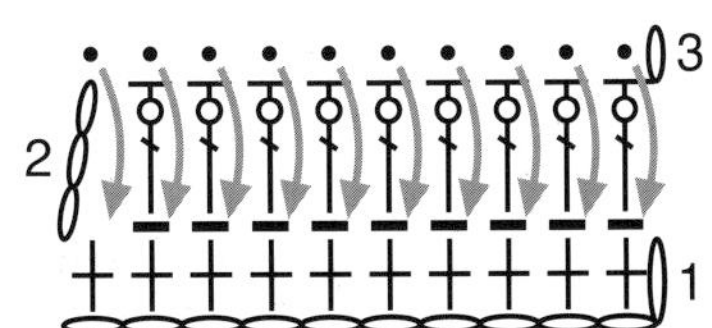

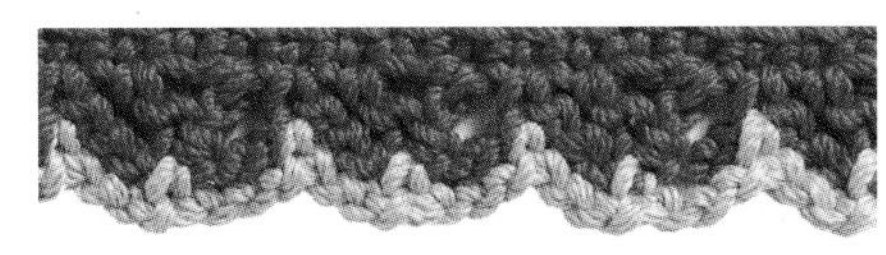

Cluster arch edging

Multiple of 4 sts + 1 st (add 1 st for base chain).

Special abbreviation:

Dc2tog = 1dc into next st until 1 loop of st remains, skip 1 st, 1dc into next until 1 loop of st remains on hook, yo and through all 3 loops on hook.

Note: work foundation row if working from a base chain.

Foundation row: Using A, 1sc into 2nd ch from hook and each ch to end, turn.

Row 1 (RS): Ch1, 1sc into 1st st, *ch3, dc2tog, ch3, 1sc into next st; rep from * to end. Fasten off. Do not turn.

Join in B into 1st sc st.

Row 2: Ch1, 1sc into 1st sc, *ch3, skip 3 ch, 1sc into next dc2tog, ch3, skip 3 ch, 1sc into next sc; rep from * to end. Fasten off.

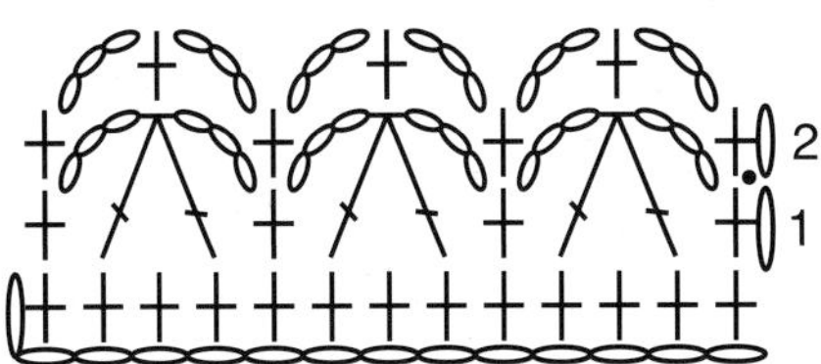

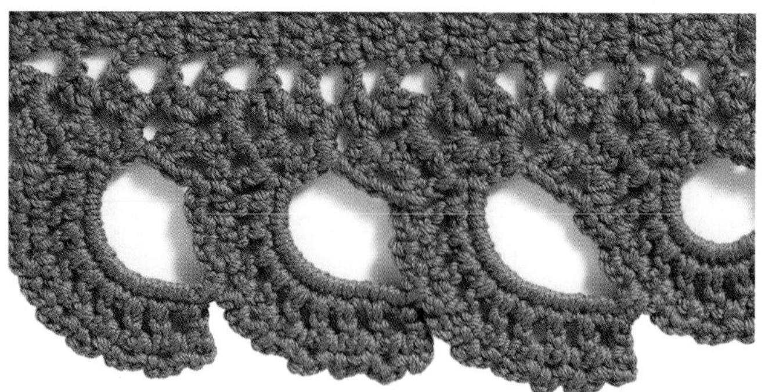

Quarter-roundel edge

Worked lengthwise.

Row 1 (RS): Ch15, 1dc into 6th ch from hook, ch2, skip 3 ch, (2tr, ch3, 2tr) into next ch, ch2, skip 2 ch, 1dc into each of next 3 ch, turn.

Row 2: Ch3 (count as 1dc), skip st at base of ch, 1dc into each of next 2 dc, ch2, skip ch-2 sp and next 2 dc, (2dc, ch3, 2dc) into next ch-3 sp, ch10, skip ch-2 sp and next dc, 1sc into ch-6 sp, turn.

Row 3: Ch1, 18sc into ch-10 sp, ch2, skip 2 dc, (2dc, ch3, 2dc) into next ch-3 sp, ch2, skip 2 dc and ch-2 sp, 1dc in each of next 2 dc, 1dc into top of tch, turn.

Row 4: Ch3, (count as 1dc), skip st at base of ch, 1dc into each of next 2 dc, ch2, skip ch-2 sp and next 2 dc, (2dc, ch3, 2dc) into next ch-3 sp, ch2, skip 2 dc, 1dc into next ch-2 sp, [ch1, skip next sc, 1dc into next sc] 9 times, turn.

Row 5: [Ch3, 1sc in next ch-1 sp] 9 times, ch2, skip 1 dc, ch-2 sp and 2 dc, (2dc, ch3, 2dc) into next ch-3 sp, ch2, 1dc in each of next 2 dc, 1dc into top of tch, turn.

Row 6: Ch3 (count as 1dc), skip st at base of ch, 1dc into each of next 2 dc, ch2, skip ch-2 sp and next dc, (2dc, ch3, 2dc) into next ch-3 sp, ch10, skip next dc, ch-2 sp and next ch-3 sp, 1sc into ch-3 sp, turn.

Rep rows 3–6 until required length is reached, ending with a row 5. Fasten off.

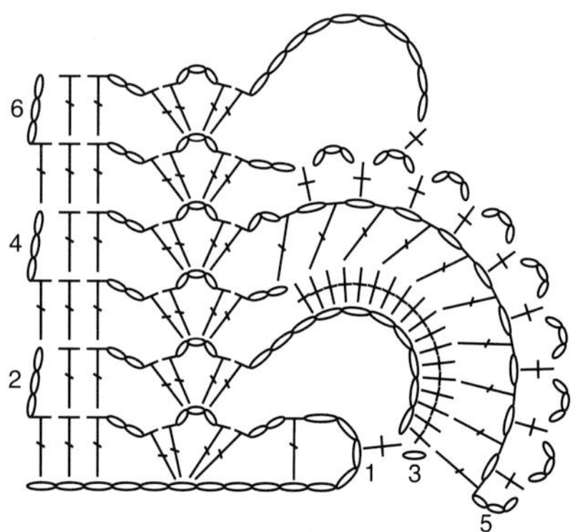

Floral diamonds

Worked lengthwise.

Special abbreviation:

Bobble = work 3dc into next ch or st indicated until 1 loop of each remains on hook, yo and draw through all 4 loops on hook.

Row 1 (RS): *Ch5, 1 bobble into 5th ch from hook; rep from * until required length is reached, with an even number of bobbles, do not turn but rotate work by 90 degrees and proceed to work along one long edge.

Row 2: Ch7, 1 bobble into base of 1st bobble, *ch7, 1sc into base of next bobble **, ch7, 1 bobble into base of next bobble; rep from * ending last rep at **, do not turn but rotate work by 180 degrees and proceed to work along the other long edge.

Row 3: Rep row 2, ending with last sc in top of last bobble, turn at end of row.

Row 4: Slip st into each of next 3 ch, ch7 (count as 1dc, ch4), *1dc in each of next 2 sps **, ch7; rep from * ending last rep at **, ch4, 1dc into 4th ch of tch, turn.

Row 5: *Ch5 (count as 1dc, ch2), 1dc in ch-4 sp, ch2, 1dc in each of next 2 dc, [ch2, 1sc in ch sp] twice, ch2, 1dc in each of next 2 dc; rep from * to last dc, ch2, 1sc in ch sp, ch2, 1dc in 3rd ch of tch.

Fasten off.

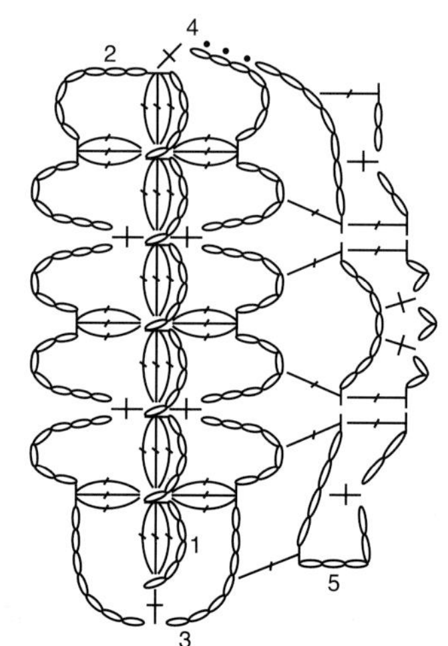

French square edging

Multiple of 9 sts (1 motif for each repeat).

Special abbreviation:

Puff st = [yo, insert hook into sp, yo and draw loop through] 4 times, yo and draw through all loops on hook.

Motif

Base ring: ch6, join with slip st to form ring.

Round 1 (RS): Ch4 (count as 1dc, ch1), [1dc into ring, ch1] 11 times, slip st to 3rd of ch-4 tch. (12 sps)

Round 2: Slip st into next sp, ch3, work puff st into same sp (counts as puff st), *ch2, work puff st into next sp, ch3, 1tr into next dc, ch3, work puff st into next sp, ch2**, puff st into next sp; rep from * twice more and from * to ** again, slip st to top of 1st puff st.

Header

With RS facing, join in yarn through top of tr at corner of square.

Row 1: Ch1, 1sc into top of same tr, *ch7, counting along the edge of the motif, skip next ch-3 sp and next ch-2 sp, 1dtr into next ch-2 sp along motif edge, 1dtr into the corresponding ch-2 sp on next motif, ch7, working along the edge of the motif, 1sc into next tr on corner, counterclockwise from last dtr; rep from * until all squares have been joined, turn.

Row 2: Ch1, work 1sc into each st to end, turn.

Row 3: Ch2, work 1hdc into each st to end, turn.

Row 4: Ch2, work 1hdc into back bar (below top loops) of each st to end. Fasten off.

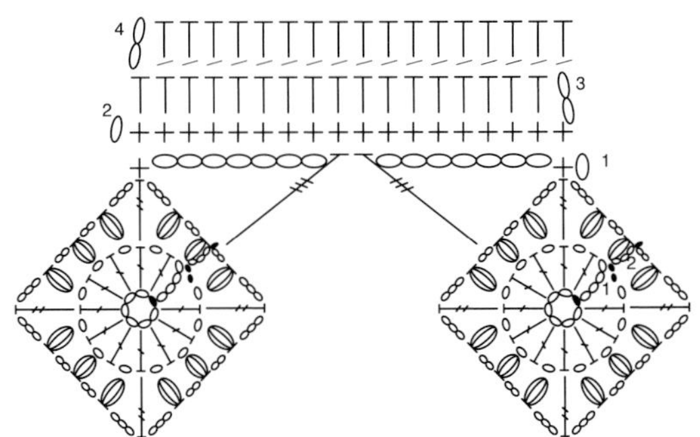

Rose garden

Note: all the roses shown are worked from the same pattern but the number of rounds worked has been varied. The number of rounds worked for each rose motif is as follows: right, all five rounds; middle, rounds 1–4 only; left, rounds 1–2 only.

Motif

Wind the yarn 3 or 4 times around a finger, remove the loop from finger and fasten with a slip st.

Round 1: Ch1, 24sc into ring, slip st to 1st sc.

Round 2: Ch6 (count as hdc, ch4), skip next 2 sc, 1hdc into next sc, [ch4, skip 2 sc, 1hdc into next sc] 6 times, ch4, slip st to 2nd ch of ch-6 tch.

Round 3: Ch4, working in sc in round 1, behind sts in round 2, skip 3 sc, 1hdc into next st, *ch3, skip next 2 sc, 1hdc into next sc; rep from * 6 times more, ch3, sl st into 2nd ch of 1st ch-4 tch, turn.Working back along the two rounds of chains just worked, work following two rounds:

Round 4: (1sc, 1hdc, 3dc, 1hdc, 1sc) into each ch-3 sp from round 3, slip st to 1st sc.

Round 5: Slip st into last ch-4 sp of round 2, (1sc, 1hdc, 3dc, 1hdc, 1sc) into each ch-4 sp from round 2, slip st to 1st sc. Fasten off. Slip stitch motifs to fabric.

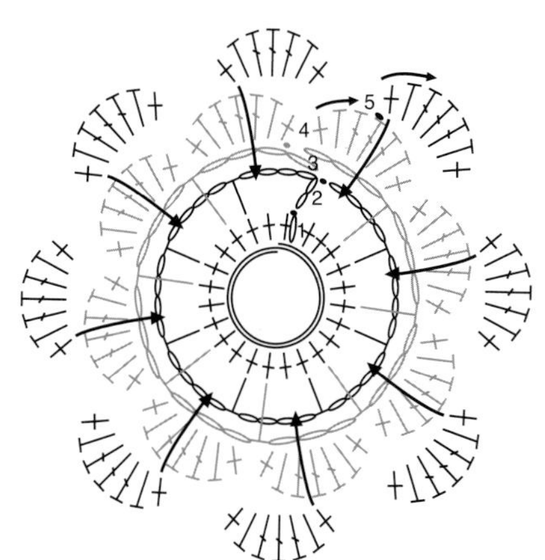

Slip stitch edge

Multiple of any number of sts (add 1 st for base chain).

Note: this edging is worked onto a background fabric of double crochet stitches.

Row 1 (RS): 1sc into 2nd ch from hook, 1sc into each ch or equivalent interval to end, turn.

Row 2: Ch1, 1sc into back loops of eachsc to end. Fasten off. Do not turn. Return to start of row 2. Join yarn under front loop of 1st sc.

Row 3: Ch1, 1sc into front loops of each sc to end. Fasten off. Do not turn. Return to start of row. Join in contrasting yarn into inside top loop of 1st st of row 2, ch1. Rotate the work through 90 degrees so the 2 rows of sc st are parallel and running away from you. Position yarn so it is lying between the 2 rows of sc.

Row 4: *Insert hook from top to bottom through inside top loop of sc from 1st row, insert hook from top to bottom through inside top loop of sc from row 2, yo, complete a slip st; rep from * to end.
Fasten off.

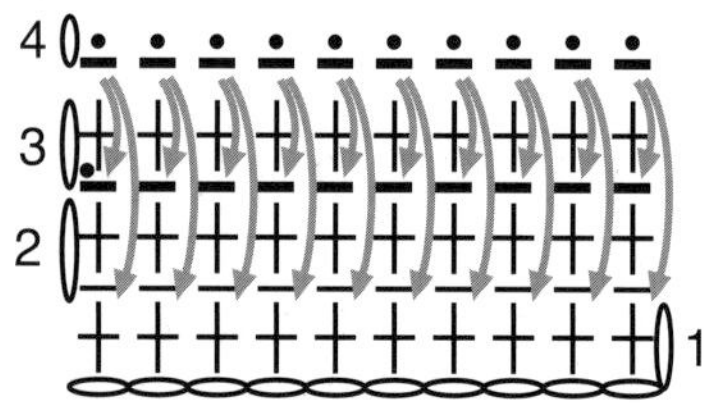

Picot twist

Multiple of 2 sts + 1 st (add 1 st for base chain).

Row 1 (RS): 1sc into 2nd ch from hook and each ch to end, turn.

Row 2: Ch3, 1sc into back loop of 1st st, *ch3, 1sc into front loop of next st, ch3, 1sc into back loop of next st; rep from * to end.
Fasten off.

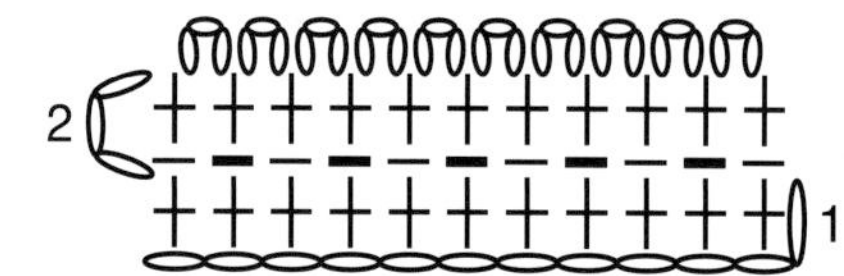

Dandelion dangle

Multiple of 17 sts + 12 sts (add 2 sts for base chain).

Row 1 (RS): Skip 3 ch (count as 1dc), 1dc into next ch, work 1dc into each ch to end, turn.

Row 2: Ch2, work 1hdc into each st to end, turn.

Row 3: Ch3 (count as 1dc), skip st at base of ch, work 1dc in each of next 11 sts, *skip next 2 hdc, work into next hdc ([1dc, ch24, slip st into back of 1st ch] 8 times, 1dc), skip 2 hdc, 1dc in each of next 12 sts; rep from * to end.
Fasten off.

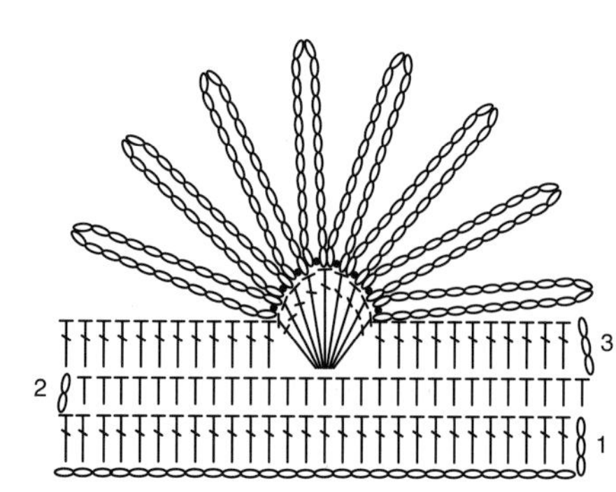

Undulating fringe

Multiple of 3 sts (add 1 st for base chain).

Row 1 (WS): Skip 2 ch (count as 1hdc), 1hdc into next ch, 1hdc into each ch to end, turn.

Row 2: Ch4 (count as 1tr), 1tr into each st to end, turn.

Row 3: Ch2 (count as 1hdc), 1hdc into each st to end, turn.

Row 4: *Ch16, slip st into back bump of 2nd ch from hook, 1 slip st into back bump of each ch, 1 slip st into next hdc, ch12, slip st into back bump of 2nd ch from hook, 1 slip st into back bump of each ch, 1 slip st into next hdc, ch8, slip st into back bump of 2nd ch from hook, 1 slip st into back bump of each ch, 1 slip st into next hdc; rep from * to end.

Fasten off.

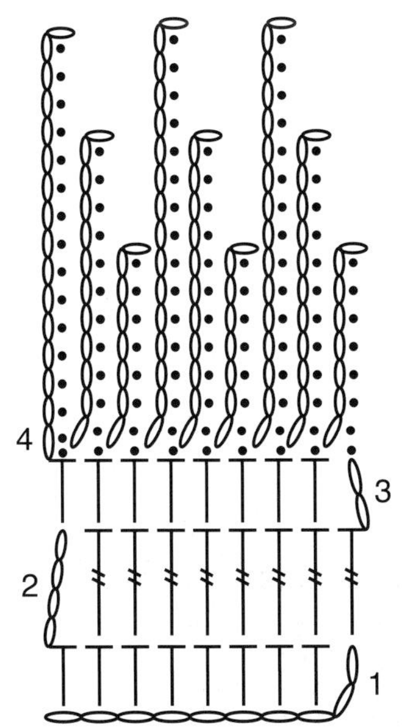

Loop ruffle

Worked lengthwise over 7 sts (add 2 sts for base chain).

Special abbreviations:

Tr/rf (raised treble crochet at the front of the fabric) = yo twice, insert hook from in front and from right to left around the stem of the appropriate stitch, and complete stitch normally.

Tr/rb (raised treble crochet at the back of the fabric) = yo twice, insert hook from behind and from right to left around the stem of the appropriate stitch, and complete stitch normally.

Row 1: Skip 3 ch (count as 1dc), 1dc into next ch, 1dc into each ch to end, turn.

Row 2: Ch3, [tr/rf around next st, tr/rb around next st] twice, tr/rf around next st, 1dc into top of tch, *yo twice, insert hook from front to back around post of last st, yo, and complete a tr st; rep from * 8 more times, turn.

Row 3: Skip 1st 9 tr, slip st into top of last dc forming ring of tr, ch3, slip st into base of last tr of ring, [tr/rf around next st, tr/rb around next st] twice, tr/rb around next st, 1dc onto top of tch, turn.

Rep rows 2–3 until required length is reached, ending with a row 2.

Fasten off.

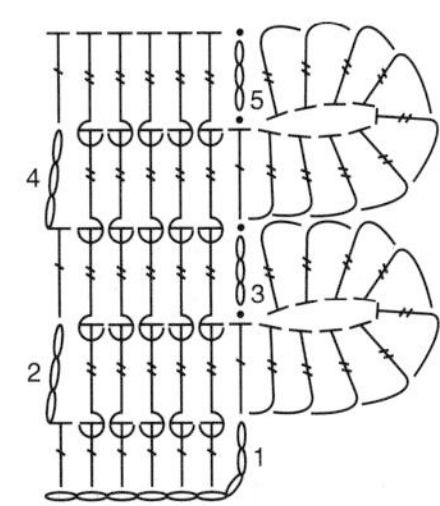

Chain arch edging

Multiple of 2 sts + 1 st (add 1 st for base chain).

Note: work foundation row if working from a base chain.

Foundation row: 1sc into 2nd ch from hook and each ch to end, turn.

Row 1 (RS): Ch1, 1sc into 1st st, *ch3, skip 1 st, 1sc into next st; rep from * to end.

Fasten off.

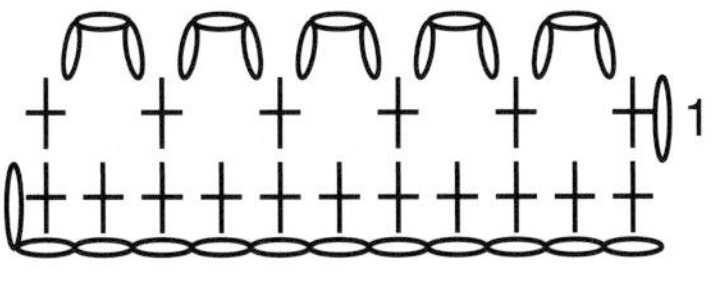

Cartwheel fringe

Multiple of 13 sts +7 sts (1 motif for each repeat).

Special abbreviations:

Tr/rf (raised treble crochet at the front of the fabric) = yo twice, insert hook from in front and from right to left around the stem of the appropriate stitch, and complete stitch normally.

Tr/rb (raised treble crochet at the back of the fabric) = yo twice, insert hook from behind and from right to left around the stem of the appropriate stitch, and complete stitch normally.

Motif

Base ring: Ch4, join with slip st to form ring.

Round 1: Work 8sc into ring, slip st to 1st sc.

Round 2: Ch5 (count as 1hdc, ch3), skip sc at base of ch-5, hdc into next sc, *ch3, hdc into next sc; rep from * 5 more times, ch3, slip st to 2nd ch of ch-5 tch. Each hdc forms a spoke.

Round 3: Ch1, 1sc into 1st st, *4sc into next ch-3 sp, 1sc into next hdc; rep from * around, omitting last sc, slip st to 1st sc. Fasten off.

Header

Foundation chain: Ch7, *tr/rb around a hdc of a motif, ch4, tr/rb around next spoke of same motif, ch7; rep from * to end, turn.

Row 1: Ch3, skip 3 ch (count as 1dc) and 1dc into next ch, 1dc into each of next 5 ch, *tr/rb around post of next st, 1dc in each of next 4 ch, tr/rb around post of next st, 1dc into each of next 7 ch; rep from * to end, turn.

Row 2: Ch3 (count as 1dc) skip dc at base of ch, 1dc into each of next 6dc, *tr/rf around post of next st, 1dc in each of next 4 ch, tr/rf around post of next st, 1dc into each of next of next 7 dc; rep from * to end. Fasten off.

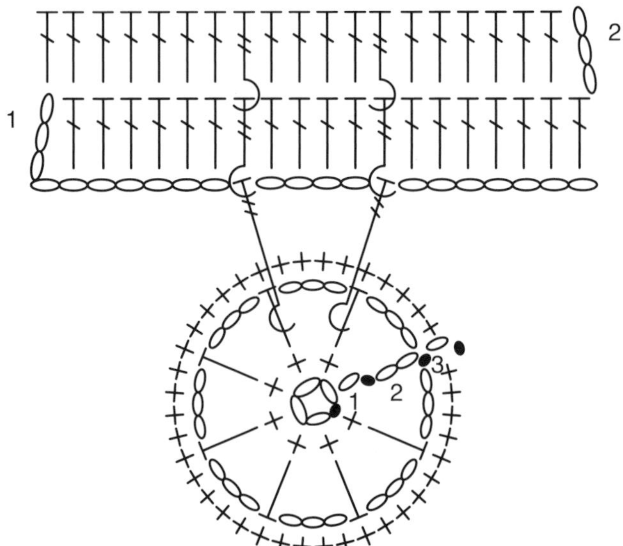

Jekyll border

Multiple of 24 sts +1 st (add 4 sts for base chain).

Special abbreviations:

Dc2tog = work 2dc into next st until 1 loop of each remains on hook, yo and through all 3 loops on hook.

Bobble = work 4dc into next st until 1 loop of each remains on hook, yo and through all 5 loops on hook.

Group = work 1dc into next st, into same st as last dc work [ch1, 1dc] twice.

Row 1 (RS): Skip 4 ch (count as 1dc, ch1), 1dc into next ch, skip 2 ch, 1sc into next ch, skip 2 ch, 1 group into next ch, skip 2 ch, 1sc into next ch, skip 2 ch, 5dc into next ch, *skip 2 ch, 1sc into next ch, [skip 2 ch, 1 group into next ch, skip 2 ch, 1sc into next ch] 3 times, skip 2 ch, 5dc into next ch; rep from * to last 12 ch, skip 2 ch, 1sc into next ch, skip 2 ch, 1 group into next ch, skip 2 ch, 1sc into next ch, skip 2 ch, into last ch work (1dc, ch1, 1dc), turn.

Row 2: Ch1, 1sc into 1st dc, 1 group into next sc, 1sc into center dc of next group, skip 1 dc, 2dc into each of next 5 dc, *1sc into center dc of next group, [1 group into next sc, 1sc into center dc of next group] twice, skip 1 dc, 2dc into each of next 5 dc; rep from * to last group, 1sc into center dc of next group, 1 group into next sc, skip (1 dc, 1 ch), 1sc into next ch, turn.

Row 3: Ch4 (count as 1dc, ch1), 1dc into 1st sc, 1sc into center dc of 1st group, ch2, skip next (1 ch, 1 dc, 1 sc), [1 bobble between next pair of dc, ch2] 5 times, *1sc into center dc of next group, 1 group into next sc, 1sc into center dc of next group, ch2, [1 bobble between next pair of dc, ch2] 5 times; rep from * to last group, 1sc into center dc of last group, into last sc work, (1dc, ch1, 1dc), turn.

Row 4: Ch1, 1sc into 1st dc, *ch4, 1dc into next ch-2 sp, [ch4, 1dc into top of next bobble, ch4, 1dc into next ch-2 sp] 5 times, ch4, 1sc into center dc of next group; rep from * to end, placing last sc into 3rd ch of ch-4 tch.

Fasten off.

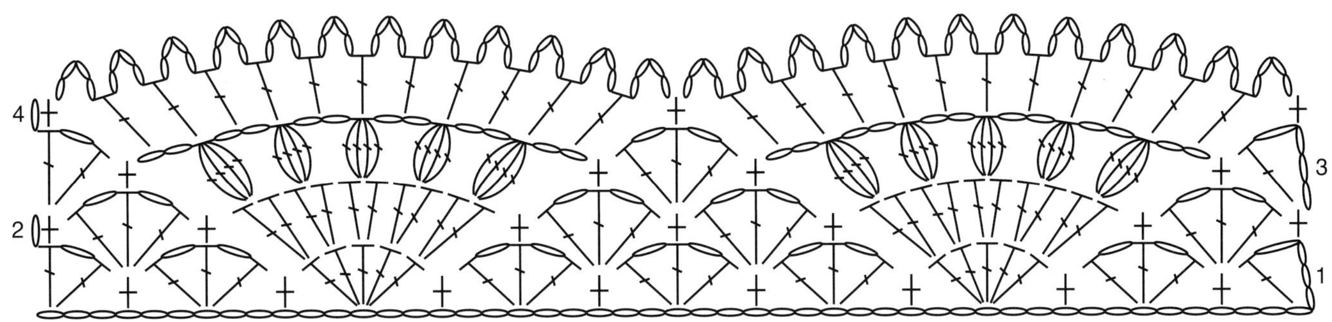

Corded edging

Multiple of any number of sts (add 1 st for base chain).

Special abbreviation:

Reverse sc = working from left to right, 1sc into st to the right, keeping the working yarn to the left of hook.

Row 1 (RS): 1sc into 2nd ch from hook, work 1sc into each ch to end. Do not turn.

Row 2: Ch1, *1 reverse sc into next st to right; rep from * to end.

Fasten off.

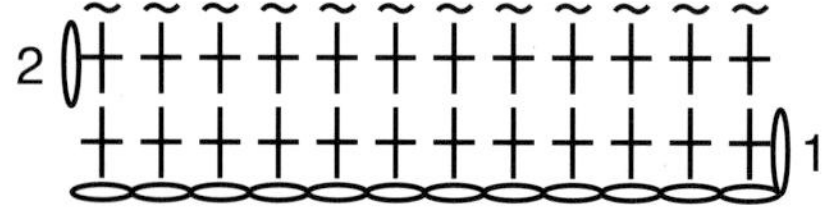

Diagonal spike edge

Multiple of 4 sts + 2 sts (add 2 sts for base chain).

Special abbreviation:

Sdc (spike double crochet) = yo, insert hook from front to back round 1st dc of previous 3dc block worked, yo, draw loop through and up so as not to crush 3dc block, [yo, draw through 2 loops] twice.

Row 1: Skip 3 ch (count as 1dc), 1dc into next ch, *1dc into next ch, ch3, slip st into 3rd ch from hook, 1dc into next ch, work 1Sdc, skip 1 ch, 1dc into next ch; rep from * to end.

Fasten off.

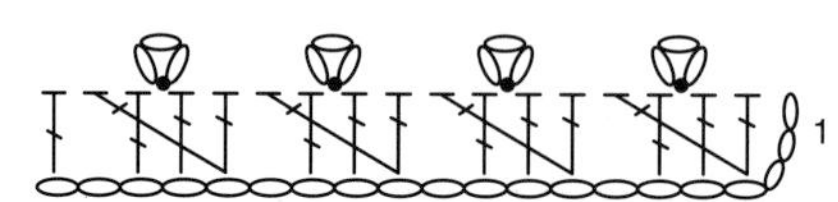

Fan frills

Worked lengthwise.

Row 1 (RS): Ch9, slip st to join.

Row 2: Ch4 (count as 1tr), 12tr into ring, turn.

Row 3: Ch4 (count as 1dc, ch1), [1dc into sp between 2 tr, ch1] 11 times, 1dc into sp between last tr and tch, turn.

Row 4: [Ch4, 1sc into next ch-1 sp] 12 times, turn.

Row 5: Ch6, skip ch-4 sp, 1sc into next ch-4 sp, turn.

Row 6: Ch4 (count as 1tr), 12tr into ch-6 sp, turn.

Row 7: Ch4 (count as 1dc, ch1), [1dc into sp between 2 tr, ch1] 11 times, 1dc into sp between last tr and tch, 1 slip st into 5th ch-4 sp of row 5, turn.

Row 8: [Ch4, 1sc into ch-1 sp] 12 times, turn.

Rep rows 5–8 until required length is reached.

Rotate work by 90 degrees and work along the edge without scallops.

Header

Next row: Ch3 (count as 1dc), 1dc into equivalent st interval to end.

Fasten off.

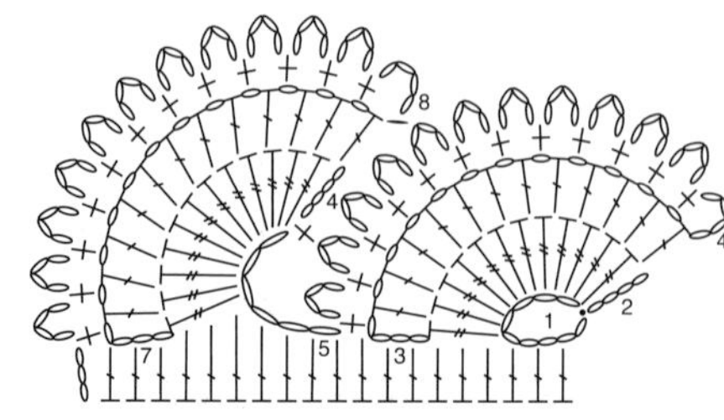

Simple ruffle

Multiple of 2 sts + 1 st (add 1 st for base chain).

Row 1 (RS): Skip 2 ch, (count as 1hdc), 1hdc into next ch, 1hdc into each ch to end, turn.

Row 2: Ch3 (count as 1dc), 1dc into back bar under top loops of each hdc to end, turn.

Row 3: Ch2 (count as 1hdc), 1hdc into each dc to end, turn.

Row 4: Ch1, 1sc into back bar under top loops of each hdc to end, turn.

Row 5: Ch3 (count as 1dc), 1dc into st at base of ch, *3dc into next sc, 2dc into next sc; rep from * to end, turn.

Row 6: Ch1, 1sc into each dc to end. Fasten off.

Long loop fringe

Multiple of 2 sts + 1 st (add 1 st for base chain).

Using yarn A, work a base chain the required length.

Row 1 (RS): Skip 2 ch (count as 1hdc), 1hdc into next ch, 1hdc into each ch to end, turn. Join in yarn B.

Row 2: Using yarn A, ch2 (count as 1hdc), *using yarn B, yo, insert hook into next st, draw yarn through st, drop yarn B, carry yarn A over yarn B, using yarn A, yo, draw through all loops on hook, using yarn A, yo, insert hook into next st, draw yarn through st, drop yarn A, carry yarn B over yarn A, using yarn B, yo, draw through all loops on hook; rep from * to end, turn. Fasten off yarn B.

Row 3: Using yarn A, *ch10, 1sc into front loop of next hdc with yarn A top loops; rep from * to end, do not turn.

Fasten off yarn A.

Return to start of row 3. Rejoin yarn B under back loop of 1st hdc with yarn B top loops.

Row 4: Using yarn B, *ch14, 1sc into front loop of next hdc with yarn B top loops; rep from * to end. Fasten off.

Strip loops

Multiple of 6 sts + 3 sts (add 1 st for base chain).

Row 1 (RS): 1sc into 2nd ch from hook, work 1sc into each ch to end, turn.

Row 2: Ch1, 1sc into each sc to end, turn.

Row 3: Ch1, slip st into 1st st, *[ch12, slip st into 3rd ch from hook, slip st into each of rem ch, slip st into next sc] twice, insert hook through ch-2 sp at end of last tail and into next st, yo, draw loop through all the layers and loop on hook, pass 1st tail through loop just created, insert hook through ch-2 sp at end of 1st tail and into next st, yo, draw loop through all the layers and loop on hook**, slip st in each of next 3 sc; rep from * ending last rep at **, slip st into last st.

Fasten off.

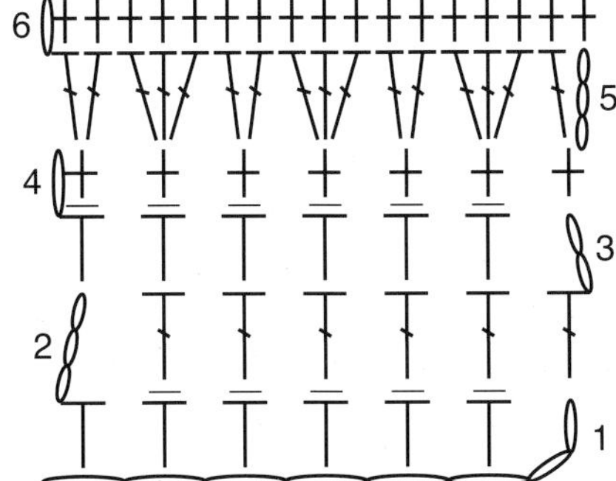

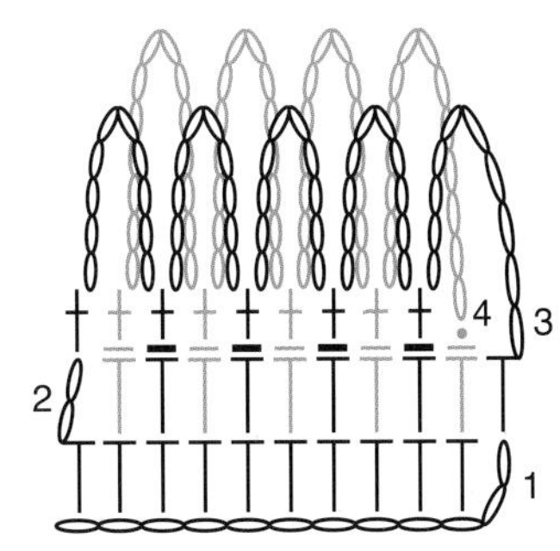

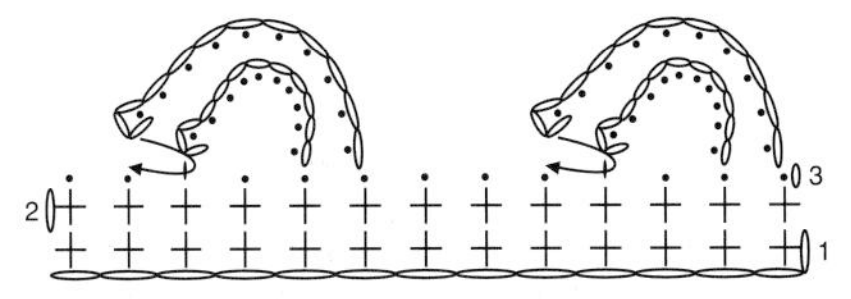

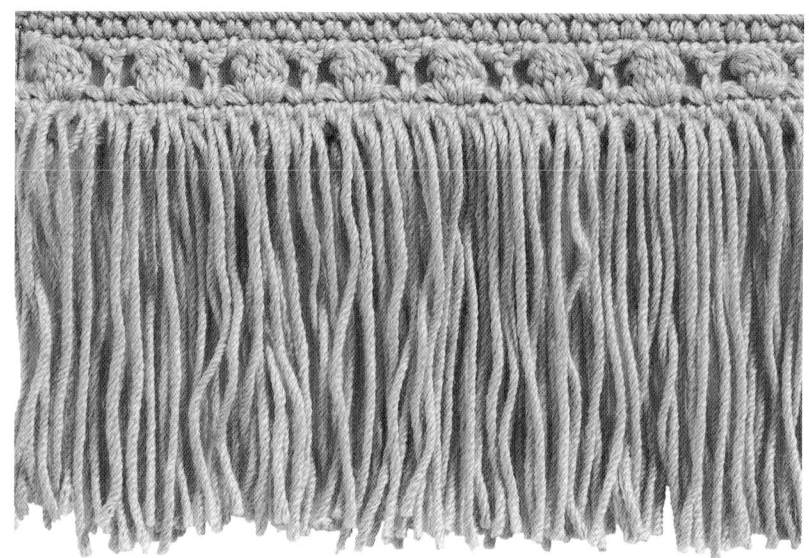

Fringe of strands

Multiple of 4 sts + 1 st (add 1 st for base chain).

Special abbreviation:

Bobble = work 3dc into next ch or st indicated until 1 loop of each remains on hook, yo and through all 4 loops on hook.

Note: using a piece of thick card slightly deeper than the required fringe, wrap yarn round the card, periodically cutting the yarn along one edge to create strands. For a thicker fringe, use more strands in some or all of the strand chains in row 2.

Row 1 (RS): 1sc into 2nd ch from hook, 1sc into back bump of each ch to end, turn.

Row 2: With WS facing, remove hook from the working loop, *insert hook through next st, place the center of a folded strand over hook, and draw through the loop on the hook, pass the ends through the loop and hang the strands down to the RS; rep from * to end. Do not turn.

Row 3 (WS): Position hook back through the working loop, ch1, *1sc into each st inserting hook through same sts that were worked in row 2, between the strands looped through each st; rep from * to end, do not turn.

Row 4: With WS facing, remove hook from the working loop, *insert hook through next st, place the center of a folded strand over the hook, and draw through the loop on the hook, pass the ends through the loop and hang the strands down to the RS; rep from * to end, turn.

Row 5 (RS): Place hook back through the working loop, ch1, *1sc into each st inserting hook through the same sts that were worked in row 4, between the strands looped through each st; rep from * to end, turn.

Row 6 (WS): Ch1, *insert hook through foundation ch ch-loops and next st, yo, to complete a sc st; rep from * to end, turn.

Row 7: Ch4 (count as 1dc, ch1), *skip 1 sc, 1 bobble into next sc, ch1, skip 1 sc, 1dc into next sc **, ch1; rep from * ending last rep at **, turn.

Row 8: Ch1, *1sc in next dc, 1sc in ch sp, 1sc in bobble, 1sc in ch sp; rep from * to last ch sp, 1sc into tch, turn.

Row 9: Ch1, 1sc into each dc to end.

Fasten off.

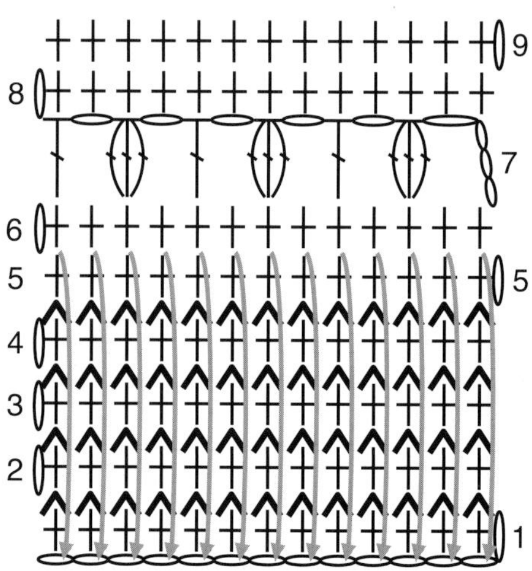

Cable edge

Worked lengthwise over 10 sts (add 1 st for base chain).

Special abbreviations:

Tr/rf (raised treble crochet at the front of the fabric) = yo twice, insert hook from in front and from right to left around stem of appropriate stitch, and complete stitch normally.

Tr/rb (raised treble crochet at the back of the fabric) = yo twice, insert hook from behind and from right to left around the stem of the appropriate stitch, and complete stitch normally.

Note: in this pattern, the stitch behind the tr/rb is to be skipped.

Row 1 (RS): 1sc into 2nd ch from hook, work 1sc into each ch to end, turn.

Row 2: Ch2 (count as 1st hdc), hdc in each sc to end, turn.

Row 3: Ch2 (count as 1st hdc), tr/rf around next st, hdc in next st, tr/rf around each of next 4 sts, hdc in next st, tr/rf around next st, hdc in top of tch, turn.

Row 4: Ch2 (count as 1st hdc), tr/rb around next st, hdc in next st, tr/rb around each of next 4 sts, hdc in next st, tr/rb around next st, hdc in top of tch, turn.

Row 5: Ch2 (count as 1st hdc), tr/rf around next st, hdc in next st, skip next 2 sts, tr/rf around each of next 2 sts; next, working in front of 2 sts just worked, tr/rf around each of 2 skipped sts, hdc in next st, tr/rf around next st, hdc in top of tch, turn.

Row 6: Ch2 (count as 1st hdc), tr/rb around next st, hdc in next st, tr/rb around each of next 4 sts, hdc in next st, tr/rb around next st, hdc in top of tch, turn.

Rep rows 3–6 until required length is reached, ending with a row 6.

Next row: Ch2 (count as 1st hdc), hdc in each sc to end, turn.

Next row: 1sc into 2nd ch from hook, work 1sc into each ch to end, turn.

Fasten off.

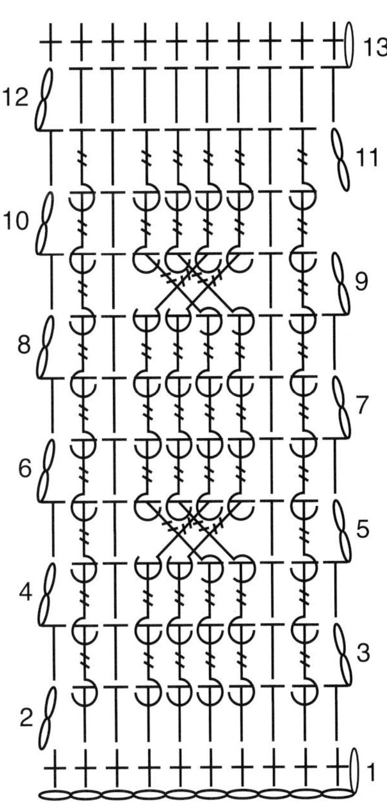

Cluster diamonds

Worked lengthwise.

Row 1 (WS): Ch20, 1sc into 11th ch from hook, skip 2 ch, 5dc into next ch, skip 2 ch, 1sc into next ch, ch5, skip 2 ch, 1sc into next ch, turn.

Row 2: Ch3, 5dc into 1st st, 1sc into next ch-5 sp, ch5, skip 2 dc, 1sc into next dc, ch5, 1sc into 3rd ch of tch, turn.

Row 3: Ch7, 1sc into next ch-5 sp, ch5, 1sc into next ch-5 sp, 5dc into next sc, skip 2 dc, 1sc into next dc, skip 2 dc, 5dc into top of tch, turn.

Row 4: Ch1, slip st into each of next 2 dc, 1sc into next dc, skip 2 dc, 5dc into next sc, skip 2 dc, 1sc into next dc, ch5, 1sc into next ch-5 sp, ch5, 1sc into 3rd ch of tch, turn.

Row 5: Ch7, 1sc into next ch-5 sp, 5dc into next sc, 1sc into next ch-5 sp, ch5, skip 1 sc and 2 dc, 1sc into next dc, turn.

Rep rows 2–5 until required length is reached, ending with a row 5.

Fasten off.

Crow's foot edging

Multiple of 5 sts (add 1 st for base chain).

Special abbreviation:

Spc (spike cluster) = insert hook through fabric 3 times, first to right, then below, then to left of next st, each time yo, drawing yarn up to height of edging row, insert hook into next st, yo, draw loop through (5 loops on hook), ending yo, draw through all loops.

Row 1 (RS): 1sc into 2nd ch from hook, work 1sc into each ch to end, turn.

Row 2: Ch1, 1sc into 1st st, work 1sc into each st to end, turn.

Rep row 2 twice more.

Row 5: Ch1, 1sc into each of 1st 2 sts, *1Spc over next st, 1sc into next of each 4 sts; rep from* to end, omitting 2sc at end of last rep.

Fasten off.

Close fan ruffle

Multiple of any number of sts (add 1 st for base chain).

Row 1 (RS): Skip 2 ch, (count as 1hdc), 1hdc into next ch, 1hdc into each ch to end, turn.

Row 2: Ch2 (count as 1hdc), 1hdc in each st to end, turn.

Rep row 2.

Row 4: Ch3 (count as 1dc), 3dc into base of ch, *4dc into front loop of next hdc; rep from * to end, turn.

Row 5: 4dc into unworked top loop (now front loop) of each hdc of row 3.

Fasten off.

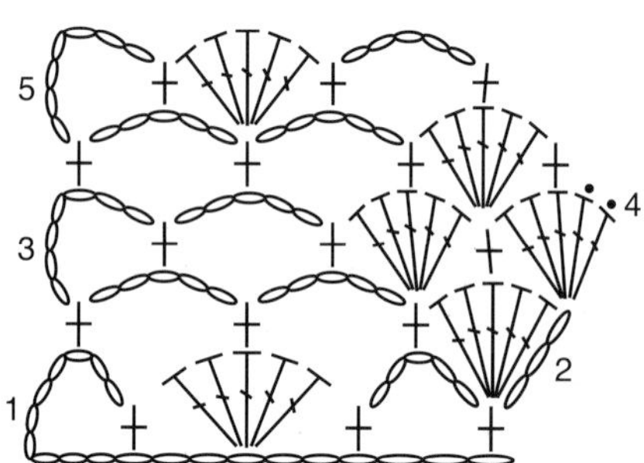

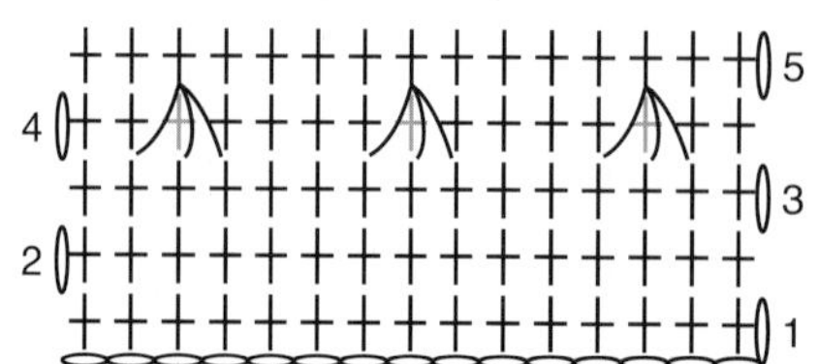

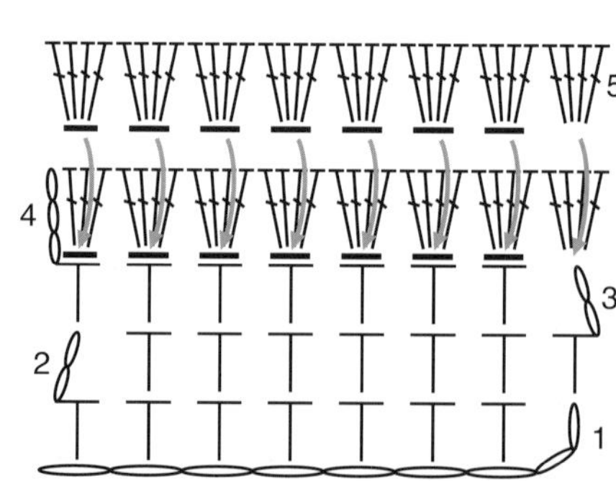

Simple chain loops

Multiple of 4 sts + 1 st (add 1 st for base chain).

Row 1 (RS): 1sc into 2nd ch from hook, work 1sc into each ch to end, turn.

Row 2: Ch1, 1sc into 1st sc, *ch5, skip 3 sc, 1sc into next sc; rep from * to end, turn.

Row 3: Ch1, 1sc into 1st sc, *ch7, 1sc into next sc; rep from * to end.

Fasten off.

Faux knitted rib

Worked lengthwise over any number of sts (add 1 st for base chain).

Row 1 (RS): Skip 2 ch, (count as 1hdc) 1htr into next ch, 1hdc into each ch to end, turn.

Row 2: Ch2, 1hdc into back bar under top loops of each hdc to end, turn.

Rep row 2 until required length is reached.

Fasten off.

Picot points

Multiple of 5 sts + 1 st (add 1 st for base chain).

Special abbreviations:

Ch-5 picot = ch5, slip st into back bar of 3rd ch from hook; **ch-6 picot** = ch6, slip st into back bar of 3rd ch from hook.

Row 1 (RS): 1sc into 2nd ch from hook, work 1sc into each ch to end, turn.

Row 2: Ch1, 1sc into 1st sc, * ch-5 picot, ch3, skip next 4 sc, 1sc into next sc; rep from * to end, turn.

Row 3: Ch1, 1sc into 1st sc, *ch-6 picot, ch4, 1sc into next sc; rep from * to end.

Fasten off.

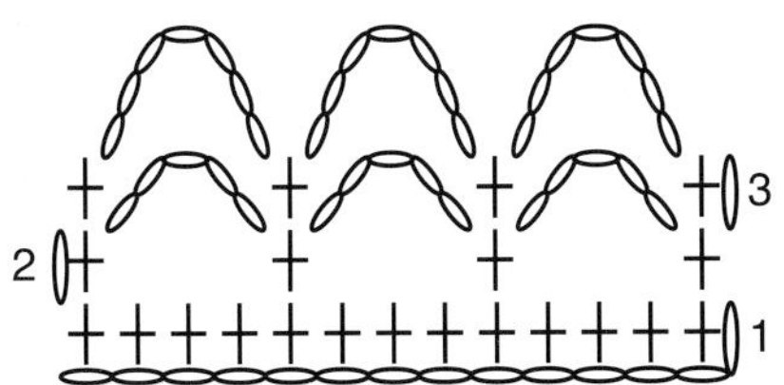

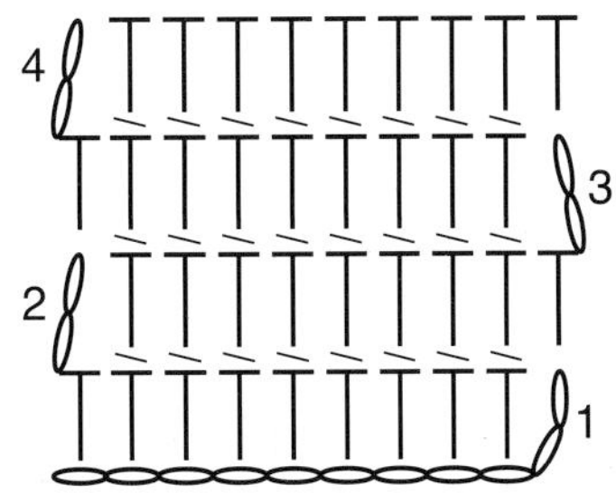

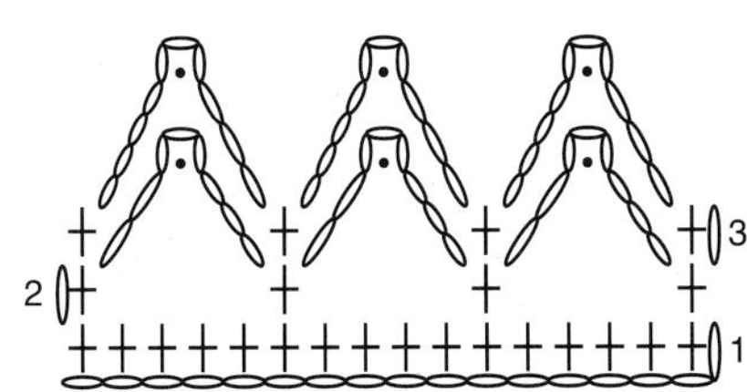

Filet triangles

Worked lengthwise.

Row 1 (RS): Ch12, 1dc into 4th ch from hook, 1dc in each of next 2 ch, ch2, 1dc into same ch as last dc, ch2, skip 2 ch, 1dc into each of next 4 ch, turn.

Row 2: Ch3 (count as 1dc), 1dc into each of next 3 dc, [ch2, 1dc into next dc] twice, 1dc in each of next 2 dc, 1dc into top of tch, turn.

Row 3: Ch3 (count as 1dc), 1dc into each of next 3 dc, ch2, 1dc into same st as last dc, [ch2, 1dc into next dc] twice, 1dc in each of next 2 dc, 1dc into top of tch, turn.

Row 4: Ch3 (count as 1dc), 1dc into each of next 3 dc, [2dc into next sp, 1dc into next dc] 3 times, 1dc in each of next 2 dc, 1dc into top of tch, turn.

Row 5: Ch3 (count as 1dc), 1dc into each of next 3 dc, ch2, 1dc into same st as last dc, ch2, skip 2 dc, 1dc in each of next 4 dc, turn.

Rep rows 2–5 until required length is reached, ending with a row 4.

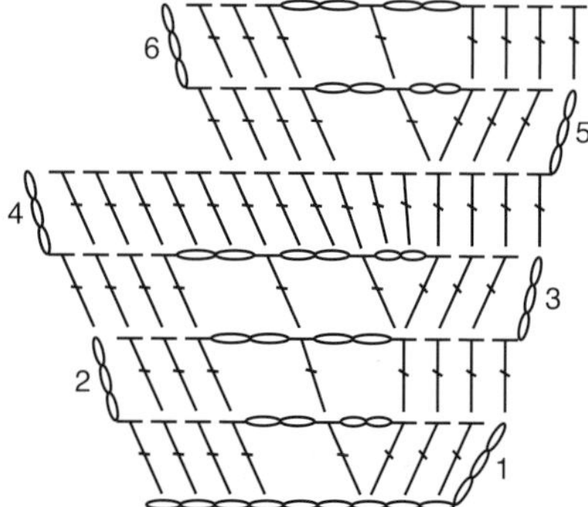

Ridged trimming

Worked lengthwise over any number of sts (add 1 st for base chain).

Row 1 (RS): 1sc into 2nd ch from hook, 1sc into each ch to end, turn.

Row 2: Ch1, 1sc into back loop of each sc to end, turn.

Rep row 2 until required length is reached. Do not turn but rotate the work by 90 degrees and proceed to work along one long edge.

Header

Row 1: Ch3 (count as 1dc), 1dc into edge st at end of each previous row to end, turn.

Row 2: Ch3 (count as 1dc), 1dc into each dc to end.

Fasten off.

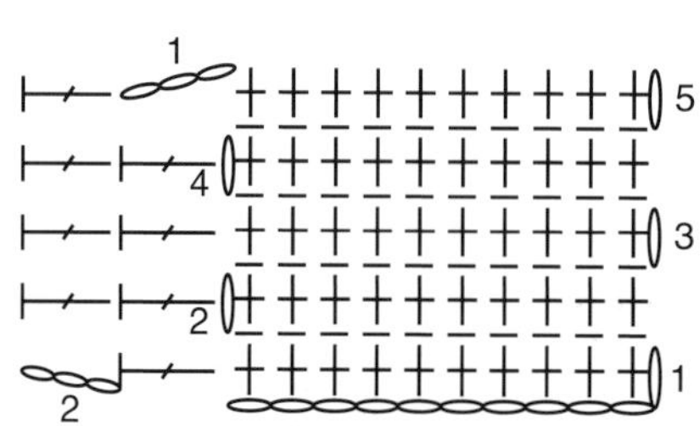

Flower border

Multiple of 9 sts + 1 st (1 motif for each repeat).

Motif

Base ring: Ch8, join with slip st.

Round 1: Ch3 (count as 1dc), 1dc into ring, [ch6, 3dc into ring] 5 times, ch6, 1dc into ring, slip st to top of ch-3 tch.

Round 2: *Ch1, (1sc, 1hdc, 7dc, 1hdc, 1sc) into next ch-6 sp, ch1, skip 1 dc, 1 slip st into next dc; rep from * 5 more times placing last slip st into top of ch-3 tch of previous round.

Fasten off.

Header

With RS facing join yarn to back bar of center dc of motif petal.

Row 1: Ch1, 1sc same place as yarn has been joined, ch8, sc into back bar of center dc of next petal, *ch9, sc into back bar of center tr of petal of next flower, ch8, sc into back bar of center dc of next petal; rep from * until all the flowers have been joined, turn.

Row 2: Ch3 (count as 1dc) 1dc into back loop of each ch or sc to end of row, 1dc in last sc, turn.

Row 3: Ch4, *skip 1 st, 1dc into next dc, ch1; rep from * to last 2 dc, skip 1 dc, 1dc into top of tch. Fasten off.

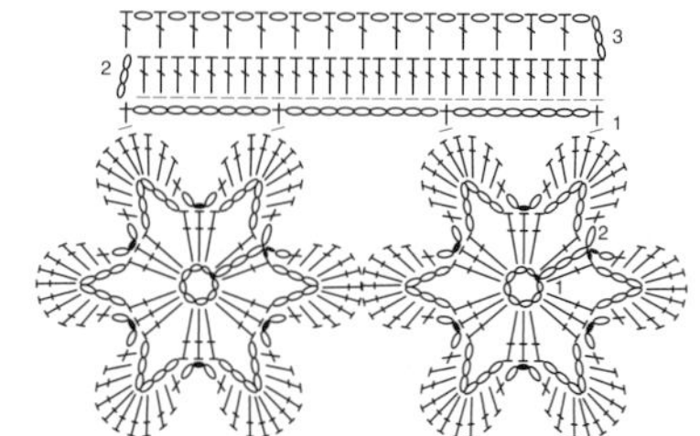

Three-picot feathers

Multiple of 10 sts + 7 sts (add 1 st for base chain).

Row 1 (WS): 1sc into 2nd ch from hook, 1sc into next ch, ch6, skip 3 ch, *1sc into each of next 7 ch, ch6, skip 3 ch; rep from * to last 2 ch, 1sc into each of last 2 ch, turn.

Row 2: Ch1, 1sc into 1st sc, *into next ch-6 arch work (1sc, 1hdc, 5dc, 1hdc, 1sc)**, ch7; rep from * ending last rep at **, work 1sc into last sc, turn.

Row 3: Ch5, skip 1st 5 sts, work 1sc into next dc, [ch3, 1sc] 3 times into same st as last sc, *ch3, (1sc, ch3, 1sc) into next ch-7 arch, ch3, skip next 4 sts, 1sc into next dc, [ch3, 1sc] 3 times into same st as last sc; rep from * to last 5 sts, ch5, slip st into last sc. Fasten off.

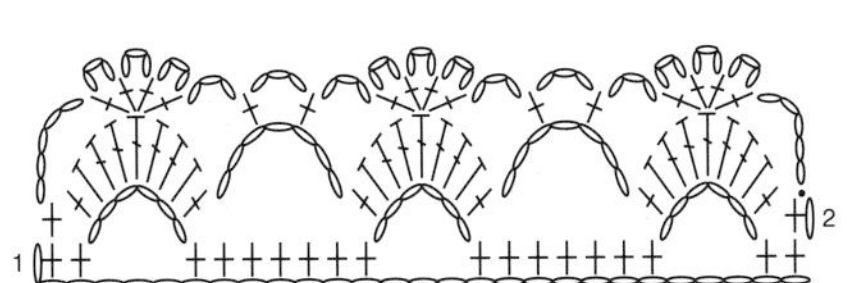

Double corded edging

Multiple of any number of sts (add 1 st for base chain).

Special abbreviation:

Reverse sc = working from left to right, 1sc into st loop specified of the st to the right, keeping the working yarn to the left of the hook.

Row 1 (RS): 1sc into 2nd ch from hook, work 1sc into each ch or equivalent interval to end. Do not turn.

Row 2: Ch1, *1 reverse sc back under front loop only of next st to right; rep from * to end. Fasten off. Do not turn.

Rejoin yarn into left edge though back loop of 1st st.

Row 3: Ch1, *1 reverse sc back under back loop only of next st to right; rep from * to end. Fasten off.

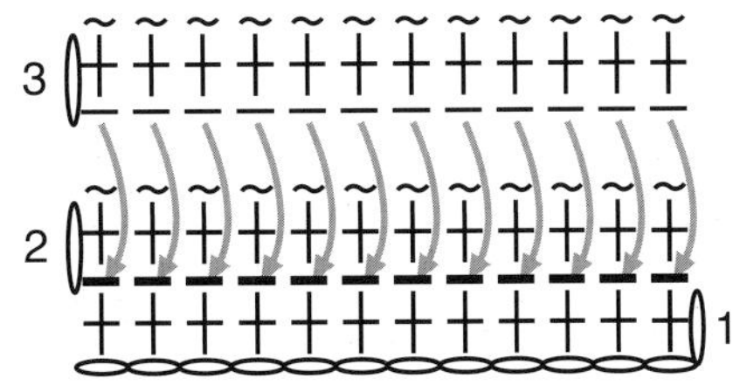

Slip stitch strands

Multiple of any number of sts.

Note: wrap yarn around a piece of card, periodically cutting the yarn along one edge to create strands.

Foundation chain: Ch1, *place the center of a folded strand over the hook, and draw through the loop on the hook, ch1 using the working yarn; rep from * to required edging length, turn.

Row 1: Ch1, *skip ch made with the strand, insert hook under and around next ch and complete a sc; rep from * to last ch, 1sc into last ch, turn.

Row 2: Ch1, 1sc into each stitch to end. Fasten off.

Pull all the strands tight and trim the ends.

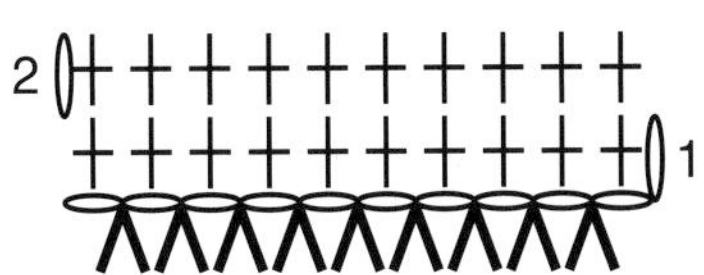

On the fold

Multiple of 14 sts + 2 sts (add 1 st for base chain).
(1 motif for each repeat).

Motif

Base ring: Ch4, join with slip st.

Round 1: Ch4 (count as 1dc, ch1), [1dc into ring, ch1] 7 times, slip st to 3rd ch of tch. (8 sps)

Round 2: Ch1, 1sc into same place as ch-1, [ch3, skip 1 ch, 1sc into next dc] 8 times omitting sc at end of last rep, slip st to 1st sc.

Round 3: Slip st into each of next 2 ch, ch1, 1sc into same sp as ch1, [ch6, 1sc into next ch-3 sp] 8 times omitting sc at end of last rep, slip st to 1st sc.

Round 4: Slip st into each of next 3 ch, ch1, 1sc into same sp as ch-1, [ch6, 1sc into next ch-6 sp] 8 times omitting sc at end of last rep, slip st to 1st sc.

Round 5: Ch1, 1sc into 1st sc, *(2dc, ch4, 2dc) into next sp, 1sc into next sc; rep from * 7 more times omitting sc at end of last rep, slip st to 1st sc. Fasten off.

Header

Row 1 (RS): 1sc into 2nd ch from hook, work 1sc into each ch to end, turn.

Hold the motif with WS facing and the motif towards the back, work from far right of the motif.

Row 2: Ch3 (count as 1dc) skip st at base of ch, 1dc into next st, using the diagram and the grey dots as a guide to st positions, work from right to left into the motif and the next st on the 1st row, *1dc into next 3 sts, 1dc into ch sp, 1dc into next 4 sts indicated, 1dc into ch sp, 1dc into each of last 3 sts indicated, 1dc into next 2 sts on 1st row; rep from * across each motif to end.

Row 3: Ch2, work 1hdc into each st to end, turn.

Row 4: Ch2, work 1hdc into back bar (below top loops) of each st to end. Fasten off.

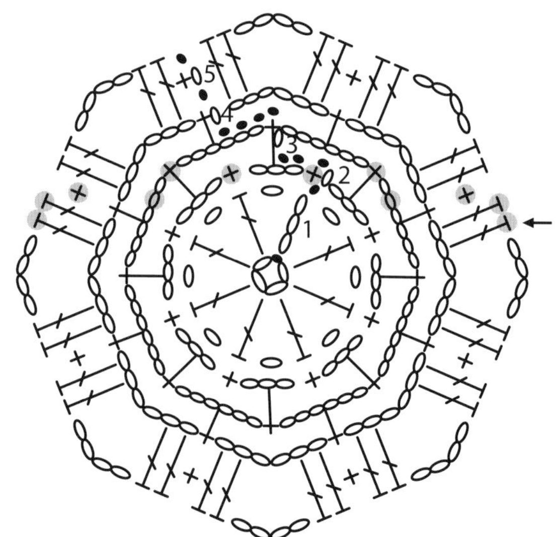

Scroll ruffle

Multiple of 7 sts + 6 sts (add 1 st for base chain).

Special abbreviations:

Dc2tog = work 1dc into next 2 sts indicated until 1 loop of each remains on hook, yo and draw through all 3 loops on hook;

Dc3tog = work 1dc into next 3 sts indicated until 1 loop of each remains on hook, yo and draw through all 4 loops on hook.

Row 1 (RS): Skip 2 ch (count as 1hdc), 1hdc into next ch, 1hdc into each ch to end, turn.

Row 2: Ch1, 1sc into each st to end, turn.

Row 3: Ch2 (count as 1hdc), 1hdc into each sc to end, turn.

Rep row 2.

Row 5: Ch3, skip 1st sc, 1dc into next sc, *ch1, skip 1 sc, dc3tog into next 3 sts; rep from * to last 3 sts, skip 1 st, dc2tog into next 2 sts, turn.

Row 6: Ch1, 1sc into 1st st, ch7, *1sc into next dc3tog, ch7; rep to last dc, 1sc into top of tch, turn.

Row 7: Ch3, (2dc, ch3, 3dc) into next ch-7 sp, *ch2, 1sc into next ch-7 sp, ch2, (3dc, ch3, 3dc) into next ch-7 sp; rep from * to end, turn.

Row 8: Ch1, *1sc into each of next 3 dc, 5sc into next ch-3 sp, 1sc into each of next 3 dc**, 2sc into next ch-2 sp, skip next sc, 2sc into next ch-2 sp; rep from * ending last rep at ** with last dc in top of tch, turn.

Row 9: Ch4, 1tr into each of next 2 sc, place st marker, *2dc into each of next 5 sc, place st marker**, 1tr into each of next 10 sc; rep from * ending last rep at **, 1tr into each of last 3 sts, turn. On following row, work 2tr into each tr between st markers.

Row 10: Ch4, 1tr into each of next 2 tr, *2tr into each of next 10 tr**, 1tr into each of next 10 tr; rep from * ending last rep at **, 1tr into each of next 2 tr,1tr in top of tch, turn. Fasten off.

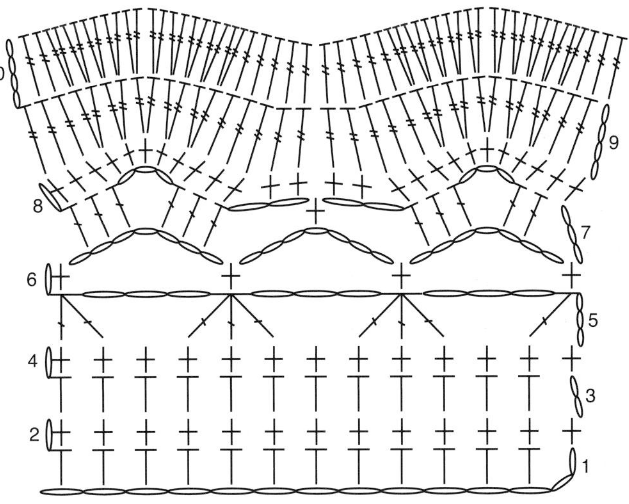

Zinnia zigzag

1 motif for each repeat

Special abbreviations:

Ch-4 picot = ch4, slip st in 1st ch for picot.

Ch-3 picot = ch3, slip st in 1st ch for picot.

Note: join the motifs by the ch-3 picots at the tip of the leaves progressing from right to left.

First motif

Base ring: Ch8, join with slip st to form ring.

Round 1: Ch3 (count as 1dc), 1dc in ring, [ch-4 picot, 2dc in ring] 8 times, ch-4 picot, join with slip st to top of ch-3, ch5, *ch5, ch-3 picot, ch2, skip 1 ch, 1dc into next ch, 1tr into each of next 2 ch, 1dc into following ch**, slip st into next ch; rep from * ending last rep at **, slip st into base of last leaf. Fasten off.

Second motif

Base ring: Ch8, join with slip st to form ring.

Round 1: Ch3 (count as 1dc), 1dc in ring, [ch-4 picot, 2dc in ring] 8 times, ch-4 picot, join with slip st to top of ch-3, ch10, ch-3 picot, ch2, skip 1 ch, 1dc into next ch, 1tr into each of next 2 ch, 1dc into following ch, slip st into next ch, ch5, ch2, drop loop from hook, insert hook in picot at tip of leaf of last motif and in dropped loop, draw loop through, ch1, complete ch-3 picot, ch1, skip 1 ch, 1dc into next ch, 1tr into each of next 2 ch, 1dc into following ch, slip st into base of last leaf.

Fasten off.

Rep 2nd motif until required length is reached.

Odd-ball edge

Multiple of 8 sts + 7 sts (add 1 st for base chain).

Special abbreviations:

Beg-popcorn = work 7dc into indicated sp, remove hook from working loop, insert hook under top loops of tch, hook the working loop and draw this through the top loops to draw the popcorn closed, ch1. **8dc-popcorn** = work 8dc into indicated sp, remove hook from working loop, insert hook under top loops of 1st of the dc sts just worked, hook the working loop and draw this through the top loops to draw the popcorn closed, ch1.

Motif

Base ring: Ch5, join with slip st.

Round 1: Ch1, 12sc into ring, slip st to 1st sc.

Round 2: Working into back loop only of each sc, ch12, slip st into 1st sc, *slip st into next sc, ch12, slip st into same sc; rep from * to end, slip st to 1st sc.

Round 3: Working into front loop only of each sc in round 1, ch8, slip st into 1st sc, *slip st into next sc, ch8, slip st into same sc; rep from * to end, slip st to 1st sc. Fasten off.

Header

Row 1 (RS): 1sc into 2nd ch from hook, 1sc into each ch to end, turn.

Row 2: Ch2, work 1hdc into each st to end, turn.

Rep row 2 once more.

Row 4: Ch1, 1sc into 1st st, *ch4, skip 1 hdc, 1sc into next hdc; rep from * to end.

Row 5: Ch3, beg-popcorn into next ch-4 sp, *ch3, (1dc, ch2, 1dc) into next ch-4 sp, ch3, 8dc-popcorn into next ch-4 sp, ch3, (1dc, ch3, join to any ch-12 loop of next motif, slip st into 3rd ch from header) into next ch-4 sp, ch3, 8dc-popcorn into next ch-4 sp; rep from * to end. Fasten off.

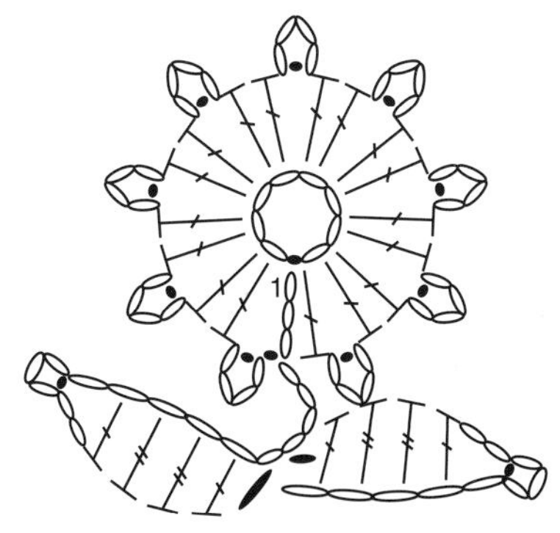

Zinnia zigzag

Layered shells

Multiple of 5 sts + 1 st (add 2 sts for base chain).

Row 1: Skip 3 ch (count as 1dc), 1dc into next ch, work 1dc into each ch to end, turn.

Row 2: Ch2, 1hdc into each st to end, turn.

Row 3: Ch1, 1sc into 1st st, ch5, skip 4 hdc, 1sc into next st; rep from * to end, turn.

Row 4: Ch1, 1sc into 1st st, *(1sc, 1hdc, 1dc, ch3, slip st into 3rd ch from hook, 1dc, 1hdc, 1sc) into next ch-5 sp; rep from * to last sc, 1sc into next sc, turn.

Row 5: Ch1, 1sc into 1st st, working behind shells in row 4, 1hdc into each of next 4 hdc skipped on row 3, *ch1, working behind shells in row 4, 1hdc into each of next 4 hdc skipped on row 3; rep from * to last sc, 1sc into next sc, turn.

Row 6: Ch1, 1sc into 1st st, 1sc into each st and ch sp to end of row, turn.

Row 7: Ch1, 1sc into 1st st, *ch5, skip 4 sc, 1sc into next st; rep from * to end, turn.

Row 8: Ch1, 1sc into 1st st, *(1sc, 1hdc, 3dc, 1hdc, 1sc) into next ch-5 sp; rep from * to last sc, 1sc into next sc, turn.

Row 9: Ch1, 1sc into 1st st, working behind shells in row 8, 1hdc into each of next 4 sc skipped on row 7, *ch1, working behind shells in row 8, 1hdc into each of next 4 sc skipped on row 7; rep from * to last sc, 1sc into next sc, turn.

Rep rows 6–8 once more.

Fasten off.

Odd-ball edge

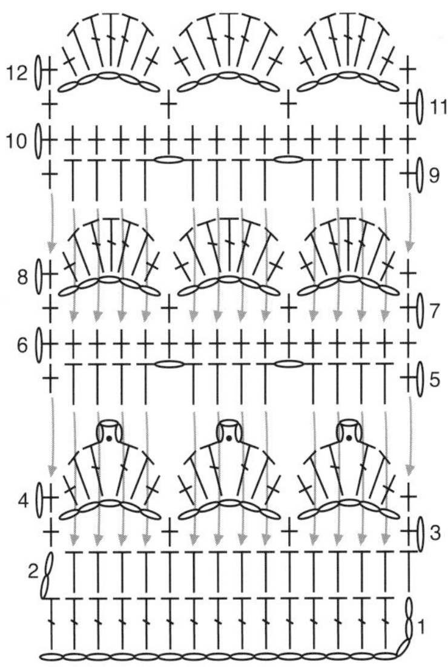

Layered shells

Hardy edge

Multiple of 6 sts + 2 sts (add 1 st for base chain).

Row 1 (WS): 1sc into 2nd ch from hook, work 1sc into each ch to end, turn.

Row 2: Ch3 (count as 1dc), skip 1st sc, 1dc into next sc, *ch1, skip 1 sc, 1dc into each of next 2 sc; rep from * to end, turn.

Row 3: Ch5 (count as 1dc, ch2), 1sc into next ch sp, *ch4, 1sc into next ch sp; rep from * to last 2 sts, ch2, 1dc into 3rd ch of ch-3 tch, turn.

Row 4: Ch1, 1sc into 1st dc, *work 5dc into next ch-4 sp, 1sc into next ch-4 sp; rep from * to end, placing last sc into 3rd ch of ch-5 tch. Fasten off.

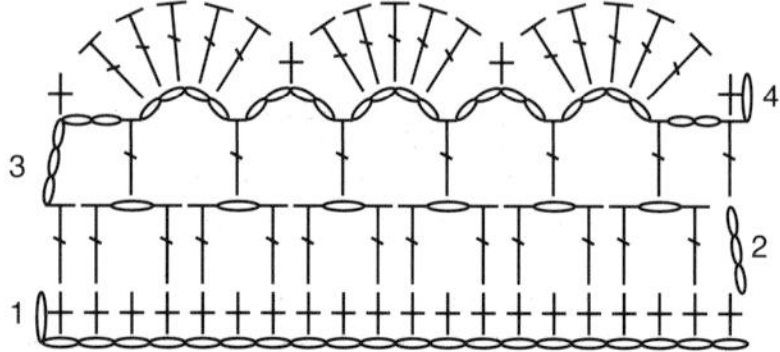

Little triangle points

Multiple of 4 sts + 1 st (add 1 st for base chain).

Special abbreviation:

Pyramid = ch6, 1sc into 3rd ch from hook, 1dc into each of next 3ch.

Note: work foundation row if working from a base chain.

Foundation row: 1sc into 2nd ch from hook and each ch to end, turn.

Row 1 (RS): Ch1, 1sc into 1st st, or join into an edge, ch1, 1sc into starting point; counting either sts or equivalent interval, *work a pyramid, skip 3 sts, 1sc into next st; rep from * to end.

Fasten off.

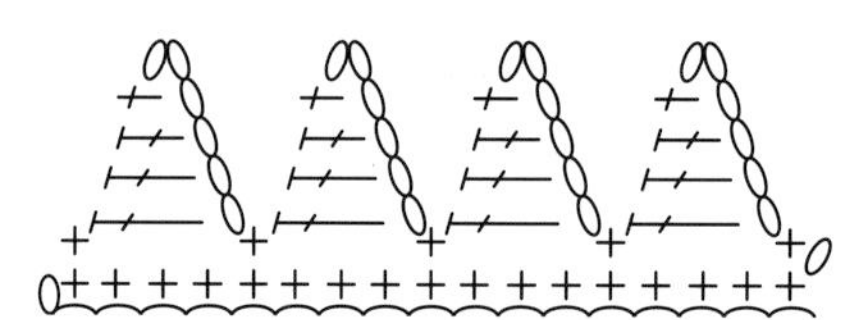

Papyrus fans

Multiple of 10 sts + 1 st (add 1 st for base chain).

Special abbreviation:

Bobble = work 3dc into next space until 1 loop of each remains on hook, yo and through all 4 loops on hook.

Row 1 (WS): 1sc into 2nd ch from hook, work 1sc into each ch to end, turn.

Row 2: Ch5 (count as 1tr, ch1), work [1tr, ch1] twice into 1st sc, skip 4 sc, 1sc into next sc, *ch1, skip 4 sc, into next sc work [1tr, ch1] 5 times, skip 4 sc, 1sc into next sc; rep from * to last 5 sc, ch1, skip 4 sc, work 1tr into last sc, ch1, into same st as last tr work (1tr, ch1, 1tr), turn.

Row 3: Ch1, 1sc into 1st tr, *ch2, into next sc work [1dtr, ch2] 4 times, skip 2 tr, 1sc into next tr; rep from * to end, placing last sc into 4th ch of ch-5 tch, turn.

Row 4: Ch1, 1sc into 1st sc, *ch4, skip next sp, 1 bobble into next ch-2 sp, [ch3, 1 bobble into next ch-2 sp] twice, ch4, 1sc into next sc; rep from * to end.

Fasten off.

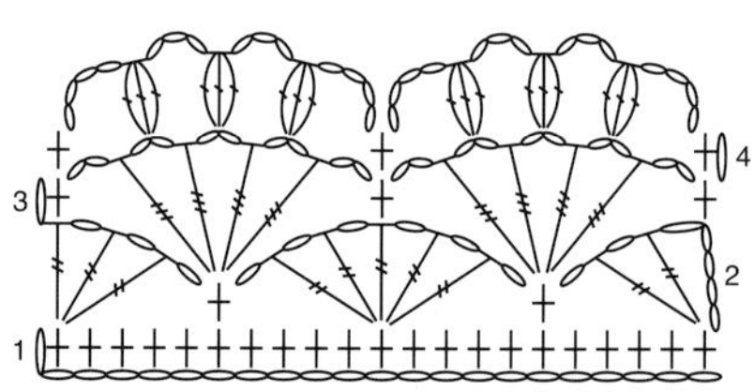

Catherine wheels

Multiple of 10 sts + 6 sts (add 1 st for base chain).

Special abbreviation:

Cluster = work (yo, insert hook, yo, draw loop through, yo, draw through 2 loops) over the number of sts indicated, yo, draw through all loops on hook.

Note: work foundation row if working from a base chain.

Foundation row: 1sc into 2nd ch from hook and each ch to end, turn.

Row 1 (WS): Ch1, 1sc into 1st 2 sts, *skip 3 sts, 7dc into next st, skip 3 sts, 1sc into each of next 3 sts; rep from * to last 4 sts, skip 3 sts, 4dc into last ch, turn.

Row 2: Ch1, 1sc into 1st st, 1sc into next st, *ch3, 1 cluster over next 7 sts, ch3, 1sc into each of next 3 sts; rep from * to last 4 sts, ch3, 1 cluster over last 4 sts, skip tch, turn.

Row 3: Ch3 (count as 1dc), 3dc into 1st st, *skip 3 ch, 1sc into each of next 3 sc, skip 3 ch, 7dc into loop that closed next cluster; rep from * to end in last cluster, skip 3 ch, 1sc into each of last 2 sc, skip tch.

Fasten off.

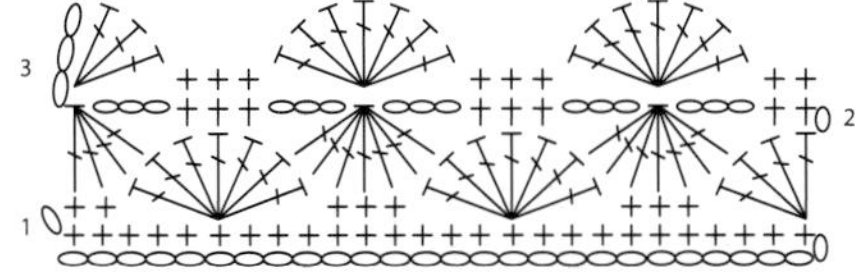

Chain ruffle

Multiple of any number of sts (add 1 st for base chain).

Row 1 (RS): 1sc into 2nd ch from hook, work 1sc into each ch to end, turn.

Row 2: Ch2 (count as 1hdc), 1hdc into front loop each sc to end, turn.

Row 3: Ch1, 1sc into back bar under top loops of each hdc to end, turn.

Rep rows 2–3 then rep row 2.

Row 7: Ch1, 1sc into 1st st, *ch4, 1sc into next sc; rep from * to end, turn.

Row 8: Ch1, 1sc into 1st st, *ch6, 1sc into next sc; rep from * to end, turn.

Row 9: Ch1, 1sc into 1st st, *ch8, 1sc into next sc; rep from * to end, turn.

Row 10: Ch1, 1sc into 1st st, *ch10, 1sc into next sc; rep from * to end, turn.

Fasten off.

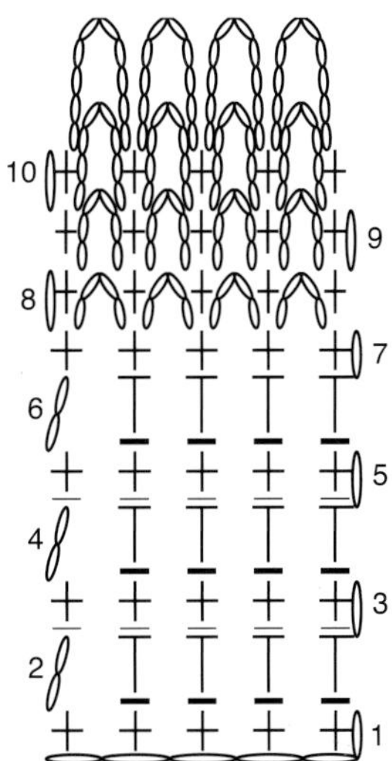

Double chain arch edging

Multiple of 3 sts + 2 sts (add 1 st for base chain).

Note: work foundation row if working from a base chain.

Scs of row 2 are always worked immediately to left of scs of row 1 into 1st of 2 skipped sts of the foundation row or equivalent intervals.

Foundation row: 1sc into 2nd ch from hook and each ch to end, turn.

Row 1 (RS): Using A, ch1, 1sc into 1st st, *ch5, skip 2 sts, 1sc into next st: rep from * to end, ending with 1 st unworked.

Fasten off. Do not turn.

Row 2 (RS): Join B at right into 2nd st of foundation row or edge, picking up yarn and drawing through the ch-5 loop of row 1 (so as not to enclose it), work 1sc into same place, *place hook over top of ch-5 loop, yo from behind loop, draw yarn through loop on hook, ch4, remove hook from working loop, insert hook through next ch-5 loop, pick up working loop again, 1sc into next st; rep from * to end.

Fasten off.

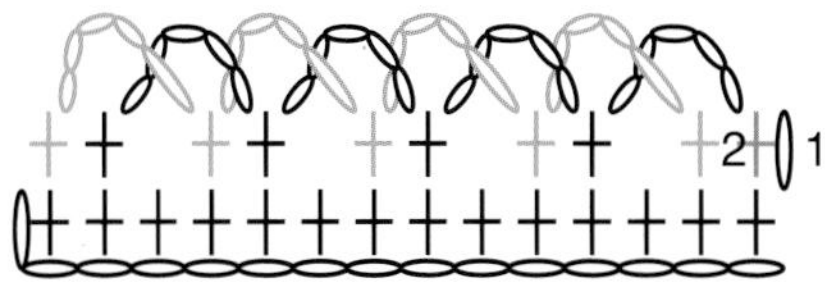

Filet ruffle

Multiple of 4 sts + 1 st (add 3 sts for base chain).

Special abbreviation:

Dc2tog = work 1dc into each of next 2 ch or sts indicated until 1 loop of each remains on hook, yo and through all 3 loops on hook.

Row 1 (RS): Skip 5 ch (count as 1dc, ch1), 1dc into next ch, *ch1, skip 1 ch, 1dc into next ch; rep from * to end, turn.

Row 2: Ch4 (count as 1dc, ch1), 1dc into next dc, *ch1, 1dc into next dc; rep from * to end, turn.

Rep row 2 a further 3 times.

Row 6: Ch3, *dc2tog in next 2dc; rep from * to end, 2nd dc of last dc2tog worked into 3rd ch of ch-4 tch, turn.

Row 7: Ch1, 1sc into each st to last dc2tog, do not sc into tch, turn.

Row 8: Ch1, 1sc into each st to end, turn. Rep row 8 twice more. Fasten off.

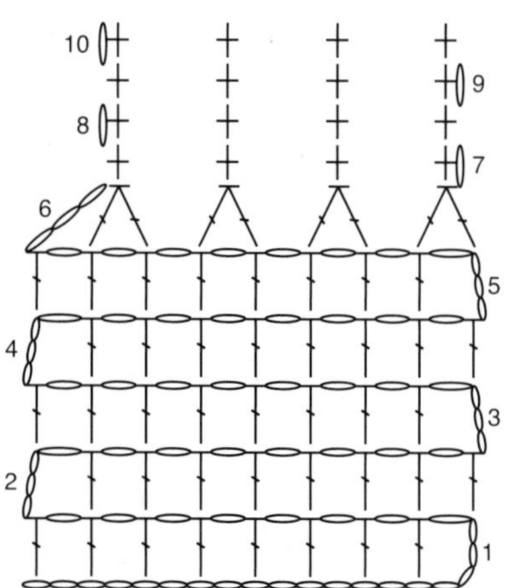

Picot sprigs

Multiple of 6 sts + 2 sts (add 1 st for base chain).

Special abbreviation:

Picot = ch3, slip st into 3rd ch from hook.

Row 1 (WS): 1sc into 2nd ch from hook, work 1sc into each ch to end, turn.

Row 2: Ch5 (count as 1dc, ch2), skip 1st 3 sc, 1sc into next sc, work 3 picots, 1sc into next sc, *ch5, skip 4 sc, 1sc into next sc, work 3 picots, 1sc into next sc; rep from * to last 3 sc, ch2, 1dc into last sc, turn.

Row 3: Ch1, 1sc into 1st dc, *ch8, 1sc into next ch-5 arch; rep from * to end, placing last sc into 3rd ch of ch-5 tch, turn.

Row 4: Ch1, 1sc into 1st sc, *11sc into next ch-8 arch, 1sc into next sc; rep from * to end.

Fasten off.

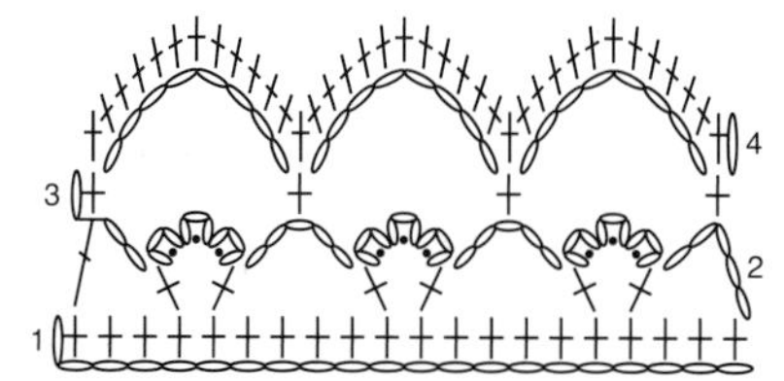

Beaded loops

Multiple of 3 sts.

Note: thread beads onto yarn before starting.

Foundation chain (WS): Ch3, *slide 3 beads to base of hook, ch3; rep from * until required length is reached, turn.

Row 1: Ch1, 1sc into front loop of 2nd ch from hook, 1sc through front loop of each ch to end.

Fasten off.

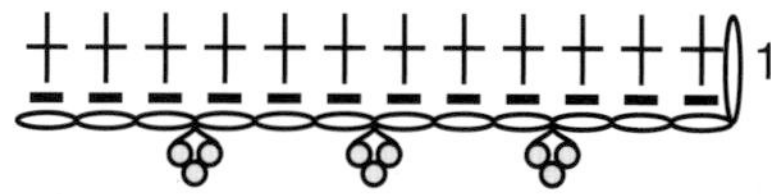

Two-tone braid

Multiple of 2 sts + 1 st (add 1 st for base chain).

Row 1 (RS): 1sc into 2nd ch from hook, work 1sc into each ch to end, turn.

Row 2: Ch2, 1hdc into each st to end, turn.

Fasten off yarn A, join in yarn B.

Row 3: Ch1, 1sc into 1st st, *skip 1 hdc from row 2, 1dc into equivalent sc on row 1, 1sc into next st in row 2; rep from * to end.

Fasten off.

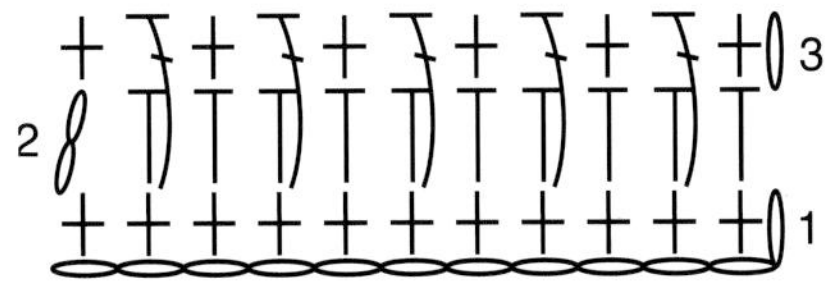

Bullion scrolls

Worked lengthwise over 10 sts (add 2 sts for base chain).

Special abbreviations:

Bullion stitch = yo hook 10 times, insert hook into ch or st indictated, yo, ease the loop through all the loops on hook, ch1.

bullion group = work 1dc, [1 bullion st, 1dc] 3 times, into ch or st indicated.

Shell = work [3dc, ch2, 3dc] into ch or st indicated.

Row 1 (RS): Skip 3 ch (count as 1dc), 1dc into next ch, skip 3 ch, work a bullion group into next ch, skip 3 ch, work a shell into last ch, turn.

Row 2: Ch7, 3dc into 4th ch from hook, 3dc into each of next 3 ch, shell into ch-2 sp at center of next shell, ch3, 1sc into 2nd bullion at center of next group, ch3, skip next 3 sts, 1dc into next dc, 1dc into top of tch, turn.

Row 3: Ch3 (count as 1dc), skip 1st st, 1dc into next st, skip 3 ch, bullion group into next sc, skip 3 ch, shell into ch-2 sp at center of next shell, turn.

Rep rows 2–3 until required length is reached, ending with a row 2.

Fasten off.

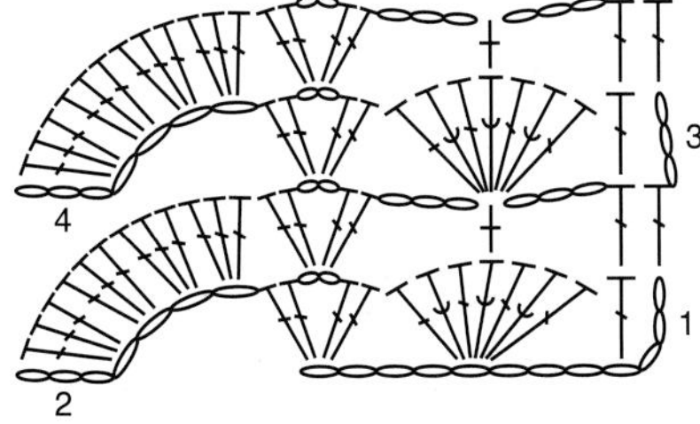

Curling petals

1 motif for each repeat

Note: pattern is worked in a spiral, do not join at the end of rounds 1–6. The leaves are from the Leaf layer edging on page 261, with the round of picots omitted.

Base ring: Ch6, join with slip st.

Round 1: 8sc into ring.

Round 2: 3sc in each st. (24 sts)

Rounds 3–4: 1sc in each st.

Round 5: *1sc in next sc, 2sc in next sc; rep from * around. (36 sts)

Round 6: 1sc in each st.

Round 7: *Ch9, slip st in 2nd ch from hook, 1sc in next ch, 1dc in each of next 3 ch, 1tr in each of next 3 ch, skip next 3 sts of previous round, slip st in next st; rep from * around, join with slip st. (9 petals)

Slip stitch motifs to fabric. Fasten off.

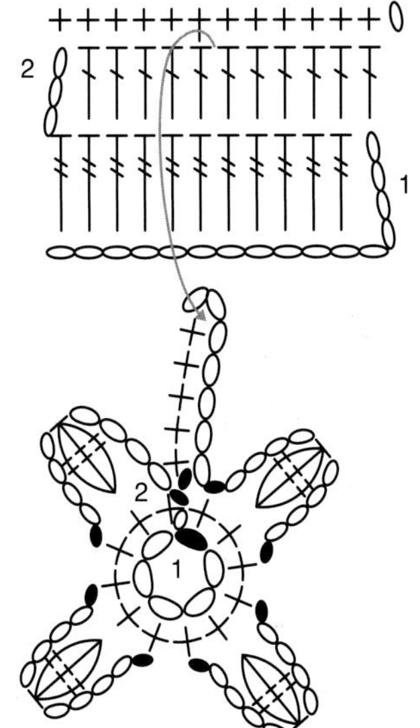

Fringed arches

Multiple of 9 sts + 1 st (add 1 st for base chain).

Row 1 (WS): 1sc into 2nd ch from hook, *ch3, skip 3 ch, 1sc into next ch, ch7, 1sc into next ch, ch3, skip 3 ch, 1sc into next ch; rep from * to end, turn.

Row 2: Ch1, 1sc into 1st sc, *skip 3 ch, work 13dc into next ch-7 arch, skip 3 ch, 1sc into next st; rep from * to end, skip tch, turn.

Row 3: Ch5, skip 1st sc and next 5 dc, *1sc into next dc, ch5, skip 1 dc, 1sc into next dc, ** ch5, skip (next 5 dc, 1 sc and 5 dc); rep from * ending last rep at **, skip next 5 dc, ch4, 1sc into last sc. Fasten off.

Tassel

Using a piece of thick card slightly deeper than the required tassel, wrap yarn round the card until required tassel thickness is reached. Note the number of wraps made. Cut the yarn along one edge to create strands, fold the bunch of strands in half and loop through the arch from the RS to the WS. Pass the ends through the loop created in the middle of the strands, neaten the strand loop and gently pull the ends to tighten the loop. Trim the ends.

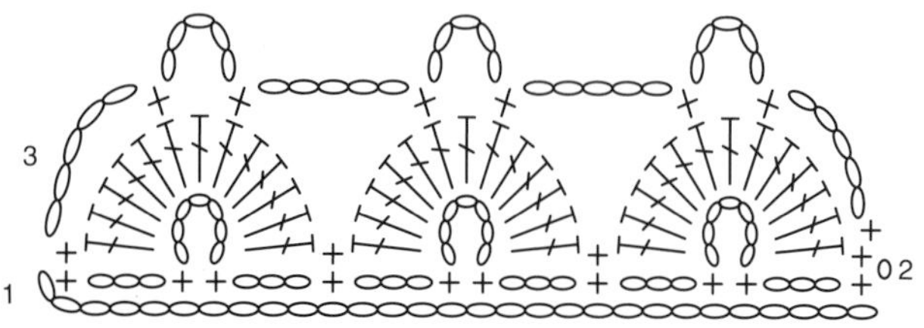

Floral fringe

Multiple of 6 sts (add 3 sts for base chain).
(1 less motif than number of repeats on the header).

Special abbreviation:

Bobble = 3tr into next sc until 1 loop of each remains on hook, yo and draw through all 4 loops on hook.

Motif

Base ring: Ch5, join with slip st.

Round 1: Ch1, 12sc into ring, slip st into 1st sc.

Round 2: *Ch4, 1 bobble into next sc, ch4, slip st into each of next 2 sc; rep from * 3 more times, skipping 1 slip st at end of last rep, ch7, 1sc into 3rd ch from hook, 1sc into each of next 4 ch, slip st into 1st sc on 1st round. Fasten off.

Header

Row 1: Skip 4 ch, work 1tr into next ch from hook, work 1tr in each ch to end, turn.

Row 2: Ch3 (count as 1dc), 1dc in each of next 5 tr, *drop loop from hook, insert hook through picot at end of stem of 1st motif and in dropped loop, draw loop through, 1dc in each of the next 6 tr; rep from * to end, turn.

Rows 3–4: Ch1, work 1sc into each st to end, turn. Fasten off.

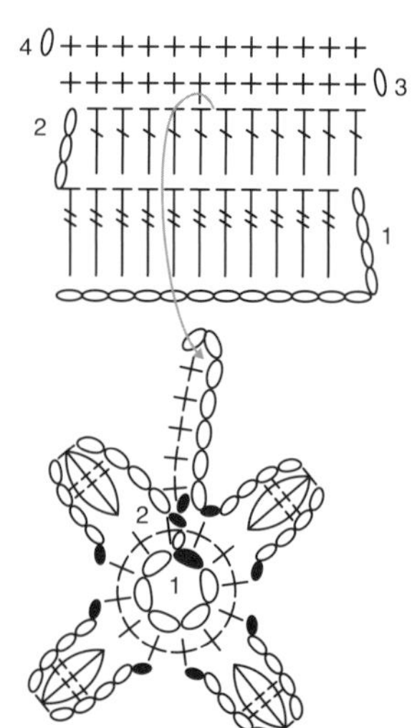

Bell ruffle

Multiple of 6 sts + 1 st (add 1 st for base chain).

Special abbreviations:

Dc/rf (raised double crochet at the front of the fabric) = yo, insert hook from in front and from right to left around the stem of the appropriate stitch, and complete stitch normally.

Dc/rb (raised double crochet at the back of the fabric) = yo, insert hook from behind and from right to left around the stem of the appropriate stitch, and complete stitch normally.

Row 1 (RS): Skip 2 ch, (count as 1hdc), 1hdc into next ch, 1hdc into each ch to end, turn.

Row 2: Ch2, *1dc/rf around next st, 1dc/rb around next st; rep from * to last 2 hdc, 1dc/rf around next st, 1hdc into top of tch, turn.

Row 3: Ch2, *1dc/rb around next st, 1dc/rf around next st; rep from * to last 2 sts, 1dc/rb around next st, 1hdc into top of tch, turn.

Row 4: Ch2, *[1dc/rf around next st, 1dc/rb around next st] twice, 1dc/rf around next st, ch1, 3hdc into next st, ch1; rep from * to last 6 sts, [1dc/rf around next st, 1dc/rb around next st] twice, 1dc/rf around next st, 1hdc into top of tch, turn.

Row 5: Ch2 *[1dc/rb around next st, 1dc/rf around next st] twice, 1dc/rb around next st, ch1, 1hdc into next ch sp, 1hdc into each of next 3 hdc, 1hdc into next ch sp; rep from * to last 6 sts, [1dc/rb around next st, 1dc/rf around next st] twice, 1dc/rb around next st, 1hdc into top of tch, turn.

Row 6: Ch2, *[1dc/rf around next st, 1dc/rb around next st] twice, 1dc/rf around next st, ch1, 1hdc into next ch sp, 1hdc into each of next 5 hdc, 1hdc into next ch sp; rep from * to last 6 sts, [1dc/rf around next st, 1dc/rb around next st] twice, 1dc/rf around next st, 1hdc into top of tch, turn.

Row 7: Ch2, *[1dc/rb around next st, 1dc/rf around next st] twice, 1dc/rb around next st, ch1, 1hdc into next ch sp, 1hdc into each of next 7 hdc, 1hdc into next ch sp; rep from * to last 6 sts, [1dc/rb around next st, 1dc/rf around next st] twice, 1dc/rb around next st, 1hdc into top of tch, turn.

Row 8: Ch2, *[1dc/rf around next st, 1dc/rb around next st] twice, 1dc/rf around next st, ch1, 1hdc into next ch sp, 1hdc into each of next 9 hdc, 1hdc into next ch sp; rep from * to last 6 sts, [1dc/rf around next st, 1dc/rb around next st] twice, 1dc/rf around next st, 1hdc into top of tch, turn. Fasten off.

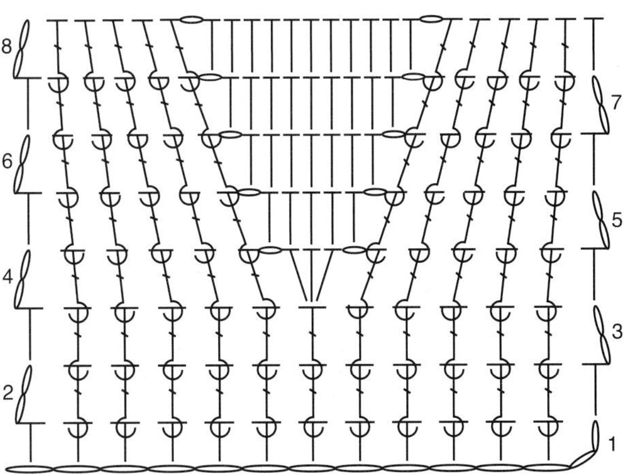

Arching spans

Multiple of 7 sts + 1 st (add 2 sts for base chain).

Row 1 (RS): Skip 3 ch (count as 1dc), 1dc into next ch, work 1dc into each ch to end, turn.

Row 2: Ch1, 1sc into each of 1st 2 dc, *ch7, skip 4 dc, 1sc into each of next 3 dc; rep from * to end, omitting 1sc at end of last rep and placing last sc into top of ch-3 tch, turn.

Row 3: Ch1, 1sc into each of 1st 2 sc, *7sc into ch-7 arch, 1sc into each of next 3 sc; rep from * to end, omitting 1sc at end of last rep, turn.

Row 4: Ch7 (count as 1tr, ch3), skip 1st 4 sc, 1sc into each of next 3 sc, *ch7, skip 7 sc, 1sc into each of next 3 sc; rep from * to last 4 sc, ch3, 1tr into last sc, turn.

Row 5: Ch1, 1sc into tr, 3sc into 1st arch, 1sc into each of next 3 sc, *7sc into next ch-7 arch, 1sc into each of next 3 sc; rep from * to last arch, 3sc into last arch, 1sc into 4th ch of ch-7 tch.

Fasten off.

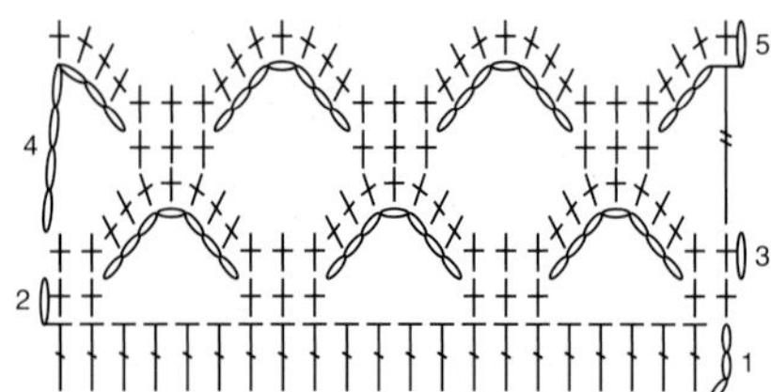

Picots with chain texture

Multiple of 12 sts + 11 sts (add 1 st for base chain).

Note: work foundation row if working from a base chain.

Foundation row: 1sc into 2nd ch from hook and each ch to end, turn.

Row 1 (RS): Ch1, 1sc into 1st st, or join into an edge, ch1, 1sc into starting point, counting either sts or equivalent interval, [ch5, skip 4 ch, 1sc into next ch] twice, *[ch5, 1sc into next ch] twice, [ch5, skip 4 ch, 1sc into next ch] twice; rep from * to end, turn.

Row 2: Ch6 (count as 1dc, ch3), 1sc into 1st ch-5 arch, *ch3, 1sc into next ch-5 arch; rep from * to end, ch3, 1dc into last sc, turn.

Row 3: Ch1, 1sc into 1st dc, *ch5, skip ch-3 arch, 1sc into next ch-3 arch, into same arch as last sc work [ch5, 1sc] twice, ch5, skip ch-3 arch, 1sc into next ch-3 arch; rep from * to end, working last sc into 3rd ch of tch.

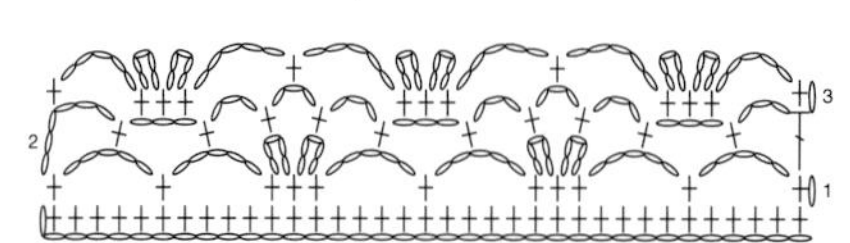

Romanesque arches

Multiple of 10 sts + 1 st (add 1 st for base chain).

Row 1 (RS): 1sc into 2nd ch from hook, work 1sc into each ch to end, turn.

Row 2: Ch3 (count as 1dc), skip 1st sc, 1dc into each of next 3 sc, *ch3, skip 3 sc, 1dc into each of next 7 sc; rep from * to end, omitting 3dc at end of last rep, turn.

Row 3: Ch1, 1sc into each of 1st 4 dc, 3sc into next ch-3 sp, *1sc into each of next 7 dc, 3sc into next ch-3 sp; rep from * to last 4 dc, 1sc into each of next 3 dc, 1sc into 3rd ch of tch, turn.

Row 4: Ch1, 1sc into 1st sc, ch2, skip 2 sc, 1sc into next sc, ch8, skip 3 sc, 1sc into next sc, *ch5, skip 5 sc, 1sc into next sc, ch8, skip 3 sc, 1sc into next sc; rep from * to last 3 sc, ch2, 1sc into last sc, turn.

Row 5: Ch1, 1sc into 1st sc, 19dc into ch-8 arch, *1sc into next ch-5 sp, 19dc into next ch-8 arch; rep from * to last ch-2 sp, 1sc into last sc.

Fasten off.

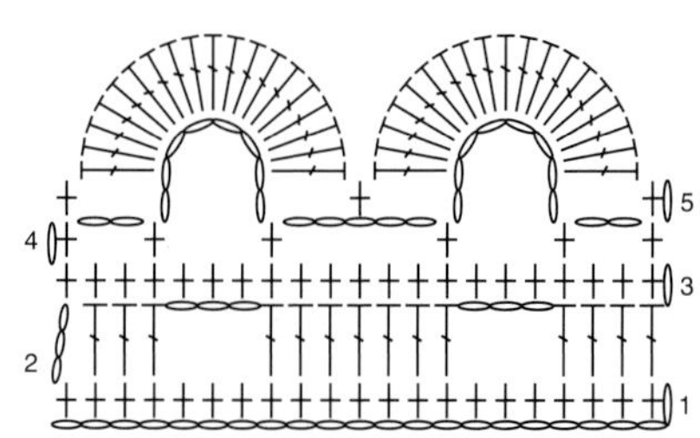

Raised-stitch rib

Worked lengthwise over any number of sts (add 2 sts for base chain).

Special abbreviation:

Dc/rf (raised double crochet at the front of the fabric) = yo, insert hook from in front and from right to left around the stem of the appropriate stitch, and complete stitch normally.

Row 1: Skip 3 ch (count as 1dc), 1dc into each ch to end, turn.
Row 2: Ch2, work 1dc/rf around each st until tch, 1hdc into top of tch, turn.
Rep row 2 until required length is reached.
Fasten off.

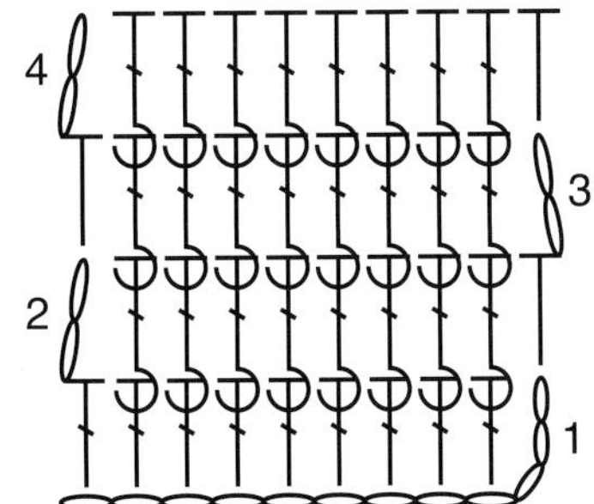

Open fans

Multiple of 10 sts + 1 st (add 1 st for base chain).

Special abbreviation:

Dc2tog = work 2dc into next ch-3 arch until 1 loop of each remains on hook, yo and through all 3 loops on hook.
Row 1 (WS): 1sc into 2nd ch from hook, *ch3, skip 3 ch, 1sc into next ch, ch3, skip 1 ch, 1sc into next ch, ch3, skip 3 ch, 1sc into next ch; rep from * to end, turn.
Row 2: Ch1, 1sc into 1st sc, *ch1, skip next ch-3 sp, dc2tog into next ch-3 arch, into same arch as last dc2tog work [ch3, dc2tog] 4 times, ch1, skip next ch-3 sp, 1sc into next sc; rep from * to end, turn.
Row 3: Ch7 (count as 1tr, ch3), skip next ch-3 arch, 1sc into next ch-3 arch, ch3, 1sc into next ch-3 arch, ch3, skip next ch-3 arch, 1tr into next sc, *ch3, skip next ch-3 arch, 1sc into next ch-3 arch, ch3, 1sc into next ch-3 arch, ch3, skip next ch-3 arch, 1tr into next sc; rep from * to end.
Fasten off.

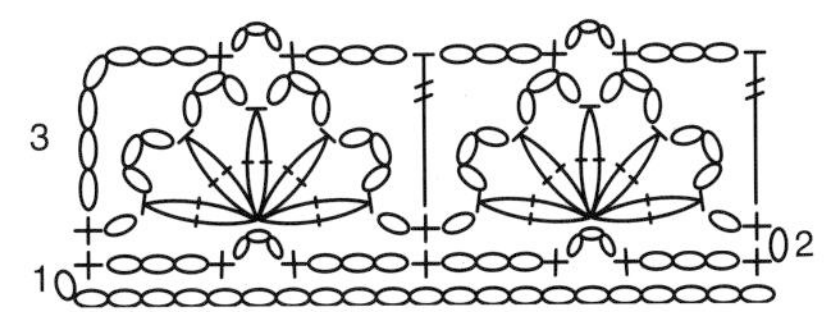

Puff stitch jewels

Multiple of 4 sts + 1 st (add 1 st for base chain).

Special abbreviations:

Sc3tog = work 1sc into next 3 ch or sts indicated until 1 loop of each remains on hook, yo and through all 4 loops on hook. **Hdc5tog (puff st)** = work 5hdc into next st indicated, until 2 loops from each remains on hook (in other words, [yo, insert hook, yo, draw loop through] 5 times]) yo and through all 11 loops on hook.
Row 1 (RS): 1sc into 2nd ch from hook, work 1sc into each ch to end, turn.
Row 2: Ch8 (count as 1dc, ch5), skip 1st 4 sts, 1dc into next st, *ch5, skip 3 sts, dc into next st; rep from * to end, turn.
Row 3: Ch3 (count as 1dc), 1hdc into 1st st, *1sc into next ch, sc3tog over next 3 ch, 1sc into next ch, (1hdc, 1dc **, 1hdc) into next st; rep from * ending last rep at **, turn.
Row 4: Ch3 (count as 1dc), skip 1st 3 sts, *(1tr, ch3, 1tr) into next sc3tog, skip 2 sts**, work hdc5tog into next dc; rep from * ending last rep at **, 1dc into top of tch.
Fasten off.

Diamonds and fans

Multiple of 6 sts (add 1 st for base chain).

Special abbreviations:

Dc2tog = work 1dc into each of next 2 sts until 1 loop of each remains on hook, yo and through all 3 loops on hook.

Cluster = work 1dc into each of next 5 sts until 1 loop of each remains on hook, yo and through all 6 loops on hook.

Half cluster = work 1dc into each of next 3 sts until 1 loop of each remains on hook, yo and through all 4 loops on hook.

Note: work foundation row if working from a base chain.

Foundation row: 1sc into 2nd ch from hook and each ch to end, turn.

Row 1 (RS): Ch3 (count as 1dc), or join into an edge and ch3; counting either sts or equivalent interval, work dc2tog working into 1st 2 sts, *ch3, 1sc into next st, turn, ch1, 1sc into last sc worked, 3sc into last ch-3 sp formed, [turn, ch1, 1sc into each of the 4sc] 3 times, work 1 cluster over next 5 sts; rep from * to end, working half cluster at end of last rep, turn.

Row 2: Ch4 (count as 1tr), work 2tr into top of 1st half cluster, skip 3 sc, 1sc into next sc, *5tr into top of next cluster, skip 3 sc, 1sc into next sc; rep from * to last dc2tog, 3tr into top of tch, turn.

Row 3: Ch3 (count as 1dc), skip 1st tr, work dc2tog over next 2 tr, *ch3, 1sc into next sc, turn, ch1, 1sc into last sc worked, 3sc into last ch-3 sp formed, [turn, ch1, 1sc into each of the 4sc] 3 times, work 1 cluster over next 5 tr; rep from * to end, and working half cluster at end of last rep placing last dc of half cluster into top of tch. Fasten off.

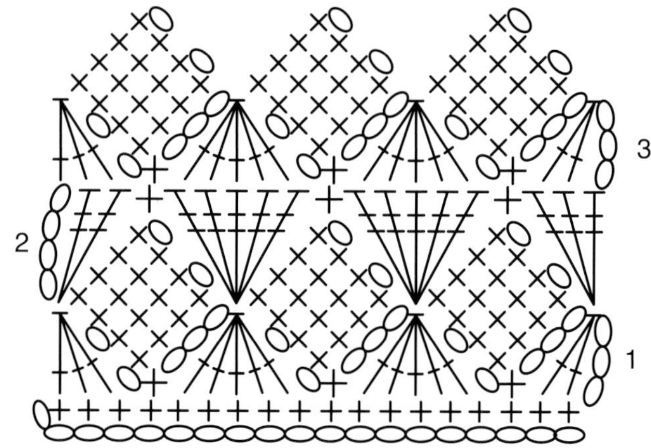

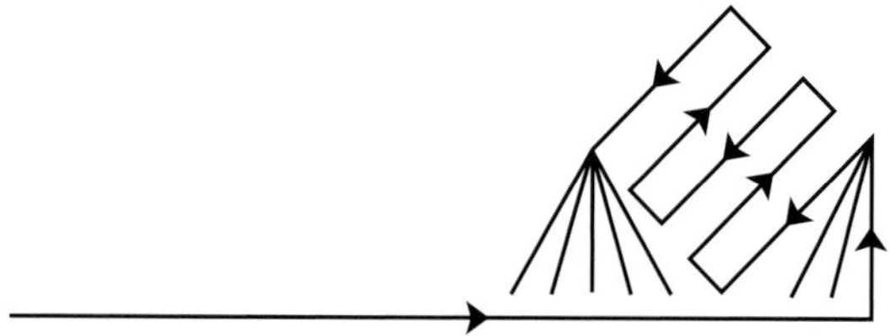

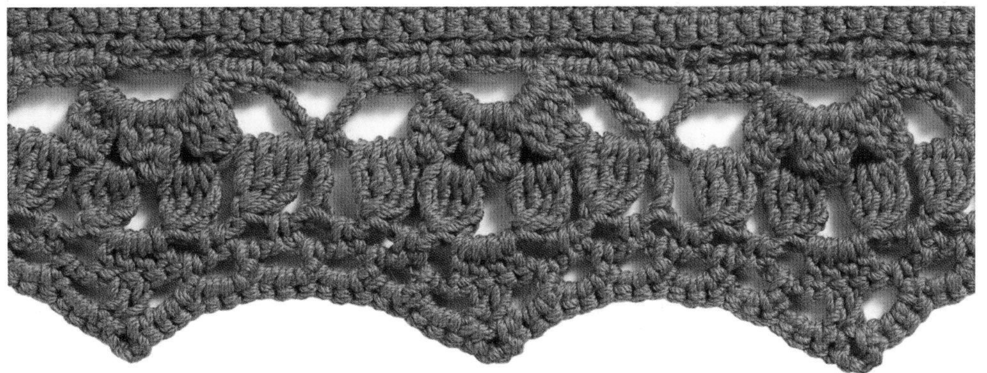

Grand bobbles

Multiple of 16 sts + 1 st (add 1 st for base chain).

Special abbreviation:

Bobble = 4tr into arch until 1 loop of each remains on hook, yo and through all 5 loops on hook.

Row 1 (WS): 1sc into 2nd ch from hook, work 1sc into each ch to end, turn.

Row 2: Ch1, 1sc into 1st sc, *ch3, skip 3 sc, 1sc into next sc; rep from * to end, turn.

Row 3: Ch1, 1sc into 1st sc, ch1, 1sc into 1st sp, *ch3, 1sc into next sp; rep from * to last sc, ch1, 1sc into last sc, turn.

Row 4: Ch6 (count as 1dc, ch3), skip 1st sc, 1sc into next sc, 3sc into next ch-3 sp, 1sc into next sc, *ch6, 1sc into next sc, 3sc into next ch-3 sp, 1sc into next sc; rep from * to last sc, ch3, 1dc into last sc, turn.

Row 5: Ch1, 1sc into 1st dc, *ch4, work 1 bobble into next ch-6 arch, into same arch as last bobble work [ch3, 1 bobble] twice, ch4, 1sc into next ch-6 arch; rep from * to end, placing last sc into 3rd ch of ch-6 tch, turn.

Row 6: Ch7 (count as 1tr, ch3), *work 1 bobble into next ch-4 arch, ch3, [1 bobble into next ch-3 arch, ch3] twice, 1 bobble into next ch-4 arch, ch3, 1tr into next sc, ch3; rep from * to end, omitting ch3 at end of last rep, turn.

Row 7: Ch1, 1sc into 1st tr, ch1, [1sc into next arch, ch3] twice, 4dc into next arch, *ch3, [1sc into next arch, ch3] 4 times, 4dc into next arch; rep from * to last 2 arches, [ch3, 1sc into next arch] twice, ch1, 1sc into 4th ch of ch-7 tch, turn.

Row 8: Ch1, 1sc into 1st sc, ch3, [1sc into next ch-3 arch, ch3] twice, skip 1 dc, 1dc into each of next 2 dc, *ch3, [1sc into next arch, ch3] 5 times, skip 1 dc, 1dc into each of next 2 dc; rep from * to last 2 ch-3 arches, ch3, [1sc into next arch, ch3] twice, 1sc into last sc, turn.

Row 9: Ch1, 1sc into 1st sc, work 3sc into each of next 3 arches, 1sc into next dc, ch3, 1sc into next dc, *3sc into each of next 6 arches, 1sc into next dc, ch3, 1sc into next dc; rep from * to last 3 arches, 3sc into each of last 3 arches, 1sc into last sc. Fasten off.

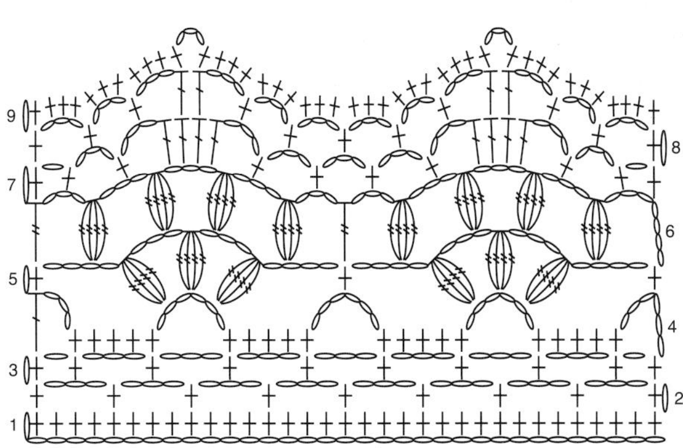

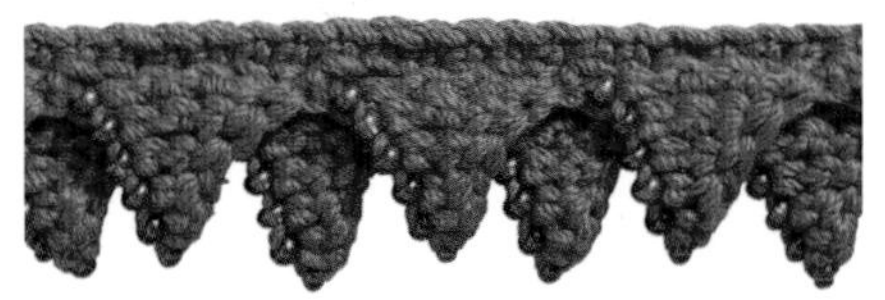

Beaded triangles

Multiple of 6 sts + 1 st (add 1 st for base chain).

Special abbreviation:

Pb (place bead) = slide next bead along yarn to base of hook.

Note: thread beads onto yarn before starting.

Row 1 (RS): 1sc into 2nd ch from hook, work 1sc into each ch to end, turn.

Row 2: Ch1, 1sc into 1st sc, *[pb, ch1] 6 times, work 1sc into 2nd ch from hook, then working 1 st into each of next 4 ch work 1hdc, 1dc, 1tr and 1dtr, skip 5 sc on previous row, 1sc into next sc; rep from * to end. Fasten off. Do not turn.

Rejoin yarn, with WS facing, in 3rd skipped sc under 1st triangle.

Row 3: Ch1, 1sc into 3rd skipped sc, *[pb, ch1] 6 times, work 1sc into 2nd ch from hook, then working 1 st into each of next 4 ch work 1hdc, 1dc, 1tr and 1dtr, skip 5 sc on previous row, 1sc into next sc; rep from * to end to within last 3 sts. Fasten off.

Zigzag dainty

Multiple of 6 sts + 1 st (add 1 st for base chain).

Special abbreviation:

Bobble = work 3dtr into next st until 1 loop of each remains on hook, yo and through all 4 loops on hook.

Row 1 (RS): 1sc into 2nd ch from hook, work 1sc into each ch to end, turn.

Row 2: Ch8 (count as 1dc, ch5), skip 1st 6 sc, 1dc into next sc, *ch5, skip 5 sc, 1dc into next sc; rep from * to end, turn.

Row 3: Ch6 (count as 1tr, ch2), work 1 bobble into 1st dc, *into next dc work (1 bobble, ch5, 1 bobble); rep from * to last dc, into top of tch work (1 bobble, ch2, 1tr), turn.

Row 4: Ch1, 1sc into 1st tr, *ch7, 1sc into next ch-5 arch; rep from * to end, placing last sc into 4th ch of ch-6 tch, turn.

Row 5: Ch1, 1sc into 1st sc, *9sc into next ch-7 arch, 1sc into next sc; rep from * to end.

Fasten off.

Pintuck ridges

Multiple of any number of sts (add 1 st for base chain).

Row 1 (WS): 1sc into 2nd ch from hook, 1sc into each ch to end, turn.

Row 2: Ch1, 1sc into front loop of each sc to end, turn.

Row 3: Ch1, 1sc into unworked top loop (now front loop) of each sc of 1st row, turn.

Row 4: Ch1, 1sc into each sc of row 3 to end, turn.

Row 5: Ch1, 1sc into each sc to end, turn.

Rep rows 2–5 twice more.

Fasten off.

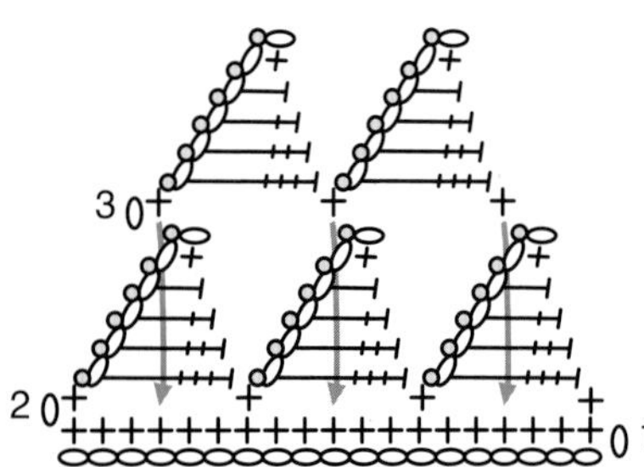

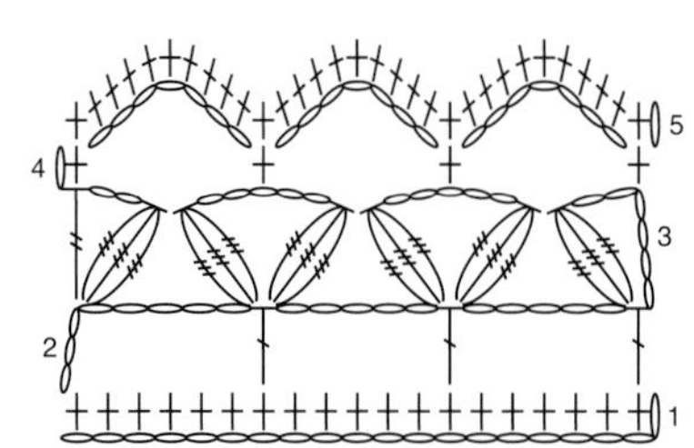

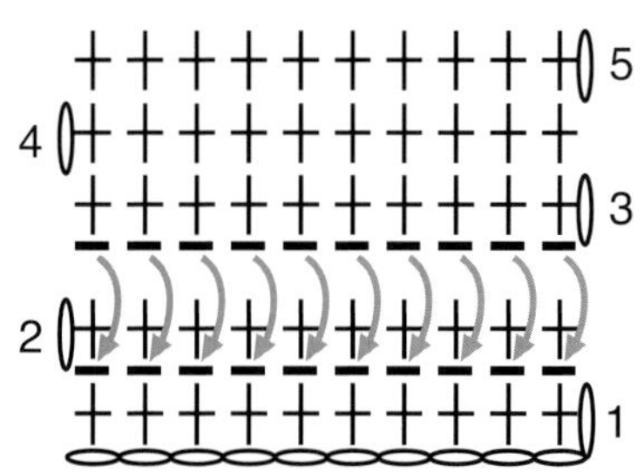

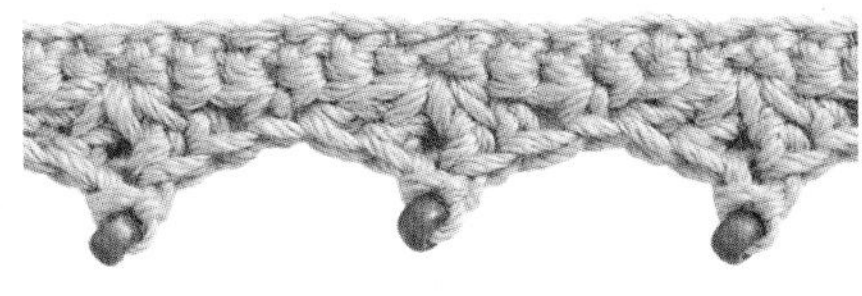

Crowned zigzag

Multiple of 9 sts + 1 st (add 4 sts for base chain).

Special abbreviation:

Bobble = work 3dtr into next st until one loop of each remains on hook, yo and through all 4 loops on hook.

Row 1 (WS): Skip 7 ch (count as 1dc, ch2), 1dc into next ch, *ch2, skip 2 ch, 1dc into next ch; rep from * to end, turn.

Row 2: Ch3 (count as 1dc), skip next sp, work 1 bobble into next sp, [ch6, 1dc into 1st of these ch] 3 times, 1 bobble into same sp as last bobble, *skip 2 sps, work 1 bobble into next sp, [ch6, 1dc into 1st of these ch] 3 times, 1 bobble into same sp as last bobble; rep from * to last sp, skip 2 ch, 1dc into next ch.

Fasten off.

Shells with bead drops

Multiple of 5 sts (add 1 st for base chain).

Special abbreviation:

Pb (place bead) = slide next bead along yarn to base of hook.

Note: thread beads onto yarn before starting.

Row 1 (RS): 1sc into 2nd ch from hook, work 1sc into each ch to end, turn.

Row 2: Ch1, 1sc in 1st st, *skip 2 sc, (2dc, ch2, pb, slip st into 2nd ch from hook, 2dc) into next sc, skip 1 sc, sc into next sc; rep from * to end.

Fasten off.

Fan edge

Multiple of 8 sts + 1 st (add 4 sts for base chain).

Row 1 (RS): Skip 9 ch (count as 1dc, ch3), 1dc into next ch, *ch3, skip 3 ch, 1dc into next ch; rep from * to end, working a multiple of 2 ch-sps, turn.

Row 2: Ch1, 1sc into 1st dc, *ch2, into next dc work (3tr, ch3, 3tr), ch2, 1sc into next dc; rep from * to end, placing last sc into 4th ch of tch, turn.

Row 3: Ch1, 1sc into 1st sc, *ch5, 1sc into next ch-3 sp, ch5, 1sc into next sc; rep from * to end, turn.

Row 4: Ch1, 1sc into 1st sc, *ch4, 1sc into next sc; rep from * to end, turn.

Row 5: Ch1, 1sc into 1st sc, *ch3, into next sc work (3tr, ch3, 3tr), ch3, 1sc into next sc; rep from * to end.

Fasten off.

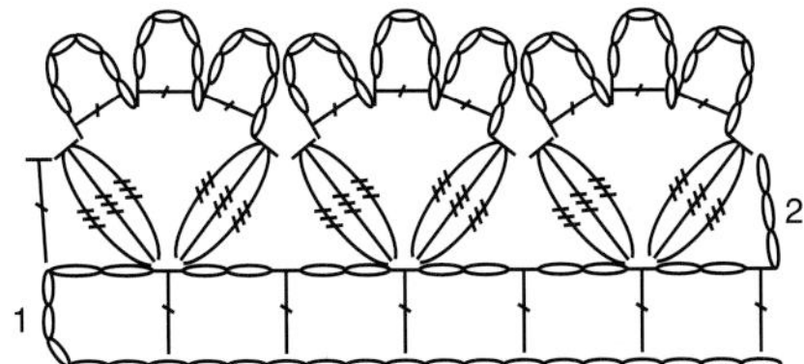

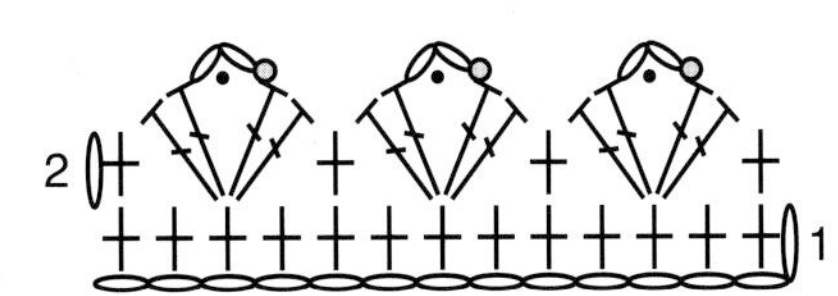

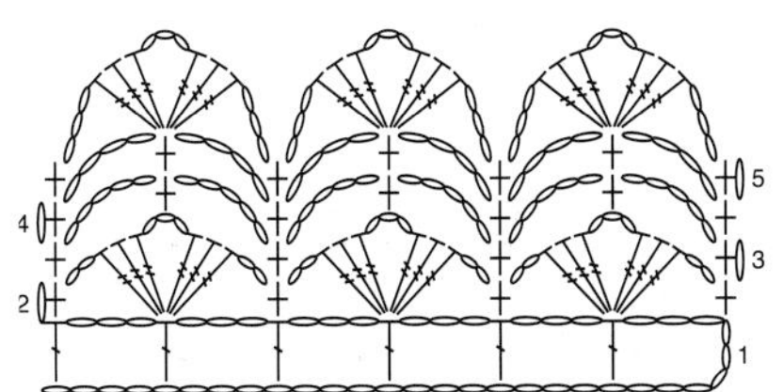

Heart frill

Multiple of 3 sts + 2 sts (add 1 st for base chain).

Special abbreviations:

Picot = ch6, 1sc in 4th ch from hook; **3tr-cluster** = yo twice, insert hook into same place as last slip st, yo and pull through, [yo and pull through 2 loops on hook] twice, [yo twice, insert hook into next tr, yo and pull through, (yo and pull through 2 loops on hook) twice] twice, yo and pull through last 4 loops on hook; **Left-cluster** = [yo twice, insert hook into next tr, yo and pull through, (yo and pull through 2 loops on hook) twice] 3 times, yo twice, insert hook into same tr, yo and pull through, [yo and pull through 2 loops on hook] twice, yo and pull through last 5 loops on hook. **Right-cluster** = yo twice, insert hook into next tr, yo and pull through, [yo and pull through 2 loops on hook] twice, yo twice, insert hook into same tr, yo and pull through, [yo and pull through 2 loops on hook] twice, [yo twice, insert hook into next tr, yo and pull through, (yo and pull through 2 loops on hook) twice], twice, yo and pull through last 5 loops on hook.

Row 1 (RS): 1sc into 2nd ch from hook, work 1sc into each ch to end, turn.

Row 2: Ch4 (count as 1tr), 2tr into base of tch, *ch3, skip 2 sc, 3tr into next sc; rep from * to end of row, turn.

Row 3: Ch4 (count as 1tr), 1tr into base of tch, *1tr into next tr, 2tr into next tr, picot, ch2, 2tr into next tr; rep from * to last 2 tr, 1tr into next tr, 2tr into top of tch, turn.

Row 4: Ch4 (count as 1tr), 1tr into base of tch, *1tr into each of next 3 tr, 2tr into next tr, ch9, 2tr into next tr; rep from * to last 4 tr, 1tr into each of next 3 tr, 2tr into top of tch, turn.

Row 5: Ch4 (count as 1tr), 3tr-cluster *ch5, 1slip st into next tr, ch5, left-cluster, ch6, skip 4 ch, (1sc, ch4, 1sc) into next ch, ch6, skip 4 ch, right-cluster; rep from * to last 4 tr, ch5, 1 slip st into next tr, ch5, 1 left-cluster over next 3 tr. Fasten off.

Diamond braid

Multiple of 6 sts + 3 sts (add 1 st for base chain).

Special abbreviation:

Bobble = work 3dc into next st until 1 loop of each remains on hook, yo and through all 4 loops on hook;

cluster = work 1tr into next ch sp until 2 loops remain on hook, 3dc into top of next bobble until 1 loop of each remains on hook (5 loops on hook), skip ch-1 sp, 1tr into next ch sp until 6 loops remain on hook, yo and through all 6 loops on hook.

Row 1 (WS): 1sc into 2nd ch from hook, work 1sc into each ch to end, turn.

Row 2: Ch4 (count as 1dc, ch1), skip 1st 4 sc, 1tr into next sc, work (ch1, 1 bobble, ch1, 1tr) into same st as last tr, ch1, *skip 5 sc, 1tr into next sc, work (ch1, 1 bobble, ch1, 1tr) into same st as last tr, ch1; rep from * to last 4 sc, 1dc into last sc, turn.

Row 3: Ch6 (count as 1dc, ch3), *1 cluster, ch5; rep from * to end, working 1st tr of each cluster into same ch sp as last tr of previous cluster and omitting 2 ch at end of last rep, 1dc into 3rd ch of ch-4 tch, turn.

Row 4: Ch1, 1sc into 1st dc, 3sc into 1st ch-3 sp, 1sc into top of 1st cluster, *5sc into next ch-5 sp, 1sc into top of next cluster; rep from * to last sp, 3sc into last sp, 1sc into 3rd ch of ch-6 tch. Fasten off.

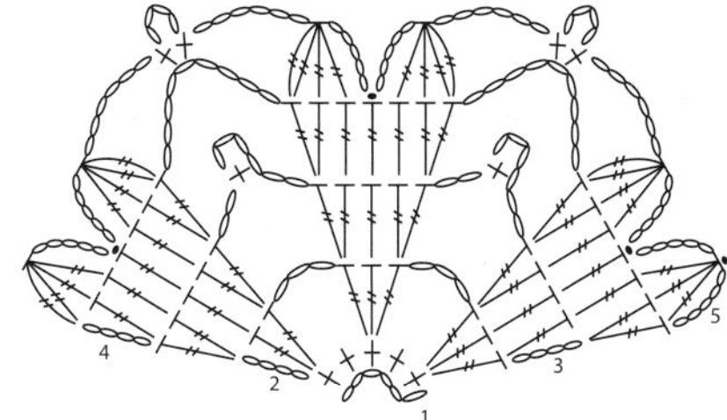

Heart frill

Pineapple edge

Worked lengthwise over 10 sts (add 1 for base chain).

Special abbreviation:

4dc-bobble = work 4dc into next st until 1 loop of each remains on hook, yo and through all 5 loops on hook.

Row 1 (WS): Skip 1 ch, 1sc into next ch, ch3, skip 1 ch, 1sc into next ch, ch4, skip 4 ch, 1dc in each of next 3 ch, turn.

Row 2: Ch3 (count as 1dc), skip 1st dc, 1dc in each of the next 2 dc, ch2, 1sc into ch-4 sp, ch1, 7dc into ch-3 sp, turn.

Row 3: Ch3, 4dc-bobble into 1st dc, [ch3, skip 1 dc, 4dc-bobble into next dc] 3 times, ch1, skip next ch-2 sp, 1dc in each of next 2 dc, 1dc into top of tch, turn.

Row 4: Ch3 (count as 1dc), skip 1st dc, 1dc into each of next 2 dc, ch2, 1sc into next ch-3 sp, [ch4, 1sc in next ch-3 sp] twice, turn.

Row 5: Slip st into each of next 2 ch, ch2, 1dc into next sc, ch2, 1dc into same st as last dc, ch2, 1sc into next ch sp, ch3, skip next ch-2 sp, 1dc in each of next 2 dc, 1dc into top of tch, turn.

Row 6: Ch3 (count as 1dc), skip 1st dc, 1dc into each of next 2 dc, ch2, skip next ch-3 sp, 1sc into next ch-2 sp, ch1, 7dc into ch-2 sp, turn.

Rep rows 3–6 until required length is reached.

Fasten off.

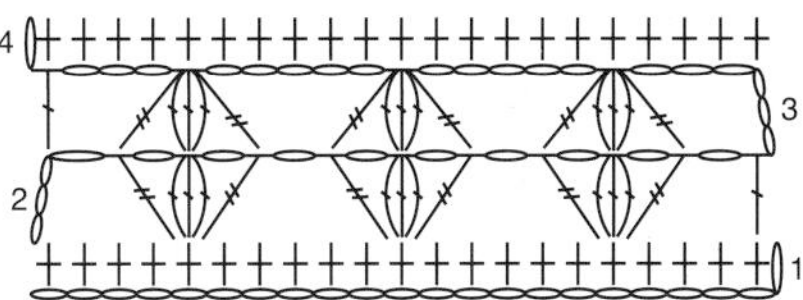

Diamond braid

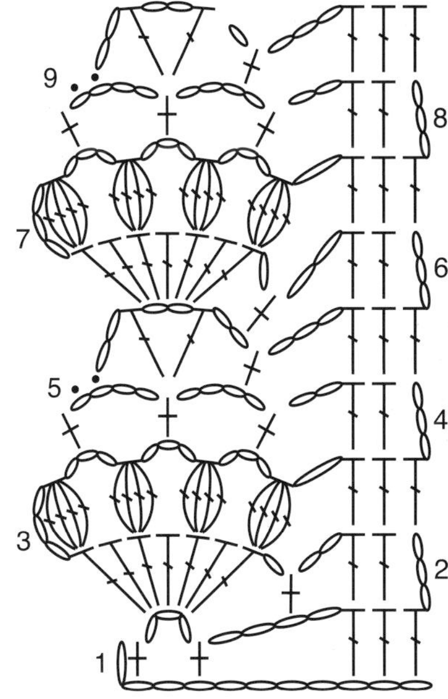

Pineapple edge

Crown ruffle

Multiple of 5 sts + 4 sts (add 1 st for base chain).

Row 1 (RS): 1sc into 2nd ch from hook, *ch7, skip 2 ch, 1sc into next ch**, ch3, skip 1 ch, 1sc into next ch; rep from * ending last rep at **, turn.

Row 2: Ch1, * work [2sc, ch3] 5 times in next ch-7 sp, 2sc into the same ch-7 sp **, ch3, skip next ch-3 sp; rep from * ending last rep at **, turn.

Row 3: Ch1, slip st into 1st ch sp, 1sc into same ch sp, *ch7, skip next 3 ch-3 sps, 1sc into next ch sp**, ch3, skip next ch sp, 1sc into next ch sp; rep from * ending last rep at **.

Rep rows 2–3 and then row 2 once more. Fasten off.

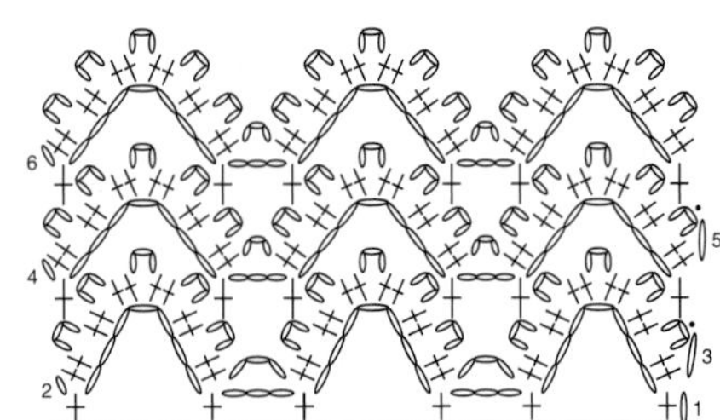

Astrakhan edge

Any number of sts (add 2 sts for base chain).

Note: work all rows with RS facing, i.e. work even-numbered rows from left to right.

Row 1 (RS): Skip 3 ch (count as 1dc), 1dc into next ch, work 1dc into each ch to end. Do not turn.

Row 2: *Ch7, slip st into front loop only of next dc to right; rep from * ending ch7, slip st into top of tch at beg of row. Do not turn.

Row 3: Ch3 (count as 1dc), skip st at base of ch, 1dc into back loop only of next and each st of second-to-last row to end. Do not turn.

Rep rows 2–3 until required depth is reached, ending with a row 3.

Finishing row: Turn, ch2 (count as 1hdc), work 1hdc in each st to end.

Fasten off.

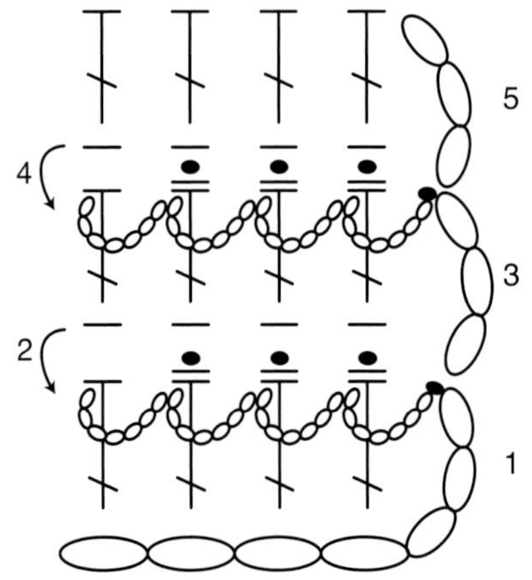

Bobble delight

Multiple of 6 sts + 5 sts (add 1 st for base chain).

Special abbreviation:

Bobble = work 4dtr into ch until 1 loop of each remains on hook, yo and through all 5 loops on hook.

Row 1 (RS): 1sc into 2nd ch from hook, work 1sc into each ch to end, turn.

Row 2: Ch6 (count as 1dc, ch3), skip 1st 4 sc, 1dc into next sc, *ch1, skip 1 sc, 1dc into next sc, ch3, skip 3 sc, 1dc into next sc; rep from * to end, turn.

Row 3: Ch1, 1sc into 1st dc, *ch4, skip ch, 1 bobble into next ch, ch4, 1sc into next dc, ch1, skip ch, sc in next dc; rep from * to end, omitting last ch and sc and working final sc into 3rd ch of ch-6 tch.

Fasten off.

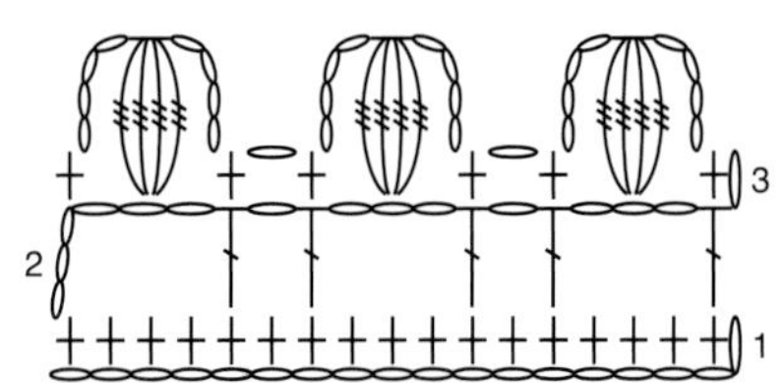

Chain wave

Multiple of 4 sts + 1 st (add 3 sts for base chain).

Row 1 (RS): Skip 5 ch (count as 1dc, ch1), 1dc into next ch or join into an edge and ch3, counting either ch or equivalent interval, *ch1, skip 1 ch, 1dc into next ch; rep from * to end, turn.

Row 2: Ch1, 1sc into 1st dc, *ch5, skip 1 dc, 1sc into next dc; rep from * to last dc, ch5, skip 1 dc and 1 ch, 1sc into next ch, turn.

Row 3: Ch1, 1sc into 1st sc, work 7sc into each ch-5 arch to end, 1sc into last sc, turn.

Row 4: Ch5 (count as 1dc, ch2), skip 1st 4 sc, 1sc into next sc, *ch3, skip 6 sc, 1sc into next sc; rep from * to last 4 sc, ch2, 1dc into last sc, turn.

Row 5: Ch1, 1sc into 1st dc, ch5, 1sc into ch-2 sp, into each sp work (1sc, ch5, 1sc) to end, placing last sc into 3rd ch of ch-5 tch. Fasten off.

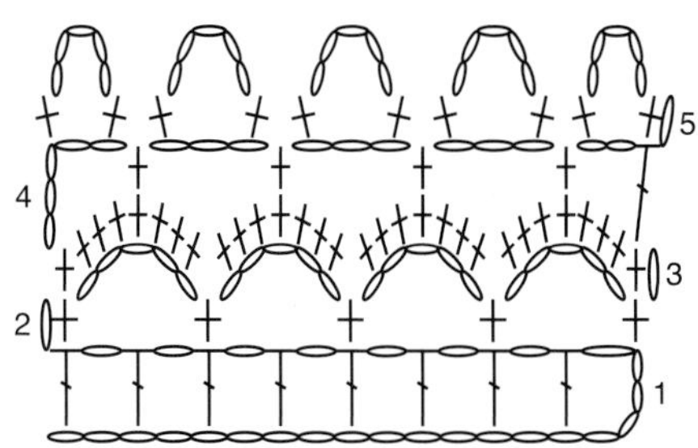

Peacock fans

Multiple of 9 sts + 4 sts (add 1 st for base chain).

Special abbreviation:

Dc2tog = work 1dc into each of next 2 dc until 1 loop of each remains on hook, yo and through all 3 loops on hook.

Row 1 (RS): 1sc into 2nd ch from hook, work 1sc into each ch to end, turn.

Row 2: Ch1, 1sc into 1st sc, ch2, skip 2 sc, 1sc into next sc, *skip 2 sc, 5dc into next sc, skip 2 sc, 1sc into next sc, ch2, skip 2 sc, 1sc into next sc; rep from * to end, turn.

Row 3: Ch1, 1sc into 1st sc, ch2, *1dc into next dc, [ch1, 1dc into next dc] 4 times**, 1sc into next ch-2 sp; rep from * ending last rep at **, ch2, 1sc into last sc, turn.

Row 4: Ch3 (count as 1dc), [1dc into next dc, ch2] 4 times, *dc2tog, ch2, [1dc into next dc, ch2] 3 times; rep from * to last dc, work 1dc into next dc until 2 loops remain on hook, 1dc into last sc until 3 loops remain on hook, yo and through all 3 loops, turn.

Row 5: Ch1, 1sc into 1st st, 3sc into 1st ch-2 sp, *ch7, 3sc into next ch-2 sp; rep from * to end, 1sc into top of tch.

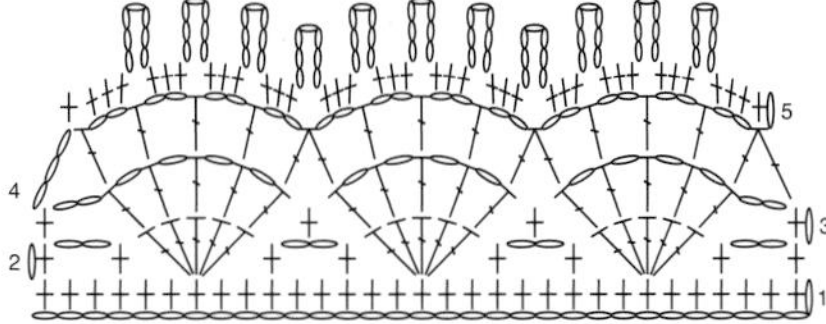

Bobble sprigs

Multiple of 11 sts + 1 st (add 2 sts for base chain).

Special abbreviation:

Bobble = work 3dtr into ch-3 loop until 1 loop of each remains on hook, yo and through all 4 loops on hook.

Row 1 (RS): Skip 3 ch (count as 1dc), 1dc into next ch, work 1dc into each ch to end, turn.

Row 2: Ch1, 1sc into 1st dc, *ch9, slip st into 3rd ch from hook, ch7, skip 10 dc, 1sc into next dc; rep from * to end, placing last sc into top of tch, turn.

Row 3: Ch5, *work 1 bobble into next ch-3 loop, ch5, into same loop as last bobble work (1 bobble, ch5, 1 bobble), 1dtr into next sc; rep from * to end. Fasten off.

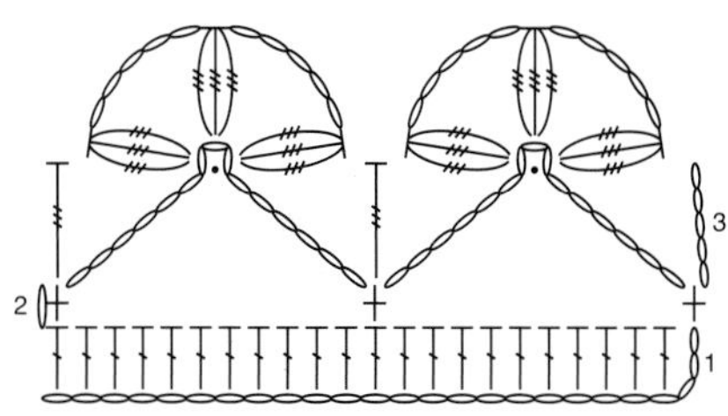

Cavalier frill

Multiple of 20 sts (add 4 sts for base chain).

Special abbreviations:

Dc2tog = work 2dc into next st until 1 loop of each remains on hook, yo and through all 3 loops on hook.

Bobble = work 3dc into next st until 1 loop of each remains on hook, yo and through all 4 loops on hook.

Row 1 (RS): Skip 6 ch (count as 1dc, ch3), 1sc into next ch, ch5, skip 3 ch, 1sc into next ch, ch1, skip 3 ch, into next ch work [1 bobble, ch1] 3 times, *skip 3 ch, 1sc into next ch, [ch5, skip 3ch, 1sc into next ch] 3 times, ch1, skip 3 ch, into next ch work [1 bobble, ch1] 3 times; rep from * to last 9 ch, skip 3 ch, 1sc into next ch, ch5, skip 3 ch, 1sc into next ch, ch2, 1dc into last ch, turn.

Row 2: Ch1, 1sc into 1st dc, ch5, 1sc into 1st ch-5 arch, ch2, [1 bobble into next ch sp, ch2] 4 times, *1sc into next ch-5 arch, [ch5, 1sc into next ch-5 arch] twice, ch2, [1 bobble into next ch sp, ch2] 4 times; rep from * to last 2 arches, 1sc into next ch-5 arch, ch5, skip 2 ch, 1sc into next ch, turn.

Row 3: Ch5 (count as 1dc, ch2), 1sc into 1st ch-5 arch, ch3, [1 bobble into next ch sp, ch3] 5 times, *1sc into next ch-5 arch, ch5, 1sc into next ch-5 arch, ch3, [1 bobble into next ch sp, ch3] 5 times; rep from * to last arch, 1sc into last arch, ch2, 1dc into last sc, turn.

Row 4: Ch1, 1sc into 1st dc, skip ch-2 sp, *ch4, [1 bobble into next ch sp, ch4] 6 times, 1 sc into next ch-5 arch; rep from * to end, placing last sc into 3rd ch of ch-5 tch, turn.

Row 5: Ch5 (count as 1dc, ch2), skip 1st ch-4 sp, 1sc into next ch-4 sp, [ch5, 1sc into next ch-4 sp] 4 times, *ch1, into next sc work [1dc, ch1] twice, skip next ch-4 sp, 1sc into next ch-4 sp, [ch5, 1sc into next ch-4 sp] 4 times; rep from * to last ch-4 sp, ch2, 1dc into last sc, turn.

Row 6: Ch3 (count as 1dc), into 1st dc work (1dc, ch1, 1 bobble), ch1, 1sc into next ch-5 arch, [ch5, 1sc into next ch-5 arch] 3 times, *ch1, skip next ch sp, into next ch sp work [1 bobble, ch1] 3 times, 1sc into next ch-5 arch, [ch5, 1sc into next ch-5 arch] 3 times; rep from * to last sp, ch1, into 3rd ch of ch-5 tch work (1bobble, ch1, dc2tog).

Fasten off.

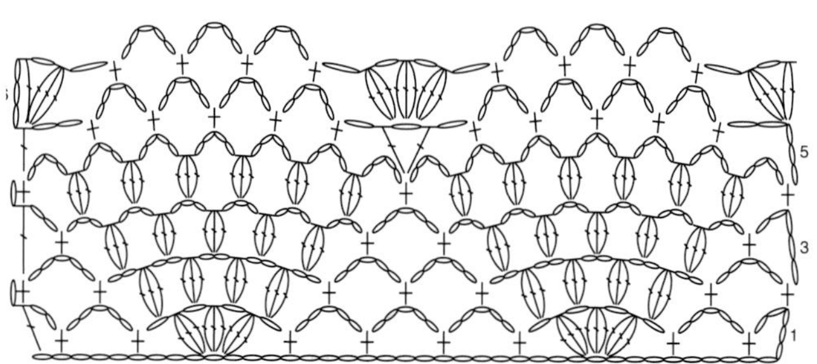

Applied shamrock

1 motif for each repeat.

First motif

Base ring: Ch9, join with slip st.

Round 1: Ch1, 16sc into ring, slip st to 1st sc.

Round 2: Ch5 (count as 1tr), 2tr into same st as last slip st, 3tr into next sc, [ch7, skip 2 sc, 3tr into each of next 2 sc] 3 times, ch7, slip st to top of ch-5 tch.

Round 3: Ch1, 1sc into same st as last slip st, *1dc into next tr, 2dc into next tr, ch4, slip st through top of last dc (picot), 2dc into next tr, 1dc into next tr, 1sc into next tr, 7sc into next ch-7 sp, 1sc into next tr; rep from * 3 times more, skipping 1sc at end of last rep, slip st to 1st sc.

Fasten off.

Second motif

Base ring: Ch9, join with slip st.

Round 1: Ch1, 16sc into ring, slip st to 1st sc.

Round 2: Ch5 (count as 1tr), 2tr into same st as last slip st, 3tr into next sc, [ch7, skip 2 sc, 3tr into each of next 2 sc] 3 times, ch7, slip st to top of ch-5 tch.

Round 3: Ch1, 1sc into same st as last slip st, *1dc into next tr, 2dc into next tr, ch4, join motifs as follows: drop loop from hook, insert hook in far right picot of last motif and in dropped loop, draw loop through, ch1, sl st through top of last dc, 2dc into next tr, 1dc into next tr, 1sc into next tr, 7sc into next ch-7 sp, 1sc into next tr; continue around same as 1st motif, skipping 1sc at end of last rep, slip st to 1st sc. Fasten off.

Rep 2nd motif but joining through the lower picot of every second motif.

Position along an edge as shown in the photograph and whip stitch to secure.

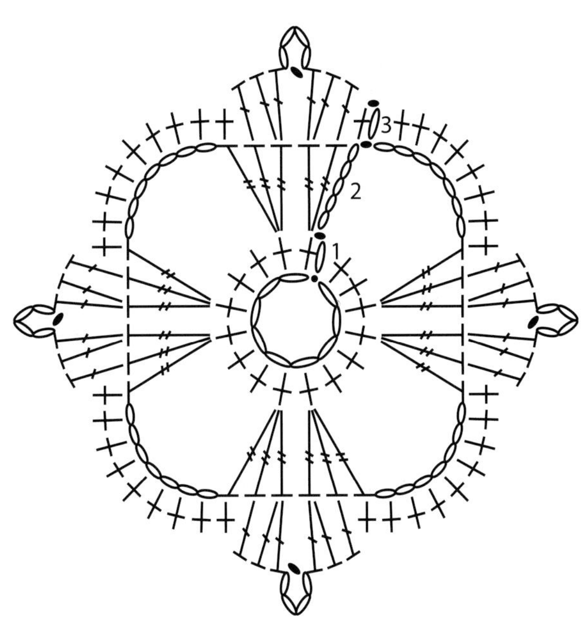

Tamed chevron

Multiple of 12 sts (add 2 sts for base chain).

Special abbreviation:

Dc2tog = work 1dc into next 2 ch or sts indicated until 1 loop of each remains on hook, yo and through all 3 loops on hook.

Row 1 (WS): Skip 3 ch (count as 1dc), 2dc into next ch, *1dc into each of next 3 ch, dc2tog twice, 1dc into each of next 3 ch, ** [2dc into next ch] twice; rep from * ending last rep at **, 2dc into last ch, turn.

Row 2: Ch1, 1sc into 1st st, *ch11, skip 11 sts, 1sc into next st; rep from * to end, working last sc into top of tch, turn.

Row 3: Ch1, 1sc into 1st st, *11sc into ch-11 sp, 1sc into next sc; rep from * to end, turn.

Row 4: Ch1, work 1sc into back loop of each st to end, turn.

Row 5: Ch3, work 1dc into each st to end. Fasten off.

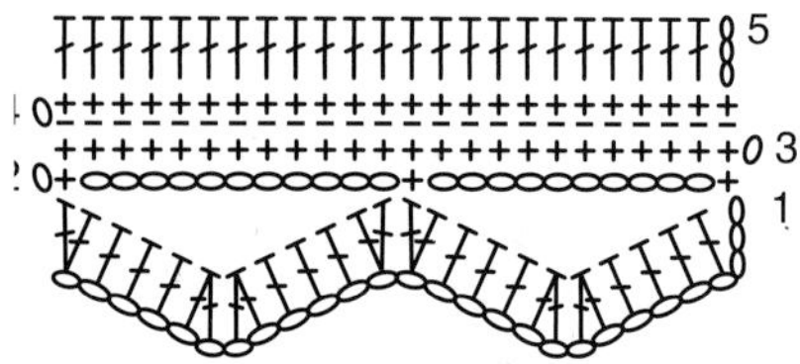

Long-stitch points

Multiple of 4 sts + 3 sts (add 1 st for base chain).

Special abbreviation:

Tr2tog 2 rows below = work 1tr into same st as last tr until last loop of tr remains on hook, skip 3 sts, work 1tr into next skipped st 2 rows below until last loop of tr remains on hook, yo and through all 3 loops.

Note: work foundation row if working from a base chain.

Foundation row: 1sc into 2nd ch from hook and each ch to end, turn.

Row 1 (RS): Ch1, 1sc into each of next 3 sts, *ch1, skip 1 st, 1sc into each of next 3 sts; rep from * to end, turn.

Row 2: Ch3 (count as 1dc), skip 1st sc, work 1dc into each st to end (working into actual st of each ch, not into ch sp), turn.

Row 3: Ch1, 1sc into 1st dc, 1tr into 1st skipped foundation row st, skip 1 dc on row 2, 1sc into next dc, ch1, skip 1 dc, 1sc into next dc, *tr2tog 2 rows below, skip 1 dc on row 2, 1sc into next dc, ch1, skip 1 dc, 1sc into next dc; rep from * to last 2 dc, 1tr into same ch as 2nd leg of last tr2tog, skip 1 dc, 1sc into top of tch. Fasten off.

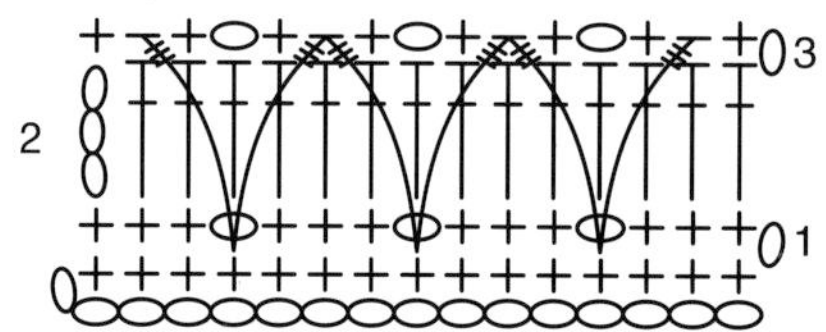

Chain swag

Multiple of 8 sts + 1 st (add 1 st for base chain).

Special abbreviation:

Triple loop = slip st into next sc, [ch7, 1 slip st] 3 times into same sc.

Row 1 (WS): 1sc into 2nd ch from hook, work 1sc into each ch to end, turn.

Row 2: Ch1, work 1sc into each sc to end, turn.

Row 3: Ch1, 1sc into each of 1st 3 sc, *ch9, skip 3 sc, 1sc into each of next 5 sc: rep from * to end, omitting 2sc at end of last rep, turn.

Row 4: Ch1, 1sc into each of 1st 2 sc, *ch5, 1sc into next ch-9 arch, ch5, skip 1 sc, 1sc into each of next 3 sc; rep from * to end, omitting 1sc at end of last rep, turn.

Row 5: Ch1, 1sc into 1st sc, *ch5, skip 1 sc, 1sc into next sc; rep from * to end, turn.

Row 6: Ch1, 1sc into 1st sc, *ch5, work 1 triple loop into next sc, ch5, 1sc into next sc; rep from * to end.

Fasten off.

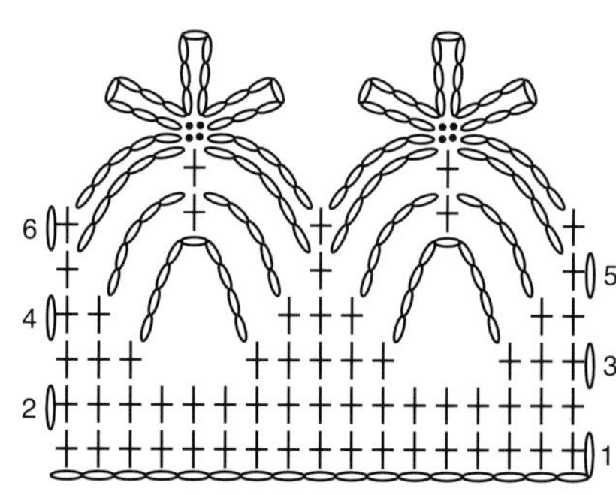

edgings & trims

Textured diamond edge

Multiple of 6 sts + 1 st (add 1 st for base chain).

Note: work rows 1–2 in color A and row 3 in color B. Work foundation row if working from a base chain.

Foundation row: 1sc into 2nd ch from hook and each ch to end, turn.

Row 1 (WS): Ch1, slip st into 1st st, *ch3, skip 2 sts, 1dc into next st, ch3, skip 2 sts, slip st into next st; rep from * to end, turn.

Row 2: Ch4 (count as 1dc, ch1), 1dc into 1st slip st, *skip ch-3 sp, slip st into next dc**, skip ch-3 sp, work (1dc, ch1, 1dc, ch1, 1dc) into next slip st; rep from * ending last rep at ** in last dc, skip ch-3 sp, work (1dc, ch1, 1dc) into last slip st, turn.

Fasten off. Join in yarn B.

Row 3: Ch6 (count as 1dc, ch3), skip (1st st, 1ch and 1dc), slip st into next slip st, *ch3, skip 1 dc and 1 ch, 1dc into next dc, ch3, skip 1 ch and 1 dc, slip st into next slip st; rep from *, ch3, skip 1 dc and 1 ch, 1dc into next ch of tch.

Fasten off.

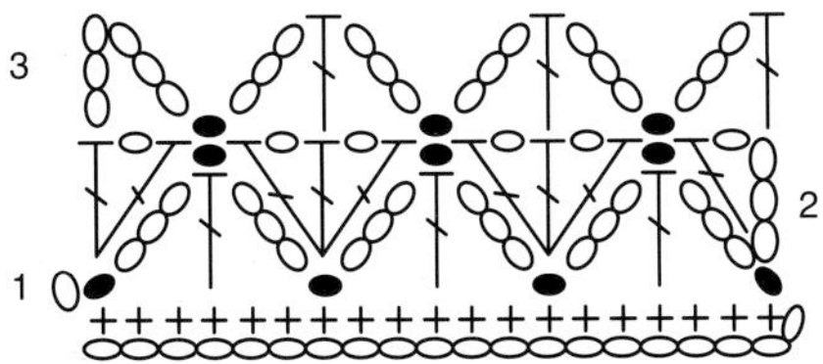

Bullion stitch balls

Multiple of 5 sts + 3 sts (add 1 st for base chain).

Special abbreviation:

Bullion st = yo 5 times, insert hook into ch or st indicated, yo, ease the loop through all the loops on hook, ch1.

Row 1 (WS): 1sc into 2nd ch from hook, work 1sc into each ch to end, turn.

Row 2: Ch1, *1sc in each of next 4 sc, ch9 (stem made), slip st into 4th ch from hook (picot made) turn, ch2 (tch) [1 bullion st] 5 times into picot, slip st in top of tch, slip st into top of each bullion st, slip st in each ch of stem, 1sc into next sc; rep from * to last 3 sc, 1sc into each of next 3 sc.

Fasten off.

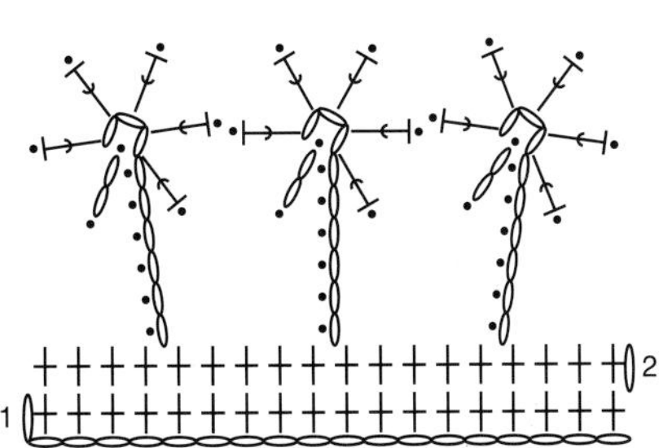

Pretty pockets

Multiple of 3 sts + 1 st (add 2 sts for base chain).

Special abbreviation:

Pgr (pocket group) = work (1sc, 1hdc, 3dc) around stem of indicated st.

Row 1 (WS): Skip 3 ch (count as 1dc), 1dc into next ch, work 1dc into each ch to end, turn.

Row 2: 1pgr around 1st st, skip 2 sts, slip st into top of next st, *1pgr around same st as slip st, skip 2 sts, slip st into top of next st; rep from * to end.

Fasten off.

Brontë fan

Multiple of 17 sts + 2 sts (add 1 st for base chain).

Special abbreviation:

Bobble = work 3dc into next space until 1 loop of each remains on hook, yo and through all 4 loops on hook.

Row 1 (RS): 1sc into 2nd ch from hook, work 1sc into each ch to end, turn.

Row 2: Ch1, work 1sc into each sc to end, turn.

Row 3: Ch1, work 1sc into each of 1st 8 sc, *ch4, skip 3 sc, 1sc into each of next 14 sc; rep from * to last 11sc, ch4, skip 3 sc, 1sc into each of last 8 sc, turn.

Row 4: Ch3 (count as 1hdc, ch1), skip 1st 2 sc, 1sc into each of next 3 sc, ch1, into next ch-4 sp work [1dc, ch1] 6 times, skip 3 sc, 1sc into each of next 3 sc, *ch3, skip 2 sc, 1sc into each of next 3 sc, ch1, into next ch-4 sp work [1dc, ch1] 6 times, skip 3 sc, 1sc into each of next 3 sc; rep from * to last 2 sc, ch1, 1hdc into last sc, turn.

Row 5: Ch1, 1sc into 1st hdc, ch2, [1 bobble into next ch sp, ch2] 7 times, *1sc into next ch-3 arch, ch2, [1 bobble into next ch sp, ch2] 7 times; rep from * to last 3 ch, skip 1 ch, 1sc into next ch, turn.

Row 6: Ch1, 1sc into 1st sc, 2sc into 1st ch-2 sp, 1sc into top of 1st bobble, 2sc into next ch-2 sp, [ch3, 2sc into next sp] twice, ch5, [2sc into next sp, ch3] twice, 2sc into next sp, 1sc into top of next bobble, 2sc into next sp, *skip 1 sc, 2sc into next sp, 1sc into top of next bobble, 2sc into next sp, [ch3, 2sc into next sp] twice, ch5, [2sc into next sp, ch3] twice, 2sc into next sp, 1sc into top of next bobble, 2sc into next sp; rep from * to last sc, 1sc into last sc. Fasten off.

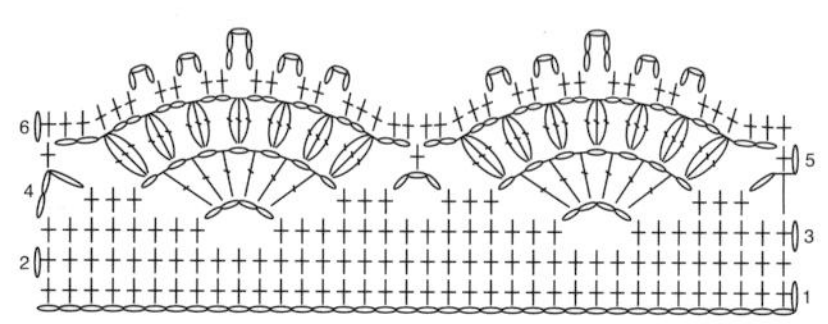

Relief chain arches

Multiple of 8 sts + 1 st (add 1 st for base chain).

Row 1 (WS): 1sc into 2nd ch from hook, 1sc into each of next 2 ch, *ch7, skip 3 ch**, 1sc into each of next 5 ch; rep from * ending last rep at ** when 3 ch remain, 1sc into each of last 3 ch, turn.

Row 2: Ch3 (count as 1dc), skip st at base of ch, 1dc into each of next 2 sts, *going behind ch-7 loop work 1tr into each of next 3 base ch**, 1dc into each of next 5 sc; rep from * ending last rep at ** when 3 sts remain, 1dc into each of last 3 sts, skip tch, turn.

Row 3: Ch1, 1sc into 1st st, *ch7, skip 3 sts, 1sc into next st at same time catching in ch-7 loop of second-to-last row, ch7, skip 3 sts, 1sc into next st; rep from * to end, turn.

Row 4: Ch3 (count as 1dc), skip st at base of ch, *going behind ch-7 loop of last row work 1tr into each of next 3 sts of second-to-last row, 1dc into next sc; rep from * to end, skip tch, turn.

Row 5: Ch1, 1sc into each of 1st 2 sts, *1sc into next st at same time catching in ch-7 loop of second-to-last row, ch7, skip 3 sts, 1sc into next st at same time catching in center of ch-7 loop of second-to-last row**, 1sc into each of next 3 sts; rep from * ending last rep at ** when 2 sts remain, 1sc into each next st, 1sc into tch.

Fasten off.

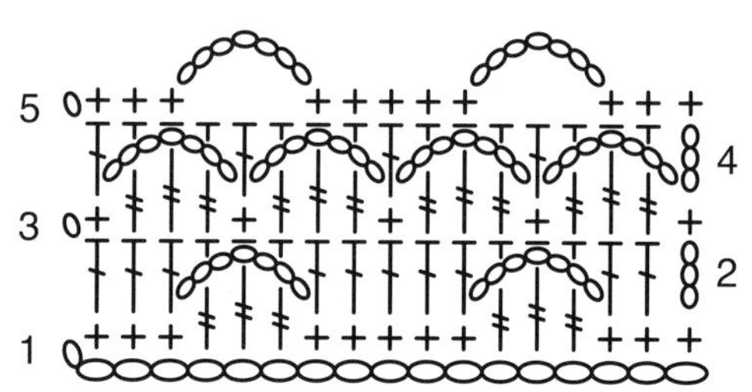

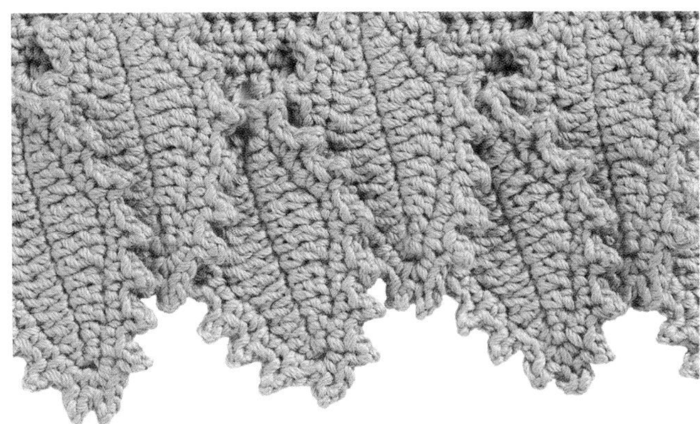

Star fringe

1 motif for each repeat
Note: pattern is worked in a spiral. Do not join at the end of each round.

First motif
Base chain: Ch2.
Round 1: 5sc in 2nd ch from hook.
Round 2: 3sc in each sc. (15 sts)
Round 3: [1sc in next st, ch6, slip st in 2nd ch from hook, 1sc in next ch, 1hdc in next ch, 1dc in next ch, 1tr in next ch, 1tr in bottom of base sc, skip 2 sc] 5 times, slip st in 1st sc. Fasten off.

Second motif
Round 1: 5sc in 2nd ch from hook.
Round 2: 3sc in each sc. (15 sts)
Round 3: [1sc in next st, ch6, drop loop from hook, insert hook in any point picot of 1st motif and in dropped loop, draw loop through, slip st in 2nd ch from hook, 1sc in next ch, 1hdc in next ch, 1dc in next ch, 1tr in next ch, 1tr in bottom of base sc, skip 2 sc] 5 times, slip st in 1st sc. Fasten off.
Skipping one point to the left of last joining, rep 2nd motif until required length is reached.
Position along an edge as shown in the photograph and whip stitch to secure.

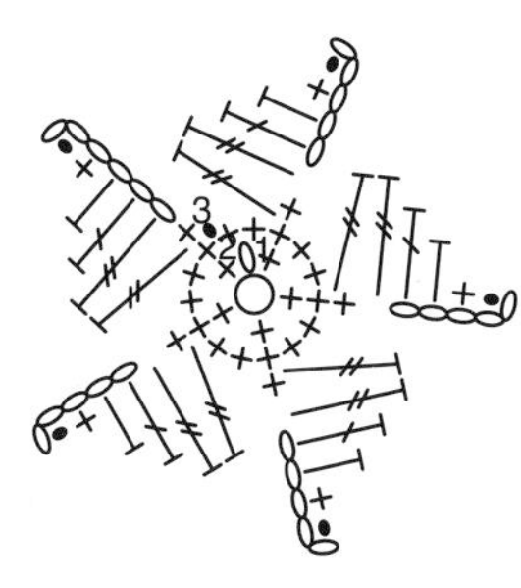

Leaf layer

Multiple of 12 sts.
Special abbreviation:
Picot = ch3, slip st into 1st of these ch; **leaf** = ch15, work in a spiral as follows: slip st into 2nd ch from hook, slip st into each of next 12 ch, ch1, 1sc into base of ch, working 1 st into each ch, work 1hdc, 3dc, 4tr, 3dc, 1hdc and 1sc, ch3, then working 1 st into each slip st on other side of base chain, work 1sc, 1hdc, 3dc, 4tr, 3dc, 1hdc, 1sc, ch3, 1sc into 1st sc at beg of spiral, 1sc into next hdc, 1 picot, [1sc into each of next 2 sts, 1 picot] 6 times, (1sc, ch4, slip st into 3rd ch from hook, ch1, 1sc) into ch-3 sp at point of leaf, [1 picot, 1sc into each of next 2 sts] 7 times, slip st into ch-3 sp.

Row 1 (RS): * Work leaf, ch10; rep from * to end.
Row 2: Ch4 (count as 1tr), skip 4 ch, 1tr into next ch, 1tr into each st to end, turn.
Row 3: Ch2 (count as hdc), skip st at base of ch, hdc into each st to end, turn.
Row 4: Ch1, 1sc into each st to end, turn.
Row 5: Ch4, (count as 1tr), skip st at base of ch, tr into each of next 5 sc, *work leaf, 1tr into each of next 6 sc; rep from * to end, turn.
Row 6: Ch2 (count as hdc), skip st at base of ch, hdc into each st to end, turn. Fasten off.

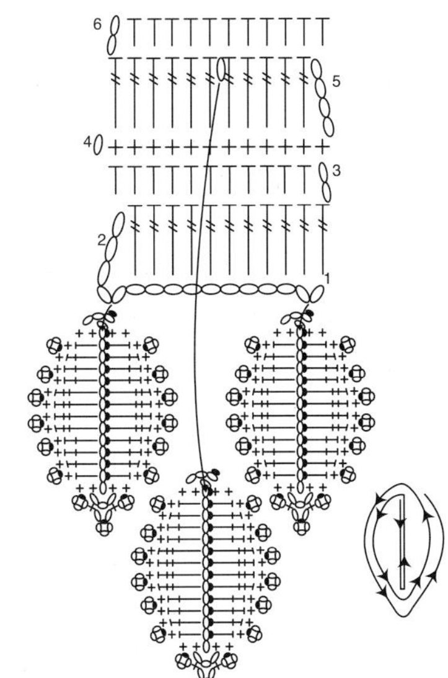

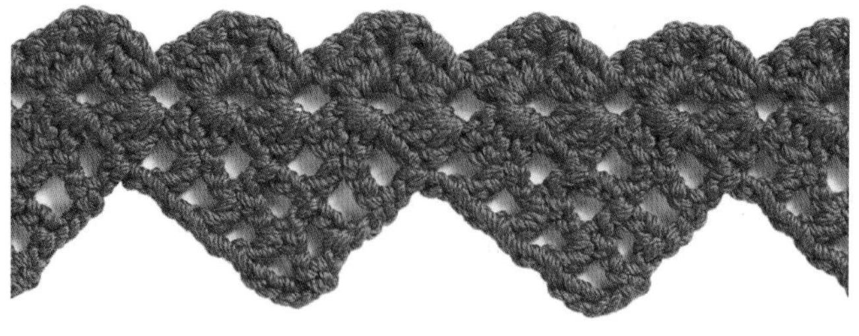

Filet points

Worked lengthwise.

Row 1 (RS): Ch5, 2dc into 4th ch from hook, ch3, 3dc into next ch, turn.

Row 2: Ch5 (count as 1dc, ch2), skip 3 dc, (3dc, ch3, 3dc) into next ch-3 sp, ch2, skip 2 dc, 1dc into top of tch, turn.

Row 3: Ch5 (count as 1dc, ch2), skip ch-2 sp, 1dc into next dc, ch2, skip 2 dc, (3dc, ch3, 3dc) into next ch-3 sp, turn.

Row 4: Ch5 (count as 1dc, ch2), skip 3 dc, (3dc, ch3, 3dc) into next ch-3 sp, ch2, skip 2 dc, 1dc into next dc, ch2, skip ch-2 sp, 1dc into next dc, ch2, skip 2 ch, 1dc into 3rd ch of tch, turn.

Row 5: Ch5 (count as 1dc, ch2), skip ch-2 sp, 1dc into next dc, [ch2, skip ch-2 sp, 1dc into next dc] twice, ch2, skip 2 dc, (3dc, ch3, 3dc) into next ch-3 sp, turn.

Row 6: Ch5 (count as 1dc, ch2), skip 3 dc, (3dc, ch3, 3dc) into next ch-3 sp, ch2, skip 2 dc, 1dc into next st, turn.

Rep rows 3–6 until required length is reached, ending with a row 5. Fasten off.

Little curls

Multiple of 4 sts + 1 st (add 1 st for base chain).

Row 1 (RS): 1sc into 2nd ch from hook, work 1sc into each ch to end, turn.

Row 2: Ch6 (count as 1dc, ch3), skip 1st 4 sc, 1dc into next sc, *ch3, skip 3 sc, 1dc into next sc; rep from * to end.

Row 3: Ch1, 1sc into 1st dc, *ch3, 1dc into next sp, ch3, work 7dc over stem of dc just worked, 1sc into next dc; rep from * to end, placing last sc into 3rd ch of ch-6 tch.

Fasten off.

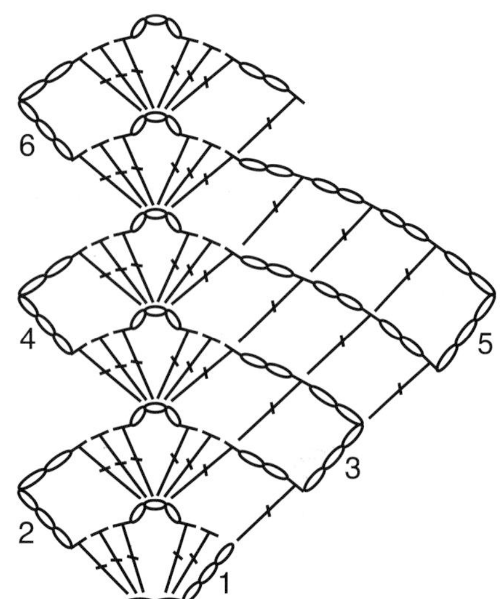

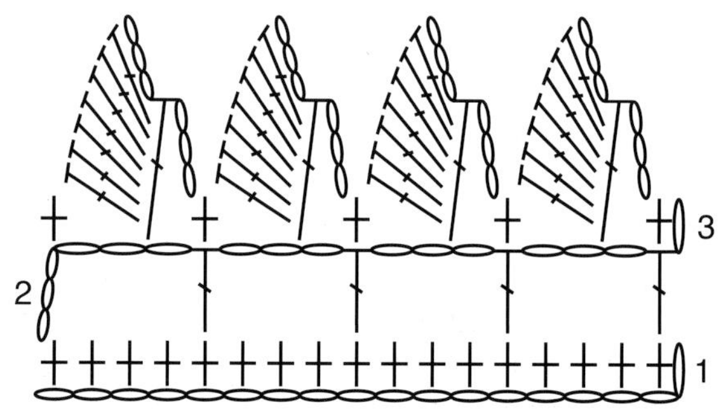

Large loop buttonhole

Multiple of 8 sts + 7 sts (add 1 st for base chain).

Suggestion: work a small sample as described and then adjust the spacing, and so the multiple, to suit the project.

Row 1 (WS): 1sc into 2nd ch from hook, work 1sc into each ch to end, turn.

Row 2: Ch1, 1sc into each st to end, turn.

Row 3: Ch1, 1sc into each of 1st 7 sts, *ch5, skip 1 sc, 1sc into each of next 7 sc; rep from * to end, turn.

Row 4: Ch1, 1sc into each of 1st 5 sts, *skip 2 sc, 1dc into ch-5 sp, [ch1, 1dc] 4 times in same ch-5 sp as last dc, skip 2 sc, 1 sc into each of next 3 sc; rep from * to last 2 sts, 1sc in each of next 2 sc.

Fasten off.

Zigzag popcorns

Multiple of 10 sts + 3 sts (add 1 st for base chain).

Special abbreviations:

5dc-popcorn = work 5dc into indicated st, remove hook from working loop, insert hook under top loops of 1st of the dc sts just worked, hook the working loop and draw this through the top loops to draw the popcorn closed, ch1.

Tr/rf (raised treble crochet at the front of the fabric) = yo twice, insert hook from in front and from right to left around the stem of the appropriate stitch, and complete stitch normally.

Tr/rb (raised treble crochet at the back of the fabric) = yo twice, insert hook from behind and from right to left around the stem of the appropriate stitch, and complete stitch normally.

Note: work foundation row if working from a base chain.

Foundation row: 1sc into 2nd ch from hook and each ch to end, turn.

Row 1 (RS): Ch3 (count as 1dc), 1dc into each of next 2 sts, *ch2, skip 3 sts, 5dc-popcorn into next st, ch1, 5dc-popcorn into next st, ch1, skip 2 sts, 1dc into each of next 3 sts; rep from * to end, turn.

Row 2: Ch3 (count as 1dc), skip 1st st, 1tr/rb around next st, 1dc into next st, *ch3, skip ch-1 sp and 5dc-popcorn, 2sc into next ch-1 sp, ch3, skip 5dc-popcorn and ch-2 sp, 1dc into next st, 1tr/rb around next st, 1dc into next st; rep from * ending last rep in top of tch, turn.

Row 3: Ch3 (count as 1dc), skip 1st st, 1tr/rf around next st, 1dc into next st, *ch2, skip ch-3 sp, 5dc-popcorn into next sc, ch1, 5dc-popcorn into next sc, ch1, skip ch-3 sp, 1dc into next st, 1tr/rf around next st, 1dc into next st; rep from * ending last rep in top of tch.

Fasten off.

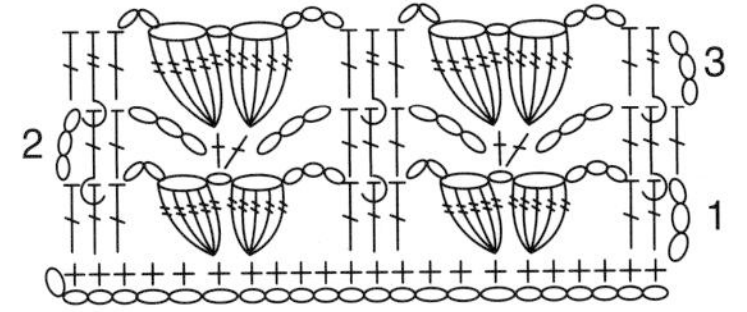

Double chevron

Multiple of 16 sts + 1 st (add 2 sts for base chain).

Special abbreviations:

Cluster = work 1dc into same arch as last 3dc until 2 loops remain on hook, skip 1 sc, work 1dc into next arch until 3 loops remain on hook, yo and through all 3 loops on hook;

Bobble = work 3tr into next sc until 1 loop of each remains on hook, yo and through all 4 loops on hook.

Row 1 (RS): Skip 3 ch (count as 1dc), 1dc into next ch, 1dc into each of next 6 ch, work 3dc into next ch, 1dc into each of next 6 ch, *work 1dc into next ch until 2 loops remain on hook, skip 1 ch, 1dc into next ch until 3 loops remain on hook, yo and through all 3 loops on hook, work 1dc into each of next 6 ch, 3dc into next ch,

1dc into each of next 6 ch; rep from * to last 2 ch, work 1dc into next ch until 2 loops remain on hook, 1dc into last ch until 3 loops remain on hook, yo and through all 3 loops (cluster made at end of row), turn.

Row 2: Ch1, work 1sc into each st to last dc, skip last dc, 1sc into top of tch, turn.

Row 3: Ch4, work 1tr into 1st sc (half bobble made at beg of row), ch2, 1 bobble into same sc as half bobble, ch4, skip 7 sc, 1sc into next sc, *ch4, skip 7 sc, work 1 bobble into next sc, into same sc as last bobble work [ch2, 1 bobble] twice, ch4, skip 7 sc, 1sc into next sc; rep from * to last 8 sc, ch4, work 1 bobble into last sc, ch2, work 2tr into same sc as last bobble until 1 loop of each remains on hook, yo and through all 3 loops on hook (half bobble made at end of row), turn.

Row 4: Ch3 (count as 1dc), 1dc into top of 1st half bobble, work 2dc into ch-2 sp, 1dc into next bobble, 3dc into next ch-4 arch, 1 cluster, 3dc into same arch as 2nd leg of last cluster, *1dc into top of next bobble, 2dc into ch-2 sp, 3dc into top of next bobble, 2dc into next ch-2 sp, 1dc into top of next bobble, 3dc into next ch-4 arch, 1 cluster, 3dc into same arch as 2nd leg of last cluster; rep from * to last bobble, 1dc into last bobble, 2dc into next ch-2 sp, 2dc into top of half bobble, turn.

Row 5: Ch1, 1sc into each st to end, placing last sc into top of tch.

Fasten off.

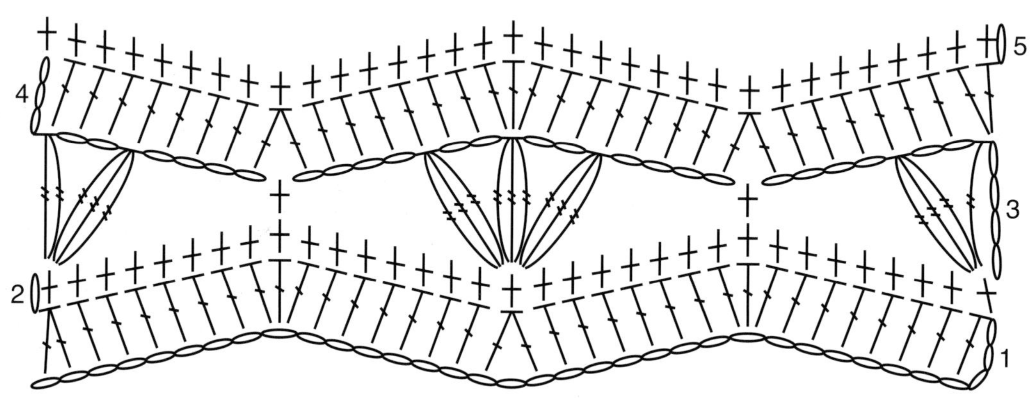

Grand popcorn fans

Worked lengthwise.

Special abbreviations:

Popcorn at beg of row = ch3, work 6dc into 1st sp, drop loop from hook, insert hook from front into top of ch-3, pick up dropped loop and draw through, ch1 to secure.

7dc-popcorn = work 7dc into next sp, drop loop from hook, insert hook from front into top of 1st of these dc, pick up dropped loop and draw through, ch1 to secure.

Ch10 and join into a ring with a slip st.

Row 1 (RS): Ch3 (count as 1dc), work 14dc into ring, turn.

Row 2: Ch5 (count as 1dc, ch2), skip 1st 2 dc, 1dc into next dc, [ch2, skip 1 dc, 1dc into next dc] 6 times placing last dc into 3rd ch of ch-3 tch, turn.

Row 3: Work 1 popcorn at beg of row, [ch3, 7dc-popcorn into next ch-2 sp] 6 times, turn.

Row 4: Ch10, skip 1st 2 ch-3 sps, work (1sc, ch5, 1sc) into next ch-3 sp, turn.

Row 5: Ch3 (count as 1dc), work 14dc into ch-5 sp, turn.

Rep rows 2–5 until required length is reached, ending with row 3. Do not turn work but continue along side edge as follows:

Final row 1: Ch3, 1sc into sp formed at beg of row 2 of pattern, *ch5, 1sc into sp formed at beg of row 4 of pattern, ch5, 1sc into sp formed at beg of row 2 of pattern; rep from * to end, turn.

Final row 2: Ch1, 1sc into 1st sc, *5sc into ch-5 sp, 1sc into next sc; rep from * to end.

Fasten off.

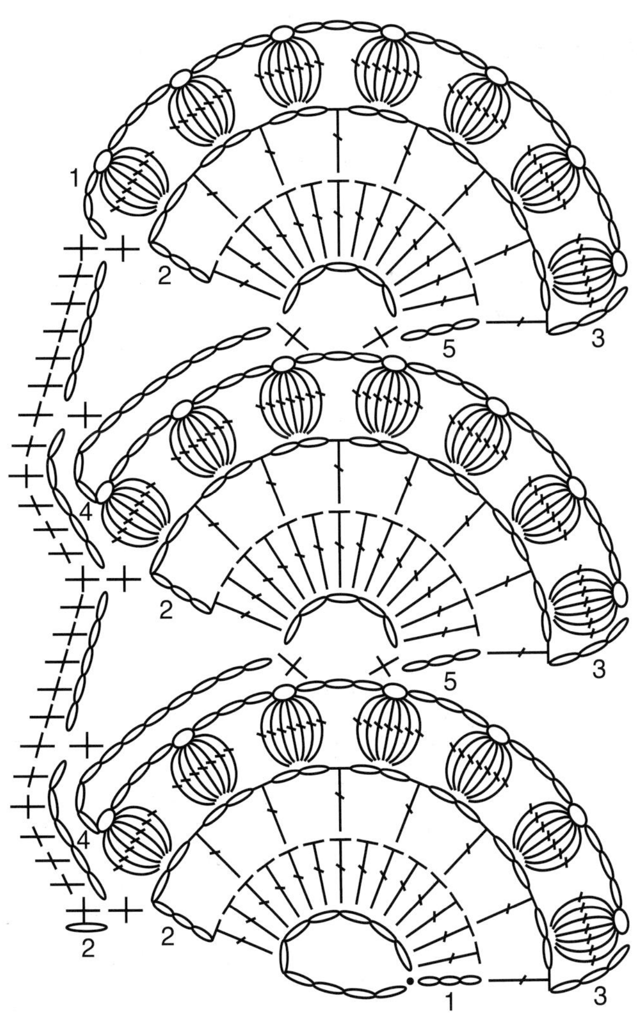

Pintuck edge

Multiple of any number of sts (add 1 st for base chain).

Using yarn A work a base ch to required length.

Row 1 (RS): 1sc into 2nd ch from hook, work 1sc into each ch to end, turn.

Row 2: Ch3 (count as 1dc), skip st at base of ch, 1dc into front loop of each sc to end, turn.

Fasten off yarn A. Join in yarn B.

Row 3: Ch3 (count as 1dc) skip st at base of ch, 1dc into back loop of each dc to end, turn.

Row 4: Ch1, *insert hook through next dc and corresponding back loop from the st on row 2, yo, draw loop through the layers, yo, to complete a sc; rep from * to end. Fasten off.

Dainty points

Worked lengthwise over 12 sts (add 2 sts for base chain).

Row 1 (RS): Skip 2 ch, 1sc into next ch, 1hdc into next ch, 1dc into next ch, 1tr into next ch, [ch1, skip 1 ch, 1tr into next ch] twice, ch2, skip 2 ch, 1tr into each of last 2 ch, turn.

Row 2: Ch1, 1sc into each of 1st 2 tr, 1sc into ch-2 sp, ch4, 1sc into same sp as last sc, 1sc into next tr, 1sc into ch sp, 1sc into next tr, turn.

Row 3: Ch7, work 1sc into 3rd ch from hook, 1hdc into next ch, 1dc into next ch, 1 tr into next ch, ch1, 1tr into next sc, ch1, skip 1 sc, 1tr into next sc, ch2, skip 2 sc, 1tr into each of last 2sc, turn.

Rep rows 2–3 until required length is reached. Fasten off.

Beaded dash

Multiple of 2 sts + 1 st (add 1 st for base chain).

Special abbreviation:

Beaded-dc = yo, insert hook into next st, yo, draw loop through, slide bead along yarn to base of hook, yo, draw yarn through 2 loops, slide bead along yarn to base of hook, yo, draw yarn through remaining 2 loops.

Note: thread beads onto yarn before starting.

Row 1 (RS): 1sc into 2nd ch from hook, work 1sc into each ch to end, turn.

Row 2: Ch3 (count as 1dc), *1 beaded-dc into next sc, 1dc in next sc; rep from * to end, turn.

Row 3: 1slip st into front loop of each st to end of row. Fasten off.

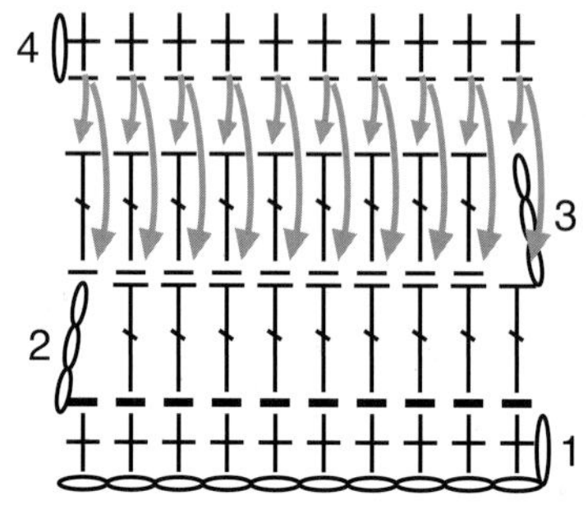

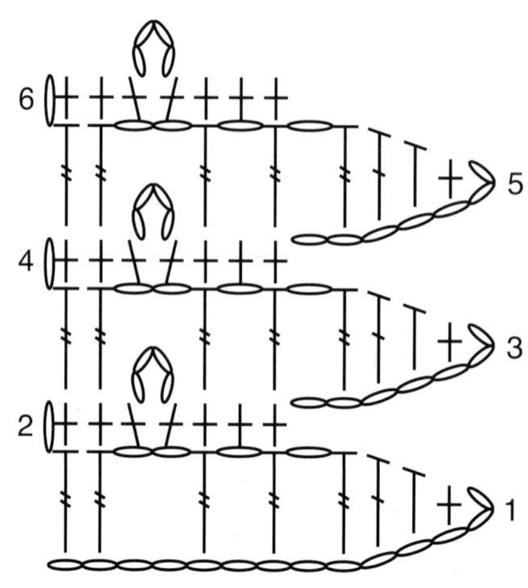

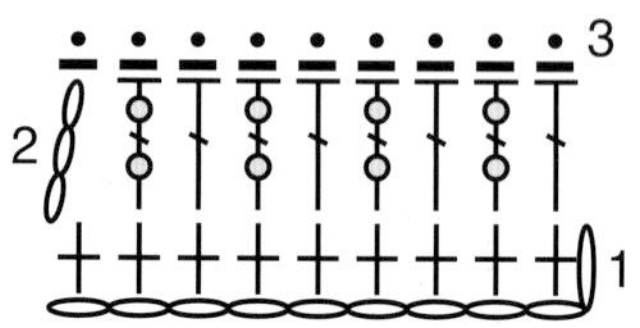

Zigzag border

Multiple of 6 sts + 1 st (add 1 st for base chain).

Special abbreviations:

Dtr-grp (double treble group) = work 3dtr into next sc until 1 loop of each remains on hook, yo and through all 4 loops on hook.

Double dtr-grp (double double treble group) = work 3dtr into same sc as last group until 1 loop of each remains on hook (4 loops on hook), skip 5 sc, into next sc work 3dtr until 1 loop of each remains on hook, yo and through all 7 loops on hook.

Row 1 (RS): 1sc into 2nd ch from hook, work 1sc into each ch to end, turn.

Row 2: Ch1, work 1sc into each sc to end, turn.

Row 3: Ch5 (count as 1dtr), skip 1st 3 sc, work 1 dtr-grp into next sc, ch5, *1 double dtr-grp, ch5; rep from * to last 3 sc, into same sc as last grp work 3dtr until 1 loop of each remains on hook (4 loops on hook), 1dtr into last sc until 5 loops remain on hook, yo and through all 5 loops, turn.

Row 4: Ch1, 1sc into top of 1st grp, 5sc into ch-5 arch, *1sc into top of next grp, 5sc into next ch-5 arch; rep from * to last grp, 1sc into top of tch, turn.

Row 5: Ch1, work 1sc into each sc to end. Fasten off.

Maids in a row

Multiple of 8 sts + 1 st (add 1 st for base chain).

Row 1 (RS): 1sc into 2nd ch from hook, work 1sc into each ch to end, turn.

Row 2: Ch1, 1sc into each of 1st 4sc, into next sc work (1sc, ch7, 1sc), *1sc into each of next 7 sc, into next sc work (1sc, ch7, 1sc); rep from * to last 4 sc, 1sc into each of last 4 sc, turn.

Row 3: Ch3 (count as 1dc), skip 1st sc, *1sc into next sc, 9sc into next arch, skip 3 sc, 1sc into next sc, 1dc into next sc; rep from * to end, turn.

Row 4: Ch1, 1sc into 1st dc, *ch4, skip 5 sc, into next sc work (1sc, ch5, 1sc), ch4, skip 5 sc, 1sc into next dc; rep from * to end, placing last sc into top of tch, turn.

Row 5: Ch1, 1sc into 1st sc, *3sc into next ch-4 arch, 5sc into next ch-5 arch, 3sc into next ch-4 arch, 1sc into next sc; rep from * to end. Fasten off.

Montana trail

Multiple of 12 sts + 7 sts (add 4 sts for base chain).

Special abbreviation:

Tr2tog = work 2tr into next st until 1 loop of each remains on hook, yo and through all 3 loops on hook.

Row 1 (RS): Skip 7 ch, 1dc into next ch, *ch2, skip 2 ch, 1dc into next ch; rep from * to end, turn.

Row 2: Ch1, 1sc into 1st dc, *ch9, skip 1 dc, into next dc work (1sc, ch4, tr2tog), skip 1 dc, into next dc work (tr2tog, ch4, 1sc); rep from * to last 2 sps, ch9, skip 1 dc, skip next 2 ch, 1sc into next ch, turn.

Row 3: Ch10, 1sc into 1st ch-9 arch, *ch4, work (tr2tog, ch4, 1slip st, ch4, tr2tog) into next tr2tog, ch4, 1sc into next ch-9 arch; rep from * to end, ch4, 1trtr into last sc, turn.

Row 4: Ch1, 1sc into 1st trtr, *ch5, skip next 2 ch-4 sps, 1sc into next tr2tog; rep from * to end, placing last sc into 6th ch of ch-10 tch, turn.

Row 5: Ch5 (count as 1dc, ch2), 1dc into next ch-5 arch, ch2, 1dc into next sc, *ch2, 1dc into next ch-5 arch, ch2, 1dc into next sc; rep from * to end. Fasten off.

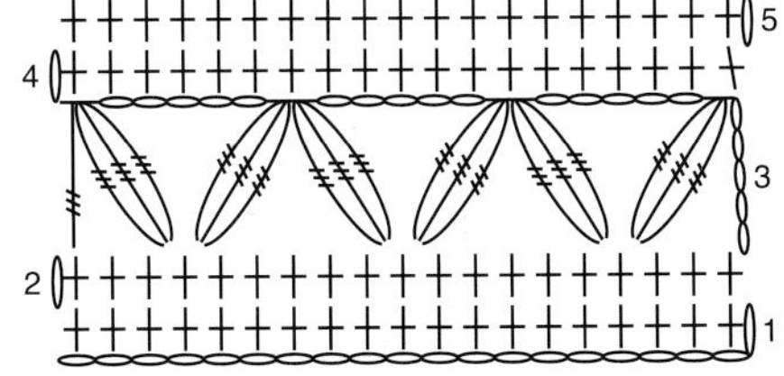

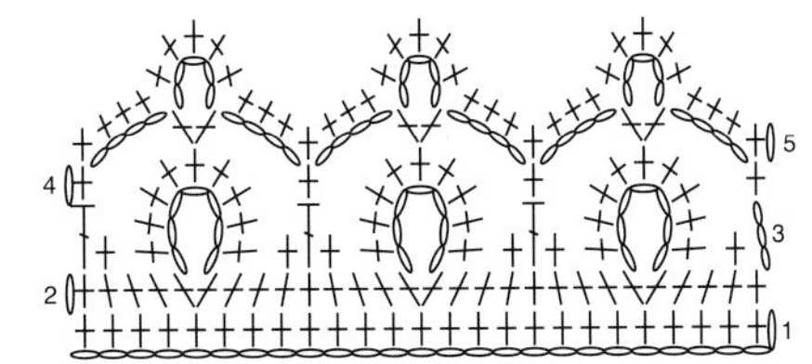

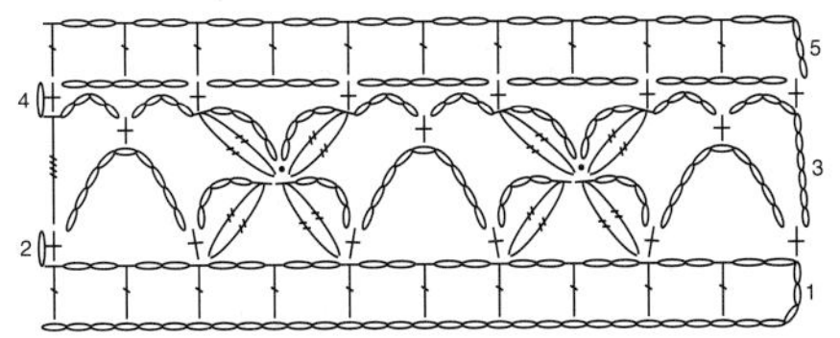

Lacy tangle

Multiple of 13 sts + 6 sts (add 3 sts for base chain).

Row 1 (RS): Skip 3 ch (count as 1dc), 3dc into next ch, skip 4 ch, 4dc into next ch, *ch3, skip 3 ch, 1sc into next ch, ch3, skip 3 ch, 4dc into next ch, skip 4 ch, 4dc into next ch; rep from * to end, turn.

Row 2: Ch3 (count as 1dc), 3dc into 1st dc, skip 6 dc, work 4dc into next dc, *ch3, 1sc into next sc, ch3, 4dc into next dc, skip 6 dc, 4dc into next dc; rep from * to end, placing last group of 4dc into top of ch-3, turn.

Row 3: Ch6 (count as 1dc, ch3), work 1sc between next 2 groups of 4dc, *ch3, skip 3 dc, 4dc into next dc, skip next 2 ch-3 sps, 4dc in next dc, ch3, 1sc between next 2 groups of 4dc; rep from * to last group, ch3, 1dc into top of tch. Fasten off.

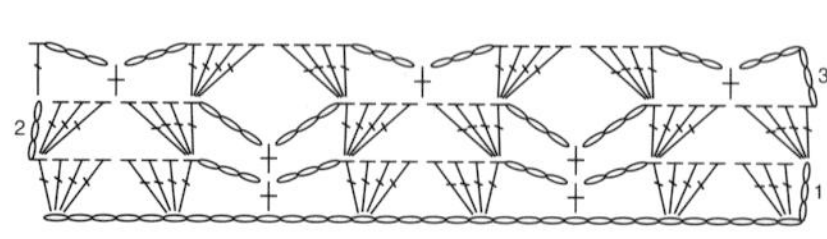

Chain buttonhole

Multiple of 8 sts + 5 sts (add 1 st for base chain).

Special abbreviation:

Picot = ch3, slip st into 3rd ch from hook.

Suggestion: work a small sample as described and then adjust the spacing, and so the multiple, to suit the project.

Row 1 (RS): 1sc into 2nd ch from hook, work 1sc into each ch to end, turn.

Row 2: Ch1, 1sc into front loop of each st to end, turn.

Row 3: Ch1, 1sc into each of 1st 5 sts, *ch7, skip 3 sc, 1sc into each of next 5 sc; rep from * to end, turn.

Row 4: Ch1, 1sc into each of 1st 4 sts, *ch3, skip 1 sc and 3 ch, 1sc into next ch, 1 picot, ch3, skip 3 ch and 1 sc, 1sc into each of next 3 sc; rep from * to last st, 1sc into next sc. Fasten off.

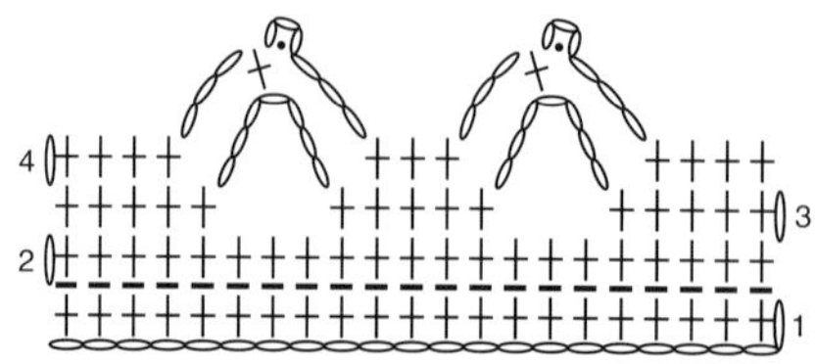

Loopy edge

Multiple of 2 sts + 1 st (add 1 st for base chain).

Note: for plain loop stitch do not cut loops. The loops are on the back of the fabric as you are working.

Special abbreviation:

Loop st = using the left-hand finger to control loop size, insert hook, pick up both threads of the loop, and draw these through; wrap yarn from the ball over hook and draw through all the loops on hook to complete.

Row 1 (RS): 1sc into 2nd ch from hook, work 1sc into every ch to end, turn.

Row 2: Ch1, sc into 1st st, *work loop stitch into next st, sc into next st; rep from * to end, turn.

Row 3: Ch1, 1sc into every st to end, turn.

Rep rows 2–3 until required depth is reached.

Last row: Ch1, work 1sc into every st to end. Fasten off.

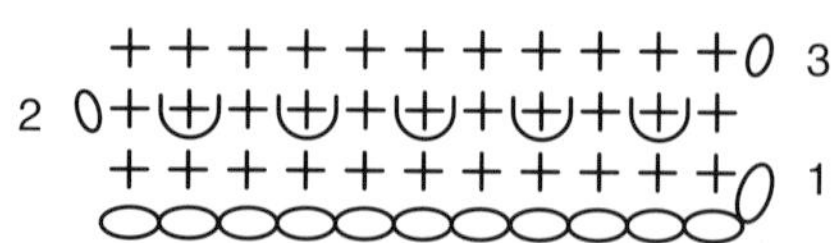

Popcorn wave

Multiple of 10 sts + 1 st (add 1 st for base chain).

Special abbreviation:

5dc-popcorn = work 5dc into indicated st, remove hook from working loop, insert hook under top loops of 1st of dc sts just worked, hook the working loop and draw this through top loops to draw the popcorn closed, ch1.

Note: work foundation row if working from a base chain.

Foundation row: 1sc into 2nd ch from hook and each ch to end, turn.

Row 1 (RS): Ch6 (count as 1dc, ch3), skip 4 sts, 1sc into next st, 1sc into each of next 2 sts, *ch3, skip 3 sts, 5dc-popcorn into next st, ch3, skip 3 sts, 1sc into each of next 3 sts; rep from * to last 4 sts, ch3, skip 3 sts, 1dc into last st, turn.

Row 2: Ch1, 1sc into 1st st, *1sc into next arch, ch3, skip 1 sc, 5dc-popcorn next sc, ch3**, 1sc into next arch, 1sc into next 5dc-popcorn; rep from * ending last rep at **, skip 2 ch of tch-arch, 1sc into each of next 2 ch. Fasten off.

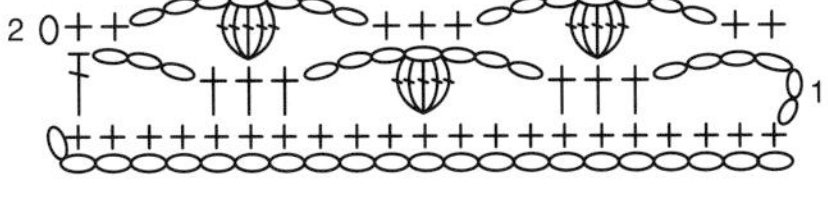

Cross-topped fans

Multiple of 4 sts + 1 st (add 1 st for base chain).

Special abbreviation:

Cross2tr = skip 3 dc, work 1tr into next dc, ch2, working behind last tr work 1tr into 1st of skipped dc.

Note: work foundation row if working from a base chain.

Foundation row: 1sc into 2nd ch from hook and each ch to end, turn.

Row 1: Ch3 (count as 1dc), skip next st, work 4dc into next st, *skip 3 sts, 4dc into next ch; rep from * to last 2 sts, skip 1 st, 1dc into last st, turn.

Row 2: Ch3 (count as 1dc), skip st at base of ch, *cross2tr; rep from * to end, 1dc into top of tch, turn. Fasten off.

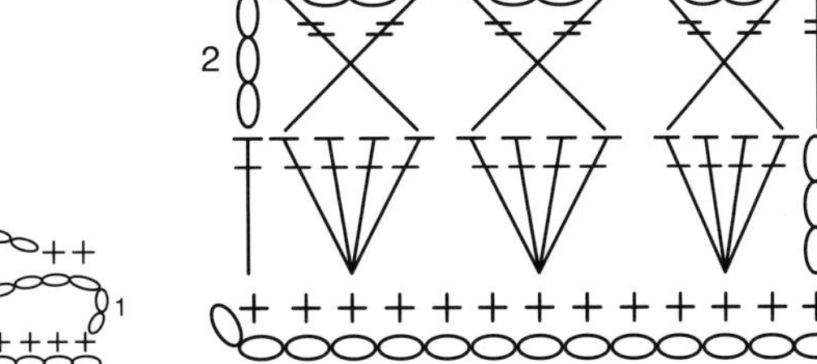

Back-and-forth ruffle

Multiple over any number of sts (add 3 sts for base chain).

Row 1: Skip 4 ch (count as 1tr), 1tr into next ch, or join into an edge and ch4; work 1tr into each ch or equivalent interval to end, turn.

Row 2: Ch4 (count as 1tr), 1tr into each st to end, do not turn but rotate work by 90 degrees so the length worked is lying towards the back and st just worked is at the bottom right. Henceforth a row is 2tr lying horizontally, top to base, top to foundation ch.

Row 3: Ch3, *work 6dc around post of 1st tr, 1dc into base, 6dc around post of next tr in row, 1dc into base of st in next row, 6dc around post of tr just worked into, 1dc into top of same tr, 6dc around post of next tr, 1dc into top of st in next row; rep from * to end, omitting last dc in last rep. Fasten off.

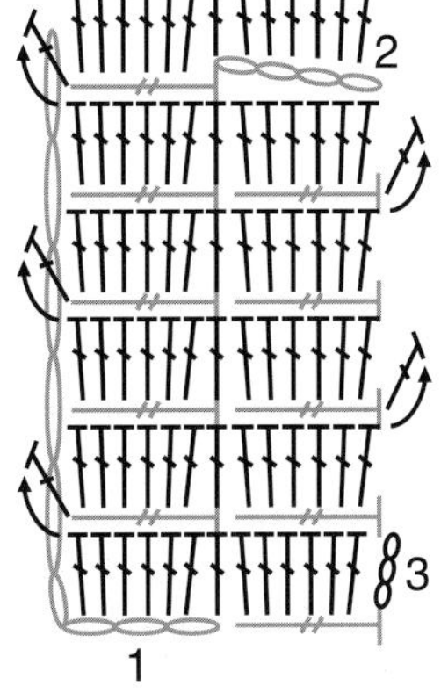

Hanging blocks

Multiple of 6 sts + 1 st (add 1 st for base chain).

Special abbreviation:

Wedge picot = ch6, 1sc into 2nd ch from hook, 1hdc into next ch, 1dc into next ch, 1tr into next ch, 1dtr into next ch.

Note: work foundation row if working from a base chain.

Foundation row: 1sc into 2nd ch from hook and each ch to end, turn.

Row 1 (RS): Ch1, 1sc into 1st st, *1 wedge picot, skip 5 sts, 1sc into next st; rep from * to end, turn.

Row 2: Ch5, *1sc into top of wedge picot, over next ch-5 at underside of wedge picot work 1sc into next ch, 1hdc into next ch, 1dc into next ch, 1tr into next ch, 1dtr into next ch, ch5, 1sc in next sc**, ch5; rep from * ending last rep at **. Fasten off.

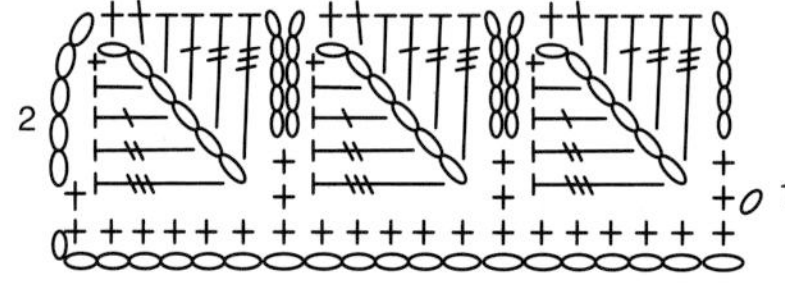

Gentle wave

Multiple of 14 sts + 1 st (add 1 st for base chain).

Note: work foundation row if working from a base chain.

Foundation row: 1sc into 2nd ch from hook, work 1sc into each ch to end, turn.

Row 1 (RS): Ch1, 1sc into 1st st, or join into an edge and work ch1, 1sc into starting point; counting either sts or equivalent interval, *over next 14 sts, 1sc into next st,

[1hdc into next st] twice, [1dc into next st] twice, ch1, [1tr into next st, ch1] 3 times, [1dc into next st] twice, [1hdc into next st] twice, [1sc into next st] twice; rep from * to end. Fasten off.

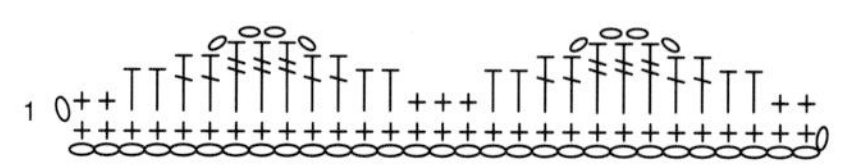

Diamond edge

Multiple of 9 sts + 2 sts (add 2 sts for base chain).

Row 1 (RS): Skip 3 ch (count as 1dc), 1dc into next ch, work 1dc into each ch to end, turn.

Row 2: Ch1, 1sc into 1st dc, ch1, 1sc into next dc, ch9, skip 7 dc, 1sc into next dc, *ch3, 1sc into next dc, ch9, skip 7 dc, 1sc into next dc; rep from * to end, ch1, 1sc into top of ch-3 tch, turn.

Row 3: Ch1, 1sc into 1st sc, 1sc into 1st ch sp, *5dc into next ch-9 arch, ch2, into same arch as last 5dc work (1sc, ch2, 5dc), 1sc into next ch-3 arch; rep from * to end, placing last sc into last ch sp, 1sc into last sc, turn.

Row 4: Ch9 (count as 1dtr, ch4), 1sc into next ch-2 sp, ch3, 1sc into next ch-2 sp, *ch9, 1sc into next ch-2 sp, ch3, 1sc into next ch-2 sp; rep from * to last 5dc, ch4, 1dtr into last sc, turn.

Row 5: Ch3 (count as 1dc), 5dc into ch-4 arch, 1sc into next ch-3 arch, *5dc into next ch-9 arch, ch2, into same arch as last 5dc work (1sc, ch2, 5dc), 1sc into next ch-3 arch; rep from * to last arch, 5dc into last arch, 1dc into 5th ch of ch-9 tch. Fasten off.

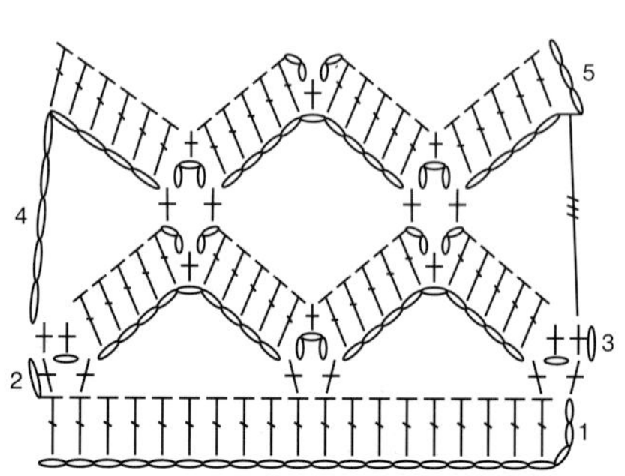

Slanting shells

Multiple of 4 sts + 1 st (add 1 st for base chain).

Special abbreviations:

Shell = work (1sc, ch3, 3dc) in ch or st indicated.

Dc2tog = work 1dc into next 2 ch or sts indicated until 1 loop of each remains on hook, yo and through all 3 loops on hook.

Row 1 (WS): Work 1 shell into 2nd ch from hook, *skip 3 ch, work a shell into next ch; rep from * to last 4 ch, skip 3 ch, 1sc into last ch, turn.

Row 2: Ch3, 1dc into 1st sc st at base of ch, *skip 3 sts, 1sc into top of ch-3 loop**, work a V st of (1dc, ch1, 1dc) into next sc; rep from * ending last rep at **, 2dc into last sc, skip tch, turn.

Row 3: Ch3, 3dc into 1st st, skip next st, *work a shell into next sc, skip next V st; rep from * ending 1sc into last sc, ch3, dc2tog over last dc and top of tch.

Fasten off.

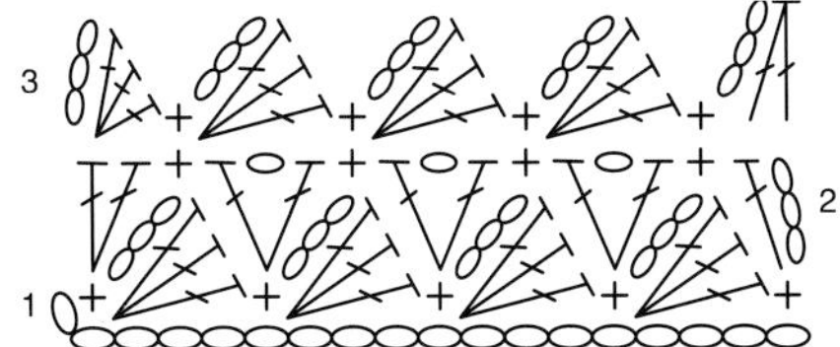

Unpicked fringe

Multiple of any number of sts (add 2 sts for base chain).

Note: This edging does unravel with age and hard wear. For extra strength, work a row of running stitch along the top of the posts of the double crochets of row 1. Using waste yarn work a base ch to required length.

Foundation row: Skip 3 ch (count as 1dc), 1dc into each ch to end, turn.

Join in working yarn.

Row 1: Ch3 (count as 1dc), 1dc into each st to end, turn.

Row 2: Ch1, 1sc into each st to end.

Cut the waste yarn through the posts of each dc and remove it. Fasten off.

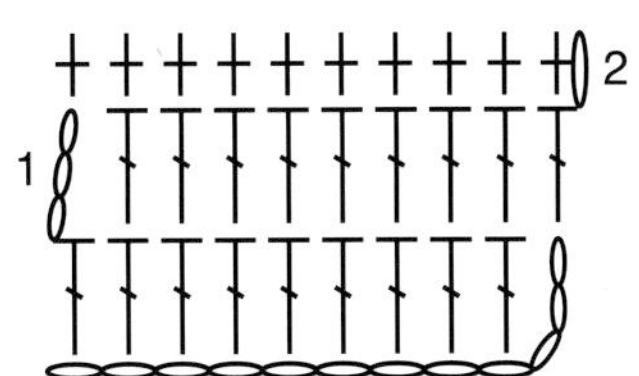

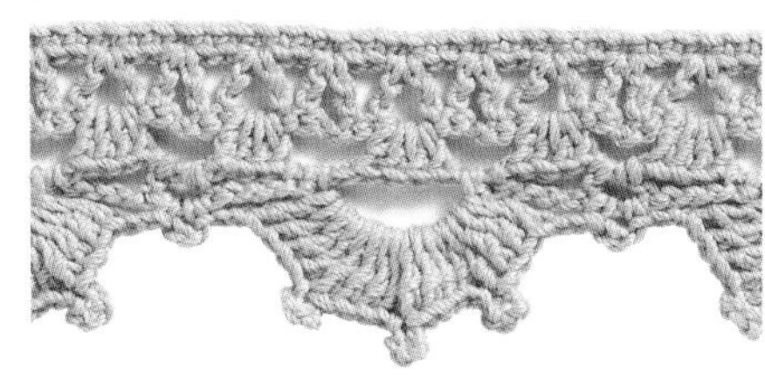

Fan flair

Multiple of 18 sts + 17 sts (add 1 st for base chain).

Row 1 (RS): 1sc into 2nd ch from hook, work 1sc into each ch to end, turn.

Row 2: Ch4 (count as 1tr), *skip next 2 sc, work (1tr, ch2, 1tr) into next sc; rep from * to last 2 sc, 1tr into last sc, turn.

Row 3: Ch3 (count as 1dc), work 4dc into 1st ch-2 sp, *ch3, skip ch-2 sp, 4dc into next ch-2 sp; rep from * to end, 1dc into 4th ch of ch-4 tch, turn.

Row 4: Ch6 (count as 1dc, ch3), 2sc into 1st ch-3 sp, ch7, 2sc into next ch-3 sp, *ch3, into next ch-3 sp work (1dc, ch2, 1dc), ch3, 2sc into next ch-3 sp, ch7, 2sc into next ch-3 sp; rep from * to last 5 sts, ch3, 1dc into 3rd ch of ch-3 tch, turn.

Row 5: Ch1, 1sc into 1st dc, ch2, into ch-7 arch work 4tr and [ch5, slip st into 1st of these ch, 4tr] 3 times, ch2, *skip ch-3 sp, into next ch-2 sp work (1sc, ch3, 1sc), ch2, into ch-7 arch work 4tr and [ch5, slip st into 1st of these ch, 4tr] 3 times; rep from * to last sp, ch2, 1sc into 3rd ch of ch-6 tch.

Fasten off.

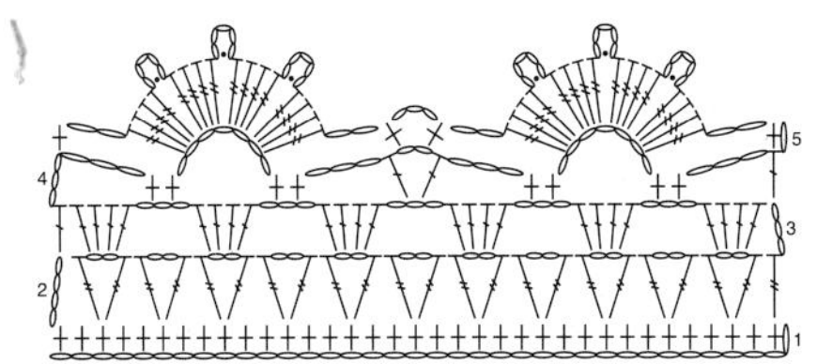

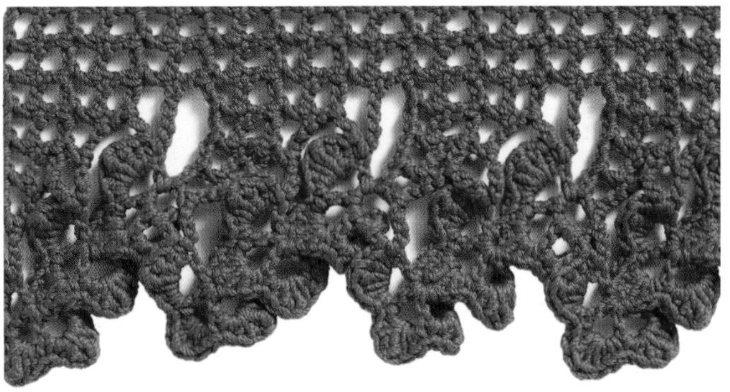

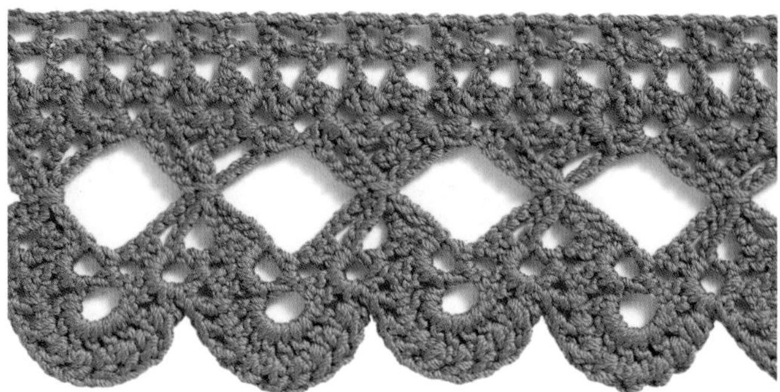

Floral trellis

Worked lengthwise over 28 sts (add 3 sts for base chain).

Row 1 (RS): Skip 6 ch, work 1dc into next ch from hook, [ch2, skip 2 ch, 1dc into next ch] 8 times, turn. (9 sps)

Row 2: Ch5 (count as 1dc, ch2), skip 1st dc, 1dc into next dc, [ch2, 1dc into next dc] 3 times, ch5, skip next 4 sps, 1dc into next sp, work [ch3, 1dc] 3 times into same sp as last dc, turn.

Row 3: Ch1, 1sc into 1st dc, into 1st ch-3 sp work (1hdc, 1dc, 1tr, 1dc, 1hdc, 1sc), into next ch-3 sp work (1sc, 1hdc, 1dc, 1tr, 1dc, 1hdc, 1sc), into next ch-3 sp work (1sc, 1hdc, 1dc, 1tr, 1dc, 1hdc), 1sc into next dc, ch5, 1dc into next dc, [ch2, 1dc into next dc] 4 times placing last dc into 3rd ch of ch-5 tch, turn.

Row 4: Ch5 (count as 1dc, ch2), skip 1st dc, [1dc into next dc, ch2] 4 times, 1dc into ch-5 sp, ch7, skip 1st group of 7 sts, work 1dc into tr at center of next group of 7 sts, [ch3, 1dc] 3 times into same st as last dc, turn.

Row 5: Ch1, 1sc into 1st dc, into 1st ch-3 sp work (1hdc, 1dc, 1tr, 1dc, 1hdc, 1sc), into next ch-3 sp work (1sc, 1hdc, 1dc, 1tr, 1dc, 1hdc, 1sc), into next ch-3 sp work (1sc, 1hdc, 1dc, 1tr, 1dc, 1hdc), 1sc into next dc, ch5, 1dc into ch-7 sp, [ch2, 1dc into next dc] 6 times placing last dc into 3rd ch of ch-5 tch, turn.

Row 6: Ch5 (count as 1dc, ch2), skip 1st dc, [1dc into next dc, ch2] 6 times, 1dc into ch-5 sp, ch7, skip 1st group of 7 sts, work 1dc into tr at center of next group of 7 sts, [ch3, 1dc] 3 times into same st as last dc, turn.

Row 7: Ch1, 1sc into 1st dc, into 1st ch-3 sp work (1hdc, 1dc, 1tr, 1dc, 1hdc, 1sc), into next ch-3 sp work (1sc, 1hdc, 1dc, 1tr, 1dc, 1hdc, 1sc), into next ch-3 sp work (1sc, 1hdc, 1dc, 1tr, 1dc, 1hdc), 1sc into next dc, ch5, 1dc into ch-7 sp, [ch2, 1dc into next dc] 8 times placing last dc into 3rd ch of ch-5 tch, turn.

Rep rows 2–7 until required length is reached, ending with a row 7. Fasten off.

Light shell frill

Worked lengthwise.

Row 1 (WS): Ch26, 1dc into 8th ch from hook, ch2, skip 2 ch, 2dc into next ch, ch3, 2dc into next ch, ch9, skip 10 ch, 2dc into next ch, ch3, 2dc into next ch, leaving 2 ch unworked, turn.

Row 2: Ch6, skip 2 dc, (1dc, ch3, 1dc) into next ch-3 sp, ch9, skip ch-9 sp and 2 dc, (2dc, ch3, 2dc) into next ch-3 sp, ch2, skip 2 dc and ch sp, 1dc into next st, ch2, skip 2 ch, 1dc into next ch of ch-5 tch, turn.

Row 3: Ch5 (count as 1dc, ch2), skip 1 dc at base of ch, 1dc into next dc, ch2, skip ch-2 sp and 2 dc, (2dc, ch3, 2dc) into next ch-3 sp, ch9, skip 2 dc and ch-9 sp, (2dc, ch3, 2dc) into next ch-3 sp, [ch1, 1dc] 7 times into ch-6 sp, ch1, 1sc into last ch of foundation ch or in following repeats into last dc of last fan motif, turn.

Row 4: Ch4, skip ch-1 sp, [1sc into next ch-1 sp, ch3] 6 times, 1dc into next ch-1 sp, (1dc, ch3, 1dc) into next ch-3 sp, ch9, skip 2 dc and ch-9 sp, (2dc, ch3, 2dc) into next ch-3 sp, ch2, skip 2 dc and ch-2 sp, 1dc into next st, ch2, 1dc into 3rd ch of ch-5 tch, turn.

Row 5: Ch5 (count as 1dc, ch2), skip 1dc at base of ch, 1dc into next dc, ch2, skip ch-2 sp and dc, (2dc, ch3, 2dc) into next ch-3 sp, ch4, 1sc around last 3 ch-9 strands, ch4, skip next dc, (2dc, ch3, 2dc) into next ch-3 sp, turn.

Rep rows 2–5 until required length is reached.

Fasten off.

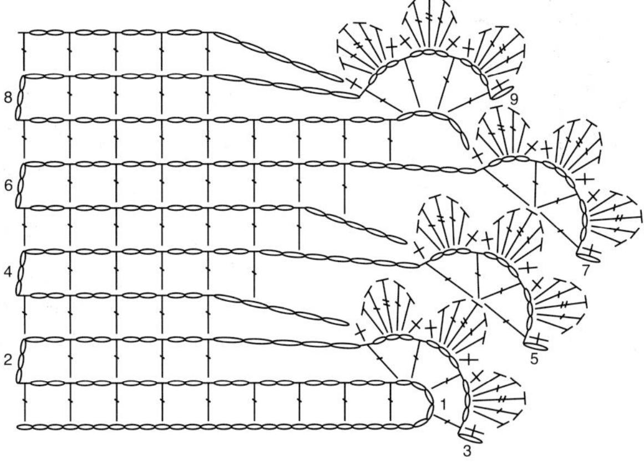

Floral trellis

Triangle edge

Multiple of 19 sts (1 motif for each repeat).

Motif

Base ring: Ch6, join with slip st to form a ring.

Round 1: Ch4 (count as 1dc, ch1), 1dc into ring, *[ch2, 1dc, ch1, 1dc] 5 times, ch2, slip st to 3rd ch of tch.

Round 2: Ch1, *1sc into next sp, [1dc, 1ch] twice into next sp, 1dc into same sp; rep from * 5 more times, slip st to 1st sc.

Round 3: Ch3 (count as 1sc, ch1), *[1sc into next ch-1 sp, ch1] twice, (1tr, ch1, 1dtr, ch5, 1dtr, ch1, 1tr) into next sc for a corner group, [ch1, 1sc into next ch-1 sp] twice, ch1**, 1sc into next sc, ch1; rep from * once more, then from * to ** again, slip st to 3rd ch of tch.

Fasten off.

Header

With WS facing and using the diagram as a guide, rejoin yarn in corner ch-5 sp to the far right of the 1st motif.

Row 1: Ch3 (count as 1dc), 1dc into the corner-sp, 1dc into next 2 sts [1dc into next ch-1 sp, 1dc into next st] 5 times, 1dc into next ch-1 sp, 1dc into next 2 sts, 2dc into the corner-sp, *2dc into the corner-sp of next motif, 1dc into next 2 sts, [1dc into next ch-1 sp, 1dc into next st] 5 times, 1dc into next ch-1 sp, 1dc into next 2 sts, 2dc into the corner-sp; rep from * across each motif to end.

Row 2: Ch2, work 1hdc into each st to end, turn.

Row 3: Ch1, 1sc into back loop of each st to end, turn.

Rows 4–6: Ch1, 1sc into each st to end, turn.

Fasten off.

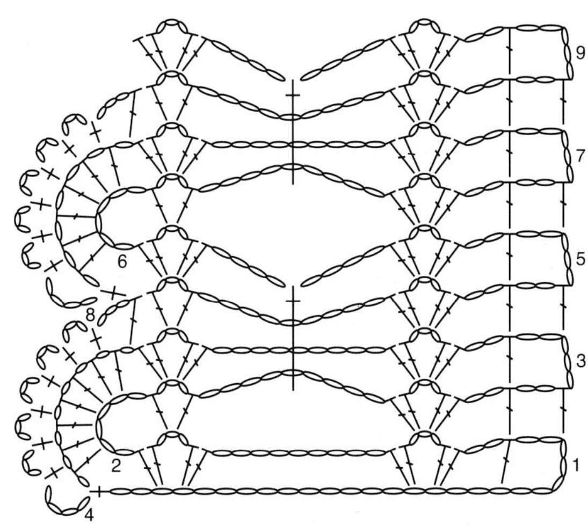

Light shell frill

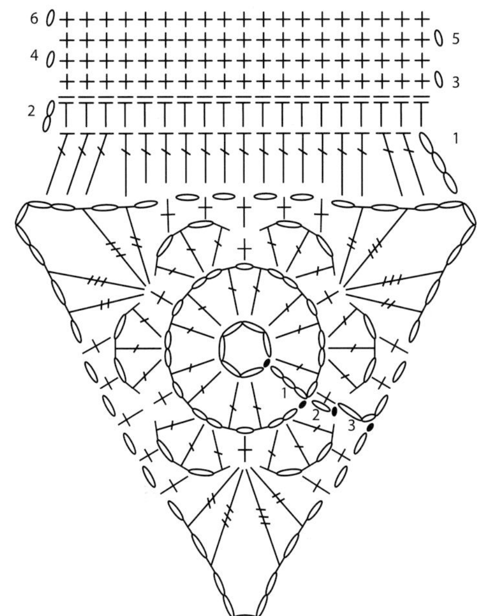

Triangle edge

Simple beaded edge

Any number of sts (add 1 st for base chain).

Special abbreviation:

Pb (place bead) = slide next bead along yarn to base of hook.

Note: thread beads onto yarn before starting.

Row 1 (RS): 1sc into 2nd ch from hook work 1sc into each ch to end, turn.

Row 2: Ch1, pb, 1sc into 1st sc, *pb, 1sc in next sc; rep from * to end.

Fasten off.

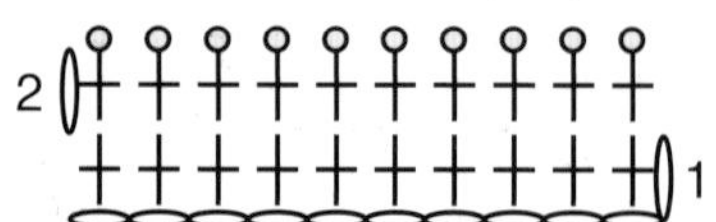

Flying diamonds

Multiple of 6 sts + 1 st (add 1 st for base chain).

Note: work foundation row if working from a base chain.

Foundation row: 1sc into 2nd ch from hook and each ch to end, turn.

Row 1 (RS): Ch6 (count as 1dc, ch3), skip 1st 3 sts, 1sc into next st, (1dc, ch-3 sp formed at beg of row), turn, ch1, 1sc into dc just worked, 3sc into ch-3 sp, [turn, ch1, 1sc into each of the 4 sc] 3 times, skip next 2 sts on foundation row, 1dc into next st, *ch3, miss next 2 sts on foundation row, 1sc into next st, turn, ch1, 1sc into sc just worked, 3sc into ch-3 sp, [turn, ch1, 1sc into each of the 4 sc] 3 times, skip next 2 sts on foundation row, 1dc into next st; rep from * to end.

Fasten off.

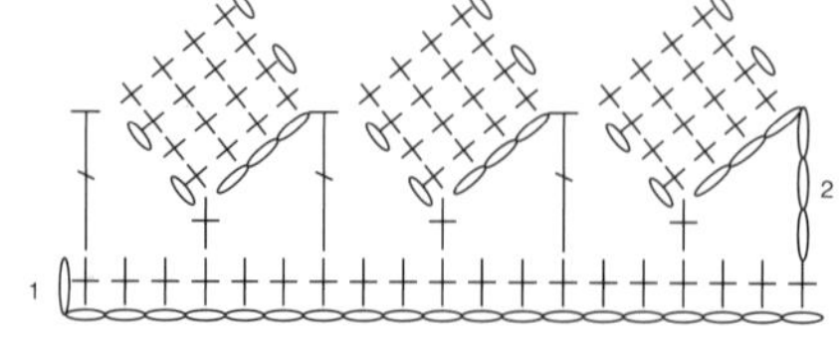

Two-row bobbles

Multiple of 6 sts +1 st (add 4 sts for base chain).

Special abbreviations:

Shell = work (dc2tog, 1dc, dc2tog) all into next st.

Group = into 1st dc2tog of shell work 2dc until 1 loop of each remains on hook (3 loops on hook), 1dc into dc of same shell until 4 loops remain on hook, into 2nd dc2tog of shell work 2dc until 1 loop of each remains on hook, yo and through all 6 loops.

Row 1 (RS): Skip 7 ch (1dc, ch-2 sp at beg of row), 1dc into next ch, or join into an edge and ch5, skip 2 st equivalent sp, 1dc in next st equivalent sp; counting either ch or equivalent interval, *ch1, skip 2 ch, work 1 shell into next ch, ch1, skip 2 ch, 1dc into next ch; rep from * to last 3 ch, ch2, skip 2 ch, 1dc into last ch, turn.

Row 2: Ch5 (count as 1dc, ch2), skip 1st dc, 1dc into next dc, ch2, *work 1 group over next shell, ch2, 1dc into next dc, ch2; rep from * to last dc, skip 2 ch, 1dc into next ch.

Fasten off.

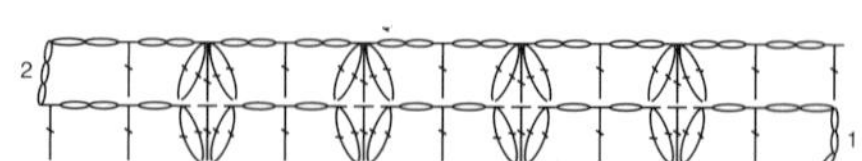

Honeycomb edge

Multiple of 5 sts + 1 st (add 1 st for base chain).

Row 1 (RS): 1sc into 2nd ch from hook, work 1sc into each ch to end, turn.

Row 2: Ch1, 1sc into each of 1st 2 sc, *ch5, skip 2 sc, 1sc into each of next 3 sc; rep from * to end, omitting 1sc at end of last rep, turn.

Row 3: Ch1, 1sc into 1st sc, *5sc into next ch-5 arch, skip 1 sc, 1sc into next sc; rep from * to end, turn.

Row 4: Ch6 (count as 1tr, ch2), skip 1st 2 sc, 1sc into each of next 3 sc, *ch5, skip 3 sc, 1sc into each of next 3 sc; rep from * to last 2 sc, ch2, 1tr into last sc, turn.

Row 5: Ch1, 1sc into 1st tr, 2sc into ch-2 sp, skip 1 sc, 1sc into next sc, *skip 1 sc, 5sc into next ch-5 arch, skip 1 sc, 1sc into next sc; rep from * to last ch-2 sp, 2sc into last sp, 1sc into 4th ch of tch. Fasten off.

Single rib edging

Multiple of 2 sts (add 2 sts for base chain).

Special abbreviations:

Dc/rf (raised double crochet at the front of the fabric) = yo, insert hook from in front and from right to left around the stem of the appropriate stitch, and complete stitch normally.

Dc/rb (raised double crochet at the back of the fabric) = yo, insert hook from behind and from right to left around the stem of the appropriate stitch, and complete stitch normally.

Row 1 (WS): Skip 3 ch (count as 1dc), 1dc into next ch or join into an edge and ch3; work 1dc into each ch or equivalent interval to end, turn.

Row 2: Ch2 (count as 1dc), skip 1st st at base of ch, *1dc/rf around next st, 1dc/rb around next st; rep from * ending 1dc into top of tch, turn.

Rep row 2 until required depth is reached. Fasten off.

Arrowhead fans

Multiple of 10 sts + 1 st (add 2 sts for base chain).

Row 1 (RS): Skip 3 ch (count as 1dc), 1dc into next ch, work 1dc into each ch to end, turn.

Row 2: Ch1, 1sc into each of 1st 3 dc, *ch2, skip 2 dc, into next dc work [2dc, ch2] twice, skip 2 dc, 1sc into each of next 5 dc; rep from end, omitting 2sc at end of last rep and placing last sc into top of tch, turn.

Row 3: Ch1, 1sc into each of 1st 2 sc, *ch3, skip next ch-2 sp, into next ch-2 sp work (3dc, ch2, 3dc), ch3, skip 1 sc, 1sc into each of next 3 sc; rep from * to end, omitting 1sc at end of last rep, turn.

Row 4: Ch1, 1sc into 1st sc, *ch4, skip next ch-3 sp, into next ch-2 sp work (4dc, ch2, 4dc), ch4, skip 1 sc, 1sc into next sc; rep from * to end, turn.

Row 5: Ch1, 1sc into 1st sc, *ch5, skip next ch-4 sp, into next ch-2 sp work (4dc, ch2, 4dc), ch5, 1sc into next sc; rep from * to end. Fasten off.

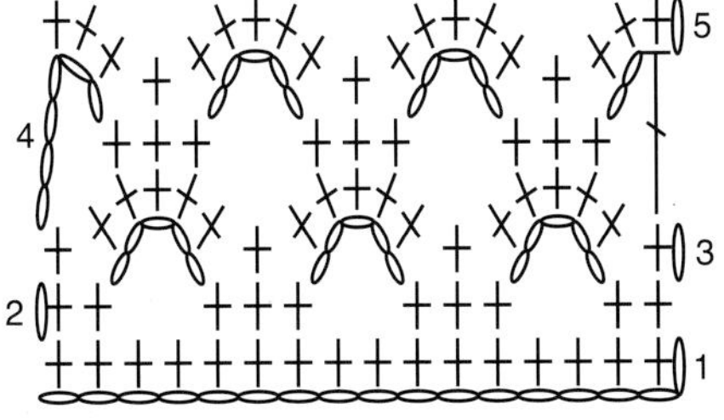

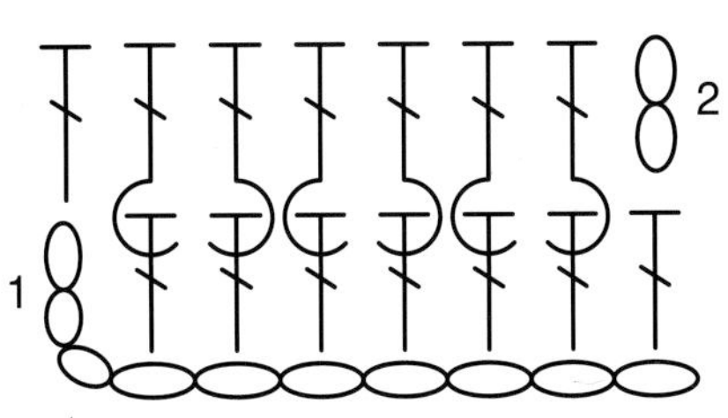

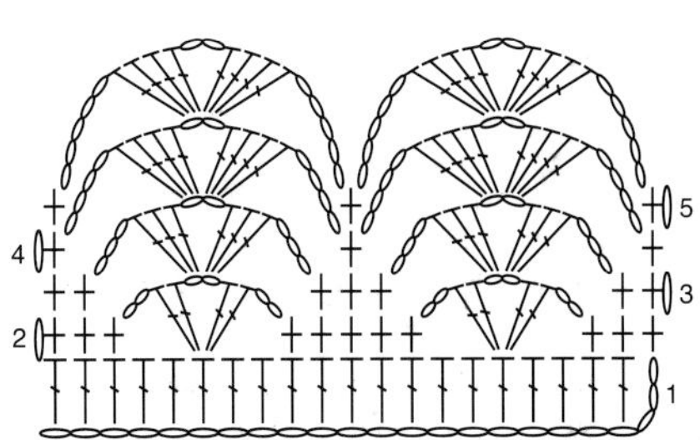

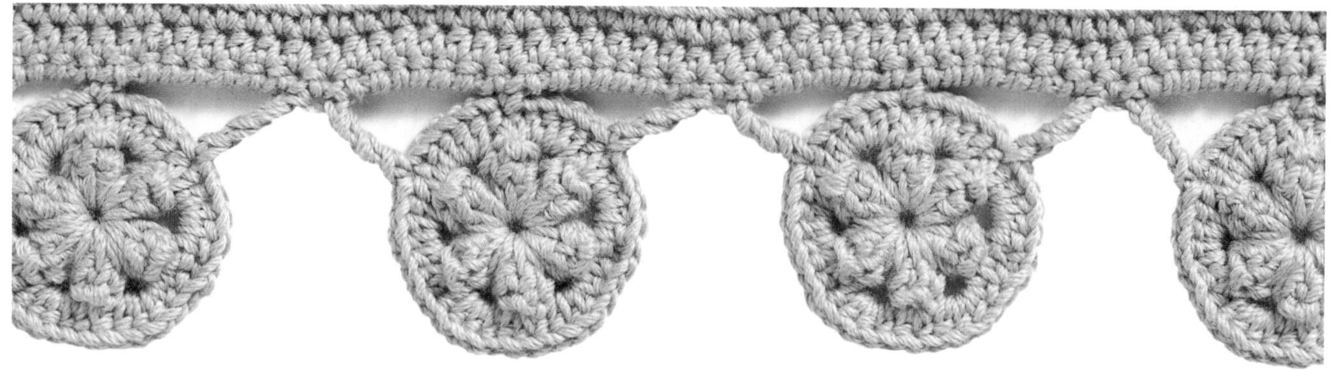

Medallion dangle

Multiple of 14 sts (1 motif for each repeat).

Special abbreviation:

4dc-popcorn = work 4dc into indicated st, remove hook from working loop, insert hook under top loops of 1st of dc sts just worked, hook the working loop and draw this through top loops to draw the popcorn closed, ch1.

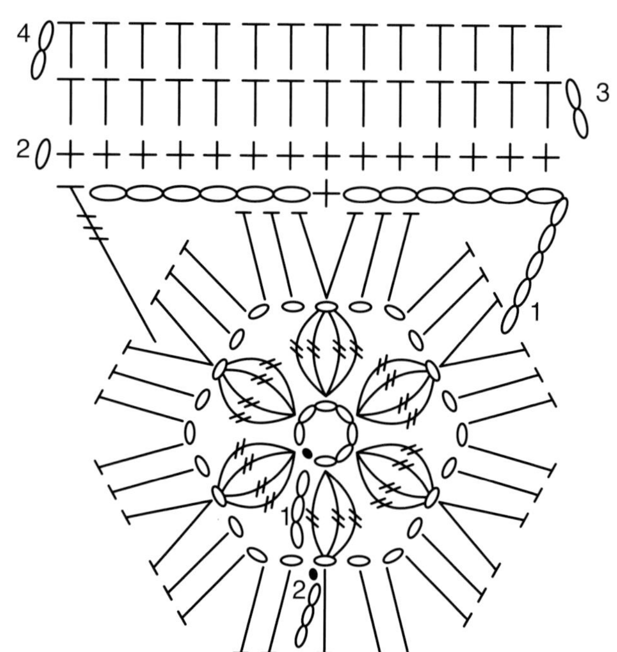

Motif

Base ring: Ch7, join with slip st.

Round 1: Ch3, 3dc into ring, remove hook and insert through top of ch-3 tch and into loop and draw through loop on hook (popcorn made), ch3, [4dc-popcorn into ring, ch3] 5 times, slip st to top of 1st popcorn.

Round 2: Ch2, (count as 1hdc) 1hdc into same place as slip st, *4hdc into next ch-3 sp, 2hdc into top of next popcorn; rep from *4 more times, 4hdc into ch-3 sp, slip st to top of ch-3. Fasten off.

Header

Rejoin yarn with a slip st between any 2hdc group on the 1st motif.

Row 1: Ch11 (count as 1dtr, ch6), *skip next 6 hdc, 1sc between next 2hdc group of motif, ch6, skip next 6 hdc, 1dtr between next 2hdc group of motif, 1dtr between any 2hdc group of next medallion, ch6; rep from * to the last motif, skip next 6 hdc, 1sc between next 2hdc group of motif, ch6, skip next 6 hdc, 1dtr between next 2hdc group of motif, turn.

Row 2: Ch1, 1sc into dtr, 6sc into ch-6 sp, *1sc into next sc, 6sc into ch-6 sp, 1sc in each of next 2 dtr, 6sc in next ch-6 sp; rep from * to last sc, 1sc into next sc, 6sc into ch-11 sp, 1sc into 4th ch of tch, turn.

Rows 3–4: Ch2, work 1hdc into each st to end, turn. Fasten off.

Chain walk

Multiple of 8 sts + 1 st (add 1 st for base chain).

Special abbreviation:

Bobble = work 4dc into next st until 1 loop of each remains on hook, yo and through all 5 loops on hook.

Row 1 (WS): 1sc into 2nd ch from hook, work 1sc into each ch to end, turn.

Row 2: Ch4 (count as 1dc, ch1), skip 1st 2 sc, 1 bobble into next sc, ch1, skip 1 sc, 1dc into next sc, *ch1, skip 1 sc, 1 bobble into next sc, ch1, skip 1 sc, 1dc into next sc; rep from * to end, turn.

Row 3: Ch1, work 1sc into each dc, ch sp and bobble to end, working last 2sc into 4th and 3rd ch of tch, turn.

Row 4: Ch1, 1sc into each of 1st 3 sc, *ch5, skip 3 sc, 1sc into each of next 5 sc; rep from * to end, omitting 2sc at end of last rep, turn.

Row 5: Ch1, 1sc into each of 1st 2 sc, *ch3, 1sc into ch-5 arch, ch3, skip 1 sc, 1sc into each of next 3 sc; rep from * to end, omitting 1sc at end of last rep, turn.

Row 6: Ch1, 1sc into 1st sc, *ch3, 1sc into next ch-3 arch, 1sc into next sc, 1sc into next ch-3 arch, ch3, skip 1 sc, 1sc into next sc; rep from * to end, turn.

Row 7: Ch5 (count as 1dc, ch2), 1sc into next ch-3 arch, 1sc into each of next 3 sc, 1sc into next ch-3 arch, *ch5, 1sc into next ch-3 arch, 1sc into each of next 3 sc, 1sc into next ch-3 arch; rep from * to last sc, ch2, 1dc into last sc, turn.

Row 8: Ch1, 1sc into 1st dc, *ch3, skip 1 sc, 1sc into each of next 3 sc, ch3, 1sc into next ch-5 arch; rep from * to end, placing last sc into 3rd ch of ch-5 tch, turn.

Row 9: Ch1, 1sc into 1st sc, *1sc into next ch-3 arch, ch3, skip 1 sc, 1sc into next sc, ch3, 1sc into next ch-3 arch, 1sc into next

Double loops

Multiple of 3 sts (add 1 st for base chain).

Row 1 (RS): 1sc into 2nd ch from hook, 1sc into back bump of each ch to end, turn.

Row 2: Ch1, 1sc into each of 1st 3 sc, *ch4, 1sc into each of next 3 sc; rep from * to end, turn.

Row 3: Ch1, 1sc in each of 1st 2 sts, *skip 1 sc, 1dc in ch-4 sp, [ch3, slip st in 3rd ch from hook, 1dc in ch-4 sp] 4 times, skip 1 sc, 1sc into next sc; rep from * to last sc, 1sc in last sc.

Fasten off. Do not turn work.

With edge just worked hanging downwards, rejoin yarn under far right ch loop of foundation ch.

Rep rows 1–3 along this edge. Fasten off.

Curlicue

Worked lengthwise over 8 sts (add 2 sts for base chain).

Row 1 (WS): Ch9, 1hdc into 3rd ch from hook, *ch1, skip 1 ch, 1hdc into next ch; rep from * to end, turn.

Row 2: Ch2, 1hdc into 1st ch sp, *ch1, 1hdc into next ch sp; rep from to end, turn.

Rep row 2.

Row 4: Ch2, 1hdc into 1st ch sp, *ch1, 1hdc into next ch sp; rep from to end, ch20, turn.

Row 5: 3dc into 4th ch from hook, 3dc into back bump of next 15 ch, (1dc, 1hdc, 1sc) into next ch, *ch1, 1hdc into next ch sp; rep from * to end.

Rep rows 2–5 until required length is reached. Fasten off.

Flower trail

Worked lengthwise.

Note: on row 2 check that each Base flower unit is not twisted before you work into it.

Row 1 (RS): Ch7, *slip st into 4th ch from hook, ch3, into ring just formed work a Base flower unit of (2dc, ch3, slip st, ch3, 2dc)**, ch10; rep from * ending last rep at ** when edging is required length, then keep same side facing and rotate so as to be able to work along underside of Base flower units.

Row 2 (RS): *Ch3, slip st into ch ring at center of Flower, ch3, (2dc, ch3, slip st, ch3, 2dc) all into same ring, skip 2 ch of base chain that connects units, slip st into next ch**, ch2, skip 2 ch, slip st into next ch; rep from * into next and each Base flower unit to end, ending at **. Fasten off.

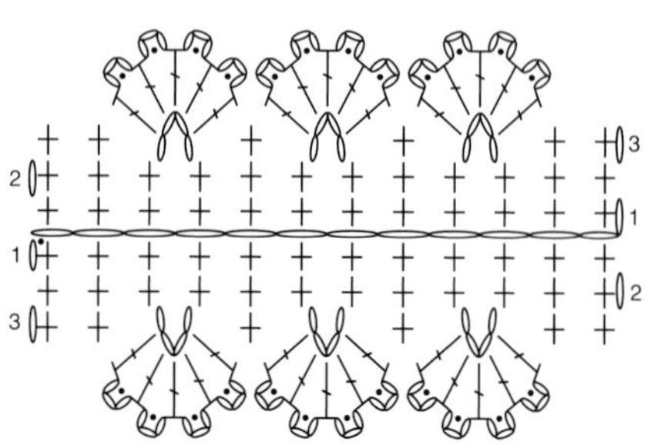

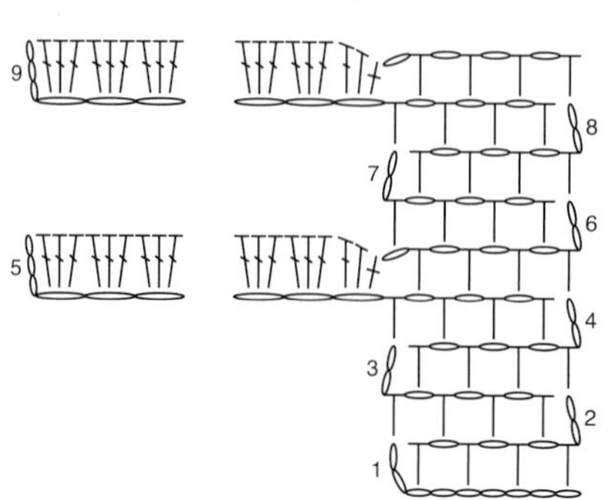

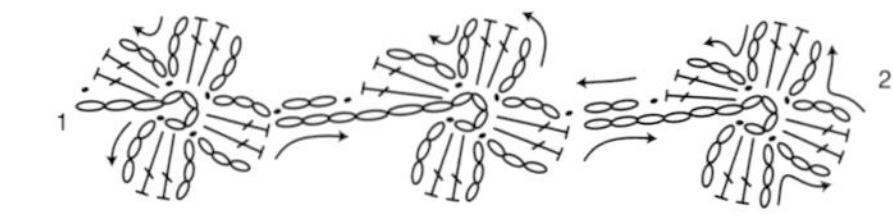

Roundel run

1 motif for each repeat.

Buckle motif

Round 1: Ch18, slip st to 1st ch, turn and ch7, slip st to opposite side of circle.

Round 2: Slip st into next ch, 1sc into each of 18 ch around, slip st to 1st sc. Fasten off.

Rep Buckle motif until required length is reached.

Linking motif

Round 1: Ch18, thread the ch under the cross bar of two Buckle motifs, join with slip st.

Round 2: Ch1, 1sc into each ch around, slip st to 1st sc.

Fasten off.

Rep Linking motif until all Buckle motifs are joined.

Using some of the yarn ends, whip stitch to secure to edge.

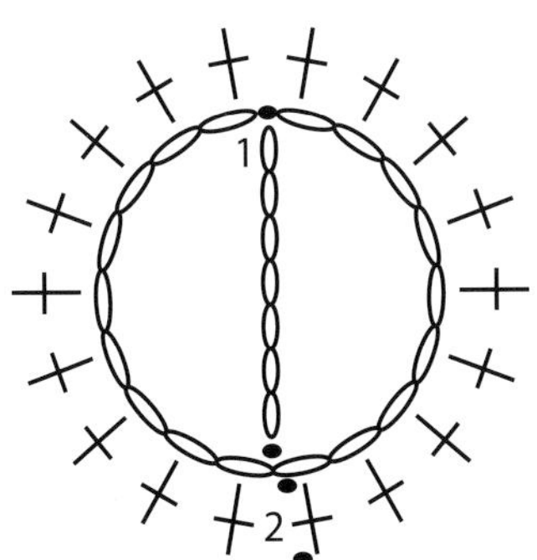

Snowdrop picots

Worked lengthwise.

Ch4 (count as 1dc, ch1).

Row 1 (WS): Work 2dc into 1st of these ch, ch2, 3dc into same ch as last 2 dc, turn.

Row 2: Ch8, slip st into 6th ch from hook, ch7, slip st into same ch as last slip st, ch5, slip st into same ch as last 2 slip sts, ch2, 3dc into ch-2 sp of next shell, ch2, 3dc into same sp as last 3dc, turn.

Row 3: Slip st into each of 1st 3 dc, ch3 (count as 1dc), 2dc into ch-2 sp, ch2, 3dc into same sp as last 2dc, turn.

Rep rows 2–3 until required length is reached, ending with a row 2. Do not turn work but continue along side edge as follows:

Final row: *Ch3, 1sc into top of tch beg of next fan, ch3, 1sc into 1st slip st at beg of next fan; rep from * to last fan, 1sc into top of ch-4 tch of row 1. Fasten off.

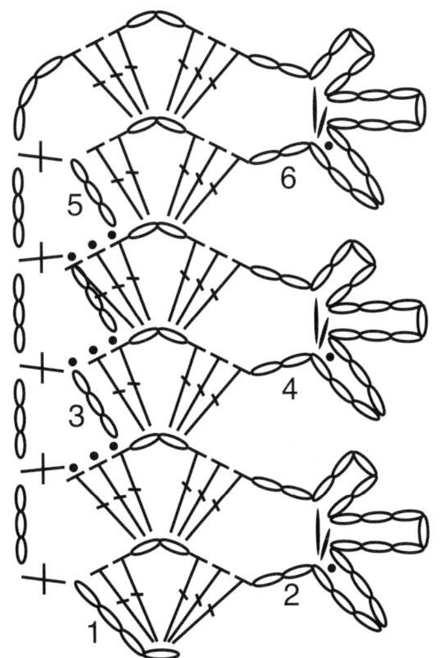

Popcorn cobbles

Multiple of 4 sts + 1 st (add 1 st for base chain).

Special abbreviation:

5dc-popcorn = work 5dc into indicated st, remove hook from working loop, insert hook under top loops of 1st of the dc sts just worked, hook the working loop and draw this through top loops to draw the popcorn closed, ch1.

Note: work foundation row if working from a base chain.

Foundation row: 1sc into 2nd ch from hook and each ch to end, turn.

Row 1 (RS): Ch1, 1sc into 1st st, *ch3, 5dc-popcorn into same place as previous sc, skip 3 sts, 1sc into next st; rep from * to end, turn.

Row 2: Ch3 (count as 1dc), skip 1st st, *1sc into each of next 2 ch, 1hdc into next ch, 1dc into next sc; rep from * to end, skip tch, turn.

Row 3: Ch1, 1sc into 1st st, *ch3, 5dc-popcorn into same place as previous dc, skip next 3 sts, 1sc into next dc; rep from * ending last rep in top of tch, turn.

Rep rows 2–3 once more. Fasten off.

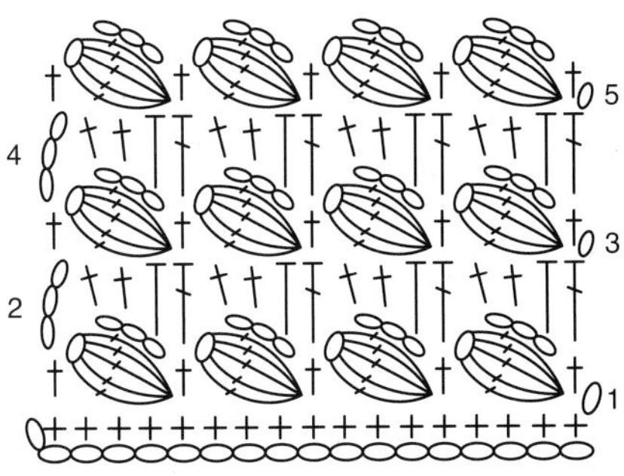

Fan parade

Multiple of 16 sts + 1 st (add 2 sts for base chain).

Special abbreviation:

Cluster = work 2dtr into next st until 1 loop of each remains on hook, yo and through all 3 loops on hook.

Row 1 (RS): Skip 3 ch (count as 1dc), 1dc into next ch, *ch1, skip 1 ch, 1dc into next ch; rep from * to last ch, 1dc into last ch, turn.

Row 2: Ch3 (count as 1dc), skip 1st dc, 1dc into each of next dc, ch sp and dc, ch5, skip 2 sps, 1tr into next sp, ch5, skip 2 dc, 1dc into next dc, *[1dc into next sp, 1dc into next dc] 3 times, ch5, skip 2 sps, 1tr into next sp, ch5, skip 2 dc, 1dc into next dc; rep from * to last 3 sts, 1dc into next sp, 1dc into next dc, 1dc into top of ch-3 tch, turn.

Row 3: Ch3, skip 1st dc, 1dc into each of next 2 dc, ch7, 1sc into next tr, ch7, *skip 1dc, 1dc into each of next 5 dc, ch7, 1sc into next tr, ch7; rep from * to last 4 sts, skip 1dc, 1dc into each of next 2 dc, 1dc into top of ch-3 tch, turn.

Row 4: Ch3, skip 1st dc, 1dc into next dc, ch7, into next sc work (1sc, ch5, 1sc), ch7, *skip 1dc, 1dc into each of next 3 dc, ch7, into next sc work (1sc, ch5, 1sc), ch7; rep from * to last 3 sts, skip 1 dc, 1dc into next dc, 1dc into top of ch-3 tch, turn.

Row 5: Ch6 (count as 1dc, ch3), *skip ch-7 arch, work 1 cluster into ch-5 arch then [ch1, 1 cluster] 4 times into same arch, ch3, skip 1 dc, 1dc into next dc, ch3; rep from * to end, omitting ch-3

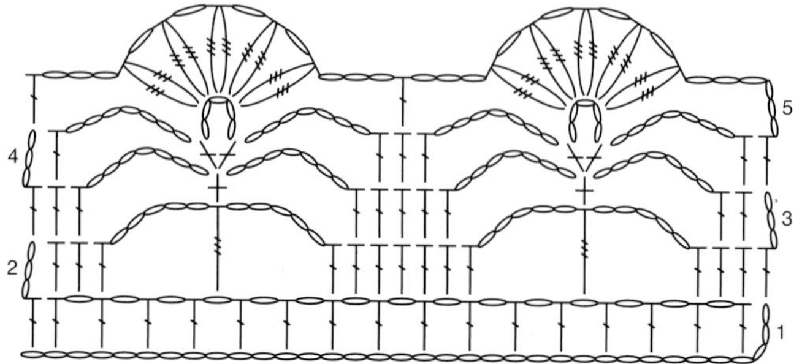

Heart filet

Worked lengthwise over 27 sts (add 4 sts for base chain).

Special abbreviations:

Open mesh = ch1, skip 1 ch or dc, 1dc into next dc st;

Solid mesh = 1dc into next ch sp or st, 1dc into next dc st;

lacet (worked over 2 mesh blocks) = row 1: ch2, skip 1 ch or dc, 1sc into next ch or st, ch2, skip 1 ch or dc, 1dc into next dc st; row 2: ch3, skip next 2 ch-2 sp, 1dc into next dc st.

Note: read the chart from right to left on odd numbered rows and left to right on even numbered rows.

Row 1 (RS as chart): Skip 6 ch, 1dc into next ch (1st mesh completed), continue to end of row using the chart as reference and counting each ch as either a sp or a st, turn.

Row 2: Ch3 (count as 1dc), continue to end of row, work last dc into top of tch, turn.

Row 3 (increase row): Ch8, skip 6 ch, 1dc into next ch (1st mesh completed), continue to end of row, turn.

Continue to follow the chart, ch3 (count as 1dc) at beg of row, start increase rows as row 3 and work last dc into into top of tch before turning. Rep rows 2–19 until required length is reached. Fasten off.

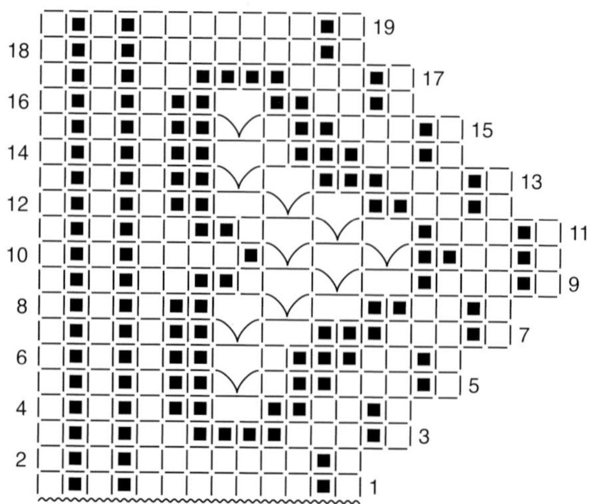

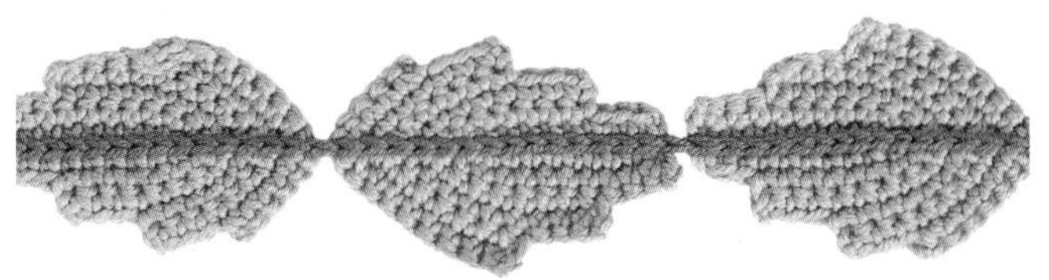

Leaf fall

1 motif for each repeat.

Motif

Base chain: Ch11.

Row 1 (RS): Skip 2 ch (count as 1sc), 1sc into each ch to last ch, work 3sc into last ch for point, then work back along underside of base chain with 1sc into each ch to end, turn.

Row 2: Ch1 (count as 1sc), skip 1 st, 1sc into each st up to st at center of point, work 3sc into center st, 1sc into each st to last 3 sts and tch, turn.

Rows 3–6: As row 2.

Fasten off.

To join the motifs

Arrange the motifs in a line as shown in the photograph, join the contrasting yarn into the outer point, either at tip or base, of the 1st motif, then, with the working yarn beneath the motif or beneath the motif and the fabric on which it is to appear, and the hook above, slip st along the line of the base chain which forms the center spine of the motif. When the end of the 1st motif is reached continue in the same way across the next motif.

Continue until required length is reached. Fasten off.

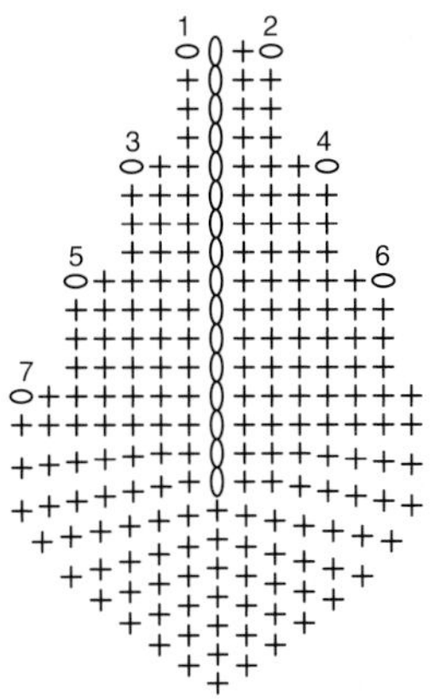

Gwenyth's cable edging

Worked lengthwise over 12 sts (add 2 sts for base chain).

Special abbreviations:

Tr/rf (raised treble crochet at the front of the fabric) = yo twice, insert hook from in front and from right to left around the stem of the appropriate stitch, and complete stitch normally.

Tr/rb (raised treble crochet at the back of the fabric) = yo twice, insert hook from behind and from right to left around the stem of the appropriate stitch, and complete stitch normally.

Row 1 (WS): Skip 3 ch (count as 1dc), 1dc into next ch, work 1dc into each ch to end, turn.

Row 2: Ch3 (count as 1dc), skip 1st st, 1tr/rf around next st, 1dc into next st, skip next 3 sts, 1dtr into each of next 3 sts, going behind last 3dtr work 1dtr into each of 3 sts just skipped, 1dc into next st, 1tr/rf around next st, 1dc into top of tch, turn.

Row 3: Ch3 (count as 1dc), skip 1st st, 1tr/rb around next st, 1dc into next st, skip next 3 sts, 1dtr into each of next 3 sts, going in front of last 3dtr work 1dtr into each of 3 sts just skipped, 1dc into next st, 1tr/rb around next st, 1dc into top of tch, turn.

Rep rows 2–3 until required length is reached, ending with a row 3. Fold the edging strip in half lengthwise and work along the length as follows:

Finishing row: Ch3, *work 2dc round post of last st or tch and round tch or 1st st at beg of same row; rep from * to end. Fasten off.

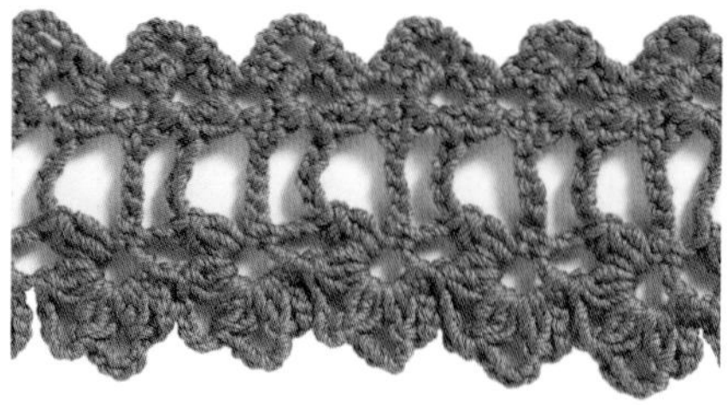

Six-point snowflake

Multiple of 3 sts + 2 sts (add 1 st for base chain).

Special abbreviation:

Picot = ch4, slip st into 4th ch from hook.

Row 1 (RS): Skip 2 ch (count as 1hdc), 1hdc into next ch, 1hdc into each ch to end, turn.

Row 2: Ch2 (count as 1hdc), *1hdc into next hdc, 1 picot, ch8, slip st into 8th ch from hook, ch10, slip st into 10th ch from hook, ch14, slip st into 14th ch from hook, 3 picots, ch4, (for the following picots, work on the other side of the picots just made and slip st into base ch of respective picot of the other side after completing each one), 3 picots, ch14, slip st into 14th ch from hook, ch10, slip st into 10th ch from hook, ch8, slip st into 8th ch from hook, 1 picot, slip st on top of hdc just made, 1hdc into each of next 2 sts; rep from * to end.

Fasten off.

Highland edge

Worked lengthwise.

Special abbreviations:

2dc-cluster = work 2dc into next space until 1 loop of each remains on hook, yo and draw through all 3 loops on hook.

3dc-cluster = work 3dc into next space until 1 loop of each remains on hook, yo and draw through all 4 loops on hook.

Row 1 (RS): Ch12, 2dc into 6th ch from hook, ch3, 2dc into same ch as last 2dc, ch5, skip 5 ch, 1sc into next ch, ch5, 1sc into same ch as last sc, turn.

Row 2: Ch4, work 2dc-cluster into 1st ch-5 sp, work [ch5, 3dc-cluster] 3 times into same ch-5 sp, ch5, skip next ch-5 sp, skip 2 dc, work into ch-3 sp (2dc, ch3, 2dc) turn.

Row 3: Ch5, skip 2 dc, work into the ch-3 sp (2dc, ch3, 2dc), ch5, skip next ch-5 sp, 1sc into next ch-5 sp, ch5, 1sc into same ch sp as last sc, turn.

Rep rows 2–3 until required length is reached, ending with a row 2. Fasten off.

Leaf filet

Worked lengthwise over 19 sts (add 4 sts for base chain).

Special abbreviations:

Open mesh = ch1, skip 1 ch or dc, 1dc into next dc st.

Solid mesh = 1dc into next ch sp or st, 1dc into next dc st.

Note: read the chart from right to left on odd numbered rows and left to right on even numbered rows.

Row 1 (RS as chart): Skip 6 ch, 1dc into next ch (1st mesh completed), continue to end of row using chart as reference and counting each ch as either a sp or a st, turn.

Row 2: Ch3 (count as 1dc), continue to end of row, work last dc into top of tch, turn.

Continue to foll the chart, ch3 (count as 1dc) at beg of each row, and work last dc into top of tch before turning.

Rep chart rows 2–7 until required length is reached. Fasten off.

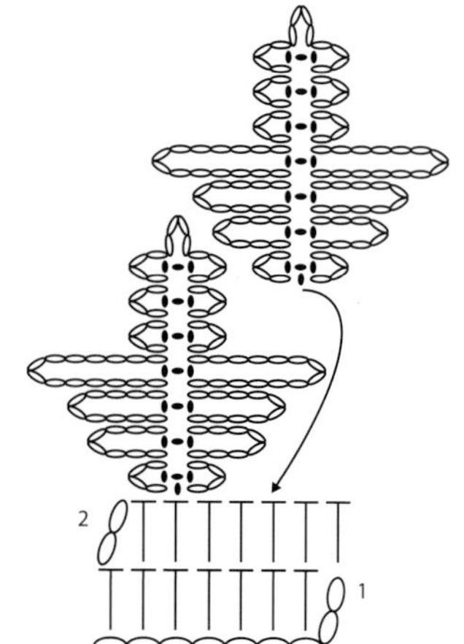

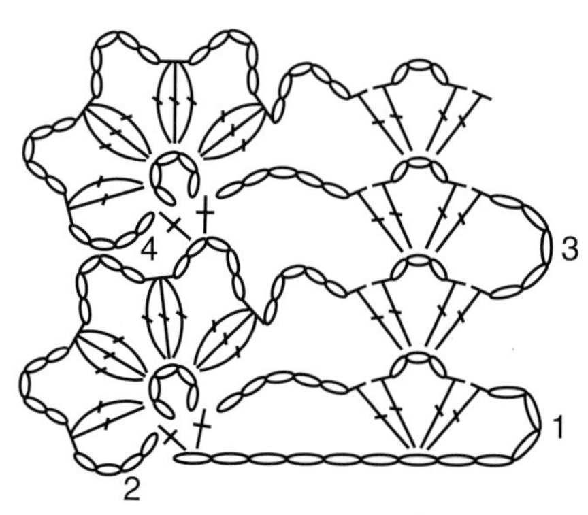

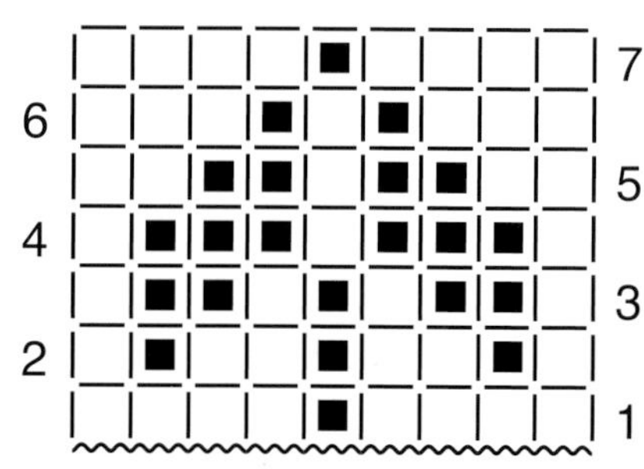

Ric-rac

Worked lengthwise.

Special abbreviation:

Shell = work (1sc, ch2, 1sc) into next space indicated.

Row 1 (RS): *Ch3, 1 shell into 3rd ch from hook, turn.

Row 2: Ch2, 1 shell into ch-2 sp of previous shell, turn.

Rep row 2 until required length is reached. Fasten off.

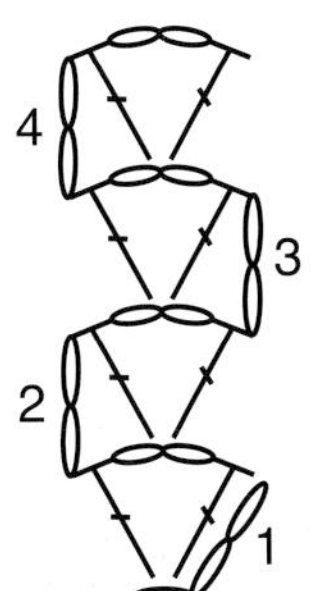

Beaded diamond picot

Multiple of 7 sts + 1 st (add 1 st for base chain).

Special abbreviation:

Pb (place bead) = slide next bead along yarn to base of hook.

Note: work foundation row if working from a base chain. Thread beads onto yarn before starting.

Foundation row: 1sc into 2nd ch from hook and each ch to end, turn.

Row 1 (WS): Ch1, 1sc into 1st st, *ch2, pb, ch3, pb, ch2, skip 6 sts, 1sc in next st; rep from * to end, turn.

Row 2: Ch2, pb, ch3, pb, ch2, 1sc in ch sp between beads of previous row, *ch2, pb, ch3, pb, ch2, 1sc in ch sp; rep from * to last ch-3 sp, ch2, pb, ch2, dc in sc.

Rep row 2 until required depth is reached. Fasten off.

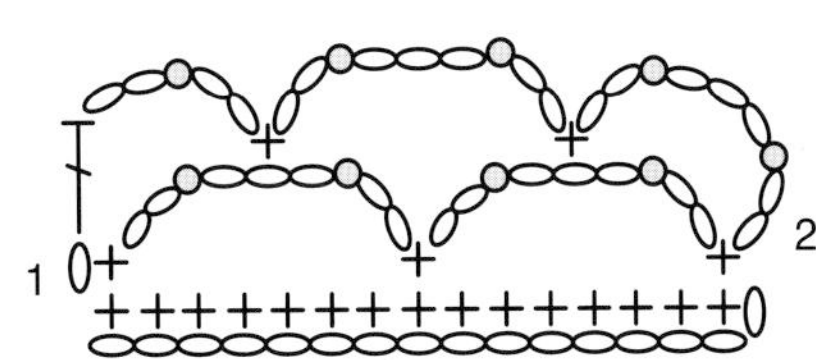

Bunched fringe

Worked lengthwise over 5 sts (add 1 st for base chain).

Row 1 (WS): Ch6, 1sc into 2nd ch from hook, 1sc into each ch to end, turn.

Row 2: Ch1, 1sc into each sc to end, turn.

Row 3: Ch1, 1sc into each sc to end, ch24, turn.

Row 4: Skip next 24 ch, 1sc into each sc to end, turn.

Rep rows 3–4 twice more.

Row 9: Ch1, 1sc into each sc to end, ch8, starting from back, wrap ch-8 around the ch-24 loops, slip st into 1st ch, turn.

Rep rows 2–9 until required length is reached. Fasten off.

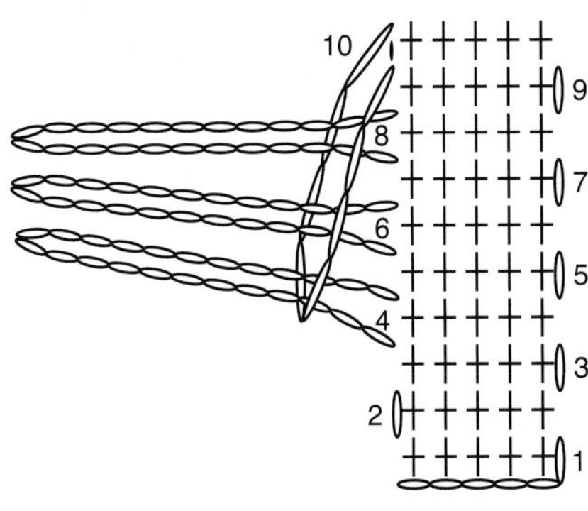

Clematis

Multiple of 20 sts (add 1 st for base chain).
1 motif for each repeat.

Motif

Row 1 (petals): *Ch20, skip 2 ch, 1sc into each of next 2 ch, 1hdc into next ch, 1dc into each of next 2 ch, 1tr into each of next 2 ch, holding back last loop of each tr work 1tr into each of next 2 ch, yo and draw through all 3 loops on hook, 1dc into each of next 3 ch, 1hdc into next ch, slip st into each of last 5 ch; rep from * 5 more times. (6 petals)

Row 2 (flower base): Ch1, 1sc in base of each of 6 petals, ch5, turn.

Row 3: Holding back last loop of each tr work 1tr into each of 1st 5 sc, 2tr into last sc, yo and through all 8 loops on hook, turn.

Row 4: Ch5, slip st into top of the flower base. Fasten off.

Header

Using contrasting yarn to that of the motifs,

Row 1: Skip 2ch, 1hdc into each ch to end, turn.

Row 2: Ch2, work 1hdc into each st to end, turn.

Rep row 2 a further 3 times.

Fasten off yarn, join in yarn matching the motifs.

Row 6: Ch2, work 1hdc into each st to end, turn.

Row 7: Ch2, 1hdc into each of next 9 sts, *yo, insert hook through ch-5 sp on base of motif and through next st, complete st as for a hdc, 1hdc in each of next 20 sts; rep from * to last 10 sts, 1hdc into each st to end.

Join in contrasting yarn.

Row 8: Ch2, work 1hdc into each st to end, turn.

Rep row 8 until required depth is reached. Fasten off.

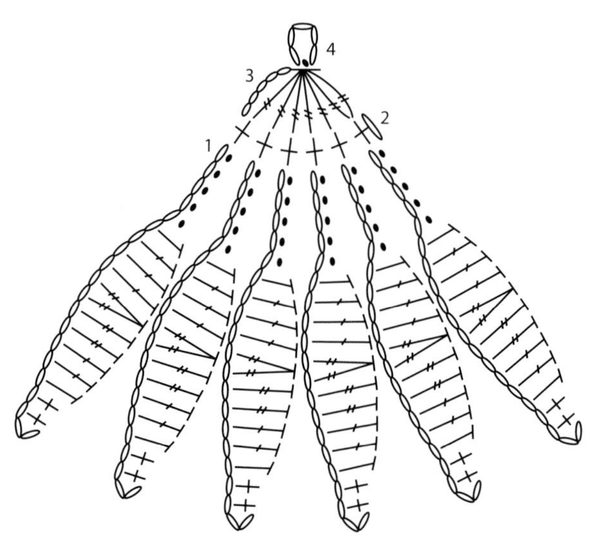

Bobble dainty

Multiple of 5 sts + 1 st (add 1 st for base chain).

Special abbreviation:

4dc-popcorn = work 4dc into next sc, drop loop from hook, insert hook from front into top of 1st of these dc, pick up dropped loop and draw through dc, ch1 to secure the popcorn.

Row 1 (RS): 1sc into 2nd ch from hook, work 1sc into each ch to end, turn.

Row 2: Ch4 (count as 1hdc, ch2), skip 1st 2 sc, 1sc into next sc, *ch5, skip 4 sc, 1sc into next sc; rep from * to last 2 sc, ch2, 1hdc into last sc, turn.

Row 3: Ch1, 1sc into 1st hdc, ch3, 1 popcorn into next sc, ch3, *1sc into next ch-5 arch, ch3, 1 popcorn into next sc, ch3; rep from * to last sp, 1sc into 2nd ch of ch-4 tch. Fasten off.

Simple buttonhole

Multiple of 8 sts + 5 sts (add 1 st for base chain).

Suggestion: work a small sample as described and then adjust the spacing, and so the multiple, to suit the project.

Row 1 (RS): 1sc into 2nd ch from hook, work 1sc into each ch, to end, turn.

Row 2: Ch2, 1hdc into each st to end, turn.

Row 3: Ch1, 1sc into each of 1st 5 sts, *ch3, skip 3 hdc, 1sc into each of next 5 hdc; rep from * to end, turn.

Row 4: Ch2, 1hdc into each st or ch to end.

Fasten off.

Simple shell edging

Multiple of 4 sts + 1 st (add 1 st for base chain).

Note: work foundation row if working from a base chain.

Foundation row: 1sc into 2nd ch from hook and each ch to end, turn.

Row 1 (RS): Ch1, 1sc into 1st st, or join into an edge and ch1, 1sc into starting point; counting either sts or equivalent interval, *skip 1 st, 5dc into next st, skip 1 st, 1sc into next st; rep from * to end. Fasten off.

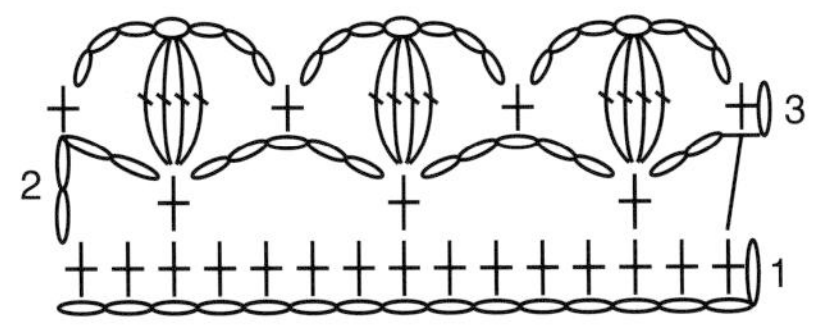

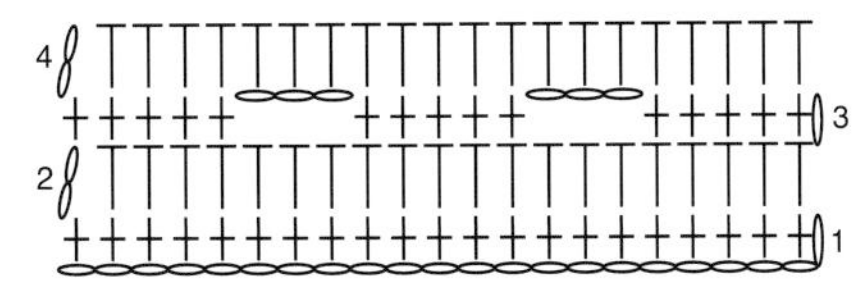

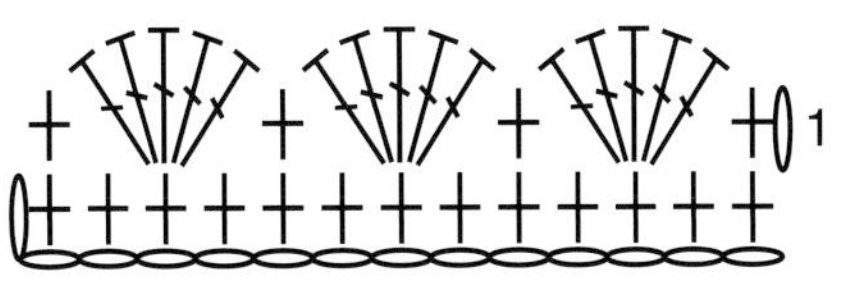

Index

acrobatic stitch 57
African violet 208
aligned cobble stitch 116
aligned puff stitch 117
alternating spike stitch I 117
alternating spike stitch II 117
alternative double crochets 44
Amanda whorl 174
anemone 189
applied shamrock 257
appliqué square 184
Aquarius stitch 204
Aran style 60
arcade diamond 162
arch gallery 118
arched lace stitch 113
arching spans 246
arrowhead fans 275
astrakhan edge 254
astro motif 197
astro waves 175
astrolabe motif 165

back-and-forth ruffle 269
back and front loop single crochet 36
back and front loop half double crochets 37
back loop single crochet 35
back loop half double crochets 37
Baltic square 132
bar stitch 127
barnacle motif 170
basket stitch 52
basketweave stitch 101
beaded dash 266
beaded diamond picot 283
beaded edge, simple 274
beaded loops 242
beaded pintuck 221
beaded triangles 250
bean cluster 179
begonia square 191
begonia wheel 146
bell ruffle 245
bird of paradise 182
block and offset shell stitch 116
blossom 183
boat steer 173
bobble 23
bobble dainty 285
bobble delight 254
bobble sprigs 255
boxed block stitch 106
boxed puff stitch 119
boxed shell stitch 38
briar rose 168
broadway 48
Brontë fan 260
broomstick lace 118
bullion scrolls 243
bullion stitch balls 259
bull's eye 209
bunched fringe 283
buttercup 210
buttonhole, simple 285

cabbage patch 62
cable edge 231
Canterbury bell 160
carpet bag stitch 124
cartwheel fringe 226
Catherine medallion 216
Catherine wheel 241
Catherine wheel I 84
Catherine wheel II 84
Catherine wheel III 85
cavalier frill 256
celestial cluster 178
Celtic motif 175
chain arch edging 225
chain buttonhole 268
chain loops, simple 233
chain ruffle 241
chain stitch (ch) 10, 30
chain swag 258
chain walk 277
chain wave 255
chart distortions 32
chevron stitch 62
chevron stitch I 110
chevron stitch II 110
Christmas rose square 130
chrysanthemum 182
circle of life 209
citrus ring 155
clematis 284
clockwork 144
close chevron stitch 49
close fan ruffle 232
cluster arch edging 221
cluster diamonds 232
cluster wheel 145
clusters 22
color 17, 20, 28
column and bowl 124
column stitch 124
connected spiral 52
cool design 100
corded edging 228
corded ridge stitch 64
cranesbill lace square 132
crinkle stitch 106
crochet hooks 8–9
cross panel 172
cross-topped fans 269
crossbill stitch 99
crossed cluster stitch 107
crossed lace loop stitch 122
crossed puff cables 114
crossed ripple stitch 112
crossed stitches 25, 30
crossed double crochet 90
crosshatch stitch I 90
crosshatch stitch II 90
crown pattern 66
crown puff lattice 77
crown ruffle 254
crowned zigzag 251
crow's foot edging 232
crow's foot lattice 80
crumpled griddle stitch 72
crunch stitch 72
crunchy chevron stitch 58
crystal hexagon 172
crystal motif 164
crystal snowflake 163
curlicue 278
curling petals 243

dahlia 211
dainty points 266
daisy bloom 195
daisy cluster square 142
daisy motif 204
daisy time 139
daisy wheel square 145
dandelion 135
dandelion dangle 224
decorative button 219
decreasing 21
desert garden 217
diagonal shell stitch 108
diagonal spike edge 228
diagonal spike stitch 116
diamond braid 252
diamond cluster motif 138
diamond edge 270
diamonds and fans 248
doily square 203
dots and diamonds 61
double chain arch edging 241
double chevron 264
double corded edging 235
double crochet (dc) 12, 30, 34
double crochet arch ground 102
double crochet cluster stitch I 68
double crochet cluster stitch II 69
double crochet cluster stitch III 69
double lattice stitch 74
double loops 278
double crochet square I 129
double crochet square II 129
double crochet V stitch 126
double treble (dtr) 14, 30
double treble cluster 30
Druid motif 211
Dutch medallion 194

eastern star 147
edging, decorative 36
elephant's ear 161
embossed motif 214
embossed pockets 76
eyelet square 190

fabric, making 16–21
fan and V stitch 98
fan edge 251
fan flair 271
fan frills 228
fan parade 280
fan trellis stitch 42
fantail stitch 76
fastening off 17
faux knitted rib 233
fern leaf 199
filet crochet 22
filet points 262
filet ruffle 242
filet triangles 234
five branches 166
five-point star 155
five-point starfish 209
5-star marguerite stitch 125
flame stitch 93
Flemish motif 173
fleur de lys stitch 46
la fleur de vie 188
floral diamonds 222
floral fringe 244
floral lace 207
floral trellis 272
floret stitch I 71
floret stitch II 71
floret stitch III 71
floribunda 136
flower border 234
flower crystal 156
flower hexagon 140
flower in hexagon 210
flower square 148
flower trail 278
flying diamonds 274
flying shell stitch 64
forked cluster stitch 58
foundation chain 16, 36
four petal 146
framed star 200
French square 130
French square edging 223
fringe of strands 230
fringed arches 244
front loop double crochet 36
frozen star 151
fur stitch 41

galaxy motif 172
garden balsam 142
garden party 216
gardenia bloom 169
garland pattern 104
gauge 20
Gemini 179
Gemini spoke 208
genesa crystal 200
gentle wave 270
geometric circle 170
global connection 43
grand bobbles 249
grand popcorn fans 265
granite wheel 169
granny Jane 212
granny Mae 206
granny square 168
granny wheel square 218
granule stitch 54
green leaf 160
griddle stitch 72
grit stitch I 119
grit stitch II 119
grouped relief strands 220
groups 22
Gwenyth's cable 113
Gwenyth's cable edging 281

half moon stitch 66
half double crochet (hdc) 12, 24, 30, 34
half double crochet cluster stitch I 56
half double crochet cluster stitch II 56
half double crochet cluster stitch III 56
half double crochet popcorn 31
half double crochet puff stitch 31
Halley's comet 145
hamster wheel 183
hanging blocks 270
hardy edge 240
heart filet 280
heart frill 252
herringbone half double crochets 40
herringbone double crochets 41
hexagon stitch 105
Highland edge 282
honeycomb edge 275

hotcross bun stitch 109
hydrangea 171

ice crystal 164
Incan star 147
increasing 21
interlocking block stitch I 111
interlocking block stitch II 111
interlocking diamonds 80
interlocking shell stitch 126
interweave stitch 96
Irish crochet 26–7
Italian square 131

Jekyll border 227
joining in new yarn 17

lacy tangle 268
lacy wave stitch 120
large loop buttonhole 263
layered shells 239
lazy wheel 176
leaf fall 281
leaf filet 282
leaf layer 261
leaf over 198
leafhopper stitch 47
leafy pinwheel 219
light shell frill 272
linked trebles 44
linked half double crochets 39
little curls 262
little gem 162
little triangle points 240
long loop fringe 229
long-stitch pintucks 220
long-stitch points 258
long wave stitch 75
loop ruffle 225
loop stitch 41
loopy edge 268

Magdalene motif 190
magic circle 160
maids in a row 267
mandala 204
marguerite stitch 30, 38
mat stitch 62
Maui orchid 194
Maui wheel 195
mayfair square 169
medallion dangle 276
Mediterranean circle 210
mirror stitch 59
mixed cluster stitch 35
Montana trail 267
Moorish medallion 149
morning glory 218

mosaic tile 158
multi-colored parquet stitch 39
nanna square 198
Norman arch stitch 98

octagon, plain 218
odd-ball edge 238
odd forked cluster stitch 115
offset V stitch 127
old American square 195
on the fold 236
open fan stitch 96
open fans 247
open shell and picot stitch 48
open shell with picot 221
orchid blossom 205
Orient motif 211

padding threads 27
painter's palette 129
papyrus fans 240
patchwork, basic 122
pattern repeats 20
patterns, working from 28–9
peacock fan stitch 114
peacock fans 255
pebble lace stitch 67
peephole chevron stitch 53
petal pattern I 88
petal pattern II 89
petal pattern III 89
petal stitch 115
petit point 194
picot 24, 29, 30, 31
picot edging 220
picot fan stitch 120
picot points 233
picot ridge stitch 49
picot sprigs 242
picot twist 224
picot V stitch 127
picots with chain texture 246
pineapple edge 253
pintuck edge 266
pintuck ridges 250
plain trellis stitch 57
polygon, easy 217
popcorn cluster 205
popcorn cobbles 279
popcorn trefoil 150
popcorn wave 269
popcorn wheel square 171
popcorns 23, 30
posey 208
prairie motif 192
pretty pockets 259
primula circle 147
puff stitch 24

puff stitch jewels 247
puff stitch plaits 121
puff stitch square 144
pulsar motif 185

quarter-roundel edge 222

rack stitch 97
raised chevron stitch 103
raised-stitch rib 247
relief arch stitch 63
relief chain arches 260
ric-rac 283
ridged chevron stitch 42
ridged string network 51
ridged trimming 234
ring web 170
ripple stitch I 94
ripple stitch II 94
ripples 202
Romanesque arches 246
rose garden 223
rose square 133
roundel run 279
ruffle, simple 229
ruled lattice 45
Russian square 156

samosa motif 178
Saturn motif 134
scallop flower 161
scalloped circle 155
scroll ruffle 237
sedge stitch 45
shallow double crochet 36
shamrock 183
shamrock motif 217
sharp chevron stitch 47
shell and V stitch 108
shell edging, simple 285
shell filigree stitch 89
shells 22
shells and popcorns 213
shells with bead drops 251
showtime 186
sidesaddle cluster stitch 100
sidesaddle shell stitch 112
silt stitch 86
singles and doubles 108
single crochet 11, 30
single crochet cluster stitch I 50
single crochet cluster stitch II 50
single crochet cluster stitch III 50
single crochet cluster stitch IV 51
single rib 78
single rib edging 275

six-point motif 182
six-point snowflake 282
six-point snowflake motif 215
six-spoked wheel 196
slanting shells 271
slip knot 10
slip stitch (slip st) 11, 30
slip stitch edge 224
slip stitch strands 235
slot stitch 73
smooth wave stitch 86
snail shell 181
snowdrop picots 279
snowflake I 152
snowflake II 152
solar system 184
solid shell stitch 81
solidarity plaque 201
Solomon's knot 15, 30, 68
sow thistle square 137
spandrel motif 143
Spanish square 187
spatter pattern 51
spider square 158
spike cluster stitch 123
spiked squares 121
spiral hexagon 171
spiral pentagram 153
spring zinnia 136
springtime 168
springtime blossom 198
star bright 190
star fringe 261
star hexagon 216
starfish 191
starting chains 16, 20, 29
starting off 10–15
strip loops 229
summer garden motif 219
summer spiral 191
sun fire 161
sunflower 202
swirl motif 205
sylvan circles 167
symbols 32

tamed chevron 258
tea rose 177
textured diamond edge 259
Thai orchid 134
theatre box 79
thistle pattern 70
three-and-two stitch 126
three-picot feathers 235
tools 8–9
tooth pattern 54
tortoise shell 104
track stitch 111
traditional hexagon I 154
traditional hexagon II 154

traditional square I 128
traditional square II 128
traffic lights 188
tread pattern 109
treasury 199
treble (tr) 14, 30, 35
treble bobble 31
treble picot string network 53
trefoil I 139
trefoil II 139
triangle edge 273
tribal star 179
trinity stitch I 95
trinity stitch II 95
triple treble 14, 30
triple picot V stitch 118
tristar 159
tulip cable 87
Tunisia flower 206
two-color star 157
two-row bobbles 274
two-tone braid 243
two-tone hexagon 146

undulating fringe 225
unpicked fringe 271

vintage square 148
viola 141

wagon wheel 192
water wheel 193
wattle stitch 57
wave and chevron stitch 78
wavy shell stitch I 82
wavy shell stitch II 82
webbed flower 199
wedge stitch I 65
wedge stitch II 65
wheatsheaf 83
wide trebles 40
windmills 180
window pane 178
woven shell stitch 83

yarn 8–9, 17, 93, 128, 140
yarn over (yo) 10, 29

zeros and crosses stitch 55
zigzag border 267
zigzag dainty 250
zigzag double string network 91
zigzag lozenge stitch 43
zigzag pip stitch 74
zigzag popcorn 263
zigzag popcorn network 125
zigzag rib 92
zinnia zigzag 238

Acknowledgments

Thanks to Kate Haxell and Erika Knight for selecting and compiling the stitches.

Thanks to Nicola Hodgson for putting together this volume.

Crocheters: Sharon Brant, Melina Kalatzi, Heather Stephenson

Photography: Geoff Dann, Holly Jolliffe, Michael Wicks

Stitch diagrams: Karen Manthey

Technical editor: Luise Roberts